HOMOSEXUALITY IN GREECE AND ROME

Homosexuality in Greece and Rome

A Sourcebook of Basic Documents

Edited by

Thomas K. Hubbard

UNIVERSITY OF CALIFORNIA PRESS

Berkeley   Los Angeles   London

The publisher gratefully acknowledges

the generous contribution to this book

provided by Joan Palevsky.

———◆———

University of California Press
Berkeley and Los Angeles, California

University of California Press, Ltd.
London, England

© 2003 by the Regents of the University of California

Library of Congress Cataloging-in-Publication Data

Homosexuality in Greece and Rome : a sourcebook of basic documents /
edited by Thomas K. Hubbard.
p.   cm. — (Joan Palevsky imprint in classical literature)
Includes bibliographical references and index.
ISBN 978-0-520-23430-7 (pbk. : alk. paper)
1. Homosexuality—Greece—History—Sources.   2. Homosexuality—Rome—
History—Sources.   3. Greece—Social life and customs.   4. Rome—
Social life and customs.   I. Hubbard, Thomas K.   II. Series.
HQ76.3G8 H66   2003
306.76'6'0937—dc21   2002013904

Manufactured in the United States of America
12   11   10   09   08
10   9   8   7   6   5   4   3

The paper used in this publication is both acid-free and totally chlorine-free (TCF).
It meets the minimum requirements of ANSI/NISO Z39.48-1992 (R 1997)
(*Permanence of Paper*). ∞

CONTENTS

TRANSLATION CREDITS

1.4–27 Translated by Diane J. Rayor. © 1991 by The Regents of the University of California.

1.37–62, 1.64–69, 1.71, 1.74–76, 1.79–83 Translated by Peter Bing and Rip Cohen. © 1991 from *Games of Venus*, by Peter Bing and Rip Cohen. Reproduced by permission of Routledge, Inc., part of the Taylor & Francis Group.

1.87 Translated by Frank Nisetich, *Pindar's Victory Songs*, pp. 82–85. © 1980 The Johns Hopkins University Press. Colometry revised by the editor.

2.1 Translated by Harold North Fowler. Reprinted by permission of the publishers and the Trustees of the Loeb Classical Library from *Plutarch, Moralia*, volume 10, pp. 9–11 odd, Loeb Classical Library Volume 321, Cambridge, Mass.: Harvard University Press, 1936. The Loeb Classical Library ® is a registered trademark of the President and Fellows of Harvard College.

2.2 Translated by Steven Lattimore, *Thucydides: The Peloponnesian War*. © 1998. Reprinted by permission of Hackett Publishing Company, Inc. All rights reserved.

2.3 Translated by J. L. Lightfoot, *Parthenius of Nicaea*, p. 321. © J. L. Lightfoot 1999. Reprinted by permission of Oxford University Press.

2.4, 2.6–8, 2.10 Translated by Andrew Lear.

2.12–14 Translated by David Leitao.

2.16 Translated by David Brooks Dodd.

2.17 Translated by Marcel Widzisz.

2.19, 2.21 Translated by Andrew Dalby.

2.28 Translated by William Morison.

3.1–10 Translated by Alan H. Sommerstein, *The Comedies of Aristophanes*, volume 2, *The Knights*, pp. 17, 27, 45, 47, 51, 77, 79, 91, 125, 127, 139.

© Alan H. Sommerstein 1981. Reprinted by permission of Aris & Phillips, Ltd.

3.11 Translated by Alan H. Sommerstein, *The Comedies of Aristophanes,* volume 3, *The Clouds,* pp. 103–17 odd. © Alan H. Sommerstein 1982. Reprinted by permission of Aris & Phillips, Ltd.

3.12 Translated by Alan H. Sommerstein, *The Comedies of Aristophanes,* volume 4, *The Wasps,* p. 101. © Alan H. Sommerstein 1983. Reprinted by permission of Aris & Phillips, Ltd.

3.13 Translated by Alan H. Sommerstein, *The Comedies of Aristophanes,* volume 6, *The Birds,* pp. 29, 31. © Alan H. Sommerstein 1987. Reprinted by permission of Aris & Phillips, Ltd.

3.14 Translated by Alan H. Sommerstein, *The Comedies of Aristophanes,* volume 8, *The Thesmophoriazusae,* pp. 21–47 odd. © Alan H. Sommerstein 1994. Reprinted by permission of Aris & Phillips, Ltd.

3.15 Translated by Alan H. Sommerstein, *The Comedies of Aristophanes,* volume 9, *The Frogs,* pp. 41, 43. © Alan H. Sommerstein 1996. Reprinted by permission of Aris & Phillips, Ltd.

3.21 Translated by Ralph Rosen.

3.23 Translated by Jeffrey Rusten.

3.28 Translated by Niall W. Slater.

3.30–31 Translated by Jeffrey Rusten.

4.1–2 Translated by Michael de Brauw.

4.3–4 Translated by S. C. Todd, *Lysias.* © 2000. By permission of the University of Texas Press.

4.6 Translated by Michael de Brauw.

4.7 Translated by Christopher Carey, *Aeschines.* © 2000. By permission of the University of Texas Press.

4.11 Translated by Benjamin Dollar.

4.12 Translated by Norman W. De Witt and Norman J. De Witt. Reprinted by permission of the publishers and the Trustees of the Loeb Classical Library from *Demosthenes,* volume 7, pp. 43–65 odd, Loeb Classical Library Volume 374, Cambridge, Mass.: Harvard University Press, 1949. The Loeb Classical Library ® is a registered trademark of the President and Fellows of Harvard College.

4.13 Translated by John J. Winkler. © 1989 by The Regents of the University of California.

5.1–3 Translated by Andrew Lear.

5.4 Translated by Rosamond Kent Sprague, in J. M. Cooper, *The Complete Works of Plato.* © 1997 by Hackett Publishing Company, Inc. Reprinted by permission of Hackett Publishing Company, Inc. All rights reserved.

5.5 Translated by Stanley Lombardo, in J. M. Cooper, *The Complete Works of Plato.* © 1997 by Hackett Publishing Company, Inc. Reprinted by permission of Hackett Publishing Company, Inc. All rights reserved.

5.6 Translated by Mark Warren.

5.7 Translated by Tom Griffith. © Tom Griffith 1986. Reprinted by permission of The Regents of the University of California.

5.8 Translated by Nigel Nicholson.

5.9 Translated by Alexander Nehamas and Paul Woodruff, *Plato: Phaedrus.* © 1995 by Alexander Nehamas and Paul Woodruff. Reprinted by permission of Hackett Publishing Company, Inc. All rights reserved.

5.10–14 Translated by David Leitao.

5.15 Translated by W. H. S. Jones. Reprinted by permission of the publishers and the Trustees of the Loeb Classical Library from *Hippocrates,* volume 4, pp. 267–71 odd, Loeb Classical Library Volume 150, Cambridge, Mass.: Harvard University Press, 1931. The Loeb Classical Library ® is a registered trademark of the President and Fellows of Harvard College.

5.16 Translated and annotated by Lesley Dean-Jones.

5.20–22 Translated by Mark Warren.

6.1–8 Translated by Benjamin Acosta-Hughes.

6.9–14 Translated by Daryl Hine. Reprinted with the permission of Scribner, a Division of Simon & Schuster, from *Theocritus: Idylls and Epigrams* by Daryl Hine. © 1982 Daryl Hine.

6.16–19 Translated by Diane J. Rayor. © 1991 by The Regents of the University of California.

6.20 Translated by Guy Davenport, from *7 Greeks,* © 1995 by Guy Davenport. Reprinted by permission of New Directions Publishing Corp.

6.24–33, 6.35–37, 6.39–59, 6.62–69, 6.71–77, 6.79–90 Translated by Benjamin Acosta-Hughes.

7.1 Translated by Amanda Krauss.

7.2–5 Translated by Benjamin Dollar.

7.7–15 Translated by Timothy J. Moore.

7.17 Translated by Benjamin Dollar.

7.18–19 Translated by Amanda Krauss.

7.20–21 Translated by Benjamin Dollar.

7.34–36 Translated by Andrew Lear.

7.39–51 Translated by Peter Green. **7.39–41** were originally published in *Arion* ser. 3, 6.1 (1998) 79–80 and **7.48** in *Arion* ser. 3, 5.2 (1997) 161–65.

7.52 Translated by Benjamin Dollar.

7.54 Translated by Mark Warren.

7.55–56, 7.59 Translated by Amanda Krauss.

7.60, 7.64 Translated by Mark Warren.

8.1 Translated by Andrew Lear.

8.4 Translated by Paul Alpers. © 1979 by The Regents of the University of California.

8.5–11 Translated by Ned W. Tuck.

8.12–14 Translated by Diane Arnson Svarlien.

8.16–17 Translated by Robert Fitzgerald. From *The Aeneid by Virgil.* © 1980, 1982, 1983 by Robert Fitzgerald. Used by permission of Random House, Inc.

8.19–22 Translated by Diane Arnson Svarlien.

9.1 Translated by Andrew Lear.

9.2–4 Translated by Benjamin Dollar.

9.7 Translated by Andrew Lear.

9.8 Translated by Benjamin Dollar.

9.9 Translated by John B. Stillwell.

9.13 Translated by Cora E. Lutz. © 1947 by Yale University Press. Used by permission of the publisher.

9.14 Translated by R. Bracht Branham and Daniel Kinney. © J. M. Dent 1996. Reprinted by permission of The Orion Publishing Group, Ltd.

9.15 Translated by Andrew Lear.

9.18–31 Translated by Amy Richlin. **9.25** and **9.31.7–12** were previously published in *The Garden of Priapus,* revised edition by Oxford University Press. © 1992 by Amy Richlin.

9.34 Translated by Benjamin Dollar.

9.38–39 Translated by Niall Rudd, *Juvenal: The Satires,* pp. 9–14 and 80–85. © Niall Rudd 1991. Reprinted by permission of Oxford University Press.

10.3 Translated by W. C. Helmbold. Reprinted by permission of the publishers and the Trustees of the Loeb Classical Library from *Plutarch, Moralia,* volume 9, pp. 307–47 odd, Loeb Classical Library Volume 425, Cambridge, Mass.: Harvard University Press, 1961. The Loeb Classical Library ® is a registered trademark of the President and Fellows of Harvard College.

10.4 Translated by Nigel Nicholson.

10.5 Translated and annotated by Lesley Dean-Jones.

10.6–7 Translated by John Erler.

10.8 Translated by Nigel Nicholson.

10.9–10 Translated by M. D. Macleod. Reprinted by permission of the publishers and the Trustees of the Loeb Classical Library from *Lucian,* volume 7, pp. 379–83 and 417–25 odd, Loeb Classical Library Volume 431, Cambridge, Mass.: Harvard University Press,1961. The Loeb Classical Library ® is a registered trademark of the President and Fellows of Harvard College.

10.11–13 Translated by B. P. Reardon. © 1989 by The Regents of the University of California.

10.14 Translated by Marcel Widzisz.

10.15 Translated by P. G. Walsh, *Apuleius: The Golden Ass,* pp. 154–58. © P. G. Walsh 1994. Reprinted by permission of Oxford University Press.

10.16 Translated by Graham Anderson. © 1989 by The Regents of the University of California.

10.17–18 Translated by John J. Winkler. © 1989 by The Regents of the University of California.

10.19 Translated by Christopher Gill. © 1989 by The Regents of the University of California.

10.20 Translated by John J. Winkler. © 1990 from *The Constraints of Desire,* by John J. Winkler. Reproduced by permission of Routledge, Inc., part of the Taylor & Francis Group.

10.22–23 Translated by Marcel Widzisz.

10.34–35 Translated by E. N. O'Neil. From H. D. Betz, ed., *Greek Magical Papyri in Translation.* © 1986 by the University of Chicago. Used by permission of The University of Chicago Press.

10.36 Translated by Robert W. Daniel and Franco Maltomini, *Supplementum Magicum,* volume 1, pp. 137–39. © 1990 by Westdeutscher Verlag GmbH. Used by permission of the publisher.

10.37 Translated by M. D. Macleod. Reprinted by permission of the publishers and the Trustees of the Loeb Classical Library from *Lucian,* volume 8, pp. 151–235 odd, Loeb Classical Library Volume 432, Cambridge, Mass.: Harvard University Press, 1967. The Loeb Classical Library ® is a registered trademark of the President and Fellows of Harvard College.

10.38–41 Translated by Jean Rhys Bram, *Ancient Astrology: Theory and Practice,* pp. 94, 164, 214, 261–62. © 1975 by Jean Rhys Bram. Used by permission of William Andrew, Inc.

All remaining selections are translated by the editor.

PREFACE

Ancient Greece and Rome have often been invoked as models of advanced civilizations that accorded same-gender relations considerably higher status and freedom of display than most subsequent Western societies did until very recently. While some aspects of this idealized image may require contextualization and modification, the appeal the ancient paradigm has had for gays and lesbians of many generations makes it worthy of serious investigation. This book brings together, in as complete a form as is possible in a single affordable volume, the literary and documentary evidence concerning same-gender eroticism in ancient Greece and Rome, as well as a limited, but representative, sample of artistic evidence. This sourcebook does not include selections that were clearly written under Christian influence, since early Christian expressions on this subject merit an anthology of their own. Some works that are readily available in a variety of affordable paperback editions, such as Plato's *Symposium,* are extracted here, even though a reading of the whole is recommended. This volume's goal is to stimulate further exploration by curious readers who may not be immersed in the cultural history of Greece and Rome, and at the same time also offer revelations to more experienced students of antiquity, either by acquainting them with unfamiliar texts, by summarizing the current state of scholarship on texts, or by piecing the evidence together in new ways.

Too often theories have been erected on the basis of a fairly limited range of texts, and generalizations have been made without due regard for the diversity of chronological, geographical, generic, and ideological factors that frame and differentiate those texts. This volume aims to present as wide a range of evidence as possible, including texts that have often been overlooked. The short introduction to each text contextualizes it in terms of date and, where necessary, its position within a larger work. The longer chapter introductions relate it to other texts of the same genre or period to reconstruct its broader ideological significance. The footnotes are geared to a general undergraduate audience that has little previous knowledge of classical civilization and may need explanation of basic cultural artifacts or historical references. The notes also include points of interpretation, which should interest both the general and the more knowledgeable reader. The general introduction to the volume is not in any sense meant to be a definitive or complete treatment of the subject; instead, it addresses a handful of critical issues on which I believe that popular misconceptions are common and can be corrected by reference to some of the evidence presented in this volume. More than the chapter or selection introductions, it represents a distillation of my personal views on points of controversy. For balance and different constructions of the evidence, readers are enthusiastically referred to the works of Sir Kenneth Dover, John Boswell, Michel Foucault, and David M. Halperin, which have much to recommend them despite my disagreement with many of their fundamental premises.

Thanks and acknowledgment are owed to many for their support and advice. Bill Germano and David Halperin gave valuable feedback at an early stage in this project's conceptualization. David Konstan, Jeffrey Henderson, Marilyn Skinner, and John Kirby also offered advice and support at critical points. Acknowledgment is made to the University Co-operative Society Subvention Fund and to the Department of Classics at the University of Texas, Austin, for providing financial assistance to defray the costs of securing permissions to reprint material, where suitable modern and explicit translations already existed. I thank the department's chair, Cynthia Shelmerdine, for pointing me in the direction of these sources, as well as supporting my petition for a leave during fall semester 2000, funded by the University Research Institute, and a research assistant, funded by the Graduate School. I owe much to the proofreading, bibliographical, and computing skills of my assistant, Raymond Kim, and I truly feel that the project could not have been completed in the time it was without his efficiency and dedication. I also thank the departmental staff for their patience and assistance: Chris Williams and David Lummus for help with digitizing photographs, Kathryn Samec for dealing with a rather complicated series of payment requests, and Debbie Coleman for what must have seemed like an interminable series of faxes and long-distance telephone calls.

I thank Alan Shapiro, Steven A. White, Veronika Grimm, David Martinez, and Heinrich von Staden for offering advice on various points that touched their respective areas of expertise. My gratitude goes to Michael Gagarin and Jeffrey Rusten for allowing me access to unpublished translations over which they had editorial control. But above all, I owe a debt of thanks to the many colleagues, former colleagues, graduate students, former students, and recognized experts who agreed to contribute new translations of material to this volume. The work would not have been possible without them. In many cases we went through several drafts together as we attempted to strike the delicate balance between fidelity to the original and felicity of English expression, further complicated by my demands for uniformity within the volume on certain semantic issues. Some—such as Nigel Nicholson, Benjamin Acosta-Hughes, and Andrew Dalby—were willing to translate substantial chunks of additional material on short notice; others—such as David Leitao, Lesley Dean-Jones, Tim Moore, and Mark Warren—made valuable recommendations concerning additional passages that proved worthy of inclusion. Many made detailed suggestions for annotation, and to all of them I owe the most profound gratitude for their generosity and forbearance. I also wish to thank Jennifer Eastman, Seth Schein, and Paul Cartledge for their careful perusal of the entire manuscript, which saved me from numerous errors and obscurities. Last, but not least, I owe an especially large debt to Kate Toll, an old friend who shepherded the project through the editorial process at University of California Press with a competence, efficiency, and enthusiasm at which I can only marvel. This project has in every sense been a collaborative and collective undertaking. I can only hope that everyone will find the whole to be worthy of the individual parts they contributed.

Austin, Texas
April 2001

Introduction

The term "homosexuality" is itself problematic when applied to ancient cultures, inasmuch as neither Greek nor Latin possesses any one word covering the same semantic range as the modern concept. The term is adopted in this volume not out of any conviction that a fundamental identity exists between ancient and modern practices or self-conceptions, but as a convenient shorthand linking together a range of different phenomena involving same-gender love and/or sexual activity. To be sure, classical antiquity featured a variety of discrete practices in this regard, each of which enjoyed differing levels of acceptance depending on the time and place. The pedagogical pederasty common among Greek men and freeborn adolescents was not the same as relationships between men and adolescent slaves or male prostitutes. "Platonic love" was not the same as a physically consummated relationship. Age-differential pairings were not the same as age-equal relations, whether between adults or adolescents. Same-gender love among males was not the same as that among females. Nevertheless, there are clear links among these disparate phenomena that justify their treatment in a single volume, since the ancient sources themselves frequently treat them together as social practices that were comparable and easily confused, though not identical. Even in modern society, "homosexual" is a somewhat unsatisfactory and abstract catch-all for a plethora of practices and subcultures: flaming queens, leather daddies, chickenhawks, bull dykes, lipstick lesbians, and Log Cabin Republicans could not be more different, but even they find it convenient to posit a certain affinity in counterdistinction to the dominant heterosexual culture.

Sexual Preference

The field of Gay Studies has, virtually since its inception, been divided between "essentialists," those who believe in an archetypal pattern of same-gender attraction that is universal, transhistorical, and transcultural, and "social constructionists," those who hold that patterns of sexual preference manifest themselves with different significance in different societies and that no essential identity exists between practitioners of same-gender love in, for instance, ancient Greece and postindustrial Western society.[1] Some social constructionists have even gone so far as to deny that sexual preference was a significant category for the ancients or that any kind of subculture based on sexual object-choice existed in the ancient world.[2]

Close examination of a range of ancient texts suggests, however, that some forms of sexual preference were, in fact, considered a distinguishing characteristic of individuals. Many texts even see such preferences as inborn qualities and thus "essential" aspects of human identity: the earliest philosophical account of male sexual passivity, from the pre-Socratic philosopher Parmenides (**10.5.134–35**), traces it to a failure of male and female seed to blend properly at the moment of conception. Other medical writers consider effeminacy in men and masculinity in women to be genetically determined (**5.15**). Aristotle (**5.13**) and his followers (**5.16**) believe that the desire to be penetrated anally arises from physiological deformity, either a congenital defect or something occurring through "abuse" as a child. Similarly, physiognomic writers (**10.6–7**) hold that effeminacy and sexual passivity can be betrayed by visible physical traits, implying that the behavior stems from an organic etiology. Later astrological texts (**10.38–41**) consider all manner of sexual preferences to be determined by the position of heavenly bodies at one's birth. The Roman fabulist Phaedrus (**9.5**) and the Greek comic poet Aristophanes (as recorded in Plato, **5.7.189–93**) both produce mythological accounts explaining the origin of different sexual orientations in the prehistory and creation of the human race. In the context of these theories, it should not surprise us to see the late Greek novelist Longus introduce a character as "a pederast by nature" (**10.19.11**).

Even our earliest literary source for homosexuality, the iambic poet Archilochus in the early seventh century B.C.E., speaks of men with different *natures* and therefore different sexual preferences (**1.1**). Somewhat later, Theognis seems conscious of boy-love as a distinctive lifestyle not shared

---

1. One of the most systematic expositions of an essentialist view is in the work of Boswell (1980); Halperin (1990) 15–53 provides an eloquent social constructionist response, which is in turn countered by Thorp (1992). See also the valuable collection of essays by Stein (1992), including Boswell's response to his critics, and the survey of Lambert and Szesnat (1984).

2. See especially Halperin (1990) 15–40, following the inspiration of Foucault (1986) and (1988).

by all men (**1.73, 1.78**) and compares it favorably to love of women (**1.77**). Similarly, the early-fifth-century lyric poet Pindar contrasts men devoted to women with those who appreciate boys (**1.85**) and generalizes that "different loves tickle the fancies of different folks" (**1.86**). An interesting black-figure pyxis from the mid-sixth century (figs. 4a, b), perhaps used for storing cosmetics, displays three panels corresponding to the same three erotic combinations conceptualized by Aristophanes in Plato's *Symposium:* man-woman, woman-woman (4a), and man-boy (4b). In *Wasps*, Aristophanes assures his audience that his tastes are not pederastic (**3.12**), and comedy generally ridicules those who seem exclusively or excessively devoted to boys or men (**3.11, 3.14, 3.19–20, 3.23–24, 3.31**), as if to imply that their preferences were not the norm, but they were nevertheless a recognizable group in ancient Athens. Roman satirical texts from authors such as Petronius (**9.14**), Martial (**9.25**), and Juvenal (**9.39**) recognize that some men were genuinely incapable of sex with women.

During the Roman period, sexual preference came to be contested as an object of active debate between those who preferred women and those who liked boys. In some cases the comparison is uncomplimentary to both and reflects indifference (**7.14, 7.27**), but in most cases partisans praise boys as natural and undemanding (**6.63, 6.70, 7.25**) or women for their mutual pleasure (**8.19**). The most extensive and formalized debates are recorded by later authors such as Plutarch (**10.3**), Achilles Tatius (**10.18**), and an imitator of Lucian (**10.37**): the parties sometimes become quite heated in their ridicule and even disgust for the other position. These late texts represent the most polarized development of a fundamental contrast in identities that in some form goes back to our earliest literary evidence from archaic Greece.

Not only was there a widespread perception that individuals were characterized by their sexual preference, but there is considerable evidence that like-minded individuals congregated in social venues conducive to pursuing their mutual interests. In early Greece, athletics was practiced in the nude at least in part to showcase the beauty of young male bodies in motion:[3] this aesthetic dimension of athletics is confirmed by the characteristic preference for male nudes in archaic and classical sculpture. It should therefore come as no surprise that the *palaestra* (a privately owned wrestling school, as opposed to public gymnasia) was a favorite gathering place for upper-class adolescent boys and their older admirers (**3.11–12, 5.4–5**). Pindar (**1.86**)

3. There has been much discussion of the interrelation between athletic and artistic nudity, both of which may be outgrowths of Greek initiatory practice, as was, in some views, Greek pederasty. See especially the discussions of Bonfante (1989), Stewart (1997) 24–42, and Golden (1998) 65–69; the last gives a brief survey of previous scholarship on the question. On the general nexus between initiation, pederasty, and Greek athletics, see Scanlon (2002) and Hubbard (2003).

makes it clear that athletic success would render a boy or young man more attractive to potential lovers of both genders and all age-groups; Xenophon's *Symposium* (**5.8**) is set at a party the wealthy Callias gives in honor of the Panathenaic victory of his beloved, the adolescent athlete Autolycus. Gymnastic venues are especially frequent in visual representations of courtship on Greek vases (see especially figs. 11, 12b, 24b, c; the strigils hanging on the wall in figs. 16, 19, and 20 may also suggest a gymnastic background).

Artistic evidence also suggests that the symposium, or drinking party, was a locus of homosexual admiration, courtship, and even sexual acts (see figs. 5a, b for the latter, fig. 23 for the former).[4] The tragedian Sophocles ogled cute serving boys (**2.21.603**), and in myth Ganymede was brought to Olympus to be the cupbearer of the gods and Zeus' favorite. As figure 23 shows, serving boys would often tend to their duties naked. That Plato and Xenophon both set dialogues on love (**5.7–8**) at such gatherings is significant. Most male homoerotic lyric poetry was probably intended for delivery in such a setting. **1.85**, **1.88**, and **1.89** are *skolia* (drinking songs) that may have been meant for recitation at banquets as an expression of homosocial values common to men of the upper class.

Less elaborate social venues also existed for fulfilling basic physical appetites. The comic poets (**3.19, 3.24**) refer to isolated spots on the outskirts of Athens frequented by men looking for other men, and a massive conglomeration of pederastic graffiti at a single location on the island of Thera (**2.22**) suggests an established gathering place for men and boys. That such discreet meeting places existed implies extensive word-of-mouth networks. In Rome, even as early as 200 B.C.E., a certain street was known to be frequented by male prostitutes specializing in both active and passive roles (**7.10**). Some men are reported to have sought company among sailors in a district near the Tiber river (**8.3**) and others were even picked up in the public baths (**9.14.92**). Juvenal (**9.39.132–33**) refers to scratching one's head with a single finger as a sign used by men of homosexual inclinations. Such evidence has convinced some critics that Rome featured a fairly well-developed homosexual subculture, despite the generally negative valuation that society placed on any man or boy who ever adopted a passive role.[5]

Varieties of Same-Gender Attraction

It is often assumed that same-gender relationships followed a stereotypical pattern and set of protocols in ancient society: in classical Greece this would

---

4. On the pederastic and initiatory significance of the symposium, see especially Levine (1985) 176–80, Winterling (1990), and Bremmer (1990).

5. See Richlin (1993) and Taylor (1997). However, see the objections of C. A. Williams (1999) 218–24.

take the form of pedagogical pederasty associating a man (usually before the age of marriage) and a freeborn boy, while in Rome, a merely physical relationship between an adult citizen and a young slave. The texts, however, reveal a much wider diversity of relationships in terms of both age and status. While these "non-normative" relationships are sometimes attacked in the texts as eccentric or inappropriate, even the "normative" forms of same-gender involvement are treated with hostility by certain sources. What the evidence establishes is that a variety of behaviors occurred with sufficient frequency to be worthy of notice, even if disapprobatory.

Greek homosexual activity, despite popular misconceptions, was not restricted to man-boy pairs. Vase-painting shows numerous scenes where there is little or no apparent difference in age between the young wooer and his object of courtship (see figs. 12a, b, 24a, b, c), as well as graphic scenes of sexual experimentation between youths (see figs. 8, 15). Early poets such as Theognis (**1.41, 1.65**) and Pindar (**1.86**) make it clear that youths were attracted to and slept with other youths of the same age. Plato tells us that the young Charmides' beauty provoked the admiration and love of everyone present, even the youngest boys (**5.4.154**). In the *Phaedrus,* Socrates quotes the proverb "youth delights youth" to imply that young men would prefer companions of their own age to older lovers (**5.9.240**). Xenophon shows Critobulus in love with Cleinias, a youth of the same age or perhaps even a bit older (**5.8.4.23**). Timarchus' lover, Misgolas, appears to be the same age (**4.7.49**). In the Hellenistic period Meleager attests that boys were attractive to boys (**6.40**), and Quintilian worries about older boys corrupting younger boys in Roman schools (**9.34**). If interpretations of Alcman's *First Maidens' Song* (**1.4**) as a ritualized lesbian betrothal are correct, the two young women paired in that performance appear to be age-equal, in which case female homoeroticism also did not always conform to the age-differential stereotype (for artistic evidence, see figs. 3, 4a, 9, 13).

Although a youth's attractiveness was thought by many to cease with the growth of his beard and body hair, the window of attraction varied to some degree according to individual preferences. The youths named as men's favorites in Athenian oratory (Theodotus in **4.4**, Timarchus in **4.7**, and Aristion in **4.10**) are all *meirakia,* a term generally used of those in the eighteen to twenty-one age-group. Philosophers, in fact, preferred older youths, who were capable of a higher level of intellectual engagement (**5.7.181, 5.24, 10.10**); the early Stoics thought that a suitable beloved could be as old as twenty-eight (**5.25**). Aristotle (**5.14**) claims that relationships based on love of character often continued after the loss of the beloved's youthful beauty. Xenophon reports that Menon, a Thessalian general, had a bearded beloved (**2.6**); similarly, Philostratus praises his beloved's beard (**10.29**). In the Hellenistic period, some lovers swore continued attraction even well into their loved one's adulthood (**6.65–66, 6.89**); others preferred boys as young as twelve (**6.59–60, 6.73–74**). In Roman times, we have more than one account of soldiers being the object of sexual attention by superior officers (**7.3, 7.21**); the elderly emperor Galba is said to have preferred mature and masculine men (**9.15**), and Nero supposedly "married" a freedman named Doryphorus (**9.7**). However, other wealthy Romans are reported to have had their favorite slaves castrated in order to maintain their youthful appearance artificially (**9.4, 9.10**).

The fact that some youths continued to take the part of the beloved even after reaching physical maturity raises the question whether it was because they derived pleasure from the passive role. Medical texts certainly recognize that some men did so (**5.16, 10.5**). Aristophanes invokes the tragic poet Agathon as the paradigm of a man who cultivated a youthful and even feminine appearance in order to remain sexually attractive to other adult men (**3.14**); later biographical sources report that he was the lifelong companion of Pausanias, who appears as his lover in Plato's *Symposium*. Theopompus (**3.24**) suggests that Agathon was not the only such character. However, excessive concern with maintaining an attractive appearance was not necessarily a sign of sexual passivity, but could also have been meant to make an active pederast more appealing to boys, as suggested by Pherecrates' effeminate perfume-seller (**3.23**) or Xenophon's Critobulus (**5.8.4**). Indeed, plays such as Aristophanes' *Knights* (**3.1–10**) and *Clouds* (**3.11**) show characters alternating between active and passive roles, suggesting that the dividing line between lover and beloved was perhaps not always so distinct; compare **6.76** and **6.84** from the Hellenistic age.

In the Roman period we hear from a variety of texts about adult men who preferred the passive role. The comic poets and satirists tell us that there were male prostitutes who specialized in taking the active role in anal sex for the benefit of such men (**7.10, 7.30–31, 9.20, 9.24, 9.39**). Martial refers to a man who used his slave for the same purpose (**9.21**). Seneca tells us that one Hostius Quadra set up a room full of distorting mirrors to make the organs of men penetrating his various bodily orifices appear larger (**9.9**). The desire to be penetrated is often associated with playing a woman's role: the emperors Nero (**9.7**) and Elagabalus (**10.22–23**) are both reported to have pretended they were female in the company of their masculine favorites. Ovid (**8.20**) ridicules husbands who make themselves more hairless than their wives in order to attract other men; the comic poet Novius (**7.32**) tells us of men who depilate their buttocks to smooth the way. An invective poem attributed to Vergil (**8.3**) associates ritual transvestism at the Cotytia with sexual passivity; Apuleius (**10.15**) narrates a story about effeminate eunuch priests of Cybele who lure a young peasant into their midst and then force him to be serviced orally by the whole troupe. One should not necessarily assume from the number of references that such behavior was more common in Rome than it was in Greece: it may be that sexual passivity on the part of free citizen males was even more offensive to Roman sensibilities (for which it was not acceptable even in free youths) and hence became a potent satirical topos for moral disorder and inversion of values, as is suggested by the uniformly hostile tone of the sources.

Greek and Latin shared a term for such men: *kinaidos/cinaedus*. It may have been used as early as Archilochus (**1.3**). Its first certain attestations in Aristophanes (*Clouds* 448 and *Birds* 429) are not distinctively sexual; it just appears as one of many terms of abuse for rascality. But by the fourth century its meaning is more specific: the orator Aeschines abuses Demosthenes as one, and Plato has Socrates refer to their life as "terrible and shameful and to be pitied" (**5.6**). The exact meaning of the word, however, is still disputed: while some Roman texts clearly associate it with sexual passivity (e.g., **7.44, 8.3, 9.14.21, 9.16.2319b**), Martial associates it with eunuchs (**9.28**), and other texts, with adulterers (**7.26, 7.46**). Cicero said Verres was "masculine among women" and an "unchaste little lady among men" (**7.57**); similar statements were made concerning Caesar (**7.36**), suggesting that homosexual passivity and heterosexual promiscuity were not inconsistent. The late astrological writer Firmicus Maternus associates the word with effeminate men who are actors and dancers, but makes it clear that they may be either married heterosexuals or pederasts (**10.40**). It therefore seems unwise to limit the term *kinaidos/cinaedus* to the sexually passive: its range seems potentially to include anyone who is perceived as sexually excessive or deviant. I have therefore adopted the somewhat unsatisfactory translation "pervert" in numerous passages throughout this volume, inasmuch as that English word combines the same vagueness of reference with an equally strong element of censure and disapproval. The *cinaedi* as a group are too often mentioned to be merely imaginary projections, however embroidered with fiction each individual story may be.[6] Antiquity, like our own society, had its share of sexual dissidents and nonconformists.

Varieties of Moral Judgment

Just as sexual behavior in Greece and Rome was irreducible to any single paradigm, moral judgments concerning the various species of same-gender interaction were far from uniform. The widespread notion that a "general acceptance" of homosexuality prevailed is an oversimplification of a complex *mélange* of viewpoints about a range of different practices, as is the dogma that a detailed regimen of protocols and conventions distinguished "acceptable" from "unacceptable" homosexual behaviors.[7] There was, in

6. See Winkler (1990) 45–54, Richlin (1993), Taylor (1997) 338–57, and C. A. Williams (1999) 172–224; the last has a particularly valuable discussion of the word's range and associations.

7. For the former view, see Boswell (1980) 61–87; the latter view is implied by Foucault (1986).

fact, no more consensus about homosexuality in ancient Greece and Rome than there is today. In these heavily discourse-oriented cultures, as in our own, sexual dissidence was a flash point of ideological contention.

In Greece, suspicion of homosexual relations of any sort seems most pronounced in those genres of discourse that are designed to appeal to the masses' resentment of sociopolitical elites: iambic poetry (**1.1–3**), comedy (chapter 3), forensic oratory (chapter 4), and popular street preaching (**5.17–18**). Such class-based hostility is already evident in our earliest literary evidence for homosexuality, the barbed lampoons of Archilochus (**1.1–3**), a self-proclaimed bastard and spokesman for the common man. Similarly, comic drama of the fifth and fourth centuries satirizes the excesses and follies of the city's intellectual and political leaders, typically showing them foiled or defeated by a protagonist who in some sense represents the average citizen. Although there is no question that comic invective holds the greatest scorn for effeminates and/or sexual passives (**3.8, 3.10, 3.14, 3.21–24, 3.32**), adult effeminacy was merely seen as the most extreme and visible manifestation of an institution (pederasty) that, even when practiced in a "normative" way, effeminized, prostituted, and corrupted adolescents who were one day destined to become the city's leaders. Active/passive roles were widely imagined as interchangeable (e.g., in Aristophanes' *Knights* [**3.1–10**] or *Clouds* [**3.11**]), in part because any active pederast had himself most likely played the passive role at some point in his development. Hence, active boy-lovers are themselves a target of satire (**3.7, 3.11–13, 3.18, 3.20, 3.23, 3.27, 3.29, 3.31, 3.33**) just as often as men who take a passive role. Boys are frequently accused of being prostitutes, but it is apparent that comedy expands the notion of "prostitution" to encompass virtually all the forms of gift-exchange that characterized traditional pederastic courtship (**3.17**; compare figs. 4b, 6–8, 16–17, 19–21) and even the offer of entertainment and a fancy meal (**3.25–26, 3.30**), staples of the upper-class homosocial symposium. In contrast, boys who sell themselves for money out of genuine need are treated more sympathetically (**3.9, 3.16**).

Athenian forensic oratory also appealed to a mass audience, since its goal was to persuade a jury composed of a cross section of the city's male citizen population. Arguments based on an opponent's bad character were commonplace, and charges of prostitution are frequent (**4.1, 4.6–8**), perhaps appealing to popular suspicions concerning politicians' venality. However, these charges are never based on any evidence more specific than that a man was known to keep the company of older men in his youth. Although formal legal contracts exchanging such long-term companionship for money were not unknown (**4.4.22**), merely benefiting from extravagant dinners and entertainment was considered equivalent to a form of payment in oratory (**4.7.75–76**), as it was in comedy. But even pederastic involvements, whether active or passive, that did not involve prostitution were thought to prejudice a jury against an opponent, and were thus brought up even when strictly irrelevant to a case (**4.2–3, 4.5, 4.10–11, 4.13**); the defendant in **4.4**, an active pederast, admits his involvement only with the greatest embarrassment and fear that it will prejudice the judges against him.

The sum of this evidence, together with the association of pederasty with upper-class venues like the symposium and wrestling school, suggests that it was primarily an upper-class phenomenon, at least in Athens; only men with a certain amount of wealth, leisure, and education were in a position to provide boys with the attention and courtship gifts they might expect, whether tangible or intangible. The majority of Greek men lived close to the subsistence level and had neither the time nor the wherewithal for such pursuits.

Even within elite intellectual circles there were many Greeks who had their doubts about any physically consummated form of pederasty. Xenophon's *Memorabilia* (**5.1–3**) presents a Socrates who cautions his young followers against pederastic involvements; and Xenophon's *Symposium* (**5.8**) seems to place a higher valuation on heterosexuality at the end. "Platonic love," as articulated in Plato's *Symposium* (**5.7**) and *Phaedrus* (**5.9**), attempts to rehabilitate pederastic desire by sublimating it into a higher, spiritual pursuit of Beauty in which the sexual appetite is ultimately transcended. The idea of a chaste pederasty gained currency in other fourth-century authors (**4.7.136–57, 4.12, 5.14**), and may have some precedent in Spartan customs (**2.9–12**), but Plato's last work, the *Laws* (**5.10–11**), appears to abandon it and present an entirely negative view. Even in the *Phaedrus*, Lysias' speech and Socrates' first speech flesh out serious and specific reflections on the harm that the wrong kind of pederasty could do a boy, suggesting that the concept of Platonic love was developed as a response to widespread censure. Texts such as the comic fragment **3.29** show that even in Plato's own day, some were skeptical whether such a chaste pederasty could exist in reality; later satirical texts (**6.48, 9.38, 10.10**) take it for granted that these philosophical pretensions were fraudulent covers.

Censure of same-gender relations in Roman culture was differently motivated: class considerations played less of a role, and the inappropriateness of sexual passivity for a Roman male, even during his youth, is the central theme of many texts (**7.1–6, 7.9, 7.13, 7.18, 7.21, 7.30–32, 7.34–38, 7.43–44, 7.57–58, 7.60–62, 7.64, 8.1, 8.3, 8.20, 9.3, 9.9, 9.21, 9.30, 9.35–37, 9.39, 10.21–23**). Some texts go further and condemn active forms of pederasty, even when practiced with a slave or foreigner: this preference is either impugned as Greek and un-Roman (**7.17, 7.48, 7.52–55**) or singled out as a sign of luxury and self-indulgence (**7.19, 7.59, 9.1, 9.4, 9.10, 9.19–20, 10.1–2, 10.4, 10.8**). Roman oratory, like its earlier Greek counterpart, assumes an audience that is generally hostile to all forms of homosexuality, whether active or passive (**7.19–20, 7.59–64, 9.2, 9.4, 9.35–37;** cf. **10.1–2** for later Greek oratory under the Roman Empire). Despite the libertarian utterances of some early Stoics (**5.21–22**), Stoic philosophy of the Roman period was profoundly negative concerning any form of sex that could be considered "against Nature" (**9.10–13, 10.1, 10.4, 10.8**), a philosophical objection some sources advanced even during the Greek period (**4.11, 5.10–11, 5.17.65**). On the other hand, comic and satiric authors such as Plautus (**7.11–12, 7.15**) or Martial (**9.22, 9.28, 9.31**) did not find fault with pederastic attentions devoted to slaves, just as Aristophanes (**3.10**) did not. That the only positively valued same-gender relationships were those with slaves (and even those were questioned by some) reveals a culture whose discursive organs were even more uncomfortable with homosexuality than the Greeks' were, however many members of Roman society may have been involved with its practice.

Power Dynamics

The perception that Greek pederasty usually conformed to an age-differential model with the older partner as active wooer and the younger as the passive object of pursuit has led some scholars to see the active/passive polarity as fundamental to the significance of pederasty as a social institution.[8] That the older partner is typically the insertive agent in sexual acts depicted on Greek vases has led to claims that phallic penetration was an index of sociopolitical empowerment, and that boys, as passive "victims" of penetration (considered isomorphic to exploitation) were parallel to women, slaves, and foreigners as instrumental foils to the adult citizen males who wielded the political franchise and thereby the right to phallic supremacy.

However, one finds little support for this interpretation in the textual evidence, and even the iconographic tradition points toward a different conclusion: most man-boy couples are engaged in frontal and intercrural (i.e., "between the thighs") penetration, not oral or anal acts, and if anything, it is the man's awkward and distorted posture that shows signs of discomfort in an attempt to accommodate himself to his younger and usually shorter partner (see figs. 4b, 6–8, 20). The focus of erotic attention is usually not the boy's anus, but his developing penis, which the lover either fondles (figs. 6, 7, 10a, b, 12a, 20) or gazes at (figs. 17, 23); in other words, the interest is not in the boy as a passive receptacle, but as a young male who is himself budding and maturing into an active agent with sexual capabilities. Boys seemed quite free either to refuse or joyfully to accept men's advances (see

---

8. See Dover (1978) 84–91, 100–109; Halperin (1990) 15–40; Winkler (1990) 45–70. This view is frequently attributed to Foucault (1986), but in fact plays a fairly minor role in his treatment of Greek sexuality: for Foucault, the fundamental dichotomy is between being active (i.e., in control) or passive (i.e., controlled) in relation to one's own appetites. For a more detailed review of arguments against this position, see Hubbard (1998b) and Davidson (2001).

figs. 12c, 22 for rejection, figs. 10b, 19, 20 for what is clearly eager acceptance); in addition, a range of responses between outright rejection and full acceptance was available to boys (see Iconographic Conventions, below). Where oral or anal penetration occurs in Attic vase-painting, as might be expected if the point were to emphasize the active partner's power and control, the partners are either heterosexual or age-equal males (see figs. 8, 14, 15; figs. 5a, b actually show an unbearded youth penetrating a bearded man). Indeed, the realization that age-equal activity was not uncommon, as we have shown, profoundly undercuts any interpretation of Greek homosexuality in terms of "victim categories." Figure 24a shows two youths on pedestals, a self-confident musician in contraposto and a hesitant admirer about to offer him a crown; the admirer is on a slightly lower pedestal and bends his head down, as if to express shyness and diffidence.

To the extent that literary texts display a power differential, it is rather to emphasize the powerlessness and even emotional helplessness of the lover and a privileged position of control occupied by the beloved youth: this configuration permeates Greek lyric texts from the archaic to the Hellenistic period (**1.32–33, 1.35, 1.38–39, 1.42, 1.45–46, 1.54–55, 1.59–62, 1.64– 67, 1.70, 1.72–73, 1.75–76, 1.82–83, 1.85, 6.6, 6.10, 6.12–14, 6.25, 6.31, 6.35–36, 6.39, 6.41–44, 6.56, 6.72**; compare also Greek-influenced Roman texts such as **7.50, 8.4, 8.12**). Even poems in which a lover congratulates himself on becoming free of a youth's tyranny (**1.40, 1.43, 1.56, 1.69, 1.81**) or admonishes the youth to beware of the future (**1.49, 1.63, 6.26, 6.29–30, 6.32, 6.45, 6.51, 6.55, 6.68, 6.71, 6.80–81**) reflect a sense of desperation on the part of an unsuccessful lover. These protestations should not be dismissed as merely hollow convention.

Whatever advantage an older lover might have in experience, social connections, or verbal charm (see **1.34**), the youth had the countervailing power of Beauty on his side, which was a rarer commodity. Simple demographic reckoning tells us that eligible youths in that short-lived, but most desirable, window of efflorescence (from about fourteen to eighteen) were far fewer in number than the adult lovers who might pursue them (Greek men typically did not marry until their thirties). And even among the demographically eligible, many boys would either not be interested or would be closely guarded by their fathers or pedagogues (slave attendants); others would prefer the company of youths closer to their own age (as implied by Socrates' proverb "youth delights youth"). It was emphatically a seller's market. Vases seldom show more boys than wooers, but often the reverse (see figs. 4b, 6–8, but fig. 19 does show a crowd of boys); vases often show boys rejecting advances or acting noncommittal (for the former, see figs. 12c, 22; for the latter, see the boys on the far right in figs. 16, 17). Boys like Lysis and Charmides are surrounded by a mob of admirers in Plato's dialogues (**5.4– 5**), and even the hypothetical boy addressed in Lysias' and Socrates' discourses in the *Phaedrus* (**5.9**) is assumed to have his choice among several lovers and non-lovers (the latter being a less emotionally heated version of the former). Theognis continually complains of his many rivals for Cyrnus' favor (**1.39–40, 1.46–47, 1.52–53, 1.55–56, 1.64–65, 1.81**). The young Timarchus certainly had no shortage of older companions who were willing to pay extravagantly for the pleasure of his company (**4.7**). Lysias' *Against Simon* (**4.4**) narrates the conflict of two men who come to blows over a boy's favor. Plutarch tells us that the adolescent Alcibiades had many lovers who willingly put up with outrageous treatment at his hands, so great was their devotion (**2.5**). The most desirable boys were precisely those from elite families, like Alcibiades or Timarchus, and the goal of a pedagogical mentorship was not to objectify and subordinate them, but to advance their socialization into the elite male world of the symposium and athletics, and eventually politics and the life of the mind. Indeed, it was to make them as much like their lover as possible, a true mirror image. Only in this sense did a lover have a power over his beloved, but any beloved who did not appreciate the model his lover offered or who did not like the way he was treated in any other respect could easily find another lover, and the evidence is that they frequently did, even with no provocation.

Since our literary remains are overwhelmingly the work of adult men, boys' authentic voices from antiquity are rare, but two graffiti do appear to be written by boys: **2.22.549** proclaims a boy's pride in his beauty and pleasure in being courted by men, and **2.23.924** praises his lover's courage. Plato (**5.9.255**) views a boy's reciprocal affection for his lover as a common enough phenomenon to need philosophical explanation; Aristotle (**5.12, 5.14**) regards such reciprocal love as desirable and not uncommon, even though the source of pleasure each partner would derive from the relationship might be different. That the poets complain about the absence of mutual love more than they celebrate its fulfillment (however, see Asclepiades' epigram **6.2** or Anacreon's **1.34**) does not disprove its existence; one misses only what one sees that others sometimes possess. The poets' attention to the power of a beautiful boy's eyes to attract, captivate, and even inflame (**1.35, 1.85, 6.34–35, 6.39–41, 6.44, 6.56, 6.72**) suggests that boys also were perceived as active agents of vision and judgment concerning the qualities of their suitors.

If the Greeks' principal interest in pederasty were as an institutionalized phallic confirmation of the sociopolitical supremacy of adult citizen males, one would expect far more attention to pederastic relationships with slaves, as in Rome, or with lower-class boys. But as we have seen, it was boys of the best families who were most likely to attract admirers. Slaves are relatively seldom mentioned as objects of interest in classical Greek texts, and where they are, it is usually someone else's slave, as with Anacreon's interest in Smerdis (**1.29**) or Sophocles' in one of Hermesileus' slaves (**2.21.603–4**). In Xenophon's *Symposium* (**5.8.4.52–54**), the Syracusan entertainer worries that other men may attempt to sleep with his slave, but has no scruples about sleeping with the boy himself. In Greek comedy, an attractive slave boy is presented as an appropriate object of attention (**3.10**); we also hear of lower-class youths selling themselves through prostitution (**3.9, 3.17**). The availability of slaves to their own masters was considered unremarkable, although technically Athenian slaves did enjoy the protection of laws against rape (**4.7.15–17**); the attention of outsiders to one's slaves was more questionable. Neither slaves nor lower-class boy prostitutes become the object of discursive elaboration or erotic imagination to nearly the same extent as boys of good family who freely choose to enter into a pederastic liaison.[9]

In the Roman period, however, relationships with slaves received far more attention and became the normative image of pederasty. Some republican sources criticize expenditure on attractive Greek slaves as extravagant and unbefitting Roman simplicity (**7.17, 7.19, 7.63**); in imperial texts influenced by Stoicism this political critique is replaced by a moral critique of the slave's treatment (**9.1, 9.4, 9.10, 9.13**). Men's involvement with their own slave boys was frequently objectionable to their wives (see **7.47, 9.14.74– 75, 9.31**), which may be evidence of considerable personal intimacy and affection in such relationships. Statius' funeral eulogy for the dead slave boy of Flavius Ursus (**9.32**) illustrates just how deep the emotional attachment might be.

Even in master-slave relations, the dynamic was not necessarily one of unchecked power to dominate: Cicero reportedly complained that his slave Tiro refused his kisses (**7.65**), and Martial praises as his ideal boy slave one who will take the initiative in lovemaking and "act more like a free man than his master" (**9.22**). One master calls his slave a friend and companion, comparing his status to that of a Homeric squire serving a warrior-king (**6.87**). Many slave relationships would not involve the slave's own master, but someone outside the household: while some slaves were clearly vulnerable to threats and abusive treatment from outsiders (**9.33**), more often they need to be courted and persuaded (**6.77**). Many slave owners might object to their slaves becoming the object of other men's attentions (**9.28**).

Roman comedy gives slave characters significant roles and thereby supplies them a fictive voice to express their view of the sexual relationship into which they might be compelled. In Plautus' *Rope* (**7.7**), a slave feels fortunate to have a master who does not engage in such practices, and in *Pseudolus* (**7.12**), a slave feels humiliated by the implication that he had serviced his master when he was a boy. But earlier in the same play (**7.11**) an unattractive slave boy laments that he does not have a lover who can provide him

---

9. For a review of the limited evidence we have about the role of slaves in classical Greek homosexuality, see Golden (1984).

gifts and attention. In *The Persian* (**7.8**), a favorite slave hopes to obtain free-dom as a result of his relationship with his master. Haterius' much-derided statement (**9.3**) that sexual submission was a "necessity" for a slave and a "duty" for a freedman implies that many freedmen attained their status pre-cisely through submitting to their master's attentions. The rich freedman Trimalchio in Petronius' *Satyricon* boasts of having been his master's pet for fourteen years (**9.14.75–76**), to the extent that he could manipulate his mas-ter into not only freeing him, but even making him the principal heir of a vast estate. This evidence, even when drawn from fictional sources, suggests that the Romans themselves did not see slave-oriented pederasty in terms of power dynamics so much as an opportunity for slaves to improve their status.

Origin and Chronological Development

Most previous discussions of Greek and Roman homosexuality, although distinguishing between the two cultures, tend to treat each culture syn-chronically, as if attitudes and practices were relatively uniform over time.[10] However, reflection on the various social practices of homosexuality and swings in public attitudes toward it in Western societies just in the second half of the twentieth century should caution us against such static assump-tions in the case of ancient societies, which bore witness to many equally wrenching social and political transformations. One advantage of gather-ing texts together in the format this volume provides is that it allows de-tailed consideration of significant chronological developments within both Greece and Rome.

The origin of institutionalized homosexual practices in Greece has been a matter of considerable speculation and controversy, with some scholars tracing it back to Indo-European or Minoan origins.[11] Ancient texts vari-ously credit the Spartans (**2.10–13**) or Cretans (**2.15–16, 5.10–11**) with a special role as early practitioners, particularly in what may be initiatory con-texts. Some lyric texts (**1.4–27, 1.87**) and the Thera graffiti (**2.22**) may sup-port an initiatory interpretation.[12] The earliest artistic evidence (figs. 1–2) is Cretan and suggests a partnership of younger and older warriors. Aristotle (**2.15**) connects the introduction of the practice with overpopulation and the desire for a lower birthrate, possibly through delayed marriage. Our earliest textual evidence is from the early seventh century (**1.1–3, 2.22**), al-though Plutarch (**2.1**) relates an incident that, if historical, must have oc-curred around 735–730 B.C.E. There is no clear evidence for homosexual-

---

10. A notable exception in this regard is E. Cantarella (1992).
11. See the bibliographical note to chapter 2.
12. See the bibliographical notes to chapters 1 and 2.

ity in the epic poetry of Homer and Hesiod,[13] which could support a thesis of seventh-century origins, possibly in response to population issues.

The evidence is far more substantial for the fifth century and later, when one can note a progressive diminution in the status of pederasty at Athens, apparently in conjunction with the growth and radicalization of the democracy. In the earliest decades of the fifth century stands the legend of the tyrannicides Aristogeiton and Harmodius (**1.89, 2.2**, fig. 18), who are credited (falsely) with a decisive role in overthrowing the Peisistratid dynasty and inaugurating democratic self-governance. Their legend should be seen as an attempt to situate the practice of upper-class pederasty within the emergent democratic ideology. Art historians have noted that scenes of uninhibited pederastic courtship and sex are common on Athenian vases until about 460 (see figs. 4–17, 19–22), parallel to the celebration of pederastic love in the lyric poets; afterward, however, such representations (and, indeed, even explicit heterosexual scenes) virtually disappear in favor of much more coded arrangements, as in figs. 23–24.[14] This movement away from a libertine and hedonistic artistic style toward more prudish and "family-oriented" modalities seems to parallel the sexual conservatism and enforcement of moral norms evident in comedy and oratory of the late fifth and early fourth centuries, which, as we have seen, appeal emphatically to popular tastes and democratic values. Indeed, Thucydides' demythologizing critique of the Aristogeiton and Harmodius legend (**2.2**) should be interpreted in the same light. The ethics of self-restraint in regard to boys that is praised by Xenophon (**2.9–10, 5.1–3, 5.8**) also attests a growing moral problematization of pederasty in this period. It may not be incorrect to read the evolution of "Platonic love" in fourth-century texts as an attempt to rehabilitate pederasty by imagining a more modest and ethically acceptable form of the institution within a social environment that increasingly marginalized traditional pederasty as both nondemocratic (i.e., upper-class) and corrupting (i.e., teaching venality).[15]

In Rome attitudes toward homosexuality experienced equally significant chronological developments. Our earliest literary evidence, the comedies of Plautus (**7.7–15**), from around 200 B.C.E., take a fairly benign view of pederastic liaisons as long as they involve slaves. However, the comedies of Pomponius and Novius (**7.28–33**) and the satires of Lucilius (**7.23–27**), from about a century later, take on a sharper tone, emphasizing male pros-

---

13. The date of the Homeric epics is disputed, but is most commonly thought to be c. 700 B.C.E. Clarke (1978a) has suggested that the Achilles-Patroclus relationship in the *Iliad* may be erotic, as it certainly was for Aeschylus (**2.21.602; 5.7.180**). Against this view, see Barrett (1981) and Patzer (1982) 94–98. See also the discussion of Halperin (1990) 75–87.

14. See Shapiro (1981).

15. See Hubbard (2000) for a fuller exposition of this historical development.

titution, effeminacy, and free men who abandon their proper roles. During the second century B.C.E., a number of moralistic texts and utterances reject male love altogether, even involving slaves (**7.17, 7.19**), or worry about the effeminization of Roman manliness (**7.18, 7.20**) under the growing influence of Greek cultural mores. This contrast between Greek and Roman, together with the perception, which may or may not have been historically accurate, that pederasty was imported into Rome from Greece, also becomes a leitmotif in late republican discourse (**7.48, 7.52–55, 7.63**). Cicero feels free to use any association with homosexuality against his rhetorical opponents (**7.57–64**). It should not surprise us that sexuality became problematized at a time when Rome's national identity and political system were undergoing such profound transformations: indeed, the poet Catullus uses metaphors of sexual domination to express the loss of political liberty with the demise of the Republic (**7.43–44, 7.46**).

By the Augustan period, however, Rome's political destiny appeared settled and Greek cultural influence was taken for granted. Even if pederasty in the Greek style was still not fully assimilated, it appears to have been considered less of a threat. In moral and satirical texts of the first century C.E. and later, same-gender relations are often the focus of critical comment, but Greek influence is no longer the issue so much as the morally debilitating effects of wealth, power, and appetitive excess, all tendencies observable at the acme of the Roman Empire and embodied in the personae of the emperors. More detailed discussion of these developments in both Greek and Roman moral attitudes is better left to the introductions to the individual chapters.

Lesbianism

The vast majority of documents from antiquity were written by men, and to the extent that we have evidence about female sexuality, it is usually filtered through male biases. Our knowledge of female homoerotic practices is therefore less satisfactory than we might wish, since these by definition occurred in contexts from which males were excluded. Some of our earliest evidence comes from the late-seventh-century poetry of Sappho (**1.5–27**), which does express a genuinely female point of view. The social context of her involvement with what appear to be younger girls is disputed, however, with various scholars reconstructing initiatory, educational, or symposiastic milieus; Alcman's *First Maidens' Song* (**1.4**) may provide a contemporary parallel for female homoerotic pairing as an initiatory ritual, but this text is also hotly disputed. Anacreon (**1.31**) and possibly Archilochus (**1.3**) show knowledge of "lesbians" as a special class of women. Plutarch (**2.13**) tells us that female pederasty was practiced in Sparta alongside male pederasty. Greek authors who believe in some form of genetic determination of sexual identity, such as Hippocrates (**5.15**) or Aristophanes in Plato's *Symposium* (**5.7.189–93**), clearly include mannish or lesbian women as well as effeminate or homosexual men; this view may go back to Parmenides in the early fifth century (**10.5.134–35**).

As might be expected, the iconographic evidence for female homoeroticism is limited, but it does exist and some is quite early. A seventh-century plate from the island of Thera (fig. 3), where we know male pederasty was practiced in the same period (see **2.22**), shows two women with crowns, one touching the chin of the other in the courtship gesture frequently attested on archaic male courtship vases (see figs. 4b, 6, 7, 10a; for the crowns, see figs. 7, 11, 24a). On the black-figure pyxis discussed earlier, which illustrates on three separate panels the three forms of eroticized gender-pairing, the two women (fig. 4a) are wrapped together in a large tapestry or coverlet, as if to display together a product that characterizes the principal female domestic/economic activity—weaving. Another scene of female intimacy is depicted by figure 13, which some have interpreted as one woman masturbating another, but others have taken to be depilation or perfuming of the woman's genitals; the vessel the standing woman holds may be either a wine cup or a container for the perfume. Even under the latter scenario, however, the scene is still one of eroticized female intimacy. Figure 9 shows two women embracing and offering a hare to Dionysus, suggesting that the release of inhibitions offered by the celebration of the Bacchic mysteries and other all-female rituals might be a context for female homoeroticism. In all these scenes, the women appear to be equal in age and stature. With the possible exception of figure 3, gift-exchange is not emphasized, and with the possible exception of figure 13, the sexual dimension of their relationship is understated and implied.

In the Hellenistic period, Herondas, a writer of satirical mimes, suggests that the female poet Nossis may have had a particular need for a dildo (**6.20**). Although Nossis' poetry is not explicitly homoerotic, it does exhibit a keen appreciation of female beauty, and she declares Sappho as her model (**6.16–19**). From Greco-Roman Egypt in the second to third centuries C.E., we have two magical spells (**10.34, 10.36**) attempting to bind one woman to another, which confirm that such relationships actually took place and could be quite intense and passionate. Male authors from the Hellenistic (**6.1**) through the Roman periods (**9.2, 9.11, 9.18, 9.26–27, 10.5.132–33, 10.9, 10.37.28**) for the most part take an extremely hostile view of female homoeroticism as the worst perversion of natural order. Ovid's story of Iphis and Ianthe (**8.21**) treats sympathetically a girl's attraction to another girl, but denies the possibility of a true lesbian relationship by transforming one of the girls into a boy at the end.

Iconographic Conventions

Artistic evidence for both male (fig. 2) and female homoeroticism (fig. 3) goes back to the seventh century B.C.E., and perhaps even as far as Minoan times (fig. 1).[16] The most abundant evidence, however, is Athenian vase-painting from the sixth and fifth centuries (figs. 4–17, 19–24); for this period it is an indispensable supplement to the literary material in reconstructing social practices. Like literary evidence, it needs to be interpreted as an ideal projection in many cases, rather than as unmediated transcription of contemporary realia. Even so, the variety of acts, positions, and practices portrayed on vases suggest a representational aesthetics that was not merely conventional. The limitations of the present volume prevent anything that even approaches an exhaustive catalogue or discussion of artistic evidence.[17] Instead, I have attempted to present one or two examples of characteristic or significant scenes from various artistic media.

One of the most common motifs on Athenian vases is what is generally labeled as "courtship" of boys or youths by men or, in some cases, by youths who are scarcely much older. Gifts might include hares (figs. 8, 16, 17, 19), deer (fig. 7), fighting cocks (figs. 4b, 6, 7, 17), crowns (figs. 7, 11, 24a), flowers (figs. 6, 17), mantles (perhaps fig. 12b), slabs of meat (fig. 21), or even a bag of coins (fig. 16), suggesting that the dividing line between gift-giving and prostitution might be tenuous. The presence of lyres in many scenes suggests that musical ability was a major source of appeal in youths (figs. 12c, 22, 23, 24a; cf. figs. 25, 26a from the Roman period, the former actually showing a scene of pederastic musical instruction). The progression beyond mere courtship to actual physical contact is depicted with great variety. In addition to chin-touching gestures (figs. 4b, 6, 7, 10a, 12d), one finds lovers touching boys' shoulders (figs. 10a, b, 12d, 22), buttocks (fig. 6), and fondling their penises (figs. 6, 7, 10a, b, 12a, 20).

Some vases display multiple pairs of lovers in different stages of seduction: for example, figure 7 shows on the left an ithyphallic man merely touching the youth's chin as the youth walks away with his gift, but the pair on the right stand closer together as the man fondles the youth's penis, and the central pair have progressed to the point of full intercrural intercourse. In figure 11, the youth on the right merely looks at a naked boy exercising, but the youth on the left crowns a boy, who stands still to accept the award,

---

16. See Koehl (1986).

17. Such a work still remains to be assembled. Numerous illustrations are available in Dover (1978) and in Koch-Harnack (1983), who provides the most complete study of courtship conventions to date. For other recent work on pederasty in Greek vase-painting, see Shapiro (1981), (1992), and (2000); Hupperts (1988); Kilmer (1997); and K. De Vries (1997). For iconographic evidence of female homoeroticism, see Rabinowitz and Auanger (2002), especially 106–66 and 211–55.

and the central pair is again privileged as the most advanced, inasmuch as the youth embraces the boy and positions his head to join in a kiss.

The wine cooler by Smikros displays four pairs in a continuous wrap-around sequence, ranging from clear rejection of the suitor by a fully clothed boy who walks away (fig. 12c) to a youth who places one hand on a boy's shoulder and reaches for his chin with the other (fig. 12d) to a youth who reaches out to touch another's penis (fig. 12b—the beloved here opens up his mantle to reveal his naked body to his wooer and reciprocates by touching the wooer's arm) to a pair who embrace and kiss as the lover fondles the boy's penis (fig. 12a). It may be significant that the two pairs who are furthest advanced in their contact and reciprocation are the two who appear to be closest to each other in age and stature, as if to imply that boys are more likely to accept physical intimacy with youths who are closer in age to themselves.

On two cups by Macron we see the use of clothing to designate varying degrees of engagement or interest: in figure 17, the man on the right offers a flower or crown to an unresponsive boy who remains tightly wrapped in his mantle, whereas the youth in the center offers a hare to a boy who reaches out to accept it and throws back his garment enough to reveal his shoulder and breast, and the boy on the left opens up his clothing to reveal a view of his entire body to the youth who offers him a cock and visibly looks down to examine his penis. The more flesh is revealed, the more responsive a boy appears to be; interestingly, the more the boys reveal also corresponds to the value of the gifts offered, but it also bears noting that the least responsive boy is the one with the greatest age difference relative to his suitor (compare the little boy on the left in fig. 19, tightly wrapped in his cloak). We see the same use of clothing in figure 16, where the boy who has accepted a hare throws back his cloak, whereas the two boys on each side keep their clothes tightly wrapped around their arms; however, the boy on the left does acknowledge his suitor's money bag by looking up to reciprocate the suitor's gaze and parting his lips as if to speak, in contrast to the boy on the right, who modestly looks down and keeps his lips closed (compare the boys on the right and left in fig. 11). Reciprocal eye contact (or the lack of it) also appears to be a significant motif in the later work of the Eretria Painter (figs. 24a, b, c) and his contemporaries.

Depictions of explicit sexual acts do not always come in a courtship context. When they do, they usually involve fondling a boy's penis or frontal intercrural penetration. The one exception (fig. 8) involves a contrast between a bearded lover and youth on the left, engaged in the usual intercrural posture, and two unbearded youths on the right, engaged in anal intercourse. In the latter pair, the active partner is stouter and larger than the youth he is penetrating, but this difference is not necessarily an index of age, since he is in fact stouter than the bearded man on the left. Is the contrast between a more mature suitor who knows the conventions better and a less-experienced lover who plugs away with less heed of his favorite's comfort? Or is it the case of a younger and more athletic lover whose favorite is willing to give him more?

The other context in which one finds explicit sexual action is *komastic,* that is, involving drunken parties or revels. Figure 5a shows a line of men dancing up to a wine bowl. Immediately to the left of the wine bowl a bearded man penetrates a sexually indeterminate figure from the rear; the ithyphallic man behind him seems to be waiting for his turn to do the same, as perhaps the rest of the figures in the line hope to do. To the right of the wine bowl, a bearded man reaches into the bowl to ladle out its contents while an unbearded youth penetrates him anally. Clearly, wine loosens sexual inhibitions (as Anacreon reminds us in **1.30**), and in a state of intoxication one can ignore all the conventional proprieties and rules about who penetrates whom or where one is supposed to place one's organs. Similarly, figure 15 shows seven age-equal youths engaged in a wild naked dance combined with sexual horseplay: one youth, who stares directly at us, as if inviting us to join, places his penis between the buttocks of two others, while another ithyphallic youth approaches from the left with outstretched arms, perhaps offering himself to be fellated by the youth next to him, but clearly intending to join the fun in some form. Such naked dances of youths, although usually without the overtly sexual element, are common in *komastic* settings, with drinking accoutrements frequently depicted. Let us not forget that this scene appears on a wine cup. This sexual abandon under the influence of Dionysus, the god of wine, is represented mythologically by the revel of satyrs (Dionysus' male followers) in figure 14: here we see bearded, adult figures engaged in fellatio, upside-down anal intercourse, and even bestiality (as one satyr attempts to penetrate a sphinx). The presence of a grapevine in the background punctuates the influence of wine in releasing men to fulfill their animal natures (represented by the satyrs' horse-tails and pointed ears). Figure 9 shows Dionysus producing a similar, if more understated, effect on women.

CHAPTER 1

Archaic Greek Lyric

Homoerotic themes abound in Greek lyric poetry from the seventh to the early fifth centuries B.C.E., and this material provides our earliest literary evidence. As with all literary and artistic works, one must take into account that the texts are not a direct transcription of social realities, but are idealized projections. Nevertheless, they reflect an aristocratic culture in which homosexual relations were at home in the symposium, athletics, and even civic/religious ritual.

The earliest surviving lyric poetry is by Archilochus, active on the islands of Paros and Thasos in the first half of the seventh century B.C.E. Although he actually wrote in a variety of meters, he is usually called an "iambic" poet, because that meter was especially associated with the harsh satire and invective for which he is best known. Archilochus' poetic persona presumes to represent the grumblings of the common man against the wealthy and powerful; his attacks on practitioners of same-gender love (**1.1–3**) should perhaps be understood in this context.

Alcman was a choral poet of the late seventh century, active in Sparta, which at that time may have been a very different society from the austere, rigidly disciplined military state known in later Greek history. He is most famous for his "maidens' songs." A papyrus preserves a large portion of one (**1.4**): the style appears obscure, allusive, and gossipy. The poem gives the impression of having been composed for a specific performance by a particular group of girls, but the names could be ritual pseudonyms assumed by different choruses. Critics have not implausibly supposed the performance to be part of a female initiation ceremony or cult, perhaps celebrating a union of the two most prominently featured girls, Hagesichora and Agido. A marital context may also be indicated by the narration of a Spartan myth about Castor and Polydeuces' quest to marry the daughters of

Leucippus. If the initiatory interpretation of this complex poem is correct, it could provide evidence for lesbian unions as a ritualized preparation of adolescent girls for later heterosexual marriage. In this case, the girls seem to be age-equals.

This type of ceremonial initiation in advance of marriage may also be the context for the nearly contemporary poems by Sappho of Lesbos, many of which treat female homoeroticism in explicit terms. Sappho certainly did not view herself as offering an alternative to heterosexual marriage; she was herself married and had a daughter named Cleis. Some of her poems seem to have been choral wedding hymns celebrating heterosexual marriage (**1.8, 1.22**), often in a bawdy and suggestive way (**1.21, 1.24**); others explore a young girl's feelings over the loss of virginity (**1.18, 1.19, 1.20, 1.23**). The poems seem resigned to the inevitability of the women being separated, no matter how great their love (see especially **1.9, 1.16, 1.17**), but recognize that a bond of sweet memories of pleasant times spent together will continue to unite them (**1.13, 1.14, 1.16, 1.17**). **1.14** identifies Sappho's relationship quite clearly as one with a young girl; **1.5** implies that Sappho's young beloved is someone who has not yet learned what it is like to be a pursuing agent in a love relationship, but who soon will. These female relationships therefore seem to conform to the same age-differential pattern as was common with male pederasty.

Some critics see the context of Sappho's social circle as musical and educational rather than initiatory; several older critics even went so far as to deny any physical involvement with the girls she addresses. One recent critic has speculated that there existed a society of female symposia on archaic Lesbos similar to male drinking parties, but there is no convincing parallel for such an institution anywhere in Greece. Wine and banquet imagery play comparatively little role in Sappho's poetry. The world she evokes is rather one of outdoor freedom amid the splendor and sensual delights of an open and bountiful Nature. In this realm her sensibilities and fineness of expression excel those of any male counterpart.

Anacreon and Ibycus were both associated with the court of Polycrates, the tyrant who ruled Samos from about 535 to 522 B.C.E. and was an illustrious patron of the arts. Anacreon's poems (**1.29–34**) tend to be witty and epigrammatic. Ibycus' work (**1.35–36**) at its best can be richly sensuous and lyrical. Testimonia tell us that he also wrote narrative poems telling of the mythological loves of Zeus for Ganymede and Talos for Rhadamanthys (frr. 289, 309 PMG). Like Sappho, both poets stress the lover's sense of helplessness and lack of self-control.

The same theme is featured in Theognis' many epigrams addressed to the boy Cyrnus. The Theognid collection (**1.37–83**) is one of our most extensive samples of Greek shorter verse, indeed the only one, aside from Pindar's odes for athletes, to survive as an actual manuscript, rather than as fragmentary papyri or quotations preserved by other authors. However, it is considered by many critics not to be the work of a single poet, but to represent several generations of wisdom poetry gathered together at Megara and attributed to the name of "Theognis," who may or may not have been an actual poet of the sixth century. What can be said about this corpus is that it presents a unified persona and set of attitudes, particularly in regard to the pederastic theme: cynical, quarrelsome, resentful, ever ready to accuse, but nevertheless helplessly devoted. Most of the poems in the corpus are not specifically amatory, but are social, political, or ethical precepts transmitted to Cyrnus as part of his formation into an adult Megarian aristocrat in Theognis' own image. Theognis' ever-gnawing suspicion of Cyrnus' promiscuous flirtations with less worthy men may function as an allegory for his anxiety that the Megarian body politic has deserted aristocrats like himself in favor of an endless succession of "new men," whose wealth is based on trade and commerce. The pederastic, pedagogical, and political levels are all mutually imbricated in this collection.

From Simonides of Ceos (556–468 B.C.E.) we have an intriguing new fragment (1.84) in which he imagines himself, possibly in the afterlife, in the embraces of the fair young Thessalian prince Echecratidas. That pederastic motifs could be employed without embarrassment in praise of the rich and mighty is also suggested by a fragment of Ibycus (fr. 282[a] PMG, not in this collection) in which the physical beauty of the young Polycrates is praised and compared to that of the heroes at Troy. Pindar of Thebes (518–c. 440 B.C.E.) wrote as one of his earliest commissions a choral ode for the adolescent athlete Hippocleas (1.86), in which he also praises the Thessalian prince Thorax, who was apparently the boy's lover and patron.

Even though Pindar declared that pederastic poems written out of personal devotion to a boy are now passé (*Isthmian* 2.1–11), he found ample opportunity to incorporate pederastic themes into his poetry. Admiration for the naked bodies of youthful athletes is a leitmotif throughout Pindar's encomiastic work. One of the most significant Pindaric texts is 1.87, a choral ode for Hieron, the ruler of Syracuse, which narrates the myth of Poseidon's love for the boy Pelops. The myth clearly exhibits an initiatory structure and significance: the boy's pederastic interlude with Poseidon is presented as enabling his later marriage to Hippodameia, and proves to be the critical transition between his childhood in Lydia and his claim to adult stature as a superior athletic competitor who can vanquish Hippodameia's cruel and tyrannical father.

To summarize, archaic Greek lyric generally describes age-differential pederastic relations, although there is some evidence for relations or attractions among age-equal youths in Alcman (1.4), Theognis (1.41, 1.65), and Pindar (1.86). Only one text seems unequivocally to describe attraction to a slave (Anacreon 1.29), but Anacreon's Cleobulus or Ibycus' Euryalus could also very well be slaves. Older lovers frequently describe themselves as at the mercy of their beloved or even captivated, but their disadvantage is sometimes counterbalanced by warnings that youth's glory is brief or that time will soon put the beloved in a position like their own (**1.5, 1.41, 1.62, 1.63, 1.67**). Significantly, we find nascent in these poets a consciousness of sexual preference as something distinctive: different people enjoy different erotic pleasures, and boy-love is not universal (Archilochus **1.1**; Theognis **1.73, 1.77, 1.78**; Pindar **1.85, 1.86**).

Bibliographical Note

On archaic Greek lyric and homosexuality generally, see Buffière (1980) 239–77, E. Cantarella (1992) 12–16, and especially Percy (1996) 95–184, although the last is sometimes prone to press the evidence too far.

On homosexual themes in Archilochus, see Burnett (1983) 74–75.

For the interpretation of Alcman's *First Maidens' Song* as a same-sex betrothal, see Gentili (1988) 73–77, drawing on the important work of Calame (1997), especially 207–63, concerning the poem's initiatory character; Calame, however, sees the homosexual element as a bond between the chorus-leader and younger girls of the chorus. See, in addition, the detailed commentary on the poem in Calame (1983), and the remarks of Lasserre (1974) 5–10, 30–33. Parker (1993) 325–31 insists that the erotic language of this poem pertains only to relationships among the age-equal chorus members themselves. Others have seen the context of the poem as entirely heterosexual, either as a wedding hymn for Hagesichora (Griffiths [1972]) or as an advertisement of the girls' attractiveness to a male audience (Clark [1996], Stehle [1997] 30–39, 73–88). On the relation of the myth to the rest of the poem, see Robbins (1994) and Too (1997).

For the theory that Sappho was engaged in a voluntary female initiation process, see Hallett (1979), Burnett (1983) 209–28, Gentili (1988) 77–89, and Calame (1997) 249–52. For Sappho's circle as educational, see Merkelbach (1957). For a critical history of these and other constructions of Sappho's social context, see Parker (1993); however, his own view of a society of age-equal relationships amid female symposia is no less speculative and is attacked by Lardinois (1994). For a good general introduction to Sappho's work, see Williamson (1995); for a more personal view from a Marxist/feminist perspective, see du Bois (1995). See also Burnett (1983) 229–313 and Snyder (1997) for readings of the major poems. For a collection of several important articles, all previously published, see Greene (1996a). In addition to these, see Svenbro (1984) on **1.5, 1.7**, and **1.9**; Greene (2002) on **1.5, 1.7**, and **1.16**; Wills (1967) and Race (1989) on **1.7**; Privitera (1969), Devereux (1970), McEvilley (1978), and Latacz (1985) on **1.9**; Carey

(1978) and Hague (1984) on **1.17**. On Sappho's later reputation and literary influence, see De Jean (1989), Greene (1996b), and Prins (1999).

On erotic themes in Anacreon, see Goldhill (1987) and Gentili (1988) 89–104. On transvestism and possible satire against effeminates, see Slater (1978), Brown (1983), and S. D. Price (1990), but it is unclear whether the fragment in question (fr. 388 PMG) has anything to do with homosexuality.

On Theognis' pederastic poems, see Lewis (1985) and Edmunds (1987). Vetta (1980) provides extensive commentary on all the poems of "book 2" (see **1.44**). Hunter (1993b) and Mace (1996) discuss Simonides, **1.84**.

For Pindar's use of erotic motifs to celebrate boy victors in his epinician odes, see von der Mühll (1964), Lasserre (1974) 17–20, Crotty (1982) 92–103, Instone (1990), Steiner (1998) 136–42, and Hubbard (2003). N. Nicholson (2000) shows how these motifs are extended to adult patrons as well. N. Nicholson (1998) shows how expressions of pederastic desire in Pindar and Theognis confirm authorial assertions of truth and sincerity. On **1.85** and **1.86**, see Hubbard (2002). On innovative and traditional elements in the Pelops myth of **1.87**, see Kakridis (1930), Köhnken (1974), and Howie (1983). On its application to the praise of Hieron, see Cairns (1977) and Burgess (1993). For its initiatory structure and significance, see Sergent (1986) 57–78 and Hubbard (1987). Gerber (1982) provides a detailed commentary.

On the Harmodius song, see Ehrenberg (1956) and the items noted in the bibliographical note of chapter 2.

1.1 Archilochus, fragment 25.1–5 West

The following fragment comes from a tattered papyrus first published in 1954. Italicized words are editorial conjecture.

. . . man's nature *is not the same,*
But each man delights his heart in something different.
. . . cock pleases Melesander,
. . . pleases the shepherd Phalangius.
No prophet other than I tells this to you.

1.2 Archilochus, fragment 117 W

Sing of Glaucus the horn-molder.[1]

---

1. The scholiast who quotes this fragment takes "horn-molder" as a reference to a man who braids his long hair into a pointed "horn," an affected archaic hairstyle, but Archilochus may also mean this phrase in an obscene sense (horn = penis). In either case, the line may be meant as a parody of the first line of Homer's *Iliad*.

1.3 Archilochus, fragment 294 W

The following are not the actual words of Archilochus but a quotation from the late oracle-critic Oenomaus, invoking Archilochus' familiar subject matter.

What do you bid us to do, if we are to appear worthy of your hospitality? Are we, in the style of Archilochus, in metrical form, to revile women who don't wish to marry us[2] and grab hold of perverts *(kinaidoi)*, since they are by far the basest among all other base men?

1.4 Alcman, *First Maidens' Song* 34–101

This song was probably performed in Sparta by a female chorus (or two semichoruses) led by Hagesichora and Agido. Some commentators consider it to be an initiation rite, perhaps even a betrothal of the two chorus leaders. The poem is preserved on a papyrus that breaks off abruptly after v. 101. The first thirty-three lines are very fragmentary: they seem to narrate a story from Spartan mythology, the killing of the ten sons of King Hippocoon by their cousins Castor and Polydeuces, who were rival suitors for the same pair of maidens. V. 34 begins by justifying the act.

. . . they suffered unforgettably
After contriving evil deeds—   35
There is a vengeance of the gods—
But he is blessed, who with wisdom
Weaves his day to the end
Without tears. And I sing
Of Agido's radiance: I see   40
Her as the sun, which Agido
Calls as witness to shine
For us. Yet for me either to praise
Or blame her, the glorious chorus leader[3]
In no way allows, but she herself   45
Stands out just as if someone
Should set among the herds a horse,

---

2. This could be a reference to Archilochus' attacks on the daughters of Lycambes. According to legend, one of the daughters was engaged to the poet until her father broke off the engagement. But given the emphasis on the women's own volition and their juxtaposition with male *kinaidoi,* this could also be a reference to lesbianism.

3. Hagesichora, whose name means "leader of the chorus/dance."

Sturdy, prize-winning, thunderhoofed,
From dreams beneath the rock.[4]

Don't you see? The racer   50
Is Enetic,[5] but the hair
Of my cousin
Hagesichora blooms
Like pure gold,
And her silver face—   55
Why should I tell you clearly?
Here is Hagesichora,
But the second after Agido in beauty
Will run as a Kolaxian horse with an Ibenian:
For these Peleiades,[6] rising through ambrosial   60
Night like the star Sirius,[7]
While we bring the robe[8] to Orthria,[9]
Fight with us.

Neither could such an abundance
Of purple exist as to defend us,   65
Nor an intricate snake[10]
All gold, nor Lydian
Headband, the delight
Of dark-eyed girls,
Not Nanno's hair,[11]   70
Nor even divine Areta,

4. An ancient note in the papyrus says this refers to afternoon dreams of a man who sleeps in the shade of a rock; other commentators think that the Greek word may be a dialectal variant for "winged" dreams.

5. I.e., Venetian: the flatlands of the northern Adriatic were a famous horse-raising area in antiquity.

6. The "Doves," a cluster of six stars visible just before dawn in the late spring sky: some commentators take this as a metaphorical name for Hagesichora and Agido (who are imagined as outshining the rest of the chorus), while others take it as the name of a rival chorus.

7. An exceptionally bright star: the comparison intensifies the brilliance attributed to the Peleiades, which are actually much fainter.

8. The Greek word may also mean "plow," which would be an appropriate offering if this ceremony is part of a spring fertility ritual. But robes were common offerings to goddesses as well.

9. Probably the dawn goddess, to be identified with Aotis in v. 88. The chorus' fight with the Peleiades could be meant to represent the battle between night and dawn.

10. Probably a bracelet or armlet.

11. This and the following names may be those of the other chorus members. Aenesimbrota may be the chorus trainer.

Not Sylacis and Clesisera;
Nor once at Aenesimbrota's will you say:
"Oh that Astaphis be mine,
May Philylla look over   75
And Damareta and desired Ianthemis"—
But Hagesichora overwhelms me.

For isn't lovely-ankled
Hagesichora here?
She remains beside Agido   80
And praises our feasts.
O gods, receive their *prayers:*
From gods come success
And fulfillment. Chorus leader,
I would speak—myself a girl   85
Screeching in vain, an owl
From a rafter—still I want most
To please Aotis,[12] since she has been
The healer of our toils;
But through Hagesichora young women   90
Enter into desired peace.[13]

For . . . by the trace-horse[14]
.   .   .   .

And on a ship one must
Listen above all to the navigator.   95
Yet she is *not* more musical
Than the Sirens:[15]
They are goddesses, but instead of eleven
These ten girls sing;[16]

12. See n. 9.
13. Probably a metaphor for victory in choral competition. Compare the battle metaphor
of v. 63.
14. In a four-horse chariot team, the trace-horse was the one on the outside and opposite to the direction of turns in the course; it therefore had to be the strongest and swiftest of
the four horses. Here, it is probably a metaphor for the chorus leader, just like the navigator
in v. 95.
15. Divine temptresses who lured sailors to shipwreck with their beautiful songs.
16. This chorus apparently consisted of ten girls—Hagesichora, Agido, and perhaps the
eight named in vv. 70–76. The sense of the ten being equal to eleven may be that Hagesichora
is so good as to take the place of two.

She sings like a swan on the streams   100
Of Xanthus.[17] The one with alluring golden hair . . .

1.5 Sappho, fragment 1 Voigt

This text is probably a complete poem in the genre of a "cletic hymn," summoning a god's presence.

On the throne of many hues, immortal Aphrodite,
Child of Zeus, weaving wiles—I beg you
Not to subdue my spirit, Queen,
    With pain or sorrow,
But come—if ever before[18]   5
Having heard my voice from far away
You listened, and leaving your father's
    Golden home you came
In your chariot yoked with swift, lovely
Sparrows bringing you over the dark Earth,   10
Thick-feathered wings swirling down
    From the sky through mid-air,
Arriving quickly—you, Blessed One,
With a smile on your unaging face
Asking again what I have suffered   15
    And why I am calling again
And in my wild heart what did I most wish
To happen to me: "Again whom must I persuade
Back into the harness of your love?
    Sappho, who wrongs you?   20
For if she flees, soon she'll pursue;
She doesn't accept gifts, but she'll give;
If not now loving, soon she'll love
    Even against her will."
Come to me now again, release me from   25
This pain, everything my spirit longs
To have fulfilled, fulfill, and you
    Be my ally.

17. A fabled river in Asia Minor.
18. This is a typical convention of Greek prayers called a *hypomnesis,* a reminder of past services either by the supplicant to the divinity or vice versa.

1.6 Sappho, fragment 2 V

Come to me from Crete to this holy
Temple, to the apple grove,
The altars smoking
   With frankincense,
Cold water ripples through apple   5
Branches, the whole place shadowed
In roses, from the murmuring leaves
   Deep sleep descends,
Where horses graze, the meadow blooms
Spring flowers, the winds   10
Breathe softly . . .

. . . . . .

Here, Cypris,[19] after gathering . . .
Pour into golden cups
Nectar lavishly   15
   Mingled with joys.

1.7 Sappho, fragment 16 V

Some say an army of horsemen, others
Say foot-soldiers, still others, a fleet,
Is the fairest thing on the dark Earth.
   I say it is whatever one loves.
Everyone can understand this—   5
Consider that Helen, far surpassing
The beauty of mortals, leaving behind
   The best man of all,[20]
Sailed away to Troy. She had no
Memory of her child or dear parents,   10
Since she was led astray
(two missing verses)
. . . lightly
. . . reminding me now of Anactoria   15
   being gone,
I would rather see her lovely step

---

19. An alternate name for Aphrodite, the love goddess, derived from her birth on the island of Cyprus.
20. Her husband, Menelaus, the king of Sparta.

And the radiant sparkle of her face
Than all the war-chariots in Lydia[21]
   And soldiers battling in shining bronze.   20

1.8 Sappho, fragment 30 V

The following fragment comes from a wedding hymn. Italicized words are editorial conjecture.

Night . . .
Virgins . . .
Celebrate all night . . .
May sing of your love and
The violet-robed bride.
But once roused, go *call*
The unwed men your age
So we may see *less* sleep
Than the clear-voiced *bird*.

1.9 Sappho, fragment 31 V

To me it seems
That man[22] has the fortune of the gods,
Whoever sits beside you, and close,
   Who listens to you sweetly speaking
And laughing temptingly;   5
My heart flutters in my breast,
Whenever I look quickly, for a moment—
   I say nothing, my tongue broken,
A delicate fire runs under my skin,
My eyes see nothing, my ears roar,   10
Cold sweat rushes down me,
   Trembling seizes me,
I am greener than grass,
To myself I seem
Needing but little to die.   15
   But all must be endured, since . . .

21. A kingdom in northwestern Asia Minor, at this time known for its magnificent wealth.
22. Possibly the girl's husband or fiancé.

1.10 Sappho, fragment 34 V

The stars around the fair moon
Hide away their radiant form
Whenever in fullness she lights
    The Earth . . .[23]

1.11 Sappho, fragment 36 V

I both desire and pursue . . .

1.12 Sappho, fragment 47 V

Love shook my senses,
Like wind crashing on mountain oaks.

1.13 Sappho, fragment 48 V

You came and did *well;* I felt for you
And you cooled my spirit burning with desire.

1.14 Sappho, fragment 49 V

I loved you, Atthis, once long ago . . .
You seemed to me a small child and without charm.

1.15 Sappho, fragment 55 V

Sappho addresses a female rival. It is unclear whether their dispute was poetic or amatory.

When you die you'll lie dead; no memory of you,
No desire will survive, since you've no part
Of the Pierian roses.[24] But once gone,
You'll flutter among the obscure,[25]
Invisible still in the house of Hades.

---

23. This image may be meant to describe a woman whose beauty outshines all others, as with the beauty comparisons of Alcman's *First Maidens' Song.*
   24. Another name for the Muses was the Pierides.
   25. Souls of the dead were sometimes imagined as having wings.

1.16 Sappho, fragment 94 V

"I simply wish to die."
Weeping she left me
And said this too:
   "We've suffered terribly.
   Sappho, I leave you against my will."   5
I answered, "Go happily
   And remember me,
   You know how we cared for you;
If not, let me remind you
   . . . the lovely times we shared.   10
   Many crowns of violets,
Roses and crocuses
   . . . together you set before me,
   And many scented wreaths
Made from blossoms   15
   Around your soft throat . . .
   . . . with pure, sweet oil
. . . you anointed me,
   And on a soft, gentle bed . . .
   You quenched your desire . . .   20
. . . no holy site . . .
   We left uncovered,
   No grove . . . dance
. . . sound

1.17 Sappho, fragment 96 V

In this poem, Sappho consoles her friend Atthis for the loss of a girl who has gone to Sardis, presumably to be married.

   . . . Sardis[26] . . .
Often holding her thoughts here

. . . .

   You, like a goddess undisguised,
   But she rejoiced especially in your song.   5
Now she stands out among
   Lydian women as after sunset
   The rose-fingered moon
Exceeds all stars; light

26. The capital of Lydia (see n. 21).

Reaches equally over the brine sea   10
  And thick-flowering fields,
A beautiful dew has poured down,
  Roses bloom, tender parsley
  And blossoming honey clover.
Pacing far away, she remembers   15
  Gentle Atthis with desire,
  Perhaps . . . consumes her delicate soul;
To go there . . . this not
  Knowing . . . much
  She sings . . . in the middle.   20
It is not easy for us to rival
  The beautiful form of goddesses,
  . . . you might have . . .
(two lines are missing)
  And . . . Aphrodite
. . . poured nectar from
  A golden . . .
  . . . with her hands Persuasion . . .

1.18 Sappho, fragment 105(a) V

The sweet apple reddens on a high branch,
High upon highest, missed by the apple-pickers:
No, they didn't miss, so much as couldn't touch.[27]

1.19 Sappho, fragment 105(b) V

Herdsmen crush under their feet
A hyacinth in the mountains; on the ground
Purple blooms . . .[28]

1.20 Sappho, fragment 107 V

Do I still desire virginity?

1.21 Sappho, fragment 111 V

Raise high the roof
  —Hymen!—

---

27. The image may be a metaphor for an untouched virgin.
28. Some see the image as one of virginity violated.

You carpenter men.
　—Hymen!—
The bridegroom approaches like Ares,[29]
　—Hymen!—
Much bigger than a big man.[30]

1.22 Sappho, fragment 112 V

Happy bridegroom, the marriage that you prayed for
Has been fulfilled—you have the girl you prayed for.
Your form is graceful, eyes . . .
Gentle, and love flows over your alluring face
. . . Aphrodite has honored you above all.

1.23 Sappho, fragment 114 V

BRIDE: Virginity, virginity, where have you gone, leaving me behind?
VIRGINITY: Never again will I come to you, never again.

1.24 Sappho, fragment 115 V

With what, dear bridegroom, can I fairly compare you?
With a slender sapling I shall best compare you.[31]

1.25 Sappho, fragment 130(b) V

Atthis, for you the thought of me has become hateful,
And you fly off to Andromeda.

1.26 Sappho, fragment 147 V

I say someone in another time will remember us.

1.27 Sappho, fragment 168(b) V

The moon and Pleiades have set.
Half the night is gone.

---

29. The god of war, an imposing masculine figure.
30. Wedding songs often feature teasing obscenity: the reference here may be to the groom's erect member.
31. See n. 30.

Time passes.
I sleep alone . . .

1.28 Solon, fragment 25 West

Solon was a prominent Athenian statesman and lawgiver active in the first quarter of the sixth century. He transmitted many of his moral and political precepts in verse, but the authenticity of short aphorisms like this one is uncertain; many similar aphorisms are found in the Theognid corpus.

. . . While one loves boys among the lovely flowers of youth,[32]
    Desiring their thighs and sweet mouths.

1.29 Anacreon, fragment 347 *Poetae Melici Graeci*

Athenaeus (12.540e) and Aelian (VH 9.4) record that Anacreon's praise of the boy Smerdis provoked the jealousy of the tyrant Polycrates, who ordered the boy's long hair cut off. The beginning of the fragment is missing.

. . . *(you lack)* the hair, which once shaded
    Your neck in abundance.
But now you are smooth-browed,
And your hair, falling into rough hands,
Has tumbled down in a heap .   5
    Into the black dust.[33]
Bravely did it meet the slash of steel.
But I am wasted away with sorrow.
For what can one do,
    When one fails even for Thrace?[34]   10

1.30 Anacreon, fragment 357 PMG

This text, probably a complete poem, is a cletic hymn (see 1.5 and 1.6) to Dionysus, the god of wine. But the poem functions as a riddle, since the god's identity and relevance are not revealed until the end. Drunkenness will make the boy more receptive.

Lord, with whom Eros the subduer
And the dark-eyed Nymphs

---

32. The Greek is ambiguous: it could be the lover who is described as still young, or the boys.
33. The phraseology is typical of dying soldiers in epic poetry.
34. Smerdis was a slave from Thrace (see Antipater of Sidon, *AP* 7.27.6). Anacreon's effort to intervene on his behalf was apparently futile.

And rosy-skinned Aphrodite
Play, you roam about
The lofty mountain peaks.   5
I beseech you, please come to us
Well disposed, and hear
    Our prayer with favor.
Become a good advisor to Cleobulus,[35]
That he accept my love,   10
    O Dionysus.

1.31 Anacreon, fragment 358 PMG

Once again golden-haired Eros,
Hitting me with a purple ball,
Calls me out to play
    With a fancy-sandaled maid.
But she, haling from   5
Well-endowed Lesbos,[36] finds fault
With my hair, for it's white.
    She gapes open-mouthed at another *girl*.[37]

1.32 Anacreon, fragment 359 PMG

I love Cleobulus,
I am mad for Cleobulus,
I gaze at Cleobulus.

1.33 Anacreon, fragment 360 PMG

Boy with a maiden's glance,
I seek you out, but you hear not,
Unknowing that you are the charioteer
Of my soul.

---

35. There may be a pun on Cleobulus' name, composed of the Greek roots *kleo-* (famous) and *boul-* (advice).

36. Inasmuch as Lesbos was Sappho's home, Lesbian girls might legitimately be suspected of Sapphism.

37. The Greek is ambiguous: the feminine adjective could denote another girl, but it could as well denote another's hair (also a feminine noun); in the latter case the reference could be to a younger man's dark hair, or to *another kind of* hair (i.e., pubic hair). Like **1.30**, the poem may be intended as a riddle.

1.34 Anacreon, fragment 402(c) PMG

Boys would love me for my words,
For I sing graceful things and I know how to say graceful things.

1.35 Ibycus, fragment 287 PMG

Eros, melting me once more with his gaze
From under dark lids,[38]
With all manner of charms throws me again
Into the boundless nets of the Love Goddess.
I tremble at him as he comes,   5
Like an old prize horse who knows the yoke
And unwilling goes into the swift chariot race
   One more time.

1.36 Ibycus, fragment 288 PMG

Euryalus, offspring of the blue-eyed Graces[39]
And care of the fair-haired Seasons,
The Love Goddess and tender-eyed Seduction
Nurtured you among rosebuds.

1.37 Theognis 87–90

Don't caress me with words, your heart and mind in another place,
   If you love me and your heart is true.
Love me with a pure heart or renounce me,
   Start a fight, hate me openly.

1.38 Theognis 371–72

Don't drive me back to the wagon, pricking hard—I won't go,
   Cyrnus, though you drag me all too deeply into your love.

---

38. Archaic Greek thought held that vision occurred through beams of fiery particles emitted from the eyes and bounced off objects.

39. Three goddesses personifying beauty, charm, and grace. They are frequently depicted as dancers.

1.39 Theognis 695–96

I can't give you everything you want, heart,[40]
　　Be patient. You're not the only lover of pretty boys.

1.40 Theognis 959–62

While I alone was drinking from that deepwater spring
　　The water seemed to me sweet and fine.
But now it's muddied, the water's mingled with water—
　　I'll drink from another spring or stream.

1.41 Theognis 1063–70

In youth you can sleep the night through with a friend,[41]
　　Unloading the desire for lusty action,
And you can go wooing and sing to a flute-girl's tune—　　　1065
　　No other thing is more thrilling than these
For men and women. What are wealth and honor to me?
　　Pleasure conquers all—and merrily.
Mindless men and fools weep for the dying
　　Instead of the blossom of youth that's falling.　　　1070

1.42 Theognis 1091–94

My heart's in pain because of my love of you,
　　For I can't either hate or love,
Knowing it's hard when a man's your friend
　　To hate him, and hard to love him if he doesn't want.

1.43 Theognis 1097–1100

Already I've risen up on wings like a bird
　　From a great marsh, leaving a rotten man behind,
Breaking the bond. And you, who've lost my love,
　　Will know one day how wise I was.

---

40. Self-address to one's vital organs (heart, soul, head) is a common convention in Greek lyric.
41. The Greek makes it clear that the friend is an age-equal.

1.44 Theognis 1231–34

Lines 1231–1389 of the Theognid collection are almost entirely concerned with the relationship of Theognis and Cyrnus. Our manuscripts label them as "book two" of Theognis' elegies, but their collection into a separate book was probably the work of later Christian scholars who wanted to segregate the most explicitly pederastic poems from the rest of the corpus.

Merciless Eros, the Frenzies cradled you and gave you suck,
  Because of you Troy's citadel was crushed,[42]
Theseus, great son of Aegeus, was crushed,[43] and Ajax crushed,
  The noble son of Oileus, by your recklessness.[44]

1.45 Theognis 1235–38

Boy, my passion's master, listen. I'll tell no tale
  That's unpersuasive or unpleasant to your heart.
Just try to grasp my words with your mind. There is no need
  For you to do what's not to your liking.

1.46 Theognis 1238a–1242

Don't leave the friend you have to find another,
  Yielding to the words of vulgar men.
You know, they'll often lie to me about you,
  To you about me. Don't listen to them.
You'll take pleasure in this love that's gone,
  And that one will elude your mastery.

1.47 Theognis 1243–44

"Let's love long."[45] Then go be with others.
  You are a trickster, fidelity's antitype.

---

42. A reference to the passion of Helen and Paris as the cause of the Trojan War.

43. Theseus, along with his friend Peirithous, went to the Underworld to rape Persephone, the Queen of the Dead. According to some accounts, he was confined there and could not return. Alternatively, the reference could be to his second wife, Phaedra, who attempted to seduce and then falsely accused his son Hippolytus.

44. Ajax raped the Trojan princess Cassandra in a shrine of Athena and was later punished for the impiety by being drowned in a storm at sea.

45. These words must be understood as an expression of Cyrnus, to which Theognis makes a bitter reply. An alternate translation, preferred by some commentators, is "let's be friends at a distance." This way the whole couplet represents the feelings of Theognis.

1.48 Theognis 1245–46

Water and fire will never mix. And we shall never be
    True to each other and kind.

1.49 Theognis 1247–48

Think about my hatred, and the crime. Know in your gut
    That I will pay you for this wrong as I am able.

1.50 Theognis 1249–52

Boy, you're like a horse.[46] Just now sated with seed,
    You've come back to my stable,
Yearning for a good rider, fine meadow,
    An icy spring, shady groves.

1.51 Theognis 1253–56

Happy the man who's got boys for loving and single-foot horses,[47]
    Hunting dogs and friends in foreign lands.
The man who doesn't love boys and single-foot horses
    And dogs, his heart will never know pleasure.[48]

1.52 Theognis 1257–58

Boy, you're like those adrift in risks,
    Your mood now friendly to some, now others.

1.53 Theognis 1259–62

Boy, you were born good-looking, but your head
    Is crowned with stupidity.
In your brain is lodged the character of a kite,[49] always veering,
    Bending to the words of other men.

---

46. Horses were usually the property of only the very wealthy in Greece and thus had aristocratic associations.

47. Horses' hooves are not cloven like those of cattle.

48. These two couplets may be variants of the same aphorism, rather than a continuous poem. Since the Theognid manuscripts do not mark clear divisions between poems, this must be a matter of editorial judgment.

49. A raptor. Some kites hunt flying, constantly roaming around, rather than watching for prey from a perched location.

1.54 Theognis 1263–66

Boy, you paid back a bad exchange for kindness.
  No thanks from you for favors.
You've never given me pleasure. And though I've often
  Been kind to you, I never won your respect.

1.55 Theognis 1267–70

Boy and horse, a similar brain: the horse
  Doesn't cry when its rider lies in the dust;
No, it takes on the next man, once it's sated with seed.
  Same with a boy: whoever's there he loves.

1.56 Theognis 1271–74

Boy, your slutting around has wrecked my affection,
  You've become a disgrace to our friends.
You dried my hull for a while. But I've slipped out of the squall
  And found a port as night came on.

1.57 Theognis 1275–78

Eros, too, rises in season, when the Earth
  Swells and blooms with Spring flowers.
Then Eros leaves Cyprus, that lovely island,[50]
  And goes among men, scattering seed on the ground.

1.58 Theognis 1278a–78b

Whoever offered you advice about me also urged you
  To leave behind our love and go your way.

1.59 Theognis 1279–82

I won't mistreat you even if the deathless gods
  Would treat me better, pretty boy.
And I don't sit in judgment on petty errors.
  Pretty boys get away with doing wrong.

---

50. The birthplace of Aphrodite, the love goddess and mother of Eros.

1.60 Theognis 1283–94

Boy, don't wrong me—I still want to
    Please·you—listen graciously to this:
You won't outstrip me, cheat me with your tricks.   1285
    Right now you've won and have the upper hand,
But I'll wound you while you flee,[51] as they say
    The virgin daughter of Iasius,
Though ripe, rejected wedlock with a man
    And fled; girding herself, she acted pointlessly,   1290
Abandoning her father's house, blond Atalanta.[52]
    She went off to the soaring mountain peaks,
Fleeing the lure of wedlock, golden Aphrodite's
    Gift. But she learned the point she'd so rejected.

1.61 Theognis 1295–98

Boy, don't stir my heart with rotten anguish,
    Don't let your love whisk me off
To Persephone's halls.[53] Beware the anger of the gods
    And men's talk. Think gentle thoughts.

1.62 Theognis 1299–1304

Boy, how long will you be on the run? I'm following,
    Tracking you down. I only wish I'd reach the end
Of your anger. But you, lusting and headstrong,
    Run off reckless as a kite.
Stop now, do me a favor. You won't
    Hang on to the gift of Cypris,[54] violet-wreathed, much longer.

1.63 Theognis 1305–10

Knowing in your heart that the flower of lovely youth
    Is briefer than a footrace, loosen my chain.

---

51. This may be a double entendre implying "I'll penetrate you from the rear."

52. The mythological huntress spurned marriage and challenged suitors to a footrace, killing them as she overtook them from behind. She was finally defeated by Melanion, who delayed her by dropping three golden apples that distracted her attention. Here the speaker vows to Cyrnus that he will not be outrun like Atalanta's suitors, but will himself be the one to overtake from behind.

53. The Underworld.

54. See n. 19 above.

For even you, mightiest of boys, may some day be compelled
    And meet the hard work of the Love Goddess,
Even as I do now with you. Beware!
    A boy's wickedness may one day conquer you.

1.64 Theognis 1311–18

You haven't fooled me, boy—I'm on your trail—
    You've stolen off to your new fast friends,
And thrown my love away in scorn.
    But you were no friend of theirs before.
No, out of them all, I thought it was you I'd made a trusted
    Mate. And now you hold another love.
I, who served you well, am laid low. Looking at you
    No one on Earth would want to love a boy.

1.65 Theognis 1319–22

Boy, since the goddess Cypris gave you a lusty
    Grace, and your beauty's every boy's concern,[55]
Listen to these words and for my sake take them to heart—
    Knowing how hard it is for a man to bear desire.

1.66 Theognis 1323–26

Cyprian, end these pains, scatter the cares
    That eat my soul, turn me back to merriment.
End this awful anxiety, be merciful,
    And let me act wisely now that my youth is gone.

1.67 Theognis 1327–34

Boy, as long as your cheek is smooth, I'll never
    Stop praising you, not even if I have to die.
For you to give still is fine, for me there's no shame in asking,
    Since I'm in love. At your knees . . . I beg,
Respect me, boy, give pleasure, if you're ever
    To have the gift of Cypris with her wreath of violets,

---

55. In other words, Cyrnus' beauty arouses desire even among boys his own age.

When it's you who's wanting and approach another. May the goddess
   Grant that you get exactly the same response.

1.68 Theognis 1335–36

Happy the lover who has a workout when he gets home
   Sleeping all day with a beautiful boy.

1.69 Theognis 1337–40

I no longer love the boy, I've kicked away terrible pains
   And fled in joy from crushing sorrows.
I've been freed from desire by Cytherea[56] of the lovely wreath.
   Boy, you hold no charm for me at all.

1.70 Theognis 1341–50

Alas! I love a smooth-skinned boy, who to all friends
   Displays me against my will.
But I'll put up with it and not hide. Much is compelled, even unwilling.
   For I was not shown tamed by an unappealing boy.
Boy-love is a delight, since even the son of Cronus,   1345
   King of the gods, once came to love Ganymede,
And seizing him, brought him up to Olympus and made him
   Eternal in the lovely flower of boyhood.[57]
So, Simonides,[58] don't wonder that even I
   Was shown to be tamed by love of a comely boy.   1350

1.71 Theognis 1351–52

Boy, don't go reveling, heed an old man.
   Reveling's not good for a young man.

1.72 Theognis 1353–56

Bitter and sweet, pleasant and harsh is the love of youths,
   Cyrnus, till it be achieved.

---

56. Another name for Aphrodite, based on her cult on the island of Cythera.

57. Zeus sent his eagle to carry up to Olympus the beautiful Trojan prince Ganymede, to
whom he gave immortal youth and a position as cupbearer to the gods.

58. Probably addressed to the poet Simonides of Ceos (556–468 B.C.E.), the author of **1.84**.

If achieved, it becomes sweet, but if a man pursues
And achieves not, it is the most grievous of all.

1.73 Theognis 1357–60

For boy-lovers a yoke lies on the neck, uncomfortable,
A difficult memory of erstwhile welcome.
For a man who toils to win a boy must lure him into love
Like a hand into a blazing fire of vine twigs.

1.74 Theognis 1361–62

A ship, you struck a rock and missed my love's haven,
Boy, laid hold of a rotten hawser.

1.75 Theognis 1363–64

I'll never hurt you, even when I'm gone; and no one
Will talk me out of loving you.

1.76 Theognis 1365–66

Prettiest, most desirable of boys—
Stick around and listen to me a bit.

1.77 Theognis 1367–68

With a boy there must always be mutual favor. But to a woman
No one's a trusted mate; she always loves the one who's there.

1.78 Theognis 1369–72

Boy-love is nice to have, nice to put aside;
It is easier to be found than to achieve.
Countless ills hang on it, countless gains,
But there is some charm even in this.

1.79 Theognis 1373–74

You've never waited for my sake, no, you always
Chase eagerly after every message.

1.80 Theognis 1375–76

Happy the lover of boys who doesn't know the sea
And worry, there on the waves, about the coming night.[59]

1.81 Theognis 1377–80

Being good-looking and loving vice, you hang out with worthless
Men, and for this you get ugly reproaches,
Boy. But though I lost your love against my will,
I've won, can act a free man.

1.82 Theognis 1381–85

Men thought you came with the gift of the golden
Cyprian. Yet the gift of the violet wreathed
Can be the hardest load men have
If the Cyprian doesn't give hardship some relief.

1.83 Theognis 1386–89

Cyprian Cytherea with your web of cunning, Zeus did you honor
By giving you this transcendent gift;
You master men's clever minds, and there is none
So strong and skilled that he can flee.

1.84 Simonides, fragment 22.9–18 West²

*This fragment comes from two tattered papyri, which in 1992 were pieced together
and assigned to Simonides. The first eight lines are very fragmentary, but seem to describe the speaker reaching a pleasant, forested island, possibly the Isle of the Blessed
(an afterlife paradise).*

And seeing blond Echecratidas[60] with my eyes,
  I would take his hand,   10
While he drips the flower of youth from his comely skin
  And alluring desire from his eyelids.
And I would luxuriate, reclining with the boy among flowers,
  Clearing away from my face white hair and wrinkles,

---

59. Storms at sea were supposed to be especially common at night. But the couplet could
also suggest worry about whom the boy might be sleeping with back home. Maritime trade was
generally disparaged by landed aristocrats.

60. Echecratidas was a Thessalian prince for whose family Simonides wrote poems.

Plaiting a flowery crown . . .   15
  . . . lovely, new-grown on his locks.
Steering an eloquent tongue in my mouth . . .
  . . . clear, alluring . . .

1.85 Pindar, fragment 123 Snell–Maehler

*This short skolion (a drinking song for performance at symposia) praises the beauty of
the boy Theoxenus. Some critics have supposed it to be Pindar's personal declaration
of love, but it was more likely commissioned by the boy's lover and the first-person voice
is meant to express the erotic attraction of any man who likes boys. Pindar's lyric poems are built out of metrically equivalent stanzas ("strophe" and "antistrophe") followed by a stanza in a different meter (the "epode").*

[*strophe*] One must pluck loves, my heart, in due season and at the
        proper age.
Ah! But any man who catches with his glance
The bright rays flashing from Theoxenus' eyes[61]
And is not tossed on the waves of desire,
Has a black heart of adamant or iron   5
    [*antistrophe*] Forged in a cold flame, and dishonored by Aphrodite of
        the arching brow
Either toils compulsively for money
Or, as a slave, is towed down a path utterly cold
By a woman's boldness.
But I, by the will of the Love Goddess, melt   10
    [*epode*] Like the wax of holy bees stung by the sun's heat,
Whenever I look upon the fresh-limbed youth of boys.
And surely even on the isle of Tenedos
Seduction and Grace dwell
In the son of Hagesilas.   15

1.86 Pindar, *Tenth Pythian Ode* 55–68

*This is from Pindar's earliest datable poem, publicly celebrating the footrace victory of
the boy Hippocleas in the Pythian games of 498 B.C.E. The poem may have been commissioned by the Thessalian prince Thorax, whom an ancient commentator identifies
as the young athlete's lover.*

61. In other words, any man who sees Theoxenus looking back at him. See n. 38.

[strophe 4] When Ephyrean[62] choristers pour out   55
My sweet voice around the Peneius,[63]
I expect by my songs to make the crowned Hippocleas
Still more splendid to look upon to both his age-mates and older men,
And a heartthrob for young maids. For
Different loves tickle the fancies of different folks.   60
    [antistrophe 4] Whatever each man reaches for,
If he wins it, let him hold as his desire an ambition near at hand;
Things a year in the future are impossible to foreknow.[64]
I have relied on the kind hospitality of Thorax, who, bustling about for
        my sake,
Yoked this four-horse chariot of the Muses,[65]   65
Favoring one who favors him, giving willing guidance to one who
        guides him.
    [epode 4] To one who tests it, gold is revealed on the touchstone—
So too an upright mind.[66]

1.87 Pindar, *First Olympian Ode*

This poem was commissioned in 476 B.C.E. to celebrate the Olympic horse-race victory of Hieron, monarch of Syracuse, the most powerful Greek city in Sicily. In the poem Pindar tells the myth of the sea-god Poseidon's love for the young Pelops.

[strophe 1] Water is preeminent and gold, like a fire burning in the night,
outshines all possessions that magnify men's pride.
But if, my soul, you yearn
to celebrate great games,
look no further for another star   5
shining through the deserted ether brighter than the sun,
or for a contest mightier than Olympia—
where the song has taken its coronal design of glory,
plaited in the minds of poets as they come,

---

62. Ephyre was an ancient name of the Thessalian city of Krannon.

63. The main river of Thessaly.

64. The poet appears to be exhorting the boy not to be tempted by the other erotic opportunities that may be presented to him in his newly acquired glory, but to stick with his present good, namely Thorax.

65. This expression is probably a metaphor for commissioning the present poem.

66. In other words, Thorax' virtue and devotion are proven by commissioning this poem (putting his gold to the test).

calling on Zeus' name,[67]   10
to the rich radiant hall of Hieron
    [antistrophe 1] who wields the scepter of justice in Sicily,
reaping the prime of every distinction.
And he delights
in the flare of music,   15
the brightness of song
circling his table from man to man. Then take the Dorian lyre[68] down
        from its peg
if the beauty of Pisa[69] and of Pherenicus[70]
somehow cast your mind under a gracious spell,
when by the stream of Alpheus,   20
keeping his flanks ungrazed by the spur,
he sped and put his lord in the embrace of power—
    [epode 1] Syracusan knight and king, blazoned with glory
in the land of Pelops:[71]
Pelops, whom Earth-cradling Poseidon loved,   25
since Clotho[72] had taken him out of the pure cauldron,
his ivory shoulder gleaming in the hearth-light.
Yes! marvels are many, stories starting from mortals somehow stretch
        truth
to deception woven cunningly on the loom of lies.
    [str. 2] Grace, the very one who fashions every delight for mortal
        men,   30
by lending her sheen to what is unbelievable,
often makes it believed.
But the days to come
are the wisest witness.
It is proper for a man to speak well of the gods—the blame will be less.   35
Pelops, I will tell your story differently from the men of old.[73]

---

67. Zeus was the patron god of the Olympic games.

68. Syracuse was originally settled by Dorian colonists from Corinth. The dialect of Pindar's poems is also mainly Doric.

69. Pisa was the city closest to Olympia, Alpheus a nearby river.

70. The name of Hieron's horse, literally "Victory-bringer."

71. As the myth goes on to narrate, Pelops became the king of Elis, the region around Olympia, and eventually of the entire Peloponnese, which was named after him.

72. One of the three Fates, the goddesses who determine one's life span at the moment of one's birth.

73. Pindar is calling attention to the fact that he is challenging the traditional version of the myth, which holds that Pelops was killed and served by his father as food to the gods and was then subsequently recooked and reanimated in another cauldron, with an ivory shoulder to replace the one that had been eaten. Pindar claims instead that Tantalus' crime was theft of the gods' nectar and ambrosia, and that the story about Pelops being eaten was an invention

Your father Tantalus had invited the gods
to banquet in his beloved Sipylus,
providing a stately feast in return for the feast they had given him.
It was then Poseidon seized you,   40
  [ant. 2] overwhelmed in his mind with desire, and swept you on
        golden mares
to Zeus' glorious palace on Olympus,
where, at another time,
Ganymede came also
for the same passion in Zeus.[74]   45
But after you had disappeared and searchers again and again returned
        to your mother
without you, then one of the neighbors, invidious, whispered
that the gods had sliced you limb by limb
into the fury of boiling water,
and then they passed morsels of   50
your flesh around the table and ate them.
  [ep. 2] No! I cannot call any of the blessed gods a savage: I stand apart.
Disaster has often claimed the slanderer.
If ever the watchlords of Olympus honored a man,
this was Tantalus. But he could not digest   55
his great bliss—in his fullness he earned
the doom that the father poised above him,
the looming boulder which, in eternal distraction, he strains to heave
        from his brow.[75]
  [str. 3] Such is the misery upon him,
a fourth affliction among three others,[76] because he robbed the
        immortals—   60
their nectar and ambrosia,
which had made him deathless,
he stole and gave to his drinking companions.
But a man who hopes to hide his doings from the gods is deluded.
For this they hurled his son Pelops back   65
among the short-lived generations of men.

---

of envious neighbors after Poseidon abducted him. Vv. 25–27 seem to imply that in Pindar's
version, Pelops had the ivory shoulder from birth. Some commentators believe that Poseidon's
love for Pelops was also Pindar's innovation.

74. See n. 57 above.

75. One version of Tantalus' punishment in Hades was that he had to stand underneath a
cliff that was about to crumble.

76. The three other punishments were Tantalus' perpetual thirst and hunger, and his son
being dismissed from Olympus.

But when he grew toward the time of bloom
and black down curled on his cheeks,
he thought of a marriage there for his seeking—
    [ant. 2] to win from her Pisan father[77] the girl Hippodameia.   70
Going down by the dim sea, alone in the dark,
he called on the god of the trident,
loud-pounding Poseidon,
who appeared and stood close by.
"If in any way," Pelops said to him, "the gifts of Aphrodite count in my
        favor,   75
shackle the bronze spear of Oenomaus,
bring me on the swiftest chariot
to Elis, and put me within the reach of power,
for he has slain thirteen suitors now,
and so he delays his daughter's marriage.   80
    [ep. 3] Great danger does not come upon the spineless man,
and yet, if we must die, why squat in the shadows,
coddling a bland old age, with no nobility, for nothing?
As for me, I will undertake this exploit.
And you—I beseech you: let me achieve it."   85
He spoke, and his words found fulfillment: the god made him glow
        with gifts—
a golden chariot and winged horses never weary.
    [str. 4] He tore the strength from Oenomaus and took the maiden
        to his bed.
She bore him six sons, leaders of the people, intent on prowess.
Now in the bright blood rituals   90
Pelops has his share,
reclining by the ford of Alpheus.[78]
Men gather at his tomb, near the crowded altar. The glory
of the Olympiads shoots its rays afar in his races,
where speed and strength   95
are matched in the bruise of toil.
But the victor, for the rest of his life,
enjoys days of contentment,
    [ant. 4] as far as contests can assure them. A single day's blessing
is the highest good a mortal knows. I must crown him   100
now to the horseman's tune,

77. Oenomaus, the king of Elis, who challenged suitors for his daughter's hand to a deadly
chariot race.
    78. A reference to the sacrifice at the shrine of Pelops that began the Olympic games every
four years.

in Aeolean rhythms,[79]
for I believe the shimmering folds of my song
shall never embrace a host
more lordly in power or perception of beauty.   105
Hieron, a god is overseer to your ambitions,
keeping watch, cherishing them as his own.
If he does not abandon you soon,
still sweeter the triumph I hope
    [*ep. 4*] will fall to your speeding chariot,[80] and may I be the one
        to praise it,   110
riding up the sunny Hill of Cronus![81]
The Muse is tempering her mightiest arrow for me.
Men are great in various ways, but in kingship the ultimate crest is
        attained.
Peer no farther into the beyond.
For the time we have, may you continue to walk on high, and may I
        for as long   115
consort with victors, conspicuous for my skill among Greeks everywhere.

1.88 *Carmina Popularia,* fragment 873 Poetae Melici Graeci

This anonymous skolion, according to Plutarch, celebrates the legendary love of a Chalcidian soldier and a boy who saw him die in battle during the Lelantine War (in the eighth century B.C.E.).

You boys who have a share of the Graces and noble fathers,
Do not begrudge the company of good men during your hour of youth.
For together with courage Eros, the limb-loosener,[82]
Flourishes in the cities of the Chalcidians.

1.89 *Carmina Popularia,* fragment 893 PMG

This anonymous skolion celebrates a famous pair of lovers in Athenian history, the tyrannicides Harmodius and Aristogeiton (on whom see 2.2 and fig. 18). The song exists in several versions; it was probably current soon after the Cleisthenic reforms of 507 B.C.E.

---

79. The meter of this poem is similar to that used by poets writing in the Aeolic dialect, such as Sappho.

80. Chariot victories involving a team of four horses were even more prestigious than victories in the single-horse race, such as Hieron has won this time.

81. A small hillock inside the Olympic complex.

82. An epithet also used of Sleep and Death.

In a myrtle branch I'll carry my sword,[83]
Like Harmodius and Aristogeiton
When they killed the tyrant
And made Athens a land of equal laws.[84]

83. The myrtle branch was part of the sacrificial ceremony during which the assassination of Hipparchus took place.

84. In other words, a land where all men were equal before the law. The overthrow of the Peisistratids is generally credited as the starting point of Athens' development into a truly democratic state.

CHAPTER 2

Greek Historical Texts

This chapter brings together texts from a variety of sources and dates—historiography, biography, anecdotes, political theory, and inscriptions, both official and unofficial. Some texts, such as Plutarch (c. 100 C.E.) and Aelian (c. 200 C.E.), are much later than the events they describe and must be treated with appropriate caution, even though they are surely based on the work of earlier, now lost historians. But even fourth-century B.C.E. historians who recorded contemporary events, such as Theopompus, give highly colored and rhetorical narratives and must also be approached with some measure of skepticism. Ancient historians were fond of illustrating points through moral examples, both positive and negative, and many of the anecdotes preserved here are of this character. Read as illustrations of the historian's own ideology (or those of his sources or audience), these stories have greater value than as records of historical fact.

One common story pattern is of pederastic couples whose love and desire to impress one another led them to sacrifice themselves courageously in assassinating, or attempting to assassinate, a tyrant (**2.2, 2.3, 2.21.602;** cf. **5.7.182**). The paradigm here, of course, is the Athenian story of Harmodius and Aristogeiton, whose actions were popularly supposed to have resulted in the overthrow of the Peisistratid tyrants in the late sixth century. However, Thucydides (**2.2**) and Aristotle (*Athenian Constitution* 18.1–19.1, not in this volume) both offer consciously demythologizing accounts of the incident that demonstrate its relative unimportance in the ultimate overthrow of the tyranny; as Thucydides notes, the tyrant Hippias' cruelty actually grew worse after the assassination of his brother. What is significant, therefore, is not the incident itself, but the fact that it was interpreted so widely to have a greater significance than it did: one can perhaps see an attempt by mainly upper-class enthusiasts of pederasty (whose sympathies might otherwise be suspected of being undemocratic) to contextualize their practices as integral with Athens' developing democratic constitution by granting pederasty a prominent place in the democracy's foundational mythology.

A variant of this story pattern is that of the lustful tyrant (**2.1, 2.3, 2.20;** in **2.19** even the slave of a tyrant assumes this role) whose outrages may trigger vengeance. In some stories (**2.7**, Phalaris in **2.21.602**, or Alexander in **2.21.603**), a despot is softened by seeing the devotion of a pederastic couple. Xenophon composed an interesting dialogue involving the tyrant Hieron of Syracuse (**2.4**), who complains that a tyrant's life is unhappy because he cannot be loved in return. Xenophon's *Agesilaus* (**2.9**) presents a portrait of an ideal ruler as one who may feel attraction to a boy, but restrains himself from any physical expression. This paradigm is consistent with the negative view of physical love between males suggested in Xenophon's philosophical works (**5.1–3, 5.8**). His portraits of Menon the Thessalian (**2.6**) and the Median relative of Cyrus (**2.8**) provide clear examples of men who cannot restrain themselves.

The Spartan king Agesilaus is a model of the qualities of self-discipline that were admired in Spartan culture as a whole: applied to pederasty, this took the form of man-boy relationships that allegedly abstained from any sexual contact (**2.10–13**). Plutarch (**2.12**) reveals that these relationships began at the age of twelve and were part of a generalized communal responsibility in raising children; in **2.13** he tells us that similar relationships existed between women and girls. Aelian (**2.11**) informs us that Spartan boys were not haughty toward lovers like boys in Athens and other places, because they needed lovers to "inspire" them (literally "breathe [virtue] into" them); see also **6.10.13**. Some scholars have interpreted this term as possible evidence for an earlier form of Dorian pederasty that was physical and involved "anal insemination" of a warrior's courage and moral qualities.

In historical times, such military bonding may have been the practice among the Boeotians, who unquestionably did practice physical love (**2.10.12, 5.7.182**). **2.14** tells of the Sacred Band, an elite military unit Plutarch believes to have been formed out of pederastic couples, on the assumption that love impels men to courageous acts in the presence of their partner.

The Cretans are often credited with the invention of pederasty (**2.15, 2.21.602, 5.10**). Aristotle (**2.15**) speculates that it was to limit the size of families and thus prevent overpopulation. Ephorus (**2.16**) describes an interesting ritual of pederastic abduction that is peculiar to Crete; many scholars have interpreted this procedure as an initiatory rite of passage into adulthood and regard it as a practice of great antiquity. Crete was often imagined as an origin for many Greek practices and beliefs, since even Greeks of the historical period recognized that the island hosted an advanced culture far older than any on the mainland. Indeed, artistic evidence (fig. 1) suggests that Minoan culture of the second millennium B.C.E. did feature some form of pederasty, particularly in military contexts; figure 2 suggests that the same institution existed in Crete of the seventh century.

Some texts also give insight into boy-love as practiced by non-Greeks: it is attributed to Persians, who supposedly learned it from the Greeks, and even some Gallic tribes (**2.8, 2.21.603**).

Ion of Chios' and Hieronymus of Rhodes' anecdotes about the tragedian Sophocles' flirtations with boys (**2.21.603–4**) give us a vivid portrait of such encounters as they occurred in Greek life. Similarly, Plutarch's account of Alcibiades' youth (**2.5**), which is not wholly unsympathetic, gives an idea of how much lovers were willing to endure at the hands of a proud and beautiful youth who embodied the crème de la crème of Athenian aristocracy.

Also providing insight into the *realia* of Greek life are a number of graffiti from different periods and locations. Among the earliest are seventh/sixth century inscriptions from the island of Thera (**2.22**). Two of these (**2.22.537a** and **538b**), written by the same man, proclaim a sexual conquest on the spot, but most are not so explicit. Several praise boys for their dancing. This emphasis, together with the proximity of the graffiti to a temple of Apollo, raises the possibility that the relationships were part of a ritualized initiation that involved musical or choral training. The graffiti from other locales are also laudatory, not sexually explicit: epithets include beautiful, sweet, ripe, wild, gracious, refined, elegant in figure and bearing, a delight to speak to, gold, silver. Two graffiti (**2.22.549, 2.23.924**) are interesting in that they seem to have been written by beloved boys themselves, although we cannot discount the possibility that they were written by lovers in the persona of their boyfriends. Some acclamatory graffiti at Nemea (**2.25**) are significant in virtue of their location in a tunnel leading into the stadium: it was apparently a practice of some men to carve the names of their favorite boy athletes into stone to preserve them for posterity in a visible and prominent location frequented by visitors from all over Greece. One does sometimes find inscribed on Athenian vases as early as the second quarter of the seventh century sexually explicit boasts or slanders against boys or perhaps men (**2.27**), but these are far less common than the usual laudatory formula ". . . is beautiful."

Finally, there is a Hellenistic law from the Macedonian town of Beroea (**2.28**) regulating qualifications for entry into the public gymnasium and stipulating that young men are to be kept away from boys. This law may represent a legislative attempt to protect boys from corrupting influences, but it could also be simply a set of organizational rules dividing the young into age classes and maintaining a certain country-club exclusivity for the gymnasium.

Bibliographical Note

For general surveys of Greek historical texts, see Meier and de Pogey-Castries (1930) 41–105, 158–68, and Buffière (1980) 49–236.

On the legend of Harmodius and Aristogeiton and its significance in Athenian democratic culture, see Podlecki (1966), Fehr (1984), Lavelle (1986), and Monoson (2000). See also Wohl (1999), who treats this story as well as offering ideas on the sexual ambiguity of Alcibiades as a destabilization of Athenian values.

On Spartan pederasty in historical times, see the important study of Cartledge (1981). Bethe (1907) is responsible for the theory that "anal insemination" was a Dorian practice, which is modified by Patzer (1982), who regards it as an archaic practice common to all Greeks; see Percy (1996) 27–35 for a succinct history of the controversy about this theory, and 73–92 for his own view of Spartan pederasty. See also Dover (1978) 185–96. Leitao (2002) argues that the Sacred Band of Thebes was not in fact organized on the basis of pederastic couples, as Plutarch imagines. On the relation of pederasty to military organization, see also Ogden (1996). On Xenophon specifically, see Hindley (1994) and (1999).

Bremmer (1980) and Sergent (1986) 7–54 see in the Cretan abduction ceremony an initiatory rite of Indo-European origins; this theory has been criticized by Dover (1988) 115–34 and Percy (1996) 19–26. See Bremmer (1989) for other ethnographic parallels. Koehl (1986) argues for a Minoan origin based on artistic parallels (principally fig. 1). On the other hand, Dodd (2000) takes a more skeptical view of Ephorus' evidence and shows how it is colored by contemporary Athenian views of pederasty. Percy (1996) 59–72 credits Aristotle's theory about a Cretan origin of pederasty as an institutionalized effort at population control and dates the phenomenon to the seventh century B.C.E.

On the Thera graffiti, see Hiller von Gaertringen (1897) 21–28, who connects them with the festival of Carneian Apollo; see also Brongersma (1990). Dover (1978) 112–14, 122–24 regards the more graphic graffiti as boasts and slanders. For the inscriptions on Athenian vases, see Lang (1976) 11–15. On the graffiti at Nemea, see Miller (1979) 99–101; on those at Thasos, Garlan and Masson (1982) and Taillardat (1983).

On the significance of the gymnastic law of Beroea, see Moretti (1982) 48–54, who regards it as an attempt to protect the young from seduction, and E. Cantarella (1992) 28–34. See Gauthier and Hatzopoulos (1993) for a detailed commentary.

2.1 Plutarch, *Love Stories* 2.772E–773B

Plutarch tells the story of an Argive family that settled in Corinth. These events, if historical, would have occurred around 735–730 B.C.E. The story is alluded to by Alexander of Aetolia, an early Hellenistic poet.

[772] This Melissus had a son named Actaeon, the handsomest and most modest youth of his age, who had many lovers, chief of whom was Archias, of the family of the Heracleidae,[1] in wealth and general influence the most outstanding man in Corinth. Now when he could not gain the boy by persuasion, he determined to carry him off by force. So he got together a crowd of friends and servants, went as in a drunken frolic to the house of Melissus, and tried to take the boy away. But his father and his friends resisted, the neighbors also ran out and pulled against the assailants, [773] and so Actaeon was pulled to pieces and killed; the assailants thereupon went away. But Melissus took his son's body and exhibited it in the market-place of the Corinthians, demanding the punishment of the men who had done the deed; but the Corinthians merely pitied him and did nothing further. So, being unsuccessful, he went away and waited for the Isthmian festival,[2] when he went up upon the temple of Poseidon, shouted accusations against the Bacchiadae and reminded the people of his father Habron's benefactions,[3] whereupon, calling upon the gods to avenge him, he threw himself down from the rocks. Not long afterwards the city was afflicted by drought and pestilence, and when the Corinthians consulted the oracle concerning relief, the god replied that the wrath of Poseidon would not relax until they inflicted punishment for the death of Actaeon. Archias knew of this, for he was himself one of those sent to consult the oracle, and voluntarily refrained from returning to Corinth. Instead, he sailed to Sicily and founded Syracuse. There he became the father of two daughters, Ortygia and Syracusa, and was treacherously murdered by Telephus, who had been his beloved and had sailed with him to Sicily in command of a ship.

1. Archias was a member of the ruling clan of Corinth, the Bacchiadae, who, like most Dorian noble families, traced their descent back to the Heracleidae, sons of Heracles.

2. A springtime athletic festival celebrated every two years in Corinth. Poseidon was the patron god. Although it later became one of the four great pan-Hellenic games, at this time it was probably only a local event.

3. Melissus' father, Habron, had warned the Corinthians of a treacherous plot against their army by the Argive king, Pheidon.

2.2 Thucydides 6.54.1–4, 6.56.1–59.2

This account of the assassination of Hipparchus, brother of the Athenian tyrant Hippias, in 514 B.C.E., comes as a digression in Thucydides' narrative of events in 415, when many Athenians suspected an oligarchical coup and return to tyranny.

[54] For the exploit of Aristogeiton and Harmodius was undertaken because of a love affair, and by describing it in full I will show that neither other sources nor the Athenians themselves say anything accurate about their own tyrants or about the incident. For after Peisistratus died at an advanced age while holding the tyranny,[4] it was not Hipparchus, as widely believed, but Hippias as the oldest who took his place. When Harmodius was conspicuous in his youthful prime, Aristogeiton, an Athenian and a citizen of the middle class, possessed him as a lover. Harmodius, after he was propositioned by Hipparchus and refused him, denounced him to Aristogeiton. And he, with a lover's outrage, fearing Hipparchus' rank and a possible abduction by force, immediately plotted, as far as one of his class could, to overthrow the tyranny. Meanwhile, Hipparchus, after he had again propositioned Harmodius with no greater success, was unwilling to use force yet arranged to insult him in a surreptitious way, as though it were quite unconnected. . . .

[56] Harmodius, then, who had refused his advances, he insulted just as he had planned; after enlisting his sister, a maiden, to carry a basket in a certain procession,[5] they expelled her saying that they had not enlisted her in the first place, because of her unworthiness. While Harmodius was resentful, Aristogeiton on his account became very much more enraged as well, and after they had made their other arrangements with those taking part in the deed, they awaited the Great Panathenaea,[6] which was the only day that those citizens who escorted the procession assembled in arms without becoming suspect. They themselves were to begin, and the others were supposed to join in the attack immediately by attending to the mercenaries. The members of the conspiracy were not many, for reasons of security; they hoped that if even a few acted boldly, those with no advance knowledge, since they even had weapons, would want to take part in their own liberation then and there.

---

4. Peisistratus was tyrant twice between 561 and 556 and again from 546 to 527.

5. Maidens would often serve as *kanēphoroi* in sacred processions, carrying food offerings to the gods in baskets on their heads.

6. An Athenian festival celebrated in the late summer of every fourth year, including athletic and musical contests as well as public ceremonies and processions. It was a larger, and pan-Hellenic, version of Athens' annual festival, the Little (or Lesser) Panathenaea, which is also sometimes called simply the Panathenaea.

[57] And when the festival came around, Hippias was outside with the bodyguard in what is known as the Kerameikos[7] arranging how each part of the procession was to go forth; and Harmodius and Aristogeiton, with their daggers now, were advancing for the deed. And when they saw a member of their own conspiracy talking informally with Hippias (who was approachable to everyone), they were alarmed and thought that they had been informed on and were just on the point of being arrested. Accordingly, they hoped that if possible their revenge would come first, against their tormentor who had caused them to risk everything, and in this state they rushed inside the gates, encountered Hipparchus near what is called the Leokoreion,[8] and falling on him immediately, with no hesitation, in all the fury that a man in love and a man humiliated could feel, they stabbed until they killed him. The one, Aristogeiton, escaped the bodyguard for the moment when the crowd was milling around and later, after capture, was dealt with in no gentle way;[9] Harmodius was killed right on the spot. [58] When the news reached Hippias in the Kerameikos, he immediately proceeded not toward the incident but toward the hoplites[10] in the parade before they found out, since they were some way off, and making his face inscrutable in the presence of the calamity he ordered them to go where he had pointed to a certain spot, without their weapons. They went off, thinking that he was going to tell them something, but he, after a signal to the bodyguard to remove the weapons, picked out those he held responsible, along with anyone caught carrying a dagger; for their practice was to parade with shields and spears.[11]

[59] It was in this way, because of a lover's grievance, that both the original plot and the heedless daring of Harmodius and Aristogeiton, in the alarm of the moment, came about. After this, the tyranny took on a harsher form for the Athenians, and Hippias, now more under the influence of fear, put many citizens to death and at the same time looked around in foreign parts to see where he could find some place providing him with security if a revolution occurred.

---

7. The northwest part of Athens.

8. A shrine in the western part of the marketplace, dedicated to the daughters of the hero Leos, who were sacrificed with their father's consent when an oracle made it a condition of the city's survival.

9. Aristotle says he was tortured to determine the names of his confederates, and that he falsely accused several friends of the tyrant. Finally his insults provoked Hippias into killing him.

10. Heavy-armed infantry.

11. Aristotle here disagrees with Thucydides, claiming that the parade with weapons was a later innovation. Thucydides' version makes the Athenians prior to this incident appear more cowardly, in that they would have had opportunities to attack the tyrants, but never did.

2.3 Phanias of Eresus, Fr. 16 FHG

Phanias was a pupil of Aristotle who wrote historical treatises on tyrants in the late fourth century B.C.E. There is no other record of a tyranny at Heraclea, which was founded in 433.

In Heraclea in Italy there was a beautiful boy called Hipparinus, who came from a very good family. His lover, Antileon, tried everything, but was wholly unable to win him round. He would often dash up to the boy, who was a regular at the gymnasia, declaring that he wanted him so much that he would endure any hardship, that whatever the boy told him to do, he would fail in nothing. Now the boy asked him ironically to fetch the bell[12] from a certain rocky place that was kept under especially close guard by the Heraclean tyrant, convinced that Antileon would never manage this feat. But Antileon secretly approached the fort, lay in wait for the man who was guarding the bell, and killed him. And when he came back to the boy, the mission accomplished, the boy became very fond of him and from that time onwards they loved each other dearly. When the tyrant began to lust after the young man's beauty and was on the point of using force to abduct him, Antileon was outraged. He told the boy not to incur risks by refusal; but he himself, when the tyrant was leaving his house, rushed up and assassinated him. This done, he fled and would have escaped had he not fallen in with a flock of sheep all tied together and been captured. So once the city had returned to its original constitution the Heracleotes erected bronze statues to both men,[13] and a law was enacted that no one in the future was to drive bound sheep.

2.4 Xenophon, *Hieron* 1.29–38

This work presumes to record a dialogue between Hieron, the tyrant of Syracuse from 478 to 467 B.C.E., and the poet Simonides of Ceos, who, like Pindar, wrote encomiastic poems for him.

[29] And the tyrant is at a disadvantage in the pleasures that come from making love to boys even more than in the pleasures that come from begetting children. For we all, presumably, know that making love is by far the most pleasurable if one does it with desire.[14] [30] But desire, in general, comes to a tyrant less easily than to anybody else. For desire does not like to aim at available things, but rather at hoped-for ones. Therefore, just as someone who is unacquainted with thirst would not enjoy drinking,

---

12. Carried around by guards to send signals to other guards.

13. This parallels the bronze statues the Athenians dedicated to Harmodius and Aristogeiton after the overthrow of the tyrants.

14. The word translated as "desire" in this passage is *erōs*.

in the same way someone who is unacquainted with desire is unacquainted with the sweetest forms of love.

[31] That is what Hieron said, but Simonides, having had a laugh, said, "What is that you said, Hieron? You say that desire for boys isn't native to tyrants? How does it then come that you are in love with Daïlochus, whose nickname is 'the loveliest'"?

[32] "Because, by Zeus, Simonides," he said, "I do not desire to get from him that which I could obviously have for the asking, but rather that which a tyrant is least likely of anyone to win. [33] For certainly I love Daïlochus on account of those things that human nature compels us to seek from the beautiful. But I very much desire to get the things my love wants from a willing lover and with friendship. And I think I would want to take them from him by force less than I would want to do myself harm. [34] For I consider that to take from your enemy against his will is the sweetest of all things; but the sweetest of all charms, I think, are the charms of a boy who yields to you willingly. [35] For when a boy loves you in return, how sweetly he looks back at you, how sweetly he asks questions, how sweetly he answers; and the sweetest of all and the most erotic is when he fights with you and argues. [36] But to enjoy the charms of an unwilling boy," he said, "seems to me to be more like robbery than lovemaking. In fact, a robber at least gets some pleasure from his profits and from making his enemies unhappy; but for a man to take pleasure in the unhappiness of the person he loves and to be hated in return for his love and to force himself on someone he makes miserable: how could this not be a nasty, debasing experience? [37] The private citizen, as soon as the boy he loves does him a favor, has proof that the boy is being kind to him out of love, because he knows that he is doing these things under no compulsion, but it is never possible for a tyrant to feel sure that he is loved. [38] For we know that those who do things for one out of fear do everything they can to make it seem that they act out of friendship. Indeed, plots are most often formed against tyrants by none other than those who claim to love them the most."

2.5 Plutarch, *Alcibiades* 3.1–4.1, 4.3–5.3

Plutarch's biography describes the youth of the famous Athenian general Alcibiades (c. 450–404 B.C.E.).

[3.1] Among Antiphon's slanders[15] it has been written that Alcibiades ran away from home to Democrates, one of his lovers. When Ariphron[16]

---

15. The Athenian orator (d. 411) apparently wrote a speech attacking Alcibiades, which is now lost.

16. Pericles' brother and Alcibiades' tutor.

wanted to have his disappearance announced publicly by heralds, Pericles[17] did not allow it, saying, "If he is dead, it will be revealed only one day sooner, but if he is safe, his reputation for the rest of his life will not be saved." Antiphon also says that he struck and killed with a staff one of those attending him in the wrestling-school of Sibyrtius. But these things are perhaps not worthy of belief, since they were said by a man who admitted that he abused Alcibiades out of hatred.

[4.1] Soon many noble men gathered around Alcibiades and pursued him: some were clearly struck by the brilliance of his youthful prime and flattered him, but Socrates' love was a testimony to the boy's excellence of character and good birth. Seeing this appear and shine in his outward form, Socrates feared that his wealth and status, as well as the throng of citizens and foreigners with their flattery and favors, would spoil him prematurely. He undertook, as much as he could, to protect the boy and not stand by idly while a plant in bloom lost its own fruit and was ruined. . . . [4.3] Alcibiades quickly made Socrates his associate and listened to the words of a lover who did not hunt unmanly pleasure or ask for kisses and caresses, but examined the rottenness of his soul and restrained his empty and foolish vanity.

> The proud fighting-cock cowered like a slave, with lowered wing.

Alcibiades considered Socrates' activity truly a service he rendered the gods for the care and salvation of young men. [4.4] Despising himself and wondering at that man, loving his kind disposition and feeling shame before his upright character, Alcibiades without knowing it acquired an "image of love," as Plato calls it,[18] a reciprocal love, such that all men were amazed at seeing him constantly dine with, wrestle with, and even share the same tent with Socrates, while he was difficult and unmanageable for other lovers, and even altogether hostile to some, like Anytus, son of Anthemion.[19]

[4.5] For this man, Anytus, happened to be a lover of Alcibiades and, when hosting some guests to dinner, invited Alcibiades too. He refused the invitation, but getting drunk at home with his friends, made a wild procession to Anytus' house. Standing at the door to the men's dining room and seeing the tables full of silver and gold cups, he told the slaves to take half of them back to his house; he did not think it worth going in

---

17. The Athenian statesman (d. 429) became Alcibiades' guardian after the early death of his father Cleinias.

18. See 5.9.255.

19. This man was to become one of Socrates' primary accusers in 399, prosecuting him for "corrupting the youth." This anecdote, implying that his hostility to Socrates goes back to an old love rivalry, is probably a later invention.

himself, but went back home after this matter had been accomplished. When the guests were angry and said that Alcibiades had treated Anytus violently and contemptuously, Anytus replied, "No, he treated me fairly and humanely, for when it was possible for him to take everything, he left part for us."

[5.1] He also treated his other lovers in this way, except for one metic,[20] as they relate, who did not have much property, but sold all he had and brought the proceeds to Alcibiades, in the sum of 100 staters,[21] asking him to take it. Alcibiades laughed and with pleasure invited him to dinner. After feasting him and being kind, Alcibiades gave him back his money, but ordered him to outbid the tax collectors at the auction of public tax contracts on the following day.[22] [5.2] The man protested, because the purchase would cost many talents,[23] but Alcibiades threatened to whip him if he failed to do it. For he happened to have a private quarrel with the tax collectors. The next morning the metic went to the marketplace and raised the purchase price by a talent. When the tax collectors gathered around him and demanded to know his security for the bid, as if he did not have one, the man was confused and withdrew. But Alcibiades, standing up at the rear of the crowd, said to the magistrates conducting the sale, "Write my name down. He is my friend and I pledge security for him." [5.3] The tax collectors were confounded when they heard this, for they had always been accustomed to pay off loans for earlier purchases with profits on later purchases, and they did not see any way out of their bind. They tried begging the metic and even offered him money to withdraw his bid. But Alcibiades would not let him take less than a talent, and when they offered it, he ordered the metic to take it and withdraw. That man he helped in this way.

2.6 Xenophon, *Anabasis* 2.6.28

This work describes an expedition of 13,000 Greek mercenaries, in which Xenophon was a commander, assisting the younger Cyrus in a campaign to overthrow his older brother, the Persian king, and the further adventures of the mercenaries after Cyrus was killed (401–399 B.C.E.). The following extract describes an unprincipled Thessalian officer named Menon.

20. Metics were noncitizen residents of Attica, either ex-slaves or immigrants from other parts of Greece for the purpose of doing business there.

21. This is a fairly modest amount compared to Alcibiades' wealth, but was the equivalent of 5–6 years' wages for a skilled worker.

22. There was no state agency to collect taxes in Athens. Instead, it was done by private contractors who bid on the rights to collect a given tax.

23. A race was equal to three times the amount the man offered Alcibiades.

While still at the peak of youth and beauty, he obtained from Aristippus[24] the command of his mercenaries and got on very intimate terms with the barbarian Ariaios, because Ariaios enjoyed the company of beautiful youths; he himself, although beardless, had as his boy love Tharupas, whose beard was already grown.

2.7 Xenophon, *Anabasis* 7.4.7–11

[7] There was a certain Episthenes from Olynthus, a boy-lover, who, seeing a beautiful boy, just at the beginning of adolescence, holding a light Thracian shield and about to be put to death, ran up to Xenophon and appealed to him to come to the rescue of a beautiful boy. [8] So Xenophon went to Seuthes[25] and pleaded with him not to kill the boy; he also told him about Episthenes' ways, how once he had put together a company thinking of nothing but whether they were beautiful, and how, fighting with them, he had shown himself a brave man. [9] But Seuthes replied by asking, "Episthenes, would you be willing to die in place of this boy?" So Episthenes stretched out his neck and said, "Strike, if the boy wishes and will be grateful to me." [10] Seuthes then asked the boy if he should strike Episthenes instead of him. The boy would not allow it but pleaded with him to kill neither of them. Then Episthenes, throwing his arms around the boy, said, "The time has come, Seuthes, for you to fight for the boy with me; for I won't give him up to you." [11] But Seuthes laughed the matter off.

2.8 Xenophon, *Cyropaedia* 1.4.27–28

This work is a fictionalized account of the education and life of the elder Cyrus, the first king of Persia (c. 580–529 B.C.E.). It is mainly a vehicle for Xenophon to portray his image of an ideal ruler.

[27] If it is all right to bring up a story that has to do with boy-love too, it is said that when Cyrus was going away, and they were saying goodbye to each other, his relatives took their leave from him with a kiss on the mouth, as is the Persian custom; for even today the Persians still do this. A certain Median,[26] a thoroughly fine gentleman, had been smitten for quite some time with Cyrus' beauty, but when he saw his relatives kissing him, he held

---

24. A noble descendant of the Aleuadae, a Thessalian clan that long had close connections with the Persians. Cyrus gave him money to organize a mercenary army in Thessaly.

25. Seuthes II was a Thracian potentate who attempted to engage Xenophon's mercenaries in his service while they were returning to Greece through his territory.

26. A race closely related to the Persians, who before Cyrus' reign were politically dominant.

back. When the others had gone away, he went up to Cyrus and said, "Am I the only one of your relatives that you don't recognize, Cyrus?"

"What," said Cyrus, "are you too, then, a relative of mine?"

"Very much so," he said.

"Then that is why you were always looking at me," Cyrus said, "for I think I have often noticed you doing so."

"I always wanted to come up to you," he said, "but, by the gods, I was ashamed."

"But you shouldn't have been," said Cyrus, "seeing that you are a relative." And at the same time he went over and kissed him.

[28] And the Median, when he had been kissed, asked, "Is it then really the custom among the Persians to kiss your relatives?"

"Absolutely," he said, "or at least when they see each other after a long time, or when they part from each other."

"It might be time," said the Median, "for you to kiss me again: for I am already parting from you, as you see."

And so Cyrus kissed him goodbye again and went off. But they had not gone very far when the Median appeared again with his horse in a lather. When Cyrus saw him, he said, "What's this? Did you forget something that you wanted to say?"

"No, by Zeus," he said, "but I have come back after some time."

"By Zeus," Cyrus said, "cousin, after a short time, rather."

"You call it short?" the Median said. "Don't you realize, Cyrus, that you are so beautiful that the time it takes to blink seems long to me, because in that time I don't see you?"

Then Cyrus, after shedding tears, laughed and told him to go off in good spirits, because he would be with them in a little while, so he would be able to see him, if he liked, without blinking.

2.9 Xenophon, *Agesilaus* 5.4–6

Agesilaus was a king of Sparta from 399 to 360 B.C.E. and, like Cyrus, was praised by Xenophon as a model of the ideal ruler.

[4] Is it not worth mentioning his self-control in erotic matters if for no other reason than one's amazement at it? One would say that his holding off from those he did not desire was merely the act of an ordinary human. But he loved Megabates, the son of Spithridates,[27] just as the most intense character would love the most beautiful boy. When Megabates tried to kiss

27. A Persian warlord who deserted to the Spartan side during Sparta's war against Persia in 396–95.

Agesilaus (since it is the custom among the Persians to kiss those whom they honor), Agesilaus struggled with all his might not to be kissed. Isn't this a mark of temperance and exceptional high-mindedness? [5] Since Megabates took it as a slight and no longer attempted to kiss him, Agesilaus spoke to one of his friends and asked him to persuade Megabates to "honor" him again. When his friend asked whether he would kiss the boy back, if Megabates should be persuaded, Agesilaus fell silent for a moment and then said, "Not by the twin gods,[28] not even if I were to become the most handsome, strong, and swift man alive! Indeed, I swear by all the gods that I would rather fight the same struggle again than have everything I see turn to gold." [6] I am not ignorant of what some people suspect in regard to these matters. But I at least think I know that more men are able to gain mastery over their enemies than over such appetites.

2.10 Xenophon, *Constitution of the Lacedaemonians* 2.12–14

This treatise discusses Spartan customs, some of which are traced back to the legendary lawgiver Lycurgus, who is variously dated from 900 to 775 B.C.E. Many of the customs attributed to him were probably of much later origin.

[12] It seems to me that something must also be said about the love of boys; for this too has a bearing on education. The other Greeks either do as the Boeotians do, where man and boy are joined as couples and live together, or like the Eleans, who get to enjoy the charms of boys by making them grateful; there are also those who wholly prevent boy-lovers from conversing with boys.

[13] But Lycurgus' views were opposed to all of these: if a man who was decent and upright admired the soul of a boy and tried to spend time with him and to make him his friend without bringing blame on him, he approved this and called it the noblest form of education; if, on the other hand, someone seemed to lust after a boy's body, he laid down that this was the most shameful of all things and that in Lacedaemon[29] boy-lovers should keep their hands off boys just as parents do not lay hands on their own children or brothers on their own brothers.

[14] It does not, however, surprise me that certain people do not believe this: in most of the Greek cities the laws do not oppose men's desire for boys. Thus the Laconian education system, as well as that of the other Greeks, has been explained. Which of them produces men who are more

---

28. The Spartan heroes Castor and Polydeuces. Polydeuces shared his immortality with his twin brother, and they later came to be revered as gods. See ch. 5, n. 80.

29. The entire southern Peloponnesian territory governed by Sparta. Also called Laconia.

trustworthy and more modest and more self-controlled when it is necessary, anyone who is interested may judge for himself.

2.11 Aelian, *Varied History* 3.12

Aelian of Praeneste was a Stoic rhetorician active around 200 C.E. He authored miscellanies that preserve a variety of interesting anecdotes.

Handsome Lacedaemonians are neither effeminate nor arrogant toward lovers, and it is possible to learn from them something completely different than among other ripe adolescents. For they need lovers to "inspire" them[30]—this is the term among the Lacedaemonians meaning "love." Spartan love knows nothing shameful: whether a young man should dare to suffer outrage or a lover to give it, it would benefit neither to dishonor Sparta by doing so. For they would either have to leave their fatherland or, better yet, life itself.

2.12 Plutarch, *Lycurgus* 17.1

This work also discusses Spartan customs attributed to the lawgiver Lycurgus.

And when the boys reached this age [twelve], lovers from among the distinguished young men began to associate with them. The older men also turned their attention to them, making more frequent visits to their places of exercise and being present when the boys sparred and joked with one another. And they did this not as an afterthought, but because they truly believed that they were all in some way the fathers, teachers, and governors of all of the boys. As a result, there was no time or place that lacked someone to admonish and correct a boy who did wrong.

2.13. Plutarch, *Lycurgus* 18.4

Lovers shared in the reputation of their boyfriends, whether good or bad. And it is said that once, when a boy uttered a dishonorable sound in a fight, his lover was fined by the magistrates. Love was so esteemed among them that girls also became the erotic objects of noble women. But rivalries were not permitted: rather, men who had fallen in love with the same boys made it an opportunity to forge a friendship between themselves and they continued to work together to make their beloved the best he could be.

---

30. The Greek word is *eispnein* (breathe into). Some scholars see in this term the remnant of an earlier practice of imparting wisdom and virtue through seminal injection.

2.14 Plutarch, *Pelopidas* 18–19

This passage discusses the Sacred Band of Thebes, an elite military unit organized in 378 B.C.E.

[**18.1**] The Sacred Band, they say, was first organized by Gorgidas out of three hundred picked men, who were trained and fed at the city's expense. They camped out on the Theban citadel, the Cadmeia, and for this reason they were called the "City Band," for in those days the term "city" was generally applied to the citadel. [**18.2**] Some people say that this band was composed of lovers and beloveds, and tradition records a witty remark of Pammenes to this effect. He said that Homer's Nestor was not a shrewd tactician when he ordered that the Greeks be drawn up according to tribe and clan, "so that clan might aid clan, and tribe tribe,"[31] [**18.3**] and that what he should have done was station lover beside beloved. For when the going gets tough, tribesmen don't give much thought for their fellow tribesmen, nor clansmen for their fellow clansmen. But a battalion joined together by erotic love cannot be destroyed or broken: its members stand firm beside one another in times of danger, lovers and beloveds alike motivated by a sense of shame in the presence of the other. [**18.4**] And this is not surprising, when you consider that they even feel more concern for the opinions of loved ones who are absent than before others who are present. A good example is the man who pleaded with an enemy soldier who was about to slaughter him as he lay on the ground to plunge the sword through his chest "in order that my beloved not see my dead body pierced through the back and be ashamed." [**18.5**] It is said also that it was as Heracles' beloved that Iolaus joined in the hero's labors and stood by his side in battle.[32] And Aristotle says that in his own day beloveds and lovers still swore pledges of loyalty at the tomb of Iolaus (at Thebes). [**18.6**] It is therefore natural that Thebes' band was called "sacred," just as Plato too referred to the lover as a "divinely inspired friend."

[**18.7**] It is said that the band remained undefeated until the Battle of Chaeronea,[33] and that when Philip, surveying the casualties after the battle, stood at that place where the three hundred chanced to lie dead, men who

---

31. *Iliad* 2.363.

32. Iolaus was the son of Heracles' half-brother, Iphicles, and accompanied Heracles on many of his labors. His status as a beloved was probably a later interpretation of the myth, as in the case of Achilles and Patroclus.

33. This was the climactic battle between Philip of Macedon and the combined forces of Athens and Thebes (338 B.C.E.), after which Philip was able to enforce a federal constitution on the Greek states with himself as supreme leader.

had faced the Macedonian long spears and were now a jumble of bodies and armor, he was struck with admiration. And when he learned that this was the band of lovers and beloveds, he wept and exclaimed, "May utter destruction fall upon those who suppose these men did or suffered anything disgraceful!"

[19.1] The Thebans' practice of intimacy with lovers, to speak more generally, did not have its origin, as the poets say, in the passion of Laius.[34] Rather, the practice grew out of deliberate policies that the lawgivers adopted in order to temper and soften the Thebans' fiery and violent nature right from childhood. One thing they did was to introduce a major role for the flute in every aspect of work and play and, indeed, they elevated the instrument to a degree of honor and preeminence. The other was to cultivate a conspicuous reverence for love in the wrestling establishments, and thereby moderate the impetuous character of the young men. [19.2] This is also the reason for their wise decision to introduce the goddess Harmony into the city.[35] The goddess is said to be the child of Ares and Aphrodite, and their theory was that where combativeness and belligerence (i.e., Ares) consort and mingle with persuasion and charm (i.e., Aphrodite), all elements of society can be brought into the most harmonious and most orderly whole.

[19.3] Gorgidas brought this Sacred Band out into the front ranks and distributed its members over the entire length of the hoplite phalanx.[36] But in doing so he inadvertently obscured the excellent qualities of the men, and failed to take advantage of their potential for collective action, because they were mixed in with a large number of inferior troops and thus their potential effectiveness was diluted. [19.4] But Pelopidas, after they fought conspicuously at Tegyra[37] and their excellence shone forth, ceased to divide and disperse them and instead, during the greatest battles, employed them as an organic unit, a division that would enter battle before the rest of the army. [19.5] Horses run faster when they are harnessed to a chariot than when ridden individually, and it is not because they displace more air as a group as they rush forth, but because their spirit is fired by their competition with one another and by their love of victory. So too Pelopidas thought that brave men are most useful and eager for collective

34. The mythological Theban king who raped the Elean boy Chrysippus and was identified by Euripid as the originator of pederasty. He was also the father of Oedipus.

35. According to Theban myth, she was the wife of Cadmus, the founder and first king of Thebes.

36. A phalanx was a concentrated block formation of heavy infantry who held their shields contiguous in a solid line.

37. A town in northern Boeotia where Theban forces defeated the Spartans in 375 B.C.E.

action when they instill in one another a sense of rivalry to perform noble deeds.

2.15 Aristotle, *Politics* 2.10, 1272a22–26

In this chapter, Aristotle contends that the Spartans derived many of their institutions from Crete, and cites in particular the institution of common meals. In the midst of this discussion comes the following digression on pederasty.

The lawgiver[38] gave much thought to the benefits of moderation in eating and also to the isolation of women, so that they not have many children. To this end he devised intercourse with males. There will be another occasion to examine whether or not this is a bad thing.

2.16 Ephorus of Cyme, Fr. 149 *Fragmente der griechischen Historiker*

Ephorus was a historian of the mid-fourth century B.C.E. *Here he discusses the Cretan practice of ritualized pederastic abduction.*

They have a unique custom with regard to love affairs. For they do not win their boyfriends through persuasion, but through abduction. The lover warns the boy's friends and family three or more days in advance that he is going to carry out the abduction. It is most shameful for them to hide the boy or not allow him to travel the appointed road, as this is viewed as a confession that the boy is unworthy of such a lover. When they meet him, if the abductor is a man equal to or surpassing the boy in social standing and all else, they fight and pursue him only a bit, enough to fulfill what is customary, and after that they turn the boy over and enjoy the occasion. But if the abductor is unworthy, they prevent him from taking the boy. The pursuit ends when the boy is brought to the men's building[39] of the one who seized him. They think most desirable not the boy distinguished by beauty but the one distinguished by bravery and good behavior. After giving him presents, he takes the boy away to any place in the countryside he wishes, and those who were present at the abduction accompany them; after feasting and hunting together for two months—for it is not permitted to keep the boy away any longer than that—they come down to the city. The boy is set free upon receiving as gifts military equipment, an

---

38. The Cretans' legendary lawgiver was Minos, a wholly mythological figure.
39. The building where Cretan men took common meals together.

ox, a drinking cup[40]—these are the traditional gifts—and many other
things, at such expense that the lover's friends also contribute because
of the magnitude of his expenses. The boy sacrifices this ox to Zeus and
holds a feast for those who came down with him; then he gives his opinion
of his time with his lover, whether it has happened to please him or not,
for the custom gives him this prerogative, in order that, if violence has
been used against him in the course of the abduction, he have the power
at this point to avenge himself and escape. For those who are good looking and from illustrious families it is a disgrace not to get a lover, since it is
assumed that they suffer this because of their manner of living. The "side-
kicks"—this is their name for those who were abducted—receive special
honors in the dances and the most honored places at the races, and they
are permitted to outfit themselves differently from the others, in the equipment they have received from their lovers. And not only then, but also
when they are grown, they wear an outfit distinct from those of other men,
from which each of them will be recognized as *kleinos* (famous). For they
call the boyfriend a *kleinos,* and they call the lover a *philētor* (lover). These
then are their customs regarding love affairs.

2.17 Pausanias 1.30.1

Pausanias was a geographer of the second century C.E., *who wrote a detailed description of the monuments of Greece. In this section he discusses the Academy, a park
and gymnasium on the northwest edge of Athens.*

Before the entrance to the Academy is an altar to Eros that has an inscription that reads, "Charmus,[41] first of the Athenians, dedicated this to Eros."
They say that another altar in the city is called "Anteros" and that it was
a dedication from the metics,[42] because the Athenian Meles, in dishonor-
ing the metic Timagoras, who was in love with him, ordered him to throw
himself down from a rock after he had climbed to the highest part of it.
Timagoras was then unsparing of his own life and wished to please the
youth in every way and so, indeed, he went and cast himself down. But
after Meles saw that Timagoras had died, he came into such a pitch of
repentance that he fell from the same rock and thus, throwing himself

---

40. These three gifts seem to symbolize the boy's assuming adult status in three realms: war,
religion (since the ox is sacrificed), and the banquet.

41. An ally of the tyrant Peisistratus and his sons in the sixth century B.C.E.

42. Since the metics ceased to exist as a separate class by the end of the fourth century, this
dedication must be fourth century or earlier.

down, he died. And from here it has been established among the metics to honor Anteros as the avenging spirit of Timagoras.[43]

2.18 Theopompus, Fr. 225a *Fragmente der griechischen Historiker*

Theopompus was a historian of the fourth century B.C.E., *who wrote a history of contemporary Greece centering around the career of Philip of Macedon.*

Indeed, if there was anyone among the Greeks or among the foreigners lewd[44] or outrageous in character, all these were gathered at Macedon and were called "companions"[45] at the court of Philip. For Philip generally neglected those who were well behaved in their manners and who were mindful of their personal possessions, but he honored and advanced those men who spent extravagantly on their drinking and dice-games. For that very reason he not only arranged for these men to have these things but he made them "athletes" of every injustice and abomination. With what shameful or terrible deed were they not associated? From what good or serious deed were they not dissociated? Some would shave themselves and make themselves smooth, although they continued to be men. Others would mount each other although they had beards. They caroused about with two or three companions, and they would furnish the same services to those companions. From which fact one could not rightly take them to be companions, but rather courtesans,[46] and one could not call them soldiers, but rather brothel-whores. For being man-slayers by nature, they were man-sluts by habit. To put it simply, so I may cease from expatiating, and above all since so many concerns are inundating me, I consider these friends and so-called companions of Philip to have been such beasts as were neither the Centaurs who inhabited Pelion,[47] nor the Laestrygonians who settled on the plain of Leontini,[48] nor any other such creatures.

43. It is unclear whether the original sense of "Anteros" was love avenged, as Pausanias here interprets it, or love returned.

44. The Greek adjective is the rare *lastauros,* which seems to be an intensive form of *stauros,* an upright stake used especially for impalement. It therefore seems to be a metaphorical term for those characterized by habitual sexual excess.

45. The Greek word here is *hetairoi,* which is ambiguous, meaning either companions in a general sense, members of a political/social group, or male prostitutes.

46. Theopompus is here playing on the masculine and feminine forms of the word *hetairoi/ai.* The feminine form meant female prostitutes, but of a higher class than mere *pornai,* here corresponding to "man-sluts" *(andropornoi).*

47. A mythological tribe of half-human, half-equine creatures who inhabited Thessaly and were known for their crudity and lack of civilization.

48. Cannibalistic giants in Homer's *Odyssey,* who in later times were thought to be located in Sicily.

2.19 Carystius of Pergamum,
Fr. 10 *Fragmenta Historicorum Graecorum*

Carystius, a historian writing near the end of the second century B.C.E., describes events in Athens at the end of the fourth century, after the fall of the democracy to Alexander the Great's successors.

After his brother Himeraeus had been killed by Antipater,[49] Demetrius of Phalerum[50] went to live with Nicanor;[51] he had been accused of offering sacrifice to his brother's divine manifestation.[52] Then he became a friend of Cassander[53] and gained great power. At first his lunch had been only a bowl of vinegar with miscellaneous olives in it and island cheese. Once he was rich he bought Moschion, the best cook and caterer of his time, and so numerous were the dishes prepared daily for his dinners that Moschion himself, who was given the leftovers, within two years had bought three tenement blocks and was abusing freeborn boys and women of noble families. All the boys were jealous of Demetrius' boyfriend, Diognis, and so keen were they to meet Demetrius that when he had strolled about The Tripods[54] after lunch, all the most beautiful boys gathered there on the following days so as to be seen by him.

2.20 Plutarch, *Demetrius* 24.1–3

Plutarch here describes the Macedonian general Demetrius Poliorcetes, who took up residence in the Parthenon after liberating Athens from his rival, Cassander, in 304 B.C.E.

[1] Although it was fitting that he feel shame before Athena, if for no other reason than her being his elder sister (so he liked to hear her called),[55] Demetrius stained the Acropolis with so much rape of freeborn boys and

---

49. The Macedonian general who acted as regent over Greece during Alexander's campaigns in the east and after his death, until his own death in 319. Upon defeating Athens and the other Greek cities that revolted after Alexander's death, he ordered the arrest of prominent Athenian democrats in 322.

50. A student of Aristotle, who became absolute governor of Athens under Cassander from 317 to 307 and instituted extensive legal reforms.

51. Aristotle's son-in-law and a general under Alexander and Cassander.

52. In other words, he was accused of considering his dead brother a god.

53. Antipater's son and successor.

54. A street in Athens.

55. The Athenians had decreed divine status to Demetrius in thanks for his "liberating" the city. He should have felt shame before Athena because she was a chaste virgin, as emphasized by her epithet Athena Parthenos. The Parthenon was her chief temple.

citizen women that the place seemed pure in comparison when he mingled
in wild abandon with whores like Chrysis, Lamia, Demo, and Anticyra.

[2] For the city's sake it is better not to report the other affairs clearly, but
it is worthwhile not to pass over the courage and temperance of Democles.
For he was still an adolescent boy, and it did not escape Demetrius' notice
that his nickname, "Democles the fair," revealed his beauty. He was caught
by none of the many men who tried, whether offering gifts or threats, and
finally he avoided the gymnasium and wrestling-schools altogether. Instead, he made a practice of going into an establishment where he could
bathe privately. Demetrius waited for the right moment and entered when
he was alone there. [3] When the boy recognized that he was quite alone
and under the threat of force, he took the lid off the cauldron of boiling
water for the bath and leaped into it, thereby killing himself and suffering
an unworthy death, but one that he thought worthy of his fatherland and
beauty.

2.21 Athenaeus 13.601A–B, 601E–605D

Athenaeus, an author of the late second century C.E., *wrote a lengthy symposiastic
work that assembles anecdotes and quotations from a variety of earlier sources. This
section is part of a lengthy speech by Myrtilus, discussing famous boy-lovers.*

[601] Stesichorus,[56] another man of strong passions, composed the particular kind of lyrics that were called "boy songs" and "boy love." No one
used to despise those who had a passionate nature: love affairs were such
an open and everyday matter that the great poet Aeschylus, and Sophocles
too, put sexual themes on the stage in their tragedies, Aeschylus showing
Achilles' love for Patroclus, Sophocles love of the boys in *Niobe* (which is
why some people call this play *Paiderastria*)—and their audiences enjoyed
such themes.[57]

. . . And many men, overall, prefer love with boys to love with females.
In the very cities of Greece that have the best laws by comparison with
others, this is the mode of behavior that is fashionable. The Cretans, as I
told you, and the Chalcidians of Euboea, are both especially fond of love
with boys. Notice that Echemenes in *Cretan Studies* says that it was not Zeus
but Minos who stole Ganymede; while those Chalcidians, for their part,
say that it *was* Zeus, but that Ganymede was stolen from their very own

56. Principally known as a poet of long mythological dithyrambs in the late seventh and
early sixth centuries B.C.E. None of his pederastic lyrics are extant.

57. For Aeschylus' *Myrmidons*, see **5.7.180**. Extant fragments (frr. 135–37 *TGrF*) confirm
that the relationship of Achilles and Patroclus in this play was explicit and physical. In fr. 448
TGrF of Sophocles' *Niobe*, one of the dying sons of Niobe appeals to his lover for help.

territory, and they can show you the place: they call it "The Stealing," and lots of myrtles grow there. Minos even gave up his enmity with the Athenians (though it had arisen from the death of his own son) once he fell in love with Theseus;[58] he gave Theseus his daughter Phaedra to marry, so says Zenis or Zeneus of Chios in his book about Chios.

[602] Hieronymus the Aristotelian says that love with boys was fashionable because several tyrannies had been overturned by young men in their prime, joined together as comrades in mutual sympathy. In his boyfriend's presence, a lover would go through any suffering rather than have the boy think him a coward. This was demonstrated in practice by the Sacred Band, formed by Epaminondas at Thebes;[59] by the Peisistratid assassination, the work of Harmodius and Aristogeiton; and at Acragas in Sicily by the story of Chariton and Melanippus. Melanippus was the boyfriend, so says Heracleides of Pontus[60] in *On Love Affairs;* the two were discovered to be plotting against Phalaris[61] and were tortured to force them to name their accomplices. Not only did they refuse to speak, they made Phalaris so sorry for their sufferings that he released them with fulsome commendation. Apollo was pleased at this and consequently favored Phalaris by postponing his death, stating this in his response to the persons who asked the Pythian oracle how they were to go about attacking Phalaris. Apollo also pronounced an oracle about Chariton and those who were with him, giving it the form of a pentameter followed by a hexameter (the same pattern that Dionysius of Athens, called "the Bronze," was afterwards to employ in his *Elegies*).[62] This is the oracle:

Blessed were Chariton and Melanippus:
They showed mortals the way to a friendship that was divine.

The story about Cratinus of Athens is famous, too. He was a beautiful youngster at the time when Epimenides had to purify Athens of some ancient miasma[63] and was to do so by means of human blood; whereupon he

58. Minos' son Androgeus died in Attic territory, after which Minos made war on Athens and demanded an annual tribute consisting of seven Athenian youths and seven maidens, to be fed to the Minotaur. The young Theseus volunteered to go as one of the victims and killed the Minotaur. This is the only account we have of Minos falling in love with him.

59. 2.14 identifies Gorgidas as the founder. Epaminondas was a Theban general slightly later, from 371 to 362 B.C.E.

60. A fourth-century follower of Plato's school and prolific writer of dialogues.

61. The tyrant of Acragas from approximately 570 to 550 B.C.E. He reportedly tortured his victims by roasting them inside a bronze bull placed over a fire.

62. An elegiac poet of the fifth century, so named because of his role in the introduction of bronze currency.

63. Epimenides was a Cretan holy man and wonder-worker who was asked to purify Athens of the pollution it incurred when the Athenians violated oaths of safe conduct they had given

(Cratinus) volunteered himself on behalf of his homeland, so Neanthes of
Cyzicus tells us in *On Initiations,* book 2. After him his lover, Aristodemus,
also accepted death, and thus the pollution was cleansed. Because of affairs
like these, the tyrants, under threat from such conspiracies, made love
affairs with boys totally illegal and put a stop to them wherever they were
found. Some even burned and demolished the gymnasia, regarding them
as siege-works that threatened their own fortresses: Polycrates, tyrant of
the Samians, did precisely this.

Among the citizens of Sparta—so says Hagnon the Platonist—it is customary for men to keep company with [64] unmarried girls in the same way
that they do with boys elsewhere.

Now it was the lawgiver Solon who said:

> . . . sighing for thighs and for sweet lips.

Aeschylus and Sophocles were likewise explicit. In the *Myrmidons* Aeschylus said:

> You abjured the holy sacrament of the thighs!
> You spurned a profusion of kisses! [65]

Sophocles in *Women of Colchis* said of Ganymede that he

> . . . lit the fire of tyrant Zeus with his thighs.

—And, yes, I know Polemon the Traveler [66] says in *Refutations of Neanthes*
that the story of Cratinus and Aristodemus is all made up. As for you,
Cynulcus,[67] you may well think these tales are fiction, but you use them as
if they were true. Everything that there is in these poems about the love of
boys you yourself do quietly at home!—But the people who first introduced
pederasty to Greece were the Cretans, so Timaeus[68] tells us. Others say
that Laius was the first pederast: he was Pelops' guest, fell in love with

---

some conspirators who had helped Cylon seize the Acropolis with a view to establishing a
tyranny and had subsequently taken refuge at a temple of Athena. Sources differ on Epimenides' date, but the original Cylonian conspiracy is generally dated to either 636 or 632 B.C.E.

64. The verb *homilein* also has the connotation "have sex with." In this context the reference
may be to anal sex, which would be practiced as a form of birth control.

65. This is fr. 135 *TGrF.* These are the words of Achilles addressing the corpse of Patroclus,
whom he reproaches for disobeying his instructions not to attack Troy and thus abandoning
Achilles' love by dying.

66. Probably Polemon of Ilium, a Stoic geographer active around 190 B.C.E., who collected
epigraphic material.

67. The speaker of this section, Myrtilus, here addresses another one of the symposiasts, the
Cynic Cynulcus. The Cynics were generally unsympathetic to pederasty (see **5.17–18**).

68. A historian of Sicily active in the late fourth and early third centuries B.C.E. He was
known for historicizing interpretation of myths.

Pelops' son Chrysippus, [603] kidnapped the boy, put him in his chariot and escaped to Thebes; but Praxilla of Sicyon[69] says that Chrysippus' kidnapper was Zeus.

Among other peoples the Celts, in spite of the fact that their women are very beautiful, prefer boys as sexual partners. There are some of them who will regularly go to bed—on those animal skins of theirs—with a pair of lovers.[70] The Persians also have sex with boys, but they learned it from the Greeks, Herodotus says.[71]

King Alexander, too, was quite excessively keen on boys: according to Dicaearchus[72] in *On the Sacrifice at Troy*, he was so taken with the eunuch Bagoas that under the eyes of the whole theater he bent over to give him a kiss, and when the audience shouted and applauded, he very willingly bent over and kissed him again. Charon of Chalcis—so says Carystius in *Historical Notes*—had a beautiful boy who was devoted to him. Alexander remarked on his beauty during a drinking bout hosted by Craterus. Charon told his boy to give Alexander a kiss. "No!" said the king. "That would pain you more than it would please me." Although he was a passionate man, Alexander was also self-controlled as regards decency and propriety: when he had captured Dareius' daughters and wife (who was quite admirably beautiful), not only did he not have sex with them, he arranged that they should not even learn that they were captives, giving the order that they should continue to be attended just as if Dareius still ruled. That was why Dareius, when he learned of this, stretched out his hands to the Sun in prayer that *either* he *or* Alexander should be king.

Rhadamanthys the Just, says Ibycus, had Talos as his lover.[73] Diotimus says in the *Heracleia* that Heracles had made Eurystheus[74] his boyfriend and that was why he performed his labors. There is a myth that Agamemnon had Argynnus as his lover, having seen him swimming in the Cephisus, and then he drowned in it (he bathed in it often, evidently) and Agamemnon buried him and raised a shrine there to Aphrodite Argynnis. Licymnius of Chios[75] says in his *Dithyrambs* that Argynnus' lover was Hymenaeus.

69. A dithyrambic poet of the mid-fifth century B.C.E.

70. "One of each sex" is the implication. The Greek ethnonym, *Keltoi*, may mean "Celts," but is more often applied in Greek sources to the Germans.

71. Herodotus 1.135.

72. A prolific pupil of Aristotle who wrote many historical and philosophical treatises in the late fourth century. The treatise cited here described Alexander's sacrifices before the battle of Granicus.

73. Rhadamanthys was a brother of Minos whose reputation for justice resulted in his becoming a judge in the Underworld after his death. Talos was a bronze giant who guarded Crete.

74. Heracles' cousin and the King of Tiryns, at whose command he performed his legendary Twelve Labors.

75. A fifth-century dithyrambic poet and rhetorician.

King Antigonus[76] was lover of the citharode Aristocles, on whom Antigonus of Carystus, in the *Life of Zeno,* writes as follows:

> King Antigonus used to go serenading with Zeno. He once emerged from a drinking bout at dawn, hurried to Zeno's and urged him to join in serenading the citharode Aristocles, whom the king loved passionately.

Sophocles was as much a lover of young boys as Euripides was a lover of women. The poet Ion of Chios[77] writes thus in his book *Encounters.*

> The poet Sophocles I met at Chios when, as general, he was bound for Lesbos:[78] a playful man, when in wine, and clever. Hermesileus, his own friend and the consular representative of Athens, was hosting him, when there beside the fire, ready to pour out his wine, was a boy . . .[79] of course, and he said, "Do you want me to like my wine?" and the boy said yes. "Then hand me the cup slowly, and take it from me slowly." The boy was now blushing more and more, and Sophocles said to his neighbor, "Phrynichus put it so beautifully! **[604]** 'Shines on his crimson cheeks the light of love.'"[80] Whereupon the other, an Eretrian schoolmaster or else an Erythraean, replied, "Yes, you are learned in poetry, Sophocles, but all the same Phrynichus was wrong to call a beautiful boy's cheeks crimson. If the painter smeared this boy's cheeks with crimson, he would no longer seem beautiful. It's quite wrong to compare beauty with what is not beautiful." Sophocles laughed at this Eretrian: "Don't you like that line of Simonides, either, sir? 'From crimson lips the virgin's voice was raised'—yet the Greeks all think it's quite right! or the poet who spoke of 'golden-haired Apollo,'[81] although if a painter painted Apollo's hair gold and not black, so much the worse for the painting; or the poet of 'rosy-fingered,'[82] because if you dip your fingers into rose-colored paint you have the hands of a crimson-dyer, not those of a beautiful woman." They laughed, and the Eretrian was put out of countenance by this retort; Sophocles took up his conversation with the boy again. He was trying to get a bit of straw out of the wine cup with his little finger. "Do you see the bit of straw?" asked Sophocles, and the boy said he saw it. "Don't dip your finger in, then," he said. "Just blow it away instead." Then, as the boy's face approached

---

76. Antigonus Gonatas, the embattled Macedonian king of Greece from 284 to 239 B.C.E., was a great patron of art and philosophy. The Zeno referred to as his companion was Zeno the Stoic (see **5.20–25**).

77. A fifth-century poet, known to have produced tragedies in Athens between 451 and 428, but also active in other genres.

78. Sophocles was general during the Samian War, probably 441–440.

79. Something is missing in the Greek text at this point, perhaps a description of the boy.

80. Phrynichus was an early tragic poet, known to be active between 511 and 476. This line is cited earlier by Athenaeus (at 13.564F) as from his *Troilus,* describing the Trojan prince known for his beauty.

81. Pindar, *Olympian* 6.41, cf. Tyrtaeus 3.2.

82. "Rosy-fingered Dawn," as, for example, in *Odyssey* 2.1 or Hesiod, *Works and Days* 610.

the cup, Sophocles brought the cup nearer to his own lips, so that their two heads would be closer; and when they were very close, he put his arm around him and kissed him. There was applause, with laughter and shouts, at how well he had managed the boy, and Sophocles said, "I am practicing strategy, gentlemen. Pericles said that I knew how to make poetry, but not how to be a strategist. This stratagem fell out 'just right' for me, didn't it?"[83] His conversation over wine, and his behavior in daily life, were full of such clever turns; in politics, though, he was no more wise and no more effective than any other respectable Athenian.

Hieronymus of Rhodes,[84] in *Historical Notes,* says that Sophocles induced a good-looking boy to come outside the city walls to have sex with him:

This boy laid his own cloak on the ground under them, and they wrapped themselves in Sophocles' cape. After the act the boy snatched Sophocles' cape and went off leaving Sophocles his own boyish cloak. The incident was widely reported. Euripides heard of it and made a joke out of it, saying that he had had that boy too and it did not cost him anything; Sophocles had let himself go and had paid with ridicule. When Sophocles heard that, he composed an epigram against Euripides in the following sense, alluding to the story of the North Wind and the Sun, and at the same time satirizing Euripides' adulteries:

It was the Sun, and not a boy, whose heat stripped me naked;
   As for you, Euripides, when you were kissing someone else's wife
The North Wind screwed you. You are unwise, you who sow
   In another's field, to accuse Eros of being a snatch-thief.

Theopompus in his *On the Wealth Pillaged from Delphi* says **[605]** that Asopichus, the boyfriend of Epaminondas,[85] had the trophy at Leuctra depicted on his shield, that he came through astonishing perils, and that the shield had been laid in the Stoa at Delphi. In the same essay Theopompus says that Phayllus, tyrant of the Phocians, was a woman-lover and Onomarchus[86] a boy-lover: that when the son of Pythodorus of Sicyon, a beautiful boy, came to Delphi to cut off his long hair,[87] Onomarchus had sex with

83. Appropriately Sophocles uses a phrase, *kat' orthon* "just right," which was one of his own favorites in his poetry (three citations in Liddell and Scott 1925–40 s.v. *orthos* III.1.b).

84. A philosopher and literary historian active in Athens under the patronage of Antigonus Gonatas in the third century B.C.E. A pupil of the Aristotelian school, he later became an Eclectic.

85. See n. 59. His victory over the Spartans at Leuctra occurred in 371.

86. Phayllus and Onomarchus were brothers who commanded the Phocian army in the late 350s and were accused of stealing Delphic treasures to finance their efforts.

87. A ceremony performed by boys when they reach the age of eighteen.

him and gave him four gold strigils,[88] which were temple offerings of the people of Sybaris; and that Phayllus gave Deiniades' flute-girl, Bromias, a silver *karkhēsion*[89] belonging to the Phocians and a gold ivy-wreath belonging to the Peparethians. Theopompus says:

> This same girl was going to play the flute at the Pythia, but the mob put a stop to it. To Physcidas, son of Lycolas of Tricholeum, a beautiful boy, Onomarchus gave a gold bay wreath, a temple offering of the Ephesians; this same boy, taken to Philip's court by his father and prostituted there, was sent away without any presents. To Damippus, a beautiful boy, son of Epilycus of Amphipolis, Onomarchus gave a temple offering dedicated by Pleisthenes. To Pharsalia, the Thessalian dancing-girl, Philomelus gave a gold bay wreath, a temple offering of the Lampsacenes. This same girl, Pharsalia, was killed in Metapontium by the fortune-tellers in the marketplace, because of a voice that came out of the bronze bay tree that the Metapontines had set up when Aristeas of Proconnesus visited them and said that he had come from the people beyond the North Wind. As soon as they saw her entering the marketplace the fortune-tellers became mad and tore her to pieces. When the reason for this was afterwards investigated, it was determined that her death was due to the wreath, the property of a god.[90]

And so, you philosophers who disgrace the goddess Aphrodite by using her[91] unnaturally, take care that you are not destroyed in the same way. Clearchus[92] tells us:

> "Boys are beautiful only during the period when they resemble a woman," the courtesan Glycera used to say.

2.22 Graffiti from Thera = *Inscriptiones Graecae* 12.3.537–550

Some of these inscriptions may be as early as the seventh century B.C.E. *They were found on rocks in the vicinity of a temple of Apollo and gymnasium, which may, however, postdate the graffiti.*

[537a] By Delphinius Apollo, here Crimon penetrated the son of
          Bathycles, brother of . . .
[538b] Here Crimon penetrated Amotion.

---

88. Scrapers used by athletes to remove dirt and oil from their bodies after exercise.

89. An hourglass-shaped drinking cup.

90. These tales from Theopompus show that love-gifts stolen from Delphic temples brought bad luck to their possessors. In the last example, we are to understand, the offended god was found by the investigators to have driven the fortune-tellers mad and so caused the death of Pharsalia. The same story is told in a different way by Plutarch.

91. "Using Aphrodite" is metaphorical for "having sex."

92. Clearchus of Soli was a polymath active in the late fourth and early third centuries B.C.E.

[540(I)] Lacydidas is good.

[540(II)] Eumelus is the best dancer.

[540(III)] Crimon first delighted Simias with his lascivious dance.

[542] . . . loves Phanocles.

[543] Barbax both dances well and gave . . .

[546] Telecrates is a good dancer.

[547] Pykimedes is the best of the Scamotidae.[93]

[549] I, . . . , am beautiful in the eyes of all.

[550] In the presence of Dyman, son of Hermeias, . . . always offered . . .

2.23 Graffiti from Athens = *IG* 1².921–26

These were found at various places in the city and are sixth to fifth century B.C.E. in date.

[921] Arisemus is beautiful; Polytime is a whore.

[922] I don't tickle Lysanias, son of Chaerephon.

[923] . . . -ous is beautiful and a delight to speak to.

[924] Lysitheus says that he loves Micion especially of the men in the city,
    for he is courageous.

[925] Lysias is beautiful.

[926] Archias is beautiful.

2.24 Graffiti from Thasos = *Supplementum Epigraphicum Graecum* 32.847

The following, discovered in 1980, are among fifty-eight similar inscriptions on three rock faces overlooking an isolated bay. They appear to be mid-fourth century in date.

[13] Aetes is ripe, fair in the face, sweet, and gracious.[94]

[16] Aetes is refined in the face.

[22] Herophon is gold.

[26] Aetes is elegant in his figure and bearing.

[28] Anthippus is beautiful in the face.

[30] Pythion is sweet.

[36] Myiscus is wild.[95]

---

93. Apparently the name of a local family or clan.

94. The last epithet is *eucharis* in Greek. In addition to denoting grace and charm, this word may have connotations of willingness to gratify a lover, as in the verb *charizein* (to grant sexual favors).

95. The epithet here is *agrios*, which in other contexts refers to active lovers with no self-restraint.

[40] Mys is sweet.
[42] Myiscus has good rhythm.
[44] Aetes is gracious and refined.[96]
[47] Myiscus is gracious and beautiful.
[54] Myiscus is gold, fair in the face, and . . . of Hera.[97]
[57] Myiscus is my sweet.
[58] Myiscus of Thasos is silver.

2.25 Graffiti from Nemea = *SEG* 29.349

The following were written on the walls of a tunnel in the stadium at Nemea, site of a major pan-Hellenic athletic festival. They are fourth to third century B.C.E. in date.

[g] Epicrates is beautiful.
[i] Acrotatus is beautiful *(and added in a second hand)* in the opinion of the
    writer.[98]

2.26 Graffito from Mytilene = *IG* 12.2.268

Phaestas is beautiful. So says Ogesthenes, who wrote this.

2.27 Inscriptions on Athenian Vases = *Athenian Agora* 21 C

Many drinking vessels of Athenian manufacture were inscribed with boys' names and the epithet "beautiful" or the generic phrase "the boy is beautiful." Some of the more interesting variants are assembled here, ranging in date from the early seventh century to the late fifth century. We cannot exclude the possibility that some of the names refer to men rather than boys.

[1] *(second quarter of seventh century)* The boy is abominable.[99]
[5] *(late sixth century)* Titas, the Olympic victor, is anal.[100]

---

96. "Gracious" is *eucharis* (see n. 94), and "refined" is *asteios*, which literally means "of the town," as opposed to rustic.

97. Perhaps we should understand "beloved" in the gap.

98. This was the name of at least two members of a Spartan royal family, one of whom died in 305, the other around 252. The comment written by the second hand could therefore be a later political judgment, even if the original Acrotatus praised in the inscription was someone else entirely.

99. The Greek epithet is *misetos* (hateful), but is often used with connotations of sexual excess or prostitution.

100. The Greek word here is *katapugon* (oriented toward the buttocks). It seems to be used of both active and passive participants in anal sex.

[7] *(late sixth to early fifth century)* Menecrates is beautiful and dear to Lysicles.

[8] *(early fifth century)* Hegestratus had intercourse with me.

[18] *(second quarter of fifth century)* Sosias is anal. So says the one who wrote this.

[23] *(second quarter of fifth century)* Sydromachus of the gaping anus submitted.

[26] *(third quarter of fifth century)* Aristomenes is anal.

2.28 Gymnastic Law from Beroea = *SEG* 27.261, side B, 13–15, 26–32

This law, from a city in Macedonia, can be dated to the mid-second century B.C.E.

With regard to the boys, let no one of the young men approach the boys, nor let any chat with them, but if one does, let the gymnasiarch [101] punish him and let him keep the one doing it away from them. . . . With regard to those who should not have a share in the gymnasium: let neither a slave strip down for the purpose of exercise nor a freedman nor their sons nor an *apalaistros* [102] nor a male prostitute [103] nor craftsmen [104] nor a drunk nor a madman. And if the gymnasiarch knowingly permits any of those known to be such to be oiled, or if someone reveals this situation to him and proves it, let him pay a penalty of one thousand drachmas.

101. The manager of the gymnasium.

102. This is a word of uncertain meaning, but probably refers to those who are qualified to enter the gymnasium in other respects, but do not attend due to a lack of physical fitness.

103. Literally, "anyone who has ever prostituted himself."

104. Literally, anyone "using a marketplace skill," which could also refer to small vendors.

—————

CHAPTER 3

Greek Comedy

Attic (Athenian) comedy is particularly useful for the study of homosexuality in virtue of its characteristic explicitness in sexual matters. Moreover, it provides insight into what may have been prevailing popular attitudes toward the practice. The genre's assumptions are populist and anti-elite. Although the authors of comedy were themselves probably members of the educated upper class, the plays are focalized from the point of view of the average Athenian: Aristophanes' heroes are often characterized as rustics or otherwise marginalized citizens who, through their pluck and ingenuity, overthrow the city's political and intellectual leaders.

Attic comedy is generally divided into three phases: Old (486–400 B.C.E.), Middle (400–325 B.C.E.), and New (after 325 B.C.E.). Old Comedy is more politically engaged and frequently alludes to the sexual habits of well-known figures as essential character traits that reveal their overall ethos. While the plots of Middle Comedy are not as overtly political, personal satire, particularly against targets perceived as sexually deviant, continues to be common. New Comedy deals principally with plots of heterosexual romance and features little satire or interest in homosexuality.

The most conspicuous representative of Old Comedy is Aristophanes, who produced plays between 427 and 388 B.C.E., of which eleven are extant. **3.12**, from the early *Wasps*, emphasizes the poet's personal dissociation from pederastic tastes as a sign of his continuing solidarity with his theatrical public. **3.15**, from *Frogs*, identifies a hierarchy of sexual practices ranging from the most normative (heterosexuality) to the most *outré* (necrophilia), with pederasty ranged after heterosexuality and attraction to effeminate adult men coming just before necrophilia. The most extravagant and sustained portrait of such an effeminate is **3.14**, from *Thesmophoria*

Women, where we see in transvestite attire the tragic poet Agathon, the host of Plato's *Symposium* and a character known from many sources to have remained clean-shaven and to have played a boy's role with older men well into adulthood.

But even conventional pederasty does not receive positive treatment. **3.13,** from *Birds,* speculates about an ideal city where fathers would welcome suitors' interest in their sons, but this is clearly presented as the opposite of the real Athens and is the fantasy of a not very creditable character. **3.17,** from *Wealth,* implies that the gift-giving of traditional pederastic courtship was no different from giving money and that upper-class youths who expected such gifts were no better than prostitutes; even entertaining a boy at a lavish dinner is viewed as buying his favors (see **3.25, 3.26,** and **3.30**). By contrast, boys who resorted to prostitution out of real poverty are actually treated with some sympathy (see **3.9** and **3.16**). The one arguably positive allusion to pederasty (**3.10**) involves a slave boy.

Our most complete description of traditional man-boy pederasty comes in *Clouds* (**3.11**). One of the denizens of Socrates' Thinkery, named "Better Argument," describes at length the archaic ideal of modest, orderly, muscular, athletic boys who defer to their elders. "Worse Argument" counters him by justifying a life of dissolution and adultery; even if one should be punished, as adulterers sometimes were, by having radishes or other foreign objects rammed up one's anus, one would be none the worse for it, since most of Athens' intellectual and political elite are already "wide-assed" due to having engaged in pederastic relations as boys. Better Argument admits defeat in the debate, as he too belongs among this group. The implication is that having been penetrated as a boy changes one's anatomy (and character) for life, and that even active pederasts like Better Argument have never really ceased being "wide-assed" passives.

This free interchange of sex roles is also apparent in *Knights,* a play in which homosexual imagery is employed throughout as a metaphor for political exploitation and manipulation. The play involves a domestic allegory, in which the leading politicians of Athens are imagined as slaves to the master Demos (= the common people); one slave, Paphlagon (= the demagogue Cleon), has ingratiated himself with Demos and uses his position of favor to bully and dominate all the other slaves. Two of these, Demosthenes and Nicias, recruit a lowly street vendor of sausages to be even more shameless in pandering to Demos than Paphlagon and thereby to depose him from his privileged position. The play is constructed around a series of verbal duels between the two rivals, who both boast of their ability to dominate through active penetration (**3.3, 3.6, 3.7**) and at the same time to curry favor through submitting to penetration (**3.1, 3.2, 3.4, 3.5, 3.8, 3.9**). That Sausage-seller was a male prostitute in his youth (**3.5, 3.9**) is even treated as a prime qualification for becoming a political leader: he is willing to do any-thing to please Demos. As well as giving us insight into the complex political dynamics of master-slave relations in a household, this play reinforces the negative image of homosexual activity among Athens' leadership elite that we gain from the rest of Aristophanes' work.

Comedies that survive only in fragmentary form are also a rich, if much neglected, mine of information. In **3.18** and fr. 358 PCG, Aristophanes identifies pederasty as a practice characteristic of Ionians and Spartans, re-spectively; either way, it is marginalized as un-Athenian. Cratinus, an older contemporary of Aristophanes, wrote a play attacking philosophers in which homosexual inclinations are among the charges leveled against them (**3.19, 3.20**). **3.19** and **3.24** suggest that there were isolated hot spots on the edge of town where men could go to meet other men or boys, even as today cer-tain parks or public facilities have a reputation for being "active." **3.22** and **3.32** convey the view that oral sex is something particularly disgusting for both parties. **3.23** suggests that an effeminate man might also be an active pederast; the actual reason some men may have chosen to shave their beards and look like youths may have been to make themselves more attractive to youths, rather than to older men, as comedy generally implies. Active peder-asts generally come in for just as much ridicule (Cratinus, frr. 58, 104 PCG; Aristophanes, fr. 583 PCG; Teleclides, fr. 52 PCG; Plato Com., fr. 279 PCG) as boys (Crates, fr. 1 PCG) or effeminate men (**3.21**; Cratinus, fr. 11 PCG; Eupolis, frr. 177, 178, 249 PCG; Aristophanes, frr. 178, 422 PCG). Ar-istophanes' contemporary Eupolis wrote two plays (*Flatterers* and *Autolycus*) lampooning the rich Callias (host of Xenophon's *Symposium*—**5.8**) for al-lowing himself to be manipulated by boys and effeminate men.

Middle Comedy largely continues the same themes of ridicule against both effeminate men (Eubulus, frr. 10, 166 PCG; Alexis, frr. 105, 266 PCG; Timocles, fr. 5 PCG) and extravagant pederasts like Misgolas (**3.31**; Alexis, fr. 3 PCG; Timocles, fr. 32 PCG; Antiphanes wrote a whole play titled *The Pederast*). It also continued Old Comedy's interest in writing plays based on pederastic myths: Eubulus, Antiphanes, and Alcaeus each wrote a *Ganymede*, just as Strattis had written a *Chrysippus* and Plato Comicus a *Laius*. The one new theme Middle Comedy had to contribute was ridicule of Plato's dia-logues on love and the idea that there could be a chaste, philosophical Eros (see **3.27–29**).

New Comedy, largely romantic in nature, shows far less interest in homo-sexual themes, although Diphilus did apparently write a play titled *Pederasts* and **3.33** shows a character enthusing over a beautiful youth he has seen. **3.34** is a clever riddle about anal penetration, but without any element of personal satire.

Bibliographical Note

Comparatively little has been written concerning homosexuality in Greek comedy. However, see Dover (1978) 135–53. The most systematic treatment of sexuality generally in Attic comedy is Henderson (1975), with 204–20 specifically on homosexuality. Hubbard (1998b) 50–59 uses Aristophanes and the comic fragments as evidence of popular prejudices against homosexuality as an elite practice. Storey (1995) and (1998) 112, 115–18 examines some individual cases of personal satire based on gender inversion or homosexual habits.

On homosexual themes in Aristophanes' *Knights,* see Henderson (1975) 67–69. For the "lover of the people" metaphor (**3.7**) as a possible remnant of Cleon's oratory, see Connor (1971) 96–108; Monoson (1994) suggests a possible origin in Pericles' oratory. On the Sausage-seller's fellatio in **3.2** and Greek attitudes toward the practice generally, see Jocelyn (1980). On homosexuality as a sign of the city's corruption in *Clouds,* see Henderson (1975) 72–78. For a good philosophical analysis of the two competing systems of education offered by the Arguments, see Nussbaum (1980) 51–67. Fowler (1996) has argued that the women's sex strike in *Lysistrata* is predicated on the assumption that homosexuality was not an option for most Athenian men. On gender inversion and transvestism in *Thesmophoria Women,* see especially Snyder (1974), R. Cantarella (1975), Muecke (1982), and Stohn (1993); on Agathon's homosexuality, see Pretagostini (1997).

On homosexual themes in Middle and New Comedy, see Lilja (1983) 34–40.

3.1 Aristophanes, *Knights* 75–79

This play dates to 424 B.C.E. The slave Demosthenes describes Paphlagon's (= Cleon's) watchfulness and involvement in all household affairs (that is, every part of Greece).

DEMOSTHENES: That man watches over everything. He stands with one leg in Pylos[1] and the other in the Assembly, with his feet *this* far apart *[he demonstrates];* so that his ass is right in Chasmos, his hands in Extortia, and his mind in Larcenadae.[2]

---

1. Pylos, in the southwest Peloponnese, was the scene of a notable Athenian victory over the Spartans on Spartan territory, for which Cleon took credit.

2. These three names all involve puns on recognizable Greek place names. The Greek refers literally to the Chaonians, a remote people of northwestern Greece; the pun involves the verb *chaskō* (gape), a term Aristophanes frequently uses with reference to a habitually penetrated anus.

3.2 Aristophanes, *Knights* 164–67

Demosthenes tries to recruit the Sausage-seller to become a rival of Paphlagon (Cleon) by showing him all the advantages that political power brings.

DEMOSTHENES: Of all these you shall be the paramount chief, chief too of the market, the harbors, and the Pnyx.[3] You'll trample on Council and trim back the generals; you'll chain, you'll imprison, you'll . . . suck cocks in the Prytaneum.[4]

3.3 Aristophanes, *Knights* 364–65

Paphlagon and the Sausage-seller engage in a preliminary verbal duel, including this exchange.

SAUSAGE-SELLER: And I'll stuff your ass like a sausage skin.
PAPHLAGON: And I'll drag you out-of-doors by the buttocks, head downwards.

3.4 Aristophanes, *Knights* 375–81

Demosthenes adds a threat of his own against Paphlagon.

DEMOSTHENES: And, by Zeus, we'll shove a peg in his mouth as the butchers do, then pull out his tongue and take a good and proper look at him,[5] there with his gaping . . . ass, to see if he's measly.[6]

3.5 Aristophanes, *Knights* 417–28

SAUSAGE-SELLER: And, oh yeah, there are other pranks of mine, when I was a boy. I used to trick the butchers by saying this sort of thing: "Look, boys, don't you see? The new season; a swallow!" And they'd look up, and in the meantime I'd steal some of their meat.

---

3. The hill on which the Athenian Assembly (the entire citizen population) met for political purposes.

4. The town hall, where the presiding representatives of the Council and other distinguished citizens regularly dined. Here a different form of oral consumption is imagined.

5. Butchers would typically examine pigs before slaughter for signs of tapeworm, such as cysts under the tongue.

6. Since Paphlagon is here imagined as a habitual sexual passive, his anus must also be examined for signs of disease.

DEMOSTHENES: You clever bloke! That was a wise piece of planning: you stole, like people eat nettles, before the swallows came.[7]

SAUSAGE-SELLER: *And* nobody saw me doing it. But if ever any of them did, I'd hide the stuff up my crotch and swear my innocence by the gods. So that one of the politicians said, when he saw me doing that, "It's as certain as certain can be that this boy will one day hold the stewardship of the people."

DEMOSTHENES: He guessed well. But it's obvious what led him to that conclusion: the fact that you perjured yourself after committing a robbery, and that you had someone else's meat up your ass.

3.6 Aristophanes, *Knights* 719–21

Paphlagon (Cleon) boasts of his ability to control Demos (the people).

PAPHLAGON: And what is more, by Zeus, with my wizardry I can make Demos expand and contract at my pleasure.

SAUSAGE-SELLER: Even my asshole knows *that* trick.

3.7 Aristophanes, *Knights* 730–40

To resolve the dispute, they knock on Demos' door.

DEMOS: Who's doing you wrong, Paphlagon?

PAPHLAGON: I'm being assaulted on your account by this man and these youngsters.

DEMOS: For what reason?

PAPHLAGON: Because I cherish you, Demos; because I am your lover.

DEMOS: *[to Sausage-seller]* And tell me, who are you?

SAUSAGE-SELLER: This man's rival for your love; one who has long desired you and wanted to do things for your good, as have many other good and decent people. But we can't do them, because of this fellow. You're like the boys who have lovers: you don't accept those who are good and decent, but give yourself to lamp-sellers and cobblers and shoemakers and leather-mongers.[8]

---

7. Nettle tops are best eaten when young and tender, namely in the winter and early spring (i.e., before the first swallows appear). Mature plants are difficult to harvest, because they sting.

8. Cleon owned a tannery, and is therefore depicted in comedy as a shoemaker or leather-seller. Another prominent politician of the time, Hyperbolus, is depicted as a lamp-seller.

3.8 Aristophanes, *Knights* 875–80

Paphlagon and Sausage-seller compete for the favor of Demos by offering him various gifts and benefactions. Sausage-seller has just given him a new pair of shoes.

PAPHLAGON: Isn't it terrible that a pair of shoes should count for so much, when you don't recall all I have done for you? I put a stop to the buggers by erasing Grypus from the rolls.[9]

SAUSAGE-SELLER: Well, isn't it dreadful that you should indulge in this ass-snooping and "put a stop to the buggers"? And there's no room for doubt that you put a stop to them out of jealousy, for fear they should become politicians.

3.9 Aristophanes, *Knights* 1241–42

Paphlagon questions Sausage-seller to see whether Sausage-seller is the man who an oracle foretold would overthrow him.

PAPHLAGON: When you were approaching manhood, what trade did you practice?

SAUSAGE-SELLER: I sold sausages . . . and also sometimes sold myself.

3.10 Aristophanes, *Knights* 1373–87

After the final defeat of Paphlagon, Demos comes back on stage rejuvenated and announces a series of political reforms.

DEMOS: Nor is anyone to frequent the Agora[10] whose beard is not grown.

SAUSAGE-SELLER: Then where are Cleisthenes and Strato[11] going to do their shopping?

DEMOS: I mean those adolescents in the perfume-market,[12] who sit and blabber things like this: "Clever man, that Phaeax;[13] ingenious, the

---

9. Probably a reference to a historical incident in which Cleon invoked the same law Aeschines used against Timarchus (see 4.7) to have someone removed from political participation based on the charge that he had once prostituted himself.

10. The marketplace and center of the city's business activity.

11. Greek men of adult years generally wore full beards during this period. Cleisthenes and Strato were exceptional in not doing so and are repeatedly ridiculed by Aristophanes as effeminate.

12. Men who wore perfume would also be considered overly concerned with their appearance and therefore effeminate. For the perfume-seller's stall as a place of resort for affected young men, see 3.23.

13. A prominent Athenian politician during the period 424–416 B.C.E.

way he escaped death! He's cohesive and penetrative, productive of original phrases, clear and incisive, and most excellently repressive of the vociferative."[14]

SAUSAGE-SELLER: So I suppose you're give-the-fingerative to that bletherative lot?

DEMOS: No, I'll compel them all to give up moving decrees and go hunting instead.[15]

[The sausage-seller signals to a slave, and a boy brings out a camp-stool.]

SAUSAGE-SELLER: Then on those terms you can have this camp-stool, and a boy with balls to carry it about for you;[16] and should the fancy take you, you can make a camp-stool of *him*.[17]

DEMOS: Bless me, I *am* reverting to the old ways!

3.11 Aristophanes, *Clouds* 949–1113

This play was originally produced in 423 B.C.E., but this part was probably added when Aristophanes revised the play around 417. Socrates stages this debate between the Better and Worse Argument to convince the young Pheidippides to enter his school and learn his clever ways.

CHORUS: Now these two will show, who trust
    In their ultra-clever   950
    Arguments and thoughts and
    Phrase-coining cogitations,
    Which of them will prove himself
    Superior. For now everything
    Is at stake here for Learning,   955
    In regard to which, for my friends,
    This is the crunch.

CHORUS-LEADER: *[to Better Argument]* Now, you who adorned the men of old with abundance of virtuous disposition, utter forth a sound, that in which you rejoice, and describe your own nature.

---

14. The adjectives here render Greek adjectives all ending in -*ikos*. The coining of new technical vocabulary with such suffixes was characteristic of the sophists and rhetoricians who came to be prominent in Athens during this decade and who, like Socrates, had a following especially among well-educated youth.

15. A more appropriate and manly activity.

16. In other words, a masculine youth, not an effeminate or overly young boy. Athenaeus 12.512C records that it was a habit of rich Athenians to have a slave follow them about with such a stool in case they wished to stop and rest.

17. In other words, make the boy crouch in an anally receptive posture.

BETTER ARGUMENT: Very well, I will describe how the old education was managed, in the days when I and my just cause flourished and it was the done thing to be decent. First of all, it was the rule that not a sound should be heard from a boy, not a grunt; then, the boys of the neighborhood had to walk through the streets to the music-master's together and in good order and without cloaks, even if it was snowing as thick as barley groats. Then again he would teach them to learn a song by heart, and not to keep their thighs together while doing so[18]—a song such as "Pallas the terrible, sacker of cities" or "A strain that sounds afar," singing it in the mode their fathers handed down. And if any of them played the clown or introduced some convolution such as the moderns use, those annoying twists in the style of Phrynis,[19] he was thrashed hard and often for disfiguring the music. At the gymnastic trainer's the boys, when they sat down, had to cover themselves with their thighs, so as not to expose to the onlookers anything that was—cruel; and then, when they stood up again, they had to smooth the sand down, and take care not to leave behind for their lovers the impress of their manhood.[20] In those days, too, no boy would anoint himself below the navel, and so on their private parts there was a coat of dewy down like on quinces;[21] nor would he water down his voice to speak tenderly to his lover and walk along making eyes and being his own pimp. Nor was he allowed when dining to pick up a head of the radish, nor to snatch his elders' dill or celery, nor to eat dainties, nor to giggle, nor to have his legs crossed.[22]

WORSE ARGUMENT: What antiquated rot, smelling of the Dipolieia, and crawling with cicadas, Cedeides, and ritual bovicide![23]

---

18. An ancient commentator says that the concern here is about boys stimulating their genitals by rubbing their thighs together.

19. A fifth-century cithara-player known for introducing modulations and changes of rhythm into his music. In fact, he was not so newfangled, having won a victory in the Panathenaic competition of 456 B.C.E. In this speaker's opinion, music 30–40 years old is too modern.

20. The floor in a gymnasium would be covered with sand. The boys should be careful not to leave the marks of their genitals in the sand, lest they overexcite their admirers.

21. I.e., immature pubic hair bristling with sweat from exercise, not plastered down with olive oil, used as part of the cleaning process.

22. A relaxed posture. Boys were to sit straight and attentive.

23. "Cicadas" were golden brooches in the shape of cicadas used to hold long hair in a bun —a very archaic hairstyle. Cedeides was either an early dithyrambic poet or a contemporary poet with a reputation for being old-fashioned. The Dipolieia was an annual festival of Zeus that featured the slaughter of an ox followed by a bizarre ritual called the Buphonia: the sacrificer was to run away, and in his place the knife was to be put on trial and thrown into the sea. Later the ox would be stuffed and yoked to a plow. Any ritual might be considered archaic by modern sophisticates, especially such a strange one as the Buphonia, and not long after this play there was a famous scandal involving parody of the Eleusinian mysteries by members of an aristocratic club.

BETTER ARGUMENT: But what matters is that these are the ways in which my education bred the men who fought at Marathon.[24] While you teach the young of today to swaddle themselves in cloaks right from the start,[25] which makes me choke with rage, when they have to dance at the Panathenaea, and one of them holds his shield in front of his ham,[26] caring nothing for Tritogeneia.[27] So, my lad, choose me, the Better Argument, with confidence; and you will know to hate the Agora and shun the bathhouses;[28] and to be ashamed of what is shameful; and to flare up when someone makes fun of you; and to give up seats to your elders when they approach; and not to act rudely towards your own parents; nor to do anything else disgraceful that would defile the statue of Honor; nor to rush into a dancing-girl's house, lest while you're panting after that sort of thing you may have an apple thrown at you[29] by a little whore and so have your good name shattered; nor to contradict your father in anything; nor to call him Iapetus[30] and so cast his years in his teeth, those years which were spent in rearing you from a nestling.

WORSE ARGUMENT: If you follow this advice of his, my lad, then, by Dionysus, you'll become like the sons of Hippocrates,[31] and they'll call you a pap-sucker.

BETTER ARGUMENT: But you'll be spending your time in gymnasia, with a gleaming, blooming body, not in outlandish chatter on thorny subjects in the Agora like the present generation; nor in being dragged into court over some sticky, contentious, damnable little dispute; no, you will go down to the Academy,[32] and under the sacred olive-trees, wearing a chaplet of green reed, you will start a race together with a good decent companion of your own age, fragrant with green-brier and catkin-shedding poplar and freedom from cares, delighting in the season of spring, when the plane tree whispers to the elm. *[more quickly]*

24. Athens' glorious victory over the Persian invaders in 490 B.C.E., apparently a much celebrated topos of later political discourse.

25. The speaker evidently wants to see boys show more flesh and considers modern boys too ashamed of being naked.

26. "Ham" may be a slang word for penis.

27. An alternate name for Athena, whose annual festival at Athens was the Panathenaea. Among its many contests was the Pyrrhic dance, which involved naked boys performing with shields.

28. Most bathing in antiquity occurred in public establishments. The speaker considers frequent bathing an indulgence of the idle. On the Agora, see n. 10.

29. A sign of erotic attention; see 1.31. Dancing-girls were slaves and frequently prostitutes.

30. One of the Titans, i.e., the older generation of gods displaced by the Olympians.

31. Hippocrates was an Athenian general and nephew of Pericles. His sons are ridiculed in comedy as boorish and uneducated.

32. A park on the edge of town, sacred to the local hero Academus. In the fourth century it came to be the seat of Plato's school. But at this time it was more a place for physical exercise.

If you do these things I tell you, and bend your efforts to them, you will always have a shining breast, a bright skin, big shoulders, a minute tongue, a big rump and a small prick.[33] But if you follow the practices of the youth of today, for a start you'll have a pale skin, small shoulders, a skinny chest, a big tongue, a small rump, a big ham and a long . . . winded decree;[34] and he *[indicating Worse Argument]* will talk you into believing whatever is foul to be fair, and whatever is fair foul; and on top of that he will infect you with the faggotry of Antimachus.[35]

CHORUS: You who perfect yourself in wisdom,
  Wisdom the glorious, the fair and lofty,   1025
  How sweet on your words
  Is the bloom of virtue!
  Happy, indeed, I see, were they
  Who lived then, in the time of the men of old.
  [to Worse Argument] In answer to this, you with your refined and
     plausible art   1030
  Will have to say something novel; for
  The man has won great credit.

CHORUS-LEADER: It seems you will need some clever schemes against him, if you are going to overcome the man and not be a laughing-stock.

WORSE ARGUMENT: Well, actually I've been choking in my insides for some time with eagerness to make mincemeat of all this by counter-arguments. For it was for just this reason that I got the name of Worse Argument among the men of thought, because I was the first who conceived the notion of arguing in contradiction to established values and justified pleas. *[to Pheidippides]* And that is worth more than ten thousand staters,[36] to be able to choose the inferior case and yet win. Look at the way I shall examine the education in which he puts his trust. He says that first of all he won't let you bathe in hot water. Now *[to Better Argument]* on what principle do you base your objection to hot baths?

BETTER ARGUMENT: That they are a most unmanly thing, and make the man who takes them a coward.

---

33. The Greeks considered small penises more aesthetically pleasing, as can be seen from the depiction of beautiful youths in sculpture and vase painting. Large penises are reserved for satyrs, Pans, and grotesques. Large buttocks would be considered a sign of muscularity and therefore attractive.

34. In other words, he will become an orator and legal busybody, like the effeminate youths of 3.10.

35. In *Acharnians* 1150–73 Aristophanes attacks a figure of the same name as a bad poet and niggardly chorus sponsor.

36. A non-Athenian coin of high value.

WORSE ARGUMENT: Hold it! Right away I've got you held round the waist
in a grip you can't escape. Now tell me: of the sons of Zeus, whom do
you consider to have been the greatest-hearted man, tell me, and to
have performed the most labors?

BETTER ARGUMENT: For my part, I reckon no man superior to Heracles.

WORSE ARGUMENT: Well then, where have you ever seen Heraclean
baths[37] that were cold? And yet who was more manly than he?

BETTER ARGUMENT: That—that's the stuff that the young men are
always blabbering about all day, which makes the bathhouse full and
the wrestling-schools empty.

WORSE ARGUMENT: Then you object to their frequenting the Agora;
I, on the contrary, commend it. If it were something wicked, Homer
would never have described Nestor and, indeed, all his men of wisdom
as "agoretes."[38] Well, from there I shall proceed to the tongue, which my
opponent says it is not right for the young to train: I say it is right. And
again, he says one should be modest: that makes two pernicious evils.
For [to Better Argument] who is there that you have ever yet seen to derive
any benefit from being modest? Say who, and by naming him refute me.

BETTER ARGUMENT: Plenty of people. For example, Peleus got his knife
because of that.[39]

WORSE ARGUMENT: A knife? A charming profit the poor devil made! Now
Hyperbolus from the lamp market[40] has made a whole load of talents by
being wicked, but never a knife, by Zeus, no!

BETTER ARGUMENT: And also Peleus got to marry Thetis because of his
virtue.[41]

WORSE ARGUMENT: Yes, and then she left him and went away, because he
wasn't wanton and wasn't an enjoyable partner for an all-night session
under the covers. A woman enjoys being mauled. You're just a hulking
old Cronus.[42] [to Pheidippides] Look, my lad, at all that virtue entails, and
all the pleasures you'll be deprived of: boys, women, cottabus,[43] good

---

37. Natural hot springs, which were supposed to have been created by the gods for Heracles to bathe in.

38. The Homeric word *agorētēs* refers to an orator. In Homeric times, the *agora* would have
been a meeting place and thus the site of political or judicial deliberations, not a marketplace.

39. Peleus was staying with King Acastus of Iolcus, whose wife attempted to seduce him.
When Peleus rejected her advances, she falsely accused him and he was punished by being
abandoned on a mountain with nothing to defend himself against wild animals. The gods rewarded his chastity by giving him a knife for self-defense.

40. See n. 8 above.

41. The Nereid Thetis was destined to bear a son greater than his father, so Zeus saw to it
that she was married to a worthy human rather than to another god.

42. The king of the Titans, the older generation of gods overthrown by Zeus.

43. A drinking game in which banqueters would try to hit a target with the lees left at the
bottom of their wine cup. See the man on the right in fig. 23.

food, drink, laughter. How can life be worth living for you if you're deprived of these? Very well; I will go on from there to the demands of nature. You've erred, you've fallen in love, you've had a bit of an affair, and then you've been caught. You're done for, because you're not able to argue. But if you become my pupil you can indulge your nature, leap and laugh, think nothing shameful. If by chance you are taken in adultery, this is what you will reply to the husband: that you have done nothing wrong. Then transfer the responsibility to Zeus, saying that even he is a slave to love and women, and how can you, a mortal, be stronger than a god? [44]

BETTER ARGUMENT: But what if, as a result of following your advice, he gets the radish treatment and is plucked and singed with ashes? [45] Will he have any argument he can use to save himself from being wide-assed?

WORSE ARGUMENT: And if he does become wide-assed, how will that harm him?

BETTER ARGUMENT: You mean, what further misfortune could he ever suffer that would be greater than that?

WORSE ARGUMENT: Well, what will you say if I confute you on this point?

BETTER ARGUMENT: I'll remain silent; what else?

WORSE ARGUMENT: Come on then, tell me: from what type of person do advocates come?

BETTER ARGUMENT: From the wide-assed.

WORSE ARGUMENT: I agree. Again, from what type do tragedians come?

BETTER ARGUMENT: From the wide-assed.

WORSE ARGUMENT: Quite right. And from what type do politicians come?

BETTER ARGUMENT: From the wide-assed.

WORSE ARGUMENT: Then do you realize that you were talking nonsense? Again, look and see which are in the majority among the audience.

BETTER ARGUMENT: There, I'm looking.

WORSE ARGUMENT: Well, what do you see?

BETTER ARGUMENT: That, heavens above! the wide-assed are the *vast* majority. At any rate, I know *that* one is, and that one over there, and that one with the long hair.

WORSE ARGUMENT: Well, what are you going to say?

BETTER ARGUMENT: We are defeated. Here, you buggers, please, for heaven's sake, take my cloak; I'm deserting to your camp! *[He throws his cloak to Worse Argument and rushes offstage.]*

---

44. Greek myth tells of countless seductions of mortal women by Zeus. For the appeal to his example, see 1.70.

45. Typical punishments for adultery would include thrusting radishes or other large objects up the adulterer's anus, tearing out his pubic hair, and burning his privates with hot ash.

WORSE ARGUMENT: *[to Strepsiades]* Well, how about it? Do you want to
take this son of yours away, or shall I teach him oratory for you?
STREPSIADES: Teach him and chastise him, and remember to give him a
sharp edge, with one side adapted to small lawsuits, while the other side
of his jaws you should whet to serve for weightier affairs.
WORSE ARGUMENT: Don't worry, you'll receive him back a skilled sophist.
PHEIDIPPIDES: *[aside]* More like a god-forsaken paleface, I should think.

3.12 Aristophanes, *Wasps* 1023–28

This play dates to 422 B.C.E. In the parabasis, a nondramatic interlude in the middle
of the play, the chorus-leader reminds the audience of Aristophanes' past dramatic
achievements and gives evidence of his solidarity with Athenian democratic values.

And when he was raised to greatness, and honored as nobody has ever
been among you,[46] he says he didn't end up getting above himself; nor did
he puff up with pride; nor did he gallivant around the wrestling-schools,
making passes;[47] and if a man who had had a lovers' quarrel pressed him
to satirize the youth concerned, he says he never complied with any such
request, having in this the reasonable purpose of not making the Muses
he employs into procurers.[48]

3.13 Aristophanes, *Birds* 127–42

This play dates to 414 B.C.E. The two protagonists, Peisetaerus and Euelpides, are
running away from Athens, where they can't stand life. They are asked what their
ideal city would be like.

TEREUS: Well, what kind of city would you most like to live in?
PEISETAERUS: One where my greatest troubles would be of this sort: one
of my friends would come to my door of a morning and say this: "In the
name of Olympian Zeus, make sure you give your children a bath and
come with them early to my place; I'm going to be celebrating a wedding.
Do this without fail; if you don't, you needn't come to me when the time
comes that I'm in trouble!"
TEREUS: By Zeus, you do love a toilsome life! *[to Euelpides]* What about you?
EUELPIDES: I fancy the same sort of thing.

---

46. With first-place victories for three of his earliest plays.

47. As numerous vases show, athletic settings were frequently the scene for admirers to approach attractive boys.

48. An ancient commentator tells us that Aristophanes is here alluding to the conduct of
his rival, the comic poet Eupolis, who wrote a play about Autolycus, the beloved of Callias (see
5.8.1.2), but this play was probably later.

TEREUS: What sort of thing?

EUELPIDES: A place where the father of an attractive boy would meet me and complain to me like this, as if I'd done him wrong: "A fine thing you did to my son, old sparkler! You met him coming away from the gymnasium after bathing, and you didn't kiss him, you didn't greet him, you didn't draw him close, you didn't finger his balls—and you an old family friend of mine!"

3.14 Aristophanes, *Thesmophoria Women* 1–276

This play (411 B.C.E.) features the tragedian Euripides, who attempts to foil a plot of the women against him because of the supposedly negative attitudes toward women that his plays have engendered. He attempts to infiltrate their meeting at the female-only Thesmophoria festival.

> *[Enter, by a side passage, Euripides and his In-law,*
> *the latter lagging a little behind and seeming fatigued.*
> *Euripides stops in front of the stagehouse.]*

IN-LAW: *[to himself]* O Zeus, is the springtime really going to come at last? That man will kill me yet, the way he's been traipsing about ever since sunrise. *[to Euripides]* Might it be possible, before I've coughed up my spleen entirely, to learn from you, Euripides, where you're taking me?

EURIPIDES: You don't have to hear it all from me, considering that you're presently going to be seeing it in person.

IN-LAW: What do you mean? Say it again. I've not got to hear it?

EURIPIDES: Not what you're going to be seeing.

IN-LAW: So I've not to see either?

EURIPIDES: Not what you've got to hear, no.

IN-LAW: What is the advice you're giving me? You do put it cleverly! You say that I mustn't either hear or see?

EURIPIDES: The point is that the two things are distinct in nature.

IN-LAW: How do you mean, distinct?

EURIPIDES: This is how they were separated originally. When in the beginning the Sky became a separate entity, and took part in begetting living, moving beings within itself, it first devised the eye "in imitation of the solar disc," whereby they should see, and as a funnel for hearing made the perforations of the ears.[49]

IN-LAW: So because of this funnel I'm not to hear or see? By Zeus, I am delighted to have learnt that! What a wonderful thing it is, I must say, this intellectual conversation!

---

49. Euripides' characters sometimes echo the doctrines of contemporary sophists or cosmologists.

EURIPIDES: Oh, you could learn a lot more things like that from me.

IN-LAW: Then is there any chance, to add to these blessings, that you could discover a way for me to learn how to—be lame in both legs?

EURIPIDES: Come over here and give me your attention.

IN-LAW: *[joining Euripides]* Here I am.

EURIPIDES: *[pointing to the door of the stage-house]* Do you see that door?

IN-LAW: By Heracles, I think I do!

EURIPIDES: Keep quiet then.

IN-LAW: I'm keeping quiet about the door.

EURIPIDES: Listen.

IN-LAW: I'm listening to the door and keeping quiet about it.

EURIPIDES: This is where the famous Agathon has his residence, the tragic poet.[50]

IN-LAW: What Agathon is that?

EURIPIDES: *[declaiming]* There is one Agathon—

IN-LAW: You don't mean the bronzed, muscular one?

EURIPIDES: No, a different one; haven't you ever seen him?

IN-LAW: Not the one with the bushy beard?

EURIPIDES: You haven't ever seen him![51]

IN-LAW: I certainly haven't—at least not that I know of.

EURIPIDES: And yet you've fucked him—but perhaps you're not aware of the fact! *[The door opens.]* Let's crouch down out of the way, because a servant of his is coming out with fire and a myrtle wreath—to make an offering, I suppose, for his master's poetry.

[Agathon's servant, who has come out of the house, advances to the stage altar, as Euripides and In-law conceal themselves.]

SERVANT: Let all the people close their lips
And speak fair; for the holy band of Muses
Is residing and composing song
Within my master's halls!
[kindling incense on the altar] Let windless heaven restrain its blasts,
Let the blue waves of the sea make no noise[52]—   45

IN-LAW: Boom di boom!

---

50. Agathon's first tragedy is recorded in 416 B.C.E. This play is five years after that, so he is still relatively young. He was famous for an elaborate antithetical style, for writing choral odes with no relevance to the dramatic plot, and for sometimes writing plays on freely invented themes with no relation to traditional mythology.

51. Agathon was notable, like Cleisthenes and Strato (see n. 11), in remaining clean-shaven even as an adult.

52. The Servant's language is hymnic in form, as if to announce the presence or invocation of a god.

EURIPIDES: *[to In-law]* Quiet! What's he saying?

SERVANT: Let the tribes of birds be lulled to sleep,
Let the feet of the beasts that range the woods
Be bound fast in stillness—

IN-LAW: Boom didi boom di boom!

SERVANT: For Agathon of the lovely language,
Our suzerain, is about—

IN-LAW: *[louder]* Not about to be fucked, is he?

SERVANT: Who is it that spoke?

IN-LAW: Windless heaven.

SERVANT: —To lay the stocks on which to commence a play.
He is bending new verbal timbers into shape,
Now gluing songs together, now fashioning them on the lathe,
And coining ideas and creating metaphors   55
And melting wax and rounding out
And casting in a mold—

IN-LAW: And sucking cocks.

SERVANT: What rustic is this that approaches these corniced walls?

IN-LAW: *[advancing upon him]* One who's ready to take you and your poet
Of the lovely language, round you up,   60
Bend you over, and then cast
This prick of mine[53] here up your cornice!

SERVANT: You certainly must have used to behave outrageously when you were young, old sir!

EURIPIDES: *[hastily coming up to them; addressing Servant]* My dear fellow, leave him be—but please, I implore you, call Agathon to come out here to me.

SERVANT: No need to implore; he'll be coming out anyway himself soon. He's starting to compose a lyric, and the thing is, being winter, it's not easy to bend and twist them into shape unless he comes outside in front in the sun.

EURIPIDES: So what should I do?

SERVANT: Just wait here, because he's coming out.

EURIPIDES: *[in tones of desperate tragic appeal]* "O Zeus, what is 't thy mind to do to me this day?"[54]

IN-LAW: *[to himself]* I want to find out, by the gods, what all this business is about. *[to Euripides]* What are you groaning for? What are you so upset about? You shouldn't be hiding it from me when you're a relation of mine.

---

53. Comic actors wore a large leather phallus stitched onto their costume, that might be lifted up for display in passages like this one.

54. Possibly a line from a lost play of Euripides.

EURIPIDES: There's terrible trouble been cooked up for me.

IN-LAW: What sort of trouble?

EURIPIDES: This day it will be decided whether Euripides is still among the living or whether he is a dead man.

IN-LAW: But how can that be? Why, the law courts won't be holding any trials today, and there isn't a sitting of Council either, because it's the middle day of the Thesmophoria.[55]

EURIPIDES: Yes, that's exactly what I'm expecting will be my ruin. The women have hatched a plot against me, and today in the Thesmophorian sanctuary they're going to hold an assembly about me with a view to my liquidation.

IN-LAW: Why, may I ask?

EURIPIDES: Because I lampoon them and slander them in my tragedies.

IN-LAW: Then you'll be getting your just deserts, by Poseidon! But in this situation, what scheme have you got?

EURIPIDES: To persuade Agathon, the tragic dramatist, to go to the Thesmophorian sanctuary.

IN-LAW: And do what, pray?

EURIPIDES: And speak in the women's assembly, saying whatever needs to be said in my defense.

IN-LAW: In his own person, or in disguise?

EURIPIDES: In disguise, wearing a woman's outfit.

IN-LAW: An elegant idea, that, and very much in your style![56] When it comes to scheming, we absolutely take the cake!

[A platform begins to roll out of the central door, on which is Agathon,
sitting on a bed. He is dressed as a woman and holds a lyre.
Scattered over the bed are a variety of clothes and accessories,
most of them feminine.]

EURIPIDES: Keep quiet!

IN-LAW: What's the matter?

EURIPIDES: Agathon's coming out.

IN-LAW: *[looking around him]* What, where is he?

EURIPIDES: Where is he? There he is—the man who's being wheeled out now.

IN-LAW: What, am I blind or something? I don't see any man here at all; what I see is Madam Cyrene![57]

[Agathon begins to half sing, half hum an elaborate wordless melody.]

---

55. A three-day festival of Demeter held in the fall. Only married women could participate.

56. Euripidean tragedy often featured the device of characters speaking in disguise.

57. A talented courtesan.

EURIPIDES: Quiet now; he's getting ready to sing a lyric.

IN-LAW: What is that tune he's warbling his way through? "Anthill Passages"[58] or what?

[In the ensuing song Agathon, singing falsetto and accompanying himself on the lyre, takes alternately the part of a Priestess and of a Chorus of Trojan maidens.]

AGATHON: *[as Priestess]* Take up, maidens, the holy torch of the Two Nether Goddesses

And in the hour of freedom dance with the loud songs of your fathers.[59]

[as Chorus] To which of the gods shall my festive song be?

Tell me, pray. My heart is eager to obey you   105

And render worship to the gods.

[as Priestess] Come now, felicitate in song

Him who draws the golden bow,

Phoebus, who established the precinct   110

Of our city in the land of the Simois.[60]

[as Chorus] Rejoice in our beautiful song,

O Phoebus, and be first to receive

This holy privilege in our fair tribute of music.

[as Priestess] And hymn the Maiden of the mountains where the oak trees grow,

Artemis, Lady of the Wild.[61]   115

[as Chorus] I follow you, glorifying the august

And blessed child of Leto,

Artemis, the virgin inviolate.

[as Priestess] And Leto, and the strains of the Asian lute, out   120

Of time and in time to your step,[62] at the beck

Of the Phrygian Graces.

[as Chorus] I give honor to our Lady Leto

And to the lute, mother of songs,

Esteemed for its loud masculine tones.   125

58. An appropriate name for a convoluted or over-complicated song.

59. The two goddesses are Demeter and Persephone, whose separation and reunion ("the hour of freedom," Persephone's release from the Underworld) were reenacted as part of the Thesmophoria ritual. Torches were a typical part of their iconography, since Demeter carried a torch to search for her lost daughter day and night.

60. The priestess is apparently Trojan. Simois is a river near Troy. Phoebus Apollo helped build the walls of Troy.

61. The sister of Apollo, also an Asiatic deity identified with Troy. She was the protector of wild animals.

62. The correlation between metrical divisions, dance movements, and syntax begins to break down.

[as Priestess] Whereby light sparkles forth in the eyes of the god,
As also by reason of your vocal attack; wherefore
Glorify Lord Phoebus!
[as Chorus] All hail, blest son of Leto!

> *[Agathon ends with a loud feminine ritual ululation.]*

IN-LAW: *[coming up to Agathon]* Holy Genetyllides,[63] how delightful that
song was! how feminacious, how fully tongued, how frenchkissy! Why,
as I listened to it I felt a tickle stealing right up my backside! And now,
young sir, I want to ask you in the style of Aeschylus, in words from the
Lycurgus plays, what manner of woman you are. "Whence comes this
epicene? What is its country, what its garb?" *[examining the objects on
the bed]* What confusion of lifestyles is this? What has a bass to say to a
saffron gown?[64] or a lyre to a hair net? What's an oil-flask[65] doing with
a breast-band? How incongruous! And what partnership can there be
between a mirror[66] and a sword? And what about yourself, young 'un?
Have you been reared as a man? Then where's your prick? Where's your
cloak? Where are your Laconian shoes? Or as a woman, was it? Then
where are your tits? What's your answer? Why aren't you saying anything?
Or shall I find you out by your song, seeing that you don't want to tell
me yourself?

AGATHON: Old man, old man, I heard your jealous censure, but I did
not feel the smart of it. I change my clothing according as I change my
mentality. A man who is a poet must adopt habits that match the plays
he's committed to composing. For example, if one is writing plays about
women, one's body must participate in their habits.

IN-LAW: So when you write a Phaedra,[67] you mount astride?

AGATHON: *[ignoring this]* If you're writing about men, your body has what
it takes already; but when it's a question of something we don't possess,
then it must be captured by imitation.

IN-LAW: Ask me over, then, when you're writing a satyr-play,[68] so I can
collaborate with you, long and hard, from the rear.

---

63. Local Attic goddesses of procreation and fertility, possibly connected with the cult of
Aphrodite.

64. The bass, or *barbiton,* was a lower-pitched version of the lyre; both instruments were
played mainly by men. Yellow gowns would be worn only by women.

65. A small portable jar of olive oil used by men to anoint themselves after exercise.

66. Mirrors were used almost exclusively by women, mainly for doing make-up.

67. The second wife of Theseus, who attempted to seduce and then falsely accused her step-
son. Both Sophocles and Euripides wrote tragedies on this theme.

68. At the City Dionysia, every tragic trilogy would be accompanied by a satyr-play, a comic
burlesque of a familiar myth, featuring a chorus of satyrs, goat-like creatures known for their
lack of sexual restraint.

AGATHON: *[again ignoring him]* And besides, it's unaesthetic to see a poet who looks like a hairy yokel. Think of the famous Ibycus, and Anacreon of Teos, and Alcaeus—the men who put the flavor into music—how they all minced and wore bandeaux in Ionian fashion.[69] And Phrynichus[70]—you must have actually heard him sing—he was an attractive man and he also wore attractive clothes, and that's why his plays were attractive too. One just can't help creating work that reflects one's own nature.

IN-LAW: Ah, that's why Philocles, who's ugly, writes ugly plays, and Xenocles, who's a wretch, writes wretched ones, and Theognis too, being a cold character, writes frigid ones.[71]

AGATHON: It's absolutely inevitable, and it's because I recognized that fact that I gave myself this treatment.

IN-LAW: *[misunderstanding him]* What treatment was it, in heaven's name?[72]

EURIPIDES: *[to In-law]* Stop yapping now. I was like that too at his age, when I was just beginning to compose.

IN-LAW: I don't envy you your upbringing, by Zeus!

EURIPIDES: Please let me say what I came here to say.

IN-LAW: Go ahead.

EURIPIDES: Agathon, "it is the mark of a wise man to be able to compress a long discourse elegantly into brief compass."[73] I have been stricken by an unprecedented disaster, and have come to you as a suppliant.

AGATHON: Of what do you stand in need?

EURIPIDES:, Today at the Thesmophoria the women are going to liquidate me, because I slander them.

AGATHON: So what assistance can we provide for you?

EURIPIDES: All the assistance in the world! If you seat yourself among the women, incognito—because anyone would think you were a woman—

---

69. Alcaeus was a contemporary of Sappho, also from Lesbos. On Ibycus and Anacreon, see ch. 1, introduction. Numerous fifth-century Athenian vases show Ionian men (including one figure labeled "Anacreon") dressed in long, flowing robes more characteristic of what Athenians would expect women to wear. This could have reflected actual Ionian fashion, but perhaps also an Athenian perception of the Ionians (who were long enslaved to the Persians) as self-indulgent, weak, and incapable of defending themselves.

70. A tragedian slightly earlier than Aeschylus; his first victory is recorded in 510 B.C.E.

71. Three minor tragedians of Aristophanes' time often ridiculed in comedy. Philocles was a nephew of Aeschylus. Theognis is not the same as the elegiac poet in ch. 1.

72. He thinks Agathon has referred to castration.

73. A line from Euripides' *Aeolus*. The following line also appears to conflate Euripidean phrases.

and answer them on my behalf, you'll save me, for sure. Only you are
capable of making a speech that's worthy of me.

AGATHON: In that case why don't you make your own defense in person?

EURIPIDES: I'll tell you. In the first place, I'm someone that people recognize; and secondly, I'm bearded and white-haired, whereas you're fresh-
faced, fair-complexioned, clean-shaven, you've a woman's voice, soft
cheeks, attractive looks. . . .

AGATHON: Euripides

EURIPIDES: Yes?

AGATHON: Did you once write: "You rejoice to see the light of day; think
you your father does not?"[74]

EURIPIDES: I did.

AGATHON: Then don't expect us to bear your troubles. We'd be quite mad
to do so. It's your business; bear it yourself as your private affair. It is
right to endure one's misfortunes, not with clever scheming but with
willing submission.

IN-LAW: Just as you, you young faggot, got your dilated asshole not by
words but by willing submission!

EURIPIDES: What is it that you're afraid of about going along there?

AGATHON: I'd be even worse torn apart than you.

EURIPIDES: How come?

AGATHON: How come? Because they think I steal women's knockturnal
business and rob them of the female's natural rights.

IN-LAW: "Steal" indeed! Get fucked, that's what you mean! But I must say
it's a fair enough excuse!

EURIPIDES: *[to Agathon]* How about it then? Will you do it for me?

AGATHON: Don't you imagine it!

EURIPIDES: *[in despair]* Thrice wretched that I am! I am absolutely
done for!

IN-LAW: *[comforting him]* Euripides—my dear, dear fellow—my kinsman
—don't give up your own cause!

EURIPIDES: So what am I to do, then?

IN-LAW: Tell him he can go to blazes, then take me and use me any way
you like.

EURIPIDES: All right then, since you're offering yourself to me, take off
that cloak.

IN-LAW: *[doing so]* There you are, it's on the ground. Here, what are you
meaning to do with me?

---

74. A line from Euripides' *Alcestis,* in which Pheres refuses his son's request that he die in
his place.

EURIPIDES: To shave off this lot *[indicating In-law's beard]* and to singe off what's down below.

IN-LAW: *[after a brief, shocked pause]* Very well, do it, if that's what you want to do. Else I ought never to have offered myself to you in the first place.

EURIPIDES: Agathon, you carry a razor all the time, so could you possibly lend us one?

AGATHON: *[pointing to one of the objects on the bed]* Take it yourself from the razor-holder here.

EURIPIDES: You're a gentleman. *[to In-law]* Sit down, and puff out your right cheek.

> *[In-law obeys, and Euripides begins to shave him.*
> *The beard is tough, and Euripides is not a skilful barber.]*

IN-LAW: He-elp!

EURIPIDES: What are you shouting about? I'll have to shove a peg in your mouth[75] if you don't keep quiet.

IN-LAW: *[nicked again]* Aagh! AAGH! *[He jumps up and starts running away.]*

EURIPIDES: Hey, you, where are you running off to?

IN-LAW: To the sanctuary of the Dread Goddesses.[76] I will not, by Demeter, stay here being cut in pieces.

EURIPIDES: You'll look plain ridiculous then, won't you, clean-shaven on one side of your face?

IN-LAW: I couldn't care less!

EURIPIDES: In the gods' name, don't desert me! Come back here.

IN-LAW: *[returning reluctantly and sitting down again]* Poor, poor me!

EURIPIDES: Stay right here, keep still, and put your head back. *[He continues shaving In-law, but when the razor gets under his chin In-law tries to turn his head away.]* What are you twisting round for? *[He turns In-law's head firmly back into position, and clamps his mouth shut with one hand while continuing to shave him with the other—and cutting him a third time.]*

IN-LAW: *[trying to scream with his mouth shut]* Mmmmmmmm!

EURIPIDES: What are you mmmmmmmming about? It's all nice and done now.

IN-LAW: *[fingering his bare cheeks and chin]* Poor me, I'll have to serve my next campaign in the Bare Skin Brigade![77]

---

75. A regular practice of butchers about to slaughter pigs; see **3.4**.

76. Often identified with the Furies, the goddesses of revenge. Their sanctuary was a place of refuge.

77. A pun on the word *psilos*, which means both "clean-shaven" and "light-armed infantry."

EURIPIDES: Don't worry! You're going to look really handsome. *[picking up a mirror from the bed]* Do you want to have a look at yourself?

IN-LAW: Bring it here, if you want.

EURIPIDES: *[holding the mirror in front of him]* Do you see yourself?

IN-LAW: No, I don't, I see Cleisthenes! [78]

EURIPIDES: Stand up, so I can singe you; [79] bend over and stay like that.

IN-LAW: *[standing up]* Heaven help me, I'm going to be made a pig of!

EURIPIDES: *[calling into the stage-house]* Someone bring me a torch or a lamp from in there. *[A torch is brought.]* Bend right over. *[In-law does so.]* Now mind the tip of your tail.

IN-LAW: I'll take care of it all right—*[Euripides rapidly singes his bottom with the torch]*—only I'm on FIRE! Help, help! Water, neighbors, water, before the flames catch hold of another ass!

EURIPIDES: Don't be frightened.

IN-LAW: What do you mean, don't be frightened? I've been burnt to the ground!

EURIPIDES: You've got nothing to worry about any more; you're through the worst part of the job.

IN-LAW: *[who has been gingerly applying his hand to the affected area, and now inspects it]* Ugh! Look at this soot! I've got all charred, all round the crotch!

EURIPIDES: Don't worry. Someone else will sponge it for you.

IN-LAW: Anyone who tries to wash my bum will live to regret it!

EURIPIDES: Agathon, since you're not prepared to offer your own person, at least please lend us a mantle and a breastband for my friend here to wear. You're not going to say you haven't got them.

AGATHON: *[waving his arm towards the bed]* Take them and use them; I don't grudge you them at all.

IN-LAW: What should I take, then?

EURIPIDES: What should you take? First take the saffron gown and put it on.

IN-LAW: *[taking gown from bed, and sniffing it]* By Aphrodite, this has a nice smell of willy! [80] *[He puts it on, not very skillfully.]* Quick, belt it up. *[Euripides belts the gown and adjusts its folds.]*

EURIPIDES: *[to Agathon]* Now pass me a breastband.

AGATHON: Here you are.

---

78. See **3.10** and n. 11.

79. Women typically used small oil lamps to singe off pubic and body hair.

80. The Greek word is *posthion*, a diminutive form of "penis," as if to imply that Agathon still has a little boy's penis, making him appropriately a sexual object like boys. Others think the point is that Agathon has been embracing young boys and his gown carries their smell.

[Euripides takes a (padded) breastband from him,
ties it round in-law, and then brings up the gown
over the breastband and pins it at the shoulders.]

IN-LAW: *[looking down]* Come on now, sort me out around the legs. *[Euripides makes sure that the lower part of the gown is hanging correctly.]*

EURIPIDES: We need a hair-net and a bandeau.

AGATHON: No, no, here's a put-on headpiece, which I wear at night.

EURIPIDES: *[taking it]* By Zeus, it's really just what's wanted!

IN-LAW: Will it fit me?

EURIPIDES: *[putting it on him and inspecting the effect]* Why, it's excellent! *[to Agathon]* Give me a mantle.

AGATHON: Take this one from the bed. *[Euripides takes mantle and puts it on In-law.]*

EURIPIDES: We need shoes.

AGATHON: *[taking off his boots]* Take these of mine. *[Euripides passes them to In-law.]*

IN-LAW: Will they fit me? *[He puts them on and finds them very roomy.]* You certainly like wearing them loose!

AGATHON: You be the judge of that. Now you've got all you need—so someone please wheel me inside, right away. *[Agathon's platform is rolled back into the stage-house, and the door closed.]*

EURIPIDES: *[stepping back and inspecting In-law]* There we are; this gentleman is now a lady—to look at, anyway. Only, if you talk, make sure you put on a good, convincing woman's voice.

IN-LAW: *[in a squeaky falsetto]* I'll try!

EURIPIDES: Off you go, then.

IN-LAW: By Apollo, I will not, not unless you swear to me—

EURIPIDES: Swear what?

IN-LAW: To help and save me by hook or by crook, if any danger befalls me.

EURIPIDES: Then I swear it by the Sky, the dwelling-place of Zeus.[81]

IN-LAW: That's no more an oath than saying "by Hippocrates' tenement block."[82]

EURIPIDES: Very well, I swear it by all the gods, the whole lot.

IN-LAW: Just remember this, then, that it was your heart that swore; it wasn't your tongue that swore nor did I ask it to.[83]

---

81. This line is quoted from Euripides' *Melanippe the Wise*. Euripides, like Socrates, was accused of inventing new gods.

82. This Hippocrates may have been Pericles' nephew, a famous Athenian general who died in 424.

83. This parodies the famous line from Euripides' *Hippolytus* (612): "My tongue has sworn, but my heart is unsworn."

3.15 Aristophanes, *Frogs* 52–70

This play dates to 405 B.C.E. The god Dionysus tells Heracles that he has conceived a sudden desire to bring the recently deceased tragic poet Euripides back from the dead.

DIONYSUS: And, anyway, on the ship I was reading *Andromeda*[84] to myself, and suddenly my heart was struck with a longing, you can't imagine how hard.

HERACLES: A longing? How big a longing?

DIONYSUS: Only a little one—the size of Molon.[85]

HERACLES: For a woman?

DIONYSUS: No, it wasn't.

HERACLES: Then for a boy?

DIONYSUS: No, by no means.

HERACLES: You mean it was for a *man?*

DIONYSUS: *[reeling in distress]* Aaaah!

HERACLES: *[matter-of-factly]* So you had it off with Cleisthenes,[86] did you?

DIONYSUS: Don't make fun of me, brother,[87] I really am in a bad way, such is the passion that's ravaging me.

HERACLES: What kind of passion, brother dear?

DIONYSUS: I can't describe it; but nonetheless I'll explain it to you by analogy. Have you, before now, ever felt a sudden desire for pea soup?

HERACLES: Pea soup? Whew *[it is almost a sigh]*, thousands of times in my life!

DIONYSUS: "Do I make clear my sense,"[88] or shall I explain it some other way?

HERACLES: Not about pea soup you needn't; I understand perfectly.

DIONYSUS: Well, that is the kind of yearning that is devouring me for— Euripides.

HERACLES: You mean even though he's *dead?*

DIONYSUS: Yes, and no man on Earth will be able to dissuade me from going in quest of him.[89]

---

84. A play of Euripides produced in 412 B.C.E.

85. An actor well known for his large stature. Dionysus' characterization of his longing as "little" is thus ironic.

86. See n. 11.

87. Dionysus and Heracles were both sons of Zeus.

88. A quotation from Euripides' *Hypsipyle.*

89. To the Underworld.

3.16 Aristophanes, *Frogs* 145–51

Heracles describes to Dionysus the terrors of the Underworld, including this place of punishment.

HERACLES: And then a vast sea of mud and ever-flowing dung, in which
there lies anyone who has ever, say, broken the laws of hospitality, or
slyly grabbed back a rent-boy's money while having it off with him, or
struck his mother, or given his father a sock in the jaw, or sworn a
perjured oath, or had someone copy out a speech by Morsimus.[90]

3.17 Aristophanes, *Wealth* 149–59

Chremylus and his slave Carion discuss the powers of the god Wealth in this play of 388 B.C.E.

CHREMYLUS: They say that the Corinthian whores[91] pay no heed, when-
ever a poor man happens to approach them, but if a rich man does so,
they wiggle their ass in his direction right away.
CARION: And they say that boys do the same thing, not for the sake of
lovers, but for money.
CHREMYLUS: Not the good and noble boys, surely, but the male whores.
For the good and noble ones don't ask for money.
CARION: What then?
CHREMYLUS: One wants a good horse, another asks for hunting dogs.
CARION: Perhaps because they are ashamed to ask for money, they cover
their baseness with pretense.

3.18 Aristophanes, *Triple Phallus* fr. 556 *Poetae Comici Graeci*

Then all the distinguished foreigners who were present followed and so-
licited him, one begging, "May 'e bring the boy and sell 'im in Chios,"[92] or
another, "May 'e sell 'im in Clazomenae," or another, "May 'e sell 'im in
Ephesus," or another, "In Abydus." Everything was "May 'e."

---

90. Not wronging a guest (hospitality), one's parents, and the gods (perjury) were the three
"unwritten laws" of Greek ethics. Doing wrong to a male prostitute hardly seems on the same
level as does copying out a speech of Morsimus, a mediocre tragic poet and the great-nephew
of Aeschylus.

91. As a major port city and trading center, Corinth was particularly well known for female
prostitution, including temple prostitution associated with the cult of Aphrodite.

92. All of the places listed are cities or islands in Ionia, the Greek-settled area on the coast
of Asia Minor. Aristophanes represents each speaker with characteristic Ionic dialect.

3.19 Cratinus, *The All-Seeing Ones* fr. 160 PCG

This play attacks the followers of the philosopher Hippon.[93]

Aristodemus,[94] like a man who behaves disgracefully among the Cimonian ruins[95] . . .

3.20 Cratinus, *The All-Seeing Ones* fr. 163 PCG

. . . for you strongly despise women and now turn to boys.

3.21 Eupolis, *The Dippers* fr. 88 PCG

This song probably comes from a scene of lewd and suggestive dancing.

. . . you who beat the drum so well
And pluck the triangle
And shake your butt
And put your legs up high.

3.22 Strattis, *Spittle* fr. 41 PCG

"I know what I'll do with him," he said in anger, "I'll do with my mouth what *the Lesbians* do."[96]

3.23 Pherecrates, *Kitchen* or *All-Night Revel* fr. 70 PCG

Athenaeus quotes this fragment as proof that perfume-selling was a disreputable occupation for a man.

What does a man have to know to be a perfume-seller, sitting up high under an umbrella,[97] providing a gathering-place for teenaged boys to

---

93. A natural philosopher with a reputation for atheism. He believed that all matter originated in moisture, and semen apparently played an important role in his physiological theory. This play may have been a model for Aristophanes' *Clouds*.

94. Aristophanes, fr. 242 PCG, refers to his name as synonymous with "asshole."

95. Apparently a reference to the ruins of the suburban estate of Cimon, a conservative leader of Athens in the 470s and 460s B.C.E. Byzantine lexica tell us that this was a public toilet; it may have also been a cruising spot for men with certain sexual tastes; the joke could also be that Aristodemus is a disgrace when compared to men like Cimon.

96. The ancient commentary that quotes this fragment says the reference is to oral sex. The island of Lesbos was particularly associated with the practice in both men and women.

97. A typically feminine accoutrement.

chatter in all day? . . . For example, no one ever saw a woman butcher or fish-seller. . . .

3.24 Theopompus, *The Mede* fr. 30 PCG

LYKABETTOS:[98] In my neighborhood those who have too long been youths[99] perform sexual favors for their age-mates.

3.25 Ephippus, *Sappho* fr. 20 PCG

When a young person comes in to eat another man's relishes and to place a noncontributory hand upon the provender, you may assume that he'll be paying the bill overnight.

3.26 Alexis, *Sleep* fr. 244 PCG

That's why this male prostitute, whenever he came to dinner with us, never ate any leeks: it was so that he wouldn't upset his lover when he gave him a kiss.

3.27 Alexis, *Helen* fr. 70 PCG

So anyone who is in love with the ripeness of human bodies and doesn't know the rest of the story is a friend not to people but to pleasure. Himself a mortal, he clearly wrongs the god Eros, because he makes all the beautiful boys mistrust him.

3.28 Alexis, *Phaedrus* fr. 247 PCG

This play as a whole seems to be a parody of Plato's dialogues on love.

PHAEDRUS: As I was coming from the Piraeus, it occurred to me to philoso-
phize about my troubles and confusion. They seem ignorant to me,
in short, these artists of Eros, when they make images of this god. It's
neither female nor male, nor again god or human, neither stupid nor
wise, but put together from everywhere, supporting many forms in one

---

98. The highest hill in Athens, on the northeast edge of the ancient city.
99. In other words, men who have shaved their beards to continue looking young even after reaching a mature age.

shape. It has the courage of a man, but a woman's timidity, the confusion of madness, but the logic of sense, a beast's violence, but the endurance of steel, and a divine pride. And these things—by Athena and the gods! I don't know exactly what it is, but, nonetheless, it's something like this, and I'm close to naming it.

3.29 Amphis, *Dithyramb* fr. 15 PCG

What do you say? Do you expect to persuade me that there is such a thing as a lover of a ripe young boy who is merely a lover of character, who overlooks his appearance and is truly modest? I am not persuaded of this any more than that a poor man who often annoys the prosperous does not want to take something.

3.30 Anaxandrides, *Odysseus* fr. 34 PCG

FISHERMAN: The beautiful artistry of painters is admired in pictures on the wall, but this art is grabbed from the casserole and disappears right out of the frying pan. For what other art, my fine fellow, are the mouths of the smart set all aflame, or is there such a crush of fingers or suffocation, if they can't gobble it up right now? And is not the only begetter of all couplings a well-stocked fish-market? Who will come to dinner for "processed" seafood or over-the-counter crowfish or sprats? That gorgeous little boy, with what incantations or what speeches is he caught, I'd like to know, if you remove the fishermen's art? That's what brings them down, conquering them with boiled heads of fish, opening under their very selves the gates of Eurotas,[100] compelling the wild thing to lie down at no cost.

3.31 Antiphanes, *Fisherwoman* fr. 27.9–18 PCG

Various species of fish are likened to famous courtesans and their lovers.

You red mullets, I've put you over on the right for handsome Callisthenes to devour; he's already devouring his estate for one of you, you know. And here's an eel with a wider back than Sinope; who will be the first to come and eat it? Misgolas, you see, is not a connoisseur of these,[101] although

---

100. The broad river that passes through Sparta.
101. Misgolas, denounced by Aeschines as one of the lovers of Timarchus (see **4.7.41–53**), does not care for female fish.

he'll make a grab for this lyrefish [102] here as soon as he sees it. The man's really keen on his secret attachments to all players of the lyre.

3.32 Archedicus, fr. 4 PCG

The following is a paraphrase, not an actual fragment.

Demochares [103] was a prostitute with the upper portions of his body and therefore unfit to blow up the sacred flame. [104]

3.33 Damoxenus, fr. 3 PCG

Damoxenus was a comic poet of the late fourth century.

A young man of perhaps sixteen or seventeen was playing ball. He was from the island of Cos, which seems to produce veritable gods. After he looked at us sitting there, whether he was catching or throwing the ball, we all cried out at the same time, ". . . What rhythm! What manner! How much poise!" In both his actions and words there appeared an awesome beauty, my dear fellows. I have never heard nor seen such grace before. I would be suffering some greater harm, if I had stayed there any longer. Even now I don't think I'm quite recovered.

3.34 Diphilus, *Theseus* fr. 49 PCG

Diphilus was one of the most prolific comic poets of the late fourth and early third centuries, much imitated in Roman comedy. The following passage is probably not a verbatim fragment, but a paraphrase describing either an event or a narrative in the play.

Three Samian girls were telling riddles while drinking at the Adonis festival. [105] The question was posed to them, what is the strongest thing of all? One girl said "Iron" and gave as her proof that men dig and cut everything with it and use it as a tool for all sorts of purposes. This seemed like a good answer, but the second girl followed her and said that the smith

---

102. A kind of flounder or flatfish. Lyre-players are almost always male.
103. A nephew of the orator Demosthenes.
104. Fire was used in a variety of religious rituals, including sacrifice. The sense is that Demochares' mouth was impure.
105. An annual spring fertility festival especially popular with women.

is much stronger, because this man in working iron could bend it, soften it, and do what he wanted with it. The third girl said that the penis is the strongest thing of all, because with this they can screw the smith and make him groan.[106]

106. There is probably a pun here on the word *stenonta* (groaning), which with an aspirated pronunciation *(sthenonta)* means "strong" or "mighty."

CHAPTER 4

Greek Oratory

Like comedy, Athenian forensic oratory gives us insight into popular attitudes toward homosexual practices. Mass juries (often as large as five hundred or one thousand) were typically comprised of a cross section of the citizen population, in which the poorer classes were far more numerous. Since Athenian juries were paid a subsistence wage, some older men may have even used jury service as a means of support. While the speechwriters and professional politicians were of well-educated, upper-class backgrounds, they had to calibrate their rhetoric to appeal to the prejudices and values of a broader audience.

While legal oratory doubtless existed as early as law courts did, it was only in the last quarter of the fifth century B.C.E. that it came to be the subject of systematic study in Athens and that speeches delivered in the courts began to be published as literary artifacts worthy of preservation. Our greatest examples of Attic oratory date from this period until Athens' loss of political liberty a century later.

Since the presiding judge's role was largely procedural and did not include ruling on evidence or interpreting the law for the jury, the nature of legal debate was very different from modern practice. Verifiable evidence and strict construction of the law were therefore less important than pandering to the jury's sympathies and seeming to be more credible than one's opponent. Hence vicious attacks on an opponent's character or family were commonplace, often with little basis in fact.

It is in this context that statements relating to an opponent's homosexual practices occur, always framed as a characteristic that will render him less appealing in the jury's eyes. In **4.2**, **4.3**, and **4.10** we see passing allusions to an opponent's pederastic liaisons, whether as active or passive partner, even though it is not directly relevant to the case. In **4.5** and **4.9** we see speakers contrast their own devotion to family with an opponent's homosexual preferences. Effeminacy is a frequent charge: in addition to **4.9** and **4.11**, see **4.7.110**, where the charge stems from having once been another man's beloved, and **4.7.131**, where it is connected with an opponent's fine clothing (as if to imply that all wealthy men are "soft" and "feminine"). But by far the most damaging charge one could make was that an opponent had been a male prostitute in his youth, since conviction on this count entailed disfranchisement of one's legal right to hold any office or address any political body, whether the Assembly, the Council, or a court. The motivation behind the law seems to have been a perception that character was constant, and a man who sold himself for money as a youth would sell his loyalty for a bribe as an adult in political office. This charge is made in passing in **4.1** and **4.8**, at greater length in **4.6** (where it is, however, still not the actual legal issue on trial), and as the focus of the entire speech in **4.7**, Aeschines' notorious prosecution of Timarchus.

None of these charges are backed with evidence, but Greek orators make free use of inference from probability: that Timarchus was extremely handsome as a young man, had lived with a succession of older men, and had a reputation for a spendthrift lifestyle add up (for Aeschines) to his having been a prostitute (see especially **4.7.75–76**). What Aeschines relies on here is a vague suspicion on the part of some poorer members of the jury that the kind of gift-giving and lavish entertainment common to all upper-class pederasty was really little more than a glorified form of prostitution; we have seen the same confusion exploited in Aristophanes (**3.17**). By this line of reasoning, virtually any upper-class politician who had been involved in a pederastic relationship when younger might plausibly be accused of prostitution. The charge was therefore a potent one to use in stirring up class envy, and Aeschines loses no opportunity to remind the jury of the inherited wealth and careless extravagance of Timarchus and his lovers, whom the orator brands as equally culpable and lacking in self-restraint.

Aeschines' speech rebuts the arguments used by Demosthenes and another orator to defend Timarchus, which allows us to reconstruct their speeches in some detail. It appears that their counter-argument was couched as a defense of pederasty as a noble and traditional practice, as if they perceived the greatest threat in Aeschines' speech not to be the actual charges of prostitution, but its appeal to more general prejudices against male love.

Lysias' *Against Simon* (**4.4**) is unique in that it features a defendant who admits to a pederastic relationship, but what is apparent is that he does so only with an acute sense of embarrassment and fear of prejudice against him (see especially **4.4.4**); contrast the relative nonchalance of the speaker in Lysias' *On a Premeditated Wound* (not in this collection), concerning a similar fight between erotic rivals over a slave woman. Although the defendant in **4.4** complains of being violently pursued and harassed by his rival for the boy, he preferred to leave Athens rather than prosecute his antagonist, so afraid was he of exposing the matter to public gossip (**4.4.9–10**). He is a wealthy citizen from a prominent family and feared prejudice from a common jury on this basis too. Now, having been sued by his opponent, he has no alternative but to appear in court.

4.12 is a special case in that it is not a speech for public delivery, but an "epideictic" oration, or display piece, in praise of an ideal youth, written in a flowery and highly mannered style for what is clearly a select literary audience. Despite its title, the "Erotic Essay" *(Erōticos)*, it is not really a work in praise of pederasty: the youth Epicrates is congratulated precisely for being open and friendly to all men, but intimate with none (**4.12.17–21**). The version of boy-love advocated here, as at the end of Aeschines' speech (**4.7.136–57**), appears to be a chaste, self-restrained, nonsexual form, consistent with the concept of Eros promulgated earlier in the fourth century by Plato.

The orators also give us a rich store of valuable information about Greek daily life and thus afford a glimpse into some details about the actual practice of Athenian pederasty not available elsewhere. For instance, **4.4.22** (see also **4.7.41**) refers to a contractual arrangement with a youth for companionship based on an up-front payment of three hundred drachmas (about a year's wages for a skilled worker). **4.2** tells us of a boy's lover being appointed his guardian in his father's will, showing that fathers sometimes did sanction and approve such relationships. **4.4**, **4.7**, and **4.10** all refer to boys or youths who live at the house of their lover; **4.7.40–41** suggests that this arrangement was ostensibly to learn a profession, but that the pedagogical relationship was also pederastic. All three of these cases (Theodotus, Timarchus, and Aristion) seem to involve *meirakia* (young men eighteen or older), suggesting that pederasty often involved post-adolescents. Interestingly, one of Timarchus' alleged lovers, Misgolas, appears to have been the same age (or possibly even younger—see n. 58). Misgolas, known also from comedy to be an active lover of boys (see **3.31**), appears to have been handsome and to have cultivated a youthful appearance (**4.7.49**), perhaps to make himself more appealing to young companions. The speaker of **4.4**, on the other hand, apologizes for being involved in such affairs at his advanced age. This new range of evidence provided by oratory shows that our stereotypical notions about the age ranges of lover and beloved may be in some need of revision; they may have been more fluid than often supposed.

Bibliographical Note

On homosexuality in Attic oratory, see Dover (1978) 19–109, Buffière (1980) 211–17, and E. Cantarella (1992) 48–53. On the relevant legal issues, see especially Rainer (1986) and D. Cohen (1991) 171–202; on male prostitution particularly, see Halperin (1990) 88–112 and Winkler (1990) 45–70, whose views are countered in E. E. Cohen (2000) 155–91. Hubbard (1998b) 59–70 connects the negative judgments in Greek oratory with appeal to popular prejudice against what was perceived as an upper-class practice.

On Lysias' *Against Simon,* see Harris (1997). For a commentary on this speech and *Against Alcibiades* I, see Carey (1989) 86–113, 141–79.

On Aeschines' *Against Timarchus,* see, in addition to Dover's lengthy treatment, Harris (1995) 101–6, who takes a very skeptical view of Aeschines' claims. Ford (1999) treats Aeschines' technique of citing and interpreting legal and poetic authority in this speech; see also Wooten (1988) 41–43. Meulder (1989) augments the old thesis of Hug (1874) about Platonic influence on Aeschines. Natalicchio (1998) 80–255 and Fisher (2001) provide well-annotated editions.

For an introduction and well-annotated edition of the *Erotic Essay,* see Clavaud (1974) 69–137, who retains this treatise as a genuine work of Demosthenes, but documents the strong influence of Plato and Isocrates; D. Brown (1977) also favors attribution to Demosthenes, and relates the work to proposed reforms of the Athenian *ephebeia* in 338/37 B.C.E. For such erotic discourses as a recognized genre, see Lasserre (1944).

4.1 Andocides, *On the Mysteries* 100–101

Dated to 399 B.C.E., this is a speech of self-defense against old charges of having participated in an aristocratic club that parodied the Eleusinian mysteries. Andocides addresses his accuser.

Now you, of all people, talk to me about the issue of political association and cast aspersions upon certain men? You? You yourself, after all, have "associated"[1] not just with one man (that would be fine), but used to offer pretty cheap rates for anyone who wanted. As these jurors know, you've lived off the lowest line of work, and this despite the fact you're so ugly. Nevertheless, gentlemen, this man dares to accuse others, even though your laws don't even grant him the right to speak in his own defense.

---

1. A pun on the Greek word *hetairos,* which can refer to either a companion, a member of a political club, or a male prostitute.

4.2 Lysias, *Against Teisis,* Fr. 17.2.1–2 Gernet–Bizos

For Archippus here, gentlemen of Athens, worked out in the same wrestling school as Teisis, the defendant in this suit, and one day the two of them became angry with each other. First they traded jibes, then they argued, and finally it came to rancor and insults. Pytheas was Teisis' lover (for you must be told the whole truth) and had been designated the young man's guardian by the will of his father. When Teisis told him about the quarreling in the gym, he, wanting to flatter the boy and to appear smart and cunning before him, instructed Teisis (as we've learned from what happened and have heard from knowledgeable sources) to reconcile with Archippus for the moment, but to watch out for a chance to catch him alone somewhere.[2]

4.3 Lysias, *Against Alcibiades* I, 25–27

This is a prosecution against the younger Alcibiades (son of the famous general) for avoiding service in the infantry by enrolling in the cavalry without the proper qualifying examination. It was tried before a special military court, probably in 395, at the beginning of the Corinthian War (395–386).

[25] When my opponent was a child, he used to drink at the house of Archedemus[3]—the man with the runny eyes, who had embezzled a great deal of your property—reclining together under the same cloak, in the sight of many people. He used to dance the *kōmos*[4] during the day and maintained a courtesan before reaching adulthood. Clearly he was emulating his ancestors,[5] in the belief that he could become famous when older only if he showed himself to be the worst of criminals when he was young. [26] He was sent for by Alcibiades[6] because he was behaving scandalously in public. How do you think you should regard a person whose behavior had scandalized even the man who taught other people such things? He plotted with Theotimus against his own father, and betrayed Orni[7]—and Theotimus, on taking over the site, first of all committed *hybris* against

---

2. The narrative proceeds to relate that Teisis invites Archippus to a party, where he ties him to a pillar and savagely whips him.

3. A popular political leader during the last years of the Peloponnesian War. Aristophanes also makes fun of his runny eyes.

4. A drunken dance, usually characteristic of late night revels.

5. His father also had a reputation for extravagant expenditures and drunken outrages as a youth. See **2.5**.

6. His father.

7. One of the elder Alcibiades' forts in Thrace, where he took refuge after his final exile from Athens in 406 B.C.E.

him[8] (now that he was in the prime of his youth), and eventually imprisoned him and tried to exact a ransom.[9] [27] However, his father hated him so much that he declared he would not even collect his bones if he died. After his father's death,[10] Archebiades[11] became his lover and paid the ransom. Not much later, after gambling away his property, he began to raid his friends' ships, using Leuke Akte[12] as his base.

4.4 Lysias, *Against Simon* 1–26, 44, 47–48

In this case, dated sometime after 394 B.C.E., the speaker (a client of Lysias) defends himself against a charge of attempted murder in a brawl over a beloved young man from Plataea named Theodotus. Cases of homicide or attempted homicide were tried before the Council of the Areopagus, which consisted of the city's former magistrates.

[1] I already knew many disreputable things about Simon, members of the Council, but I did not expect him to reach such a level of audacity that he would bring a prosecution, pretending to be the victim in an affair for which he himself deserves to be punished, and that he would appear before you after swearing such a great and serious oath.[13] [2] If anybody else were going to decide my case, I would be very worried about the danger. I know that carefully prepared tricks or mere chance can sometimes produce wholly unexpected outcomes for those on trial, but because I am appearing before you, I remain confident that I shall receive justice. [3] I am particularly upset, members of the Council, at being forced to speak about matters like this in front of you. I put up with mistreatment because I was ashamed at the prospect of many people knowing all about me. But Simon has put me under such pressure that I shall tell you the full story without hiding anything. [4] If I have done anything wrong, members of the Council, I do not expect any mercy, but if I can show that I am not guilty of any of the charges that Simon has stated on oath, even though it is obvious that I have behaved rather foolishly towards the young man, given my age, I shall ask you to think no worse of me. You know that

---

8. *Hybris* is a technical legal term for assault or any act of violence, including rape, which is probably meant here.

9. From the elder Alcibiades.

10. In 404 B.C.E. If the information Isocrates gives us about the birth date of the younger Alcibiades is correct, the boy could have been scarcely more than 13 at the time.

11. An old associate of the elder Alcibiades, indicted along with him for the scandal surrounding the parody of the Eleusinian mysteries in 415 B.C.E.

12. The "White Promontory," a name common to several locations in Greece. The reference here is to maritime piracy, which was a problem especially on trade routes to the Black Sea.

13. A special oath was sworn by all litigants and witnesses in cases of homicide or attempted homicide.

desire affects everybody and that the most honorable and restrained man is the one who can bear his troubles most discreetly. In my case, Simon here has prevented all this, as I shall show you.

[5] We were both attracted, members of the Council, to Theodotus, a young man from Plataea.[14] I expected to win him over by treating him well, but Simon thought that by behaving arrogantly and lawlessly he would force him to do what he wanted. It would be a lengthy task to list all the wrongs that Theodotus suffered at his hands, but I think you should hear the offenses he committed against me personally. [6] He found out that the young man was staying with me, and came to my house drunk one night. He knocked down the doors and made his way into the women's rooms, where my sister and my nieces were—women who have been brought up so respectably that they are ashamed to be seen even by relatives. [7] Simon, however, reached such a level of arrogance[15] that he refused to leave, until the men who were present, together with those who had accompanied him, realized that by entering the rooms of young orphaned girls he was behaving unacceptably, and threw him out by force. Far from apologizing for this outrageous conduct, he found out where I was having dinner and did something that was extraordinary and (unless you know his criminal insanity) unbelievable. [8] He called me out of the house, and as soon as I came out, he immediately tried to hit me. I defended myself, so he moved off and threw stones at me. He missed me but hit his own companion Aristocritus with a stone, injuring his forehead. [9] For my part, members of the Council, I felt this was appalling treatment, but as I said earlier, I was embarrassed by the experience and decided to put up with it. I preferred not to bring legal action over these offenses, rather than appear foolish to my fellow citizens. I knew that the affair would be seen as typical for a criminal like him but that my misfortunes would be laughed at by many of those who are always jealous of anybody who tries to play a responsible role in the city. [10] I was so unsure how to react to his lawlessness, members of the Council, that I decided it would be best to leave Athens. So I took the young man—you need to know the whole truth—and left the city. When I thought that enough time had passed for Simon to forget him and to be sorry for his earlier offenses, I returned.

14. Plataea was a town in Boeotia near the border of Attica allied with Athens during the Peloponnesian War and destroyed by Thebes in 427. The surviving Plataeans were relocated to Athens and given a special grant of citizenship, if they chose to register for it. Many commentators have assumed that Theodotus was a slave, based on a misunderstanding of section 33 (not included here), but the "little boy" referred to there must be a younger member of the speaker's household who accompanied him about town (see ch. 3, n. 16). If Theodotus were actually a slave, there would be no reason for referring to his Plataean provenance.

15. The Greek word here is *hybris*, on which see n. 8.

[**11**] I went to live in Piraeus,[16] but my opponent immediately heard that Theodotus had returned and was staying with Lysimachus, who lived close to the house he himself had rented. He called on some of his friends to help him. They began eating and drinking, and set a lookout on the roof, so that they could seize the young man when he came out. [**12**] It was at this moment that I arrived from Piraeus, and since I was passing, I called at Lysimachus' house. After a little while we came out. These men, who were by now drunk, jumped on us. Some of those present refused to join this attack, but Simon here, together with Theophilus, Protarchus, and Autocles, began dragging the young man off. But he threw off his cloak and ran away. [**13**] I reckoned he would escape, and they would be embarrassed and give up the chase as soon as they met anybody, so I went away by a different route. You see how carefully I tried to avoid them, since I thought everything they did was trouble for myself. [**14**] So where Simon claims the battle occurred, nobody on either side had his head broken or suffered any other injury. I will produce those who were present as witnesses for you.[17]

[**15**] Those who were present, members of the Council, have testified that he was the one who intentionally attacked me, not the other way around. After this, the young man ran into a fuller's shop,[18] but they charged in and started to drag him off by force. He began yelling and shouting and calling out for witnesses. [**16**] Many people rushed up, angry at what was happening, and said that it was disgraceful behavior. My opponents ignored what they said, but beat up Molon, the fuller, and several others who tried to protect Theodotus. [**17**] I was walking along by myself when I happened to meet them in front of Lampon's house. I thought it would be a terrible disgrace just to watch this lawless and violent assault on the young man, so I grabbed him. I asked why they were acting so illegally toward him, and they refused to answer. Instead, they let go of the young man and started hitting me. [**18**] A fight developed, members of the Council. The young man was throwing things at them and defending himself. They were throwing things at us, and were still hitting him, because they were drunk. I was defending myself, and the passersby were all helping us, because we were the ones being attacked. In the course of this melee, we all got our heads cracked. [**19**] As soon as they saw me after this episode, the others who had joined Simon in this drunken assault asked my forgiveness —not as victims but as wrongdoers. Since then, four years have passed,

---

16. The port of Athens, about four miles from Athens itself.
17. At this point, the speaker probably stops to allow the witnesses to give their testimony.
18. A kind of dry cleaner.

and at no time has anybody brought a prosecution against me. **[20]** My opponent, Simon, who was the cause of all the trouble, kept the peace for a while because he was afraid. However, when he heard that I had lost some private cases arising from an *antidosis,*[19] he grew contemptuous of me and recklessly forced this trial on me. To show that here too I am telling the truth, I shall produce those who were present as witnesses.[20]

[21] You have heard what happened, both from me and from the witnesses. For my part, members of the Council, I could wish Simon shared my opinions, so that you could hear both of us tell the truth and then easily make the right decision. But since he pays no attention to the oath he has sworn, I shall also try to explain to you the ways in which he has lied. **[22]** He had the nerve to claim that he gave Theodotus three hundred drachmas[21] and made an agreement with him, and that I plotted to turn the young man against him. But if this were true, he should have called for support from as many witnesses as possible and dealt with the matter according to the laws. **[23]** However, it is clear that he has never done anything of the sort. Instead, in his insolence[22] he beat up both of us, battered down the doors, and entered by night into the presence of free-born women. You should regard this, members of the Council, as the strongest evidence that he is lying to you. **[24]** Look at what he said, which is quite unbelievable: he has valued his entire property at two hundred and fifty drachmas—but it would be incredible if he hired somebody to be his boyfriend for more money than he actually possesses. **[25]** He has become so reckless that it was not enough for him simply to lie about having paid the money, but he even claims to have recovered it. And yet how can it be plausible that at one moment we should have committed the offense of which he has accused us—the alleged plot to defraud him of three hundred drachmas—but that after winning the fight we should have given him back the money, when we had received no formal release from legal charges and were under no obligation to pay? **[26]** In fact, members of the Council, he has devised and constructed the whole story. He says he paid the money, so that he would not appear to be treating the young man

19. A wealthy person subject to a liturgy (a tax levied to support a specific state enterprise, such as a ship or a chorus) could claim that another person was wealthier and thus more worthy of bearing the liturgy; if that party refused to accept the liturgy, he would have to exchange his property with the one who challenged him. This procedure was called an *antidosis,* and the lawsuits the speaker mentions may have arisen from disputes in connection with this exchange of property.

20. Again, the speaker probably stops at this point to let witnesses give their testimony.

21. The daily wage of a skilled worker in Athens of this period would be between one and two drachmas.

22. The Greek word is again *hybris,* on which see n. 8.

so outrageously in the absence of an agreement. But he claims to have got it back, because it is evident that he never brought a prosecution to claim the money and in fact made no mention of it. . . .[23]

[44] I am very confused about my opponent's character. Being in love and being a sycophant[24] do not seem to me compatible: the first is characteristic of simple people, the second of those who are particularly unscrupulous. I wish I were allowed to demonstrate his wickedness by referring to other events.[25] That way, you would recognize that it would be far more just for him to be on trial for his life than to put other people in danger of exile. . . .[26]

[47] Remember this and deliver a just verdict. Do not let me be unjustly expelled from my fatherland, for which I have faced many dangers and performed many liturgies. I have never been responsible for any harm to the fatherland, nor have any of my ancestors; instead, we have brought many benefits.[27] [48] So I rightly deserve pity from you and from others, not only if I should suffer the fate that Simon intends but simply because I have been compelled by these events to undergo such a trial.

4.5 Isaeus, *On the Estate of Aristarchus* 25

In this complicated inheritance case, dated to the period of the Theban War (378–371 B.C.E.), the plaintiff concludes by contrasting his familial piety to the lifestyle of his cousin.

Gentlemen of the jury, it is not enough for Xenaenetus to have wasted the estate of his grandfather Aristomenes on the love of boys, but now he thinks it fitting that he should manage this estate also in the same way. But I, jurymen, gave my sisters away in marriage, giving them as much dowry as I could, even though little savings belonged to me. Behaving as an orderly citizen, doing my assigned duties and serving in the army, I think it right that I should not be deprived of my mother's inheritance from her father.

---

23. The following paragraphs refute other arguments and statements made in Simon's speech of prosecution. The speaker also contends that the law against attempted homicide is not applicable in this case.

24. A malicious and habitual prosecutor of enemies.

25. Trials before the Council of the Areopagus apparently had to adhere to stricter rules of evidence than other cases.

26. He nevertheless proceeds to mention an episode in which Simon beat up his commander in the army and was censured for insubordination.

27. In other words, he and his ancestors have performed many liturgies (see n. 19) for the state. This suggests that the speaker is a wealthy man from a family of long-standing wealth.

4.6 Demosthenes, *Against Androtion* 21–32, 56–58

This speech, dated to 355 B.C.E. and written for delivery by Diodorus, prosecutes the tax collector Androtion for having made an illegal proposal. The speaker invokes the law concerning former prostitutes to argue that Androtion should not, in fact, be qualified for political participation at all.

[**21**] Now, concerning the law of prostitution, he is trying to argue that we are insulting and attacking him with vicious defamation. He says if we think the charges are true, we ought to accuse him before the Thesmothetes,[28] where we'll risk a thousand drachmas if proven wrong. But right now, according to him, we are trying to trick you by making empty charges and slanders, and to confuse you, who are not properly judges of these matters. [**22**] But I think it is first necessary for you to consider for yourselves that slander and accusation are quite distinct from proof. It is an accusation whenever someone gives a flimsy speech offering no evidence for what he claims; it is proof when someone at the same time demonstrates the truth of what he is saying. Accordingly, those proving a case must either offer evidence with which to show its credibility, or point out likelihoods, or produce witnesses. Since it is impossible to bring forth eyewitnesses of certain acts, you consider yourselves most likely to have sufficient proof of the truth whenever someone shows just one of the types of evidence. [**23**] And in this particular case, we are not giving you a probable account or circumstantial evidence, but we have a witness, an actual man, who can be challenged in court with a lawsuit and who has provided a written contract documenting Androtion's personal history. Our man makes himself fully accountable for the evidence. So when Androtion calls this slander and accusation, reply that this is proof; slander and accusation is what he is engaging in himself. And when he says we ought to have denounced him before the Thesmothetes, reply that we will, and that we are now, quite appropriately, discussing the relevant statute. [**24**] For if we were making these accusations against you in another case, you would be right to complain. But the present trial is about illegal legislation. The laws do not permit those who have lived this lifestyle to address the assembly. If we are showing that Androtion has not only spoken illegally but also lived illegally, how is it not appropriate for us to discuss the law that demonstrates this?

[**25**] And you should also understand this point: Solon, who established these laws (as well as most of our other laws), and who was a legislator not at all like the defendant, did not grant volunteer prosecutors only

---

28. The court properly charged with examining official qualifications, consisting of six of the city's highest magistrates.

one means of punishing wrongdoers for each type of offense, but many. For he knew, I think, that it was impossible for everyone in the city to be equally bold and clever, or equally cautious. And so he reasoned: if he designed methods of prosecution for only the cautious to bring charges, a lot of scum would get off easy. But if he made them for only bold and powerful speakers, private citizens would not have the same opportunity to bring charges. [26] Yet he also thought that no one should be deprived of the right to obtain redress in the way he best could. So, how is this possible? By granting many different ways of prosecuting each charge. Take theft, for example. Are you strong and confident in yourself? Make the arrest and risk a thousand drachmas. Are you rather weak? File a report with the archons[29] and they will take care of it. [27] Are you afraid of even this? Bring an indictment. Do you think yourself lacking, since you're poor and unable to pay the thousand drachmas? Sue for theft before a public arbiter and you'll risk nothing. All of these methods are different. It's the same way for prosecuting impiety: bring an indictment, sue the offender before the Eumolpidae,[30] or report him to the *basileus*.[31] And it's similar for practically all the other offenses. [28] So, suppose someone should not deny that he is a criminal, or a religious offender, or whatever he's on trial for, but claim that he ought to be let off, if, for example, he was arrested, because it was also possible for you to bring him before the arbiter, and that you therefore should have indicted him, or, if you brought him before the arbiter, that you should have arrested him, so that you would risk the thousand drachmas. Surely that defense would be a joke. For the man who has done nothing wrong must not defend himself on grounds of what kind of charge should have been brought, but rather he must show that he did not commit the crime. [29] In the same way, Androtion, don't think, following such reasoning, that you, who have served as a prostitute and who are now indicted for illegal legislation, ought to be acquitted simply because we could have also denounced you before the Thesmothetes. Instead, either show that you were never a prostitute or accept punishment for whatever legislation you wrote in spite of being that sort of man. If we don't seek to punish you in every way the laws allow, be grateful to us for every charge we overlook. But don't think, on that account, that you shouldn't be punished at all.

[30] It is also worthwhile, gentlemen of Athens, to consider the character of Solon, who wrote the law on prostitution, and to observe how much thought for the form of government he put into all his laws, and how

29. The city's nine principal magistrates, including the six Thesmothetes.

30. A clan at Eleusis, from which the *hierophant* (priest) of the Eleusinian mysteries was chosen.

31. The archon whose chief function was supervision of religious festivals.

much more concerned he was with our political way of life than with the particular offense he legislated against. You can see it everywhere, but especially in this law, which forbids those who have prostituted themselves from speaking in the assembly and writing legislation. For Solon understood that even though all of you are permitted to speak in the assembly, most of you don't. So he thought that this restriction would not be burdensome; he could have made the law much harsher, if his intention had been to punish prostitutes. [31] But he wasn't very concerned with this. Rather, he forbade these things for your sake and for your form of government. For he knew, indeed, he *knew* that the form of government most hostile to men who live disgusting lives is the one where everyone is able to speak out about the shameful things those men do. What constitution is that? Democracy. He thought it would be dangerous if there was ever at one time a group of men who were both bold and powerful speakers, but also mixed up in such shameful matters. [32] For the people could in many ways be led astray by leaders of that sort. Indeed, those men surely would try either to overthrow the democracy altogether (in oligarchies, after all, no one can defame the magistrates, even if their lives are more disgusting than Androtion's), or, by corrupting the people, to bring them down to their own level. For this reason, Solon forbade such men from taking any part in political deliberation, so that the people would not be tricked and led into error. Disregarding this law, however, the fine gentleman here not only thought it necessary to write legislation and to propose it in the assembly (when it was illegal for him to do so), but also to do these things for the sake of a law that is unconstitutional.[32]

. . . [56] Androtion was so shameless and greedy in his attitude toward you that he thought it right that his own father, who had been imprisoned on account of debt to the state treasury and who had neither paid up nor been acquitted by a jury, should escape, while any other citizen who was unable to pay his debts was dragged from his home to jail. On top of all this, since he was able to do anything, he forced an additional pledge of payment from Phanostrate and Sinope. Indeed, these women are prostitutes, but they owed no property tax. [57] So even if some people think that they were fit to suffer, surely this matter doesn't seem "fitting," that is, that certain individuals, given the chance, get so arrogant that they strut into households and make off with furniture from people who owe no taxes. Indeed, one can spot many people who are fit to suffer, or to have suffered, but the laws don't agree, nor do the customs of this government, customs that you have a duty to preserve. Rather, in these institutions

---

32. In the following sections the speaker goes on to rebut various arguments he expects Androtion to make in his defense.

there abide pity, sympathy, and all the sentiments that befit free men.
[58] The defendant, however, doesn't seem to share any of these feelings,
neither by his inborn nature nor from his upbringing. For no doubt he has
been abused and degraded many times while consorting with men who felt
no affection for him, but who could pay his rates. And as for your anger
over these matters, Androtion, you shouldn't have taken it out on any
citizen you happened to meet, or on the whores with whom you share
a profession, but on the father who raised you into this way of life.

4.7 Aeschines, *Against Timarchus* 6.2–11, 13–15, 17–20, 26–32, 37–49, 51–62.1, 70–76, 90–91, 94–96, 106–12, 119–27, 130–40, 155–60, 166–72, 185–91, 194–95

Aeschines brought this prosecution against Timarchus in 346 B.C.E. to forestall Timarchus' attempt to prosecute him for corruption in office. By demonstrating that Timarchus should under law be deprived of his rights to political participation, Aeschines could deprive him of legal standing to bring a suit; he appears to have succeeded in this case.

Consider, men of Athens, how great a concern for decency was shown by
that ancient legislator Solon, and Draco and the other legislators of that
period.[33] [7] First of all, they legislated for the decency of our children
and they laid down explicitly how the freeborn boy should live and how
he should be brought up, then secondly for young men and thirdly for the
other age-groups in succession, not only for private citizens but also for
public speakers. They wrote these laws down and entrusted them to your
care, making you their guardians.

[8] What I want to do now is to use the same order in my own speech
to you as the legislator uses in the law. First of all, I shall describe the laws
that are laid down for the good conduct of your children, then secondly
those for the young men, and thirdly in succession the laws for the other
age-groups, not only for private citizens but also for public speakers. In
this way, I think, my argument will be easiest to grasp. At the same time,
men of Athens, I also want first to give you a preliminary account of the
city's laws and then after that to examine Timarchus' character, for you
will find that his way of life has been contrary to all the laws.

[9] To start with, in the case of teachers, into whose care of necessity we
hand our children, for whom decency means a livelihood and the oppo-

---

33. Draco was the first major Athenian lawgiver, dating to the late seventh century; his law
code was notorious for its severity. Solon was a moderate reformer of the early sixth century,
who set up the constitutional foundations for the later development of Athenian democracy.

site means poverty, even so the legislator was clearly suspicious, and he lays down explicitly the time of day when a free boy should go to school, then how many other children should go there with him, and the time he should leave. [10] He forbids the teachers to open the schools and the athletic trainers to open the wrestling schools before the sun is up and instructs them to shut them before sunset. He holds seclusion and darkness in particular suspicion. As to the young pupils, he prescribes who they should be and what ages, and the official who is to be responsible for them, and provides for the oversight of slave attendants *(paidagogoi)*[34] and the celebration of the festival of the Muses in the schools and of Hermes in the wrestling schools, and finally for the company kept by the boys at school and the circular dances.[35] [11] For he instructs that the chorus producer,[36] who will be spending his own money for you, should be over forty years of age when he undertakes this task, so that he is already at the age of greatest self-control when he is in the company of your sons.

Now the clerk will read out these laws to you, to show you that the legislator believed that a boy who had been brought up properly would be a useful citizen when he reached manhood. But when the individual's nature at the outset gets a corrupt start in its education, he thought that badly brought up boys would become the sort of citizens that Timarchus here is. Read these laws to them. . . .[37]

[13] Now after this, men of Athens, he legislates for offences that, though they are grave, still (I think) occur in the city. For it was the fact that some unseemly acts actually took place that led the men of old to lay down the laws. Anyway, the law states explicitly that if any father or brother or uncle or anyone at all in the position of guardian hires a boy out as a prostitute —it does not allow an indictment to be brought against the boy in person but against the man who hired him out and the man who paid for him, the former because he hired him out and the latter, it says, because he hired him. And it has made the penalties the same for each of them, and it adds that any boy who has been hired out for prostitution is not obliged on reaching maturity to keep his father or provide him with a home; though on the father's death he is to bury him and to carry out the other customary rites. [14] Observe how fair this is, men of Athens. In life the law deprives

---

34. These would be owned by wealthy families to accompany and supervise children in public.

35. These are also known as "dithyrambs," narrative songs performed by a chorus of fifty youths at numerous public festivals, including the City Dionysia.

36. The chorus producer, or *choregus*, was a wealthy citizen who undertook the financing and training of the chorus as a voluntary liturgy (see n. 19). In some cases he would supervise the boys' training himself.

37. The actual text of the law that follows is almost certainly a later forgery by a Hellenistic editor.

him of the advantages of parenthood, as he deprived his son of the right of free speech,[38] while after death, when the recipient cannot perceive the benefit conferred on him, but it is the law and religion that receive the honor, finally it instructs the son to bury his father and to perform the other customary rites.

What other law did he lay down to protect your children? The law against procuring, to which he attached the most severe penalties, if anyone procures for prostitution a free boy or woman.

[15] What other law? The law of outrage,[39] which sums up in a single statement all such acts. In this law is written explicitly that if anyone commits outrage against a boy (and anyone who hires him commits outrage, I imagine) or man or woman, whether free or slave, or if he does anything contrary to law to any of these, it has allowed for an indictment for outrage and prescribed assessment of the penalty he is to suffer or pay. Read out the law. . . .[40]

[17] It may be that someone at first hearing might wonder why on Earth this term, "slaves," was added in the law of outrage. But if you consider it, men of Athens, you will find that it is the best provision of all. For the legislator was not concerned about slaves; but because he wanted to accustom you to keep far away from outrage on free persons, he added the prohibition against committing outrage even against slaves. Quite simply, he thought that in a democracy the man who commits outrage against anyone at all was not fit to share the rights of citizenship. [18] Please remember this too, men of Athens, that at this point the legislator is not yet addressing the boy in person but those connected with the boy—father, brother, guardian, teachers, in sum, those responsible for him. But once he is entered in the deme register[41] and knows the city's laws and is now able to determine right and wrong, the legislator from now on addresses nobody else but at this point the individual himself, Timarchus. [19] And what does he say? If any Athenian (he says) prostitutes himself, he is not to have the right to serve as one of the nine archons[42] (the reason being, I think, that these officials wear a sacred wreath), nor to undertake any priesthood, since his body is quite unclean; and let him not serve (he says) as advocate for the state or hold any office ever, whether at home or abroad, whether

---

38. A reference to the law under which Timarchus is now being examined, stipulating that one who committed acts of prostitution could not speak before the Assembly or courts.

39. The Greek word is *hybris,* for the technical sense of which, see n. 8. The following parenthesis seems to be stretching the actual application of that law.

40. See n. 37.

41. At the age of eighteen, a boy was examined by the officials of his deme (a geographical district) to insure that he was the correct age and of citizen parents belonging to that deme.

42. See n. 29.

selected by lot or elected by a vote; **[20]** let him not serve as herald, nor as envoy (nor let him bring to trial people that have served as envoys, nor let him act as a sycophant for pay),[43] nor let him voice any opinion in the Council or the Assembly[44] (not even if he is the cleverest speaker in Athens). If anyone acts against these provisions, he has allowed for indictments for prostitution and imposed the most severe penalties.[45] Read this law out to them as well, to make you aware of the noble and decent character of the established laws, against which Timarchus has dared to address the Assembly, a man whose way of life is known to you all. . . .[46]

[26] Now observe, men of Athens, the enormous difference between Solon and those great men whom I mentioned a little earlier in my speech and Timarchus. While they for their part thought it shameful to speak with their hand outside their robe, this man here, not some time ago but just the other day threw off his robe and cavorted like a pancratiast[47] in the Assembly, stripped, in such a vile and shameful physical condition on account of drunkenness and other abuses that decent men covered their faces out of shame for the city, that we take advice from people like this. **[27]** With this in mind the legislator explicitly declared who should address the people and who should not speak in the Assembly. He does not expel a man from the platform if his ancestors have not served as generals, nor if he works at some trade to provide for the necessities of life; indeed, he especially welcomes these men and this is why he repeatedly asks: "Who wishes to speak?"

[28] Which men then did he think should not speak? People who have lived a life of shame—these are the ones he does not allow to address the people. And where does he state this? When he says: "The scrutiny of public speakers: if anyone who beats his father or mother or does not keep them or provide a home speaks in the Assembly"; this man he does not allow to speak. A fine rule, by Zeus, in my personal opinion. Why?

---

43. See n. 24.

44. The Council was the principal legislative body in Athens, consisting of 500 citizens chosen annually by lot, 50 from each of the ten tribes. The Assembly was a meeting that all voting citizens were entitled to attend.

45. This is usually taken as a euphemism for the death penalty. But it is very unlikely that the law carried any penalty beyond disenfranchisement. Aeschines may be exaggerating here, as also in attributing the law to Solon.

46. See n. 37. In sections 22–25 Aeschines proceeds to emphasize the dignity appropriate to public speakers: elders are always allowed to speak first, and the men of former times were so dignified that they did not even make the kind of hand gestures common in contemporary oratory. Aeschines here appeals to prejudice against brash young men involved in politics (such as Timarchus).

47. The pancratium was the most extreme form of contact sport practiced by the Greeks. It involved a combination of free boxing, wrestling, and kicking; the only forbidden moves were biting and eye gouging. Like all gymnastic events, it would be undertaken naked.

Because if anyone mistreats the ones he should honor on a level with the gods, what sort of treatment, says the legislator, will people unconnected with him and, indeed, the city as a whole receive from him? [29] And who are the next ones he forbids to speak? "Or anyone," he says, "who has not performed all the military service he is ordered to, or has thrown away his shield," and rightly. Why exactly? Mister, when you do not take up arms for the city or because of cowardice cannot protect it, do not presume to give it advice. Who are the third group he addresses? "Or anyone who has been a prostitute," he says, "or has sold himself." For the man who has willfully sold his own body would, he thought, casually sell out the interests of the city. [30] Who are the fourth group he addresses? "Or anyone who has squandered his paternal estate," he says, "or any other property he has inherited." For he considered that the man who has mismanaged his private household would treat the city's interests in much the same way, and the legislator could not conceive that the same individual could be worthless in private life and useful to the public good, nor did he believe that a public speaker should come to the platform fully prepared in his words and not in his life. [31] He believed that statements from a good and decent man, even when expressed in a clumsy or simple way, would be of advantage to the hearers, while those from an unprincipled man who had treated his own body with contempt and disgracefully squandered his ancestral property, would not benefit the hearers even when expressed with great eloquence. [32] These then are the men he bars from the platform; these are the ones he forbids to address the people. And if anyone in defiance of these rules does not just speak but plays the sycophant and behaves unscrupulously, and the city can no longer tolerate such a man, "Let any Athenian who wishes and has the right," he says, "declare a scrutiny," and at that point he bids you to decide the case in court. And it is under this law that I have now come before you. . . .[48]

[37] But as I proposed at the beginning of my speech, now that I have spoken about the laws, I want to turn to the examination of Timarchus' way of life, so you will realize how far it differs from your laws. And I ask you, men of Athens, to pardon me if, when forced to speak about activities that by their nature are distasteful but have actually been practiced by this man, I am induced to use any expression that resembles Timarchus' actions. [38] It would not be fair for you to criticize me, if in my desire to inform you I were to use rather plain language, but rather criticize this man, if he has actually led such a life that anyone describing his behavior is unable to say what he wants to say without using expressions of this sort. But I shall avoid doing so to the very best of my ability.

48. Sections 33–36 consist of a largely irrelevant digression on those who preside over meetings of the Assembly.

[**39**] Observe, men of Athens, how reasonable I shall be in dealing with this man Timarchus. Any abuses he committed against his own body while still a boy I leave out of account. Let it be void like events under the Thirty or before Euclides,[49] or any other official time limit of this sort that has been laid down. But the acts he has committed since reaching the age of reason and as a young man and in full knowledge of the laws, these I shall make the subject of my accusations, and I urge you to take them seriously.

[**40**] Now this man first of all, as soon as he ceased to be a child, settled in the Piraeus[50] in the establishment of the doctor Euthydicus, ostensibly to learn the profession, but in reality because he had determined to sell himself, as events themselves showed. I pass over voluntarily all the merchants or other foreigners or our fellow citizens who had the use of his body during that period, so that nobody can say that I am dwelling excessively on every detail. I shall confine my account to the men in whose house he has lived, bringing shame on his own body and the city, earning a living from the very practice that the law forbids a man to engage in, or forfeit the right to address the people.

[**41**] There is a man named Misgolas, son of Eucrates of Collytus, men of Athens, a man who in other respects is decent and above criticism but has a phenomenal passion for this activity and is always in the habit of having male singers and lyre-players in his company.[51] I say this not to indulge in low gossip but so you will recognize who he is. This man, perceiving the reason for Timarchus' spending his time at the doctor's house, paid a sum of money in advance and moved Timarchus and set him up in his own house, a fine figure of a man, young and unprincipled and ready for the acts that Misgolas was eager to perform, and Timarchus to have done to him. [**42**] Timarchus had no inhibition but submitted to it, though he did not lack the resources for all reasonable needs. For his father had left him a very large estate, which he had squandered, as I shall show later in my speech. No, he did all this as a slave to the most disgraceful pleasures, gluttony and expensive eating and flute-girls and courtesans[52] and dice and the other activities that should never have control of a decent and

---

49. The Thirty Tyrants were oligarchs installed by the Spartans after Athens' defeat in the Peloponnesian War. They were overthrown in 403 B.C.E., but a general amnesty was declared. In the same year a new legal code was put into place under the archon Euclides, but its provisions were not retroactive.

50. See n. 16.

51. See **3.31**. Aeschines may also be making the point that Misgolas did not share the common taste for athletic types.

52. Flute-girls were slaves who performed at banquets, typically available as prostitutes on a fee-for-service basis. Courtesans (*hetairai*) were free women, usually from other parts of Greece, who offered high-class companionship, in some cases even of an intellectual or artistic nature. They expected lavish gifts and continuous financial support.

freeborn man. But this vile man felt no shame in abandoning his father's house and living with Misgolas, a man who was not a friend of his father nor one of his own age-group nor a guardian, no, a man who was unconnected and older than himself, a man without restraint in such activity, when he himself was young and handsome.

[43] Of the many ridiculous acts of Timarchus in that period there is one that I want to recount to you. It was during the procession for the City Dionysia, and Misgolas, the man who had taken him up, and Phaedrus,[53] son of Callias of Sphettus, were both taking part in the procession. This man Timarchus had agreed with them that he would join them in the procession, and they were busy with their preparations; but Timarchus had not returned. Angry at this, Misgolas went in search of him with Phaedrus; acting on information received, they found him dining in a lodging house with some foreign guests. Misgolas and Phaedrus threatened the foreigners and ordered them to come with them at once to the prison for corrupting a free youth; the foreigners took fright and ran off, leaving everything behind.

[44] The truth of this story is known to everyone who was familiar with Misgolas and Timarchus at that time. And I find it very gratifying that my dispute is with a man who is not unknown to you, and is known for precisely the practice on which you will be casting your vote. For in a case that concerns unknown individuals it is perhaps incumbent on the prosecutor to offer explicit proof, but where the facts are generally agreed, it is no great task in my view to act as prosecutor; for he needs only to remind his hearers. [45] Now although the matter is generally agreed, since we are in a law court, what I have done is draft a deposition for Misgolas, one that is accurate but not gross, or so I believe. The actual term for the acts he committed on this man are not included, nor have I written down anything that renders a witness admitting the truth subject to punishment under the laws;[54] what I have written is recognizable to you but without risk to the witness or disgrace.

[46] Now if Misgolas is prepared to come forward here and testify to the truth, he will be doing what is right. But if he would rather ignore the summons than testify to the truth, then you can see the whole business plainly. For if the active partner is to feel ashamed and prefer to pay one thousand drachmas to the Treasury to avoid showing his face to you,[55]

---

53. A prominent Athenian general from a wealthy family, not to be confused with the Phaedrus of Plato's dialogues.

54. In other words, the deposition Aeschines presents Misgolas avoids self-incrimination.

55. The fine if a witness ignored a formal summons and refused either to affirm the truth or to deny knowledge of the events in a prepared written deposition. The amount is equal to over a year's wages for a skilled laborer.

while the passive partner is to speak in the Assembly, it was a wise legislator who barred people as vile as this from the platform. [47] But if he
obeys the formal summons but takes the most shameless course, which is
to deny the truth on oath, with the intention of showing his gratitude to
Timarchus and at the same time demonstrating to others that he knows
how to keep such activities secret, firstly he will be harming himself and
secondly he will achieve nothing.[56] I have drafted another deposition for
the people who know that this man Timarchus abandoned his father's
house and lived with Misgolas, though the task I am attempting is, I think,
a difficult one. For I must offer as witnesses neither my own friends nor
their enemies nor people who are acquainted with neither of us, but their
friends. [48] But if it transpires that they dissuade these witnesses from
testifying (I don't think they will, anyway not all of them), this at least they
will never be able to do, eradicate the truth, nor the general report in the
city about Timarchus; I did not create this for him, he did it for himself.
For the decent man's life should be so clean that it does not allow even the
suspicion of blameworthy conduct.

[49] I want to say something else in advance, in case Misgolas obeys the
laws and your authority. There are men who by their nature differ from
others in their physical appearance as far as age is concerned. There are
some men who though young appear mature and older, while others
though old when one counts the years seem positively young. Misgolas is
one of these. He is in fact a contemporary of mine and was an ephebe[57]
with me; we are both in our forty-fifth year. And I myself have all these
grey hairs that you see, but he doesn't. Why do I give this advance warning?
So that when you suddenly see him you will not be surprised and mentally
respond: "Heracles! He is not much older than Timarchus!"[58] For it is a
fact both that his appearance is naturally like this and that Timarchus was
already a youth when Misgolas had relations with him. . . .[59]

[51] Now, men of Athens, if this man Timarchus had stayed with Misgolas and had not gone to live with anyone else, his conduct would have
been more decent, if indeed there is any decency in such behavior, and I
would have hesitated to charge him with anything beyond the frank term

56. There was apparently no formal penalty to a false disclaimer of knowledge.

57. This refers to mandatory military service between the ages of eighteen and twenty.

58. In fact, Timarchus seems also to be at least 45 at the time of this speech, judging from
his service on the Council in 361 (mentioned in section 109); one had to be at least 30 to
serve. Aeschines is apparently attempting to confuse the jurors and make Timarchus seem
younger than Misgolas, whereas they were in fact the same age. Some commentators suspect
textual corruption and think Aeschines and Misgolas were 54 rather than 45.

59. In section 50 Aeschines formally presents the written depositions to which he challenges
Misgolas and Phaedrus.

used by the legislator, that is only with having been a kept lover. For I think that this is exactly the charge for anyone who engages in this activity with a single partner but does so for pay. [52] But if, ignoring these wild men, Cedonides and Autoclides and Thersander, into whose houses he has been taken to live, I remind you of the facts and demonstrate that he has earned his living with his body not only at the home of Misgolas but in the house of another and then another, and that he went from this one to yet another, then it will be clear that he has not only been a kept lover but (and by Dionysus!—I don't think I can evade the issue all day) has actually prostituted himself. For I think that this is exactly the charge for anyone who engages in this activity casually with many partners for pay.

[53] Now when Misgolas tired of the expense and dismissed Timarchus from his house, Anticles the son of Callias of Euonymon[60] next took him up. Anticles is away in Samos as one of the colonists; but I shall tell you what happened after that. When this Timarchus left Anticles and Misgolas, he did not reflect on his conduct or turn to better ways but spent his days at the gaming house where the gambling board is set up and people engage in cockfighting and dice playing. I imagine that some of you have already seen the place or, if not, have at least heard of it. [54] One of the people who pass their time there is a man called Pittalacus; this person is a public slave of the city.[61] Now Pittalacus, who was financially well-off and had seen Timarchus passing his time there, took him up and kept him at his house. And this vile creature was not bothered even by this, that he was about to shame himself with a person who was a public slave of the city; no, his only concern was to get a backer[62] to finance his vile habits, while to questions of decency or disgrace he gave not a moment's thought. [55] Now the abuses and outrages that I have heard were committed on the person of Timarchus by this individual were such that—in the name of Olympian Zeus!—I could not bring myself to describe them to you. The acts that this man felt no shame to commit in practice are ones that I would rather die than describe clearly in words among you.

But about the same time that this man was living with Pittalacus, Hegesander sailed back to Athens from the Hellespont. I am aware that you have

60. This Callias was a Treasurer of the Athenian Empire in 410, not to be confused with the Callias of Xenophon's *Symposium* and of comedy.

61. Some skilled slaves belonged not to any individual master, but to the city, and could live quite independently, even accumulating money from business beyond their public duties. It may be that Pittalacus was actually a former slave and Aeschines is intentionally confusing the jury about his status to make Timarchus look worse.

62. Aeschines' actual word is *choregus*, on which see n. 36. Here it is metaphorical, but may imply something about the huge amount of expense involved, as well as the youth of the person sponsored.

been puzzled for some time at my failure to mention him; so notorious are the events I am about to narrate. **[56]** This Hegesander, whom you know better than I, arrived. As it happened, he had at that time sailed to the Hellespont as treasurer to Timomachus of Acharnae,[63] who served as general, and he returned to Athens the beneficiary, it is said, of Timomachus' gullibility, in possession of not less than eighty minas of silver;[64] and in a way he was not the least to blame for Timomachus' ruin. **[57]** Well-off as he was, and as a regular visitor to the house of Pittalacus, who was a gambling-partner of his, he saw Timarchus there for the first time. He was impressed and his passion was aroused and he wanted to take him into his own house; he thought, I imagine, that Timarchus' nature closely resembled his own. First of all he spoke to Pittalacus, urging him to let him have Timarchus; and when he could not persuade Pittalacus, he assailed Timarchus here in person. It did not take much argument; he persuaded him instantly. Indeed, when it comes to the actual business, his candor and openness to persuasion are remarkable; for this very reason he should properly be an object of hatred.

[58] After he had left Pittalacus and been taken in by Hegesander, Pittalacus was, I think, distressed at having spent so much money (as he saw it) to no purpose and jealous of what was going on. And he kept going to the house. And because he was annoying them, observe the great feat of Hegesander and Timarchus! At one point they and some others whose names I prefer not to mention got drunk and **[59]** burst at night into the house where Pittalacus was living. First of all they broke his equipment and threw it into the street (throwing dice and dice cups and other gaming items) and they killed the quails and cocks on which the wretched man doted, and finally they tied Pittalacus himself to a pillar and inflicted on him the worst whipping imaginable for so long that even the neighbors heard the commotion. **[60]** Next day Pittalacus, enraged at the treatment, went robeless into the Agora[65] and sat as suppliant at the altar of the Mother of the Gods. A crowd assembled, as usually happens, and Hegesander and Timarchus in panic that their vile behavior might be announced to the whole city (the Assembly was about to meet) ran up to the altar, accompanied by some of their dicing partners. **[61]** They clustered around Pittalacus and begged him to leave the altar, maintaining that the whole incident had been a drunken prank. Timarchus himself

63. An Athenian naval commander in the 360s B.C.E.

64. A small fortune (= 8000 drachmas), equivalent to over twenty years' wages for a skilled worker.

65. The central marketplace of Athens, through which people on the way to the meeting place of the Assembly would pass.

(who was not yet as ugly-looking as nowadays—heavens, no—but still serviceable) touched the fellow's chin in supplication and said he would comply with all his wishes. Eventually they induced the fellow to quit the altar on the understanding that he would receive some sort of justice. But once he left the Agora they took no further notice of him. [62] And Pittalacus, angered at the outrageous treatment, brought a suit against each of them. . . .[66]

[70] Shall I bring myself to speak a little more frankly than is in my nature? Tell me, in the name of Zeus and the other gods, men of Athens, when a man has shamed himself with Hegesander, don't you think he has played whore to a whore? What excesses of vile behavior do we suppose they did not practice when drunk and on their own? Don't you think that Hegesander, trying to compensate for his notorious activities for Leodamas,[67] which you all know of, made arrogant demands in the belief that his own past behavior would seem moderate in comparison with the extremes of Timarchus?

[71] Nonetheless, you will see that Hegesander himself and his brother Crobylus will leap up here shortly and with considerable deviousness and rhetorical skill will claim that my case is one of downright stupidity. They will demand that I present witnesses who testify explicitly where he carried out the acts and who saw and what kind of act. This I think is a scandalous demand. [72] I don't consider you so forgetful that you do not recall the laws you heard read out a little earlier, in which it is written that anyone who hires an Athenian for this activity or anyone who hires himself out is liable to the most severe penalties, the same in both cases.[68] What man is so witless that he would agree to give explicit testimony of this sort by which it is certain, if he attests the truth, that he proves himself liable to the most extreme penalties? [73] So then, all that is left is for the passive partner to admit the facts himself. But this is why he is on trial, because after engaging in this activity he addressed the Assembly in defiance of the laws. So do you want us to abandon the whole issue and not investigate? By Poseidon, we

66. Pittalacus could not have brought a suit if he were actually a slave, as Aeschines alleges, although he might have had someone bring a suit on his behalf. Sections 62–66 proceed to narrate the legal maneuvers undertaken by Hegesander and Timarchus to block Pittalacus' suit. In 67–69 Aeschines challenges Hegesander to a deposition just as he had previously done with Misgolas.

67. An Athenian politician active as early as 376, here alleged to have been Hegesander's lover.

68. In point of fact, the law that Aeschines cites in sections 19–22 deals only with those who prostitute themselves, not with those who hire them. Aeschines appears to be conflating this with the law on *hybris* that he cites in sections 15–17 in an attempt to confuse his audience. On the "most severe penalties," see n. 45.

shall really manage the city well, if when we know that acts are taking place
we are to ignore them simply because someone does not come forward in
court and testify explicitly without shame.

[74] Consider the issue on the basis of parallels; and I suppose the parallels will have to resemble Timarchus' practices. You see these men who sit
in the brothels, the ones who on their own admission practice this activity.
Yet these men, when they are required to engage in the act, still throw a
cloak over their shame and lock the doors. Now if someone were to ask
you, the men passing by in the street: "what is this person doing at this
moment?" you would immediately give the name of the act, without seeing
who had gone in; no, once you know the chosen profession of the individual you also recognize the act. [75] So you should investigate Timarchus
in the same way and not ask whether anyone saw him but if this man has
engaged in the practice. For by the gods what is one to say, Timarchus?
What would you yourself say about another person who was being tried on
this charge? What is one to say when a young lad leaves his father's house
and spends his nights in the homes of others, a lad of unusual beauty, and
enjoys lavish dinners without making any contribution and keeps flute-
players and the most expensive courtesans and plays at dice, while he pays
out nothing himself but another man pays for him?[69] [76] Does one need
to be clairvoyant? Isn't it obvious that the man who makes such enormous
demands of others must himself inevitably provide certain pleasures in
return to the men who pay out the money in advance? By Olympian Zeus,
I can find no more decorous way of referring to the grotesque acts that
you have practiced. . . .[70]

[90] If this practice is to take place, as is usually the case, secretly and
in isolated spots and private houses, and the man who possesses the full-
est knowledge, but has shamed a citizen, is to be liable to the most severe
penalties if he testifies to the truth; while the man on trial, against whom
his own life and the truth have given evidence, is to insist on being judged
on the basis not of what is known but of the depositions, the law and the
truth are destroyed and a clear route has been revealed for those guilty of
the worst felonies to be acquitted. [91] For what mugger or thief or seducer
or homicide, or anyone else who commits the gravest offences but does so
in secret, will be punished? For, in fact, those of them who are caught with

69. Athenaeus 13.572B–D quotes this section of the speech side-by-side with the comic
fragments **3.25** and **3.26** as evidence that even a good meal could be considered a form of payment for sex.

70. In sections 77–89 Aeschines argues that the jurors should not need witnesses because
they already know Timarchus' nature and laugh at him any time he is the subject of discussion
in the Assembly. He adduces as parallels trials concerning bribery or deme votes on citizen
qualifications, where witnesses are not necessary.

their guilt manifest are executed at once if they confess, but those who go undetected and deny their guilt are tried in the courts and the truth is discovered on the basis of likelihood. . . .[71]

[94] Yet a speechwriter, the one who has devised his defense, claims that I contradict myself.[72] He says that in his view it is impossible for the same man to have prostituted himself and squandered his inheritance; to have misused one's body is the conduct of a child, while to have squandered one's inheritance is the conduct of a man. Furthermore, he claims that men who shame themselves charge fees for the practice. So he is going around the Agora expressing surprise and wonderment that the same man has prostituted himself and squandered his inheritance. [95] But if anyone does not realize how the matter stands, I shall attempt to lay it out more clearly in my account. While the estate of the heiress whom Hegesander, Timarchus' husband, had married, and the money that he brought back from his period abroad with Timomachus, lasted, they indulged in enormous excess and extravagance. But when it was all gone, wasted on dicing and lavish dinners, and Timarchus had passed his prime, as one would expect, nobody would pay money any more, while his vile and unholy nature still longed for the same pleasures, and in its extreme dissipation made continuing demands on him, and he was drawn back to his daily habits; [96] at that point he turned to eating up his inheritance. And he not only ate it up, but—if one can say this—drank it up as well! And indeed he sold off each of his possessions, and not even at its true value; he could not wait for a profit or a good price but sold it for what it would realize immediately. So compelling was his haste to enjoy his pleasures . . .[73]

[106] Now he has not only devoured his inherited property but in addition all of your public property that he has had in his control. For at the young age that you see there is no office he has not held, and he acquired none of them by selection by lot or election but bought every one illegally. The majority of them I shall ignore and just mention two or three. [107] He became auditor and did enormous damage to the city by receiving bribes from people guilty of malpractice in office, though his favorite

71. In sections 92–93, Aeschines appeals to the example of the Council of the Areopagus (the homicide court) to show that witnesses or the lack of them are not always dispositive.

72. The reference here is to Demosthenes, whose credibility is undercut by being referred to as a professional speechwriter for hire. Prosecution speeches like this one were always delivered first, so it is unclear how Aeschines knew what Demosthenes was going to say: he may have heard rumors from common acquaintances, or more likely he was just guessing. It is also possible that the published version of this speech as we have it was altered to respond to arguments that the other side actually made in the courtroom.

73. In sections 97–105 Aeschines calls witnesses to prove the magnitude of Timarchus' father's estate and the fact that Timarchus now has nothing left. He also accuses Timarchus of failing to support his blind uncle, even when he begged for a state disability pension.

practice was to persecute innocent men undergoing their final audit. He was magistrate at Andros,[74] an office he bought for thirty minas, money he borrowed at a rate of eighteen percent,[75] using your allies as a means of funding his vile habits. And he displayed appetite on a scale never before seen from anyone in his treatment of the wives of free men. I present none of the men here to testify in public to the personal misfortune that he chose to conceal; I leave it to you to investigate. [108] But what do you expect? When the same man committed outrages not only on others but also on his own person while here in Athens, under the rule of law, with you watching and his enemies nearby, who could imagine that once he obtained impunity, opportunity, and public office, he would leave undone any act of the most extreme wantonness? Many times before now, by Zeus and Apollo, I have reflected on the good luck of our city, not least among many reasons for the fact that in that period no buyer could be found for the city of Andros![76]

[109] But perhaps one could argue that he was unprincipled when holding office alone but upright when he had colleagues. How could that be? This man, men of Athens, was appointed to the Council in the archonship of Nicophemus.[77] Now to attempt an account of all the crimes he committed in that year is not reasonable in a small portion of a day. But I shall give you a brief account of the ones most relevant to the charge that forms the basis of the present trial. [110] During the same archonship in which Timarchus was a member of the Council, Hegesander the brother of Croby-lus was treasurer to the goddess,[78] and in collaboration like good friends they stole a thousand drachmas from the city. A decent man, Pamphilus of Acherdus, who had quarreled with the defendant and was angry with him, observed what had happened, and during an Assembly he stood up and said, "Men of Athens, a man and a woman are between them stealing a thousand drachmas of your money." [111] When you were puzzled at what he meant by a man and a woman and what he was talking about, he paused for a moment and said: "Don't you understand what I'm saying? The man is Hegesander over there—now, though before he was himself Leodamas' woman; the woman is Timarchus here. How the money is being

---

74. An Aegean island under Athenian control during this period.

75. A normal interest rate during this period would be twelve percent. That Timarchus borrowed at a much higher rate suggests either that he was considered a credit risk or that he was spendthrift and careless about his financial transactions.

76. The implication is that if Timarchus could have sold Andros for personal profit, he would have. In point of fact, magistrates did not have impunity for their acts, but would be audited at the end of their term in office.

77. 361 B.C.E.

78. Sacred monies were held in the name of Athena Parthenos, to be used only in national emergencies. A board of ten treasurers was chosen by lot to supervise these funds.

stolen I shall tell you." Then he gave a fully informed and lucid account of
the affair. And after giving this information he said: "So what do I advise
you to do, men of Athens? If the Council convicts Timarchus of the offence,
expels him and hands him over to a law court, give them their reward,[79]
and if they don't punish him, withhold it and hold this against them until
that day." [112] When the Council next entered the Council chamber,
they expelled him in the straw vote but accepted him back in the formal
ballot. And because they did not hand him over to a law court or eject him
from the Council chamber, though it pains me to mention it, still I must
tell you that they did not receive their reward. So, men of Athens, do not
show your anger against the Council and deprive five hundred citizens
of their crown for failing to punish this man, and then yourselves acquit
him and preserve for the Assembly a public speaker who was useless to the
Council. . . .[80]

[119] That consummate speaker Demosthenes claims that you must
either expunge the laws or else you must pay no attention to my arguments.
He says he is amazed if you don't all remember that every year the Council
sells off the prostitution tax,[81] and that those who buy the right to exact
the tax do not guess but have precise knowledge of the people who engage
in this trade. While I have had the audacity to charge that Timarchus has
no right to address the people when he has prostituted himself, Demosthenes claims that the practice itself calls not for an allegation from a prosecutor but a deposition from a tax man who has collected the tax from
Timarchus. [120] Men of Athens, see whether you find the reply I make
to this simple and frank. I am ashamed for the city's sake if Timarchus,
the people's adviser, the man who has the nerve to serve on embassies to
the rest of Greece, will not attempt to cleanse his reputation of the whole
business but instead query the locations where he offered himself and
ask if the tax-collectors have ever collected the prostitution tax from him.
[121] He should abandon this line of defense for your sake. I shall offer
you another line of defense, an honorable and just one, which you should
use, if you have nothing shameful on your conscience. Steel yourself to
look the jurors in the face and say what a decent man should about his
youth: "Men of Athens, I have been reared among you, from my childhood
and adolescence, and my way of life is no secret. I am seen among you in
the Assembly. [122] And I think that, if I were addressing any other body
on the charge for which I am now on trial, your testimony would enable

79. It was customary for each year's outgoing Council to be awarded a gold crown for their
service.

80. In sections 113–15 Aeschines gives additional examples of Timarchus' corruption in
public office. In 116–18 he warns the jurors not to be misled by Demosthenes' verbal tricks.

81. Most taxes were contracted out to private tax collectors like Androtion (see 4.6).

me to refute the accuser's statements easily. I think the rest of my life
not worth living, not only if I have committed any of these acts but if it is
your belief that the life I have lived resembles the accusations made by my
opponent, and I freely offer the punishment you inflict on me as a means
for the city to defend itself in the eyes of Greece. I have not come to plead
with you for mercy; no, destroy me, if you think me this sort of man."

This, Timarchus, is the defense that befits a noble and decent man, one
who has confidence in his way of life and properly treats every attempt at
slander with contempt. [123] In contrast, the argument that Demosthenes
is trying to persuade you to use is not the speech of a free man but of a
prostitute who is quibbling about locations. But since you take refuge in
the names of the lodgings and demand that the case be proved on the basis
of the establishment where you plied your trade, once you have heard what
I am about to say you will not use this argument if you have any sense. It
is not buildings or lodgings that give their names to the occupants but
occupants who give the titles of their individual practices to their locations.
[124] Where a number of people have rented a single building divided
among them, we call it an apartment building. Where one man lives, we
call it a house. Surely if a doctor moves into one of the shops by the road-
side, it is called a doctor's surgery. If he moves out and a blacksmith moves
into the same shop, it is called a smithy. If it is a fuller, it is called a laundry,
if it is a carpenter, it is called a carpenter's shop. If a pimp and prostitutes
move in, it gets the name brothel from the trade itself. And so you have
created a lot of brothels from your skill in the profession. So then, don't
ask where you ever engaged in the acts, but defend yourself on the ground
that you have not done so.

[125] Another argument, it seems, will be offered, contrived by the same
sophist. He maintains that there is nothing more unjust than common report; and he offers examples picked up from the marketplace and entirely
consistent with his own life. . . .[82] [126] And he offers himself as example
by way of a joke, like a good-humored man making jokes about his own
way of life. "Unless," he says, "I , too, must respond to the crowd when
they call me not Demosthenes but Batalus, because my nurse gave me
this nickname."[83] So if Timarchus was beautiful and is the butt of jokes

82. Aeschines goes on to say that Demosthenes will use examples of a commonly misidentified building and statue.

83. The nickname may have meant "stammerer," referring to Demosthenes' childhood
speech impediment. But Eupolis, fr. 92 PCG, implies that it also means "anus," in which case
Aeschines' reference to Demosthenes joking about his "way of life" suggests that he also was sexually passive with other men. Other sources tell of a flute-player of this name, who was known
for effeminacy.

in slanderous distortion of the fact and not because of his own conduct, surely, says Demosthenes, he doesn't deserve to be ruined for this.

[127] Myself, Demosthenes, where dedicatory offerings and houses and possessions, in short all voiceless objects, are concerned I hear many tales of all sorts and never consistent. For they have no capacity for noble or base action; it is the man who happens to become associated with them, whoever he may be, who furnishes the common account according to the scale of his own reputation. But where men's lives and actions are concerned, of its own accord a true report spreads through the city announcing an individual's conduct to the public at large and often predicting future events too. . . .[84]

[130] So recollect, gentlemen, the report you have encountered concerning Timarchus. Isn't it the case that as soon as the name is uttered you ask the question: "Which Timarchus? The whore?" So then, if I were offering witnesses, you would believe me. Yet if I offer the god as witness, will you not believe, when in all piety one cannot charge her with false testimony? [131] As to Demosthenes' nickname, he is rightly called Batalus, by common report and not by his nurse, having earned the name for unmanly and pathic ways. For if someone were to remove these smart robes of yours and the soft tunics in which you write speeches against your friends and carry them around and place them in the hands of the jurors, I think that, if someone were to do this unannounced, they would be at a loss whether they were holding the clothing of a man or a woman.

[132] And one of the generals will take the stand for the defense, I'm told, head held high and preening himself, with the air of a man who has frequented the wrestling schools and the philosophers' haunts.[85] And he will attempt to discredit the whole basis of the dispute, maintaining that I have initiated not a prosecution but the start of an appalling coarseness. He will cite first of all your benefactors, Harmodius and Aristogeiton[86] and speak of their mutual loyalty and the good their relationship did for the city. [133] He will not shrink, they tell me, even from using the poems of Homer or the names of heroes, but will sing the praises of the friendship of Patroclus and Achilles, based on love, they say,[87] and will now eulogize beauty, as though it had not long since been considered a blessing—if it is combined with self-control. If certain people by slandering this physical

84. In sections 128–29 Aeschines quotes the poets to prove that Rumor was honored as a goddess.

85. Both places associated with promoting pederastic courtship.

86. The tyrannicides, on whom see **1.89** and **2.2**.

87. This relationship was interpreted in explicitly pederastic terms in Aeschylus' *Myrmidons;* see **2.21.601–2** and **5.7.180**.

beauty bring ruin on those who possess it, he claims, your collective vote will be at odds with your individual prayers. [134] For he finds it strange, so he says, if in the case of sons as yet unborn all of you who are about to sire children pray that they may be born noble in appearance and a credit to the city, but in the case of sons already born, who ought to be a source of pride for the city, if they stun people with their outstanding youthful beauty and become objects of lovers' rivalry, you will evidently disfranchise them under the influence of Aeschines. [135] And then he intends to make a direct attack on me, I'm told. He'll ask if I'm not ashamed to subject the practice to censure and risk, when I make a nuisance of myself in the gymnasia and have been in love with many. And finally, so certain individuals inform me, in an attempt to encourage idle laughter among you, he says he will exhibit all the erotic poems I have written to individuals and claims he will provide testimony to quarrels and blows which the practice has brought me.

[136] Personally, I neither criticize legitimate desire, nor do I allege that boys of outstanding beauty have prostituted themselves; nor do I deny that I myself have felt desire and still do. And I do not deny that the rivalries and fights which the thing provokes have befallen me. As to the poems they ascribe to me, some I admit to, but in the case of the rest I deny that their character is that presented by my opponents, who distort them. [137] According to my definition, desire for those who are noble and decent is characteristic of the generous and discerning spirit, but debauchery based on hiring someone for money I consider characteristic of a wanton and uncultivated man. And to be loved without corruption I count as noble, while to have been induced by money to prostitute oneself is shameful. The distance which separates them, the enormous difference, I shall try to explain to you in what follows. [138] Our fathers, when they were legislating about conduct and activities dictated by nature, prohibited slaves from engaging in activities which they thought should belong to free men. "A slave," says the law, "may not exercise and rub himself down with oil in the wrestling schools." It did not add further: "but the free man is to rub himself down and exercise." For when the legislators in considering the benefits derived from the gymnasia prohibited slaves from participating, they believed that with the same law in which they prohibited these they were also encouraging free men to go to the gymnasium. [139] And again the same legislator said: "A slave may not be the lover of a free boy or follow him, or he is to receive fifty blows of the public lash." But he did not forbid the free man from being a boy's lover or associating with and following him, and he did not envisage that this would prove harmful to the boy but would be testimony to his chastity. But since the boy is at this stage not responsible, and is unable to distinguish between real and false affection, it is the lover he disciplines and he postpones talk of love to the age of

reason, when the boy is older. And he considered that following and watching over a boy was the most effective way of securing and protecting his chastity. [140] In this way the city's benefactors, Harmodius and Aristogiton, those men of outstanding virtues, were brought up by that decent and lawful feeling—call it love or what you will—to be men of such merit that when their deeds are praised the panegyrics seem inadequate to their achievements. . . .[88]

[155] But I don't want to talk at excessive length about the poets. Instead I shall tell you the names of older men who are well known, and young men and boys. Some of these have had many lovers because of their beauty, while others are still in the bloom of youth now; but none of them has ever been exposed to the same accusations as those made against Timarchus. And in contrast I shall give you the names of men who have practiced shameful and blatant prostitution; remembering these will help you to put Timarchus in the proper category. [156] I shall start with the names of people who have lived in the honorable manner which befits free men. Men of Athens, you know that Crito, the son of Astyochus,[89] and Periclides of Perithoidae and Polemagenes and Pantaleon, the son of Cleagoras, and Timesitheus the runner were in their day the most beautiful not only of the Athenian citizens but in all Greece, and that they attracted the largest number of lovers, and the most decent. Yet nobody has ever found fault with them. [157] Again, among those who are young men or still children even now, there is Iphicrates' nephew, the son of Tisias of Rhamnus, who bears the same name as the defendant Timarchus. Though he is good-looking, he is so foreign to shameful conduct that the other day, at the Rural Dionysia during the performance of the comic plays at Collytus,[90] when the comic actor Parmeno spoke an anapaestic line to the chorus in which mention was made of certain "big Timarchian prostitutes," nobody suspected a reference to the young man; everyone saw a reference to you. So firm is your claim to the practice. And again there is Anticles the sprinter[91] and Phidias the brother of Melesias. Though I could mention still more, I shall stop there, to avoid seeming to flatter any of them with my praise.

[158] Turning to those who share Timarchus' habits, I shall avoid making enemies and speak of those who least concern me. Who among you does not know of Diophantus, known as "the orphan," who arrested the foreigner and brought him before the archon for whom Aristophon of

---

88. In sections 141–54 Aeschines quotes Homer and Euripides to show that the love they praised was chaste and noble.

89. This was a wealthy family. The rest of the names are otherwise unknown.

90. A district on the southern side of Athens.

91. An Olympic victor in the games of 340 B.C.E.

Azenia was serving as assistant. He alleged that he had been cheated of four drachmas owed for this service and cited the laws which instruct the archon to take care of orphans when he himself had broken those which cover chastity. What citizen was not offended by Cephisodorus, known as the son of Molon, who had defiled his most beautiful appearance with the most infamous acts? Or Mnesitheus, known as the cook's son, and many others whose names I purposely forget. [159] I don't want to pursue each of them by name spitefully. In fact in my love of my city I would dearly wish to have a shortage of such cases to cite. But now that we have mentioned some examples of each type, dealing separately with the objects of chaste love and those who abused their own persons, I want you now to answer this question from me: to which category do you assign Timarchus, to the people who have lovers or to the prostitutes? So then, Timarchus, do not try to desert the society you have chosen and defect to the way of life of free men.

[160] If they try to argue that a man has not prostituted himself if he did not make a contract to hire himself out, and demand that I provide documentation and witnesses to this effect, firstly remember the laws concerning prostitution; nowhere does the legislator mention contracts. He did not ask whether anyone had disgraced himself under a written contract but, however the activity takes place, he absolutely bars the man who has engaged in it from the public affairs of the city. And rightly so. If any man in his youth abandoned noble ambitions for the sake of shameful pleasure, he believed that this man should not in later years enjoy political rights. . . .[92]

[166] Yet though these issues have been defined so clearly, Demosthenes will discover many diversionary arguments. The wickedness of his statements on the main issue might not arouse so much resentment. But the irrelevant arguments he will drag in to the detriment of the city's system of justice deserve your anger. Philip will be there in plenty; and the name of his son Alexander will be thrown in too.[93] For in addition to his other faults this man is a crude and insensitive individual. [167] His offensive remarks against Philip in his speech are uncivil and inappropriate, but less serious than the wrong I am about to mention; for his abuse will be directed incontrovertibly against a man, for all that he himself is not a man. But

92. In sections 161–65 Aeschines ridicules the notion that anyone would ever use a written contract for prostitution or be willing to go to court to enforce such a contract. However, see 4.4.22 for an alleged oral contract.

93. The king of Macedon and his son, Alexander (the Great). Philip's threat to the autonomy of Athens and the other Greek states was the source of conflict between Demosthenes' and Timarchus' anti-Macedonian faction and politicians like Aeschines, who favored appeasement and negotiation.

when with the use of labored ambiguous language he drags in shameful insinuations against the boy, he makes a laughing stock of the city. **[168]** In an attempt to spoil the audit I am about to undergo for my service on the embassy, he alleges that when he was giving the Council an account of Alexander the other day, how he played the lyre to us while we were drinking and recited speeches and debated with another boy, and was telling the Council all he knew about the matter, I grew angry at the jokes against the boy as if I were not one of the envoys but a relative.[94] **[169]** In fact, I have not spoken with Alexander, naturally, because of his youth. But Philip I praise right now for his auspicious statements. If his conduct towards us matches his present promises, he will make it a safe and easy task to praise him. I criticized Demosthenes in the Council chamber not out of a desire to curry favor with the boy but because I felt that if you listened to such things the city would appear to share the speaker's lack of decency.

[170] But in general, men of Athens, you should not admit lines of defense irrelevant to the main issue, first of all because of the oaths you have sworn, and secondly to avoid being misled by a fellow who is a master of the art of speaking. I shall take my story back a little to give you the information. When Demosthenes had squandered his inheritance,[95] he went round the city hunting for rich young orphans whose fathers were dead and whose mothers were in charge of the property. I shall omit many of them and mention one of the victims of appalling treatment. **[171]** He noticed a household which was rich but badly run. The head of the house was a proud but unintelligent woman, but the property was handled by a half-mad orphaned youth, Aristarchus the son of Moschus. He pretended to be in love with this young man, drew him into this intimate relationship, and filled him full of false hopes that he would very soon be a leading public speaker, and he showed him a list of names.[96] **[172]** And he encouraged and taught him to commit acts of a sort that the young man is now in exile from his fatherland, while this man, having got hold of the money which was to support Aristarchus in his exile, has robbed him of three talents; and Nicodemus of Aphidna[97] has been violently murdered by Aristarchus, with both his eyes gouged out, poor wretch, and the tongue cut out with

---

94. Demosthenes would appear to be implying that Aeschines was sexually attracted to Alexander, who was only ten at the time of the embassy.

95. In fact, Demosthenes had been defrauded of his inheritance by corrupt guardians, whom he later prosecuted with only partial success.

96. Presumably names of Demosthenes' former pupils who had become successful politicians.

97. A political enemy of Demosthenes, who indicted Demosthenes for failure to perform military service.

which he exercised free speech in confidence in the laws and in your authority. . . .[98]

[185] So then, this was the view of your fathers on the issues of shame and honor. Will *you* acquit Timarchus, a man guilty of the most shameful practices? A man, with a male body, who has committed the offences of a woman? Which of you then, if he catches his wife in misconduct, will punish her? Who will not seem stupid, if he shows anger at a woman who does wrong according to her nature but uses as his adviser[99] a man who had abused himself against nature. [186] What will be the state of mind of each of you when he goes home from court? The man on trial is not obscure; he is well known. And the law on the scrutiny of public speakers is not a poor one but quite excellent. It is to be expected that boys and young men will ask their relatives how the case has been judged. [187] So what will you say, you who now have the power to vote, when your sons ask you if you convicted or acquitted? The moment you admit to acquitting him, won't you overturn the whole educational system? What's the use in keeping slave chaperones or appointing gymnastic trainers and teachers for our children, when the men who have been given responsibility for the laws are deflected from their duty when faced with disgraceful acts?

[188] I also find it surprising, men of Athens, if you, who hate brothel keepers, intend to let go people who have voluntarily prostituted themselves. Evidently this same man, who will not be allowed to obtain the priesthood of any of the gods, since under the laws his body is unclean, will draft in the text of decrees prayers to the Solemn Goddesses[100] for the good of the city. Then why be amazed at the failure of public policy, when speakers like this man attach their names to decisions of the people? Shall we send abroad as envoy a man whose life at home has been disgraceful and entrust to him our most important interests? What would a man not sell when he has sold off the abuse of his person? Who would this man pity when he has shown no pity for himself?

[189] Which of you is unfamiliar with the disgusting conduct of Timarchus? In the case of people who exercise, even if we don't attend the gymnasia, we can recognize them from a glance at their fit condition. In the same way we recognize men who have worked as prostitutes from their shameless and impudent manner and from their general behavior even

---

98. In sections 173–79, Aeschines again warns the jurors not to be distracted by Demosthenes' attempts to introduce the Macedonian issue. In sections 180–81 he praises the Spartans for not allowing unworthy men to advise them, and in 182–84 he praises the ancient Athenians for valuing chastity in their women and children.

99. On political matters.

100. The Furies, who came to be symbols of moral conscience and punishment of wrongdoers.

if we're not present at their activities. For if a man has shown contempt for the laws and for morality on the most important issues, he has a certain attitude of mind which is visible from his disorderly manner.

[**190**] You will find that it is men such as this more than all others who have destroyed cities and have themselves encountered the worst disasters. Don't imagine, men of Athens, that wrongdoing has its origins in the gods and not in the willfulness of men, or that Furies punish men guilty of impiety, as in the tragedies, and punish them with burning brands. [**191**] No, unrestrained physical pleasures and a feeling that nothing is ever enough, these are what recruit to gangs of robbers, what fill the pirate ships, these are each man's Fury; these are what drive him to slaughter his fellow-citizens, serve tyrants, conspire to overthrow democracy. They take no account of the shame or the consequences for themselves; it is the pleasure success will bring that mesmerizes them. So eradicate natures such as this, men of Athens, and turn the ambitions of young men toward virtue. . . .[101]

[**194**] Timarchus has three kinds of supporting speakers to help him, those who have squandered their inheritance with their daily expenditures, those who have misspent their youth and abused their bodies and are afraid not for Timarchus but for themselves and their way of life, in case they are brought to trial at some point, and others who are people without any restraint who have made unrestricted use of men like him and whose motive is that trust in the aid they offer will make people more ready to do wrong. [**195**] Before you listen to their speeches in support of Timarchus, remember their way of life. Tell the ones who have done wrong to their own bodies not to pester you but to stop addressing the people; for the law does not examine the conduct of private citizens but public men. Tell the ones who have squandered their inheritance to work and make their living in some other way. And tell the hunters of the young men who are easily caught to turn their attentions to foreigners and resident aliens; then they won't be deprived of their chosen passion and your interests will not be damaged.[102]

4.8 Demosthenes, *On the Corrupt Embassy* 287

In 343 B.C.E., the prosecution that Timarchus had been blocked from bringing against Aeschines finally came to trial, this time with Demosthenes as the accuser. In it, he alludes to Aeschines' case against Timarchus.

---

101. Aeschines proceeds to warn that Timarchus' acquittal would send a bad message and inspire others like him.

102. A brief concluding summary follows in section 196.

The man who proposed the law against exporting arms to Philip in wartime, under penalty of death, has been outraged and destroyed.[103] This man who surrendered the arms of your allies to Philip[104] was his accuser, and spoke about prostitution, O land and gods, when he has two brothers-in-law at whom you would scream if you saw them—the repugnant Nicias, who hired himself out to Chabrias for a trip to Egypt, and the accursed Cyrebio,[105] who dances drunkenly in the Dionysiac procession without wearing a comic mask. And what is worse, he dared to speak about prostitution while aware of his own brother Aphobetus.[106] Indeed, all those words about prostitution flowed forth on that day like water trying to move upstream.

4.9 Aeschines, *On the Embassy* 179

This comes near the end of Aeschines' speech of self-defense in the same case.

There are people here to join me in imploring you: my father—do not deprive him of his hopes for his old age; my brothers, who would not want to live if I were taken from them; my in-laws; and these little children who do not yet recognize the danger but who will be pitiful if anything befalls me. I beg and implore you to give careful thought to them and not hand them over to their enemies or to this unmanly and effeminate person.[107]

4.10 Aeschines, *Against Ctesiphon* 162

Dated to 330 B.C.E., this case stands as the culmination in the long feud of Aeschines and Demosthenes. On technical grounds, Aeschines prosecutes Ctesiphon for having proposed a crown to honor Demosthenes' career of service to the Athenian state, but the speech is really aimed at Demosthenes throughout.

For according to the crew of the *Paralus*[108] and the envoys who went to Alexander[109] (and the incident is entirely credible), there's a certain Aris-

---

103. Timarchus.

104. Demosthenes blames Aeschines for the betrayal of the Phocians to Philip of Macedon in the Peace of Philocrates; the present prosecution is predicated on the assumption that Aeschines was bribed to do so.

105. The in-law's real name was Epicrates. "Cyrebio" is a nickname meaning "cattle feed." Aeschines denies the incident, but does admit that his brother-in-law is "easily led."

106. Aeschines' youngest brother, who had a prominent political career as a custodian of public funds and envoy to the Persian king.

107. Demosthenes.

108. An Athenian ship used for special ceremonial and diplomatic duties.

109. Alexander the Great, who at this time was in Persia.

tion of Plataea, the son of Aristobulus the pharmacist, no doubt known to some of you. This young man was once outstandingly beautiful and lived for a long time in Demosthenes' house—as to what he did and what was done to him, the allegations vary, and it would be quite improper for me to discuss the matter. This man, so I am told, is trying to ingratiate himself with Alexander, who does not know his background and his way of life, and is seeking out his company. And through him Demosthenes has sent letters to Alexander and so has achieved some immunity and a reconciliation for himself and has engaged in a great deal of flattery.

4.11 Hyperides, fr. 215 C

The date and target of this fragment are unknown, but Hyperides was known to be politically active especially in the period from 343 to 322 B.C.E.

Finally, what if the judge in this case I am arguing were Nature, which has divided the male personality from the female in such a way that it allots to each its own work and duty? If I were to show you that this man abused his body by treating it like a woman's, would Nature not be utterly astonished if anyone did not judge it the greatest gift that he was born a man, but hastened to turn himself into a woman by a corrupted gift of Nature?

4.12 Ps.-Demosthenes, *Erotic Essay* 1–32

This display piece, probably dating to the period of Demosthenes, praises an ideal youth. The oral delivery implied at the beginning is a dramatic fiction.

[1] Well, since you wish to hear the essay, I shall bring it out and read it aloud; but first you must understand its purpose. The writer's desire is to praise Epicrates, whom he thought to be the most charming young man in the city, although there were many fine gentlemen among those of his own age, and to surpass them even more in understanding than in beauty of person. Observing also that, generally speaking, most erotic compositions attach shame rather than honor to those about whom they are written, he has taken precautions that this should not happen in his case, and has written only what he says he is convinced of by his judgment, believing that an honest lover would neither do anything shameful nor request it. [2] Now, that part of my essay which you may find to be the most erotic, so to speak, is on this topic, but the rest of it in part praises the lad himself and in part counsels him about his education and his design for living. The whole essay is written as one would put it into a book, because discourses intended to be delivered ought to be written simply and just as one might speak offhand, while those of the other kind, which are planned to last longer, are properly composed in the manner of poetry and ornately, for

it is the function of the former to win converts and of the latter to display one's skill. Accordingly, to avoid spoiling the essay for you or rehearsing my own opinions about these questions, I ask you to lend your attention, since you are immediately going to hear the essay itself, because Epicrates is also at hand, whom I wished to hear it.

[3] Observing that certain of those who are loved and possess their share of good looks make the right use of neither one of these blessings, but put on grand airs because of the comeliness of their appearance and exhibit reluctance to associate with their admirers, and so far fail in judging what is best that, because of those who pervert the thing,[110] they assume a surly attitude toward those also who desire to associate with them from pure motives, I concluded that such young men not only defeat their own interests but also engender evil habits in the rest, [4] and that the high-minded should not follow their foolish example, bearing in mind particularly that, since actions are not absolutely either honorable or shameful but for the most part vary according to the persons concerned, it is unreasonable to adopt the same attitude toward both classes of men, and secondly, that it is the height of absurdity to envy those who have a host of firm friends but to repulse their admirers, who are a separate group and alone feel drawn by nature, not toward all, but only to the beautiful and modest.

[5] Moreover, although those who have never yet seen such a friendship turn out well or have severely condemned themselves on the ground that they would be incapable of associating innocently with casual acquaintances, it is perhaps not unreasonable to entertain this prejudice; but for those so disposed as yourself, who have not utterly refused to hear how very many benefits accrue through love without shame and have lived the rest of their lives with the utmost circumspection, it is not reasonable to have even a suspicion that they would do anything shameful. [6] Consequently I have felt all the more moved to write this essay, feeling sure I should not fail to secure two most honorable rewards. For when I have described the good qualities you possess, I hope that at one and the same time I shall prove you to be worthy of admiration and myself not senseless if I love you, being what you are; and secondly, in tendering the advice that is most urgently needed I believe I shall present proof of my own goodwill and furnish a basis for our mutual friendship.

[7] And yet it does not escape me that it is difficult to describe your character in keeping with your deserts and that it is more hazardous still to give advice when the adviser is bound to make himself answerable for his advice to the one who accepts it. It is my judgment, however, that, while it becomes the recipients of merited eulogies to baffle by the excess of

---

110. Through mere physical gratification.

their real virtue the ability of those who praise them, yet in my counsel
I shall not miss the mark, being well aware that no advice could be innocently carried out if proffered by men who are senseless and quite ruined
by incontinence, not even if they advise supremely well, but that not even
the advice that is only moderately pondered can altogether miss the mark
if tendered by men who choose to live pure and self-disciplined lives.

[8] Cherishing such hopes I enter upon my theme. All men would agree
with me, I believe, that it is of the utmost importance for young men of
your age to possess beauty in respect of person, self-discipline in respect of
soul, and manliness in respect of both, and consistently to possess charm in
respect of speech. As for these two kinds of qualities, natural and acquired,
Fortune has so generously blessed you with nature's gifts that you consistently enjoy distinction and admiration, and the other kind you are bringing to such perfection through your own diligence that no fair-minded
person could have fault to find with you. [9] And yet what ought he to
possess who is worthy of the highest eulogies? Must he not manifestly be
loved by the gods and among men be admired, for some qualities on his
own account, for others because of his good fortune? Now the longer list
of your virtuous qualities it will perhaps be fitting to describe summarily
later on, but the praise I have to utter for each of the gifts of Fortune I shall
now try to declare with truthfulness.

[10] I shall begin by praising that quality of yours which all who see you
will recognize first, your beauty, and the hue of your flesh, by virtue of which
your limbs and your whole body are rendered resplendent. Wondering
what fitting comparison for this I may offer, I find none, but it is my privilege to request those who read this essay to see you and contemplate you,
so that I may be pardoned for declaring that I have no suitable simile. [11]
For to what could anyone liken something mortal which arouses immortal
longing in the beholder, the sight of which does not satiate, and when
removed from sight lingers in the memory, which in human form possesses
a natural beauty worthy of the gods, like a flower in its comeliness, beyond
suspicion of imperfections? Furthermore, it is impossible to impute to your
person even those blemishes which in the past have marred many another
who has shared in beauty. [12] For either through ungainliness of mien
they have ruined all their natural comeliness or through some unfortunate
mannerism have involved their natural attractions in the same disfavor.
By none of these could we find your person afflicted, for whichever of the
gods it was that took forethought for your person has so diligently guarded
you against all such mishaps as to leave nothing calling for criticism and
to render your general appearance superb. [13] Moreover, since the face
is the most conspicuous of the parts that are seen, and of the face itself
the eyes, even more in these did the god reveal the goodwill that he had
toward you. For he not only furnished you with eyes adequate to perform

the necessary functions but, although the virtue of some men is not recognized even from their actions, of your character he has placed in a clear light the fine qualities through the evidence of your glance, displaying it as gentle and kind toward those who look at you, dignified and serious toward those who converse with you, manly and proper to all men.

[14] And here is a matter that may be particularly surprising. For while other men are assumed to be mean-spirited because they are gentle and to be arrogant because they are dignified, and are thought overbearing because they are manly, and stupid because they keep quiet, Fortune in your case has taken qualities so mutually contradictory and caused them all to be properly harmonized, as if fulfilling a prayer or wishing to set an example for others, but not framing a mere mortal nature, as was her usual way.

[15] Now if it were possible to do justice to such beauty as yours in words, or if this were the only quality of yours worthy of praise, we should think it necessary to omit praise of none of your good points; but as things are, I am afraid that we may find our hearers refusing to hear praise of your other merits and that we may defeat ourselves by harping on this theme. [16] For how could anyone overdo the verbal description of your appearance, since not even works of art executed by the skill of the best masters could do more than justice to it? Nor is this astonishing; for works of art have a motionless aspect, so that it is uncertain what they would look like if they possessed life, but your personality enhances in your every action the superb comeliness of your body. Only this much, therefore, I have to say in praise of your beauty, omitting a great deal.

[17] As for discreetness of conduct, it is my privilege to pass the finest of compliments, namely, that though such youthfulness readily invites scandal, it has been your lot to be praised instead. For so far from overstepping the mark, you have chosen to live more prudently than expected of your years. Of this the most convincing evidence is your deportment toward others; for although many make your acquaintance, and reveal characters of every kind and sort, and all seek to entice you into intimacies, you have so managed such people that all are content to feel friendship for you. [18] This is an index of those whose choice it is to live in the esteem and affection of men. And yet some men in the past have been well thought of who have advised against welcoming the company of all comers, as is also true of some who have taken their advice. For they claim that it is necessary either to humor low-minded people and so be maligned among the multitude, or else to be constantly on guard against such reproaches and so incur the dislike of such acquaintances themselves. [19] Personally I think you deserve to be eulogized all the more for this reason, that, while the other lads think it one of the impossible things to please men of every type, you have so surpassed these as to have risen superior

to all the difficult and troublesome people, allowing the others no reason even for suspecting immoral relations[111] with any and overcoming your annoyance with them by the adaptability of your manners.

[20] Now touching your admirers, if it is right to speak also of these, you seem to me to deport yourself so admirably and sensibly toward them, that, though most of them cannot be patient even with the object of their preference, you succeed in pleasing them all exceedingly. And this is a most unmistakable proof of your goodness; for not one finds himself disappointed of favors from you which it is just and fair to ask, but no one is permitted even to hope for such liberties as lead to shame. So great is the latitude your discreetness permits to those who have the best intentions; so great is the discouragement it presents to those who would fling off restraint. [21] Furthermore, while the majority of men, when young, seek a reputation for prudence by keeping silent, you are so superior to them in natural gifts that you gain men's good opinion of you not less by your speech and demeanor in casual company than by all your other merits; so great is the grace and charm of your words whether in jest or in earnest. For you are ingenuous without doing wrong, clever without being malicious, kindly without sacrifice of independence, and, taking all in all, like a child of Virtue sired by Love.

[22] Turning now to courage—for it will not do to omit this either, not because I would intimate that your character does not still admit of great development nor that the future will fail to furnish richer material for eulogy to those who wish to praise you, but rather that words of praise mean most at your age when to do no wrong is the best hope for other lads —your courage a man might extol on many other grounds but especially because of your training for athletic sports, of which you have a multitude of witnesses. [23] And perhaps it is in place first to say that you have done well in choosing this kind of contest. For to judge rightly when one is young what line of action one should pursue is the token of an honest soul and of sound judgment alike, and on neither ground would it be right to omit praise of your choice.

You, therefore, being well aware that slaves and aliens share in the other sports but that dismounting[112] is open only to citizens and that the best men aspire to it, have eagerly applied yourself to this sport. [24] Discerning, moreover, that those who train for the foot-races add nothing to their courage nor to their morale either, and that those who practice boxing and the like ruin their minds as well as their bodies, you have singled out

---

111. The Greek here literally means "make a mistake together with someone else."

112. A special type of ceremonial chariot race in the Panathenaea, in which an athlete wearing armor would at intervals dismount from a racing chariot, run beside it for a distance, and then remount it, still at full speed.

the noblest and grandest of competitive exercises and the one most in harmony with your natural gifts, one which approximates to the realities of warfare through the habituation to martial weapons and the laborious effort of running, in the magnificence and majesty of the equipment simulates the might of the gods, [25] presents besides the most delectable spectacle, embraces the largest number and the greatest variety of features and has been deemed worthy of the most valuable prizes. For, apart from those offered, getting the drill and practice in such exercises itself will possess glamour as no paltry prize in the eyes of those who are even moderately ambitious for excellence. The best evidence for this may be found in the poetry of Homer, in which he represents the Greeks and barbarians warring against one another with this equipment. I may add that even now it is customary to employ it in contests in Greek cities, and not in the meanest cities but in the greatest.

[26] So admirable is your choice of sport and so approved among all men. Believing also, as you do, that it is futile to desire the things most worthwhile, or yet to be physically endowed for all sorts of feats, unless the soul has been prepared for an ambitious career, at the very outset you exhibited diligence in the training grounds, nor in the real tests were you disappointing, but you gave extraordinary proof of the distinction of your natural gifts and particularly of the courage of your soul in the games. [27] I hesitate to begin treating this topic for fear words may fail me in the description of what took place on that occasion, but nevertheless I shall not pass it over; for it is a shame to refuse a report of what enthralls us as spectators.

Were I to describe all the contests an unseemly length would perhaps accrue to this essay, but by recalling a single example in which you especially distinguished yourself I shall demonstrate the same truth and be found to make a more reasonable use of the patience of my hearers. [28] When the teams had been started and some had leaped to the fore and some were being reined in,[113] you, prevailing over both, first one and then the other, in proper style, seized the victory, winning that envied crown in such fashion that, glorious as it was to win it, it seemed the more glorious and astounding that you came off safely. For when the chariot of your opponents was bearing down upon you head-on[114] and all thought the momentum of your horses beyond checking, you, aware that some drivers, though no danger should threaten, become overanxious for their own safety, not only did you not lose your head or your nerve, but by your

113. Some charioteers would restrain the horses at first with the intention of leaving them more energy for the end of the race.

114. After turning around the post at the end of the track, chariots would be racing in opposite directions, which could easily cause accidents on a narrow track.

courage got control of the impetus of your team and by your speed passed even those contenders whose luck had suffered no setback. [29] What is more, you caused such a revolution in men's minds that, though many keep insisting that nothing in equestrian contests affords such delight as a crash, and seem to speak the truth, in your case all the spectators, on the contrary, were afraid that some such accident might befall you. Such good-will and eagerness for your success did your personality awaken in them.

[30] They had good reason to feel so, for while it is a splendid thing to become distinguished for some one excellence, it is still more splendid to combine all the qualities of which a man of sense might justly feel proud. From the following examples this will be clear: we shall find that Aeacus and Rhadamanthys[115] were beloved by the gods for their discretion, Heracles, Castor and Pollux for their courage, and Ganymede, Adonis,[116] and others like them for their beauty, so that I at any rate am not astonished at those who covet your friendship but at those who are not so disposed. For when some, through sharing in one or another of the qualities I have mentioned, have been deemed worthy of the company of the gods, surely to a mere mortal it is the height of desire to become the friend of one who has become the proud possessor of all good qualities. [31] Certainly your father and mother and the rest of your kinsmen are rightly envied because you so far surpass those of your own age in excellence, but still more enviable are those whom you, who have been deemed worthy of such blessings, select from the whole number to be your friends, judging them worthy of your companionship. And since Fortune has appointed the former to share your affection, but the latter their own fine qualities have recommended in addition, [32] I do not know whether to call these young men admirers or unique for their sound judgment. For, as I think, Fortune, scorning base men and wishing to arouse the minds of the good, at the very outset made your nature beautiful, not for a life of pleasure, to be beguiled thereto, but serviceable for a virtuous life, to have happiness therein.[117]

4.13 Achilles Tatius, *Leucippe and Clitophon* 8.9

This excerpt, from a Greek romance of the third/fourth century C.E., narrates a legal dispute that closely parallels the conventions of earlier Attic oratory.

The priest stepped forward. He was by no means an incompetent speaker, an emulator in particular of Aristophanic comedy. He began to speak in

115. Two heroes who became judges in the Underworld because of their reputation for justice.

116. The male beloveds of Zeus and Aphrodite, respectively.

117. The remaining twenty-five sections of the discourse exhort Epicrates to the study of philosophy.

the urbane style of comedy, attacking the sexual integrity of Thersandros. "To insult the goddess by such an uncontrolled harangue against her clean-living servants [118] is the work of an impure mouth. Not only here but everywhere he goes, this man's tongue is coated with rank insolence. As a youth he was on intimate terms with many well-endowed men, spending his youthful beauty all on them. His looks exuded piety; he acted the role of chastity, pretending a very hot desire to be cultivated. When he found men who would exercise him to this end, he would kneel at their feet and bend over double to please them. He left his father's house and rented a little bedroom where he set up shop, specializing in the old Greek lays (Homer, I mean), and was receptive to all who might serve him and give him what he wanted. He was supposed to be developing his mind, but this was just a cover for a dissolute life. In the gymnasia we couldn't help but notice how he oiled his body, that special way he shinnied on the pole, and how in wrestling with the boys he always clung more tightly to the ones who were more manly. So much for his physical activities.

"This went on while his youthful beauty lasted. When he became a man, he exposed everything that he had concealed before. He neglected the rest of his body, which was worn out anyway, and concentrated on the tongue, whetting it for disgusting activities, and used his mouth in shameless ways, insulting everyone, parading his shamelessness on his very face. This man was not ashamed to slander in your presence (and so inelegantly at that!) a man whom you have honored with the priesthood. If I had lived in some other land and not with you, I would have to defend myself and my ways of life. But since you know that my behavior is very far removed from his blasphemies, let me speak to you instead about the specific accusations. . . ."

118. The novel's chaste hero and heroine, Clitophon and Leucippe, who have taken refuge in the sanctuary of the virgin goddess Artemis at Ephesus.

CHAPTER 5

Greek Philosophy

Same-gender love among males is a recurring topic in Greek philosophical discourse of the fourth century B.C.E. and later. While later satirical texts (e.g., **5.25, 9.38, 10.10**) attribute this interest to a predilection among the philosophers themselves, it is more likely a reflection of the erotic preference that prevailed among the target audience of philosophical education during this period: wealthy, elite males, particularly the unmarried young. Philosophical schools were with rare exception homosocial fraternities with a pedagogical mission, and were thus not far removed from the milieu of pedagogical pederasty either in popular imagination or in fact.

The circle of young men who gathered around Socrates during the last third of the fifth century, as recorded in the works of both Xenophon (**5.1–3, 5.8**) and Plato (**5.4–5, 5.7, 5.9**), reflect a culture in which intimate male attachments, even among age-equals (see **5.4.154, 5.8.4.23, 5.9.240**), were taken for granted as part of the social landscape. While passages such as **5.4** and **5.5** clearly show Socrates himself frequenting the gymnasium and enjoying the company of beautiful boys, Xenophon (**5.1–3**) depicts a Socrates who firmly disapproves of any actual physical involvement with them; Alcibiades' biographical account of Socrates in Plato's *Symposium* (**5.7.216–19**) indicates the same ethic of abstinence. Xenophon's *Memorabilia* is often assumed to be the most reliable source for the words and doctrines of the historical Socrates, but even this work is animated by an apologetic intent to clear Socrates of the charges that led to his condemnation, notably "corrupting the youth." And while early Platonic dialogues such as the *Charmides* and *Lysis* are, with some justification, thought to reflect Socratic method and teachings more than later dialogues, even they present fictionalized situations and should be used with great caution.

Plato's *Symposium* (5.7) is thought to be a work of Plato's "middle" period, perhaps within a few years of 380 B.C.E. It is interesting not only as a vivid dramatic depiction of Athenian intellectuals at ease in the period immediately before the religious scandals and anti-intellectual backlash of 415 but also as a dialogue featuring varying points of view about Eros, defined principally (but not solely) in pederastic terms. The speeches can be seen as a sequence of partial and imperfect understandings leading up to Socrates' climactic discourse, which records something like what may have been Plato's own view. Phaedrus' short oration uses mythological examples to explore the nature of love but bogs down in confusion over the identity of "lover" and "beloved": every one of his examples fails to illustrate his thesis that only a lover will die for one. Pausanias' speech differentiates between higher and lower forms of Eros, the former character-based, spiritual, and only homoerotic, the latter purely carnal; what Pausanias fails to address directly, however, is to what extent a spiritual relationship can also be carnal. The physician Eryximachus does deal with the bodily effects of these two forms of Eros, but on the basis of an abstract Empedoclean doctrine of harmony and disharmony. Aristophanes' speech relates an etiological myth explaining sexual orientation as an inherent trait determined by one's descent from primordial double-humans, with love as a yearning for one's ancestral lost half. Agathon delivers a paean to the god Eros as the most beautiful of all beings. Socrates refutes this portrait by showing that the force of love should not be confused with the object of love, but he does pick up Agathon's emphasis on beauty, as well as elements of the other speeches, to forge the image of a "ladder of love" (5.7.211), whereby beautiful bodies guide one to appreciation of beautiful character, leading to appreciation of beautiful arts, and ultimately to an understanding of Beauty as an ideal form. What is not completely clear from Socrates' speech is whether the lower stages of this process (bodily love) are to be excluded or merely passed through on one's spiritual quest for higher beauty. Alcibiades' subsequent narrative about Socrates' disinterest in the physical might suggest the former.

Xenophon's *Symposium* (5.8) seems to have been written as a response to Plato's on several points, not the least being the higher prestige it accords heterosexual love. Pederasty is criticized for not affording mutual pleasure (5.8.8.21) and for often separating a boy from the authority of his father (5.8.8.11 and 19). Interestingly, Critobulus' speech (5.8.4.10–18) shows that even active pederasts prided themselves on a beautiful appearance, even to the point of vanity.

Plato's *Phaedrus* (5.9) is generally thought to be somewhat later than his *Symposium,* since it articulates a more developed theory of forms, with Eros as a remembrance of the soul's fleeting glimpse of ideal Beauty before its birth into a body. We also find in **5.9.255** an account of mutual and reciprocal love between man and boy, absent in Socrates' *Symposium* speech. In addition, this dialogue features an interesting essay attributed to the orator Lysias, in which he argues that a boy would do better to grant his company (and presumably sexual favors, although this is not altogether clear) to a "non-lover" rather than to a lover, that is, to a man who is rational rather than emotionally possessive.

One of Plato's last works is the *Laws* (**5.10–11**), which aims to design the constitution of an ideal state that explicitly outlaws all sexual relations among males. This rejection of physical gratification (an issue only ambiguously addressed in the *Symposium*) may be foreshadowed in the *Phaedrus* (especially **5.9.254–56**), which designates a physically consummated love as inferior to a Platonic relationship. Even the early *Gorgias* (**5.6**) treats *kinaidoi*, men who are sexually excessive and/or passive, as unspeakable monsters.

Aristotle also devalues the physical side of male love, considering love of character longer lasting than love of bodies (**5.14**) and mutual affection more important than physical consummation (**5.12**). **5.13** and the post-Aristotelian **5.16** ponder what causes some men to enjoy passive sexual intercourse. It is held to be either a natural disposition due to physiological abnormalities or a habit engendered by "abuse" during early puberty. The earlier Hippocratic **5.15** suggests that gender confusion might be genetically determined at the moment of conception, a view that may go as far back as the early-fifth-century pre-Socratic philosopher Parmenides (see **10.5.134–35**).

The other philosophical schools of the fourth century also have interesting perspectives. Not surprisingly, the Cyrenaics (or "hedonists") saw nothing wrong with physical enjoyment of beautiful boys, and also seem to have made no distinction in value between boys and women (**5.19**). The Cynics were a diverse group, but most visible as roving popular philosophers and homeless street preachers, what we today might call "urban performance artists," who praised a life based on bare satisfaction of natural instincts and held in contempt all manifestations of luxury and civilized pretense. The earliest Cynics did not write treatises, but their thought is preserved in the form of barbed aphorisms and anecdotes (**5.17–18**): it is no surprise that pederasty, as a characteristic upper-class refinement with no basis in "nature," was one of their targets, and they frequently attempted to dissuade young men from making themselves objects of attention. Interestingly, they considered men who were overly concerned with their appearance equally likely to be sexual passives and adulterers, in some cases both.

The Stoics, a philosophical school founded by Zeno of Citium around 300 B.C.E., offer some particularly puzzling reflections. Zeno was originally a student of the Cynics, as may be reflected in some iconoclastic statements rejecting conventional tenets of sexual morality (**5.21–22**). However, other statements and anecdotes reflect that Zeno himself, although oriented to young men, was self-restrained (**5.23**) and believed in the love of youths based only on character (**5.20**). Some texts suggest that the Stoics favored loving older youths (up to the age of twenty-eight!), who were capable of philosophical education, rather than adolescent boys (**5.24–25**; compare Pausanias in **5.7.181**). It could be that Zeno's doctrine differentiated between sex, which could be satisfied indiscriminately, and love, which should be more selective and self-restrained; indeed, **5.21** may mean to suggest that sex and love have nothing to do with each other. However, we should also not underestimate the fact that some of the more provocative doctrines ascribed to the Stoics are recorded in hostile sources.

Zeno's contemporary Epicurus, who followed in the footsteps of the Cyrenaics much as Zeno did of the Cynics, had nothing distinctive to say about male love, but Epicurean doctrine generally emphasized the greatest pleasure with the least pain and thus in erotic matters encouraged either freedom from appetites or satisfaction of appetites (pleasure) without emotional involvement (pain), a position not unlike that attributed to Lysias in the *Phaedrus*.

Bibliographical Note

For general surveys of homosexuality in Greek philosophical texts, see Dover (1978) 153–70, Buffière (1980) 391–480, E. Cantarella (1992) 54–69, Nussbaum (1994) 1555–97. Meier and de Pogey-Castries (1930) 106–57 include various biographical anecdotes about the loves of ancient philosophers. For general treatments of Plato's theory of love and desire, see Gould (1963), Halperin (1985), Kahn (1987), Santas (1988) 14–96, and A. W. Price (1989) 1–102.

On desire in the *Lysis,* see Versenyi (1975), Glidden (1981), Osborne (1994) 56–61, Adams (1995), and Reshotko (1997). Bolotin (1979) 63–225 offers a detailed philosophical commentary on the dialogue.

For a similar commentary on the *Symposium,* see Allen (1991). Rosen (1968), Dorter (1969), and Penwill (1978) provide detailed readings focusing on the interrelations between the speeches; Brenkman (1977) offers a deconstructive reading of the tension between the dialogue's philosophical content and literary form, which are related in a more constructive way by Halperin (1992). On Phaedrus' and Pausanias' speeches, see Nola (1990); on Aristophanes' speech, see Dover (1966), Hani (1982), and Halperin (1990) 18–21. On Agathon's speech and Socrates' response to it, see Stokes (1986) 114–82. Of course, Diotima's speech has received the most serious philosophical attention: see Cornford (1950) 68–80, Neumann (1965), White (1989), Irigaray (1994), and Sier (1997). Osborne (1994) 86–116 questions whether it really embodies Plato's own views. Allen and

Welton (1996) treat Alcibiades' actions as an attempt to prove Socrates' fallibility; Nussbaum (1986) 165–99 accords this speech a prominent position in reasserting the importance of loving the individual as against the impersonal Love that is advocated by Diotima. Edmonds (2000) treats it in terms of role reversal between lover and beloved. D. T. Steiner (1996) treats the image of the Silenus statue at the beginning of Alcibiades' speech.

On the relative dates of Xenophon's and Plato's *Symposium*, see Flacelière (1961) and Dover (1965), who date Plato earlier; Wimmel (1957), who cautiously dates Xenophon earlier; and Thesleff (1978), who dates only chapters 1–7 of Xenophon earlier, but see 8–9 as a response to Plato. Flacelière interprets Xenophon's dialogue as a feminist response to Plato's work, which showed Socrates as more indulgent toward pederasty than Xenophon believed he was. On Xenophon's judgment of male love, see Hindley (1999).

For detailed studies of the *Phaedrus*, see Ferrari (1987), Griswold (1996), and G. Nicholson (1999); Rossetti (1992) assembles the proceedings of an international colloquium on the dialogue, with many interesting contributions. Hackforth (1952), G. J. de Vries (1969), and Rowe (1986) provide philosophical commentaries. Döpp (1983), Dalfen (1986), and Görgemanns (1998) consider whether the speech attributed to Lysias is genuinely his, with Döpp and Görgemanns supporting the attribution; Rosen (1979) treats the speech philosophically. Brown and Coulter (1979) see Socrates' first speech as modeled on the techniques of Isocrates. Nussbaum (1986) 200–33 reads the *Phaedrus* as a work more tolerant of human appetites and "madness" than the earlier *Republic;* Rowe (1990) counters this view.

One of the major controversies in criticism of Plato's erotic doctrine concerns the importance of individuals. In a seminal article, Vlastos (1973) 3–34 argues that Plato attached little importance to love of the individual for his own sake, since individuals are by definition flawed and imperfect. He is substantially followed by Nussbaum (1986) 165–99, but Kosman (1976), Levy (1979), A. W. Price (1981), Roochnik (1987), Gill (1990), and White (1990) offer various counter-arguments; A. W. Price (1991) replies to Nussbaum.

Another debated issue has been whether Plato's philosophical doctrine has any inherent connection to the pederastic model assumed in his dialogues: Vlastos (1973) 38–42 and Joó (1997) assert that the doctrine could just as well apply to love of women in a different cultural context; Nicolai (1998) denies it. Du Bois (1985) and Halperin (1990) 113–51 both argue for an appropriation of the female even within the homoerotic discourse of Plato's work; see also Plass (1978) and Pender (1992) for the metaphor of spiritual pregnancy. Keller (1985) 21–32, Halperin (1986), and Foley (1998) examine Plato's move toward a concept of reciprocal love at variance with some assumptions about contemporary cultural practice.

Nussbaum (1994) 1570–81, 1623–39 maintains that the *Phaedrus* and *Laws* condemn heterosexual and homosexual acts equally. Rist (1997) strongly disagrees, and discerns in the *Laws* evidence for a growing hostility toward homosexual sex. However, Brès (1973) 78–84, 229–32, 364–66, and 375–78 argues that the sex-negativity of the *Laws* is not inconsistent with Plato's earlier doctrine. Wallace (1997) embeds the sexual doctrines of the *Laws* in what he sees as a conservative aristocratic reaction against moral license in the mid-fourth century. On the terminology of *erōs, epithumia,* and *philia,* that bulks large in the *Laws,* see Hyland (1968) and Cummins (1981).

On Aristotle's discussion of homosexual love, see A. W. Price (1989) 236–49 and Capriglione (1999).

Schofield (1991) 22–56 embeds Zeno's ideas on homosexual practice within his communistic political system. For further consideration of Stoic erotic doctrine, see Nussbaum (1995) and Inwood (1997).

5.1 Xenophon, *Memorabilia* 1.2.29–31

This work records historical anecdotes about Socrates' interaction with his pupils. Its overall intention was to defend Socrates against the charges on which he was condemned to death in 399 B.C.E.: corrupting the young and denying the gods of the city.

[29] But if, even though he himself did nothing wicked, he praised others when he saw them doing shameful things, he would rightly be censured. When, however, he perceived that Critias[1] was in love with Euthydemus and trying to take advantage of him in the way men do when they make use of boys' bodies for sexual pleasure, he tried to dissuade him by saying that it was not worthy of a free man or of a gentleman to beg from his beloved, in whose eyes he wanted to seem praiseworthy, pleading like a beggar and beseeching him to give him something it is ignoble to give. [30] And as Critias did not listen to him and was not dissuaded, they say that Socrates, in front of many people, including Euthydemus, said that it seemed to him that Critias was in the state of mind of a pig, for he desired to rub up against Euthydemus just as piglets do against stones. [31] From this day on Critias hated Socrates.

---

1. A onetime pupil of Socrates who later became one of the Thirty Tyrants, an oligarchical regime installed by Sparta in 404 B.C.E., after Athens' defeat in the Peloponnesian War, but overthrown soon afterward. Socrates' condemnation came in the aftermath of reprisals against the Thirty and those who collaborated with them. Critias' amoral character was supposed by his opponents to be due to Socrates' iconoclastic teachings.

5.2 Xenophon, *Memorabilia* 1.3.8–14

[8] Socrates advised that one abstain resolutely from sex with beautiful boys; for he said it was not easy for a man who engaged in such things to behave moderately. Indeed, when he heard that Crito's son Critobulus had kissed Alcibiades' son,[2] who was a beautiful boy, he asked Xenophon, with Critobulus present, [9] "Tell me, Xenophon, did you not consider Critobulus one of the moderate rather than the rash, and one of the cautious rather than the thoughtless and foolhardy?"

"Yes, indeed," said Xenophon.

"Well, consider him, instead, as thoroughly hot-headed and reckless: he is the kind of man who would do somersaults on a bed of knives or jump into a fire."

[10] "Why, what did you see him doing," said Xenophon, "that you have accused him of such things?"

"Was he not," he said, "so bold as to kiss Alcibiades' son, a boy with a beautiful face and right in the bloom of boyhood?"

"Well, if that," said Xenophon, "is the kind of thing that the foolhardy do, I think I too might be such a fool as to risk it."

[11] "Unhappy man, what do you think you would experience by kissing a beautiful boy—if not instantly becoming a slave instead of a free man, spending money on harmful pleasures, having no time to give thought to anything fine and noble and being forced to pursue things that not even a madman would pursue?"

[12] "By Heracles," said Xenophon, "what a terrible power you say a kiss has!"

"And do you wonder at that?" said Socrates, "Do you not know that tarantulas, although they are only as large as a half-obol piece,[3] only have to take hold of men with their mouths in order to crush them with pain and drive them out of their minds?"

"Yes, by Zeus," said Xenophon, "but that is because tarantulas inject something into their sting."

[13] "Foolish man," said Socrates, "do you think that the beautiful, when kissing, do not inject something, just because you don't see it? Do you not know that this beast, which they call 'beautiful' and 'in bloom,' is so much more dangerous than tarantulas, since tarantulas need to take hold of a man, but this beast, without taking hold of him—if the man only

---

2. This would be the younger Alcibiades, whom Lysias (4.3) identifies as the beloved of many men. However, in 5.8.4.12–26, Critobulus is in love with Cleinias, the younger cousin of the general Alcibiades. In that passage, Critobulus praises himself as a man of great personal beauty.

3. A very small coin.

looks at it—injects such a powerful substance that even from far away it makes him go mad? Indeed, I advise you, Xenophon, whenever you see someone beautiful, to flee from him as fast as you can; you, on the other hand, Critobulus, I advise to go abroad for a year. For it is more likely that you would get better if you went for such a long time."

[14] Indeed, this is how he thought that those who were not in firm control of their sex drive must deal with sex: they should conduct themselves in such a way that the soul would not allow it, unless the body were in urgent need, and that the soul would not object, if the body's need were real. In this regard he had evidently trained himself to resist the most beautiful and most in bloom more easily than others resist the ugliest and least blooming.

5.3 Xenophon, *Memorabilia* 2.6.28–33

[28] "But take heart, Critobulus," Socrates said, "try to become a noble man and when you have, make an effort to catch friends among the noble and fair. Perhaps I too could help you in the pursuit of such gentlemen, as I am wholly involved in the erotic. Indeed, it is amazing how, when I desire someone, I set off heart and soul after getting the ones I love to love me in return, and the ones I long for to long for me in return, and the ones I desire to be with to desire my company as well. [29] And I see that you will need to do this too, when you desire to make friendships with people. So do not hide from me with whom it is you want to be friends: my efforts at pleasing those who please me have, I think, given me some experience in the pursuit of men."

[30] "Yes, precisely, Socrates," Critobulus said, "it is these lessons that I have desired for a long time, especially if the same skill will serve with those who are noble in soul and those who are fair of body."

[31] "But Critobulus," said Socrates, "the skill I teach does not help one to get the fair to submit to one's will by laying hands on them. I am convinced, indeed, that the reason men fled from Scylla[4] is that she laid hands on them; the Sirens,[5] on the other hand, laid hands on no one but rather sang to one and all from afar, and that is why, they say, everyone submitted to their charm and, through listening to them, were enchanted."

[32] "Agreed, then," said Critobulus, "that I will not put my hands on anyone; if you know anything that is good for acquiring friends, teach me."

---

4. A mythological monster in the *Odyssey*, who had six heads on long necks and snatched sailors off ships that passed her cliff.

5. Also creatures of the *Odyssey*, these three bird-women sang beautiful melodies to lure sailors to shipwreck on the shallow rocks surrounding their beach.

"Will you then also not," said Socrates, "put your mouth to theirs?"

"Don't worry," said Critobulus, "I will not put my mouth to anyone's, unless he is fair."

"Right at the start, Critobulus," he said, "you have said the opposite of what you ought to say. The fair do not submit to such things, while the ugly allow it happily because they think they are considered fair for their souls."

[33] "Agreed, then, that I will kiss the fair once," said Critobulus, "and that I will cover the noble with kisses, go on and teach me about catching friends."

"When, in that case, Critobulus," Socrates said, "you want to make friends with someone, will you allow me to reveal to him that you admire him and desire to be his friend?"

"Reveal away," said Critobulus, "I do not know of anyone who dislikes admirers."

5.4 Plato, *Charmides* 153A–155D

Socrates narrates this encounter to an unnamed interlocutor.

[153] We got back the preceding evening from the camp at Potidaea,[6] and since I was arriving after such a long absence I sought out my accustomed haunts with special pleasure. To be more specific, I went straight to the palaestra of Taureas[7] (the one directly opposite the temple of Basile), and there I found a good number of people, most of whom were familiar, though there were some, too, whom I didn't know. When they saw me coming in unexpectedly, I was immediately hailed at a distance by people coming up from all directions, and Chaerephon,[8] like the wild man he is, sprang up from the midst of a group of people and ran towards me and, seizing me by the hand, exclaimed, "Socrates! How did you come off in the battle?" (A short time before we came away there had been a battle at Potidaea and the people at home had only just got the news.)

And I said in reply, "Exactly as you see me."

"The way we heard it here," he said, "the fighting was very heavy and many of our friends were killed."

"The report is pretty accurate," I said.

"Were you actually in the battle?" he said.

---

6. A city in northern Greece and the site of a revolt (432–431 B.C.E.) that was one of the alleged causes of the Peloponnesian War.

7. A private wrestling school. As in 3.11 and 3.12, these were frequently places of social activity for youths and their admirers.

8. Socrates' closest associate, ridiculed along with him in Aristophanes' *Clouds*.

"Yes, I was there."

"Well, come sit down and give us a complete account, because we've had very few details so far." And while he was still talking he brought me over to Critias,[9] the son of Callaeschrus, and sat me down there.

When I took my seat I greeted Critias and the rest and proceeded to relate the news from the camp in answer to whatever questions anyone asked, and they asked plenty of different ones.

When they had had enough of these things, I in my turn began to question them with respect to affairs at home, about the present state of philosophy and about the young men, whether there were any who had become distinguished for wisdom or beauty or both. [154] Whereupon Critias, glancing towards the door and seeing several young men coming in and laughing with each other, with a crowd of others following behind, said "As far as beauty goes, Socrates, I think you will be able to make up your mind straight away, because those coming in are the advance party and the admirers of the one who is thought to be the handsomest young man of the day, and I think that he himself cannot be far off."

"But who is he," I said, "and who is his father?"

"You probably know him," he said, "but he was not yet grown up when you went away. He is Charmides, the son of my mother's brother Glaucon, and my cousin."[10]

"Good heavens, of course I know him," I said, "because he was worth noticing even when he was a child. By now I suppose he must be pretty well grown up."

"It won't be long," he said, "before you discover how grown up he is and how he has turned out." And while he was speaking Charmides came in.

You mustn't judge by me, my friend. I'm a broken yardstick as far as handsome people are concerned, because practically everyone of that age strikes me as beautiful. But even so, at the moment Charmides came in he seemed to me to be amazing in stature and appearance, and everyone there looked to me to be in love with him, they were so astonished and confused by his entrance, and many other lovers followed in his train. That men of my age should have been affected this way was natural enough, but I noticed that even the small boys fixed their eyes upon him and no one of them, not even the littlest, looked at anyone else, but all gazed at him as if he were a statue. And Chaerephon called to me and said, "Well, Socrates, what do you think of the young man? Hasn't he a splendid face?"

"Extraordinary," I said.

---

9. See n. 1.

10. Charmides would later become a key partisan of the Thirty Tyrants. He was also Plato's uncle.

"But if he were willing to strip," he said, "you would hardly notice his face, his body is so perfect."

Well, everyone else said the same things as Chaerephon, and I said, "By Heracles, you are describing a man without an equal—if he should happen to have one small thing in addition."

"What's that?" asked Critias.

"If he happens to have a well-formed soul," I said. "It would be appropriate if he did, Critias, since he comes from your family."

"He is very distinguished in that respect, too," he said.

"Then why don't we undress this part of him and have a look at it before we inspect his body? Surely he has already reached the age when he is willing to discuss things."

"Very much so," said Critias, "since he is not only a philosopher but also, [155] both in his own opinion and that of others, quite a poet."

"This is a gift, my dear Critias," I said, "which has been in your family as far back as Solon. But why not call the young man over and put him through his paces? Even though he is still so young, there can be nothing wrong in talking to him when you are here, since you are both his guardian and his cousin."

"You are right," he said, "we'll call him." And he immediately spoke to his servant and said, "Boy, call Charmides and tell him I want him to meet a doctor for the weakness he told me he was suffering from yesterday." Then Critias said to me, "You see, just lately he's complained of a headache when he gets up in the morning. Why not pretend to him that you know a remedy for it?"

"No reason why not," I said, "if he will only come."

"Oh, he will come," he said.

Which is just what happened. He did come, and his coming caused a lot of laughter, because every one of us who was already seated began pushing hard at his neighbor so as to make a place for him to sit down. The upshot of it was that we made the man sitting at one end get up, and the man at the other end was toppled off sideways. In the end he came and sat down between me and Critias. And then, my friend, I really was in difficulties, and although I had thought it would be perfectly easy to talk to him, I found my previous brash confidence quite gone. And when Critias said that I was the person who knew the remedy and he turned his full gaze upon me in a manner beyond description and seemed on the point of asking a question, and when everyone in the palaestra surged all around us in a circle, my noble friend, I saw inside his cloak and caught on fire and was quite beside myself. And it occurred to me that Cydias was the wisest love-poet when he gave someone advice on the subject of beautiful boys and said that "the fawn should beware lest, while taking a look at the lion, he should provide part of the lion's dinner," because I felt as if I had been snapped up by such a creature. All the same, when he asked me if I knew the headache remedy, I managed somehow to answer that I did.[11]

5.5 Plato, *Lysis* 203A–207C, 221D–223A

Again, Socrates narrates this encounter to an unnamed interlocutor.

[203] I was on my way from the Academy straight to the Lyceum,[12] following the road just outside and beneath the wall; and when I got to the little gate by Panops' spring, I happened to meet Hippothales, Hieronymus' son, and Ctesippus of Paeania, and with them some other young men standing together in a group. Seeing me coming, Hippothales said,

"Hey, Socrates, where are you coming from and where are you going?"

"From the Academy," I said, "straight to the Lyceum."

"Well, come straight over here to us, why don't you? You won't come? It's worth your while, I assure you."

"Where do you mean, and who all are you?"

"Over here," he said, showing me an open door and an enclosed area just facing the wall. "A lot of us spend our time here. [204] There are quite a few besides ourselves—and they're all good-looking."

"What is this, and what do you do here?"

"This is a new wrestling school," he said, "just built. But we spend most of our time discussing things, and we'd be glad to have you join in."

"How very nice," I said. "And who is the teacher here?"

"Your old friend and admirer, Mikkos."

"Well, God knows, he's a serious person and a competent instructor."

"Well, then, won't you please come in and see who's here?"

"First I'd like to hear what I'm coming in for—and the name of the best-looking member."

"Each of us has a different opinion on who that is, Socrates."

"So tell me, Hippothales, who do you think it is?"

He blushed at the question, so I said, "Aha! You don't have to answer that, Hippothales, for me to tell whether you're in love with any of these boys or not—I can see that you are not only in love but pretty far gone, too. I may not be much good at anything else, but I have this god-given ability to tell pretty quickly when someone is in love, and who he's in love with."

---

11. Socrates goes on to describe a doctrine of holistic medicine, in which health of the body is based on balance and temperance within the soul. This leads to an inquiry on the nature of temperance, a quality Critias praises in his cousin Charmides.

12. The Academy was a public park and gymnasium to the northwest of Athens, the Lyceum a public gymnasium just outside the eastern wall of the city, named after its proximity to the sanctuary of Apollo Lyceus. The latter was a particularly favored place for Socrates to meet his followers; the Academy, of course, later became the seat of Plato's school.

When he heard this he really blushed, which made Ctesippus say, "O very cute, Hippothales, blushing and too embarrassed to tell Socrates the name. But if he spends any time at all with you he'll be driven to distraction hearing you say it so often. We're all just about deaf, Socrates, from all the 'Lysis' he's poured into our ears. And if he's been drinking, odds are we'll wake up in the middle of the night thinking we hear Lysis' name. As bad as all this is in normal conversation, it's nothing compared to when he drowns us with his poems and prose pieces. And worst of all, he actually sings odes to his beloved in a weird voice, which we have to put up with listening to. And now when you ask him the name he blushes!"

"Lysis must be pretty young," I said. "I say that because the name doesn't register with me."

"That's because they don't call him by his own name much. He still goes by his father's name, because his father is so famous. I'm sure you know what the boy looks like; his looks are enough to know him by."

"Tell me whose son he is," I said.

"He's the oldest son of Democrates of Aexone."

"Well, congratulations, Hippothales, on finding someone so spirited and noble to love! [205] Now come on and perform for me what you've performed for your friends here, so that I can see if you know what a lover ought to say about his boyfriend to his face, or to others."

"Do you think what he says really counts for anything, Socrates?"

"Are you denying that you are in love with the one he says you are?"

"No, but I am denying that I write love poems about him and all."

"The man's not well, he's raving," Ctesippus hooted.

"O.K., Hippothales," I said. "I don't need to hear any poems or songs you may or may not have composed about the boy. Just give me the general sense, so I'll know how you deal with him."

"Well why don't you ask Ctesippus? He must have total recall of it all, from what he says about it being drummed into his head from listening to me."

"You bet I do," Ctesippus said, "and it's pretty ridiculous, too, Socrates. I mean, here he is, completely fixated on this boy and totally unable to say anything more original to him than any child could say. How ridiculous can you get? All he can think of to say or write is stuff the whole city goes around singing—poems about Democrates and the boy's grandfather Lysis and all his ancestors, their wealth and their stables and their victories at the Pythian, Isthmian, and Nemean Games in the chariot races and the horseback races.[13] And then he gets into really ancient history. Just the day

---

13. Conventional encomiastic topics such as were typical in Pindar's odes for victorious athletes, which also feature myths linking ancestors to the gods and heroes.

before yesterday he was reciting some poem to us about Heracles being entertained by one of their ancestors because he was related to the hero— something about him being a son of Zeus and the daughter of their deme's founding father—old women's spinning-songs, really. This is the sort of thing he recites and sings, Socrates, and forces us to listen to."

When I heard that I said, "Hippothales, you deserve to be ridiculed. Do you really compose and sing your own victory ode before you've won?"

"I don't compose or sing victory odes for myself, Socrates."

"You only think you don't."

"How is that?" he asked.

"You are really what these songs are all about," I said. "If you make a conquest of a boy like this, then everything you've said and sung turns out to eulogize yourself as victor in having won such a boyfriend. But if he gets away, then the greater your praise of his beauty and goodness, [206] the more you will seem to have lost and the more you will be ridiculed. This is why the skilled lover doesn't praise his beloved until he has him: he fears how the future may turn out. And besides, these good-looking boys, if anybody praises them, get swelled heads and start to think they're really somebody. Doesn't it seem that way to you?"

"It certainly does," he said.

"And the more swell-headed they get, the harder they are to catch."

"So it seems."

"Well, what do you think of a hunter who scares off his game and makes it harder to catch?"

"He's pretty poor."

"And isn't it a gross misuse of language and music to drive things wild rather than to soothe and charm?"

"Well, yes."

"Then be careful, Hippothales, that you don't make yourself guilty of all these things through your poetry. I don't imagine you would say that a man who hurts himself, by his poetry, is at all a good poet—after all, he does hurt himself."

"No, of course not," he said. "That wouldn't make any sense at all. But that's just why I'm telling you all this, Socrates. What different advice can you give me about what one should say or do so his prospective boyfriend will like him?"

"That's not easy to say. But if you're willing to have him talk with me, I might be able to give you a demonstration of how to carry on a conversation with him instead of talking and singing the way your friends here say you've been doing."

"That's easy enough," he said. "If you go in with Ctesippus here and sit down and start a conversation, I think he will come up to you by himself. He really likes to listen, Socrates. And besides, they're celebrating the festival of Hermes,[14] so the younger and older boys are mingled together. Anyway, he'll probably come up to you; but if he doesn't, he and Ctesippus know one another because Ctesippus' nephew is Menexenus, and Menexenus is Lysis' closest companion. So have Ctesippus call him if he doesn't come by himself."

"That's what I'll have to do," I said and, taking Ctesippus with me, I went into the wrestling school, followed by the others. When we got inside we found that the boys had finished the sacrifice and the ritual and, still all dressed up, were starting to play knucklebones.[15] Most of them were playing in the courtyard outside, but some of them were over in a corner of the dressing room playing with a great many knucklebones, which they drew from little baskets. [207] Still others were standing around watching this group, and among them was Lysis. He stood out among the boys and older youths, a garland on his head, and deserved to be called not only a beautiful boy but a well-bred young gentleman. We went over to the other side of the room, where it was quiet, sat down, and started up a conversation among ourselves. Lysis kept turning around and looking at us, obviously wanting to come over, but too shy to do so alone. After a while Menexenus, taking a break from his game in the court, came in and when he saw Ctesippus and me, he came to take a seat beside us. Lysis saw him and followed over, sitting down together with Menexenus next to him, and then all the others came too. When Hippothales (let's not forget about him) saw that a small crowd had gathered, he took up a position in the rear where he thought Lysis wouldn't see him—afraid he might annoy him—and listened from his outpost.

Then I looked at Menexenus and asked him, "Son of Demophon, which of you two is older?"

"We argue about that," he said.

"Then you probably disagree about which one has the nobler family, too," I said.

"Very much so," he said.

"And likewise about which one is better looking." They both laughed.

"Naturally, I won't ask which of you two is richer. For you two are friends, isn't that so?"

"Definitely," they said.

"And friends have everything in common, as the saying goes; so in this respect the two of you won't differ, that is, if what you said about being friends is true."

They agreed. . . .

14. The patron god of gymnasia and wrestling schools, usually represented in Greek art of this period as an athletic youth.

15. These would be used as dice. Typically, four would be thrown together: the luckiest throw was with all the numbers different, the unluckiest with all the numbers being one.

The dialogue proceeds to discuss the nature of love and friendship without any satis-factory definition being reached. Finally Socrates asks Lysis:

[**221**] "Then can it really be, as we were just saying, that desire is the cause of friendship, and that what desires is a friend to that which it desires, and is so whenever it does so? And that what we were saying earlier about being a friend was all just chatter, like a poem that trails on too long?"

"There's a good chance," he said.

"But still," I said, "a thing desires what it is deficient in. Right?"

"Yes."

"And the deficient is a friend to that in which it is deficient."

"I think so."

"And it becomes deficient where something is taken away from it."

"How couldn't it?"

"Then it is what belongs to oneself, it seems, that passionate love and friendship and desire are directed towards, Menexenus and Lysis."

They both agreed.

"And if you two are friends with each other, then in some way you natu-rally belong to each other."

"Absolutely," they said together.

[**222**] "And if one person desires another, my boys, or loves him pas-sionately, he would not desire him or love him passionately or as a friend unless he somehow belonged to his beloved either in his soul or in some characteristic, habit, or aspect of his soul."

"Certainly," said Menexenus, but Lysis was silent.

"All right," I said, "what belongs to us by nature has shown itself to us as something we must love."

"It looks like it," he said.

"Then the genuine and not the pretended lover must be befriended by his boy."

Lysis and Menexenus just managed a nod of assent, but Hippothales beamed every color in the rainbow in his delight.

Wanting to review the argument, I said, "It seems to me, Lysis and Me-nexenus, that if there is some difference between belonging and being like, then we might have something to say about what a friend is. But if belong-ing and being like turn out to be the same thing, it won't be easy to toss out our former argument that like is useless to like insofar as they are alike. And to admit that the useless is a friend would strike a sour note. So if it's all right with you, I said, since we are a little groggy from this discussion, why don't we agree to say that what belongs is something different from what is like?"

"Certainly."

"And shall we suppose that the good belongs to everyone, while the bad is alien? Or does the bad belong to the bad, the good to the good, and what is neither good nor bad to what is neither good nor bad?"

They both said they liked this latter correlation.

"Well, here we are again, boys," I said. "We have fallen into the same arguments about friendship that we rejected at first. For the unjust will be no less a friend to the unjust, and the bad to the bad, as the good will be to the good."

"So it seems," he said.

"Then what? If we say that the good is the same as belonging, is there any alternative to the good being a friend only to the good?"

"No."

"But we thought we had refuted ourselves on this point. Or don't you remember?"

"We remember."

"So what can we still do with our argument? Or is it clear that there is nothing left? I do ask, like the able speakers in the law courts, that you think over everything that has been said. If neither the loved nor the loving, nor the like nor the unlike, nor the good, nor the belonging, nor any of the others we have gone through—well, there have been so many I certainly don't remember them all any more, but if none of these is a friend, then I have nothing left to say."

[223] Having said that, I had a mind to get something going with one of the older men there. But just then, like some kind of divine intermediaries, the guardians of Menexenus and Lysis were on the scene. They had the boys' brothers with them and called out to them that it was time to go home. It actually was late by now. At first our group tried to drive them off, but they didn't pay any attention to us and just got riled up and went on calling in their foreign accents. We thought they had been drinking too much at the Hermaea and might be difficult to handle, so we capitulated and broke up our party. But just as they were leaving I said, "Now we've done it, Lysis and Menexenus—made fools of ourselves, I, an old man, and you as well. These people here will go away saying that we are friends of one another—for I count myself in with you—but what a friend is we have not yet been able to find out."

5.6 Plato, *Gorgias* 494C–495A

Socrates questions the aristocratic youth Callicles, who argues that Nature allows to the strong unlimited enjoyment of whatever they have the strength to take and that self-restraint is therefore unnecessary.

SOCRATES: [494] So first off, tell me whether even the man who has an itch and scratches it, being able to keep scratching without end, scratching continually throughout his life, is living happily.

CALLICLES: How extraordinary you are, Socrates, and quite a crowd seducer!

SOCRATES: Exactly, Callicles! That's how I drove both Polus and Gorgias[16] into feeling panic and shame. But not you. You wouldn't feel panic or shame; for you are a real man. However, just answer the question.

CALLICLES: Then pay attention. I state that even a man who scratches would be living pleasantly.

SOCRATES: So if indeed pleasantly, wouldn't he also be living happily?

CALLICLES: For sure!

SOCRATES: Is it when he scratches just his head—or can I ask you about something else? See, Callicles, what you would answer if someone were to ask all the questions, which logically follow these questions. And the climax of this line of questioning, the life of perverts *(kinaidoi)*, isn't this life terrible and shameful and to be pitied? Or would you dare call these men happy, just as long as they have what they want in abundance?

CALLICLES: Aren't you ashamed, Socrates, to bring our discussion to such matters?

SOCRATES: Now am I the one who brings it there, noble Callicles? Or is it that man who couldn't determine which kinds of pleasure are good and which are bad, and would claim that those, who get their pleasure similarly without any restraint, in whatever way they get pleasure, [495] are happy? But now then, tell me another thing. Do you claim that what is pleasant and what is good are the same thing, or is there anything pleasant which is not good?

CALLICLES: Certainly, to keep from contradicting my own argument by claiming that they are different, I'll say that they are the same.[17]

5.7 Plato, *Symposium* 178A–185C, 189C–193D, 199E–212C, 216A–219E

This dialogue describes a dinner party held at the house of the tragic poet Agathon on the occasion of his first dramatic victory, in 416 B.C.E. Following a suggestion by his beloved Phaedrus, Eryximachus proposes that each guest deliver a speech in praise of the god Eros. The speeches are recounted many years later by a character named

---

16. Socrates' two earlier interlocutors in the dialogue: Gorgias of Leontini, the sophist and rhetorician, and his pupil.

17. Socrates goes on to demonstrate that pleasure and the good are not the same, but some pleasures are bad.

Apollodorus, who was not present but heard about the party from a guest named Aristodemus.

[**178**] They all agreed with Socrates, and told Phaedrus[18] to start. Aristodemus couldn't remember the exact details of everybody's speech, nor in turn can I remember precisely what he said. But I can give you the gist of those speeches and speakers which were most worth remembering.

Phaedrus, as I said, began something like this: "Eros is a great god, a marvel to men and gods alike. This is true in many ways, and it is especially true of his birth. He is entitled to our respect, as the oldest of the gods, as I can prove. Eros has no parents, either in reality or in works of prose and poetry. Take Hesiod,[19] for example. All he says is that in the beginning there was Chaos '. . . and then came the full-breasted Earth, the eternal and immovable foundation of everything, and Eros.'[20] Acusilaus[21] agrees with Hesiod, that after Chaos there were just these two, Earth and Eros. And then there's Parmenides'[22] theory about his birth, that 'Eros was created first of the Gods.' So there is widespread agreement that Eros is of great antiquity. And being very old he also brings us very great benefits. I can see nothing better in life for a young boy, as soon as he is old enough, than finding a good lover, nor for a lover than finding a boyfriend. Love, more than anything (more than family, or position, or wealth), implants in men the thing which must be their guide if they are to live a good life. And what is that? It is a horror of what is degrading, and a passionate desire for what is good. These qualities are essential if a state or an individual is to accomplish anything great or good. Imagine a man in love being found out doing something humiliating, or letting someone else do something degrading to him, because he was too cowardly to stop it. It would embarrass him more to be found out by the boy he loved than by his father or his friends, or anyone. And you can see just the same thing happening with the boy. He is more worried about being caught behaving badly by his admirers than by anyone else. So if there were some way of arranging that a state, or an army, could be made up entirely of

18. Phaedrus would be exiled soon after the dramatic date of this dialogue for suspected participation in the religious scandals of 415 B.C.E., which had strong overtones of denying and disrespecting the city's traditional religious cults.

19. An early epic poet (probably late eighth or early seventh century) whose *Theogony* gives a systematic genealogy of the gods.

20. In fact, it is not all he says. Phaedrus leaves out lines 118 and 119 of the *Theogony*. But such an ellipsis is not unusual in quotations of verse from memory.

21. An early fifth-century genealogist.

22. A metaphysical philosopher of the early fifth century whose theories about Being and Seeming were particularly influential on Plato. His philosophical poem uses many allegorical figures.

pairs of lovers, it is impossible to imagine a finer population. They would avoid all dishonor, and compete with one another for glory: in battle, this kind of army, though small, fighting side by side could conquer virtually the whole world.[23] [179] After all, a lover would sooner be seen by anyone deserting his post or throwing away his weapons, rather than by his boyfriend. He would normally choose to die many times over instead. And as for abandoning the boy, or not trying to save him if he is in danger—no one is such a coward as not to be inspired with courage by Eros, making him the equal of the naturally brave man. Homer says, and rightly, that god breathes fire into some of his heroes. And it is just this quality, whose origin is to be found within himself, that Eros imparts to lovers.

"What is more, lovers are the only people prepared to die for others. Not just men, either; women also sometimes. A good example is Alcestis, the daughter of Pelias.[24] She alone was willing to die for her husband. He had a father and mother but she so far surpassed them in devotion, because of her passion for him, that she showed them to be strangers to their son, relations in name only. In so doing she was thought, by men and gods alike, to have performed a deed of supreme excellence. Indeed, the gods were so pleased with her action that they brought her soul back from the underworld—a privilege they granted to only a fortunate handful of the many people who have done good deeds. That shows how highly even the gods value loyalty and courage in love. Orpheus, the son of Oeagrus, on the other hand, was sent away from the underworld empty-handed; he was shown a mere phantom of the woman he came to find, and not given the woman herself.[25] Of course, Orpheus was a musician, and the gods thought he was a bit of a coward, lacking the courage to die for his love, as Alcestis did, but trying to find a way of getting into the underworld alive. They punished him further for that, giving him death at the hands of women.[26]

"In contrast, the man whom the gods honored above all was Achilles, the son of Thetis.[27] They sent him to the Islands of the Blessed. His mother

23. This is often supposed to be an allusion to the Sacred Band of Thebes, founded in 378 B.C.E. (see **2.14**). However, Phaedrus refers to it as a hypothetical army.

24. The wife of Admetus. Admetus was allowed to defer his own death if he could find someone to die in his place. This story is the subject of a tragedy by Euripides.

25. The great musician of Greek myth. The usual story is that his music so charmed the gods of the Underworld that they allowed him to bring his wife back to the living with him on the condition that he not look back at her until fully emerged from the Underworld, a stipulation he violated at the last minute. Phaedrus' version of the story is otherwise unattested.

26. He was torn apart by Thracian Maenads, female devotees of Dionysus.

27. The son of a goddess (Thetis), and hero of the *Iliad*, who in some accounts went to an island paradise after his early death.

had warned him that if he killed Hector he would himself be killed, but if he didn't, he would return home and live to a ripe old age. Nevertheless, out of loyalty to his lover Patroclus he chose without hesitation to die— [180] not to save him, but to avenge him; for Patroclus had already been killed. The gods were full of admiration, and gave him the highest possible honor, because he valued his lover so highly.

"Incidentally, Aeschylus' view, that it was Achilles who was in love with Patroclus, is nonsense.[28] Quite apart from the fact that he was more beautiful than Patroclus (and than all the other Greek heroes, come to that) and had not yet grown a beard, he was also, according to Homer, much younger.[29] And he must have been younger because it is an undoubted fact that the gods, though they always value courage which comes from love, are most impressed and pleased, and grant the greatest rewards, when the younger man is loyal to his lover, than when the lover is loyal to him. That's because the lover is a more divine creature than the younger man, since he is divinely inspired. And that's why they honored Achilles more than Alcestis, and sent him to the Islands of the Blessed.

"There you are then. I claim that Eros is the oldest of the gods, the most deserving of our respect, and the most useful for those men, past and present, who want to attain excellence and happiness."

That was the gist of Phaedrus' speech. After him, several other people spoke, but Aristodemus couldn't really remember what they said. So he left them out and recounted Pausanias' speech:[30]

"Phaedrus, I don't think we've been very accurate in defining our subject for discussion. We've simply said that we must make a speech in praise of Eros. That would be fine, if there were just one Eros. In fact, however, there isn't. And since there isn't, we would do better to define first which Eros we are to praise. I am going to try to put things straight, first defining which Eros we are supposed to be praising, and then trying to praise the god as he deserves.

"We are all well aware, I take it, that without Eros there is no Aphrodite. If there were only one Aphrodite, there would be one Eros. However, since there are in fact two Aphrodites, it follows that Eros likewise must be two. There's no doubt about there being two Aphrodites; the older has no

---

28. Aeschylus' tragedy *Myrmidons* dramatized this story with a clear homosexual interpretation of the relationship, which was absent in Homer. See **2.21.601–2** and frr. 135–37 *TGrF.* In Aeschylus' tragedy Achilles was the lover, Patroclus the beloved.

29. *Iliad* 11.787 makes Achilles younger, but Phaedrus exaggerates in saying "much younger."

30. A student of the sophist Prodicus, who held that we attribute divinity to forces that are useful to us. Several sources relate that Pausanias was the long-time lover of Agathon, and went with him to Macedon when life in Athens became unpleasant for them.

mother and is the daughter of Heaven. We call her Heavenly Aphrodite.[31] The younger is the daughter of Zeus and Dione, and we call her Common Aphrodite.[32] It follows that the Eros who assists this Aphrodite should also, properly speaking, be called Common Eros, and the other, Heavenly Eros. We certainly ought to praise all the gods, but we should also attempt to define what is the proper province of each.

"It is, in general, true of any activity that, simply in itself, it is neither good nor bad. [181] Take what we're doing now, for example—that is to say, drinking, or singing, or talking. None of these is good or bad in itself, but each becomes so, depending on the way it is done. Well and rightly done, it is good; wrongly done, it is bad. And it's just the same with loving, and Eros. It's not all good and doesn't all deserve praise. The Eros we should praise is the one which encourages people to love in the right way.

"The Eros associated with Common Aphrodite is, in all senses of the word, common, and quite haphazard in his operation. This is the love of the man in the street. For a start, he is as likely to fall in love with women as with boys. Secondly, he falls in love with their bodies rather than their minds. Thirdly, he picks the most unintelligent people he can find, since all he's interested in is the sexual act. He doesn't care whether it's done in the right way or not. That is why the effect of this Eros is haphazard— sometimes good, sometimes the reverse. This love derives its existence from the much younger Aphrodite, the one composed equally of the female and male elements.

"The other Eros springs from Heavenly Aphrodite, and in the first place is composed solely of the male element, with none of the female (so it is the love of boys we are talking about), and in the second place is older, and hence free from lust. In consequence, those inspired by this love turn to the male, attracted by what is naturally stronger and of superior intelligence. And even among those who love boys you can tell the ones whose love is purely heavenly. They only fall in love with boys old enough to think for themselves—in other words, with boys who are nearly grown up.

"Those who start a love affair with boys of that age are prepared, I think, to be friends, and live together, for life. The others are deceivers, who take advantage of youthful folly and then quite cheerfully abandon their victims in search of others. There ought really to be a law against loving young boys, to stop so much energy being expended on an uncertain end. After all, no one knows how good or bad, in mind and body, young boys

31. Or Uranian Aphrodite. According to Hesiod's *Theogony,* Aphrodite was born out of the bubbling foam created when the castrated genitals of Uranus (Heaven) were thrown into the sea by his son Cronus.

32. Or Aphrodite Pandemos. Dione (a feminine version of Zeus' name, which is "Dios" in its root form) is recorded as the mother of Aphrodite in Homer.

will eventually turn out. Good men voluntarily observe this rule, but the common lovers I am talking about should be compelled to do the same, just as we stop them, so far as we can, falling in love with free women. [182] They are actually the people who have brought the thing into disrepute, with the result that some people even go so far as to say that it is wrong to satisfy your lover. It is the common lover they have in mind when they say this, regarding his demands as premature and unfair to the boy. Surely nothing done with restraint and decency could reasonably incur criticism.

"What is more, while sexual conventions in other states are clear-cut and easy to understand, here and in Sparta, by contrast, they are complex. In Elis, for example, or Boeotia,[33] and places where they are not sophisticated in their use of language, it is laid down, quite straightforwardly, that it is right to satisfy your lover. No one, old or young, would say it was wrong, and the reason, I take it, is that they don't want to have all the trouble of trying to persuade them verbally, when they're such poor speakers. On the other hand, in Ionia and many other places under Persian rule,[34] it is regarded as wrong. That is because the Persians' system of government (dictatorships) makes them distrust it, just as they distrust philosophy and communal exercise. It doesn't suit the rulers that their subjects should think noble thoughts, nor that they should form the strong friendships or attachments which these activities, and in particular love, tend to produce. Dictators here in Athens learnt the same lesson by experience. The relationship between Harmodius and his lover, Aristogeiton, was strong enough to put an end to the dictators' rule.[35]

"In short, the convention that satisfying your lover is wrong is a result of the moral weakness of those who observe the convention—the rulers' desire for power, and their subjects' cowardice. The belief that it is always right can be attributed to mental laziness. Our customs are much better but, as I said, not easy to understand. Think about it—let's take the lover first. Open love is regarded as better than secret love, and so is love of the noblest and best people, even if they are not the best looking. In fact, there is remarkable encouragement of the lover from all sides. He is not regarded as doing anything wrong; it is a good thing if he gets what he wants and a shame if he doesn't. And when it comes to trying to get what he wants, we give the lover permission to do the most amazing things and

33. Elis is the territory around Olympia in the western Peloponnese. Boeotia is the area around Thebes in central Greece. Both places were despised as culturally inferior by Athenians, although Thebes had produced no less a poet than Pindar.

34. In fact, Ionia would not have been under Persian rule at the time of the dialogue's dramatic date, but it was after 387 B.C.E., which may help us date the composition.

35. On the tyrannicides, see 2.2.

be applauded for them—things which, if he did them with any other aim or intention, would cover him in reproach. [183] Think of the way lovers behave towards the boys they love—think of the begging and entreating involved in their demands, the oaths they swear, the nights they spend sleeping outside the boys' front doors, the slavery they are prepared to endure (which no slave would put up with).[36] If they behaved like this for money, or position, or influence of any kind, they would be told to stop by friends and enemies alike. Their enemies would call their behavior dependent and servile, while their friends would censure them sharply and even be embarrassed for them. And yet a lover can do all these things and be approved of. Custom attaches no blame to his actions, since he is reckoned to be acting in a wholly honorable way. The strangest thing of all is that, in most people's opinion, the lover has a unique dispensation from the gods to swear an oath and then break it. Lovers' vows, apparently, are not binding.

"So far, then, gods and men alike give all kinds of license to the lover, and an observer of Athenian life might conclude that it was an excellent thing in this city both to be a lover and to be friendly to lovers. But when we come to the boy, the position is quite different. Fathers give their sons escorts when men fall in love with them, and don't allow them to talk to their lovers—and those are the escort's instructions as well. The boy's peers and friends jeer at him if they see anything of the kind going on and when their elders see them jeering, they don't stop them or tell them off, as they should if the jeers were unjustified. Looking at this side of things, you would come to the opposite conclusion—that this kind of thing is here regarded as highly reprehensible.

"The true position, I think, is this. Going back to my original statement, there isn't one single form of love. So love is neither right nor wrong in itself. Done rightly, it is right; done wrongly, it is wrong. It is wrong if you satisfy the wrong person for the wrong reasons and right if you satisfy the right person for the right reasons. The wrong person is the common lover I was talking about—the one who loves the body rather than the mind. His love is not lasting, since *what* he loves is not lasting either. As soon as the youthful bloom of the body (which is what he loves) starts to fade, he 'spreads his wings and is off,' as they say, making a mockery of all his speeches and promises. On the other hand, the man who loves a boy for his good character will stick to him for life, since he has attached himself to what is lasting.

[184] "Our customs are intended to test these lovers well and truly, and get the boys to satisfy the good ones, and avoid the bad. That's why we

---

36. These are all topoi of erotic poetry.

encourage lovers to chase after boys, but tell the boys not to be caught. In this way we set up a trial and a test, to see which category the lover comes in, and which category the boy he loves comes in. This explains a number of things—for instance, why it's thought wrong for a boy to let himself be caught too quickly. It is felt that some time should elapse, since time is a good test of most things. Also why it is wrong to be caught by means of money or political influence—whether it's a case of the boy being threatened, and yielding rather than holding out, or a case of being offered some financial or political inducement, and not turning it down. No affair of this kind is likely to be stable or secure, quite apart from the fact that it is no basis for true friendship.

"There is just one way our customs leave it open for a boy to satisfy his lover and not be blamed for it. It is permissible, as I have said, for a lover to enter upon any kind of voluntary slavery he may choose, and be the slave of the boy he loves. This is not regarded as self-seeking or in any way demeaning. Similarly there is one other kind of voluntary slavery which is not regarded as demeaning. This is the slavery of the boy, in his desire for improvement. It can happen that a boy chooses to serve a man, because he thinks that by association with him he will improve in wisdom in some way, or in some other form of goodness. This kind of voluntary slavery, like the other, is widely held among us not to be wrong and not to be self-seeking.

"So it can only be regarded as right for a boy to satisfy his lover if both these conditions are satisfied—both the lover's behavior and the boy's desire for wisdom and goodness. Then the lover and the boy have the same aim, and each has the approval of convention—the lover because he is justified in performing any service he chooses for a boy who satisfies him, the boy because he is justified in submitting, in any way he will, to the man who can make him wise and good. So if the lover has something to offer in the way of sound judgment and moral goodness, and if the boy is eager to accept this contribution to his education and growing wisdom, then, and only then, this favorable combination makes it right for a boy to satisfy his lover. In no other situation is it right.

"Nor, in this situation, is there any disgrace in making a mistake, whereas in all other situations it is equally a disgrace to be mistaken or not. [185] For example, suppose a boy satisfies his lover for money, taking him to be rich. If he gets it wrong and doesn't get any money because the lover turns out to be poor, it is still regarded as immoral, because the boy who does this seems to be revealing his true character and declaring that he would do anything for anyone in return for money. And that is not a good way to behave. Equally, a boy may satisfy a man because he thinks he is a good man, and that he himself will become better through his friendship. If he gets it wrong, and his lover turns out to be a bad man, of little moral worth, still there is something creditable about his mistake. He too seems to have revealed his true character—namely, that he is eager to do anything for anyone in return for goodness and self-improvement. And this is the finest of all qualities.

"So it is absolutely correct for boys to satisfy their lovers, if it is done in pursuit of goodness. This is the love which comes from the heavenly goddess; it is itself heavenly, and of great value to state and individual alike, since it compels both lover and boy to devote a lot of attention to their own moral improvement. All other sorts of love derive from the other goddess, the common one.

"Well, Phaedrus, that's the best I can offer, without preparation, on the subject of Eros."

Pausanias paused (sorry about the pun—sophistic influence). After that it was Aristophanes' turn to speak. But he had just got hiccups. I don't know if it was from eating too much or for some other reason; anyway, he was unable to make his speech. . . .

Instead, the physician Eryximachus delivers a speech based on a rather abstract conception of the two forms as Eros as forces of harmony and disharmony within the human body. At the end he asks Aristophanes if his hiccups have stopped, and they have. Aristophanes continues:

[189] "Well, Eryximachus, I do intend to make a rather different kind of speech from the kind you and Pausanias made. It's my opinion that mankind is quite unaware of the power of Eros. If they were aware of it, they would build vast temples and altars to him, and make great offerings to him. As it is, though it is of crucial importance that this observance should be paid to him, none of these things is done.

"Of all the gods, Eros is the most friendly towards men. He is our helper, and cures those evils whose cure brings the greatest happiness to the human race. I'll try to explain his power to you, and then you can go off and spread the word to others.

"First of all you need to know about human nature and what has happened to it. Our original nature was not as it is now, but quite different. For one thing there were three sexes, rather than the two (male and female) we have now. The third sex was a combination of these two. Its name has survived, though the phenomenon itself has disappeared. This single combination, comprising both male and female, was, in form and name alike, hermaphrodite.[37] Now it survives only as a term of abuse.

---

37. The actual Greek word here is *androgynos*.

"Secondly, each human being formed a complete whole, spherical, with back and ribs forming a circle. They had four hands, four legs, and two faces, identical in every way, on a circular neck. They had a single head for the two faces, which looked in opposite directions; four ears, two sets of genitals, and everything else as you'd expect from the description so far. [190] They walked upright, as we do, in whichever direction they wanted. And when they started to run fast, they were just like people doing cartwheels. They stuck their legs straight out all round, and went bowling along, supported on their eight limbs, and rolling along at high speed.

"The reason for having three sexes, and of this kind, was this: the male was originally the offspring of the Sun, the female of the Earth, and the one which was half-and-half was the offspring of the moon, because the moon likewise is half-Sun and half-Earth. They were circular, both in themselves and in their motion, because of their similarity to their parents. They were remarkable for their strength and vigor, and their ambition led them to make an assault upon the gods. The story which Homer tells of the giants, Ephialtes and Otus,[38] is told of them—that they tried to make a way up to heaven, to attack the gods. Zeus and the other gods wondered what to do about them and couldn't decide. They couldn't kill them, as they had the giants—striking them with thunderbolts and doing away with the whole race—because the worship and sacrifices they received from men would have been done away with as well. On the other hand, they couldn't go on allowing them to behave so outrageously.

"In the end Zeus, after long and painful thought, came up with a suggestion: 'I think I have an idea. Men could go on existing, but behave less disgracefully, if we made them weaker. I'm going to cut each of them in two. This will have two advantages: it will make them weaker, and also more useful to us, because of the increase in their numbers. They will walk upright, on two legs. And if it's clear they still can't behave, and they refuse to lead a quiet life, I'll cut them in half again and they can go hopping along on one leg.'

"That was his plan. So he started cutting them in two, like someone slicing vegetables for pickling, or slicing eggs with a wire. And each time he chopped one up, he told Apollo to turn the face and the half-neck round towards the cut side (so that the man could see where he'd been split, and be better behaved in future), and then to heal the rest of the wound. So Apollo twisted the faces round and gathered up the skin all round to what is now called the stomach, like a purse with strings. He made a single outlet and tied it all up securely in the middle of the stomach; this we now call the navel. [191] He smoothed out most of the wrinkles and formed

---

38. Giants who attempted to scale heaven by piling mountains on top of each other.

the chest, using a tool such as cobblers use for smoothing out wrinkles in a hide stretched over a last. He left a few wrinkles, however, those around the stomach itself and the navel, as a reminder of what happened in those far-off days.

"When man's natural form was split in two, each half went round looking for its lost half. They put their arms round one another and embraced each other, in their desire to grow together again. They started dying of hunger and also from lethargy, because they refused to do anything separately. And whenever one half died and the other was left, the survivor began to look for another and twined itself about it, either encountering half of a complete woman (i.e., what we now call a woman) or half a complete man. In this way they kept on dying.

"Zeus felt sorry for them, and thought of a second plan. He moved their genitals to the front—up till then they had had them on the outside, and had reproduced, not by copulation but by discharge on to the ground, like grasshoppers. So, as I say, he moved their genitals to the front, and made them use them for reproduction by insemination, the male in the female. The idea was that if, in embracing, a man chanced upon a woman, they could produce children, and the race would increase. If man chanced upon man, they could get full satisfaction from one another's company, then separate, get on with their work, and resume the business of life.

"That is why we have this innate love of one another. It brings us back to our original state, trying to reunite us and restore us to our true human form. Each of us is a mere fragment of a man (like half a tally-stick); we've been split in two, like filleted plaice. We're all looking for our other half. Men who are a fragment of the common sex (the one called hermaphrodite) are womanizers, and most adulterers are to be found in this category. Similarly, women of this type are nymphomaniacs and adulteresses. On the other hand, women who are part of an original woman pay very little attention to men. Their interest is in women; Lesbians are found in this class. And those who are part of a male pursue what is male. As boys, because they are slices of the male, they are fond of men, and enjoy going to bed with men and embracing them. [192] These are the best of the boys and young men, since they are by nature the most manly. Some people call them immoral—quite wrongly. It is not immorality, but boldness, courage and manliness, since they take pleasure in what is like themselves. This is proved by the fact that, when they grow up and take part in public life, it's only this kind who prove themselves men.[39] When they come to manhood, they are lovers of boys, and don't naturally show any interest in marriage or

39. This corresponds to the Aristophanic notion that most prominent political leaders are homosexual in inclination: see 3.5 and 3.11. Plato, perhaps for irony's sake, presents a much more sympathetic Aristophanes.

producing children; they have to be forced into it by convention. They're quite happy to live with one another, and not get married.

"People like this are clearly inclined to have boyfriends or (as boys) inclined to have lovers, because they always welcome what is akin. When a lover of boys (or any sort of lover) meets the real thing (i.e., his other half), he is completely overwhelmed by friendship and affection and desire, more or less refusing to be separated for any time at all. These are the people who spend their whole lives together, and yet they cannot find words for what they want from one another. No one imagines that it's simply sexual intercourse, or that sex is the reason why one gets such enormous pleasure out of the other's company. No, it's obvious that the soul of each has some other desire, which it cannot express. It can only give hints and clues to its wishes.

"Imagine that Hephaestus[40] came and stood over them, with his smith's tools, as they lay in bed together. Suppose he asked them, 'What is it you want from one another, mortals?' If they couldn't tell him, he might ask again, 'Do you want to be together as much as possible, and not be separated, day or night? If that's what you want, I'm quite prepared to weld you together, and make you grow into one. You can be united, the two of you, and live your whole life together, as one. Even down in Hades, when you die, you can be a single dead person, rather than two. Decide whether that's what you want, and whether that would satisfy you.' We can be sure that no one would refuse this offer. Quite clearly, it would be just what they wanted. They'd simply think they'd been offered exactly what they'd always been after, in sexual intercourse, trying to melt into their lovers, and so be united.

"So that's the explanation; it's because our original nature was as I have described, and because we were once complete. And the name of this desire and pursuit of completeness is Eros, or love. [193] Formerly, as I say, we were undivided, but now we've been split up by god for our misdeeds —like the Arcadians by the Spartans.[41] And the danger is that, if we don't treat the gods with respect, we may be divided again, and go round looking like figures in a bas-relief, sliced in half down the line of our noses. We'd be like torn-off counterfoils. That's why we should all encourage the utmost piety towards the gods. We're trying to avoid this fate, and achieve the other. So we take Eros as our guide and leader. Let no-one oppose this aim—and incurring divine displeasure *is* opposing this aim—since if we are friends with god, and make our peace with him, we shall find and

40. The god of metalworking and skilled crafts.
41. The reference is to the Spartans' defeat of Mantinea in 385 B.C.E., dividing its population into separate villages and locations.

meet the boys who are part of ourselves, which few people these days succeed in doing.

"I hope Eryximachus won't misunderstand me, and make fun of my
speech, and say it's about Pausanias and Agathon. Perhaps they do come
in this class, and are both males by nature. All I'm saying is that in general (and this applies to men and women) this is where happiness for the
human race lies—in the successful pursuit of love, in finding the love who
is part of our original self, and in returning to our former state. This is the
ideal, but in an imperfect world we must settle for the nearest to this we
can get, and this is finding a boyfriend who is mentally congenial. And if
we want to praise the god who brings this about, then we should praise
Eros, who in this predicament is our great benefactor, attracting us to
what is part of ourselves, and gives us great hope for the future that he
will reward respect for the gods by returning us to our original condition,
healing us, and making us blessed and perfectly happy.

"There you are then, Eryximachus. There is my speech about Eros. A
bit different from yours, I'm afraid. So please, again, don't laugh at it, and
let's hear what all the others have to say—or rather, both the others, since
only Agathon and Socrates are left. . . . "

*Agathon proceeds to deliver an encomium of the god Eros in flowery and poetic lan-
guage, declaring him by far the most beautiful of the gods. Socrates questions Agathon
on this point:*

[199] "Try then to answer my question about Eros. Is Eros love of nothing,
or of something?"

"Of something, certainly."

[200] "Good. Hold on to that answer. Keep it in mind, and make a
mental note what it is that Eros is love of. But first tell me this; this thing
which Eros is love of, does he desire it, or not?"

"Certainly."

"And does he possess that which he desires and loves, or not?"

"Probably not."

"I'm not interested in probability, but in certainty. Consider this proposition: anything which desires something desires what it does not have,
and it only desires when it is lacking something. This proposition, Agathon,
seems to me to be absolutely certain. How does it strike you?"

"Yes, it seems certain to me too."

"Quite right. So would a big man want to be big, or a strong man want
to be strong?"

"No, that's impossible, given what we have agreed so far."

"Because if he possesses these qualities, he cannot also lack them."

"True."

"So if a strong man wanted to be strong, or a fast runner to be fast, or a healthy man to be healthy—but perhaps I'd better explain what I'm on about. I'm a bit worried that you may think that people like this, people having these qualities, can also want the qualities they possess. So I'm trying to remove this misapprehension. If you think about it, Agathon, people cannot avoid possession of whichever of these qualities they do possess, whether they like it or not. So obviously there's no point in desiring to do so. When anyone says, 'I'm in good health, and I also desire to be in good health,' or 'I am rich and also desire to be rich,' that is, 'I desire those things which I already have,' then we should answer him: 'what you want is to go on possessing, in the future, the wealth, health, or strength you possess now, since you have them now, like it or not. So when you say you desire what you've already got, are you sure you don't just mean you want to continue to possess in the future what you possess now? Would he deny this?"

"No, he would agree."

"But isn't this a question of desiring what he doesn't already have in his possession—that is, the desire that what he does have should be safely and permanently available to him in the future?"

"Yes, it is."

"So in this, or any other, situation, the man who desires something desires what is not available to him, and what he doesn't already have in his possession. And what he neither has nor himself is—that which he lacks—this is what he wants and desires."

"Absolutely."

"Right then, let's agree on the argument so far. Eros has an existence of his own; he is in the first place love of something, and secondly, he is love of that which he is without."

[201] "Yes."

"Keeping that in mind, just recall what you said were the objects of Eros, in your speech. I'll remind you, if you like. I think what you said amounted to this: trouble among the gods was ended by their love of beauty, since there could be no love of what is ugly. Isn't that roughly what you said?"

"Yes, it is."

"And a very reasonable statement, too, my friend. And this being so, Eros must have an existence as love of beauty, and not love of ugliness, mustn't he?"

"Yes."

"But wasn't it agreed that he loves what he lacks, and does not possess?"

"Yes, it was."

"So Eros lacks, and does not possess, beauty."

"That is the inevitable conclusion."

"Well then, do you describe as beautiful that which lacks beauty and has never acquired beauty?"

"No."

"If that is so, do you still maintain that Eros is beautiful?"

"I rather suspect, Socrates, that I didn't know what I was talking about."

"It sounded marvelous, for all that, Agathon. Just one other small point. Would you agree that what is good is also beautiful?"

"Yes, I would."

"So if Eros lacks beauty, and if what is good is beautiful, then Eros would lack what is good also."

"I can't argue with you Socrates. Let's take it that it is as you say."

"What you mean, Agathon, my very good friend, is that you can't argue with the truth. Any fool can argue with Socrates. Anyway, I'll let you off for now, because I want to pass on to you the account of Eros which I once heard given by a woman called Diotima, from Mantinea.[42] She was an expert on this subject, as on many others. In the days before the plague[43] she came to the help of the Athenians in their sacrifices, and managed to gain them a ten-years' reprieve from the disease. She also taught me about love.

"I'll start from the position on which Agathon and I reached agreement, and I'll give her account, as best I can, in my own words. So first I must explain, as you rightly laid down, Agathon, what Eros is and what he is like; then I must describe what he does. I think it'll be easiest for me to explain things as she explained them when she was questioning me, since I gave her pretty much the same answers Agathon has just been giving me. I said Eros was a great god, and a lover of beauty. Diotima proved to me, using the same argument by which I have just proved it to Agathon, that, according to my own argument, Eros was neither beautiful nor good.

"'What do you mean, Diotima,' I said, 'Is Eros then ugly or bad?'

"'Careful what you say. Do you think what is not beautiful must necessarily be ugly?'

[202] "'Obviously.'

"'And that what is not wise is ignorant? Don't you realize there is an intermediate state, between wisdom and ignorance?'

"'And what is that?'

"'Think of someone who has a correct opinion, but can give no rational explanation of it. You wouldn't call this knowledge (how can something

42. We know nothing else of this figure. She may be fictitious, localized to Mantinea because of the name's resemblance to *mantis* (prophet).

43. A reference to the great plague that broke out in 430 B.C.E., in the early part of the Peloponnesian War.

irrational be knowledge?), yet it isn't ignorance either, since an opinion which accords with reality cannot be ignorance. So correct opinion is the kind of thing we are looking for, between understanding and ignorance.'

"'That's true.'

"'So don't insist that what is not beautiful must necessarily be ugly, nor that what is not good must be bad. The same thing is equally true of Eros; just because, as you yourself admit, he is not good or beautiful, you need not regard him as ugly and bad, but as something between these extremes.'

"'Yet he is universally agreed to be a great god.'

"'By those who don't know what they are talking about, do you mean? Or those who do?'

"'I mean by absolutely everyone.'

"Diotima laughed. 'How can Eros he agreed to be a great god by people who don't even admit that he's a god at all?'

"'What people?'

"'Well, you, for one. And me, for another.'

"'What do you mean?'

"'Quite simple. The gods are all happy and beautiful, aren't they? You wouldn't go so far as to claim that any of the gods is not happy and beautiful?'

"'Good Lord, no.'

"'And you agree that "happy" means possessing what is good and beautiful?'

"'Certainly.'

"'But you have already admitted that Eros lacks what is good and beautiful, and that he desires them because he lacks them.'

"'Yes, I have.'

"'How can he be a god, then, if he is without beauty and goodness?'

"'He can't, apparently.'

"'You see, even you don't regard Eros as a god.'

"'What can Eros be, then? A mortal?'

"'Far from it.'

"'What, then?'

"'As in the other examples, something between a mortal and an immortal.'

"'And what is that, Diotima?'

"'A great spirit, Socrates. Spirits are midway between what is divine and what is human.'

"'What power does such a spirit possess?'

"'He acts as an interpreter and a means of communication between gods and men. He takes requests and offerings to the gods, and brings back instructions and benefits in return. Occupying this middle position he plays a vital role in holding the world together. He is the medium of all prophecy and religion, whether it concerns sacrifice, forms of worship, incantations, or any kind of divination or sorcery. There is no direct contact between god and man. [203] All association and communication between them, waking or sleeping, takes place through Eros. This kind of knowledge is knowledge of the spirit; any other knowledge (occupational or artistic, for example) is purely utilitarian. Such spirits are many and varied, and Eros is one of them.'

"'Who are his parents?'

"'That is not quite so simple, but I'll tell you, all the same. When Aphrodite was born, the gods held a banquet, at which one of the guests was Resource, the son of Ingenuity. When they finished eating, Poverty came begging, as you would expect (there being plenty of food), and hung around the doorway. Resource was drunk (on nectar, since wine hadn't been invented), so he went into Zeus' garden, and was overcome by sleep. Poverty, seeing here the solution to her own lack of resources, decided to have a child by him. So she lay with him, and conceived Eros. That's why Eros is a follower and servant of Aphrodite, because he was conceived at her birthday party—and also because he is naturally attracted to what is beautiful, and Aphrodite is beautiful.

"'So Eros' attributes are what you would expect of a child of Resource and Poverty. For a start, he's always poor, and so far from being soft and beautiful (which is most people's view of him), he is hard, unkempt, barefoot, homeless. He sleeps on the ground, without a bed, lying in doorways or in the open street.[44] He has his mother's nature, and need is his constant companion. On the other hand, from his father he has inherited an eye for beauty and the good. He is brave, enterprising and determined —a marvelous huntsman, always intriguing. He is intellectual, resourceful, a lover of wisdom his whole life through, a subtle magician, sorcerer and thinker.

"'His nature is neither that of an immortal nor that of a mortal. In one and the same day he can be alive and flourishing (when things go well), then at death's door, later still reviving as his father's character asserts itself again. But his resources are always running out, so that Eros is never either totally destitute or affluent. Similarly he is midway between wisdom and folly, as I will show you. [204] None of the gods searches for wisdom, or tries to become wise—they are wise already. Nor does anyone else wise search for wisdom. On the other hand, the foolish do not search for wisdom or try to become wise either, since folly is precisely the failing which

---

44. An allusion to the poetic topos of a forlorn lover camping out on the doorstep of his beloved. See section 183.

consists in not being fine and good or intelligent, and yet being quite satisfied with the way one is. You cannot desire what you do not realize you lack.'

"'Who then are the lovers of wisdom,[45] Diotima, if they are neither the wise nor the foolish?'

"'That should by now be obvious, even to a child. They must be the intermediate class, among them Eros. We would classify wisdom as very beautiful, and Eros is love of what is beautiful, so it necessarily follows that Eros is a lover of wisdom (lovers of wisdom being the intermediate class between the wise and the foolish). The reason for this, too, is to be found in his parentage. His father is wise and resourceful, while his mother is foolish and resourceless.

"'Such is the nature of this spirit, Socrates. Your views on Eros revealed a quite common mistake. You thought (or so I infer from your comments) that Eros was what was loved, rather than the lover. That is why you thought Eros was beautiful. After all, what we love really *is* beautiful and delicate, perfect and delightful, whereas the lover has the quite different character I have outlined.'

"'Fair enough, my foreign friend, I think you're right. But if that's what Eros is like, what use is he to men?'

"'That's the next point I want to explain to you, Socrates. I've told you what Eros is like, and what his parentage is; he is also love of what is beautiful, as you say. Now let's imagine someone asking us, "Why is Eros love of the beautiful, Socrates and Diotima?" Let me put it more clearly: what is it that the lover of beauty desires?'

"'To possess it.'

"'That prompts the further question, what good does it do someone to possess beauty?'

"'I don't quite know how to give a quick answer to that question.'

"'Well, try a different question, about goodness rather than beauty: Socrates, what does the lover of goodness want?'

"'To possess it.'

"'What good will it do him to possess it?'

"'That's easier. It will make him happy.'

[205] "'Yes, because those who are happy are happy because they possess what is good. The enquiry seems to have reached a conclusion, and there is no need to ask the further question, "If someone wants to be happy, why does he want to be happy?"'

"'True.'

---

45. The Greek word here is *philosophountes,* which can also be translated as "those who practice philosophy."

"'Do you think this wish and this desire are common to all mankind, and that everyone wants always to possess what is good? Or what do you think?'

"'I think it is common to all men.'

"'In that case, Socrates, why do we not describe all men as lovers, if everyone always loves the same thing? Why do we describe some people as lovers, but not others?'

"'I don't know. I agree with you, it *is* surprising.'

"'Not really. We abstract a part of love, and call it by the name of the whole—love—and then for the other parts we use different names.'

"'What names? Give me an example.'

"'What about this? Take a concept like creation, or composition. Composition means putting things together, and covers a wide range of activities. Any activity which brings anything at all into existence is an example of creation. Hence the exercise of any skill is composition, and those who practice it are composers.'

"'True.'

"'All the same, they aren't all called composers. They all have different names, and it's only one subdivision of the whole class (that which deals with music and rhythm) which is called by the general name. Only this kind of creation is called composing, and its practitioners composers.'

"'True.'

"'Well, it's the same with love. In general, for anyone, any desire for goodness and happiness is love—and it is a powerful and unpredictable force. But there are various ways of pursuing this desire—through money-making, through physical fitness, through philosophy—which do not entitle their devotees to call themselves lovers, or describe their activity as loving. Those who pursue one particular mode of loving, and make that their concern, have taken over the name of the whole (love, loving and lovers).'

"'You may well be right.'

"'There is a theory that lovers are people in search of their other half.[46] But according to my theory, love is not love of a half, nor of a whole, unless it is good. After all, men are prepared to have their own feet and hands cut off, if they think there's something wrong with them. They're not particularly attached to what is their own, except in so far as they regard the good as their own property, and evil as alien to them. [206] And that's because the good is the only object of human love, as I think you will agree.'

"'Yes, I certainly do agree.'

"'Can we say, then, quite simply, that men love the good?'

---

46. This is, of course, the theory implied in Aristophanes' myth.

"'Yes.'

"'And presumably we should add that they want to possess the good?'

"'Yes, we should.'

"'And not merely to possess it, but to possess it forever.'

"'That also.'

"'In short, then, love is the desire for permanent possession of the good.'

"'Precisely.'

"'If this is always the object of our desire, what is the particular manner of pursuit, and the particular sphere of activity, in which enthusiasm and effort qualify for the title "love"? What is this activity? Do you know?'

"'No, I don't. That's why I find your knowledge so impressive. In fact, I've kept coming to see you, because I want an answer to just that question.'

"'Very well, I'll tell you. The activity we're talking about is the use of what is beautiful for the purpose of reproduction, whether physical or mental.'

"'I'm no good at riddles. I don't understand what you mean.'

"'I'll try to make myself clearer. Reproduction, Socrates, both physical and mental, is a universal human activity. At a certain age our nature desires to give birth. To do so, it cannot employ an ugly medium, but insists on what is beautiful. Sexual intercourse between man and woman is this reproduction. So there is the divine element, this germ of immortality, in mortal creatures—that is, conception and begetting. These cannot take place in an uncongenial medium, and ugliness is uncongenial to everything divine, while beauty is congenial. Therefore procreation has Beauty as its midwife and its destiny, which is why the urge to reproduce becomes gentle and happy when it comes near beauty: then conception and begetting become possible. By contrast, when it comes near ugliness it becomes sullen and offended, it contracts, withdraws, and shrinks away and does not beget. It stifles the reproductive urge, and is frustrated. So in anyone who is keen (one might almost say bursting) to reproduce, beauty arouses violent emotion, because beauty can release its possessor from the agony of reproduction. Your opinion, Socrates, that love is desire for beauty, is mistaken.'

"'What is the correct view, then?'

"'It is the desire to use beauty to beget and bear offspring.'

"'Perhaps.'

"'Certainly! And why to beget? Because begetting is, by human standards, something eternal and undying. [207] So if we were right in describing love as the desire always to possess the good, then the inevitable conclusion is that we desire immortality as well as goodness. On this argument, love must be desire for immortality as much as for beauty.'

"Those were her teachings, when she talked to me about love. And one day she asked me, 'What do you think is the reason for this love and this desire? You know how strangely animals behave when they want to mate.

Animals and birds, they're just the same. Their health suffers, and they get all worked up, first over sexual intercourse, and then over raising the young. For these ends they will fight, to the death, against far stronger opponents. They will go to any lengths, even starve themselves, to bring up their offspring. We can easily imagine human beings behaving like this from rational motives, but what can be the cause of such altruistic behavior in animals? Do you know?'

"'No, I don't.'

"'Do you think you can become an expert on love without knowing?'

"'Look, Diotima, I know I have a lot to learn. I've just admitted that. That's why I've come to you. So please tell me the cause of these phenomena, and anything else I should know about love.'

"'Well, if you believe that the natural object of love is what we have often agreed it to be, then the answer is not surprising, since the same reasoning still holds good. What is mortal tries, to the best of its ability, to be everlasting and immortal. It does this in the only way it can, by always leaving a successor to replace what decays. Think of what we call the life span and identity of an individual creature. For example, a man is said to be the same individual from childhood until old age. The cells in his body are always changing, yet he is still called the same person, despite being perpetually reconstituted as parts of him decay—hair, flesh, bones, blood, his whole body, in fact. And not just his body, either. Precisely the same happens with mental attributes. Habits, dispositions, beliefs, opinions, desires, pleasures, pains and fears are all varying all the time for everyone. [208] Some disappear, others take their place. And when we come to knowledge, the situation is even odder. It is not just a question of one piece of knowledge disappearing and being replaced by another, so that we are never the same people, as far as knowledge goes: the same thing happens with each individual piece of knowledge. What we call studying presupposes that knowledge is transient. Forgetting is loss of knowledge, and studying preserves knowledge by creating memory afresh in us, to replace what is lost. Hence we have the illusion of continuing knowledge.

"'All continuous mortal existence is of this kind. It is not the case that creatures remain always, in every detail, precisely the same—only the divine does that. It is rather that what is lost, and what decays, always leaves behind a fresh copy of itself. This, Socrates, is the mechanism by which mortal creatures can taste immortality—both physical immortality, and other sorts. (For immortals, of course, it's different.) So it's not surprising that everything naturally values its own offspring. They all feel this concern, and this love, because of their desire for immortality.'

"I found these ideas totally novel, and I said, 'Well, Diotima, that's a very clever explanation. Is it really all true?' And she, in her best lecturer's man-

ner, replied, 'There can be no question of it. Take another human characteristic, ambition. It seems absurdly irrational until you remember my
explanation. Think of the extraordinary behavior of those who, prompted
by Eros, are eager to become famous, and "amass undying fame for the
whole of time to come." For this they will expose themselves to danger even
more than they will for their children. They will spend money, endure any
hardship, even die for it. Think of Alcestis' willingness to die for Admetus,
or Achilles' determination to follow Patroclus in death,[47] or your Athenian
king Codrus and his readiness to give up his life for his children's right to
rule.[48] Would they have done these things if they hadn't thought they were
leaving behind them an undying memory which we still possess of their
courage? Of course not. The desire for undying nobility, and the good
reputation which goes with it, is a universal human motive. The nobler
people are, the more strongly they feel it. They desire immortality.

"'Those whose creative urge is physical tend to turn to women, and
pursue Eros by this route. The production of children gains them, as they
imagine, immortality and a name and happiness for themselves, for all
time. In others the impulse is mental or spiritual—[209] people who
are creative mentally, much more than physically. They produce what
you would expect the mind to conceive and produce. And what is that?
Thought, and all other human excellence. All poets are creators of this
kind, and so are those artists who are generally regarded as inventive.
However, under the general heading "thought," by far the finest and most
important item is the art of political and domestic economy, what we call
good judgment, and justice.

"'Someone who, right from his youth, is mentally creative in these areas,
when he is ready, and the time comes, feels a strong urge to give birth, or
beget. So he goes around, like everyone else, searching, as I see it, for a
medium of beauty in which he can create. He will never create in an ugly
medium. So in his desire to create he is attracted to what is physically
beautiful rather than ugly. But if he comes across a beautiful, noble, well-
formed mind, then he finds the combination particularly attractive. He'll
drop everything and embark on long conversations about goodness with
such a companion, trying to teach him about the nature and behavior of
the good man. Now that he's made contact with someone beautiful, and
made friends with him, he can produce and bring to birth what he long

47. Note that Diotima is here interpreting the motives of these heroes differently from
Phaedrus: they die for immortal fame, not for a lover.

48. A mythological ruler. An oracle proclaimed that the Dorian invaders of Attica would
prevail only if they avoided killing the king. Codrus heard of the oracle and, in disguise, provoked the Dorians into killing him.

ago conceived. Present or absent, he keeps it in mind, and joins with his friends in bringing his conception to maturity. In consequence such people have a far stronger bond between them than there is between the parents of children; and they form much firmer friendships, because they are jointly responsible for finer, and more lasting, offspring.

"'We would all choose children of this kind for ourselves, rather than human children. We look with envy at Homer and Hesiod, and the other great poets, and the marvelous progeny they left behind, which have brought them undying fame and memory: or, if you like, at children of the kind which Lycurgus left in Sparta,[49] the salvation of Sparta and practically all Greece. In your city, Solon is highly thought of, as the father of your laws, as are many other men in other states, both Greek and foreign. They have published to the world a variety of noble achievements, and created goodness of every kind. There are shrines to such people in honor of their offspring, but none to the producers of ordinary children.

"'You, too, Socrates, could probably be initiated this far into knowledge of Eros. [210] But all this, rightly pursued, is a mere preliminary to the full rites, and final revelation, which might well be beyond you. Still, I'll tell you about it, so that if I fail, it won't be for want of trying. Try to follow, if you can.

"'The true follower of this subject must begin, as a young man, with the pursuit of physical beauty. In the first place, if his mentor advises him properly, he should be attracted, physically, to one individual; at this stage his offspring are beautiful discussions and conversations. Next he should realize that the physical beauty of one body is akin to that of any other body, and that if he's going to pursue beauty of appearance, it's the height of folly not to regard the beauty which is in all bodies as one and the same. This insight will convert him into a lover of all physical beauty, and he will become less obsessive in his pursuit of his one former passion, as he realizes its unimportance.

"'The next stage is to put a higher value on mental than on physical beauty. The right qualities of mind, even in the absence of any great physical beauty, will be enough to awaken his love and affection. He will generate the kind of discussions which are improving to the young. The aim is that, as the next step, he should be compelled to contemplate the beauty of customs and institutions, to see that all beauty of this sort is related, and consequently to regard physical beauty as trivial.

"'From human institutions his teacher should direct him to knowledge, so that he may, in turn, see the beauty of different types of knowledge.

49. I.e., the Spartan constitution, which was much admired as a model of good government.

Whereas before, in servile and contemptible fashion, he was dominated by the individual case, loving the beauty of a boy, or a man, or a single human activity, now he directs his eyes to what is beautiful in general, as he turns to gaze upon the limitless ocean of beauty. Now he produces many fine and inspiring thoughts and arguments, as he gives his undivided attention to philosophy. Here he gains in strength and stature until his attention is caught by that one special knowledge—the knowledge of a beauty which I will now try to describe to you. So pay the closest possible attention.

"'When a man has reached this point in his education in love, studying the different types of beauty in correct order, he will come to the final end and goal of this education. Then suddenly he will see a beauty of a breathtaking nature, Socrates, the beauty which is the justification of all his efforts so far. [211] It is eternal, neither coming to be nor passing away, neither increasing nor decreasing. Moreover it is not beautiful in part, and ugly in part, nor is it beautiful at one time, and not at another; nor beautiful in some respects, but not in others; nor beautiful here and ugly there, as if beautiful in some people's eyes, but not in others. It will not appear to him as the beauty of a face, or hands, or anything physical nor as an idea or branch of knowledge, nor as existing in any determinate place, such as a living creature, or the Earth, or heaven, or anywhere like that. It exists for all time, by itself and with itself, unique. All other forms of beauty derive from it, but in such a way that their creation or destruction does not strengthen or weaken it, or affect it in any way at all. If a man progresses (as he will do, if he goes about his love affairs in the right way) from the lesser beauties, and begins to catch sight of this beauty, then he is within reach of the final revelation. Such is the experience of the man who approaches, or is guided towards, love in the right way, beginning with the particular examples of beauty, but always returning from them to the search for that one beauty. He uses them like a ladder, climbing from the love of one person to love of two; from two to love of all physical beauty; from physical beauty to beauty in human behavior; thence to beauty in subjects of study; from them he arrives finally at that branch of knowledge which studies nothing but ultimate Beauty. Then at last he understands what true Beauty is.

"'That, if ever, is the moment, my dear Socrates, when a man's life is worth living, as he contemplates Beauty itself. Once seen, it will not seem to you to be a good such as gold, or fashionable clothes, or the boys and young men who have such an effect on you now when you see them. You, and any number of people like you, when you see your boyfriends and spend all your time with them, are quite prepared (or would be, if it were possible) to go without food and drink, just looking at them and being with them. But suppose it were granted to someone to see Beauty itself quite clearly, in its pure, undiluted form—not clogged up with human flesh and coloring, and a whole lot of other worthless and corruptible matter. No, imagine he were able to see the divine Beauty itself in its unique essence. [212] Don't you think he would find it a wonderful way to live, looking at it, contemplating it as it should be contemplated, and spending his time in its company? It cannot fail to strike you that only then will it be possible for him, seeing Beauty as it should be seen, to produce, not likenesses of Goodness (since it is no likeness he has before him), but the real thing (since he has the real thing before him); and that this producing, and caring for, real Goodness earns him the friendship of the gods and makes him, if anyone, immortal.'

"There you are, then, Phaedrus and the rest of you. That's what Diotima said to me, and I, for one, find it convincing. And it's because I'm convinced that I now try to persuade other people as well that man, in his search for this goal, could hardly hope to find a better ally than Eros. That's why I say that everyone should honor Eros, and why I myself honor him, and make the pursuit of Eros my chief concern, and encourage others to do the same. Now, and for all time, I praise the power and vigor of Eros, to the limits of my ability.

"That's my speech, Phaedrus. You can take it, if you like, as a formal eulogy of Eros. Or you can call it by any other name you please. . . ."

After this speech, the handsome young general Alcibiades bursts into the party with several drunken companions and a female prostitute. He is asked to give a speech on Eros and begins by comparing Socrates to an impudent satyr[50] with a unique power over him. He explains:

[216] "He forces me to admit that with all my faults I do nothing to improve myself, but continue in public life just the same. So I tear myself away, as if stopping my ears against the Sirens;[51] otherwise I would spend my whole life there sitting at his feet. He's the only man who can appeal to my better nature (not that most people would reckon I *had* a better nature), because I'm only too aware I have no answer to his arguments. I know I should do as he tells me, but when I leave him I have no defense against my own ambition and desire for recognition. So I run for my life, and avoid him, and when I see him, I'm embarrassed, when I remember conclusions we've reached in the past. I would often cheerfully have seen

50. A part-human, part-goat creature of enormous sexual energy, known for complete lack of inhibition.

51. Socrates apparently used this metaphor of himself. See Xenophon's account in **5.3.31** and n. 5.

him dead, and yet I know that if that did happen, I should be even more upset. So I just can't cope with the man.

"I'm by no means the only person to be affected like this by his satyr's music, but that isn't all I have to say about his similarity to those figures I likened him to, and about his remarkable powers. Believe me, none of you really knows the man. So I'll enlighten you, now that I've begun.

"Your view of Socrates is of someone who fancies attractive men, spends all his time with them, finds them irresistible—and you know how hopelessly ignorant and uncertain he is. And yet this pose is extremely Silenus-like.[52] It's the outward mask he wears, like the carved Silenus. Open him up, and he's a model of restraint; you wouldn't believe it, my dear fellow-drinkers. Take my word for it, it makes no difference at all how attractive you are, he has an astonishing contempt for that kind of thing. Similarly with riches, or any of the other so-called advantages we possess. He regards all possessions as worthless, and us humans as insignificant. No, I mean it, he treats his whole life in human society as a game or puzzle.

"But when he's serious, when he opens up and you see the real Socrates —I don't know if any of you has ever seen the figure inside. I saw it once, and it struck me as utterly godlike and golden and beautiful and wonderful. In fact, I thought I must simply do anything he told me. [**217**] And since I thought he was serious about my good looks, I congratulated myself on a fantastic stroke of luck, which had given me the chance to satisfy Socrates, and be the recipient, in return, of all his knowledge. I had, I may say, an extremely high opinion of my own looks.

"That was my plan, so I did what I had never done up to then—I sent away my attendant, and took to seeing him on my own. You see, I'm going to tell you the whole truth, so listen carefully, and you tell them, Socrates, if I get anything wrong. Well, gentlemen, I started seeing him—just the two of us—and I thought he would start talking to me as lovers do to their boyfriends when they're alone together. I was very excited. But nothing like that happened at all. He spent the day talking to me as usual, and then left. I invited him to the gymnasium with me, and exercised with him there, thinking I might make some progress that way. So he exercised and wrestled with me, often completely on our own, and (needless to say) it got me nowhere at all. When that turned out to be no good, I thought I'd better make a pretty determined assault on the man, and not give up, now that I'd started. I wanted to find out what the trouble was. So I asked him to dinner, just like a lover with designs on his boyfriend.

52. Silenus was the chief of the satyrs—usually represented as short, fat, and bald, like Socrates. Earlier in his speech, Alcibiades described hollow Silenus statuettes one could buy that opened up to reveal smaller figures.

"He took some time to agree even to this, but finally I did get him to come. The first time he came, he had dinner, and then got up to go. I lost my nerve, that time, and let him go. But I decided to try again. He came to dinner, and I kept him talking late into the night. When he tried to go home, I made him stay, saying it was too late to go. So he stayed the night on the couch next to mine. There was no one else sleeping in the room.

"What I've told you so far I'd be quite happy to repeat to anyone. The next part I'm only telling you because (a) I'm drunk—'in vino veritas,' and all that—and (b) since I've started praising Socrates, it seems wrong to leave out an example of his superior behavior. Besides, I'm like someone who's been bitten by an adder. They say that a man who's had this happen to him will only say what it was like to others who've been bitten; they're the only people who will understand, and make allowances for, his willingness to say or do anything, such is the pain. [218] Well, I've been bitten by something worse than an adder, and in the worst possible place. I've been stung, or bitten, in my heart or soul (whatever you care to call it) by a method of philosophical argument, whose bite, when it gets a grip on a young and intelligent mind, is sharper than any adder's. It makes one willing to say or do anything. I can see all these Phaedruses and Agathons, Eryximachuses, Pausaniases, Aristodemuses and Aristophaneses here, not to mention Socrates himself and the rest of you. You've all had a taste of this wild passion for philosophy, so you'll understand me, and forgive what I did then, and what I'm telling you now. As for the servants, and anyone else who's easily shocked, or doesn't know what I'm talking about, they'll just have to put something over their ears.

"There we were, then, gentlemen. The lamp had gone out, the slaves had gone to bed. I decided it was time to abandon subtlety, and say plainly what I was after. So I nudged him. 'Socrates, are you asleep?' 'No.' 'Do you know what I've decided?' 'What?' 'I think you're the ideal person to be my lover, but you seem to be a bit shy about suggesting it. So I'll tell you how I feel about it. I think I'd be crazy not to satisfy you in this way, just as I'd do anything else for you if it was in my power or in my friends' power. Nothing matters more to me than my own improvement, and I can't imagine a better helper than you. Anyone with any sense would think worse of me for not giving a man like you what he wants than most ignorant people would if I did give you what you want.'

"Socrates listened to this. Then, with characteristic irony, he replied. 'My dear Alcibiades, you're certainly nobody's fool, if you're right in what you say about me, and I do have some power to improve you. It must be remarkable beauty you see in me, far superior to your own physical beauty. If that's the aim of your deal with me, to exchange beauty for beauty, then you're trying to get much the better of the bargain. You want to get real beauty in exchange for what is commonly mistaken for it, like Diomedes getting gold armor in return for his bronze.[53] Better think again, however. [219] You might be wrong about me. Judgment begins when eyesight starts to fail, and you're still a long way from that.'

"I listened, then said: 'Well, as far as I am concerned, that's how things stand. I've told you my real feelings. You must decide what you think best for yourself and for me.' 'That's good advice. We must think about it some time, and act as seems best to us, in this matter as in others.'

After this exchange, thinking my direct assault had made some impact, I got up, before he could say anything more, wrapped my cloak around him (it was winter), and lay down with him under his rough cloak. I put my arms round him. I spent the whole night with him, remarkable, super-human being that he is—still telling the truth, Socrates, you can't deny it —but he was more than equal to my advances. He rejected them, laughed at my good looks, and treated them with contempt; and I must admit that, as far as looks went, I thought I was quite something, members of the jury. (I call you that, since I'm accusing Socrates of contempt.) In short, I prom-ise you faithfully, I fell asleep, and when I woke up in the morning I'd slept with Socrates all night, but absolutely nothing had happened. It was just like sleeping with one's father or elder brother.

"Imagine how I felt after that. I was humiliated and yet full of admira-tion for Socrates' character—his restraint and strength of mind. I'd met a man whose equal, in intelligence and control, I didn't think I should ever meet again. I couldn't have a row with him; that would just lose me his friendship. Nor could I see any way of attracting him. I knew money would make as little impression on him as Trojan weapons on Ajax,[54] and he'd already escaped my one sure means of ensnaring him. I didn't know what to do, and I went around infatuated with the man. No one's ever been so infatuated. . . . "[55]

5.8 Xenophon, *Symposium* 1.1–2.9, 4.10–28, 4.52–54, 8.1–9.7

This work was probably written as Xenophon's response to Plato's Symposium. *It in-cludes conversation on a variety of ethical topics in addition to love.*

[1.1] It is, I believe, important to record what fine and noble men do, not only when they are serious, but also when they are at play. That this is true

---

53. An allusion to Diomedes and Glaucus' exchange of armor as friendship gifts when they meet on the battlefield in *Iliad* 6.232–36. Homer comments that Glaucus was a fool to give up the more valuable armor.

54. A stalwart Greek warrior in the *Iliad*, who carried a massive shield impervious to enemy weapons.

55. Alcibiades goes on to tell of Socrates' indifference to physical discomfort during his military service. After Alcibiades' speech, the party eventually breaks up.

was made clear to me by an event in which I took part, and I would like to describe that event here.

[1.2] It was the day of the horse races at the Great Panathenaic Games.[56] Still a boy, Autolycus had won the pancratium,[57] and Callias, the son of Hipponicus, who was in love with him, had brought him to the see the show.[58] When the horse races had ended, Callias went off to his house in the Piraeus[59] with Autolycus and Autolycus' father, and Niceratus[60] also went along with him. [1.3] But when he saw Socrates together with Critobulus, Hermogenes, Antisthenes, and Charmides,[61] he told a slave to escort Autolycus and the others and went up to Socrates and his companions and said, "What luck to have met you! [1.4] I am about to give a dinner for Autolycus and his father, but my provisions would, I think, appear much more impressive if my dining room were adorned with men such as yourselves whose souls are pure, rather than with generals, cavalry commanders, and those with their eyes set on public office."

[1.5] Socrates replied, "You always make fun of us and look down on us because you have paid a lot of money to Protagoras, Gorgias, Prodicus,[62] and many others to gain wisdom, while we, as it were, grow our own philosophy."

[1.6] "It is true," said Callias, "that before now I have kept it hidden from you that I have many wise things to say, but now, if you will join me, I will show you that I deserve very considerable respect."

[1.7] At first, as you might expect, Socrates and his friends thanked Callias for the invitation, but did not commit themselves to attending the dinner. But when it became clear that Callias was most distressed that they would not go with him, they followed along. Others then came along too, some after exercising and being rubbed down, others having also taken

---

56. These occurred every four years at Athens and included athletic competition as well as civic sacrifices and processions. They did not have the same stature as the pan-Hellenic games at Olympia and Delphi, but were prominent among local contests.

57. On this event, see ch. 4, n. 47. Autolycus' victory is dated to 422 B.C.E. and was commemorated by a statue in the Prytaneum (town hall). He was the subject of a comedy by Eupolis, and in 404 was executed by the Thirty Tyrants.

58. Callias was an extravagantly wealthy Athenian from a prominent family with a long history of sponsoring chariot teams in the races. He would be about thirty at the time of this dialogue.

59. See ch. 4, n. 16. The racecourse was nearby.

60. Son of the prominent general and conservative statesman Nicias. He had some reputation as a performer of epic verse, and was also killed by the Thirty Tyrants.

61. For Critobulus as a notable boy-lover and a companion of Socrates, see 5.2 and 5.3. On Charmides as a youthful beauty, see 5.4. Hermogenes was a less affluent brother of Callias, and Antisthenes was a pupil of Socrates who went on to found the Cynic school.

62. Professional sophists who charged for their lessons, unlike Socrates.

a bath. [1.8] Autolycus sat by his father, while the others, as is proper, reclined.[63]

Anyone watching the events would at once have realized that beauty is by nature something like a king, especially when someone has won modesty and temperance to go with it, as Autolycus then had. [1.9] For first of all, just as when a light appears in the night and all eyes are drawn toward it, so then did Autolycus' beauty draw everyone's gaze toward him, and second, there was no one among those who looked whose soul was not affected by him. Some became quieter, others moved more gracefully. [1.10] All who are possessed by a god are certainly worthy of study, but those possessed by most gods become more severe in their faces, more frightening in their voices, and more impetuous in their actions, while those possessed by modest Love show a greater kindness in their eyes and a greater softness in their voices, and carry themselves in ways more fitting of a free man. This is how Callias was then, because of Love, and so offered to that god's devotees an object worthy of study.

[1.11] They were all eating in silence, just as if ordered by a master, when Philip the jester knocked at the door and told the gatekeeper to announce who he was and why he wanted to be let in. He said that he had come fully equipped with everything necessary—necessary, that was, to eat someone else's food—and that his slave was much weighed down by being loaded with nothing, not even breakfast. [1.12] When he heard him, Callias said, "Gentlemen, it would be a shame to begrudge him a roof, so let him come in." At the same time he looked over to Autolycus, evidently to see how he liked the joke.

[1.13] Philip stopped at the hall where the dinner was and said, "You all know that I am a jester. I have come here in good spirits, presuming that it is funnier to come to dinner without an invitation than with one."

"Lie down then," said Callias. "For the people here have taken their fill of seriousness, as you can see, but are perhaps somewhat in need of laughter."

[1.14] As they ate, Philip immediately tried to make a joke; that was, after all, the only reason why he received invitations to dinner. When he stirred no laughter, he was clearly aggrieved. Again a little while later, he wanted to make another joke, but when the guests did not even laugh at him then, he at once ceased eating, covered his head and lay down. [1.15] "What is the matter?" asked Callias. "Are you in pain?"

---

63. At a banquet, adult guests would typically recline on couches, sometimes in pairs, with portable tables of food set in front of them. Boys would sit in a respectful posture and listen quietly.

"Yes, by Zeus, great pain," he said groaning. "When laughter is gone from mankind, my livelihood is ruined. I used to be invited to dinner so that my fellow diners might enjoy themselves by laughing at me, but why will anyone invite me now? I cannot be serious, any more than I can live forever, and no one will invite me in expectation of a return invitation, since everyone knows that it has never been my custom, not even once, to bring dinner to my house." As he said these things, he blew his nose and it was obvious from the noise that he was crying. [1.16] So everyone comforted him, saying that they would laugh next time and told him to eat. Critobulus, however, burst out laughing at his weeping, and when Philip heard the laughter, he uncovered his head, bade himself take heart, now that he would certainly have a part to play in future engagements,[64] and went back to eating.

[2.1] When the tables had been taken away and when they had poured libations and sung a hymn to Apollo, a Syracusan came in to entertain them. He brought with him a flute-girl, a dancing-girl (one of those skilled in juggling tricks), and a boy who was both very beautiful and very good at playing the lyre and dancing. The Syracusan made his living by putting on these performances at dinner parties as if they were public shows. [2.2] But when the flute-girl played her flute and the boy played his lyre, both were thought most appropriate entertainment, and so Socrates said, "By Zeus, Callias, you have provided the perfect feast. Not only did you set before us a meal that no one could criticize, but you also provide us with the sweetest sights and sounds."

[2.3] "Then what if someone were also to bring us perfume, so that we might feast with fine fragrances too?" said Callias.

"A very bad idea," said Socrates. "For, just as the clothes that are proper for a woman are different from the clothes that are proper for a man, so the fragrances that fit a woman are different from those that fit a man. For the fact is no man is rubbed down with an expensive perfume for another man's sake, and what need of additional perfume do married women have, especially if they are recently married like the wives of Niceratus here and Critobulus? [2.4] They smell of it already. But the smell of olive oil in the gymnasia is sweeter to us than the smell of perfume is to married women, and its absence is more greatly missed. The fact is that every man, whether slave or free, when once anointed with perfume, immediately smells the same, but the odors that come from the labors of a free man require at the least studied application and a long period of practice if they are to smell sweet and free."

---

64. Philip compares his fear of hunger to a soldier's fear of battle. The word for engagements, *sumbolai*, can refer to both battles and the contributions made by individuals to a common dinner.

"So that may be so for youths, but what about those of us who no longer exercise? What should we smell of?" asked Lycon.[65]

"Of noble character, by Zeus," said Socrates.

"And where should someone get this ointment?"

"Not, by Zeus, from the perfume shops."

"So where then?"

"Theognis said,

You will learn noble things from noble people, but if with bad
You mix, you will lose even the sense you now have."[66]

[2.5] "Do you hear this, my son?" said Lycon.

"He does," said Socrates. "And he puts it to use. At any rate, when he wanted to win the pancratium, with your help he considered *who was the best at that sport and associated with him, and now if he wants to live a noble life, he will consider* once again with you who seems to be the best at practicing this and will associate with him."

[2.6] At this many spoke up. "Where will he find someone to teach this?" asked one. Another said that it could not be taught, while a third said that, if anything could be learned, this could. [2.7] "Since this matter is disputed," said Socrates, "let us put it aside for a later date and complete now what we have before us. For I see that the dancing-girl here has taken up position and someone is bringing her some hoops."

[2.8] After this the other girl began to play her flute for the dancer, and someone standing next to the dancer passed her the hoops until she had twelve. She took them and as she danced she threw them whirling upwards, judging what height she needed to throw them so as to catch them in time to the music. [2.9] And Socrates said, "It is obvious from what this girl does, as well as from many other things, that a woman's nature is in no way inferior to a man's, but lacks only good sense and strength. So, if any of you has a wife, be confident that you can teach her whatever you want her to know for your purposes."

After they watch more entertainments, Callias proposes that each guest tell what he takes the greatest pride in. Critobulus explains that it is his physical beauty:

[4.10] Critobulus said, "Shall I now tell you the reasons why I am proud of my beauty?"

"Do," they said.

"If, indeed, I am not, as I think, beautiful, then you could all be justly

---

65. Autolycus' father. One of Socrates' accusers at his trial in 399 was named Lycon; it is uncertain whether he is the same man, but Xenophon may be ironically grouping together men who later became enemies (as with Charmides, a supporter of the Thirty Tyrants, and Autolycus and Niceratus, both executed under the Thirty).

66. Theognis 35–36, addressed to Cyrnus.

accused of dishonesty. For, although no one calls upon you to do so, you are always saying on oath that I am beautiful, and I believe you. For I consider you gentlemen. [4.11] If then I am truly beautiful and you suffer the same experience before me that I suffer before those that seem beautiful to me, then I swear by all the gods that I would not swap the kingdom of Persia for my beauty. [4.12] For my part, I now watch Cleinias[67] with more pleasure than I watch all other beautiful things in the world; I would agree to be blind to all other things before I would agree to be blind to him, though he is only one person. I am vexed at the night and at my sleep because I do not see him, and I genuinely feel grateful to the day and the sun because they reveal Cleinias to me.

[4.13] "We beautiful ones should be proud of this too, that, while the strong man must labor to obtain good things, the brave man to face danger and the clever man to make speeches, the beautiful man may achieve everything without disturbing his peace. [4.14] Although well aware that wealth is a sweet thing to have, I for one would more happily give my possessions to Cleinias than take more from someone else, and more happily be a slave than a free man, if Cleinias would wish to be my master. With more ease would I labor for him than rest and with more pleasure would I face dangers on his behalf than live a life without danger. [4.15] Consequently, Callias, if you are proud because you can make men more just,[68] I can more justly induce men to adopt every virtue. For, because we beautiful ones inspire[69] something in lovers, we make them more liberal with their possessions, harder working and keener to gain honor in the face of danger, and further more modest and self-controlled, since they feel especially ashamed about what they want. [4.16] And they are mad too who do not choose beautiful people to be their generals.[70] I would even go through fire with Cleinias, and I know that you too would come with me. Thus, Socrates, no longer trouble yourself over whether my beauty will benefit mankind at all.

[4.17] "Nor should one dishonor beauty in this way, on the grounds that it swiftly passes its prime, since, just as there are beautiful boys, so there are beautiful young men, beautiful adults, and beautiful old men. My evidence is that beautiful old men are selected to carry the olive branches for Athena,[71] as if beauty accompanies every time of life.

67. This Cleinias was the younger cousin of Alcibiades; he is perhaps misidentified as his son in 5.2 and 5.3.
68. Callias claimed in section 4.1–5 (not included here) that he made men more just by giving them money and thus releasing them from the constraints of poverty.
69. This may allude to the Spartan concept of the lover as "inspirer" (*eispnēlos*) of the beloved, on which see 2.11 and 6.10.13. Here Critobulus inverts the concept by making the beloved the "inspirer" of the lover.
70. Perhaps a reference to Alcibiades himself, well known for his good looks.
71. At the Panathenaic festival.

[4.18] "And, if it is sweet to obtain what one desires from one who willingly gives it, I know that right now, without even speaking, I could persuade this boy and this girl to kiss me sooner than you could, Socrates, even if you were to give a very long and clever speech."

[4.19] "What do you mean?" said Socrates. "Are you implying by your boast that you are more beautiful than I?"

"Certainly, by Zeus," said Critobulus. "Otherwise I would be uglier than all the Silenuses[72] in the satyr-plays."

[4.20] "Well then," said Socrates, "be sure to remember to set up this beauty contest[73] when all the conversations before us have concluded. And let not Alexander, Priam's son,[74] judge us, but these very people whom you think desire to kiss you."

[4.21] "Would you not entrust the judging to Cleinias, Socrates?" he said.
He replied, "Will you not stop thinking about Cleinias?"

"But if I do not speak his name, do you think I would be thinking about him any less? Do you not know that I have such a clear image of him in my soul that, if I were a sculptor or a painter, I could make a likeness of him no less from that image than by looking at him?"

[4.22] Socrates answered, "Why, then, if you have so exact an image of him, do you trouble me by taking me to places where you will see him?"

"Because, Socrates, the sight of him has the power to make me happy, while the sight of the image provides no pleasure, but causes only longing."

[4.23] Hermogenes said, "Socrates, I do not consider it appropriate for you to overlook the fact that Critobulus has been so driven out of his senses by love."

"Do you think," said Socrates, "that he has been in this condition ever since he associated with me?"

"If not, since when?"

"Do you not see that the soft hair has recently crept alongside this one's ears, while it already climbs from Cleinias' chin towards the back.[75] Critobulus here was mightily inflamed before, when he went to the same school as Cleinias, [4.24] and it was because he saw this that his father gave him to me, in the hope that I might be able to help. And he is already much

72. See n. 52. Satyr-plays were humorous mythological burlesques that accompanied the performance of a tragic trilogy at the City Dionysia.

73. The Panathenaea featured a male beauty contest called the *euandria*. We also know of kiss contests in Megara, on which see **6.10.27–37**.

74. Usually known as Paris. He judged the beauty contest among Aphrodite, Athena, and Hera that ultimately led to the Trojan War.

75. This suggests that Critobulus and Cleinias were both adolescents: if anything, Cleinias may have actually been a bit older. However, the interpretation of the Greek is disputed: others take the reference to be to hair on the nape of Cleinias' neck. And 2.3 tells us that Critobulus is already married! Perhaps Critobulus is exaggerating his youthful appearance to imagine himself as more like his beloved.

better. For before, like those who look at Gorgons,[76] he stared like a stone and was nowhere absent from Cleinias' side, but now I have even seen him blink. [4.25] By the gods, my friends, I believe that, between ourselves, he had, in fact, even kissed Cleinias, and there is no more terrible fuel to the fire of love than this. For it knows no satisfaction and offers sweet hopes. [4.26] It is for this reason that I say that anyone who hopes to be able to control himself should keep away from kissing those in the bloom of youth."

[4.27] Charmides said, "But why, Socrates, do you make such efforts to scare us, your friends, away from beautiful boys, when, while you were both looking for something in the same book at the school, I saw you, by Apollo, holding your head against Critobulus' head and your bare shoulder against his bare shoulder?"

[4.28] "Alas," said Socrates, "from these events I have had a sharp pain in my shoulder for more than five days, as if bitten by a snake, while in my heart I thought I had been stung. But now, Critobulus," he said, "before all these witnesses I publicly proclaim that you should not touch me before you have grown as much hair on your chin as on your head."

In this way, they mixed in jests with their serious observations.

Others explain their sources of pride, until Charmides turns to the Syracusan:

[4.52] "But you, man of Syracuse," said Charmides, "what are you proud of? The boy, presumably?"

"No, by Zeus, not at all. I am instead extremely anxious about him. For I see people plotting to destroy him."

[4.53] "Heracles!" Socrates said when he heard this. "What has your boy done that is in their view so wrong that they wish to kill him?"

"They do not wish to kill him," he said, "but to persuade him to sleep with them."

"And if this happened, you would presumably think that he had been destroyed?"

"Well, yes, by Zeus," he said, "absolutely."

[4.54] "Is it not the case that you sleep with him?" he asked.

"Yes, by Zeus. All night and every night."

"By Hera," said Socrates, "You are very lucky to have been born with a body of such a constitution that you alone do not destroy those you sleep with. You should, I conclude, at least take great pride in your body, if in nothing else."

---

76. Three winged women with snake hair who turned to stone anyone who looked at them.

Other speeches are delivered. Finally, the beauty contest between Critobulus and So-
crates is judged, with Critobulus the victor. Socrates suggests that the Syracusan pre-
pare a new kind of entertainment for the guests, and the conversation continues:

[8.1] . . . Socrates once more broached a new subject. "Given that a
mighty god is present," he said, "a god as old as the eternal gods but most
youthful in appearance, a god who extends everywhere but is seated in
the soul of man, given his presence, gentlemen, should we not make
mention of Love, especially as we are all devotees of this god? [8.2] For I
cannot name a time when I was not in love with someone and I know that
Charmides here has had many lovers and on occasion even felt desire for
them himself. Critobulus too already desires others, though still himself
desired. [8.3] And we can add Niceratus who, I hear, both loves his wife
and is loved by her. And who of us does not know that, whatever nobility
of character is, Hermogenes wastes away from love of it? Do you not see
how serious is his brow, how still his gaze, how measured his words, how
soft his voice, and how happy his disposition? And that, though he considers the most holy gods his friends, he does not ignore us humans at all?
Are you, Antisthenes, the only one who is not in love?"

[8.4] "By the gods, not at all," he said, "I am very much in love with you."

Pretending to be coy as a joke, Socrates said, "Don't bother me now.
[8.5] As you can see, I am doing something else."

Antisthenes replied, "It is so obvious that you are always acting as your
own pimp when you do such things. You never converse with me; sometimes your 'demonic sign' [77] provides the excuse, while at other times you
are focused on something else."

[8.6] "By the gods, Antisthenes," said Socrates, "please don't knock me
around. Every other harsh action I am happy to endure and will continue
to do so. But," he said, "let us hide your love from public view, since you
love not my soul, but my handsome body. [8.7] But as for you, Callias, the
whole city knows that you love Autolycus, and many from outside of it too,
I suspect, since you have famous fathers and are also distinguished yourselves. [8.8] I have always admired your natural disposition, but now I
admire it even more when I see you in love not with someone who revels
in luxury and is weakened by softness, but with someone who displays to
all his strength, endurance, courage, and temperance. To desire such
qualities gives an indication of the nature of the lover also. [8.9] Whether
there is one Aphrodite, or two, Heavenly Aphrodite and Common Aphrodite,[78] I am not sure; for Zeus has many names, but is considered one god.

77. A kind of inner voice Socrates sometimes claimed to hear. Every individual was thought
to have a tutelary spirit (or *daimon*) who watched over him.

78. An allusion to Pausanias' speech in Plato (5.7.180–81).

I am sure, however, that there are separate altars and temples for each of the two, as well as separate offerings, those for Common Aphrodite as wanton as those for Heavenly Aphrodite are holy. [8.10] You would guess that Common Aphrodite delivers love of the body, and Heavenly Aphrodite love of the soul, of friendship and of noble deeds. It is by this second sort of love, Callias, that I think you are possessed. [8.11] My judgment is based on the noble character of the boy you love and on my observation that you include the boy's father in your dealings with him. Nothing in such relationships should be kept hidden from the father by a noble lover."

[8.12] Hermogenes said, "By Hera, Socrates, I am impressed by many of the things you do, but I am particularly impressed that now, at the same time that you flatter Callias, you are also teaching him what sort of a person he should be."

"True," he said, "and to gratify him further, I will also offer evidence that the love of the soul is much better than the love of the body. [8.13] We all know that an association that excludes friendship is not worth mentioning. Well, to feel such friendship is a necessity for those who admire character—a necessity that is called sweet and voluntary—while many of those who desire the body find fault with and detest the ways of those they love. [8.14] If they love both the mind and the body, the flower of youth is, I think, swiftly past its prime, and when this is gone, the friendship must wither away with it. Yet the longer the soul proceeds after wisdom, the more worthy of love it becomes.

[8.15] "Moreover, you can have too much contact with physical beauty; you will feel the same way about your favorite as you do about food when you are full. But love of the soul is pure and so is harder to satisfy. This is not because, as one might suppose, it offers fewer of Aphrodite's charms. No, our prayer that the goddess confer her charms on our words and deeds is clearly answered. [8.16] For no argument is needed to prove that to feel admiration and love for a boy is the mark of a soul that flowers with the beauty of freedom and with a modest and noble character, of a soul that is at once a leader among its peers and kind in addition; but I will now prove that we should expect such a lover to be loved in return by his favorite.

[8.17] "First of all, how could someone fail to like a man whom he knew to think him fine and noble? Second, how could a boy fail to like a man whom he saw taking more pains over his fine upbringing than his own pleasures? Furthermore, how could a boy fail to like a man whose friendship he was convinced would not lessen, even if his beauty faded, either from advancing age or sickness? [8.18] And surely those who love each other must enjoy looking at each other, must happily converse together, must trust each other and be trusted, must look out for each other and take pleasure in happy outcomes, but feel pain when someone slips? Surely they must be happy to be together when both are healthy, but then, if one of the two falls sick, surely they will spend even more time together and think even more about each other when they are apart than when they are together? Are not all these things the charms that Aphrodite offers? At any rate, it is because of actions such as these that they will continue both to love friendship and to practice it into old age.

[8.19] "But why should a boy return the love of a man who is wholly focused on the body? Because that man gets what he desires for himself, but gives to the boy only the greatest of reproaches? Or is it because he keeps his favorite's family from knowing what he is keen to get from him? [8.20] Moreover, the fact that he does not force the boy, but persuades him, makes him more loathsome, since he who uses force reveals himself to be wicked, but he who uses persuasion corrupts the soul of the one he persuades. [8.21] And what of the boy who sells his youth for money? How will he love the buyer any more than one who trades and sells in the marketplace loves his customers? No, because he is in his prime while his buyer is past his, because he is beautiful while his buyer is no longer so, and because his buyer feels attracted while he does not, he will feel no friendship towards him. For, unlike a woman, a boy does not share in the pleasures of the sexual act with a man, but soberly watches him as he is made drunk by Aphrodite. [8.22] Consequently it should come as no surprise if he soon disdains his lover.

"Further, on examination one will find that nothing savage has been caused by those who love each other for their characters, while many unholy acts have been committed by those in a shameless relationship.

[8.23] "I will now demonstrate that it is the mark of a servile mind to spend time with a man who loves the body more than the soul. If a man teaches a boy to say and do what is right, he will be justly honored, as Chiron and Phoenix were honored by Achilles,[79] but if he desires his body, he can expect to be treated like a beggar. After all, he trails after him, always asking and begging for a kiss or a caress.

[8.24] "If I speak boldly, do not be surprised. The wine urges me on, and the love that always dwells with me goads me to speak freely against the love that is its opponent. [8.25] For the fact is, someone who pays attention to outward appearances seems to me to be like someone who rents an estate. His efforts are not directed to making the property worth more, but to gathering as great a harvest as possible. But someone whose goal is friendship is more like someone who owns his own fields; at any rate, he adds what he can from his resources to make his beloved worth more.

---

79. Chiron and Phoenix were tutors of Achilles. Phoenix was an elderly servant in the house of Achilles' father; Chiron the centaur educated Achilles in his cave during the hero's early childhood.

[8.26] "Furthermore, if a favorite knows that whoever is sufficiently attractive physically will dominate his lover, he is likely to be slack in the rest of his conduct. But if he knows that he will not keep his lover's friendship unless he is good and noble, he is more likely to concern himself with virtue. **[8.27]** The greatest benefit that falls to the man who seeks to make a good friend out of his favorite is that he must himself also practice virtue. For it is impossible for him to make the one he is with good if he himself is doing wicked things, or to make his beloved self-controlled and modest if he exhibits shamelessness and incontinence.

[8.28] "Callias, I wish to show you from myths that not only men, but also gods and heroes consider love of the soul more important than intimacy with the body. **[8.29]** Zeus, for example, left all the mortal women that he loved for their external appearance to remain as mortals, even though he coupled with them, but made all those he admired for their souls immortal. These include Hercules and the Dioscuri,[80] and others are mentioned also. **[8.30]** I further contend that Ganymede was also brought to Olympus by Zeus for his soul, not for his body. His very name suggests this. In Homer we find the phrase, 'He rejoices to hear,' meaning that he enjoys hearing, and elsewhere, I think, 'Having close-packed counsels in his mind,' meaning that he has clever ideas in his mind.[81] So, since his name is composed of these two elements, rejoicing and counsel, Ganymede stands revealed as honored among the gods not for the pleasures of his body, but for the pleasures of his mind.

[8.31] "Furthermore, Niceratus, Achilles is depicted by Homer gloriously avenging the dead Patroclus not because he was his favorite boy but because he was his companion.[82] Orestes and Pylades, Theseus and Pirithous,[83] and many other excellent heroes are praised for having achieved the most great and noble deeds together, not because they slept with each other, but because they admired each other. **[8.32]** And what about the noble deeds that are achieved today? Would someone not discover that these are all done by men willing to toil and expose themselves to danger for the sake of praise, and not by men accustomed to choose pleasure over glory? Yet Pausanias, the lover of the poet Agathon, has defended those

---

80. The Dioscuri were the twin Spartan heroes, Castor and Polydeuces: Polydeuces, the son of Zeus and Leda, was immortal, while Castor was the mortal son of Leda and her mortal husband. In return for their heroism, Zeus allowed them to share Polydeuces' immortality.

81. In fact, neither of these phrases as quoted occurs in Homer. The etymology posited here is formed of the verb *ganysthai* (to rejoice) and the noun *mēdea* (counsels).

82. This passage explicitly rejects the erotic interpretation of the relationship advanced by Aeschylus and cited by Phaedrus' speech in Plato (5.7.179–180).

83. Orestes grew up with Pylades, and Pylades followed him even when he was pursued all over Greece by the Furies as punishment for killing his mother. Pirithous accompanied Theseus on many adventures, including a trip to the Underworld.

who wallow in self-indulgence by saying that the most mighty army would be one composed of lovers and their favorites.[84] **[8.33]** For he said that in his opinion they would be most ashamed to desert each other—an amazing thing to say. Will those who are accustomed to ignore censure and behave shamelessly towards one another really be the most ashamed to do something shameful? **[8.34]** As evidence for his claim he added that the Thebans and Eleans have learned that it is true.[85] He said that, though they sleep with their favorites, in preparation for battle they still station them at their side. But this evidence has no application to our case, since, although this practice is normal for them, it is the object of the greatest reproach among us; and, to me at least, those who station their favorites at their sides seem to believe that, were the boys not beside them, they would not do the deeds of noble men. **[8.35]** The Spartans (who think that even someone who feels desire for the body will come to nothing fine or noble) make the objects of their love so perfectly noble that even if they are stationed with strangers, or in a different city from their lover, they are equally ashamed to desert those who are there. For they consider Modesty, not Immodesty, a goddess.[86]

[8.36] "I think we would all agree on what I am saying if we think about it in this way: in which of the two ways would you prefer a boy to be loved to whom you were to entrust your money or your children or the services that you expect to be reciprocated? For my part, I think that even the man who focuses on the external appearance of the beloved would rather entrust all these things to the boy who is loved for his soul.

[8.37] "It seems to me, Callias, that you should thank the gods that they have cast in you a love for Autolycus. For it is clear how eager for honor he is, having endured much toil and much pain in order that he might be proclaimed victorious in the pancratium. **[8.38]** But if he hopes not only to make himself and his father glorious, but also through his bravery to be able to benefit his friends and strengthen his city by raising trophies over its enemies, and in this way to become admired and well known among both Greeks and barbarians, if this is what he hopes for, surely you must realize that he would regard with the greatest respect whoever he thought would be the most helpful companion in these endeavors? **[8.39]** If you wish to satisfy him, you must study what Themistocles had to know to be able to liberate Greece, and what Pericles had to know to be considered the

---

84. In fact, it is not Pausanias, but Phaedrus, who makes this proposal (5.7.178–79).

85. Pausanias does mention the acceptability of pederasty among the Thebans and Eleans (5.7.182), but he does not do so in the context of describing their military arrangements. Xenophon is either conflating the two passages or, less probably, referring to an actual speech of the historical Pausanias.

86. For Xenophon's view of Spartan customs in this regard, see 2.9 and 2.10.

best advisor for his fatherland.[87] You must examine also how Solon's pursuit of knowledge enabled him to lay down the best laws for this city, and you must track down those practices that cause the Spartans to be considered the best leaders; after all, you are their consular representative, and their most important people are always having dinner at your house.

[8.40] "You may be sure that, if you wished, our city would soon put itself in your hands. You have the greatest advantages: you are of noble blood, a priest of the gods who have been worshipped since Erechtheus and who fought against the Persians with Dionysus as their leader;[88] you are considered to have discharged your holy office at the festival most magnificently, surpassing your predecessors; and you have a body that, although the most handsome in the city, is also able to endure toil. [8.41] And if I seem to you to speak of matters too weighty for a drinking party, do not be surprised. I have always joined the city in loving those who are noble in nature and strive eagerly after excellence."

[8.42] While the others began to discuss what had been said, Autolycus looked at Callias, and Callias, looking over to him, said, "So, Socrates, will you pimp my charms to the city,[89] so that I may go into politics and forever gain her favor?"

[8.43] "Absolutely, by Zeus," he said, "At least if men see that you care for excellence in reality and not in appearance. For, when put to the test, a false reputation is soon found out, but true nobility, so long as a god does not harm it, always confers an ever more brilliant glory through its deeds."

[9.1] The conversation stopped there. As it was now time for his walk, Autolycus rose to leave, and his father Lycon went out with him. As Lycon did so, he turned and said, "By Hera, Socrates, you seem to me to be a good and noble man."[90]

[9.2] After this, a throne was first placed in the room and the Syracusan came in and said, "Gentlemen, Ariadne is about to enter the wedding chamber she shares with Dionysus,[91] and after this Dionysus will come

---

87. Themistocles was the Athenian admiral responsible for the Persians' defeat at Salamis in 480 B.C.E.; Pericles was Athens' leading statesman at the beginning of the Peloponnesian War.

88. Callias belonged to the ancient Eleusinian clan of the Kerykes, and held the office of torch-carrier in the Eleusinian mysteries. Herodotus 8.65 tells of miraculous occurrences involving Dionysus and the other Eleusinian deities before the decisive Greek victory over the Persians at Salamis.

89. Earlier in the dialogue (4.56–64), Socrates had ironically declared that the quality he took most pride in was his ability to act as a pimp or procurer—someone who could teach men how to make themselves more attractive to the city.

90. This remark may be intended as a dramatic irony, if this Lycon is in fact the same man who accused Socrates of corrupting the youth at his trial (see n. 65).

91. Ariadne was the wife of Dionysus. A ritual at Athens' annual Anthesteria festival re-enacted their wedding.

from drinking with the gods and will go in to see her, and then they will make love to each other."

[9.3] The first thing to happen after this was that Ariadne, dressed as a bride, came in and sat on the throne. Although Dionysus could not yet be seen, a flute began to play the music of Bacchus, and then all appreciated the dancing master. As soon as she heard the music, Ariadne made it clear by her gestures that she was glad to hear it. She did not go to meet him, nor even stood up, but it was clear that she remained still only with great difficulty. [9.4] When Dionysus saw her, he danced over to her as one who was very much in love would dance and sat on her lap and, taking her in his arms, he kissed her. She looked bashful, but still returned his embrace lovingly, and as the dinner guests watched they both clapped and called for more. [9.5] But when Dionysus stood up and made Ariadne stand up with him, it was then possible to see the shapes made by those who kiss and embrace each other, and when they saw a truly beautiful Dionysus and an Ariadne truly in the bloom of youth, not play-acting, but actually kissing each other with their lips, all who were watching were aroused. [9.6] They actually heard Dionysus asking Ariadne if she loved him, and Ariadne swearing that she did so insistently that not only Dionysus, but all who were present would have sworn that the boy and the girl loved each other. For they did not seem to have been taught the poses, but seemed to have been allowed to do what they had long since desired. [9.7] And, when at length the dinner guests saw them leaving with their arms about each other to go to the marriage bed, those who were not married swore they would marry, and those who were married mounted their horses and rode off to their wives so as to enjoy the same pleasures. But Socrates and those of the others who remained went off with Callias to join Lycon and his son on their walk, and that is how the dinner ended.

5.9 Plato, *Phaedrus* 227A–257B

Socrates and Phaedrus meet on a street in Athens. The dramatic date of the dialogue is unclear.

SOCRATES: [227] Phaedrus, my friend! Where have you been? And where are you going?

PHAEDRUS: I was with Lysias, the son of Cephalus,[92] Socrates, and I am going for a walk outside the city walls because I was with him for a long time, sitting there the whole morning. You see, I'm keeping in mind the

---

92. This is Lysias the orator (4.2–4). His father, Cephalus, was a wealthy metic, at whose house Plato's *Republic* is set.

advice of our mutual friend Acumenus,[93] who says it's more refreshing to walk along country roads than city streets.

SOCRATES: He is quite right, too, my friend. So Lysias, I take it, is in the city?

PHAEDRUS: Yes, at the house of Epicrates, which used to belong to Morychus, near the temple of the Olympian Zeus.

SOCRATES: What were you doing there? Oh, I know: Lysias must have been entertaining you with a feast of eloquence.

PHAEDRUS: You'll hear about it, if you are free to come along and listen.

SOCRATES: What? Don't you think I would consider it "more important than the most pressing engagement," as Pindar says, to hear how you and Lysias spent your time?

PHAEDRUS: Lead the way, then.

SOCRATES: If only you will tell me.

PHAEDRUS: In fact, Socrates, you're just the right person to hear the speech that occupied us, since, in a roundabout way, it was about love. It is aimed at seducing a beautiful boy, but the speaker is not in love with him—this is actually what is so clever and elegant about it: Lysias argues that it is better to give your favors to someone who does not love you than to someone who does.

SOCRATES: What a wonderful man! I wish he would write that you should give your favors to a poor rather than to a rich man, to an older rather than to a younger one—that is, to someone like me and most other people: then his speeches would be really sophisticated, and they'd contribute to the public good besides! In any case, I am so eager to hear it that I would follow you even if you were walking all the way to Megara, as Herodicus[94] recommends, to touch the wall and come back again.

PHAEDRUS: What on Earth do you mean, Socrates? [228] Do you think that a mere dilettante like me could recite from memory in a manner worthy of him a speech that Lysias, the best of our writers, took such time and trouble to compose? Far from it—though actually I would rather be able to do that than come into a large fortune!

SOCRATES: Oh, Phaedrus, if I don't know my Phaedrus I must be forgetting who I am myself—and neither is the case. I know very well that he did not hear Lysias' speech only once: he asked him to repeat it over and over again, and Lysias was eager to oblige.[95] But not even that was enough for him. In the end, he took the book himself and pored over

93. A physician, the father of Eryximachus.

94. Another physician, born in Megara, which was on the isthmus some twenty-six miles from Athens.

95. Socrates here parodies the style of a forensic narrative such as one commonly finds in Lysias' speeches.

the parts he liked best. He sat reading all morning long, and when he got tired, he went for a walk, having learned—I am quite sure—the whole speech by heart, unless it was extraordinarily long. So he started for the country, where he could practice reciting it. And running into a man who is sick with passion for hearing speeches, seeing him—just seeing him—he was filled with delight: he had found a partner for his frenzied dance,[96] and he urged him to lead the way. But when that lover of speeches asked him to recite it, he played coy and pretended that he did not want to. In the end, of course, he was going to recite it even if he had to force an unwilling audience to listen. So, please, Phaedrus, beg him to do it right now. He'll do it soon enough anyway.

PHAEDRUS: Well, I'd better try to recite it as best I can: you'll obviously not leave me in peace until I do so one way or another.

SOCRATES: You are absolutely right.

PHAEDRUS: That's what I'll do, then. But, Socrates, it really is true that I did not memorize the speech word for word; instead, I will give a careful summary of its general sense, listing all the ways he said the lover differs from the non-lover, in the proper order.

SOCRATES: Only if you first show me what you are holding in your left hand under your cloak, my friend. I strongly suspect you have the speech itself. And if I'm right, you can be sure that, though I love you dearly, I'll never, as long as Lysias himself is present, allow you to practice your own speechmaking on me. Come on, then, show me.

PHAEDRUS: Enough, enough. You've dashed my hopes of using you as my training partner, Socrates. All right, where do you want to sit while we read?

SOCRATES: Let's leave the path here and walk along the Ilissus; [229] then we can sit quietly wherever we find the right spot.

PHAEDRUS: How lucky, then, that I am barefoot today—you, of course, are always so. The easiest thing to do is to walk right in the stream; this way, we'll also get our feet wet, which is very pleasant, especially at this hour and season.

SOCRATES: Lead the way, then, and find us a place to sit.

PHAEDRUS: Do you see that very tall plane tree?

SOCRATES: Of course.

PHAEDRUS: It's shady, with a light breeze; we can sit or, if we prefer, lie down on the grass there.

SOCRATES: Lead on, then.

---

96. The reference here is to the ecstatic dance of the Corybantes, mythical attendants of the Asian mother goddess, Cybele.

PHAEDRUS: Tell me, Socrates, isn't it from somewhere near this stretch of the Ilissus that people say Boreas carried Oreithuia away?[97]

SOCRATES: So they say.

PHAEDRUS: Couldn't this be the very spot? The stream is lovely, pure and clear: just right for girls to be playing nearby.

SOCRATES: No, it is two or three hundred yards farther downstream, where one crosses to get to the district of Agra. I think there is even an altar to Boreas there.

PHAEDRUS: I hadn't noticed it. But tell me, Socrates, in the name of Zeus, do you really believe that that legend is true?

SOCRATES: Actually, it would not be out of place for me to reject it, as our intellectuals do.[98] I could then tell a clever story: I could claim that a gust of the North Wind blew her over the rocks where she was playing with Pharmaceia; and once she was killed that way people said she had been carried off by Boreas—or was it, perhaps, from the Areopagus?[99] The story is also told that she was carried away from there instead. Now, Phaedrus, such explanations are amusing enough, but they are a job for a man I cannot envy at all. He'd have to be far too ingenious and work too hard—mainly because after that he will have to go on and give a rational account of the form of the Hippocentaurs, and then of the Chimera; and a whole flood of Gorgons and Pegasuses[100] and other monsters, in large numbers and absurd forms, will overwhelm him. Anyone who does not believe in them, who wants to explain them away and make them plausible by means of some sort of rough ingenuity, will need a great deal of time.

But I have no time for such things; and the reason, my friend, is this. [230] I am still unable, as the Delphic inscription orders, to know myself; and it really seems to me ridiculous to look into other things before I have understood that. This is why I do not concern myself with them. I accept what is generally believed, and, as I was just saying, I look not into them but into my own self: Am I a beast more complicated and savage than Typhon,[101] or am I a tamer, simpler animal with a share in

97. Oreithuia was the daughter of one of Athens' early mythological kings; Boreas is the spirit of the north wind.

98. Socrates here alludes to sophists like Prodicus, who attempted to give rational or allegorical explanations of myths and gods.

99. The "Hill of Ares," northwest of the Acropolis in Athens and the seat of the Council of the Areopagus.

100. Centaurs were part horse, part men; the Chimera a beast with fire-breathing lion and goat heads and a snake tail; the Gorgons were winged women with snake hair; Pegasus was a winged horse.

101. A monster with one hundred fire-breathing heads.

a divine and gentle nature? But look, my friend—while we were talking, haven't we reached the tree you were taking us to?

PHAEDRUS: That's the one.

SOCRATES: By Hera, it really is a beautiful resting place. The plane tree is tall and very broad; the chaste-tree, high as it is, is wonderfully shady, and since it is in full bloom, the whole place is filled with its fragrance. From under the plane tree the loveliest spring runs with very cool water —our feet can testify to that. The place appears to be dedicated to Achelous[102] and some of the Nymphs, if we can judge from the statues and votive offerings. Feel the freshness of the air; how pretty and pleasant it is; how it echoes with the summery, sweet song of the cicadas' chorus! The most exquisite thing of all, of course, is the grassy slope: it rises so gently that you can rest your head perfectly when you lie down on it. You've really been the most marvelous guide, my dear Phaedrus.

PHAEDRUS: And you, my remarkable friend, appear to be totally out of place. Really, just as you say, you seem to need a guide, not to be one of the locals. Not only do you never travel abroad—as far as I can tell, you never even set foot beyond the city walls.

SOCRATES: Forgive me, my friend. I am devoted to learning; landscapes and trees have nothing to teach me—only the people in the city can do that. But you, I think, have found a potion to charm me into leaving. For just as people lead hungry animals forward by shaking branches of fruit before them, you can lead me all over Attica or anywhere else you like simply by waving in front of me the leaves of a book containing a speech. But now, having gotten as far as this place this time around, I intend to lie down; so choose whatever position you think will be most comfortable for you, and read on.

PHAEDRUS: Listen, then:

"You understand my situation: I've told you how good it would be for us, in my opinion, if this worked out. [231] In any case, I don't think I should lose the chance to get what I am asking for,[103] merely because I don't happen to be in love with you.

"A man in love will wish he had not done you any favors once his desire dies down, but the time will never come for a man who's not in love to change his mind. That is because the favors he does for you are not forced but voluntary; and he does the best that he possibly can for you, just as he would for his own business.

"Besides, a lover keeps his eye on the balance sheet—where his interests have suffered from love, and where he has done well; and when

102. A river god.
103. Commentators generally understand the speaker to be asking for sex without love.

he adds up all the trouble he has taken, he thinks he's long since given the boy he loved a fair return. A non-lover, on the other hand, can't complain about love's making him neglect his own business; he can't keep a tab on the trouble he's been through, or blame you for the quarrels he's had with his relatives. Take away all those headaches and there's nothing left for him to do but put his heart into whatever he thinks will give pleasure.

"Besides, suppose a lover does deserve to be honored because, as they say, he is the best friend his loved one will ever have, and he stands ready to please his boy with all those words and deeds that are so annoying to everyone else. It's easy to see (if he is telling the truth) that the next time he falls in love he will care more for his new love than for the old one, and it's clear he'll treat the old one shabbily whenever that will please the new one.

"And anyway, what sense does it make to throw away something like that[104] on a person who has fallen into such a miserable condition that those who have suffered it don't even try to defend themselves against it? A lover will admit that he's more sick than sound in the head. He's well aware that he is not thinking straight; but he'll say he can't get himself under control. So when he does start thinking straight, why would he stand by decisions he had made when he was sick?

"Another point: if you were to choose the best of those who are in love with you, you'd have a pretty small group to pick from; but you'll have a large group if you don't care whether he loves you or not and just pick the one who suits you best; and in that larger pool you'll have a much better hope of finding someone who deserves your friendship.

"Now suppose you're afraid of conventional standards and the stigma that will come to you if people find out about this. [232] Well, it stands to reason that a lover—thinking that everyone else will admire him for his success as much as he admires himself—will fly into words and proudly declare to all and sundry that his labors were not in vain. Someone who does not love you, on the other hand, can control himself and will choose to do what is best, rather than seek the glory that comes from popular reputation.

"Besides, it's inevitable that a lover will be found out: many people will see that he devotes his life to following the boy he loves. The result is that whenever people see you talking with him they'll think you are spending time together just before or just after giving way to desire. But they won't even begin to find fault with people for spending time

---

104. Presumably a boy's chastity.

together if they are not lovers; they know one has to talk to someone, either out of friendship or to obtain some other pleasure.

"Another point: have you been alarmed by the thought that it is hard for friendships to last? Or that when people break up, it's ordinarily just as awful for one side as it is for the other, but when you've given up what is most important to you already,[105] then your loss is greater than his? If so, it would make more sense for you to be afraid of lovers. For a lover is easily annoyed, and whatever happens, he'll think it was designed to hurt him. That is why a lover prevents the boy he loves from spending time with other people. He's afraid that wealthy men will outshine him with their money, while men of education will turn out to have the advantage of greater intelligence. And he watches like a hawk everyone who may have any other advantage over him! Once he's persuaded you to turn those people away, he'll have you completely isolated from friends; and if you show more sense than he does in looking after your own interests, you'll come to quarrel with him.

"But if a man really does not love you, if it is only because of his excellence that he got what he asked for, then he won't be jealous of the people who spend time with you. Quite the contrary! He'll hate anyone who does not want to be with you; he'll think they look down on him while those who spend time with you do him good; so you should expect friendship, rather than enmity, to result from this affair.

"Another point: lovers generally start to desire your body before they know your character or have any experience of your other traits, with the result that even they can't tell whether they'll still want to be friends with you after their desire has passed. [233] Non-lovers, on the other hand, are friends with you even before they achieve their goal, and you've no reason to expect that benefits received[106] will ever detract from their friendship for you. No, those things will stand as reminders of more to come.

"Another point: you can expect to become a better person if you are won over by me, rather than by a lover. A lover will praise what you say and what you do far beyond what is best, partly because he is afraid of being disliked, and partly because desire has impaired his judgment. Here is how love draws conclusions: When a lover suffers a reverse that would cause no pain to anyone else, love makes him think he's accursed! And when he has a stroke of luck that's not worth a moment's pleasure, love compels him to sing its praises. The result is, you should feel sorry for lovers, not admire them.

105. Again, this seems to be a periphrasis for a boy's chastity or reputation.
106. Presumably sexual favors.

"If my argument wins you over, I will, first of all, give you my time with no thought of immediate pleasure; I will plan instead for the benefits that are to come, since I am master of myself and have not been overwhelmed by love. Small problems will not make me very hostile, and big ones will make me only gradually, and only a little, angry. I will forgive you for unintentional errors and do my best to keep you from going wrong intentionally. All this, you see, is the proof of a friendship that will last a long time.

"Have you been thinking that there can be no strong friendship in the absence of erotic love? Then you ought to remember that we would not care so much about our children if that were so, or about our fathers and mothers. And we wouldn't have had any trustworthy friends, since those relationships did not come from such a desire but from doing quite different things.

"Besides, if it were true that we ought to give the biggest favor to those who need it most, then we should all be helping out the very poorest people, not the best ones, because people we've saved from the worst troubles will give us the most thanks. For instance, the right people to invite to a dinner party would be beggars and people who need to sate their hunger, because they're the ones who'll be fond of us, follow us, knock on our doors, take the most pleasure with the deepest gratitude, and pray for our success. No, it's proper, I suppose, to grant your favors to those who are best able to return them, not to those in the direst need —[234] that is, not to those who merely desire the thing, but to those who really deserve it—not to people who will take pleasure in the bloom of your youth, but to those who will share their goods with you when you are older; not to people who achieve their goal and then boast about it in public, but to those who will keep a modest silence with everyone; not to people whose devotion is short-lived, but to those who will be steady friends their whole lives; not to the people who look for an excuse to quarrel as soon as their desire has passed, but to those who will prove their worth when the bloom of your youth has faded. Now, remember what I said and keep this in mind: friends often criticize a lover for bad behavior; but no one close to a non-lover ever thinks that desire has led him into bad judgment about his interests.

"And now I suppose you'll ask me whether I'm urging you to give your favors to everyone who is not in love with you. No. As I see it, a lover would not ask you to give in to all your lovers either. You would not, in that case, earn as much gratitude from each recipient, and you would not be able to keep one affair secret from the others in the same way. But this sort of thing is not supposed to cause any harm, and really should work to the benefit of both sides.

"Well, I think this speech is long enough. If you are still longing for more, if you think I have passed over something, just ask."

How does the speech strike you, Socrates? Don't you think it's simply superb, especially in its choice of words?

SOCRATES: It's a miracle, my friend; I'm in ecstasy. And it's all your doing, Phaedrus: I was looking at you while you were reading and it seemed to me the speech had made you radiant with delight; and since I believe you understand these matters better than I do, I followed your lead, and following you I shared your Bacchic frenzy.[107]

PHAEDRUS: Come, Socrates, do you think you should joke about this?

SOCRATES: Do you really think I am joking, that I am not serious?

PHAEDRUS: You are not at all serious, Socrates. But now tell me the truth, in the name of Zeus, god of friendship: Do you think that any other Greek could say anything more impressive or more complete on this same subject?

SOCRATES: What? Must we praise the speech even on the ground that its author has said what the situation demanded, and not instead simply on the ground that he has spoken in a clear and concise manner, with a precise turn of phrase? If we must, I will have to go along for your sake, since—surely because I am so ignorant—that passed me by. [235] I paid attention only to the speech's style. As to the other part, I wouldn't even think that Lysias himself could be satisfied with it. For it seemed to me, Phaedrus—unless, of course, you disagree—that he said the same things two or even three times, as if he really didn't have much to say about the subject, almost as if he just weren't very interested in it. In fact, he seemed to me to be showing off, trying to demonstrate that he could say the same thing in two different ways, and say it just as well both times.

PHAEDRUS: You are absolutely wrong, Socrates. That is in fact the best thing about the speech: He has omitted nothing worth mentioning about the subject, so that no one will ever be able to add anything of value to complete what he has already said himself.

SOCRATES: You go too far: I can't agree with you about that. If, as a favor to you, I accept your view, I will stand refuted by all the wise men and women of old who have spoken or written about this subject.

PHAEDRUS: Who are these people? And where have you heard anything better than this?

SOCRATES: I can't tell you offhand, but I'm sure I've heard better somewhere; perhaps it was the lovely Sappho or the wise Anacreon or even

107. Intoxicated followers of Dionysus were thought to go wild and lose their civilized personalities.

some writer of prose. So, what's my evidence? The fact, my dear friend, that my breast is full and I feel I can make a different speech, even better than Lysias'. Now I am well aware that none of these ideas can have come from me—I know my own ignorance.[108] The only other possibility, I think, is that I was filled, like an empty jar, by the words of other people streaming in through my ears, though I'm so stupid that I've even forgotten where and from whom I heard them.

PHAEDRUS: But, my dear friend, you couldn't have said a better thing! Don't bother telling me when and from whom you've heard this, even if I ask you—instead, do exactly what you said: You've just promised to make another speech making more points, and better ones, without repeating a word from my book. And I promise you that, like the nine archons,[109] I shall set up in return a life-sized golden statue at Delphi, not only of myself but also of you.

SOCRATES: You're a real friend, Phaedrus, good as gold, to think I'm claiming that Lysias failed in absolutely every respect and that I can make a speech that is different on every point from his. I am sure that that couldn't happen even to the worst possible author. In our own case, for example, do you think that anyone could argue that one should favor the non-lover [236] rather than the lover without praising the former for keeping his wits about him or condemning the latter for losing his— points that are essential to make—and still have something left to say? I believe we must allow these points, and concede them to the speaker. In their case, we cannot praise their novelty but only their skillful arrange- ment; but we can praise both the arrangement and the novelty of the nonessential points that are harder to think up.

PHAEDRUS: I agree with you; I think that's reasonable. This, then, is what I shall do. I will allow you to presuppose that the lover is less sane than the non-lover—and if you are able to add anything of value to com- plete what we already have in hand, you will stand in hammered gold beside the offering of the Cypselids in Olympia.[110]

SOCRATES: Oh, Phaedrus, I was only criticizing your beloved[111] in order to tease you—did you take me seriously? Do you think I'd really try to match the product of his wisdom with a fancier speech?

---

108. Pretension to lack of knowledge was the hallmark of Socrates' irony.

109. The chief magistrates of Athens, who swore an oath to dedicate such a statue if they failed to uphold the laws.

110. The rulers of archaic Corinth. Among their offerings at Olympia was an ornate chest.

111. Socrates is here ironically adopting the language of love relationships to describe the non-lover, Lysias. Nothing should be inferred about the relative ages of Lysias and Phaedrus; if anything, Phaedrus still seems to be an impressionable and confused young man, as in the *Symposium*.

PHAEDRUS: Well, as far as that goes, my friend, you've fallen into your own trap. You have no choice but to give your speech as best you can: otherwise you will force us into trading vulgar jibes the way they do in comedy. Don't make me say what you said: "Socrates, if I don't know my Socrates, I must be forgetting who I am myself," or "He wanted to speak, but he was being coy." Get it into your head that we shall not leave here until you recite what you claimed to have "in your breast." We are alone, in a deserted place, and I am younger and stronger. From all this, "take my meaning"[112] and don't make me force you to speak when you can do so willingly.

SOCRATES: But, my dear Phaedrus, I'll be ridiculous—a mere dilettante, improvising on the same topics as a seasoned professional!

PHAEDRUS: Do you understand the situation? Stop playing hard to get! I know what I can say to make you give your speech.

SOCRATES: Then please don't say it!

PHAEDRUS: Oh, yes, I will. And what I say will be an oath. I swear to you —by which god, I wonder? How about this very plane tree?—I swear in all truth that, if you don't make your speech right next to this tree here, I shall never, never again recite another speech for you—I shall never utter another word about speeches to you!

SOCRATES: My oh my, what a horrible man you are! You've really found the way to force a lover of speeches to do just as you say!

PHAEDRUS: So why are you still twisting and turning like that?

SOCRATES: I'll stop—now that you've taken this oath. How could I possibly give up such treats?

PHAEDRUS: [237] Speak, then.

SOCRATES: Do you know what I'll do?

PHAEDRUS: What?

SOCRATES: I'll cover my head while I'm speaking. In that way, as I'm going through the speech as fast as I can, I won't get embarrassed by having to look at you and lose the thread of my argument.

PHAEDRUS: Just give your speech! You can do anything else you like.

SOCRATES: Come to me, O you clear-voiced Muses, whether you are called so because of the quality of your song or from the musical people of Liguria, "come, take up my burden" in telling the tale that this fine fellow forces upon me so that his companion may now seem to him even more clever than he did before:[113]

There once was a boy, a youth rather, and he was very beautiful, and had very many lovers. One of them was wily and had persuaded him that

112. A quote from Pindar.
113. Socrates parodies epic invocations of the Muses. The reference to Liguria (i.e., southern France) is a punning etymology of the Muses' epithet *ligeiai* (clear-voiced).

he was not in love, though he loved the lad no less than the others.[114] And once in pressing his suit to him, he tried to persuade him that he ought to give his favors to a man who did not love him rather than to one who did. And this is what he said:

"If you wish to reach a good decision on any topic, my boy, there is only one way to begin: You must know what the decision is about, or else you are bound to miss your target altogether. Ordinary people cannot see that they do not know the true nature of a particular subject, so they proceed as if they did; and because they do not work out an agreement at the start of the inquiry, they wind up as you would expect—in conflict with themselves and each other. Now you and I had better not let this happen to us, since we criticize it in others. Because you and I are about to discuss whether a boy should make friends with a man who loves him rather than with one who does not, we should agree on defining what love is and what effects it has. Then we can look back and refer to that as we try to find out whether to expect benefit or harm from love. Now, as everyone plainly knows, love is some kind of desire; but we also know that even men who are not in love have a desire for what is beautiful. So how shall we distinguish between a man who is in love and one who is not? We must realize that each of us is ruled by two principles which we follow wherever they lead: one is our inborn desire for pleasures, the other is our acquired judgment that pursues what is best. Sometimes these two are in agreement; but there are times when they quarrel inside us, and then sometimes one of them gains control, sometimes the other. Now when judgment is in control and leads us by reasoning toward what is best, that sort of self-control is called 'being in your right mind'; [238] but when desire takes command in us and drags us without reasoning toward pleasure, then its command is known as 'outrageousness.'[115] Now outrageousness has as many names as the forms it can take, and these are quite diverse. Whichever form stands out in a particular case gives its name to the person who has it—and that is not a pretty name to be called, not worth earning at all. If it is desire for food that overpowers a person's reasoning about what is best and suppresses his other desires, it is called gluttony and it gives him the name of a glutton, while if it is desire for drink that plays the tyrant and leads the man in that direction, we all know what name we'll call him then! And now it should be clear how to describe someone appropriately in the other cases: call the man by that name—sister to these others—that derives from the sister of these desires that controls him at the

---

114. Socrates is here calling attention to the paradox that any presumptive "non-lover" who desires a boy's favors must really desire (and therefore in some sense "love") the boy.

115. The respective Greek terms are *sophrosynē* and *hybris*.

time. As for the desire that has led us to say all this, it should be obvious already, but I suppose things said are always better understood than things unsaid: The unreasoning desire that overpowers a person's considered impulse to do right and is driven to take pleasure in beauty, its force reinforced by its kindred desires for beauty in human bodies—this desire, all-conquering in its forceful drive, takes its name from the word for force[116] and is called *erōs*."

There, Phaedrus my friend, don't you think, as I do, that I'm in the grip of something divine?

PHAEDRUS: This is certainly an unusual flow of words for you, Socrates.

SOCRATES: Then be quiet and listen. There's something really divine about this place, so don't be surprised if I'm quite taken by the Nymphs' madness as I go on with the speech. I'm on the edge of speaking in dithyrambs[117] as it is.

PHAEDRUS: Very true!

SOCRATES: Yes, and you're the cause of it. But hear me out; the attack may yet be prevented. That, however, is up to the god; what we must do is face the boy again in the speech:

"All right then, my brave friend, now we have a definition for the subject of our decision; now we have said what it really is; so let us keep that in view as we complete our discussion. What benefit or harm is likely to come from the lover or the non-lover to the boy who gives him favors? It is surely necessary that a man who is ruled by desire and is a slave to pleasure will turn his boy into whatever is most pleasing to himself. Now a sick man takes pleasure in anything that does not resist him, but sees anyone who is equal or superior to him as an enemy. [239] That is why a lover will not willingly put up with a boyfriend who is his equal or superior, but is always working to make the boy he loves weaker and inferior to himself. Now, the ignorant man is inferior to the wise one, the coward to the brave, the ineffective speaker to the trained orator, the slow-witted to the quick. By necessity, a lover will be delighted to find all these mental defects and more, whether acquired or innate in his boy; and if he does not, he will have to supply them or else lose the pleasure of the moment. The necessary consequence is that he will be jealous and keep the boy away from the good company of anyone who would make a better man of him; and that will cause him a great deal of harm, especially if he keeps him away from what would most improve his mind—and that is, in fact, divine philosophy, from which it is nec-

---

116. In Greek, *rhōmē*.

117. Choral poems narrating a myth. By this period, the dithyrambic style came to be associated with loosely constructed free verse. Dithyrambs were also sacred to Dionysus, so Socrates may intend this as a continuation of the metaphor of Bacchic frenzy.

essary for a lover to keep his boy a great distance away, out of fear the boy will eventually come to look down on him. He will have to invent other ways, too, of keeping the boy in total ignorance and so in total dependence on himself. That way the boy will give his lover the most pleasure, though the harm to himself will be severe. So it will not be of any use to your intellectual development to have as your mentor and companion a man who is in love.

"Now let's turn to your physical development. If a man is bound by necessity to chase pleasure at the expense of the good, what sort of shape will he want you to be in? How will he train you, if he is in charge? You will see that what he wants is someone who is soft, not muscular, and not trained in full sunlight but in dappled shade—someone who has never worked out like a man, never touched hard, sweaty exercise. Instead, he goes for a boy who has known only a soft unmanly style of life, who makes himself pretty with cosmetics because he has no natural color at all. There is no point in going on with this description: it is perfectly obvious what other sorts of behavior follow from this. We can take up our next topic after drawing all this to a head: the sort of body a lover wants in his boy is one that will give confidence to the enemy in a war or other great crisis while causing alarm to friends and even to his lovers. Enough of that; the point is obvious.

"Our next topic is the benefit or harm to your possessions that will come from a lover's care and company. Everyone knows the answer, especially a lover: His first wish will be for a boy who has lost his dearest, kindliest and godliest possessions—his mother and father and other close relatives. He would be happy to see the boy deprived of them, [240] since he would expect them either to block him from the sweet pleasure of the boy's company or to criticize him severely for taking it. What is more, a lover would think any money or other wealth the boy owns would only make him harder to snare and, once snared, harder to handle. It follows by absolute necessity that wealth in a boyfriend will cause his lover to envy him, while his poverty will be a delight. Furthermore, he will wish for the boy to stay wifeless, childless, and homeless for as long as possible, since that's how long he desires to go on plucking his sweet fruit.

"There are other troubles in life, of course, but some divinity has mixed most of them with a dash of immediate pleasure. A flatterer, for example, may be an awful beast and a dreadful nuisance, but nature makes flattery rather pleasant by mixing in a little culture with its words. So it is with a mistress—for all the harm we accuse her of causing—and with many other creatures of that character, and their callings: at least they are delightful company for a day. But besides being harmful to his boyfriend, a lover is simply disgusting to spend the day with. 'Youth delights youth,' as the old proverb runs—because, I suppose, friendship grows from similarity, as boys of the same age go after the same pleasures. But you can even have too much of people your own age. Besides, as they say, it is miserable for anyone to be forced into anything by necessity—and this (to say nothing of the age difference) is most true for a boy with his lover. The older man clings to the younger day and night, never willing to leave him, driven by necessity and goaded on by the sting that gives him pleasure every time he sees, hears, touches, or perceives his boy in any way at all, so that he follows him around like a servant, with pleasure.

"As for the boy, however, what comfort or pleasure will the lover give to him during all the time they spend together? Won't it be disgusting in the extreme to see the face of that older man who's lost his looks? And everything that goes with that face—why, it is a misery even to hear them mentioned, let alone actually handle them, as you would constantly be forced to do! To be watched and guarded suspiciously all the time, with everyone! To hear praise of yourself that is out of place and excessive! And then to be falsely accused—which is unbearable when the man is sober and not only unbearable but positively shameful when he is drunk and lays into you with a pack of wild barefaced insults!

"While he is still in love he is harmful and disgusting, but after his love fades he breaks his trust with you for the future, in spite of all the promises he has made with all those oaths and entreaties [241] which just barely kept you in a relationship that was troublesome at the time, in hope of future benefits. So, then, by the time he should pay up, he has made a change and installed a new ruling government in himself: right-minded reason in place of the madness of love. The boy does not even realize that his lover is a different man. He insists on his reward for past favors and reminds him of what they had done and said before —as if he were still talking to the same man! The lover, however, is so ashamed that he does not dare tell the boy how much he has changed or that there is no way, now that he is in his right mind and under control again, that he can stand by the promises he had sworn to uphold when he was under that old mindless regime. He is afraid that if he acted as he had before he would turn out the same and revert to his old self. So now he is a refugee, fleeing from those old promises on which he must default by necessity; he, the former lover, has to switch roles and flee, since the coin has fallen the other way, while the boy must chase after him, angry and cursing. All along he has been completely unaware that he should never have given his favors to a man who was in love—and who therefore had by necessity lost his mind. He should much rather have done it for a man who was not in love and had his wits about him. Otherwise it follows necessarily that he'd be giving himself to a man who is deceitful, irritable, jealous, disgusting, harmful to his property, harmful to his physical fitness, and absolutely devastating to the cultivation of his soul, which truly is, and will always be, the most valuable thing to gods and men.

"These are the points you should bear in mind, my boy. You should know that the friendship of a lover arises without any good will at all. No, like food, its purpose is to sate hunger. 'Do wolves love lambs? That's how lovers befriend a boy!'"

That's it, Phaedrus. You won't hear another word from me, and you'll have to accept this as the end of the speech.

PHAEDRUS: But I thought you were right in the middle—I thought you were about to speak at the same length about the non-lover, to list his good points and argue that it's better to give one's favors to him. So why are you stopping now, Socrates?

SOCRATES: Didn't you notice, my friend, that even though I am criticizing the lover, I have passed beyond lyric into epic poetry?[118] What do you suppose will happen to me if I begin to praise his opposite? Don't you realize that the Nymphs to whom you so cleverly exposed me will take complete possession of me? So I say instead, in a word, that every shortcoming for which we blamed the lover has its contrary advantage, and the non-lover possesses it. Why make a long speech of it? That's enough about them both. [242] This way my story will meet the end it deserves, and I will cross the river and leave before you make me do something even worse.

PHAEDRUS: Not yet, Socrates, not until this heat is over. Don't you see that it is almost exactly noon, "straight-up" as they say? Let's wait and discuss the speeches, and go as soon as it turns cooler.

SOCRATES: You're really superhuman when it comes to speeches, Phaedrus; you're truly amazing. I'm sure you've brought into being more of the speeches that have been given during your lifetime than anyone else, whether you composed them yourself or in one way or another forced others to make them; with the single exception of Simmias the Theban,[119] you are far ahead of the rest. Even as we speak, I think, you're managing to cause me to produce yet another one.

PHAEDRUS: Oh, how wonderful! But what do you mean? What speech?

SOCRATES: My friend, just as I was about to cross the river, the familiar divine sign came to me which, whenever it occurs, holds me back from

---

118. Socrates said in 238 that he was speaking in dithyrambs, and the last line of his speech has the metrical form of an epic line.

119. Another of Socrates' companions and a major character in Plato's *Phaedo,* a dialogue on the immortality of the soul. This reference may adumbrate the discussion of the soul we are about to hear in Socrates' next speech.

something I am about to do. I thought I heard a voice coming from this very spot, forbidding me to leave until I made atonement for some offense against the gods. In effect, you see, I am a seer, and though I am not particularly good at it, still—like people who are just barely able to read and write—I am good enough for my own purposes. I recognize my offense clearly now. In fact, the soul too, my friend, is itself a sort of seer; that's why, almost from the beginning of my speech, I was disturbed by a very uneasy feeling, as Ibycus puts it, that "for offending the gods I am honored by men." But now I understand exactly what my offense has been.

PHAEDRUS: Tell me, what is it?

SOCRATES: Phaedrus, that speech you carried with you here—it was horrible, as horrible as the speech you made me give.

PHAEDRUS: How could that be?

SOCRATES: It was foolish and close to being impious. What could be more horrible than that?

PHAEDRUS: Nothing—if, of course, what you say is right.

SOCRATES: Well, then? Don't you believe that Love is the son of Aphrodite? Isn't he one of the gods?

PHAEDRUS: This is certainly what people say.

SOCRATES: Well, Lysias certainly doesn't and neither does your speech, which you charmed me through your potion into delivering myself. But if Love is a god or something divine—which he is—he can't be bad in any way; and yet our speeches just now spoke of him as if he were. That is their offense against Love. And they've compounded it with their utter foolishness in parading their dangerous falsehoods [243] and preening themselves over perhaps deceiving a few silly people and coming to be admired by them.

And so, my friend, I must purify myself. Now for those whose offense lies in telling false stories about matters divine, there is an ancient rite of purification—Homer did not know it, but Stesichorus[120] did. When he lost his sight for speaking ill of Helen, he did not, like Homer, remain in the dark about the reason why. On the contrary, true follower of the Muses that he was, he understood it and immediately composed these lines:

> There's no truth to that story:
> You never sailed that lovely ship,
> You never reached the tower of Troy.

---

120. A dithyrambic poet of the early sixth century B.C.E. His palinode, from which Socrates proceeds to quote, justified its narration of a radically new version of Helen's story, denying her presence in Troy, by claiming that she had caused the poet's blindness as a punishment for telling the traditional story about her infidelity.

And as soon as he completed the poem we call the *Palinode,* he immediately regained his sight. Now I will prove to be wiser than Homer and
Stesichorus to this small extent: I will try to offer my *Palinode to Love*
before I am punished for speaking ill of him—with my head bare, no
longer covered in shame.

PHAEDRUS: No words could be sweeter to my ears, Socrates.

SOCRATES: You see, my dear Phaedrus, you understand how shameless
the speeches were, my own as well as the one in your book. Suppose a
noble and gentle man, who was (or had once been) in love with a boy
of similar character, were to hear us say that lovers start serious quarrels
for trivial reasons and that, jealous of their beloved, they do him harm
—don't you think that man would think we had been brought up among
the most vulgar of sailors, totally ignorant of love among the freeborn?
Wouldn't he most certainly refuse to acknowledge the flaws we attributed
to Love?

PHAEDRUS: Most probably, Socrates.

SOCRATES: Well, that man makes me feel ashamed, and as I'm also afraid
of Love himself, I want to wash out the bitterness of what we've heard
with a more tasteful speech. And my advice to Lysias, too, is to write as
soon as possible a speech urging one to give similar favors to a lover
rather than to a non-lover.

PHAEDRUS: You can be sure he will. For once you have spoken in praise
of the lover, I will most definitely make Lysias write a speech on the
same topic.

SOCRATES: I do believe you will, so long as you are who you are.

PHAEDRUS: Speak on, then, in full confidence.

SOCRATES: Where, then, is the boy to whom I was speaking? Let him hear
this speech, too. Otherwise he may be too quick to give his favors to the
non-lover.

PHAEDRUS: He is here, always right by your side, whenever you want him.[121]

SOCRATES: [244] You'll have to understand, beautiful boy, that the previous speech was by Phaedrus, Pythocles' son, from Myrrhinus, while
the one I am about to deliver is by Stesichorus, Euphemus' son, from
Himera. And here is how the speech should go:

"'There's no truth to that story'—that when a lover is available you
should give your favors to a man who doesn't love you instead, because
he is in control of himself while the lover has lost his head. That would
have been fine to say if madness were bad, pure and simple; but, in fact,
the best things we have come from madness, when it is given as a gift
of the god.

---

121. Phaedrus may be ironically representing himself as a would-be beloved of Socrates,
like Alcibiades in the *Symposium.*

"The prophetess of Delphi and the priestesses at Dodona [122] are out of their minds when they perform that fine work of theirs for all of Greece, either for an individual person or for a whole city, but they accomplish little or nothing when they are in control of themselves. We will not mention the Sybil or the others who foretell many things by means of god-inspired prophetic trances and give sound guidance to many people—that would take too much time for a point that's obvious to everyone. But here's some evidence worth adding to our case: The people who designed our language in the old days never thought of madness as something to be ashamed of or worthy of blame; otherwise, they would not have used the word *manic* for the finest experts of all—the ones who tell the future—thereby weaving insanity into prophecy. They thought it was wonderful when it came as a gift of the god, and that's why they gave its name to prophecy; but nowadays people don't know the fine points, so they stick in a 't' and call it *mantic*. Similarly, the clear-headed study of the future, which uses birds and other signs, was originally called *oionoïstic*, since it uses reasoning to bring intelligence *(nous)* and learning *(historia)* into human thought; but now modern speakers call it *oiōnistic*, putting on airs with their long 'ō.' [123] To the extent, then, that prophecy, *mantic*, is more perfect and more admirable than sign-based prediction, *oiōnistic*, in both name and achievement, madness *(mania)* from a god is finer than self-control of human origin, according to the testimony of the ancient language givers.

"Next, madness can provide relief from the greatest plagues of trouble that beset certain families because of their guilt for ancient crimes: [124] it turns up among those who need a way out; it gives prophecies and takes refuge in prayers to the gods and in worship, discovering mystic rites and purifications that bring the man it touches through to safety for this and all time to come. So it is that the right sort of madness finds relief from present hardships for a man it has possessed.

[245] "Third comes the kind of madness that is possession by the Muses, which takes a tender virgin soul and awakens it to a Bacchic frenzy of songs and poetry that glorifies the achievements of the past and teaches them to future generations. If anyone comes to the gates of poetry and expects to become an adequate poet by acquiring expert

---

122. These prophetesses delivered their oracles in a trance-induced gibberish that could be understood only by the priests.

123. It was only with the new alphabet introduced at the end of the fifth century that omega (long "o") was distinguished from omicron (short "o"), which had been used to designate both vowels.

124. The reference would appear to be to epilepsy, the so-called sacred disease, the divine origins of which were debunked by Hippocratic medicine.

knowledge of the subject without the Muses' madness, he will fail, and his self-controlled verses will be eclipsed by the poetry of men who have been driven out of their minds.

"There you have some of the fine achievements—and I could tell you even more—that are due to god-sent madness. We must not have any fear on this particular point, then, and we must not let anyone disturb us or frighten us with the claim that you should prefer a friend who is in control of himself to one who is disturbed. Besides proving that point, if he is to win his case, our opponent must show that love is not sent by the gods as a benefit to a lover and his boy. And we, for our part, must prove the opposite, that this sort of madness is given us by the gods to ensure our greatest good fortune. It will be a proof that convinces the wise if not the clever.

"Now we must first understand the truth about the nature of the soul, divine or human, by examining what it does and what is done to it. Here begins the proof:

"Every soul is immortal. That is because whatever is always in motion is immortal, while what moves, and is moved by, something else stops living when it stops moving. So it is only what moves itself that never desists from motion, since it does not leave off being itself. In fact, this self-mover is also the source and spring of motion in everything else that moves; and a source has no beginning. That is because anything that has a beginning comes from some source, but there is no source for this, since a source that got its start from something else would no longer be the source. And since it cannot have a beginning, then necessarily it cannot be destroyed. That is because if a source were destroyed it could never get started again from anything else and nothing else could get started from it—that is, if everything gets started from a source. This then is why a self-mover is a source of motion. And that is incapable of being destroyed or starting up; otherwise all heaven and everything that has been started up would collapse, come to a stop, and never have cause to start moving again. But since we have found that a self-mover is immortal, we should have no qualms about declaring that this is the very essence and principle of a soul, for every bodily object that is moved from outside has no soul, while a body whose motion comes from within, from itself, does have a soul, that being the nature of a soul; and if this is so—that whatever moves itself is essentially a soul—then it follows necessarily that a soul should have neither birth nor death.

[246] "That, then, is enough about the soul's immortality. Now here is what we must say about its structure. To describe what the soul actually is would require a very long account, altogether a task for a god in every way; but to say what it is like is humanly possible and takes less time. So let us do the second in our speech. Let us then liken the soul to the

natural union of a team of winged horses and their charioteer. The
gods have horses and charioteers that are themselves all good and come
from good stock besides, while everyone else has a mixture. To begin
with, our driver is in charge of a pair of horses; second, one of his horses
is beautiful and good and from stock of the same sort, while the other
is the opposite and has the opposite sort of bloodline. This means that
chariot-driving in our case is inevitably a painfully difficult business.

"And now I should try to tell you why living things are said to include
both mortal and immortal beings. All soul looks after all that lacks a
soul, and patrols all of heaven, taking different shapes at different times.
So long as its wings are in perfect condition it flies high, and the entire
universe is its dominion; but a soul that sheds its wings wanders until it
lights on something solid, where it settles and takes on an earthly body,
which then, owing to the power of this soul, seems to move itself. The
whole combination of soul and body is called a living thing, or animal,
and has the designation 'mortal' as well. Such a combination cannot
be immortal, not on any reasonable account. In fact it is pure fiction,
based neither on observation nor on adequate reasoning, that a god is
an immortal living thing which has a body and a soul, and that these are
bound together by nature for all time—but of course we must let this
be as it may please the gods, and speak accordingly.

"Let us turn to what causes the shedding of the wings, what makes
them fall away from a soul. It is something of this sort: By their nature
wings have the power to lift up heavy things and raise them aloft where
the gods all dwell, and so, more than anything that pertains to the body,
they are akin to the divine, which has beauty, wisdom, goodness, and
everything of that sort. These nourish the soul's wings, which grow best
in their presence; but foulness and ugliness make the wings shrink and
disappear.

"Now Zeus, the great commander in heaven, drives his winged chariot
first in the procession, looking after everything and putting all things in
order. [247] Following him is an army of gods and spirits arranged in
eleven sections. Hestia [125] is the only one who remains at the home of
the gods; all the rest of the twelve are lined up in formation, each god in
command of the unit to which he is assigned. Inside heaven are many
wonderful places from which to look and many aisles which the blessed
gods take up and back, each seeing to his own work, while anyone who
is able and wishes to do so follows along, since jealousy has no place
in the gods' chorus. When they go to feast at the banquet they have a

---

125. The goddess of the hearth and thus a symbol of the home. Traditionally there were
twelve Olympians.

steep climb to the high tier at the rim of heaven; on this slope the gods' chariots move easily, since they are balanced and well under control, but the other chariots barely make it. The heaviness of the bad horse drags its charioteer toward the Earth and weighs him down if he has failed to train it well, and this causes the most extreme toil and struggle that a soul will face. But when the souls we call immortals reach the top, they move outward and take their stand on the high ridge of heaven, where its circular motion carries them around as they stand while they gaze upon what is outside heaven.[126]

"The place beyond heaven—none of our earthly poets has ever sung or ever will sing its praises enough! Still, this is the way it is—risky as it may be, you see, I must attempt to speak the truth, especially since the truth is my subject. What is in this place is without color and without shape and without solidity, a being that really is what it is, the subject of all true knowledge, visible only to intelligence, the soul's steersman. Now a god's mind is nourished by intelligence and pure knowledge, as is the mind of any soul that is concerned to take in what is appropriate to it, and so it is delighted at last to be seeing what is real and watching what is true, feeding on all this and feeling wonderful, until the circular motion brings it around to where it started. On the way around it has a view of Justice as it is; it has a view of Self-control; it has a view of Knowledge—not the knowledge that is close to change, that becomes different as it knows the different things which we consider real down here.[127] No, it is the knowledge of what really is what it is. And when the soul has seen all the things that are as they are and feasted on them, it sinks back inside heaven and goes home. On its arrival, the charioteer stables the horses by the manger, throws in ambrosia, and gives them nectar to drink besides.

[248] "Now that is the life of the gods. As for the other souls, one that follows a god most closely, making itself most like that god, raises the head of its charioteer up to the place outside and is carried around in the circular motion with the others. Although distracted by the horses, this soul does have a view of Reality, just barely. Another soul rises at one time and falls at another, and because its horses pull it violently in different directions, it sees some real things and misses others. The remaining souls are all eagerly straining to keep up, but are unable to rise; they are carried around below the surface, trampling and striking

126. The Forms, immaterial entities that are the primary object of definition and of which earthly objects are merely imperfect imitations.

127. In other words, the phenomenal world is always in a state of flux, such that constant realities (e.g., the Form of Horse) appear in different and changing manifestations (e.g., individual horses, each appearing different over time).

one another as each tries to get ahead of the others. The result is terribly noisy, very sweaty, and disorderly. Many souls are crippled by the incompetence of the drivers, and many wings break much of their plumage. After so much trouble, they all leave the sight of reality unsatisfied, and when they have gone they will depend on what they think is nourishment—their own opinions.

"The reason there is so much eagerness to see the plain where truth stands is that this pasture has the grass that is the right food for the best part of the soul, and it is the nature of the wings that lift up the soul to be nourished by it. Besides, the law of Destiny is this: If any soul becomes a companion to a god and catches sight of any true thing, it will be unharmed until the next circuit; and if it is able to do this every time, it will always be safe.[128] If, on the other hand, it does not see anything true because it could not keep up, and by some accident[129] takes on a burden of forgetfulness and wrongdoing, then it is weighed down, sheds its wings and falls to earth. At that point, according to the law, the soul is not born into a wild animal in its first incarnation; but a soul that has seen the most will be planted in the seed of a man who will become a lover of wisdom or of beauty,[130] or who will be cultivated in the arts and prone to erotic love. The second sort of soul will be put into someone who will be a lawful king or warlike commander; the third, a statesman, a manager of a household, or a financier; the fourth will be a trainer who loves exercise or a doctor who cures the body; the fifth will lead the life of a prophet or priest of the mysteries. To the sixth the life of a poet or some other representational artist is properly assigned; to the seventh the life of a manual laborer or farmer; to the eighth the career of a sophist or demagogue, and to the ninth a tyrant.

"Of all these, any who have led their lives with justice will change to a better fate, and any who have led theirs with injustice, to a worse one. In fact, no soul returns to the place from which it came for ten thousand years, since its wings will not grow before then, [249] except for the soul of a man who practices philosophy without guile or who loves boys philosophically. If, after the third cycle of one thousand years, the last-mentioned souls have chosen such a life three times in a row, they grow their wings back, and they depart in the three-thousandth year. As for the rest, once their first life is over, they come to judgment; and, once judged, some are condemned to go to places of punishment beneath the earth and pay the full penalty for their injustice, while the others are

128. In other words, it will not drop out of orbit and enter into a body.
129. I.e., by collision with other souls.
130. I.e., a philosopher or musician, who loves ideal beauty. The following hierarchy makes it clear that Plato regards representational artists as inferior, lovers of mere appearances.

lifted up by justice to a place in heaven where they live in the manner the life they led in human form has earned them. In the thousandth year both groups arrive at a choice and allotment of second lives, and each soul chooses the life it wants. From there, a human soul can enter a wild animal, and a soul that was once human can move from an animal to a human being again. But a soul that never saw the truth cannot take a human shape, since a human being must understand speech in terms of general forms, proceeding to bring many perceptions together into a reasoned unity. That process is the recollection of the things our soul saw when it was traveling with god, when it disregarded the things we now call real and lifted up its head to what is truly real instead.

"For just this reason it is fair that only a philosopher's mind grows wings, since its memory always keeps it as close as possible to those realities by being close to which the gods are divine. A man who uses reminders of these things[131] correctly is always at the highest, most perfect level of initiation, and he is the only one who is perfect as perfect can be. He stands outside human concerns and draws close to the divine; ordinary people think he is disturbed and rebuke him for this, unaware that he is possessed by god. Now this takes me to the whole point of my discussion of the fourth kind of madness—that which someone shows when he sees the beauty we have down here and is reminded of true beauty; then he takes wing and flutters in his eagerness to rise up, but is unable to do so; and he gazes aloft, like a bird, paying no attention to what is down below—and that is what brings on him the charge that he has gone mad. This is the best and noblest of all the forms that possession by god can take for anyone who has it or is connected to it, and when someone who loves beautiful boys is touched by this madness he is called a lover. As I said, nature requires that the soul of every human being has seen reality; otherwise, no soul could have entered this sort of living thing. [250] But not every soul is easily reminded of the reality there by what it finds here—not souls that got only a brief glance at the reality there, not souls who had such bad luck when they fell down here that they were twisted by bad company into lives of injustice so that they forgot the sacred objects they had seen before. Only a few remain whose memory is good enough; and they are startled when they see an image of what they saw up there. Then they are beside themselves, and their experience is beyond their comprehension because they cannot fully grasp what it is that they are seeing.

"Justice and self-control do not shine out through their images down here, and neither do the other objects of the soul's admiration; the

---

131. Phenomenal appearances in this life are "reminders" of the ideal forms glimpsed when our souls were in orbit with those of the gods.

senses are so murky that only a few people are able to make out, with difficulty, the original of the likenesses they encounter here. But beauty was radiant to see at that time when the souls, along with the glorious chorus (we[132] were with Zeus, while others followed other gods), saw that blessed and spectacular vision and were ushered into the mystery that we may rightly call the most blessed of all. And we who celebrated it were wholly perfect and free of all the troubles that awaited us in time to come, and we gazed in rapture at sacred revealed objects that were perfect, and simple, and unshakeable and blissful. That was the ultimate vision, and we saw it in pure light because we were pure ourselves, not buried in this thing we are carrying around now, which we call a body, locked in it like an oyster in its shell.

"Well, all that was for love of a memory that made me stretch out my speech in longing for the past. Now beauty, as I said, was radiant among the other objects; and now that we have come down here we grasp it sparkling through the clearest of our senses. Vision, of course, is the sharpest of our bodily senses, although it does not see wisdom. It would awaken a terribly powerful love if an image of wisdom came through our sight as clearly as beauty does, and the same goes for the other objects of inspired love. But now beauty alone has this privilege, to be the most clearly visible and the most loved. Of course a man who was initiated long ago or who has become defiled is not to be moved abruptly from here to a vision of Beauty itself when he sees what we call beauty here;[133] so instead of gazing at the latter reverently, he surrenders to pleasure and sets out in the manner of a four-footed beast, eager to make babies; and, wallowing in vice, he goes after unnatural pleasure too,[134] without a trace of fear or shame. [251] A recent initiate, however, one who has seen much in heaven—when he sees a godlike face or bodily form that has captured Beauty well, first he shudders and a fear comes over him like those he felt at the earlier time; then he gazes at him with the reverence due a god, and if he weren't afraid people would think him completely mad, he'd even sacrifice to his boy as if he were the image of a god. Once he has looked at him, his chill gives way to sweating and a high fever, because the stream of beauty that pours into him through his eyes warms him up and waters the growth of his wings.[135] Meanwhile,

132. Socrates speaks of himself and other philosophers.

133. I.e., earthly or phenomenal beauty, as opposed to the ideal Beauty of the Forms.

134. I.e., homosexual copulation. The Greek is *para physin*, which is not so much "contrary to nature" as "deviating from nature." See 5.10 for the same phrase.

135. Socrates is here relying on a theory of vision advocated by Empedocles and the atomists, holding that material films or effluences stream off all objects and enter the eyes. He also appears to be drawing on the Hippocratic theory of physical processes being determined by the circulation of fluids within the body.

the heat warms him and melts the places where the wings once grew, places that were long ago closed off with hard scabs to keep the sprouts from coming back; but as nourishment flows in, the feather shafts swell and rush to grow from their roots beneath every part of the soul (long ago, you see, the entire soul had wings). Now the whole soul seethes and throbs in this condition. Like a child whose teeth are just starting to grow in, and its gums are all aching and itching—that is exactly how the soul feels when it begins to grow wings. It swells up and aches and tingles as it grows them. But when it looks upon the beauty of the boy and takes in the stream of particles flowing into it from his beauty (that is why this is called 'desire'),[136] when it is watered and warmed by this, then all its pain subsides and is replaced by joy. When, however, it is separated from the boy and runs dry, then the openings of the passages in which the feathers grow are dried shut and keep the wings from sprouting. Then the stump of each feather is blocked in its desire and it throbs like a pulsing artery while the feather pricks at its passageway, with the result that the whole soul is stung all around, and the pain simply drives it wild—but then, when it remembers the boy in his beauty, it recovers its joy. From the outlandish mix of these two feelings—pain and joy— comes anguish and helpless raving: in its madness the lover's soul cannot sleep at night or stay put by day; it rushes, yearning, wherever it expects to see the person who has that beauty. When it does see him, it opens the sluice-gates of desire and sets free the parts that were blocked up before. And now that the pain and the goading have stopped, it can catch its breath and once more suck in, for the moment, this sweetest of all pleasures. [252] This it is not at all willing to give up, and no one is more important to it than the beautiful boy. It forgets mother and brothers and friends entirely and doesn't care at all if it loses its wealth through neglect. And as for proper and decorous behavior, in which it used to take pride, the soul despises the whole business. Why, it is even willing to sleep like a slave, anywhere, as near to the object of its longing as it is allowed to get![137] That is because in addition to its reverence for one who has such beauty, the soul has discovered that the boy is the only doctor for all that terrible pain.

"This is the experience we humans call love, you beautiful boy (I mean the one to whom I am making this speech). You are so young that what the gods call it is likely to strike you as funny. Some of the successors of Homer, I believe, report two lines from the less well known poems, of

136. Socrates is here tracing the etymology of the word *himeros* (desire) as compounded out of *meros* (particle) and *ienai* (go).

137. A reference to the poetic topos of lovers camped out at the door of the beloved's house.

which the second is quite indecent and does not scan very well.[138] They praise love this way:

> Yes, mortals call him powerful winged 'Love';
> But because of his need to thrust out the wings, the gods call him 'Shove.'

You may believe this or not as you like. But, seriously, the cause of love is as I have said, and this is how lovers really feel.

"If the man who is taken by love used to be an attendant on Zeus, he will be able to bear the burden of this feathered force with dignity. But if it is one of Ares'[139] troops who has fallen prisoner of love—if that is the god with whom he took the circuit—then if he has the slightest suspicion that the boy he loves has done him wrong, he turns murderous, and he is ready to make a sacrifice of himself as well as the boy.

"So it is with each of the gods: everyone spends his life honoring the god in whose chorus he danced, and emulates that god in every way he can, so long as he remains undefiled and in his first life down here. And that is how he behaves with everyone at every turn, not just with those he loves. Everyone chooses his love after his own fashion from among those who are beautiful, and then treats the boy like his very own god, building him up and adorning him as an image to honor and worship. Those who followed Zeus, for example, choose someone to love who is a Zeus himself in the nobility of his soul. So they make sure he has a talent for philosophy and the guidance of others, and once they have found him and are in love with him they do everything to develop that talent. If any lovers have not yet embarked on this practice, then they start to learn, using any source they can and also making progress on their own. They are well equipped to track down their god's true nature with their own resources because of their driving need to gaze at the god, [253] and as they are in touch with the god by memory they are inspired by him and adopt his customs and practices, so far as a human being can share a god's life. For all of this they know they have the boy to thank, and so they love him all the more; and if they draw their inspiration from Zeus, then, like the Bacchants,[140] they pour it into the soul of the one they love in order to help him take on as much of their own god's qualities as possible. Hera's[141] followers look for a kingly character, and once they have found him they do all the same things for him.

---

138. These lines are not elsewhere attested and may be Plato's invention.

139. The war god.

140. Ecstatic female followers of Dionysus, who become inspired with the god's energy and try to communicate it to others.

141. Zeus' wife and the queen of the gods.

And so it is for followers of Apollo [142] or any other god: They take their god's path and seek for their own a boy whose nature is like the god's; and when they have got him they emulate the god, convincing the boy they love and training him to follow their god's pattern and way of life, so far as is possible in each case. They show no envy, no mean-spirited lack of generosity, toward the boy, but make every possible effort to draw him into being totally like themselves and the god to whom they are devoted. This, then, is any true lover's heart's desire: if he follows that desire in the manner I described, this friend who has been driven mad by love will secure a consummation for the one he has befriended that is as beautiful and blissful as I said—if, of course, he captures him. Here, then, is how the captive is caught:

"Remember how we divided each soul in three at the beginning of our story—two parts in the form of horses and the third in that of a charioteer? Let us continue with that. One of the horses, we said, is good, the other not; but we did not go into the details of the goodness of the good horse or the badness of the bad. Let us do that now. The horse that is on the right, or nobler, side is upright in frame and well jointed, with a high neck and a regal nose; his coat is white, his eyes are black, and he is a lover of honor with modesty and self-control; companion to true glory, he needs no whip, and is guided by verbal commands alone. The other horse is a crooked great jumble of limbs with a short bull-neck, a pug nose, black skin, and bloodshot white eyes; companion to wild boasts and indecency, he is shaggy around the ears—deaf as a post—and just barely yields to horsewhip and goad combined. Now when the charioteer looks in the eye of love, his entire soul is suffused with a sense of warmth and starts to fill with tingles and the goading of desire. As for the horses, the one who is obedient to the charioteer is still controlled, [254] then as always, by its sense of shame, and so prevents itself from jumping on the boy. The other one, however, no longer responds to the whip or the goad of the charioteer; it leaps violently forward and does everything to aggravate its yokemate and its charioteer, trying to make them go up to the boy and suggest to him the pleasures of sex. At first the other two resist, angry in their belief that they are being made to do things that are dreadfully wrong. At last, however, when they see no end to their trouble, they are led forward, reluctantly agreeing to do as they have been told. So they are close to him now, and they are struck by the boy's face as if by a bolt of lightning. When the charioteer sees that face, his memory is carried back to the real nature of Beauty, and he sees it again where it stands on the sacred

142. The god of music and prophecy.

pedestal next to Self-control. At the sight he is frightened, falls over
backwards awestruck, and at the same time has to pull the reins back
so fiercely that both horses are set on their haunches, one falling back
voluntarily with no resistance, but the other insolent and quite unwilling. They pull back a little further; and while one horse drenches the
whole soul with sweat out of shame and awe, the other—once it has
recovered from the pain caused by the bit and its fall—bursts into a torrent of insults as soon as it has caught its breath, accusing its charioteer
and yokemate of all sorts of cowardice and unmanliness for abandoning
their position and their agreement. Now once more it tries to make its
unwilling partners advance, and gives in grudgingly only when they beg
it to wait till later. Then, when the promised time arrives, and they are
pretending to have forgotten, it reminds them; it struggles, it neighs,
it pulls them forward and forces them to approach the boy again with
the same proposition; and as soon as they are near, it drops its head,
straightens its tail, bites the bit, and pulls without any shame at all. The
charioteer is now struck with the same feelings as before, only worse,
and he's falling back as he would from a starting gate; and he violently
yanks the bit back out of the teeth of the insolent horse, only harder this
time, so that he bloodies its foul-speaking tongue and jaws, sets its legs
and haunches firmly on the ground, and 'gives it over to pain.' When
the bad horse has suffered this same thing time after time, it stops being
so insolent; now it is humble enough to follow the charioteer's warnings,
and when it sees the beautiful boy it dies of fright, with the result that
now at last the lover's soul follows its boy in reverence and awe.

[255] "And because he is served with all the attentions due a god by
a lover who is not pretending otherwise but is truly in the throes of love,
and because he is by nature disposed to be a friend of the man who is
serving him (even if he has already been set against love by school-
friends or others who say that it is shameful to associate with a lover,
and initially rejects the lover in consequence), as time goes forward he
is brought by his ripening age and a sense of what must be to a point
where he lets the man spend time with him. It is a decree of fate, you
see, that bad is never friends with bad, while good cannot fail to be
friends with good. Now that he allows his lover to talk and spend time
with him, and the man's good will is close at hand, the boy is amazed
by it as he realizes that all the friendship he has from his other friends
and relatives put together is nothing compared to that of this friend
who is inspired by a god.

"After the lover has spent some time doing this, staying near the boy
(and even touching him during sports and on other occasions), then
the spring that feeds the stream Zeus named 'Desire' when he was in
love with Ganymede begins to flow mightily in the lover and is partly

absorbed by him, and when he is filled it overflows and runs away outside him. Think how a breeze or an echo bounces back from a smooth
solid object to its source; that is how the stream of beauty goes back to
the beautiful boy and sets him aflutter. It enters through his eyes, which
are its natural route to the soul; there it waters the passages for the
wings, starts the wings growing, and fills the soul of the loved one with
love in return. Then the boy is in love, but has no idea what he loves.
He does not understand, and cannot explain, what has happened to
him. It is as if he had caught an eye disease from someone else, but
could not identify the cause; he does not realize that he is seeing himself in the lover as in a mirror. So when the lover is near, the boy's pain
is relieved just as the lover's is, and when they are apart he yearns as
much as he is yearned for, because he has a mirror image of love in him
—'backlove' [143]—though he neither speaks nor thinks of it as love, but
as friendship. Still, his desire is nearly the same as the lover's, though
weaker: he wants to see, touch, kiss, and lie down with him; and of course,
as you might expect, he acts on these desires soon after they occur.

"When they are in bed, the lover's undisciplined horse has a word to
say to the charioteer—[**256**] that after all its sufferings it is entitled to a
little fun. Meanwhile, the boy's bad horse has nothing to say, but swelling
with desire, confused, it hugs the lover and kisses him in delight at his
great good will. And whenever they are lying together it is completely
unable, for its own part, to deny the lover any favor he might beg to have.
Its yokemate, however, along with its charioteer, resists such requests
with modesty and reason. Now if the victory goes to the better elements
in both their minds, which lead them to follow the assigned regimen of
philosophy, their life here below is one of bliss and shared understanding. They are modest and fully in control of themselves now that they
have enslaved the part that brought trouble into the soul and set free
the part that gave it virtue. After death, when they have grown wings
and become weightless, they have won the first of three rounds in these,
the true Olympic Contests. There is no greater good than this that either
human self-control or divine madness can offer a man. If, on the other
hand, they adopt a lower way of living, with ambition in place of philosophy,[144] then pretty soon when they are careless because they have been
drinking or for some other reason, the pair's undisciplined horses will

143. The Greek word here is *anterōs*. For the altar to Anteros, see **2.17**.
144. Plato is here alluding to a threefold hierarchy of personality types he had earlier made
in the *Republic:* at the top, *philosophoi* (lovers of wisdom), next *philotimoi* (lovers of honor, or
ambitious men), with the lowest type being *philokerdeis* (lovers of gain).

catch their souls off guard and together bring them to commit that act which ordinary people would take to be the happiest choice of all; and when they have consummated it once, they go on doing this for the rest of their lives, but sparingly, since they have not approved of what they are doing with their whole minds. So these two also live in mutual friendship (though weaker than that of the philosophical pair), both while they are in love and after they have passed beyond it, because they realize they have exchanged such firm vows that it would be forbidden for them ever to break them and become enemies. In death they are wingless when they leave the body, but their wings are bursting to sprout, so the prize they have won from the madness of love is considerable, because those who have begun the sacred journey in lower heaven may not by law be sent into darkness for the journey under the earth; their lives are bright and happy as they travel together, and thanks to their love they will grow wings together when the time comes.

"These are the rewards you will have from a lover's friendship, my boy, and they are as great as divine gifts should be. A non-lover's companionship, on the other hand, is diluted by human self-control; all it pays are cheap, human dividends, and though the slavish attitude it engenders in a friend's soul is widely praised as virtue, [257] it tosses the soul around for nine thousand years on the Earth and leads it, mindless, beneath it.

"So now, dear Love, this is the best and most beautiful palinode we could offer as payment for our debt, especially in view of the rather poetical choice of words Phaedrus made me use. Forgive us our earlier speeches in return for this one; be kind and gracious toward my expertise at love, which is your own gift to me: do not, out of anger, take it away or disable it; and grant that I may be held in higher esteem than ever by those who are beautiful. If Phaedrus and I said anything that shocked you in our earlier speech, blame it on Lysias, who was its father, and put a stop to his making speeches of this sort; convert him to philosophy like his brother Polemarchus so that his lover here may no longer play both sides as he does now, but simply devote his life to Love through philosophical discussions."

5.10 Plato, *Laws* 636B–D

An Athenian discusses the best laws for an ideal state with a Cretan and Spartan. Here, the Athenian has asked his interlocutors which institutions of their states most give rise to the virtue of temperance, and questions the two that the Spartan has named.

The same is true of these gymnasia and common meals [145] you mentioned: in many other respects they confer benefit on the cities which have them, but they also have the troubling tendency to promote civil strife. The young men of Miletus, Boeotia and Thurii are proof of this. Moreover, it seems that this practice has undermined a law that is ancient and indeed in accord with nature, and governs the enjoyment of sexual pleasure not only by human beings but also by animals. [146] One could place the blame for this first and foremost on your two cities and on other cities that are especially devoted to gymnasia. Regardless of whether one approaches this subject in jest or in earnest, there is one thing that one must recognize and that is that the sexual pleasure experienced by the female and male natures when they join together for the purpose of procreation seems to have been handed down in accordance with nature, whereas the pleasure enjoyed by males with males and females with females seems to be beyond nature, and the boldness of those who first engaged in this practice seems to have arisen out of an inability to control pleasure. And we are unanimous in accusing the Cretans of fabricating the story of Ganymede: because they believed that their laws had come from Zeus, they have also attached this story to the god, thinking that they could reap the fruit of this pleasure and say they were following the god's example. But that is the realm of myth.

5.11 Plato, *Laws* 835E–842A

The following excerpt comes from a discussion of the best way to educate the young.

ATHENIAN: **[835]** How will the young in this city abstain from the desires that impel many to their wit's end? For these are desires from which reason, which is endeavoring to become law, bids them abstain.

It is not surprising that most forms of desire are brought under control by the laws **[836]** we set down earlier. The prohibition against excessive wealth goes a long way toward promoting self-control. And the program of education as a whole consists of laws that are conducive to these same goals. So, too, the watchful eye of the authorities, trained as it is not to look elsewhere, but to keep constant watch, particularly on the young men, constitutes a check (at least as far as humanly possible)

---

145. It was customary for the men of Sparta and the Cretan cities to dine together in a public mess hall, rather than in their own homes.

146. Or, according to some manuscripts: "Moreover, it seems that this practice, when it has been in place for a long time, has ruined the enjoyment of sexual pleasure granted in accordance with nature not only to human beings but also to animals."

on the other desires. But what about the erotic desire for male and female adolescents and the erotic desire of women for men and men for women, which have been the source of countless problems for individuals and entire cities alike? How is one to take precautions against this? What remedy could one develop for each of these forms of desire in order to avoid such a danger? The solution is by no means easy, Cleinias, and at least part of the reason is this. In our attempt to deal with many other problems, Crete and Sparta lend us considerable assistance and indeed provide us models of innovative legislation that departs radically from the practice of most Greek states. But when it comes to erotic desire —and we are alone, so we may speak frankly—Crete and Sparta take an approach that is completely the opposite of ours.

Let us suppose someone were to follow nature and set down the law that was in effect before Laius,[147] and point out that at that time it was considered proper for one to avoid engaging in sexual intercourse with males, including young males, as one does with females. And let us suppose he were to bring forth as evidence the nature of the wild animals and show that male does not touch male with such an end in mind because it is not given by nature. His argument would probably be persuasive and would certainly not harmonize with the practice of your cities.

Furthermore, these practices also run afoul of the principle that we agreed ought to be the constant focus of the lawgiver's attention, and that is the question of which laws lead to virtue and which do not. Our inquiry has in fact not wavered from this focus. Suppose we stipulate, for the sake of argument, that it would be a fine thing (or at least in no way disgraceful) for us now to adopt current sexual practice as the basis of our law: the question then would be to what extent this legislation promotes virtue. Do we think that manly character will be engendered and take root in the soul of the one who is persuaded (the beloved)? Or that the seed of self-control will take root in the soul of the persuader (the lover)? Or do we think instead that no one would ever be persuaded of this, but would believe the exact opposite? Won't everyone censure the softness of the one who gives in to pleasure and is unable to steel himself against it, and blame the one who imitates the female for his similarity to his model? Who among men will set down legislation of this sort? Practically no one, at least not if he has a notion of true law in his mind. And how do we prove the truth of our position? If we hope to embark on a proper analysis of this subject, we must examine the nature

147. The mythological king of Thebes, whose rape of the Elean boy Chrysippus was identified by Euripides as the origin of pederasty. Laius was also the king who fathered Oedipus, despite the Delphic oracle's warning, and is thus a figure for sexual incontinence.

of friendship, desire, and the types of what we call erotic desire.[148] [837]
For although there are two forms of each, and a third that is a cross
between the other two, there is a single name that encompasses them all
and this is the source of all the problems and confusion.

CRETAN: How is that?

ATHENIAN: Well, for example, we use the term *philos* to describe one who
is the friend of another who is similar or equal to him in virtue. But
we also use the term to describe the friendship the poor man feels for
the rich man, his social opposite. And when either of these two types of
friendship is intense, we call it *erōs*.

CRETAN: That's right.

ATHENIAN: Now the friendship that pairs opposites is harsh and wild and
we tend to find it lacking in mutuality, whereas the friendship between
similar people is gentle and mutual throughout life. Then there is the
type that is a mixture of these two: it is not easy to figure out what the
man who feels this third type of erotic friendship is really after, and in
fact such a lover himself is at a loss as he is dragged to opposite extremes
by the two primary forms of love, one of them commanding him to lay
his hands on youthful flesh, the other forbidding it. For one who loves
the body and hungers for youthful flesh as though it were ripe fruit
encourages himself to take his fill and attaches no value to the character of his beloved's soul. But one who considers desire for the body
incidental and is content to look at it rather than love it, and truly desires the boy's soul with his own soul, thinks that glutting body on body
is an outrage; such a man respects and indeed reveres self-control,
manliness, greatness, and prudence, and would prefer to remain continually chaste with a beloved who is chaste. This type of love, which is a
combination of the other two, is the one that we have just now described
as the third type.

Given these three types of love, we must decide the following: should
the law prohibit all of them and prevent them from coming into existence among us? Or is it clear that we would wish to have in our city the
type of love that is a love of virtue and that desires that the young man
become the best he can be, but would keep out the other two, if at all
possible? What do you think of the argument, my dear Megillus?

SPARTAN: My friend, the argument you have just made on this subject is
entirely persuasive.

ATHENIAN: It seems that I have obtained your agreement, my friend, and
this is exactly what I anticipated. I suppose there is no need, then, for

---

148. The Greek words for these three relations are respectively *philia, epithumia,* and *erōs.*
There is some overlap between the terms and the English equivalents are not exact. *Erōs* seems
to be identified as a subcategory of both *philia* and *epithumia.*

me to examine what the law of Sparta says on such matters; I need only accept your assent to the argument. As for Cleinias, I will ply him with spells at some future point and secure his assent too. But enough of what the two of you are willing to concede. Let us by all means continue to work our way through the laws.

SPARTAN: You are quite right.

ATHENIAN: Now I have ready at hand a method for establishing this law, and it is a method [838] that is to some extent easy but also extremely difficult.

SPARTAN: How do you mean?

ATHENIAN: We are aware, I suppose, that even in this day and age most humans, even though not naturally inclined to follow the law, are nevertheless easily and effectively restrained from having sexual intercourse with beautiful people, and they are restrained not unwillingly, but with their full consent.

SPARTAN: When does this happen?

ATHENIAN: When someone has a beautiful brother or sister. The same unwritten law holds also in the case of a son or daughter, and is remarkably effective in preventing one from touching persons in this category, whether it is by sleeping with them openly or in secret, or by embracing them in some other way. But in fact desire for this type of sexual intercourse does not at all occur to most people.

SPARTAN: You are right about that.

ATHENIAN: And is there not a turn of phrase that extinguishes the flames of all pleasures of this sort?

SPARTAN: What sort of phrase are you referring to?

ATHENIAN: That such behavior is impure, hateful in the eyes of the gods, and the most shameful of all shameful acts. And isn't it true that this language is so effective because no one ever contradicts it? Indeed, doesn't everyone, from the moment he is born, hear this message at all times and places, both in jokes and in the more serious discourse of tragedy, where they bring out on stage the figure of Thyestes or Oedipus or Macareus, who had secret sexual relations with his sister and, after he was detected, imposed on himself a penalty of death for his wrong-doing?[149]

SPARTAN: You are quite right, at least to the extent of saying that public opinion enjoys remarkable power, so long as no one ever attempts to aspire to anything that is not in keeping with the law.

ATHENIAN: Therefore what we have just said is correct: if a lawgiver should wish to enslave one of those desires that most enslave men, it is easy to

---

149. All three are heroes of tragedy. Oedipus, of course, was known for incest with his mother, Thyestes with his daughter, and Macareus, as we are told here, with his sister.

figure out how he would attempt it. He would consecrate this message in the eyes of everyone, the same for slave and free and children and women and the city as a whole, and in this way he will give this law the most secure foundation.

SPARTAN: That is well and good, but I'd like to know how it shall be possible ever to make everyone willing to spread this message.

ATHENIAN: You anticipated correctly. As I said, I have a method for establishing this law, and the law will prescribe that men use sexual intercourse for procreation, as in nature; that they refrain from the male, if they are to avoid intentionally killing the human race and sowing their seed, as it were, on rocks and stones, [839] where a man's fertile seed will never take root; and that they refrain from every female field in which they would not wish their seed to grow. This law, if it becomes permanent and becomes master, just as it is now master on the subject of sexual intercourse with one's parents, and if it wins a just victory also over the other pleasures, it will bring countless blessings. The first is that the law itself has been brought into line with nature. The second is its promotion of abstention from erotic frenzy and madness, all forms of adultery, and all immoderate consumption of food and drink, and its promotion of a loving bond between husbands and their wives. And there would be many other benefits, if one should be able to bring this law within one's power.

But perhaps a violent young man, filled with a lot of seed, would approach us and would, when he heard that this law was being set down, rail that the lawgivers were setting down laws which were foolish and impossible to enforce, and perhaps he would fill the whole world with his bellowing. But I already looked ahead to this possibility and made the claim that I have a method to make sure that this law remains in place once it is set down, and it is a method that is simultaneously the easiest and most difficult of all. The easy part is realizing that the law is in fact possible and how: for we are claiming that this law, if it is sufficiently consecrated, will enslave every soul and will frighten each one into complete obedience to the laws set down. But now we are faced with this problem: no one believes that this law could be established in these circumstances, just as there is doubt about whether it is possible for an entire city to maintain a system of public messes. Although such a system has been tested in practice and has become established in your cities, nevertheless your cities do not think that the extension of this practice to women has any basis in nature. For this reason, because of the power of disbelief, I have said that it is very difficult for both of these practices to become enshrined under the law.

SPARTAN: You were right to say so.

ATHENIAN: Do you want me then to summon my powers of persuasion and attempt to outline an argument that this law is not beyond the realm of human possibility, but is in fact capable of coming into existence?

SPARTAN: How could I not?

ATHENIAN: Well, do you think someone would more easily abstain from sex and willingly observe moderation in doing what the law prescribes concerning sex if he keeps his body in excellent shape like a professional athlete or if he keeps his body in poor shape?

SPARTAN: I suppose he would abstain much more easily if he kept in shape like a professional athlete.

ATHENIAN: Have we not heard of Iccus of Tarentum [150] because of his performance in the games at Olympia and elsewhere? [840] Because of his desire for victory in these contests, his skill, and the manly virtue combined with self-control which he had in his soul, he never, as the story goes, touched a woman or even a boy during the entire period of his most intense training. And much the same story is told of Crison, Astylus, Diopompus, and many others. And yet their characters were much less developed than those of our fellow citizens, Cleinias, and their bodies much more swollen with untamed energy.

CRETAN: You are correct to say that the ancients have emphatically declared the traditions associated with these athletes to be rooted in truth.

ATHENIAN: What then? Are we to say that these men, for the sake of victory in wrestling and running and other such events, had the will to abstain from the activity that is said by the masses to lead to bliss, but that our children shall be unable to persevere for the sake of a victory that is much more beautiful? Indeed, shall we not tell them that this victory is the *most* beautiful, and convey this message to them beginning in childhood using stories and sayings and songs, and essentially bewitch them into holding this belief?

CRETAN: What kind of victory are you talking about?

ATHENIAN: A victory over pleasure. We shall say that if they should become masters of this victory, they would live happily, but that if they should be mastered, the result would be exactly the opposite. Furthermore, won't fear of the impurity that comes with indulging in pleasure enable one to master those pleasures that other men, who are inferior to these fellow citizens of ours, have mastered?

CRETAN: It is likely indeed.

ATHENIAN: Well this is where we stand on the subject of this law and our difficulty comes from the moral weakness of the masses. And so I pro-

---

150. Olympic victor in the pentathlum in 476 B.C.E., credited with a medical regimen of training he later taught to others.

pose that our law ought simply to proceed on this subject by stating that our citizens must not be inferior to birds and many other animals. These animals, who are born in large flocks, live unmated, virginal, and pure until the moment they are ready to reproduce; and when they come to this stage of life, they are paired off male with female and female with male according to personal preference and live together purely and justly for the rest of time, remaining devoted to their original commitment of mutual affection. The law should point out that it is surely necessary that our fellow citizens be superior to animals. But if they are corrupted by the great number of other Greeks and non-Greeks, when they see the so-called uncontrolled Aphrodite among them and hear about her great power, and if they are thus unable to maintain self-control, it is necessary for our law guardians to become lawgivers and contrive a second law for these men.

CRETAN: [841] What law do you advise them to set down, if they are unable to make work the law which you are now proposing?

ATHENIAN: The second law will clearly be a law conceptually dependent on the first, Cleinias.

CRETAN: And what is that?

ATHENIAN: That one ought to prevent pleasure from flexing its muscle in the body and divert the flow of sexual fluid, pleasure's food, to other parts of the body by means of physical labor. This could happen if the experience of sexual pleasure was always attended by a sense of shame. For if our citizens were to have sex rarely because they felt a sense of shame, they would find pleasure a weaker mistress because they would be experiencing pleasure infrequently. Let it be enshrined for our citizens in custom and unwritten law that if a man engages in sexual intercourse, it is noble to keep it hidden, but disgraceful not to do so; complete abstention is not required. And so the law would represent a compromise standard: sexual intercourse would be sometimes disgraceful and sometimes noble. And then there is the problem of those whose natures are corrupted, people we refer to as "weaker than themselves": but there are three kinds of things that can surround these men, a single kind, as it were, and prevent them from violating the law.

CRETAN: What factors are these?

ATHENIAN: Reverence for the gods, ambition for honor, and the development of desire not for bodies but for the ways of the soul that are noble. The proposals I am now making are wishes, perhaps not unlike the wishes they make in children's stories. They would be by far the best thing that could happen to any city if the wishes should be granted. And perhaps, god willing, we could push through one of the following two regulations governing sexuality. The first regulation states that no man should dare to touch any of the noble and freeborn women except his own wife, and that none should sow illegitimate and bastard seed with concubines or non-procreative seed with males beyond nature. The second possibility is that we would forbid sex with males entirely, but that if a man had sexual intercourse with a woman with whom he was cohabiting, other than the women who came into the household accompanied by the divine rites of marriage, whether this woman is purchased or acquired in some other way, and he does not keep it hidden from all, men and women alike, perhaps we would appear to be legislating properly if we set it down that he be excluded from the city's economy of praise, on the ground that he is in fact a foreigner. Let this law—whether we call it one law or two—be set down to govern sexual intercourse [842] and all forms of erotic activity which we engage in rightly or wrongly when we consort with one another as a result of such desires.

5.12 Aristotle, *Prior Analytics* 2.22 (68a39–b7)

Aristotle gives the following example in the course of analyzing combinations of opposite propositions.

Now suppose every lover, when he experiences erotic desire, should prefer that his beloved be disposed to grant him favors (proposition A) but not in fact grant them (proposition C), rather than that the beloved actually grant favors (proposition D) but not be disposed to do so (proposition B). In this case, it is clear that it is more desirable that the beloved be disposed to grant favors (A) than that he actually grant them (D). Therefore, when one experiences erotic desire, reciprocated affection[151] from the beloved is more desirable than sexual intercourse. And therefore erotic desire is more a desire for reciprocated affection than for sex. And if it is mostly a desire for reciprocated affection, then this is its goal. Therefore sex is either not a goal at all or it is subsumed within the larger goal of reciprocated affection. And indeed it is the same with the other appetites and arts.

5.13 Aristotle, *Nicomachean Ethics* 7.5.3–5

Book 7 of this work discusses moral states to be avoided, which are generally of three types: vice, lack of restraint, and bestiality. Here he discusses some possible exceptions.

[3] Other conditions arise because of disease (and in some people because of mental illness, as in the case of the man who sacrificed his mother and ate her flesh or the man who devoured the liver of his fellow slave). Still

---

151. "Reciprocated affection" here translates various forms of *philia*, which elsewhere means simply "friendship." See n. 148.

others originate in either disease or habit, such as pulling out one's hair or biting one's nails, eating charcoal or dirt, and finally, for a male, the condition of sexual intercourse among males.[152] For while some males are subject to this condition because of a natural deformity, others are subject to it as a result of habituation, as in the case of males who are sexually abused from childhood. [4] Now no one would label men who are subject to this condition because of nature "unrestrained," just as one would not apply this label to women because they do not mount but are instead mounted. So too in the case of those who suffer a diseased condition because of habit. [5] Indeed, to be subject to any of these conditions puts one outside the definition of vice; the same holds for those subject to the bestial condition. When a man who is subject to one of these conditions is overcome by it, we do not speak of "lack of restraint" in the pure sense, but of something analogous to it. In the same way we do not refer to a man who is overcome with anger "unrestrained" pure and simple, but rather "unrestrained in respect to his anger."

5.14 Aristotle, *Nicomachean Ethics* 8.4.1–2

Book 8 of this work deals with the various forms of friendship.

[1] This type of friendship is perfect in terms both of duration and everything else, and in all cases such friends receive from each other the same thing or something quite similar, which is indeed what ought to be shared between friends. The type of friendship formed for pleasure bears similarity to this perfect type. For indeed, good men are pleasing to one another. Likewise, too, the type of friendship forged for advantage. For good men are also advantageous to one another. And it is true also in the case of men motivated by pleasure or advantage that friendships are most likely to endure when each gets the same thing from the other, such as pleasure, and also when it flows from the same source, such as happens between witty people but not between lover and beloved. For lover and beloved do not take pleasure in the same things: rather, the lover takes pleasure in gazing at his beloved, while the latter takes pleasure in the attentions of his lover. But when the beloved's youthful beauty fades sometimes the friendship too fades. For now the lover does not find the boy pleasing to look at, and the boy receives no attention. But many couples continue the relationship, if, as a result of spending time together, they come to love each other's character, because they are of similar character.

---

152. The Greek here is vague and ambiguous, but the following discussion suggests that what Aristotle really means is sexual passivity in males, as in 5.16, where we have the same division between those who are biologically determined to be this way and those who have become this way by habit since early adolescence.

[2] But if their erotic relationship is characterized by an exchange of advantage rather than pleasure, the two are less friendly toward each other and the friendship lasts less long. Those who are friends for advantage cease to be friends when it ceases to be advantageous. For they are not friends of each other but friends of profit.

5.15 Hippocrates, *On Regimen* 1.28–29

This treatise, which may not be the authentic work of Hippocrates, certainly derives from his school and probably dates to the late fifth century. It suggests that we all contain seeds of both male and female, and that the conditions of both male effeminacy and female mannishness are determined genetically.

[28] Male and female have the power to fuse into one solid, both because both are nourished in both and also because soul is the same thing in all living creatures, although the body of each is different. Now soul is always alike, in a larger creature as in a smaller, for it changes neither through nature nor through force. But the body of no creature is ever the same, either by nature or by force, for it both dissolves into all things and also combines with all things.[153] Now if the bodies secreted from both[154] happen to be male, they grow up to the limit of the available matter, and the babies become men brilliant in soul and strong in body, unless they be harmed by their subsequent diet. If the secretion from the man be male and that of the woman female, should the male gain the mastery,[155] the weaker soul combines with the stronger, since there is nothing more congenial present to which it can go. For the small goes to the greater and the greater to the less, and united they master the available matter. The male body grows, but the female body decreases into another part. And these, while less brilliant than the former, nevertheless, as the male from the man won mastery, they turn out brave, and have rightly this name. But if male be secreted from the woman, but female from the man, and the male get the mastery, it grows just as in the former case, while the female diminishes. These turn out to be effeminate men[156] and are correctly so called. These three kinds of men are born, but the degree of manliness depends upon the blending of the parts of water, upon nourishment, education, and habits. In the sequel I shall discuss these matters also.

---

153. The point is that our bodies contain both male and female seeds and are subject to change, but the soul is uniform and stable for both genders.

154. I.e., both mother and father.

155. In other words, if the male seed is more abundant.

156. The Greek word here is *androgynoi*. Some interpret this as a reference to hermaphroditism, but the word is more commonly used in Greek of effeminates.

[29] In like manner the female also is generated. If the secretion of both parents be female, the offspring prove female and fair, both to the highest degree. But if the woman's secretion be female and the man's male, and the female gain the mastery, the girls are bolder than the preceding, but nevertheless they too are modest. But if the man's secretion be female, and the woman's male, and the female gain the mastery, growth takes place after the same fashion, but the girls prove "mannish."

5.16 Ps.-Aristotle, *Problems* 4.26

Although probably not an authentic work of Aristotle, the following short treatise certainly comes from his school, reflecting the methods and assumptions of Aristotelian biology.

Why is it that some men enjoy being the passive partner in the sexual act, and some of these also find pleasure in taking an active role, but others do not?

Is it because there exists for each residue[157] a place to which it is naturally separated off in accordance with nature,[158] and at times of exertion the *pneuma*[159] as it passes out causes it to expand and helps expel it; for example, urine naturally goes to the bladder, digested food to the bowels, tears to the eyes, phlegm to the nose, blood to the veins? Well then, as in these cases, semen passes naturally to the testicles and penis.

In those in whom the passages are not in a natural condition,[160] either on account of the blocking up of those leading to the penis (as, for example, happens in the case of eunuchs and other impotent men) or for some other reason, this particular moisture flows into the anus, for this is the natural continuation of its direction of flow. An indication of this fact is that even during active penetration of another the anus contracts and the area around the anus liquefies.

Therefore, if a man overindulges as an active partner in sexual intercourse, the excess semen gathers here, so that when desire arises this area, at which the semen has collected, desires the friction.[161]

157. A "residue" is a surplus of nourishment that has been used to build and maintain the body.

158. In his biological works Aristotle spends some time arguing that residues flow naturally to certain reservoirs in the body, contrary to the Hippocratic belief that fluids were passively drawn to certain organs in the body by a type of hydraulic attraction.

159. *Pneuma* is breath that has been heated by the body to such a point of refinement that it can carry the *psychē*, or life force, and act as the instrument by which the animal's immaterial desires move the material body.

160. The previous section has briefly explained "normal" active sexuality in men. The author now moves to a consideration of men who can never take the active role.

161. This section explains why some men enjoy both active and passive roles.

Desire arises both from food and from thinking about sex.[162] For whenever a person is excited about anything, thereupon the *pneuma* also rushes to the place where this particular residue flows naturally. And if the semen is fine and full of *pneuma*, when it has passed out the tension ceases, just as it sometimes does in the case of boys and those in old age when no fluid has been separated off and when the fluid has been doused.[163] But if he experiences neither of these things he will continue to feel desire until one of them happens.

Those who are by nature effeminate are so constituted that no or little semen is separated off to the same place as in those who have a more natural constitution,[164] but it gathers in the anal region.[165] The reason is that they are constituted contrary to nature, for although they are male, they are so disposed that the passages to the testicles and penis must be defective. The defect causes either complete destruction or a twisting. The former is impossible, since then a woman would result. It is necessary then that the seminal secretion be turned aside and, of course, set in motion in some other place. And on account of this, when they take an active role, they are unsatisfied, like women. For the fluid is meager and is not ejaculated with force, and cools down quickly.

Those in whom the semen travels to the anus desire to be passive in the sexual act, those in whom the semen travels to both places to be both active and passive. In whichever place there is more fluid they desire more friction.

In some men this disposition arises from habit. For men do whatever happens to bring them pleasure and they emit semen following the same principle. Therefore, they desire to do those things through which this is brought to pass, and it is rather as though habit becomes nature. On account of this, whoever has not been accustomed to be a passive partner in sexual intercourse before puberty, but starts around puberty, because

162. The author has explained the significance of the presence of semen. He now introduces the role of *pneuma*. In Aristotle's biology it was friction on the penis that caused the *pneuma* to rush to the testicles and further "concoct" or refine the semen to the point where it too could carry *psychē* and thereby generate a new individual.

163. Before puberty the bodies of young boys do not produce seminal residue because they are not hot enough. As men cool down in old age seminal residue also ceases to be produced. However, the author here claims that in both age-groups desire can still be present, which will cause an erection that will subside only after the *pneuma* has passed out, even if there was no ejaculation of fluid.

164. The author is here using the word "nature" in two different senses: those who are "by nature effeminate" uses nature in the sense of biological causation, even if of an aberrant type, whereas "a more natural constitution" uses nature as a template of normative development.

165. This group is different than the group including eunuchs and impotent men, because this group *can* take an active role, but finds more satisfaction in a passive role.

memory is generated during the activity and pleasure comes along with the memory, on account of their habit they desire to be the passive partner as if they were naturally so constituted—frequency and habit bringing it about just as if they were naturally so inclined. If a man happens to be lustful and self-indulgent each of these comes about more quickly.

5.17 Diogenes of Sinope = Diogenes Laertius 6.46–47, 54, 65

The biographer Diogenes Laertius records a number of anecdotes and sayings attributed to Diogenes the Cynic, who was active in the mid-fourth century. Many are probably apocryphal, but they do reflect attitudes of the Cynic school.

[46] When Diogenes saw a youth who was going off to a feast with satraps,[166] the philosopher dragged him off to his friends and family and told them to keep guard over him. When a carefully dressed youth asked Diogenes something, he said he wouldn't answer unless the youth pulled up his robe and showed whether he was a man or a woman. To a youth playing cottabus[167] in the public baths he said, "The better you play, the worse it is for you."[168] [47] . . . To a youth who complained about the crowd of men who annoyed him, Diogenes said, "Stop displaying the signs of one who takes the passive role." . . . [54] When he saw a youth whose face was made pretty with cosmetics, he said, "If it's for men, you are unfortunate; if it's for women, you do wrong."[169] . . . [65] When he saw a young man acting like a woman, he said, "Aren't you ashamed of planning something worse for yourself than Nature did? For she made you a man, and you are forcing yourself to be a woman."

5.18 Bion of Borysthenes, Frr. 57, 59, 60 Kindstrand = Diogenes Laertius 4.49

A later follower of the Cynic school, Bion was a street preacher and popular philosopher to whom many witty sayings were attributed.

[fr. 57 K] He used to say on many occasions that it was preferable to give the favor of one's own youthful prime to another than to pluck it from others; for that harmed both body and soul. [fr. 59 K] He denounced

---

166. Provincial governors in the Persian Empire. Here, "satraps" may just be metonymic for wealthy and powerful men.

167. On this game, see ch. 3, n. 43.

168. In other words, he will attract more attention from suitors.

169. Since marriages were typically arranged and had nothing to do with mutual attraction, Greeks assumed that any man who tried to appear attractive to women would be an adulterer.

even Socrates, saying that if he had need of Alcibiades and held off, he was
foolish; if he didn't have need, he did nothing exceptional. . . . [fr. 60 K]
In censure of Alcibiades he said that as a youth Alcibiades drew husbands
away from their wives, and as a young man he drew wives away from their
husbands.

5.19 Theodorus of Cyrene = Diogenes Laertius 2.99–100

Theodorus was a representative of the Cyrenaic or hedonist school in the third century B.C.E.

[99] He said that a wise man will make use of those he loves openly and
without suspicion. Hence he used questions such as these:
"Would a scholarly woman be useful insofar as she is scholarly?"
"Yes."
"Would a scholarly boy or young man be useful insofar as he is scholarly?"
"Yes."
"Then wouldn't a beautiful woman be useful insofar as she is beautiful?
And wouldn't a beautiful boy or young man be useful insofar as he is
beautiful?"
"Yes."
"And wouldn't a beautiful boy or young man be useful for this purpose,
for which he is beautiful?"
"Yes."
[100] "He is useful for sexual intercourse." When these points were
granted, he pressed on: "Therefore if someone uses sexual intercourse insofar as it is useful, he doesn't err; nor if someone should use beauty insofar as it is useful, will he err."

5.20 Zeno of Citium, Fr. 248 *Stoicorum Veterum Fragmenta* = Diogenes Laertius 7.129–130

[129] It is their[170] opinion that the wise man will be the lover of those
boys who clearly exhibit by their entire appearance a nature well formed
toward excellence. Zeno says this in his *Republic*, as do Chrysippus[171] in the
first part of his *Ways to Live* and Apollodorus in his *Ethics*. [130] They define
love as the impulse toward making a friend that is caused by a beautiful
appearance, and state that it is not an impulse toward sexual intercourse,
but toward friendship.

---

170. The early and middle Greek Stoics.
171. The third head of the Stoic school after Zeno and Cleanthes (c. 282–206 B.C.E.).

5.21 Zeno of Citium, Fr. 250 = Sextus Empiricus,
Outlines of Pyrrhonism 3.245–46

[245] At any rate Zeno, the head of their school, says in his discourses on child-rearing, along with other similar statements, the following: "Penetrate the thighs of a beloved child no more and no less than those of a non-beloved child, and neither those of a female any more or any less than those of a male. Since what is fitting and appropriate for a beloved child is not different, but the same, as for a non-beloved child, and for females no differently than for males." [246] Concerning piety towards parents the same man also states, using the story of Jocasta and Oedipus, that "there was nothing terrible in Oedipus rubbing his mother. There would have been no shame had he brought her relief by rubbing a different part of her body with his hands when she was not feeling well. Was it then shameful for him to make her feel good by rubbing other parts and easing her distress, and for him to produce noble children from his mother?" Chrysippus is also of the same opinion. At least he says in his *Republic*, "I think it good to carry out these things in such a way that a mother produces children from her son and a father from his daughter and a brother from his sister; just as even now these things are not improperly the custom among many peoples."

5.22 Zeno of Citium, Fr. 253 SVF = Epiphanius,
Against Heretical Sects 3.36

Zeno of Citium, the Stoic, says that the dead ought to be thrown as food to the living instead of as food for the fire. He also says to use boys sexually without any restraint.

5.23 Zeno of Citium, Fr. 286 SVF = Diogenes Laertius 7.17

Being romantically inclined toward Chremonides and sitting next to him and Cleanthes,[172] Zeno suddenly stood up. Since Cleanthes was surprised, Zeno said, "I understand from good doctors that the best cure for swellings and inflammations is rest."[173]

5.24 Zeno of Citium, Fr. 295 SVF = Diogenes Laertius 7.18

To a boy-lover Zeno said, "Neither teachers nor people like you have any minds left, after spending all your time with little boys."

---

172. Zeno's pupil and future successor as head of the Stoic school (331–232 B.C.E.).
173. In this particular context, his swelling is an erection.

5.25 Zeno of Citium, Fr. 247 SVF = Athenaeus 13.563D–F

The following passage is an attack on the later Stoics but preserves some information about Zeno.

Myrtilus focused on the men of the Stoa, addressing them in words taken from the *Iambics* of Hermeias of Curium:

> Listen, you Styacs,[174] dealers in nonsense, tricksters in argument, who gulp down everything on the dishes before the wise man gets any, and then are caught doing the very things you don't make a song about . . .

You are boy-watchers, and that is the only way in which you rival the founder of your school, Zeno the Levantine,[175] the man who—so Antigonus of Carystus tells us in his *Life of Zeno*—never had a woman and never stopped having boys. Yes, you gabble that one should love souls and not bodies; and you also state that one may keep a boyfriend till he reaches the age of twenty-eight![176] I think Ariston of Ceos, the Aristotelian, gave a good reply (in *Love Comparisons* II) to some Athenian who had pointed to a big well-grown young man named Dorus and described him as a 'beautiful boy.' 'I think I can apply to you,' he said, 'the reply that Odysseus made to Dolon: "Indeed, your heart is hungry for big Gifts."'[177]

174. This parodic name for the Stoics puns on the Greek verb *stuein* (to have an erection).

175. A derogatory reference to Zeno's birth in Cyprus, which, although Greek, was close to Phoenicia.

176. The topic is taken up again at 564F and 565E, where Myrtilus accuses the Stoics of "taking their boyfriends about with shaven chins and fannies."

177. The allusion is to *Iliad* 10.401. He puns on the resemblance of the name Dorus to the Greek word for gift *(dōron)*.

1. Older youth and boy face each other in military costume. The Chieftain Cup (Minoan). By courtesy of the Archaeological Receipts Fund, Ministry of Culture, Hellenic Republic.

2. Older and younger ithyphallic warriors hold hands. Bronze figurine from Kato Syme, Crete (seventh century B.C.E.). © Deutsches Archäologisches Institut, Athens, neg. no. 2000/218.

3. One woman courts another with crowns.
Plate from Thera (seventh century B.C.E.).
By courtesy of the Archaeological Receipts Fund,
Ministry of Culture, Hellenic Republic.

4a. Two women wrapped together in a cloak.
Black-figured pyxis (c. 550 B.C.E.). By courtesy of the University Museums,
University of Mississippi Cultural Center. 1977.3.72.

4b. Another side of Fig. 4a: two man-youth pairs engage
in intercrural intercourse; another youth is courted.

5a. Top register shows
a drunken orgy. Black-
figured Tyrrhenian
amphora (c. 550 B.C.E.).
By courtesy of the Musée
Languedocien.

5b. Detail of Fig. 5a:
two pairs engage in
anal intercourse around
the wine bowl.

6. Multiple men court a youth with dogs and fighting cocks.
Black-figured amphora (c. 550 B.C.E.).
By courtesy of the Vatican Museums. 352 = *ABV* 134.30.

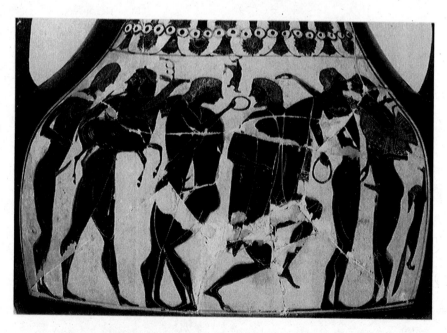

7. Two courting pairs and one engaged in intercrural intercourse.
Black-figured amphora attributed to the Berlin Painter (c. 550 B.C.E.).
© The British Museum. W39 = *ABV* 297.16.

8. Man and boy engage in intercrural intercourse, youth and boy in anal
intercourse. Black-figured kalpis (c. 550 B.C.E.).
Private collection, used with permission. Photo: Bruce White.

9. Two Maenads embrace and present an offering to Dionysus.
Black-figured amphora by Amasis (c. 530 B.C.E.). Cliché Bibliothèque
Nationale de France, Paris. 222 = *ABV* 152.25.

10a. Man fondles a boy, who makes a reciprocating gesture.
Black-figured cup (c. 520 B.C.E.). Gift of E. P. and Fiske Warren, 1908.
By courtesy of the Museum of Fine Arts, Boston. 08.292.

10b. Opposite side of Fig. 10a: boy jumps up to embrace the man.

11. Three youths admire and court three boy athletes.
Red-figured amphora attributed to the Dikaios Painter. By courtesy of the
Réunion des Musées Nationaux. Musée du Louvre, G45 = *ARV*[2] 31.4.

12a. Two youths draw together to kiss. Red-figured psykter attributed
to Smikros (c. 510 B.C.E.). Gift of Nicolas Koutoulakis.
By courtesy of the J. Paul Getty Museum, Malibu, California. 82.AE.53.

12b. Detail of another side of Fig. 12a: Hegerthos courts Andriskos and reaches toward his penis.

12c. Detail of another side of Fig. 12a: Antias walks away from Melas.

12d. Detail of another side of Fig. 12a: the vase-painter Euphronios courts "the beautiful Leagros."

13. One woman touches another's genitals. Red-figured kylix attributed to Apollodorus. By courtesy of the Soprintendenza Archeologica per l' Etruria Meridionale. Museo Nazionale Archeologico, Tarquinia Para. 333.9bis.

14. Satyrs engage in fellatio, anal intercourse, and bestiality. Red-figured kylix attributed to the Nikosthenes Painter (c. 500 B.C.E.). By courtesy of the Antikensammlung, Staatliche Museen zu Berlin—Preussischer Kulturbesitz. 1964.4 = ARV^2 1700.

15. Seven youths engage in a complex dance and orgy.
Red-figured kylix attributed to the Manner of Epileios Painter.
By courtesy of the Soprintendenza Archeologica del Piemonte.
Museo Archeologico, Torino, 4117.

16. Three men court three boys. Red-figured kylix attributed to Macron
(c. 480 B.C.E.). By courtesy of the Kunsthistorisches Museum,
Vienna. IV, 3698 = *ARV*² 471.193.

17. Three courtship pairs, with the boys showing varying degrees
of interest by their clothing. Red-figured kylix attributed to Macron
(c. 480 B.C.E.). By courtesy of the Staatliche Antikensammlungen
und Glyptothek, München. 2655 = *ARV*² 471.196.

18. The tyrannicides Aristogeiton and Harmodius.
Copy of marble sculpture by Kritios and Nesiotes (after 480 B.C.E.).
By courtesy of Alinari/Art Resource, New York.
S0018824 K22416.

19. Youths compete for a man's gift. Red-figured kylix attributed
to the Brygos Painter (c. 475 B.C.E.). By courtesy of the
Vatican Museums. H550 = ARV^2 375.68 = ARV^2 1669.1.

20. Ithyphallic man bends down to fondle a boy and allow the boy to embrace him. Detail of a red-figured kylix interior attributed to the Brygos Painter (c. 475 B.C.E.). By courtesy of the Ashmolean Museum, Oxford. 1967.304 = *ARV*² 378.137.

21. Eros carries a gift of meat from a seated man to a youth. Red-figured kylix attributed to the Telephus Painter (c. 470 B.C.E.). By courtesy of the Staatliche Antikensammlungen und Glyptothek, München. 2669 = *ARV*² 818.26.

22. A lyre-brandishing youth threatens a pursuing suitor. Red-figured pelike attributed to the Aegisthus Painter (c. 465 B.C.E.). By courtesy of the Fitzwilliam Museum, University of Cambridge. GR.26–1937 = *ARV*^{2} 506.21.

23. Banquet scene: a lyre-playing youth admires a naked serving boy, while a man playing *kottabos* reclines with a youth on the other couch. Red-figured stamnos (c. 430 B.C.E.). By courtesy of the Staatliche Antikensammlungen und Glyptothek, München. 2410.

24a. Youth with a crown admires another youth who holds a lyre.
Red-figured kylix interior attributed to the Eretria Painter (c. 425 B.C.E.).
Gift of Gilbert M. Denman, Jr. By courtesy of the
San Antonio Museum of Art. 86.134.80.

24b. Side view of Fig. 24a: two youths admire
and converse with young athletes.

24c. Opposite side of Fig. 24b: two more
youths gaze at young athletes.

25. Pan embraces the shepherd boy Daphnis and teaches him music.
Copy of marble sculpture by Heliodorus (c. 100 B.C.E.).
By courtesy of Alinari/Art Resource, New York. So105879 AN23160.

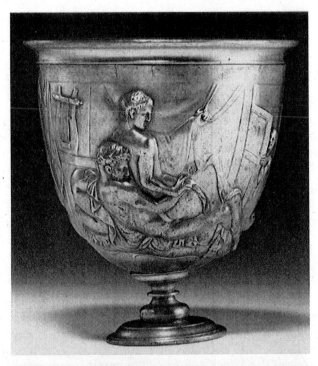

26a. Man and youth engage in anal intercourse while a slave watches through a door. The Warren Cup. Silver goblet (c. 100 c.e.). © The British Museum. 1999.4.26.1.

26b. Opposite side of Fig. 26a: man and boy engage in anal intercourse.

CHAPTER 6

Hellenistic Poetry

The Hellenistic age is generally defined as the period of Greek history from the death of Alexander the Great until the Roman conquest of Greece (323–146 B.C.E.), but in terms of literary history the period really extends much later, arguably as far as the early second century C.E. Alexander's conquests led to a diffusion of Greek culture and administrative control throughout Asia Minor, the Levant, and Egypt; these areas, together with the older Greek settlements in the west, coalesced into a cosmopolitan cultural sphere based on the Greek language and literary heritage, but no longer centered on Greece itself. The poets treated in this chapter came from a stunning variety of places: Libya (Callimachus), Sicily (Theocritus), southern Italy (Nossis), Syria (Meleager), Asia Minor (Strato), Crete (Rhianus). The most intense literary activity no longer centered upon Athens, but on the newly founded Greco-Egyptian city of Alexandria, with its splendid library and sponsorship of editorial and scholarly work on earlier texts. Egypt did not come under full Roman control until the late first century B.C.E., and even after Roman domination, the literary culture was continuous with earlier Hellenistic traditions and remained largely aloof from Latin influences.

Hellenistic poetry and art differed from that of the archaic and classical periods in the attention it gave to realism and even the grotesque in preference to idealization of the human figure and society (see, for example, the hyperrealism of fig. 25). Moreover, the scholarly culture of Alexandria produced poetry characterized by often recondite allusions to literary sources or historical and geographical minutiae. All of these features contribute to our understanding of homosexual erotics during this period.

Callimachus of Cyrene was in many ways the most influential and paradigmatic early Hellenistic poet. He is best known for championing the learned, finely polished shorter genres above more popular and ambitious forms like epic. These values of esoteric selectiveness are reflected in his erotic preferences: he does not want the boy who has been in circulation (**6.3**) or who is readily available (**6.5**), and complains of those who are ambitious for money (**6.6, 6.7**). **6.4** is an interesting meditation on the divided soul that seems to derive from the psychological doctrine of Plato's *Phaedrus*.

Theocritus of Syracuse was Callimachus' contemporary, most famous as the first "bucolic" poet: **6.9** is a splendid example of his dialogues among shepherds, in this case illustrating an embittered confrontation between an older and younger shepherd who had once been involved in a pederastic relationship. The younger (Lacon) proclaims himself now to be the lover of a boy in his own right, while the older (Comatas) has graduated to the love of women. Several of Theocritus' non-bucolic poems are also concerned with pederasty: **6.10** and **6.12** wish vainly for reciprocated love from an indifferent boy. Like Callimachus' epigram on the divided soul, **6.13** is the soliloquy of an aged lover who tries to bring himself to reason. **6.14**, possibly the work of a later imitator, tells the story of a lover who hangs himself on an indifferent youth's doorstep; the proud youth later dies when a statue of Eros topples over and falls on him.

The Hellenistic age also saw the introduction of pederastic themes into many myths: **6.11** assigns Heracles a young beloved named Hylas and adopts what many see as an ironic tone toward their love. Heracles ultimately loses the boy to some heterosexual competition and is sidetracked from his heroic mission. Phanocles (**6.15**) credits Orpheus with the invention of pederasty and sees it as an explicit alternative to the love of women. Much later, we see the epigrammatist Strato (**6.87**) attribute a pederastic relationship to the Cretan warriors Idomeneus and Meriones, who fought on the Greek side in the *Iliad*.

Literary biography was a favorite preoccupation of Hellenistic scholars, and it is to this imaginative period that we owe many of the apocryphal anecdotes about famous figures of the past. Literary forgery was not unknown, as we see with the series of epigrams attributed to Plato (**6.21–24**), depicting him as the lover of various young men represented in his dialogues, often in situations that would have been chronologically impossible. Nevertheless, the epigrams are fine specimens of a sort and incorporate Platonic imagery to good effect.

Lesbianism is less often in evidence as a theme. The male epigrammatist Asclepiades treats it very unsympathetically (**6.1**). From the poet Nossis, however, we have approximately a dozen epigrams: while none are explicitly homoerotic, in **6.16** she declares love as her theme and in **6.19** proclaims Sappho as her model. Most of the others, like **6.17–18**, show a keen appreciation of feminine beauty and grace, with no interest in men and their activities. If she wrote more explicit love poetry, it may have been lost due to the indifference or even antagonism of those responsible for the preservation and transmission of literature in the ancient world. But even without such poems, we see in Nossis a world of female homosocial intimacy, something attested in far cruder and more comic form by Herondas' dialogue between two women sharing secrets about a dildo (**6.20**), which a girl named "Nossis" is said to have borrowed, as if to imply that such an instrument were especially useful for a woman of her preferences.

The greatest flowering of Hellenistic epigram actually occurred long after the first generation of poets. The two most notable epigrammatists who treated pederastic themes were Meleager of Gadara (c. 100 B.C.E.) and Strato of Sardis, usually dated to the time of the philhellenic and homosexual Roman emperor Hadrian (early second century C.E.). Both poets edited anthologies that mixed their own work with chosen pieces by their predecessors. Epigram affords considerable insight into the social *realia* of pederasty in this period: where earlier literature had idealized the free association of man and boy as class-equals, we here find a frank emphasis on relationships with slaves (**6.77, 6.82, 6.87**) and with demanding boys whose behavior is tantamount to prostitution (**6.6, 6.7, 6.27, 6.28, 6.62, 6.78, 6.83**). The freeborn boy whose father may be an obstacle is an exception (**6.64**); however, some poems allude to teachers (**6.8**) or gymnastic trainers (**6.50, 6.79**) who have physical relations with their students, who are presumably freeborn boys.

Strato exhibits a marked preference for young boys, starting at the age of twelve (**6.60, 6.73, 6.74**): eighteen is definitely too old, and even sixteen-to seventeen-year-olds are by implication more than he can handle. **6.89** attacks a man for preferring full-grown youths. The emergence of body hair is repeatedly invoked as the decisive event in a boy's loss of attractiveness (**6.29, 6.32, 6.33, 6.54, 6.55, 6.69**). The boy is warned to take advantage of his allure while he has it, for time will soon change the equation (**6.26, 6.81**); the fragility of adolescent beauty is frequently compared to a flower's short-lived bloom (**6.30, 6.71, 6.80**). The cycle of love alluded to by Sappho (**1.5.21–24**) and Theognis (**1.63, 1.67**), in which a once arrogant youth grows older and himself falls in love, is also a leitmotif in Hellenistic epigram (**6.45, 6.51, 6.68**). On the other hand, some lovers promise a devotion that will outlast the effects of age and abide forever (**6.65, 6.66, 6.88**). The kind of mutual love vainly wished for in Theocritus (**6.10, 6.12**) is celebrated in Asclepiades (**6.2**). But others glorify easy enjoyment of multiple and various boys (**6.37, 6.38, 6.42, 6.50, 6.61, 6.86**).

Another common motif inherited from archaic poetry is that of the power of a beautiful boy's eyes, imagined as setting the lover aflame with their fiery visual rays (**6.34–35, 6.39–41, 6.44, 6.56, 6.72**). The lover's helplessness generally is assumed (**6.25, 6.31, 6.42–43**). In this context, active and passive roles often become blurred, with the boy dominant and the lover subordinated, at least until the boy loses his bloom. Some poems explore what appear to be age-equal relations between boys in which roles become readily reversible (**6.40, 6.76, 6.84**). Another theme that has some precedent in archaic poetry (**1.77, 1.85.2–9**), but becomes more prevalent in this period, is the contrast between pederasty and love of women: one finds some poets presuming to turn away from boys to women (**6.46, 6.52**), but Strato emphatically prefers boys, paradoxically both because they are more natural (**6.63, 6.70**) and because pederastic love is superior to the laws of bestial nature that govern heterosexual intercourse (**6.85**). As we shall see in chapter 10, these competing ideological positions become more rigidly polarized the later we progress.

Bibliographical Note

For a general overview of pederasty in Hellenistic poetry, see Buffière (1980) 279–324.

On Callimachus' pederastic epigrams, see G. B. Walsh (1990) 11–14, Gutzwiller (1998) 213–24, and Acosta-Hughes (2002) 224–25 and 249–51. On the much-disputed **6.3**, see Giangrande (1969), Barigazzi (1973), McKay (1974), Krafft (1977), Henrichs (1979), Schwinge (1980), Koenen (1993) 84–89, and Hubner (1996). On **6.4**, see Livrea (1996) 66–72. For Callimachus' epigram on his poverty (**6.6**), see Giangrande (1968) 135–39. On the *Iambs* (**6.7** and **6.8**), see Acosta-Hughes (2002) 195 and 235–52.

On pederastic themes in Theocritus and their background in archaic poetry, see Effe (1992a) and Hunter (1996) 167–95. On the relationship between Comatas and Lacon in *Idyll* 5, see Pretagostini (1984) and Stanzel (1995) 90–97. Giangrande (1971) contends that the speaker of *Idyll* 12 is meant to appear as a boorish rustic; on the same poem, see also Kelly (1979–80), Nethercut (1984), and G. B. Walsh (1990) 18–21. On the interrelation of the Hylas story in *Idyll* 13 with that in Apollonius Rhodius, see Köhnken (1965) 9–83 and Effe (1992b). For Theocritus' version as an ironic interpretation of the myth, see Mastronarde (1968) and Effe (1978) 60–64; however, Stanzel (1995) 229–47 and Köhnken (1996) deny ironic intent and see the story more as an illustration that love affects even demigods. For the mythological background to the story and interpretation of Hylas' rape by the nymphs as a transition to heterosexuality, see Hunter (1993a) 36–41. On the pseudo-Theocritean *Idyll* 23, see Radici Colace (1971) and Giangrande (1992) 213–20.

On the epigrams attributed to Plato, see Ludwig (1963). Skinner (1989) argues explicitly for Nossis' lesbianism. On her poetry, see also Gigante (1974) and (1981), Snyder (1989) 77–84, Skinner (1991a) and (1991b), Furiani (1991), Giangrande (1992) 220–25, and Gutzwiller (1998) 74–88. Ludwig (1968) discusses a variety of epigrams in Book 12 of the *Greek An-*

thology and shows their thematic interconnections. Tarán (1979) 7–51 studies epigrams that invoke the Ganymede theme, and in 52–114 examines the convention of the drunken revel outside a boy's (or woman's) house. Tarán (1985) looks at the motif of body hair as a warning of temporality in pederastic epigram. On Meleager's collection of erotic epigrams and its principles of arrangement, see Gutzwiller (1998) 282–301. A full-scale commentary on Meleager and the earlier epigrammatists is provided by Gow and Page (1965).

Clarke (1984) suggests a date for Strato in the first century B.C.E., rather than the orthodox Hadrianic date. Maxwell-Stuart (1972) and Clarke (1978b) and (1994) offer valuable observations on a variety of Strato's poems; Steinbichler (1998) provides detailed commentary on all of them. On **6.85** and later sexual preference debates, see Furiani (1987); on **6.89** see Ebert (1965). For an annotated edition of all the poems in Books 5 and 12 of the *Greek Anthology*, see Paduano (1989).

6.1 Asclepiades, *AP* 5.207 (7 Gow-Page)

Asclepiades was an early Alexandrian epigrammatist, who wrote in the first quarter of the third century B.C.E.

The Samian girls Bitto and Nannion[1] are not of a mind
  To meet with Aphrodite on her own terms
But desert to other practices, and not good ones.[2] Lady Cypris,
  Abhor these fugitives from your bed.

6.2 Asclepiades, *AP* 12.105 (22 GP)

I, little Eros, flown from my mother, still easy to catch,
  Do not fly high from Damis' house,
But here loving and loved without envy,
  Am not mixed with many, but am joined in spirit one with one.[3]

6.3 Callimachus, *AP* 12.43 (2 GP)

The most influential of all the Alexandrian poets, Callimachus was active during the first half of the third century B.C.E.

---

1. Elsewhere these two names are those of courtesans.
2. A reference to lesbian relations.
3. The interpretation is controversial: is Damis a boy or a lover of boys? Is Eros characterized as his lover or is he merely characteristic of the relationship between Damis and his lover?

I hate the cyclical poem,[4] nor do I enjoy
   A path that carries many hither and yon.
I despise too a promiscuous beloved, nor do I drink
   From any font. I loathe all that is common.
Lysanias, you are fair, yes, fair. Yet before uttering
   This clearly, some echo says, "He is another's."[5]

6.4 Callimachus, *AP* 12.73 (4 GP)

Half of my soul yet is a breathing thing, and half I know not
   Whether Love or Hades has snatched it, but that it is vanished.
Is it gone again to some boy? And yet frequently
   I warned, "Young men, do not receive the runaway."
Seek it at Theutimus'. For I know that one, my soul, wanders
   Somewhere near there, deserving to be stoned and sick in love.

6.5 Callimachus, *AP* 12.102 (1 GP)

The hunter, Epicydes, in the mountains seeks
   Every hare and the tracks of each roe,
Enduring frost and snow. And if someone says,
   "Look, this beast lies shot," he picks it not up.
Such too is my love. For it knows to pursue what flees
   But what lies at hand it flies by.

6.6 Callimachus, *AP* 12.148 (7 GP)

I know that my hands are empty of wealth. All the same, Menippus,
   Don't, by the Graces, tell my own dream to me.
On hearing this bitter word I am in intense pain.
   Yes, my friend, of everything from you this is the most unloving.

6.7 Callimachus, *Diegesis to Iamb* 3

This text is a later editor's summary of an invective poem.

"O would, Lord Apollo, I were when I was not."[6] He censures the era as one
of wealth rather than of virtue, and approves the one before this, which

---

4. Episodic epic poetry imitating Homer—a genre practiced by many.
5. In Greek, this phrase rhymes with the repeated word for "fair."
6. Probably the first line of *Iamb 3*.

was of the opposite frame of mind than these men (his contemporaries). And he reproves further a certain Euthydemus, on the grounds that he makes use of his beauty for profit, when he is presented by his mother to a rich man.

6.8 Callimachus, *Diegesis to Iamb* 5

This text, like the last, is a later editor's summary of an invective poem.

"O friend—for advice is a holy thing—" He attacks in iambic fashion[7] a schoolteacher, by name Apollonius, but some say a certain Cleon, because he does shameful things to his own students. In the guise of good intention, he urges him not to do this, lest he be caught.

6.9 Theocritus, *Idyll* 5

A contemporary of Callimachus, Theocritus was especially well known for his bucolic poems, purporting to be the conversations of humble shepherds. This one enacts the hostile encounter of a former lover (Comatas) and beloved (Lacon).

COMATAS: Watch out, my goats, keep away from that shepherd, the Sybarite[8] Lacon.
  He is the one who, the day before yesterday, pilfered my goatskin.
LACON: Hey! Get away from the spring, little lambs. Don't you see it's Comatas?
  That is the fellow who, the other day, made off with my Pan-pipes.
COMATAS: What sort of Pan-pipe? When did you ever, a slave of Sibyrtas,
  Get such an instrument? Why do you no longer think it sufficient
  Now to make beautiful music with Corydon, blowing his straw flute?
LACON: I mean the musical instrument Lycon once gave me, O Freedman.[9]
  What is that goatskin of yours you say Lacon made off with, Comatas?
  Tell me. Not even your master, Eumarus, has got one to sleep in.   10
COMATAS: I mean the spotted one Crocylus gave me the time that he killed a
  Goat for the nymphs as a sacrifice. You were consumed by such envy,

---

7. I.e., satirically, in the verse form of Archilochus.

8. Sybaris was a wealthy Greek city in southern Italy. Normally "Sybarite" would mean a citizen of that city, but Lacon is, of course, a slave. Comatas may therefore be using the epithet sarcastically.

9. Again, this is probably meant sarcastically, since Comatas is said two lines later to have a master.

Wretch, even then, until now you have finally left me quite naked.
LACON: Never, by Pan of the headland, did Lacon, the son of Calaethis,
Strip you of your only garment—if ever I did, my dear fellow,
May I take leave of my senses and jump off that cliff in the Crathis.[10]
COMATAS: No, my good fellow, indeed, by the nymphs of the swamp do
I swear it,
(May they continue propitious and kindly to me to the end), but
Truly Comatas did not surreptitiously pilfer your Pan-pipe.
LACON: If I believe you, in truth may I suffer the torments of
Daphnis![11]   20
But, as it is, if you're willing to wager a kid, though it's nothing
Special, I'll wage you a singing-match till you are forced to surrender.
COMATAS: Talk of the pig that once challenged Athena! But here is the
kid which
I shall put up; come along with you, wager a well-fatted lamb, then.
LACON: How, you old fox, are the stakes that we each have put up to be
equal?
Who wouldn't like to sheer wool more than hair? Why would anyone
milk a
Miserable bitch when a goat is available nursing her first-born?
COMATAS: One who believes he will vanquish his neighbor, as you do,
a hornet
Buzzing against a cicada! But seeing the kid doesn't seem a
Fair enough wager to you, here's a billy-goat. Start off the contest.   30
LACON: Not such a hurry, you aren't on fire. You will sing much more
sweetly
Seated beneath the wild olive here, under the trees of the thicket.
Here the cool water is dripping continually and the grass grows;
Here there's a bed for us both to lie down on, and crickets are chirping.
COMATAS: I'm in no hurry; and yet I am terribly hurt that you dare to
Look me so straight in the eye, even I who instructed you when you
Still were an innocent boy. You may see just what gratitude comes to—
Might as well bring up a wolf cub as rear such a puppy to eat you!
LACON: When can I even recall ever hearing or learning a single
Nice thing from you? What a jealous, obscene little manikin you are!   40
COMATAS: Once when I buggered your bum and you said that it hurt. You
may hear the
Nanny-goats bleat, but the billy-goat fucks them for all of their bleating.

10. A river that flowed through the territory of Sybaris.
11. A legendary shepherd who was either blinded for unwittingly breaking his vow of
fidelity to a nymph or who wasted away from unfulfilled love.

LACON: May you be buried no deeper than that penetration, you
　　hump-back!
　Crawl over here, I say crawl, and you'll sing your last pastoral ditty.
COMATAS: No, I won't come over there. There are oaks here and galin-
　　gale also,
　Here there are bees that go beautifully buzzing in search of the beehives;
　Here there are two cool fountains of water, and birds in the treetops
　Gurgle and twitter. The shade over here is in no way the same as
　That over there, and the pine tree above me bombards me with
　　pinecones.
LACON: If you will come over here you will tread upon lambskins and
　　woolly　　　　　　　　　　　　　　　　　　　　　　　　　　　　50
　Fleeces much softer than sleep, I assure you; but as for those smelly
　Goatskins of yours, they are ranker and stink even stronger than you do.
　Now I shall put out a great big bowl for the nymphs, of the whitest
　Milk, and I'll put out another as big full of olive oil also.
COMATAS: But if you move over here you will tread upon delicate fern and
　Blossoming basil, and here you can stretch yourself out upon goatskins
　Four times as soft as the fleeces of lambs that you have over by you.
　And I shall put out eight buckets of milk as an offering unto
　Pan,[12] and eight dishes containing eight honeycombs oozing with honey.
LACON: All right, compete over there, sing your pastoral song over there,
　　then!　　　　　　　　　　　　　　　　　　　　　　　　　　　　60
　Tread on your own territory and keep your old oak trees. However,
　Who is to judge us? If only Lycopas the oxherd would pass by!
COMATAS: Him I don't have any use for. However, if you really want to,
　We'll give a shout to that fellow, the woodman, the chap who is cutting
　Heather beyond you: it's Morson.
LACON: Let's shout to him, shall we?
COMATAS: You call him.
LACON: Come over here, my good fellow, and listen a little, I beg you.
　We are competing to see which of us is the better bucolic
　Singer. But, excellent Morson, don't judge me with too much indulgence,
　Please, neither show disproportionate favor to this other fellow.
COMATAS: No, in the name of the nymphs, my dear Morson, don't favor
　　Comatas　　　　　　　　　　　　　　　　　　　　　　　　　70
　Overmuch, nor be extremely indulgent to that other fellow.
　This is the flock of Sibyrtas of Thurii;[13] this is his shepherd;
　Whereas these goats that you see are Eumarus the Sybarite's livestock.

12. The patron god of shepherds.
13. Another Greek city in southern Italy, not far from Sybaris.

LACON: Nobody asked you, by God, if the flock were Sibyrtas' or mine, you
    Idiot! Why have you gotten so talkative all of a sudden?
COMATAS: Bless you, I never speak anything other than truth, my good
    fellow.
    I am not bragging. It's you who are so very fond of a quarrel.
LACON: If you have anything worthy of saying, then say it, and let this
    Stranger escape back to town. What a blabbermouth you are, Comatas!
COMATAS: Truly, the Muses do like me much better than Daphnis the
    poet: 80
    To them I sacrificed only the day before yesterday two goats.
LACON: Therefore Apollo must like me immensely: I'm fattening for him
    This handsome ram as his autumn festival[14] fast is approaching.
COMATAS: All of the goats that I milk except two have had twins; and the
    little
    Girl who is watching me says, "You poor man, are you milking alone,
    then?"
LACON: Shocking! But Lacon can fill just about twenty baskets with
    cream-cheese,
    And he debauches an immature boy still in bud in the bushes.
COMATAS: And Clearista keeps pelting her favorite goatherd with apples[15]
    When he goes by with his goats, and she whistles deliciously at him.
LACON: Yes, and when Cratidas hurries all glabrous to meet me, his
    shepherd,   90
    How he excites me, how glossy the hair at the nape of his neck curls!
COMATAS: Nevertheless, no mere hedge-rose or simple anemone's worthy
    To be compared to the roses that grow by the wall in their borders.
LACON: Neither are figs to be likened to acorns, for whereas the latter
    Take their thin rind from the holm-oak, the former are sweeter than
    honey.
COMATAS: Also, I'm presently going to give the dear maiden a pigeon
    Which I shall catch in a juniper bush, for it's there that it perches.
LACON: Presently I shall bestow upon Cratidas without his asking
    Delicate wool for a cloak which I freshly have shorn from the black ewe.
COMATAS: Hey, get away from that untended olive tree, kids, do your
    grazing   100
    Here as you're facing the tamarisks opposite this little hillock.
LACON: No, keep away from the oak trees, Conarus—yes, you!—and
    Cinaetha!
    Feed over there to the east, where I tell you to, just like Phalarus.

---

14. The Carneia, a festival celebrated in Dorian states at the first full moon of autumn.
15. A gesture of flirtation.

COMATAS: I have a pail that is fashioned of cypress, and also a goblet
    Carved by Praxiteles:[16] these I am keeping to give to my girlfriend.
LACON: I have a dog that is fond of the flock and can throttle a wolf, and
    Him I present to my boyfriend to hunt every manner of wild beasts.
COMATAS: Grasshoppers leaping so easily over the fence of my vineyard,
    Please do not damage the vines, which are withered and brittle already.
LACON: Notice, cicadas, how easily I can encourage this goatherd;   110
    Similarly in midsummer you, too, have encouraged the reapers.
COMATAS: How I abominate all of these bushy-tailed foxes that always
    Hang about Micon's at evening hoping to nibble his berries.
LACON: What I detest are those cockroaches greedy to gobble the giant
    Figs of Philondas, and afterwards wafted away on the breezes.
COMATAS: Don't you remember the time I was up you, and you with a
        grimace
    Wiggled your bottom deliciously, holding on tight to that oak tree?
LACON: No, that is something I do not remember at all. When Eumarus
    Tied you up here and then reamed you out thoroughly—that I
        remember.
COMATAS: Somebody's bitter already, or didn't you notice it, Morson?   120
    Better go pluck up some squills from the grave of a wise woman,[17] quickly!
LACON: Morson, you see I am certainly bothering somebody also.
    Hasten to dig up some cyclamen,[18] go to the banks of the Hales.
COMATAS: Then let the Himera flow not with water but milk, and the
        Crathis
    Redden with wine, and its reeds be productive and edible fruits, too!
LACON: So let the Sybaris trickle with honey for me; before sunrise
    There may a girl with her jug dip up honeycomb rather than water.
COMATAS: Goatwort and moon-clover—such is the fodder my goats have
        to feed on;
    Also, they trample on mastich and lay themselves down on arbutus.[19]
LACON: Honeysweet balm there is here in abundance for grazing my
        sheep on;   130
    Here does the flowering cistus abound, as abundant as roses.
COMATAS: I'm out of love with Alcippa, since yesterday she didn't kiss me
    Tenderly, holding me fast by the ears, when I gave her a pigeon.

16. Probably the famous fourth-century Athenian sculptor. If so, the boast is ignorant hy-
perbole, since he hardly would have spent his time carving goblets, nor would a poor slave like
Comatas own one if he did.

17. Squills were herbs with purgative powers. Plucked from the grave of a witch, they would
be used in apotropaic magic to ward off an enemy's curses.

18. Another herb with apotropaic powers.

19. All of these wildflowers and grasses are considered ideal for grazing goats.

LACON: I am extremely in love with Eumedes, however, for when I
   Gave him a Pan-pipe to play on he kissed me exceedingly nicely.[20]
COMATAS: Lacon, it just isn't decent or proper that jays should compete
       with
   Nightingales, hoopoes with swans. You poor wretch, you are fond of a
      quarrel.
MORSON: I am commanding the shepherd to stop, but to you, O Comatas,
   Morson is giving the lamb. When you sacrifice it to the nymphs be
   Sure that you send unto Morson immediately a nice morsel.   140
COMATAS: Yes, I will send it, by Pan! Let the whole of my flock of young
   kids now
   Snort when you see how immense is the laugh I shall have at this
      shepherd
   Lacon, because I have finally won the reward of a ewe-lamb.
   Higher than heaven I'll skip for you; be of good courage, my horned
      goats,
   I shall be washing you all in Lake Sybaris sometime tomorrow.
   You there, that white one that butts, if you mount any one of the
      she-goats
   Till I can sacrifice fairly this lamb to the nymphs, I will geld you.
   There he is, at it again! I am warning you, if I don't geld you
   May I become a Melanthius[21] rather than being Comatas.

6.10 Theocritus, *Idyll* 12

This and the remaining idylls are non-bucolic. Here the speaker addresses a beloved
boy after two days' absence.

So, you have come, my dear boy; the third night, and behold, with the
      dawn you've
Come. And yet those who desire the absent grow old in a single
Day. As the springtime is pleasanter far than the winter, and as an
Apple surpasses a sloe; as a ewe is much fleecier than her
Lamb, and a virgin is preferable to a thrice-married woman,
Just as a fawn is much lighter of foot than a calf, and the shrill-voiced
Nightingale sings so much better than all other birds put together,
So you delighted me by your appearance. I hastened toward you
Much like a wayfarer seeking the oak tree's shade in a heat wave.

---

20. Lacon here seems to forget himself and admit that he had given away to Eumedes the
pan-pipe he accused Comatas of stealing at the beginning of the poem.
   21. In *Odyssey* 22.474 Odysseus punishes the disloyal goatherd Melanthius by cutting off his
nose, ears, hands, feet, and genitals.

Would that a mutual passion inspired us equally, so that   10
We might become to all those who come after a subject of ballad:
"Splendid, indeed, were these two among lovers of earlier ages,
One, as a man from Amyclae might phrase it perhaps, The Inspirer,[22]
Whereas the other is what a Thessalian calls an Inquirer.[23]
Yoked in a common and equal affection they loved one another.
Men were of gold again,[24] when the beloved requited his lover."
Ah, Father Zeus, and you ageless immortals, if only it might be
So! and that with the elapse of two hundred or more generations
Someone might bring me these tidings in hell, from which there is no exit:
"Your sentimental attachment and that of your charming Inquirer   20
Linger on everyone's lips, and on those of the bachelors mostly."
Well, in such matters the heavenly powers are paramount: it will
Be as they wish. But for praising your beauty I surely will grow no
Pimples above my exiguous nose—the stigmata of liars.
For if you prick me a little you instantly make it all better,
Doubling my pleasure so that I come off with much more than my portion.
Champion oarsmen of Megara, excellent men of Nisaea,[25]
Blessing upon you forever because you have honored above all
Others that exile from Attica, Diocles,[26] lover of young boys.
Always about the beginning of spring at his tomb adolescents   30
Gather together in keen competition for prizes in kissing.
He who most sweetly impresses his lips on the lips of another
Heavily laden with garlands of flowers returns to his mother.
Blessed, whoever adjudges the kisses among those contestant
Boys! I imagine he supplicates bright-eyed Ganymede often
On such occasions to give him a mouth like the Lydian touchstone
Which moneychangers employ to distinguish true gold from an alloy.

6.11 Theocritus, *Idyll* 13

This idyll narrates the myth of Heracles and Hylas on the voyage of the ship Argo. The story was also told at greater length by Theocritus' contemporary Apollonius of Rhodes; it is uncertain which poet was first.

---

22. Amyclae is a town near Sparta. "Inspirer" translates the Greek *eispnēlos*, on which see **2.11**.

23. The Greek is *aitēs*. The etymology is uncertain; others translate this word as "Hearer." The sense may be that the beloved is a student to his Inspirer's teachings.

24. The reference is to a return of the Golden Age, when all was happy and prosperous.

25. Megara was the Dorian state on the isthmus north of Corinth. Nisaea was its port.

26. A mythological king of Eleusis, an Attic town close to the border with Megara, who was driven out by Theseus. He met his death while defending his beloved in battle, and the Megarians later honored him with athletic games.

We aren't the only ones, as we supposed, for whom Love was begotten,
Nicias,[27] no matter which of the heavenly powers begot him,
Nor are we, surely, the first to whom beauty appears to be beauty,
We who are mortals and cannot so much as envisage tomorrow.
Even the bronze-hearted son of Amphitryon, Heracles, he who
Challenged the savagest lion, was amorous once of a young boy,
Sweet little Hylas, who still was adorned with the ringlets of childhood,
Teaching him everything just like a father who teaches his dear son
All of the things he has learned to be, noble himself and distinguished.
So they were never apart, whether at the commencement of midday   10
Or when the morning's immaculate horses ascend into heaven,
Or at the hour when twittering chickens look forward to bedtime
Seeing the mother-hen rustling her wings on some smoke-blackened rafter.
Thereby the child would be molded according to Heracles' liking
And in this partnership finally come to authentic adulthood.
Therefore, when Jason, whose father was Aeson,[28] in search of the golden
Fleece was about to set sail, and the best of the princes were joining
Him, the elect out of every city, whoever was useful,
Then the laborious hero of many adventures arrived in
Wealthy Iolcus, the son of Alcmene, the Midean heiress.[29]   20
Hylas accompanied him to the benches of Argo, the well-manned
Ship that without even touching the slate-colored rocks in collision
Darted right through like an eagle and ran ahead into the deep and
Generous gulf of the Phasis,[30] since when the Symplegades[31] stand still.
After the rise of the Pleiades, at the beginning of summer,[32]
Just as the uttermost pastures are feeding the lambs that are newborn,
Then the divinely selected contingent of heroes considered
Sailing, and taking their places inside of the hull of the Argo
Entered the Hellespont after three days with a following south wind.

27. A physician and minor poet from Miletus to whom Theocritus also addresses three
other poems.

28. Jason was a Thessalian hero who was sent by Pelias, king of Iolcus, to retrieve from the
eastern land of Colchis a golden fleece guarded by a fire-breathing dragon. He equipped the
ship Argo and recruited the most famous heroes of his time. His story is told at length in Apollonius of Rhodes' *Argonautica*.

29. Heracles' mother, Alcmene, was the daughter of Electryon, the king of Midea in the
vicinity of Argos.

30. A river in Colchis (modern Georgia) at the other end of the Black Sea.

31. Giant cliffs bordering the entrance to the Black Sea at the Bosporus. Prior to the Argo,
they were imagined as clashing together at irregular intervals, thereby imperiling sea travel to
the north.

32. The Pleiades, or "The Doves," usually first appeared in the night sky in late April or
early May.

There they cast anchor within the Propontis, in sight of the oxen   30
Of the Cyani[33] enlarging their furrows by dragging the plowshare.
Once disembarked on the beach in their pairs they began to prepare their
Evening meal; but a communal couch was arranged for the mess-mates,
For a convenient meadow provided them plenty of thick-set
Galingale mingled with prickly sedge, which they cut for their bedding.
Golden-haired Hylas had gone with a brazen container to fetch some
Water for Heracles' supper and that of unflinching Telamon,
Both of whom dined at one table as usual, being companions.
Presently Hylas discovered a spring in a low-lying hollow
Thickly surrounded by rushes and dark blue celandine, crisp green   40
Maidenhair fern and luxuriant celery also, and dog's-tooth
Such as extends over marshes; and there in the midst of the water
Nymphs were performing a dance, those unsleeping divinities dreaded
Rurally: Eunica, Malis, and—spring in her glances—Nycheia.
Just as the youngster was dipping his practically bottomless pitcher
Eagerly into the drink he was seized by the hand by the three nymphs:
Passionate love for the Greek adolescent had panicked the tender
Hearts of all three; and their victim fell headlong into the black water,
Just as a fiery star is seen plummeting headlong from heaven
Into the sea, whereat one of the sailors exclaims to his fellows,   50
"Lighten the tackle, my lads, for the wind is propitious for sailing."
Holding the blubbering boy on their laps the solicitous nymphs were
Vainly attempting to pacify Hylas with blandishing speeches.
Meanwhile, the son of Amphitryon, worried at his disappearance,
Went in pursuit with his club, which he usually clutched in his right hand,
Also his bow, which was beautifully bent in the Scythian fashion.
"Hylas!" he shouted again and again, just as loud as his throat could
Bellow, and thrice did his boyfriend reply, but his voice underwater
Sounded so faint that he seemed to be distant although really nearby.
Like a carnivorous lion that hears in the mountains a bleating   60
Fawn and, awakening, hastens toward the convenient meal, so
Heracles, deeply disturbed by desire for the child that was missing,
Ranged through intractable thorn-bushes covering plenty of country.
Wretched are lovers! How much he endured in his wanderings through the
Woods and the mountains, with all of the business of Jason forgotten.
But though the vessel was ready, her tackle aloft and the rest all
Present, at midnight the demigods lowered the sails once again and
Waited for Heracles. Maddened, he wandered wherever his footsteps

33. These people lived on the south coast of the Propontis (the Sea of Marmara) near a
deep inlet.

Led him, a cruel divinity gnawing the heart in his bosom.
Thus it is beautiful Hylas is numbered among the immortals.   70
However, Heracles' shipmates derided the hero's desertion,
Since he abandoned the Argo with all of his sixty companions,
Coming to Colchis on foot, and the strange, inhospitable Phasis.

6.12 Theocritus, *Idyll* 29

*The following two poems are written in unusual Aeolic meters that recall the verse of
Sappho and Alcaeus. In this poem, the speaker addresses a promiscuous boy.*

In vino veritas[34] the saying goes, dear boy,
And as we're in our cups we may as well be frank.
So I'll tell you what is laid up in reason's bank
Account: you are unwilling to love me with your whole heart,
I know; but since of life I have the better part
Through your ideal form,[35] the remnant I let go.
When you are in the mood I spend a blessed day
Equal to the gods'; if you're not it's all in shadow.
How can it be right to treat an admirer so,
Giving him such pains? As a young man to his elder,   10
If you listen to me you'll do so much better
And thank me for it later. Make your only nest
In that one tree up which no uncouth creep can climb.
Now you settle on a certain branch today,
Another one tomorrow, trading this for that;
And if somebody praises your pretty face on sight,
For him you straight conceive a more than three years' friendship,
Rating your first suitor a mere three days' acquaintance.
You seem to breathe an air of super-masculine men,
But keep in love your kind, with whom you have your life.[36]   20
If you do so you'll gain a goodly reputation
About town, and Love will never treat you harshly,
Love who gaily chastens the hearts and minds of men,

---

34. "In wine is truth." This phrase is the beginning of a familiar poem by Alcaeus, also addressed to a boy.

35. The Greek word here is *idea*, which in addition to meaning "beauty" is also the technical term Plato uses to describe the Forms. An allusion to Plato's doctrine of love may be intended here.

36. There may be a problem with the text here, but as it stands, it seems to exhort the boy to stay with his equals, like the speaker, rather than seeking men of superior station (one might translate "super-human" in place of "super-masculine").

Making an old softie out of one who once was iron.
Again by your delicious lips I supplicate you,
Remember just last year how you were younger still
And before a man can spit how we grow old and wrinkled;
There is no way to keep or call youth back again
Once flown, for youth has wings upon its shoulders,
And we are much too slow to capture things that fly.   30
With such thoughts in your mind you should become more kind,
Loving me in return, your beloved[37] without any
Pretence, so that when you possess a manly beard
We'll be to one another like Achilles and his friend.[38]
But if you consign these words to the winds to waft away
And say within yourself, "Why, fiend, do you pester me?"
Though now on your behalf after the golden apples
Or Cerberus, warden of the dead, I would gladly go,[39]
Then even if you were calling at my own front door
I should not come out, having stopped my cruel longing.   40

6.13 Theocritus, *Idyll* 30

This soliloquy shows an aging lover talking to himself.

Alas for this difficult and misfortunate malaise of mine!
This is the second month a feverish passion has possessed me
For a boy of mediocre beauty, although from head to toe
He is solid charm all over, and sweet the smile upon his cheeks.
If as it is this evil sometimes grips me fast and at others
Lets go, soon there will be no respite, not enough to get to sleep.
For yesterday in passing he glanced at me through his eyelashes
Surreptitiously, ashamed to stare me straight in the face, and blushed.
Thereupon infatuation grabbed a little more of my heart
And I went home newly wounded in my susceptibility.   10
Summoning my soul, I had a lengthy discussion with myself.
"What, at it again? And what will be the limit of this distraction?
Have you not yet noticed that you have got white hairs at your temples?
It's time to be sensible. No longer youthful in appearance,
Do not misbehave like those who have barely tasted of the years.

---

37. Note that here the lover refers to himself as a beloved *(erōmenos)*, implying a complete mutuality and reciprocation of sentiment.
   38. An allusion to Achilles and Patroclus, on whom see **2.21.601-2** and **5.7.179-80**.
   39. An allusion to the last two labors of Heracles, to retrieve the apples of the Hesperides and to capture Cerberus, the three-headed watchdog of the Underworld.

And another fact escapes you: it were infinitely better
For one who's older to be a stranger to the hard loves of youth.
For such as he life hurries by like the hoofbeats of fleeting deer.
Tomorrow he will lift anchor and sail away to who knows where,
While the pick of his sweet boyhood rests with his contemporaries.[40]   20
But for such as you desire eats away at your very marrow
Whenever you remember, and many dreams at night obsess you.
Not even a year is sufficient to abate this grave disease."
In so many words, and much more besides, I upbraided my soul,
Which replied as follows: "Whoever supposes he can conquer
Devious, resourceful Love might just as easily consider
Exactly what multiple of nine the stars above us number.
Even now it is necessary for me to stretch forth my neck
As far as I can and pull his yoke whether I want to or not.
For thus, my friend, that god ordains who overthrew the mighty mind   30
Of Zeus and the Cyprian herself.[41] Me he lifts and wafts away
Light as a leaf that lives for a day at the whim of every breeze."

6.14 Ps.-Theocritus, *Idyll* 23

*This narrative starts out with the conventional scene, familiar also from heterosexual
erotic poetry, of a locked-out lover at the doorstep of his beloved. The poem probably
dates to the first century B.C.E.*

There was a passionate fellow who loved an unkind adolescent,
Decent enough in physique but his character wasn't in keeping,
For he detested his suitor and had no indulgence toward him,
Ignorant what a divinity Love is, how big are the shafts he
Wields in his hands and how sharp are the arrows he pierces the heart with.
He was immovable, whether by words or by other approaches,
Nor did he offer encouragement such as assuages the fires of
Love, not a twitch of the lip, not a gleam in his eyes or a rosy
Glow in his cheeks, not a word or a kiss to alleviate passion.
Just as a beast of the forest suspiciously glares at the huntsman,   10
So he regarded mankind altogether. His lips were farouche, and
Even his pupils possessed an inexorable, dreadful expression.
Often his face was completely transformed by extreme irritation,
And in his violent temper the color deserted his features.
Yet even so he was beautiful, so that his anger excited

---

40. In other words, a boy will prefer lovers closer to his own age.

41. Zeus fell in love with Ganymede and many mortal women, Aphrodite with Anchises and
Adonis.

Rather his lover, who finally finding he could not endure the
Furious flame of the Love goddess went and complained at the hateful
House of his love: after kissing the threshold he lifted his voice thus.
"Brutal, rebarbative boy, did a pitiless lioness nurse you,
Or are you fashioned of stone, so insensible are you to passion?   20
Now I have come with my ultimate gifts for you: here is the noose I'll
Use, for I do not desire to vex you, my lad, with the sight of
Me any longer. Instead, I am going where you have condemned me—
There, it's alleged, is the sovereign cure for the sorrows of lovers,
Namely oblivion. Yet, if I lifted that drink to my lips and
Drank every drop of it, not even then should I quench my desire.
Finally, I am resigned to begin my adieux to your doorway,
Knowing the future. The rose is exquisite which time will extinguish;
Beautiful too in the Spring is the violet—quickly it ages!
White is the lily, and yet it is withered as soon as it flowers;   30
White as the snow is, moreover, it melts just as soon as it falls. The
Beauty of boyhood is beautiful also, and lives but a short while.
Sooner or later the moment will come when you feel as a lover
Does, when your heart is aflame, and the tears that you weep will be bitter.
Nevertheless, my dear boy, you can do me an ultimate kindness.
When you emerge from your house and discover my wretched cadaver
Dangling here in the doorway, do not I beseech you just pass me
By, but remain there and weep for me briefly, and when you have
          poured this
Tribute of tears, then unfasten the rope from me, wrap me in clothing
Stripped from your limbs and conceal me, and kiss me goodbye for the
          last time   40
Granting at least my dead body the grace of your lips. Do not fear me,
I am unable to harm you: by kissing me you will dismiss me.
Hollow a burial mound for me, one that will cover my love, and
At your departure address me three times, 'You are resting in peace, friend.'
And, if you like, you may add, 'My attractive companion has perished.'
Write this inscription I'm going to scrawl on the wall of your house, too.
LOVE WAS THE DEATH OF THIS PERSONAGE. TRAVELER, DO NOT CONTINUE,
BUT AS YOU PAUSE HERE REMARK, 'HIS COMPANION WAS NOT SYMPATHETIC.'"
When he had spoken he picked up a fatal stone and he placed it
Right in the midst of the entrance not far from the wall, and he
          fastened   50
Over the lintel a slender, dependable thread, and he put his
Neck in the noose, and he kicked the support from his foot and he
          hung there
Dead. But the boy, when he opened the door and beheld the dead body
Hanged in his very own porch, was completely untroubled in spirit,

Nor did he weep for the recent fatality. Rather, defiling
All of his juvenile garments he brushed by the body and went on
To the gymnasium with its athletic equipment, and calmly
Sought out his favorite part of the swimming pool, near where a statue
Stood of the god he had flouted.[42] But just as he sprang from the marble
Pedestal into the water, the effigy toppled upon him,   60
Killing that bad adolescent. The water grew crimson. Above it
Echoed the voice of the dead boy: "Lovers, rejoice! The disdainful
One is destroyed. Let disdainers be loving, for Love is a just god."

6.15 Phanocles, Fragment 1 *Collectanea Alexandrina*

This elegiac poem narrates the love of the musician Orpheus for the winged Calais.
After the loss of his beloved wife, Eurydice, Orpheus shunned women and, according
to some, invented pederasty. Phanocles' date is uncertain, but he is most likely third
century B.C.E.

Thracian Orpheus, son of Oeagrus,
    Conceived a heartfelt love for Calais, North Wind's son,
And often sat in the shady groves singing
    His passion, nor was his heart at peace,
But sleepless cares always gnawed away at his soul,
    When he glanced at lively Calais.
The evil-plotting Bistonian women,[43] whetting their sharp swords,
    Surrounded him and killed him,
Because first among the Thracians he showed the love
    Of males and never praised desire for women.   10
They cut his head off with bronze, and then threw it
    Into the sea, nailing it fast to his Thracian lyre,
That they might both be borne together over the ocean,
    Drenched by the blue waves.
The gray sea brought them ashore on holy Lesbos.
    And since the sound of the shrill lyre reached
Over the sea and the islands and the sea-fringed beaches,
    There men buried the clear-toned head of Orpheus
And placed in his tomb the shrill lyre, which pacified
    Even the mute rocks and the hostile water of Phorcys.[44]   20

---

42. Eros. Hermes might be a more usual god to find in a gymnasium, but see **2.17** for a
statue of Eros at the entrance to the Academy gymnasium.

43. Thracian Maenads, wild and sometimes violent devotees of Dionysus.

44. A primeval sea god.

From that time songs and lovely lyre-playing
　　Hold that island, and it is the most musical of places.[45]
As the brave Thracians learned of the savage deeds of their women,
　　And terrible sorrow came over them all,
They branded their wives, that they might have a black mark
　　On their flesh and not forget their hateful carnage.
Such a penalty of that sin do the women of Thrace pay
　　Even now to the murdered Orpheus.

6.16 Nossis, *AP* 5.170 (1 GP)

Nossis was a female epigrammatist of the early third century B.C.E. *She celebrated love and female beauty and regarded herself as a successor to Sappho.*

Nothing is sweeter than love, all other riches
　　Second: even honey I've spat from my mouth.
This Nossis says: "Whomever Cypris hasn't kissed
　　Knows nothing of her flowers, what sort of roses."

6.17 Nossis, *AP* 6.353 (8 GP)

This epigram and the following one are descriptions of women's portraits, probably wall-paintings.

Melinna herself is re-created: notice the face
　　Is gentle; she seems to gaze serenely at us.
How truly the daughter resembles her mother in all—
　　How fine when children are like their parents.

6.18 Nossis, *AP* 9.605 (6 GP)

Kallo dedicated her portrait in the house of golden
　　Aphrodite, the picture painted true to life.
How gentle her stance, see how her grace blossoms!
　　Greet her with joy, for she has a blameless life.

45. Lesbos was famous for an early and rich tradition of lyric poetry, including, but not limited to, Sappho and Alcaeus.

6.19 Nossis, *AP* 7.718 (11 GP)

This poem takes the form of a grave inscription, addressed to a passer-by. It may have come at the end of Nossis' collection of poems.

Stranger, if you sail to the land of lovely dances, Mytilene,[46]
   To catch fire from the blossom of Sappho's graces,
Say that a friend to her and the Muses, the Locrian land[47]
   Bore me. And knowing my name is Nossis, go on!

6.20 Herondas, *Mimiamb* 6.17–36

Herondas was a third-century author who wrote mimes, or short satirical dialogues. In this one, Metro tries to convince her friend Koritto to tell her who manufactured a leather dildo she is reputed to possess.

METRO: You must tell me now,
   Koritto dear, who made you your dildo,
   The beautifully stitched red leather one.
KORITTO: *[agape with surprise]* But how now, when, where can you have
     seen it?
METRO: Erinna's daughter had it given her   20
   Day before yesterday, Nossis,[48] you know.
   What a beautiful present for a girl.
KORITTO: *[befuddled and alarmed]* Nossis? Who gave it to her?
METRO: If I tell, will you tell on me?
KORITTO: *[touching eyelids with fingers]* These sweet eyes, Metro!
   Koritto's mouth lets out naught.
METRO: Eubyle,
   Bitas' wife, gave it to her. Promised her,
   What's more, nobody would be the wiser.
KORITTO: Women! That woman will uproot me yet.
   I let her have it because she begged me.
   Metro, I hadn't yet used it myself!
   And she treats it like something she has found,   30
   And makes an improper present of it.
   Goodbye and goodbye to a friend like her,

---

46. The largest city on Lesbos, where Sappho resided.
47. Nossis was from Epizephyrian Locris, a Greek city on the toe of Italy.
48. A reference to the poet Nossis. Erinna, here identified as her mother, was a slightly earlier poet who also wrote epigrams, as well as a three-hundred-line poem lamenting the death of her friend Baucis.

Is what I say. She can find other friends.
She has lent my property to Nossis!
Adresteia[49] forgive me for speaking
Stronger than a woman should. But Nossis!
I wouldn't give her my old worn-out one
Even if I still had a thousand more.

6.21 Ps.-Plato, *AP* 5.78

The following four poems were attributed to Plato in a treatise by the Cyrenaic philos-
opher Aristippus designed to undercut the moral reputations of men famous for their
virtue. They probably date to the third century B.C.E.

Kissing Agathon[50] I held my soul upon my lips.
  For she came, poor wretch,[51] as though to cross unto him.

6.22 Ps.-Plato, *AP* 7.99

Some scholars think this epigram alone of the group may have been authentic.

For Hecuba and the women of Ilium the Fates assigned
  Tears, in truth, then at the hour of their birth.
But for you, Dion,[52] upon achieving the victory of noble deeds,
  The gods poured out all your far-reaching hopes.
And you lie, honored among the citizens, in your spacious fatherland,
  O Dion, who maddened my heart with love.

6.23 Ps.-Plato, *AP* 7.100

Now, when I said nothing but that Alexis[53] is fair,
  He's been seen and is the object of all eyes everywhere.
Dear heart, why point out a bone to the dogs,
  When you'll later regret it? Didn't we lose Phaedrus[54] this way?

---

49. Another name for Nemesis, the goddess of revenge.

50. The tragedian Agathon would have been older than Plato, so he can hardly have been Plato's beloved, however handsome.

51. I.e., his soul, which is a feminine noun in Greek.

52. An in-law of the Syracusan tyrants and eventual ruler of Syracuse in his own right, who became devoted to Plato's teachings after the philosopher's visit to Sicily in 389, and later studied with Plato in Athens.

53. Usually assumed to be the comic poet, who sometimes treated Platonic themes; see 3.27–28.

54. Like Agathon, Phaedrus must, in fact, have been older than Plato and could hardly have been his beloved. Clearly the author of these epigrams was merely creating fantasies.

6.24 Ps.-Plato, *AP* 7.669

My star,[55] you gaze upon the stars. Would I were Heaven,[56]
 That with many eyes I might look upon you.

6.25 Rhianus, *AP* 12.142 (10 GP)

*This poet, who was also known as the author of mythological epics, was active in the
second half of the third century B.C.E.*

Below a green plane tree Dexionicus caught
 A blackbird with lime,[57] and held it by its wings.
And the sacred bird, groaning aloud, cried out.
 But would that I, dear Love and blooming Graces,
Were both thrush and blackbird, that in his hand
 I might pour out both voice and sweet tears.

6.26 Alcaeus of Messene, *AP* 12.29 (7 GP)

This poet, not to be confused with Sappho's contemporary, was active c. 200 B.C.E.

Protarchus is handsome, but unwilling. Yet he will be willing
 Later. Youth's time with its torch is running by.[58]

6.27 Dioscorides, *AP* 12.42 (13 GP)

This epigrammatist was also probably active c. 200 B.C.E.

Look upon Hermogenes, chicken-hawk, with full hands,
 And perhaps you will achieve what your heart dreams of,
And you will relax the sullen tension of your brow. But if you go fishing
 Giving a line with no hook to the wave,
You will draw up a lot of water from the harbor. For neither shame
 Nor pity dwells within an expensive boy-toy.

---

55. Some editors read this word as the proper name Aster, reputedly another beloved of
Plato.
56. The Greek word for "heaven" is *uranus,* the same as the name of the god Uranus.
57. Lime was a sticky substance made from the bark of holly and was smeared on twigs to
catch birds.
58. A reference to relay races in which a torch is handed by one runner to the next.

6.28 Glaucus, *AP* 12.44 (1 GP)

There was a time once long ago when a quail, and a sewn ball,
    And knucklebones[59] persuaded present-loving boys.
But now it's fine food and cash. Those toys of yore
    Have no effect. Look for something else, boy-lovers!

6.29 Phanias, *AP* 12.31 (1 GP)

By Themis[60] and by this drinking cup that unsteadies me,
    Brief, Pamphilus, is the time of your love.
For already your thigh and chin bloom with hair,
    And Desire leads you for the future to other passion.[61]
But while thin traces of spark still remain for you,
    Thrust aside miserliness. For Opportunity is friend to Love.

6.30 Thymocles, *AP* 12.32 (1 GP)

You recall perhaps, you recall when I told you that sacred phrase:
    "Youth is most beautiful and most ephemeral."
Not the swiftest bird in the sky outstrips youth's beauty.
    Now see, all your petals are poured forth on the ground.

6.31 Meleager, *AP* 12.23 (99 GP)

Meleager was active c. 100 B.C.E. In addition to writing his own epigrams, he assembled a collection of earlier Hellenistic epigrams called the "Garland," including the work of Asclepiades, Callimachus, and the authors of 6.26–30. The following epigram describes his first love.

I am caught, I, who once frequently laughed
    At young men's lovelorn serenades.
Even me has winged Eros set upon your forecourt,[62]
    Myiscus, inscribing upon me SPOILS WON FROM SELF-CONTROL.

6.32 Meleager, *AP* 12.33 (90 GP)

Heraclitus was beautiful, when he once was. But now, past his youth,
    A screen of hide declares war on those who would mount from behind.

---

59. See ch. 5, n. 15.
60. The goddess of law and justice. In erotic contexts, "justice" means reciprocity.
61. Probably a reference to heterosexual love, or less likely, to his own active love of boys.
62. The area in front of the main door to the boy's house.

But, Polyxenides,[63] be not too disdainful on seeing this.
  For even on the buttocks Nemesis[64] is growing.

6.33 Meleager, *AP* 12.41 (94 GP)

No longer do I write of fair Theron, nor as before
  Is Apollodotus bright with fire, but now a burnt-out brand.
I love a female love. Let the snuggling of hairy-assed queens
  Be the concern of goat-mounting shepherds.

6.34 Meleager, *AP* 12.63 (91 GP)

Heraclitus silently speaks this line in his eyes:
  "I shall set on fire even the lightning of Zeus."
And Diodorus says this in his breast:
  "I melt even a rock when warmed by my flesh."
Wretched is he who has a torch from the eyes of one,
  And from the other a sweet fire, smoldering with desire.

6.35 Meleager, *AP* 12.72 (92 GP)

Already sweet dawn. And sleepless in the forecourt
  Damis breathes out what breath is left,
The wretch, on seeing Heraclitus. For he stood below
  The rays of that one's eyes, wax cast on burning ember.
Yet arise for me, unhappy Damis. For I too
  Bearing Love's wound, shed tears for your tears.

6.36 Meleager, *AP* 12.81 (86 GP)

You men soul-deceiving and sick in love, whoever know
  The boy-desiring flame, on tasting of that bitter honey,
Pour cold water, cold from newly melted snow,
  Quickly about my heart.
For truly I have dared to look upon Dionysius. But come,
  My fellow-slaves, and quench the fire from me before it touches my
    innards.

---

63. Apparently another boy, to whom the example of Heraclitus is addressed as a warning. His name means "with many guests," as if to suggest popularity.
  64. The goddess of revenge.

6.37 Meleager, *AP* 12.94 (76 GP)

Sweet are the chest of Diodorus, the eyes of Heraclitus,
  The speech of Dion, the back[65] of Uliades.
Yet you might touch the soft skin of the one, Philocles, and look upon
    the next,
  Speak with the third, and with the fourth do the rest. . . .
That you know how ungrudging is my mind. But if you look greedily
  Upon Myiscus, may you never again see beauty.[66]

6.38 Meleager, *AP* 12.95 (77 GP)

If the Loves cherish you, Philocles, and myrrh-breathed Seduction
  And the Graces who gather flowers of beauty,
May you hold Diodorus in your embrace, may sweet Dorotheus
  Sing across from you, and Callicrates sit on your knee.
May Dio give pleasure, stretching out your horn in his hand
  (That hits the spot!), and may Uliades retract its tip.
May Philo give you a kiss, Theron chatter,
  And may you diddle Eudemus' nipple under his cloak.
Blessed man, if the god should give you all these delights,
  What a mixed grill of boys you would cook!

6.39 Meleager, *AP* 12.101 (103 GP)

Another poem about his first love.

Myiscus struck me, unwounded yet by Desires,
  Below the breast with his eyes, and said this:
"I've taken the arrogant one. Look, that boldness below his brow
  Of scepter-bearing wisdom I now tread on with my feet."
To him, I said, hardly breathing, "You are surprised
  Dear boy? Eros drew Zeus himself down from Olympus."

6.40 Meleager, *AP* 12.109 (61 GP)

Delicate Diodorus, casting a flame upon his young age-mates,
  Has been caught by the flirtatious eyes of Timarion,[67]

65. The Greek noun *osphus* actually refers to the curve of the lower back.
66. In other words, Philocles can have any of the other boys he likes, but should keep away
from this one, whom the speaker wants for himself.
67. A female courtesan.

And retains the sweet-bitter weapon of Eros. Truly, in this I see
    A new wonder. Fire blazes bright burned by fire.

6.41 Meleager, *AP* 12.122 (85 GP)

You Graces, upon looking on handsome Aristagoras
    Face-to-face, you took him to the embrace of your soft arms.
Wherefore with his beauty he casts a flame, and speaks sweetly
    When it's right, and when he is silent he yet babbles sweetness with
        his eyes.
May he roam far from me. But what then? Like a young Zeus from
        Olympus
    The boy knows how to cast a bolt from a great distance.

6.42 Meleager, *AP* 12.157 (119 GP)

Cypris is my captain, and Eros watches the tiller,
    Holding the tip of my soul's rudder in his hand.
And Desire, breathing heavily, blows up a storm, wherefore now truly
    I swim in a sea of boys of every race.

6.43 Meleager, *AP* 12.158 (93 GP)

The goddess, mistress of Desires,[68] brought me to you, Theocles;
    Naked before you soft-sandaled Eros laid me low,
Subduing me with unbreaking rein, a stranger in a strange land.
    Yet I desire to attain a constant friendship.
But you send away me, who love you, nor does the length of time
    Assuage you nor the proofs of our common self-control.
Have mercy, lord,[69] have mercy, for a divine spirit ordained you a god.
    With you for me lie the ends of life and death.

6.44 Meleager, *AP* 12.159 (108 GP)

The cables of my life, Myiscus, are fitted to you,
    In you too is the last breath of my soul.
For yes, by your eyes, boy, which speak even to the deaf,
    And, yes, by your shining brow,

---

68. Aphrodite.

69. It is unclear whether the speaker is in this couplet addressing Eros or using liturgical language to address Theocles (whose name contains the root *theos* [god]) as a god.

If ever you cast a clouded look upon me, I see winter,
  But if you look kindly, sweet spring has bloomed.

6.45 Statyllius Flaccus, *AP* 12.12

Just now as his beard appears, Ladon, beautiful and cruel to lovers,
  Himself loves a boy. Nemesis is quick indeed.

6.46 Marcus Argentarius, *AP* 5.116

The love of women suits best those mortals,
  Whose intention in their love is serious.
But if yours is a love for the male, I know how to teach
  A cure for ridding you of your erotic affliction.
Turn fair-hipped Menophila over and imagine
  That you hold a male Menophilus in your embrace.

6.47 Addaeus, *AP* 10.20

If you see a handsome lad, strike while the iron is hot.
  Say what you're thinking, grasp his testicles full-handed.
But if you say, "I honor you, and will be like a brother to you,"
  Shame will shut you off from the road to fulfillment.

6.48 Lucillius, *AP* 11.155

This poet of the mid-first century C.E., *not to be confused with the earlier Roman satirist, wrote a series of epigrams attacking philosophers.*

This weighty adamant of virtue, this reprover of all
  In all things, this fighter with cold,
And sporter of a beard, has been caught. "At what?"
  Unsuitable to speak of. But he was caught doing the deed of the evil-
    mouthed.[70]

6.49 Alpheius of Mytilene, *AP* 12.18

Wretched are they whose life is loveless. Without desire
  Nothing is easy to say or do.

---

70. Presumably fellatio.

For I now am slow indeed. But if I should look upon Xenophilus,
   I will fly more quickly than lightning.
Wherefore I tell everyone, flee not sweet desire,
   But pursue it. Love is the whetstone of the soul.

6.50 Automedon, *AP* 12.34

Yesterday I dined with Demetrius the trainer,
   Of all men the most fortunate.
One boy lay in his lap, one hung upon his shoulder,
   One brought his food, another gave him his drink.
A much admired quartet! Said I in joke to him,
   "And at night, my friend, you train them too?"

6.51 Diocles, *AP* 12.35

Someone said once to him, once when he did not respond "hello,"
   "Yet Damon, superior with his looks, now does not even say 'hello.'
Some day he'll pay for this. Then it will be he, all hairy,
   Who will begin to greet those who do not respond."

6.52 Rufinus, *AP* 5.19

No longer am I boy-crazy as before, but now am called
   Mad for women, and now my discus is a rattle.[71]
Instead of boys' guileless skin, chalk's colors[72] have come to please me,
   And the added bloom of rouge.
Luxuriant Erymanthus[73] will feed dolphins,
   And the sea's gray wave swift deer.[74]

6.53 Scythinus, *AP* 12.232

Now you stand upright, nameless one,[75] and do not wear out,
   But are stretched tight as though you would never cease.

---

71. The *sistrum* was a musical instrument used in the worship of the Egyptian goddess Isis, whose worship was particularly popular with women throughout the Roman Empire.

72. I.e., chalk-based cosmetics.

73. A mountain in the north-central Peloponnese.

74. This expression is an example of a common figure in ancient poetry called the *adynaton*, or "world upside down," expressing a complete reversal of the expected order of things.

75. He addresses his penis. See **6.59**.

But when Nemesenus lay all of himself alongside me,
  Giving everything I wanted, you hung down dead.
Strain and burst and weep. All in vain,
  You will have no pity at my hand.

6.54 Asclepiades of Adramyttium, *AP* 12.36

Now you ask,[76] when fine down creeps
  Below your temples and sharp hairs upon your thighs.
Then you say, "For me this is sweeter." Would someone also say
  That the dry stubble is better than the smooth corn?

6.55 Anonymous, *AP* 12.39

Nicander's light is out, all his body's bloom
  Is gone, and not even the name of his charm is left,
Whom before we thought among the immortals. But think,
  Young men, only mortal thoughts. For hairs do exist.[77]

6.56 Anonymous, *AP* 12.156

My love, Diodorus, is like a spring storm in every way,
  Decided by an uncertain sea.
At one time you reveal much rain, at another you are
  As fine weather, and with your eyes you pour forth gentle laughter.
As a shipwrecked man on the sea's swell, measuring blind waves,
  I swirl wandering amidst a great storm.
But cast me a look of affection or again of hatred
  That I may know on which wave I swim.

6.57 Strato, *AP* 12.1

Strato wrote during the time of the Roman emperor Hadrian (117–38 C.E.) and compiled a collection of his own and earlier poets' pederastic epigrams. This poem is the prologue.

"Let us begin from Zeus," as Aratus has said.[78]
  But you, Muses, I do not trouble today.

---

76. In other words, now the boy begs for love.
77. A burlesque of the saying "gods do exist," a warning to the unjust.
78. A quotation from the first line of Aratus' *Phaenomena*, a Hellenistic poem on the stars. Strato's point is that Zeus is a more appropriate god to invoke in a work dealing with pederasty, since he loved Ganymede, whereas the Muses are female.

For if I love boys and it is with boys I consort,
    What does this have to do with Heliconian Muses?

6.58 Strato, *AP* 12.2

Seek not in my tablets Priam at the altars,
    Nor the sufferings of Medea and Niobe,
Nor Itys in his chambers nor the nightingales among the leaves.[79]
    For earlier men wrote of all these things abundantly.
Search rather for sweet Eros mingled with the joyful Graces,
    And Bromius.[80] These darkened brows do not suit.

6.59 Strato, *AP* 12.3

Boys' appendages, Diodorus, come in three forms[81]
    And of these you should learn the names.
For call the one with intact tip "lalou,"[82]
    "Cocco" the one just beginning to swell.
The one that already throbs at a hand's touch, call "lizard."[83]
    As for the more mature one, you know what to call it.

6.60 Strato, *AP* 12.4

I delight in the prime of a twelve-year-old,
    But thirteen is more desirable than this.
He who masters twice seven has a sweeter flower of Love;
    The one beginning thrice five is more delightful still.
The sixteenth is the year of the gods; the seventeenth
    Is not for me to seek, but for Zeus.
But if one has desire for those yet older, no longer does he play,
    But he now seeks the one "answering him back."[84]

---

79. These are all themes of epic and tragedy: Priam was the king of Troy, killed while taking refuge at an altar; Medea killed her own children; Niobe watched her children killed by Apollo and Artemis; Itys was a child killed by his mother and aunt, who subsequently were turned into birds.

80. An alternate name for Dionysus.

81. Some understand this to mean the penis at three different ages, but more likely it refers to different stages of arousal.

82. That is, the foreskin has not been retracted. This name could refer to the tip of the Greek letter lambda (λ), in other words a very small appendage.

83. "Lizard" may be an appropriate metaphor because of that animal's jerky, darting movements.

84. A Homeric formula.

6.61 Strato, *AP* 12.5

I love boys who are pale, and at the same time the honey-skinned
  And sandy haired; however I also cherish the dark ones.
I don't pass over hazel eyes, but I especially love
  Those with sparkling black eyes.

6.62 Strato, *AP* 12.6

The anus and gold have the same numerical value.[85]
  I simply found this out once by toting up the numbers.

6.63 Strato, *AP* 12.7

With a girl there's no sphincter, no simple kiss
  No natural scent of skin,
Nor that sweet dirty talk nor
  The frank expression, and an instructed girl is worse.
They're all cold from behind. But the larger problem is this—
  There is nowhere to put your wandering hand.

6.64 Strato, *AP* 12.8

I saw a boy weaving flowers with a cluster of ivy berries,
  Just as I was passing by the wreath-makers.
Nor did I pass by unwounded. I stopped and quietly said
  To him: "For how much will you sell me your flower?"
He blushed more than the buds, and with lowered head
  Said, "Go far from here, lest my father see you."
As a pretext I bought some garlands, and going home
  I garlanded the gods, praying that he be mine.

6.65 Strato, *AP* 12.9

Now you are fair, Diodorus, and ripe for lovers.
  Yet even if you marry, we will not abandon you.

85. The Greeks used letters of the alphabet to represent numbers. Therefore, any given word can be assigned a numerical value by adding up the number equivalents of each letter, which in these two words is 1,570. The epigram's point, of course, is that a boy's anus can be bought with gold.

6.66 Strato, *AP* 12.10

Although your first down, turning to hair, springs from you,
 And soft blond tendrils are upon your temples,
Not therefore do I abandon my beloved. Yet his beauty
 Is my own, even bearded, even with hair.

6.67 Strato, *AP* 12.11

Yesterday I had Philostratus for the night, but to no avail,
 Although he, how shall I put it, offered everything.
But, friends, no longer have me for a friend, but from a tower
 Cast me, since I am become too much an Astyanax.[86]

6.68 Strato, *AP* 12.16

Do not hide your love, Philocrates. The god himself
 Is able to trample on my heart.
But give me joy by giving me kisses. A time will come
 When you too will ask for these favors from others.

6.69 Strato, *AP* 12.176

Why with so gloomy an air, Menippus, are you covered down to your
 soles,
 You who before had your mantle drawn up to the back of your thighs?
And why with lowered head did you run by me, not saying anything?
 I know what you hide from me. They've come,[87] as I said they would.

6.70 Strato, *AP* 12.192

Long hair and fretted curls give me no pleasure,
 Things taught in the school of Art, not Nature.
I prefer the dusty grime of a boy fresh from the wrestling ring
 And the oil-glistened hue of his limbs' flesh.

---

86. Astyanax was the infant son of the Trojan hero Hector, who during the sack of Troy was
thrown down from the city's citadel. In this context, the poet intends a punning etymology, de-
riving his name from the verb *stuein* (to have an erection) preceded by a negative prefix *a-* (the
alpha-privative).
 87. I.e., hair on his legs.

My desire is sweet if unprettified;
　　Counterfeit beauty is the work of the female Cypris.

6.71 Strato, *AP* 12.195

Zephyr-loving [88] fields do not bud with so many flowers,
　　Spring's thick-crowded beauty,
As you will see, Dionysus, well-born boys,
　　Modeled by the hands of Cypris and the Graces.
Especially among them see how Milesius blooms,
　　As a rose resplendent with sweet-smelling petals.
But perhaps he does not know that, as a fair flower by the heat,
　　So young beauty is destroyed by a hair.

6.72 Strato, *AP* 12.196

Lycinus, god-like in form, your eyes are like sparks,
　　Or rather rays, my prince, shooting fire.
Face to face I cannot endure your gaze even a short time,
　　So do you flash lightening with both eyes.

6.73 Strato, *AP* 12.197

"Know the right time," said one of the seven sages,[89] Philippus.
　　For all things are loveliest at their prime.
Even the cucumber[90] is valued, when first seen on the garden's border,
　　But too ripe becomes fodder for pigs.[91]

6.74 Strato, *AP* 12.205

My neighbor's boy, tender everywhere, arouses me not a little.
　　And as regards his being willing, his laugh is no novice's.
Yet he is not more than twelve. Now the unripe grapes[92] are unguarded:
　　But once he matures, voilà the guards and the stakes.

---

88. Zephyr is the gentle west wind, which blows in spring.
89. The saying is ascribed to Pittacus, a moderate reformer on Lesbos in the late seventh century B.C.E., later considered one of the Seven Sages, along with his contemporary Solon of Athens.
90. Probably a metaphor for the penis.
91. "Pig" (*choiros*) was a slang term for the vagina.
92. This could be meant as a metaphor for a young boy's undeveloped testicles.

6.75 Strato, *AP* 12.207

Yesterday, as he was bathing, Diocles raised up his lizard,[93]
    "Aphrodite rising from the waves."[94]
If someone had shown it then to Paris on Ida,[95]
    He would have preferred it to the three goddesses.

6.76 Strato, *AP* 12.210

Reckon all on a bed as three in number, of whom two give it
    And two take it. I seem to be speaking of something amazing.
And, indeed, this is no lie. For one in the middle serves two,
    Giving pleasure from behind, getting it in front.

6.77 Strato, *AP* 12.211

Were I trying to convince you, still a young novice,
    You would be right to be afraid, thinking it something awful.
But if your master's bed has skilled you in this,
    Why do you grudge to grant to another what you already take as a duty?
For he, on calling you to his need, then letting you go, goes to sleep,
    Without exchanging a word with you, for he is master.
But here there is pleasure of a different kind. You will play as equal;
        mutual
Will be our chatter, and as to the rest you will be asked, not bid.

6.78 Strato, *AP* 12.212

Oh my! Why in tears again, why so downcast, little boy?
    Say it simply. Don't be pained. What do you want?
You've held out your hollow hand to me. Damned!
    Perhaps you demand payment. Where did you learn that?
No longer are slices of cake or sweet sesame enough,
    Or nuts for shooting games.
But already your mind's set on profit. Curses on the one who taught you!
    He's robbed me of my little boy.

---

93. As we see from **6.59**, this is Strato's pet term for a boy's penis that is capable of full erection.

94. A reference to the birth of Aphrodite from the foam created by the immersion of Uranus' severed genitals in the sea.

95. The Trojan prince who, on Mt. Ida, judged between the beauty of Hera, Athena, and Aphrodite.

6.79 Strato, *AP* 12.222

Once a trainer, opportunely instructing a smooth lad,
  Getting him to his knees, worked over his middle,
Touching the boy's nuts with his hand. But by chance
  The master came, seeking the boy.
Quickly the trainer, bracing him with his feet, turned the boy
  On his back and with his hand grasped the boy's throat.
However, the master, not unskilled in wrestling, said to him:
  "Stop. You are," said he, "gagging the kid."[96]

6.80 Strato, *AP* 12.234

If you boast of your beauty, know that the rose also blooms,
  But suddenly withers and is thrown out with the refuse.
For flower and beauty are of equal duration.
  Envious time causes them to wither together.

6.81 Strato, *AP* 12.235

If beauty grows old, give a share of it before it's gone.
  But if it stays, why do you fear to give what remains?

6.82 Strato, *AP* 12.236

A eunuch has pretty boys. For what use?
  And he renders them unholy harm.
Truly like the dog with roses in the manger, foolishly barking,
  He gives neither himself the benefit nor anyone else.

6.83 Strato, *AP* 12.237

Farewell, with your pretense of virtue, farewell, lowlife,
  Who just now swore never to give it.
Now swear no longer. For I know, nor do you fool me.
  I know where, how, to whom, and for how much.

6.84 Strato, *AP* 12.238

Young pups at play reciprocally offer
  Pleasure to one another in turn.

---

96. The Greek verb *pnigizeis* is a coinage combining the regular forms *pnigeis* (you choke) and *pugizeis* (you penetrate anally).

Alternately the same ones, averted, are mounted,
  Trying in turn doing and being done.
But neither is at disadvantage. For the one that earlier surrendered
  Now again stands behind.
This is the prelude at any rate. For as to exchange,
  As they say, donkey knows to scratch donkey.

6.85 Strato, *AP* 12.245

Every dumb animal only screws. But we reasoning men
  Have this over other animals,
We have discovered butt-fucking. But those who conquer women,
  They have nothing over dumb animals.

6.86 Strato, *AP* 12.246

A pair of brothers loves me. I know not which of them
  To choose as my master. For I love them both.
The one departs, the other arrives. The beauty of the one
  Is his presence, of the other, his being missed.

6.87 Strato, *AP* 12.247

As, Theodorus, Idomeneus once led from Crete
  To Troy his servant Meriones,[97]
So I have you as dexterous friend. For he
  Was now servant and now companion.
You also do for me your everyday tasks all day long.
  But at night, by Zeus, we try at Meriones.[98]

6.88 Strato, *AP* 12.248

Who can know of his beloved, whether he is past his prime,
  Since he is ever with him and never leaves him?
Who cannot give pleasure today, who gave pleasure yesterday,
  Or if he gives pleasure today, why will he not give pleasure tomorrow?

---

97. In the *Iliad*, Idomeneus is the king of Crete and Meriones his squire. This is the first allusion to their relationship as pederastic, on the model of Achilles and Patroclus.

98. There may be a pun here on the name, which is related to the Greek *mêros*, referring to the thighs and thus by implication to intercrural intercourse.

6.89 Strato, *AP* 12.255

Non-comrade, doesn't the word itself instruct you,
   Accurately derived from the verbal roots?
Dionysius, everyone is called a "boy-lover," not a "boy-ox lover."
   Can you say anything in reply?
I'm an umpire at the Pythian games, you at the Olympics;[99]
   Those whom I remove from the list you accept into competition.

6.90 Strato, *AP* 12.258

This poem probably stood as the epilogue to Strato's collection.

Perhaps someone in the future, on hearing these my trifles,
   Will think that all this suffering in love was my own.
But I inscribe letters for many other boy-lovers,
   Since this gift some god granted to me.

6.91 *Anacreontea* 17

This collection of Hellenistic verse, of mixed date, imitates the meter and themes of Anacreon.

Paint for me my friend Bathyllus
   Just as I instruct.
Make his hair sleek,
   Dark on the inside,
But sunny and bright at the ends.
   Drawing for me the free curls
And locks of his hair, leave them
   To lie as they wish, in tousled abandon.
Let a brow darker than serpents
   Encircle his forehead   10
Soft and dewy-fresh.
   Let his fierce black Gorgon eye[100]
Be mixed with serenity,
   Drawing this trait from the War God,

---

99. The Pythian games in Strato's time may have had three age classes rather than two, like the Olympics, and therefore one ceased to be eligible for competition as a "boy" at an earlier age.

100. The Gorgons were mythological monsters who turned to stone anyone they looked at or who looked at them.

That from the fair Love Goddess,
  That one may fear this
And hang upon hope from that.
  Make his downy cheek
Like a rosy red apple;
  Put in it a blush,   20
For you can, just like that of Modesty.
  I don't know how
You will render for me his lips,
  Soft and full of Seduction,
But let the image hold them
  Chattering in silence.
After his face,
  Let his ivory neck
Surpass Adonis'.[101]
  Make his breast   30
And twin hands those of Hermes.
  Give him the thighs of Pollux,
The belly of Dionysus.[102]
  Above his tender thighs,
Thighs holding fire,
  Make simple modesty
Already wanting the Love Goddess.
  You have a grudging, niggardly art,
Since you can't show the back side.
  That would be better.   40
Why should I instruct you about the feet?
  Take as much pay as you want.
Take down this image of Apollo
  And make it the model for Bathyllus.
And if you ever come to Samos,[103]
  Then draw Apollo after Bathyllus' model.

---

101. A beautiful adolescent loved by Aphrodite.

102. Hermes was the swift messenger god, Dionysus the god of wine, Pollux (a.k.a. Polydeuces) a hero famed for his skill as a boxer. All three are depicted in art as handsome young men.

103. Bathyllus is located on the island of Samos to maintain the fiction that these are verses of Anacreon, who spent much of his career at the court of Polycrates in Samos.

CHAPTER 7

Republican Rome

The Roman Republic is generally defined as the period from the expulsion of the Etruscan kings (509 B.C.E.) to the Battle of Philippi in 42 B.C.E., which ended the hopes of those who wished to restore republican government after the assassination of Julius Caesar. The Etruscans, early Rome's powerful neighbors to the north, were known to have an interest in Greek pederasty and were one of the chief export markets for Athenian vases displaying pederastic themes. Our knowledge of the early Roman Republic, however, is mostly legendary and is preserved predominately by historians writing long after the events they describe.

Our earliest evidence for homosexual acts concerns the late fourth century: **7.1** and **7.2** preserve exemplary tales, with different names and slightly different dates, explaining the abolition of debt slavery in consequence of an incident in which a creditor attempted to violate the body of a young debtor. Concerning the same period, **7.3** narrates the execution of a military officer for attempting to violate a subordinate; compare the later incident in **7.21**, where the young soldier is found to be justified in killing the officer. All of these stories serve as moral paradigms for the inviolability of a free Roman's body, regardless of poverty or low station; debt slavery was deemed unacceptable precisely because it could lead to such sexual violation. Interestingly, **7.1–3** concern young adults, not boys, as the objects of predatory lust, but the age issue is not paramount. **7.4**, an incident of uncertain date, shows that acts with freeborn Romans were considered immoral and illegal even if willingly consented to and even if the youth was a prostitute. **7.5** relates the scandal in 227 B.C.E. surrounding the tribune Scantinius Capitolinus, who was condemned for soliciting a youth of good family; his crime was considered so heinous that even the usual immunity from prosecution he would enjoy as a tribune was ignored. Scantinius' crime seems to have given his name to the later *lex Scantinia* (of 149 B.C.E.) regulating certain forms of male homosexuality. It is difficult to be sure whether any of these early incidents were historical, since our sources for all of them are Augustan or later and partake in that period's idealization of the early Republic as a time that clarified and exalted the human rights of the common man against self-aggrandizing elites.

If love of free boys was illegal, **7.6** makes the distinction that the desire for young slaves was not. We see this principle confirmed in Plautus' comedies, written at the end of the third century and in the first two decades of the second. These plays provide our earliest contemporary evidence for homosexuality, but there is some question about their value, since they are closely modeled on Greek originals and may reflect Greek social realities more than Roman. However, pederastic themes are surprisingly infrequent in our extant fragments of Greek New Comedy (Plautus' source), particularly when compared to earlier Greek comedy, so there is good reason to believe that this particular strand of reference in Plautus' work either reflects Roman realities or, at the very least, Roman perceptions of Greek realities (since the plays are always set in Greek cities). **7.7**, **7.8**, and **7.15** all assume sexual relations between master and male slave as a not unusual occurrence; in **7.8**, a slave boy even undertakes the relationship willingly and reckons it as leading to future manumission. In **7.11** a slave boy laments, with mixed feelings, his lack of a lover; in **7.12** a slave denies having ever had one, as if it were a matter of disgust. **7.10** refers to a part of town frequented by male prostitutes, both active and passive. **7.9** states clearly that free boys are off limits, but **7.13** suggests that free boys were nevertheless sometimes love objects. Where the sexual act is explicitly described, as in **7.11**, **7.12**, and **7.15**, it is anal sex. Of course, the presence of homosexual themes in Plautus should not be taken as evidence for the general acceptance or even frequency of such relations with slaves, even as Greek comedy does not necessarily convey approval of pederasty: what it may suggest is that Romans wealthy enough to own slaves did sometimes engage in physical relations with them. However, given that the settings and characters of the plays are Greek, it could also be taken as evidence that such relationships were considered "Greek" in character by a Roman audience of this time.

Terence, a comic poet of the generation after Plautus, seems to have avoided homosexual themes altogether; on the other hand, Afranius, a writer of comedy with Italic settings a bit later in the second century, is said to have filled his plays with pederastic love affairs (**7.16**). This polarization of personal tastes may simultaneously reflect the spread of the practice in Rome and a growing moral conservatism in reaction to what was interpreted in some quarters as a surfeit of luxury and Greek-inspired moral license in the wake of Rome's expansion into an overseas empire in the second century. Some Roman moralists, such as Cato the Censor (**7.17**), criticized even men's devotion to beautiful male slaves. In the mid-second century the younger Scipio and writers of his intellectual circle, such as the Greek historian Polybius, denounced the moral degeneracy they saw in a changing Rome in terms of softness, effeminacy, and sexual passivity (**7.17–18**). After Scipio's death, the popular reformer Gaius Gracchus attacked his opponents in similar terms (**7.20**), and thought it a matter of popular credit to boast that he did not surround himself with beautiful male slaves (**7.19**). What was a joke that everyone could laugh at in Plautus seems by the second century to have become deeply problematic and controversial.

At the end of the second century, the satirist Lucilius populates his poems with "beardless androgynes" (**7.26**) and boy prostitutes (**7.23–25**). And in the earliest decades of the first century a satirical emphasis on graphic homosexual acts as signs of perversity and moral abandon is also evident in the comedies of Pomponius and Novius. Unlike the work of Plautus and Terence, these plays are specifically Italic in their setting and characters. Both authors refer to freeborn men who prefer the passive role in anal sex (**7.29–32**); Pomponius even devotes a whole play to a male prostitute who specializes in penetrating such men. A leitmotif foreshadowed in Plautus (**7.14**), but more common in these poets (**7.25, 7.27, 7.33**), is the comparison of boys and women as sex objects. In some cases this juxtaposition reflects free bisexuality (**7.15, 7.27**), in others an explicit preference for boys (**7.25, 7.33**).

Some shorter verse, such as the epigram of Lutatius Catulus (**7.22**), was inspired by Hellenistic models to treat pederastic love as a positive theme, but our only author of republican lyric whose work survives in quantity, Valerius Catullus (84–54 B.C.E.), adopts a sharply satirical stance more consistent with that of Lucilius, Pomponius, and Novius than with the Hellenistic poets who were in other respects so influential on him. In **7.47** Catullus teases a bridegroom over having to give up pederasty with his favorite boy slave. Catullus' supposed boyfriend, Juventius, was a freeborn youth from an aristocratic family with branches in both Rome and Catullus' hometown of Verona; that he was not cloaked with a pseudonym, as was Catullus' girlfriend, Lesbia, suggests an intention to embarrass (see **7.23**). It is abundantly clear from poems such as **7.42, 7.49**, and **7.50** that Juventius much preferred the company of someone other than Catullus, and in **7.39** and **7.41** Catullus abuses a rival named Aurelius.

Imagery of male-to-male sexual penetration is used throughout Catullus' work as a metaphor for aggressive relations of power and domination (**7.39–41, 7.45**), even at the poet's own expense (as in **7.43**, where the provincial governor Memmius orally sodomizes Catullus) or that of the whole Roman state (as in **7.44**, where the eponymous founder Romulus is said to submit passively like a *cinaedus* while Caesar's lieutenant Mamurra plunders the provinces). **7.46** is significant in that it shows *cinaedus* to be not uniquely a term of sexual passivity but more fundamentally of sexual excess: here it is applied to the preeminently phallic Caesar and Mamurra (who himself made all of Rome a *cinaedus*). Both men are at the same time called adulterers, prolific penetrators of women (for the linkage between *cinaedi* and adultery, cf. **7.26, 7.36, 7.57**).

Catullus' most interesting poem is **7.48**, the story of a Greek youth who was once the most celebrated and courted adolescent in his city but has now gone to Phrygia to castrate himself and become a eunuch devotee of the Asian mother goddess; the poem implies a typically Roman view of Greek pederasty as an enervating and effeminizing institution that in some sense was responsible for that country's enslavement.

This contrast between Greek and Roman morality was a topos in much late republican theorizing, with pederasty as a particular flash point (**7.52, 7.54–56**; cf. **7.53**); Cicero picks up on the concerns expressed by Cato the Censor and Polybius a century earlier concerning the growth of Greek influence on Roman morals. In the free and robust political discourse of this tumultuous period in Roman history, charges concerning an opponent's involvement in homosexual relations were commonplace, whether it concerned his own passivity as a youth (**7.34–35, 7.37, 7.60–62, 7.64**), his exploitation of freeborn youths (**7.38, 7.58–59**), or his fondness for Greek slaves (**7.63**). Dio Cassius (**7.37**) tells us that even Julius Caesar, who was forgiving and tolerant of every other criticism of him, was uniquely pained by the charge that in his youth he had been the beloved of King Nicomedes of Bithynia. These charges need not be given historical credence any more than those of fourth-century Athenian oratory, but, like their Greek precedents, they bear witness to homosexuality as an area where popular suspicion of Rome's elite could be aroused and manipulated.

Bibliographical Note

For general surveys concentrating on Republican attitudes toward homosexuality, see Boswell (1980) 61–72, MacMullen (1982), E. Cantarella (1992) 97–128, and C. A. Williams (1999) 15–112. Boswell postulates an essentially tolerant attitude going back to the earliest times; MacMullen attacks this view sharply, seeing homosexuality in Rome as primarily a matter of Greek influence to which Roman morality was unsympathetic. Cantarella and Williams argue on the contrary for indigenous homosexuality independent of Greek models, as does Veyne (1985). Verstraete (1980) accepts the decisive role of Hellenizing influence but focuses on master-slave relations, which he sees in some cases as genuine emotional relationships similar to concubinage; see also Dalla (1987) 37–49. Robert (1997) 19–176 embeds the question in the broader context of evolving moral attitudes during the Republic.

Grimal (1986) 103–7 examines **7.1, 7.3, 7.4, 7.6, 7.21**, and similar stories. Lilja (1983) 106–21 treats the same episodes and others illustrating the development of Roman law during this period, including the *lex Scantinia*, on which see also Dalla (1987) 71–99 and Cantarella. Taylor (1997) 345–48 finds evidence for a growing homosexual "subculture" during the second century B.C.E.

Cody (1976) and Lilja (1983) 15–50 examine the evidence of Roman comedy and conclude that Plautus' allusions to homosexuality are his own invention, not adapted from Greek originals. See also Kwintner (1992) on oral sex in **7.11** and Taylor (1997) 341–48.

On the homoerotic poems of Catullus, see Quinn (1972) 242–56, Arkins (1982) 104–16, and Lilja (1983) 51–62. Fitzgerald (1992) 428–41 explores the programmatic significance of the homosexual dynamics in **7.39, 7.40**, and poem 50; see also Kinsey (1966) and Hallett (1996) 328–33. On **7.40** specifically, see Sandy (1971), Winter (1973), Rankin (1976), Selden (1992) 476–89, and Pedrick (1993) 182–87. For the underlying homoerotic strain in poem 50, see in addition Scott (1969a). On the homosexual imagery in the political invectives of **7.43, 7.44**, and **7.46**, see Skinner (1979). On **7.44**, see Scott (1971); on **7.45**, Scott (1969b) and Cerri (1989). For **7.48** as the story of Attis' aborted ephebic transition, see Skinner (1993) and Clay (1995); Taylor (1997) 330–37 sees the transvestite fertility cult of Cybele generally as a homosexual "subculture" within Rome.

On homosexual themes in Cicero, see Gonfroy (1978) and Lilja (1983) 88–97, 122–27. On the unreliability of the anecdotes about Caesar and the subsequent emperors, see Krenkel (1980).

7.1 Livy 8.28

Livy was a historian of the Augustan period who wrote a lengthy history of Rome from its foundation up to his own time. He often relates exemplary moral legends or anecdotes in connection with significant historical developments, as in this narrative concerning the abolition of debt slavery in 326 B.C.E.

In this year the freedom of the Roman people had a new beginning, as it were, when they abandoned the practice of slavery for debt.[1] Moreover, the law was changed on account of the notable lust and remarkable cruelty of a single moneylender. This man was Lucius Papirius, to whom C. Publilius

---

1. Men who lacked sufficient property could pledge their own bodies as collateral and thus turn themselves (and their children) into slaves in the event of non-payment.

had given himself in slavery because of his father's debt. When Publilius did this, the youth and beauty that might have been able to elicit compassion in others instead inflamed L. Papirius' thoughts toward lust and abuse. Believing that use and enjoyment of Publilius' youth was owed to him in addition to the loan, he at first endeavored to entice him with lewd proposals. Next, after Publilius refused to hear of these disgraceful suggestions, Papirius began to terrify him with threats and repeatedly reminded him of his station in life. Finally, when Papirius saw that Publilius was more mindful of his freeborn status than of his present condition, he ordered that he be stripped and given to the lash. Lacerated from the whipping, the young man ran out into the street, complaining of the cruelty and lust of his creditor. A large force of men, enraged by compassion for his young age and the indignity of the crime, as well as by consideration of their own status and that of their children, ran into the forum. Once a crowd had gathered, they proceeded to the Senate house. While the consuls,[2] drawn by the sudden riot, were calling in the Senate, they showed the young man's bloody back to the senators and threw themselves at the feet of each senator as he entered the chamber. Because of the helpless suffering of one man, an enormous form of bondage was defeated on that day, and the consuls were ordered to propose a resolution that no man could be held in shackles or prison, unless he had already been judged guilty and was waiting to pay the penalty. It was decided that a debtor's property, and not his body, was liable for the money owed. Thus, those who were indentured were set free, and precaution was taken that they would not be enslaved in the future.

7.2 Valerius Maximus 6.1.9

Valerius was a historian who wrote a book concerning "memorable sayings and deeds," probably published soon after 31 C.E. This section lists numerous moral examples illustrating the theme of chastity.

T. Veturius, still quite a young man, the son of the Veturius who had been given to the Samnites in his consulship because of a shamefully negotiated treaty,[3] had been forced on account of the collapse of his family and massive debt to give himself to P. Plotius as a surety. After Plotius whipped him like a slave when he refused to be violated, Veturius complained to the

---

2. The two chief magistrates in the Roman Republic, responsible for presiding over meetings of the Senate.

3. This Veturius was consul in 321 B.C.E. The Samnites were a people of south-central Italy who posed the chief obstacle to Roman expansion southward. The events described here can be assumed to transpire soon after Veturius' consulship.

consuls. When the consuls told the Senate about this, the Senate ordered
Plotius to be imprisoned, for they wanted chastity in Roman blood to be
safe under any circumstances.

7.3 Dionysius of Halicarnassus, *Roman Antiquities* 16.4

Dionysius was a Greek historian and rhetorician who worked in Rome during the Augustan period. Like Livy, he wrote a comprehensive history of Rome, but in the Greek language.

I will recall one more political incident that is worthy of praise from all
men, and which will make clear to the Greeks the extent of the animosity
toward wickedness in Rome and of the intolerance of men who violated
nature's universal laws. Gaius Laetorius Mergus, a man of distinguished
birth and no coward on the battlefield, had been appointed tribune of a
legion in the Samnite War.[4] He attempted for some time to persuade a
young man who was the best looking of his tentmates to offer him the
enjoyment of his body willingly. When the young man would not give in
for gifts or any other act of friendship, Laetorius was unable to control
his desire and he tried force. When everyone in the camp heard about
his transgression, the tribunes,[5] considering it a crime against the state,
charged him publicly. The people set death as the punishment, and condemned him with a unanimous vote. For they considered it unacceptable
for commanders to commit such irreparable and unnatural abuses against
free bodies that were fighting for the freedom of others.

7.4 Valerius Maximus 6.1.10

C. Fescenninus, a triumvir capitalis,[6] publicly enchained C. Cornelius, a
veteran who had undertaken the bravest military service and had four
times been awarded the honor of the First Spear by his commanders,
because he had negotiated an act of sexual immorality[7] with a freeborn
adolescent. The tribunes were summoned to his defense, not because he
denied anything about the act but because he said he was prepared to
wager that the boy was accustomed to derive profit from his body openly

4. This was probably the Second Samnite War, which took place between 327 and 304
B.C.E. Dionysius says that the events described here transpired "a few years after" those of **7.1.**

5. The ten tribunes of the people were elected to protect the interests of ordinary Romans
against abuses by magistrates or the Senate. They are to be distinguished from military tribunes, like Laetorius, who were simply military officers, usually appointed.

6. This board of three men was responsible for overseeing police and prison functions in
the city of Rome.

7. The Latin word here is the rather vague term *stuprum.*

and without pretense. But the tribunes refused to intervene. Therefore, Cornelius was forced to die in prison, for the tribunes of the people did not think it right for our republic to make contracts with brave men that they should buy favorites at home with their bravery abroad.

7.5 Valerius Maximus 6.1.7

An example of an excellent name and memorable deed follows. M. Claudius Marcellus, when he was curule aedile,[8] issued a summons for C. Scantinius Capitolinus to appear before the people on the grounds that he had accosted Marcellus' son for the purpose of sexual immorality.[9] Capitolinus insisted that he could not be compelled to appear because he held sacrosanct power,[10] and begged the help of tribunal protection. The entire college of tribunes refused to prevent the issue of chastity from being discussed. Summoned as a defendant, Scantinius was condemned by the evidence of the one witness to testify. It is agreed that the young man was brought onto the speaker's platform, hanging his head the entire time and silent; this silence, caused by shame, was extremely powerful in exacting his revenge.[11]

7.6 Plutarch, *Roman Questions* 288A

In this section, Plutarch offers various explanations of why Roman boys wore an amulet called the "bulla."

Or is it because it was not unseemly or shameful for the men of old to love male slaves who were in their season of youthful beauty, as the comedies show even today, but they emphatically kept away from free boys, and free boys bore this sign so men would not be uncertain if they encountered boys naked?[12]

7.7 Plautus, *The Rope* 1073–75

Plautus was a comic playwright active in the late third and early second centuries B.C.E. Here Trachalio, a slave, addresses the master of Gripus, another slave.

---

8. 227 B.C.E. Aediles were urban magistrates in charge of public buildings, games, and marketplaces. The curule aediles were those elected from the patrician order.

9. The Latin word is again *stuprum*.

10. Apparently as a tribune of the people, who could not be arrested. However, in this case his fellow tribunes refused to support him.

11. Plutarch adds the information that Scantinius' punishment was a large fine.

12. Presumably in a public bath, which other sources suggest could be a scene of male cruising.

TRACHALIO: Hey! I get to speak first! Please, if this guy belongs to you, stuff[13] him.

GRIPUS: What? Do you want me to get the same thing you used to get from your master? He may have been in the habit of stuffing you: our master doesn't do that to us.

7.8 Plautus, *The Persian* 284–86

Sagaristio is an adult slave, Paegnium a slave boy.

SAGARISTIO: I know all about you: you've been bedded.

PAEGNIUM: Sure have. What's it to you? At least I didn't get bedded for nothing, the way you did.

SAGARISTIO: Pretty damn sure of yourself, aren't you?

PAEGNIUM: I sure am: sure that I'm going to be free, and you'll never be.

7.9 Plautus, *Curculio* 35–38

Here a slave addresses his master.

No one forbids anyone from the public street;
As long as you don't make a path through fenced-off land,
As long as you keep away from the bride, the widow, the maiden,
The youth and free boys, love whomever you want.

7.10 Plautus, *Curculio* 482–84

The producer of the play talks about the kind of people who frequent different parts of Rome.

On the Tuscan road there are men who sell themselves, either the sort who turn themselves around for you, or who offer others an opportunity to be turned around.

7.11 Plautus, *Pseudolus* 767–87

This play is firmly dated to 191 B.C.E. The following is the speech of a young male slave.

If you're a boy, and the gods make you a pimp's slave and also make you ugly, you have a really, really hard time of it. I know that from my own

---

13. The verb *comprimere* means both "shut up" and "penetrate sexually."

experience, for that's the kind of slavery I've got here. I've got all sorts of troubles on all sides, big ones and small ones. And I can't find myself a lover anywhere, somebody to love me, so I could be cared for even a little bit. Today's the pimp's birthday. He's threatened us all, from the biggest to the smallest: he says anybody who doesn't send him a gift today is gonna be tortured and crucified tomorrow. So I've got no idea what to do. I can't do *that* thing,[14] like those slaves do, who can. But unless I send the pimp a gift today, I'll have to drink fuller's juice[15] tomorrow. Oh dear, I'm really still too small for *that* thing. But gosh, I'm so afraid of him now, if anybody gives me something to make my hand heavier, though they say *that* thing makes you groan a lot when it happens, I think I'll be able to bite down hard and bear it somehow.

7.12 Plautus, *Pseudolus* 1177–82

The pimp Ballio and the old man Simo are free adults, Harpax a slave.

BALLIO: *[addressing Harpax]* So then. When you were a boy, did you used to lie in a cradle?
SIMO: Of course he did.
BALLIO: And did you also use to—you know what I mean?
SIMO: Of course he did.
HARPAX: Are you crazy?
BALLIO: Well, did you? At night when the soldier went out on watch, and you went with him, did his sword fit in your sheath?[16]
HARPAX: Go to hell.

7.13 Plautus, *Captives* 867

Two free men converse.

HEGIO: As you wish, I willingly take it.[17]
ERGASILUS: I believe it. That's what you used to do when you were a boy.

7.14 Plautus, *Truculentus* 149–57

Astaphium is the maid of Phronesium, a courtesan. Diniarchus is one of Phronesium's lovers.

---

14. Probably a reference to anal intercourse.
15. A fuller was a dry cleaner. "Fuller's juice" is urine, which was used as a solvent. Some interpret the line as a reference to oral sex.
16. Probably a reference to anal penetration.
17. The verb *pati* can mean both "endure" (i.e., put up with something) and "take the passive role in a sexual act."

ASTAPHIUM: This field here is not farmland; it's pasture land. If it's plow-
ing you're after, you'd do better to go to boys: they're used to being
plowed.[18] Pasturage is our territory; farmland belongs to other tax
collectors.

DINIARCHUS: I'm very familiar with both types of tax collector.

ASTAPHIUM: Well, then, you must really have lots of time on your hands,
if you've managed to get into trouble both here and there. But which
do you prefer to have dealings with?

DINIARCHUS: *You*[19] are more insolent, but they are more deceitful: if you
give anything to them, it vanishes, and they themselves have nothing to
show for it. At least if *you* get something, it ends up in your bellies. All
in all I'd say they are wicked, and *you* are worthless windbags.

7.15 Plautus, *Casina* 449–66

*Olympio and Chalinus are slaves of Lysidamus. Chalinus is eavesdropping on a con-
versation between the other two, who are conspiring so that Lysidamus can have sex
with one of his wife's maids.*

OLYMPIO: Look at how obedient I've turned out to be. Thanks to me, you
can have what you've most wanted. Your heart's desire will be yours
today, and your wife won't have any idea.

LYSIDAMUS: Sh! Oh, I swear, I can hardly hold back my lips from kissing
you for what you've done today, my sweetie.

CHALINUS: *[aside]* What? You're kissing him? What's he done? What's this
"sweetie" business? I do believe, by Hercules, this guy wants to puncture
his bailiff's bladder.[20]

OLYMPIO: Oh, so you love me now.

LYSIDAMUS: Love you? I love you more than I love myself! Won't you let
me put my arms around you?

CHALINUS: *[aside]* What? Put your arms around him?

OLYMPIO: OK.

LYSIDAMUS: Oh, when I touch you, I feel like I'm licking honey.

OLYMPIO: All right, lover boy, now get off my back.

CHALINUS: *[aside]* So that's it! That's why he made him bailiff. One time I
went to fetch him home after a party, and he wanted to make me door-
keeper for the same services under the doorway.

OLYMPIO: Oh, I was so dutiful to you today and such a source of pleasure.

LYSIDAMUS: Oh, I swear by my life, I love you more than myself.

18. A reference to anal penetration.
19. The second person here is meant to denote all of womankind.
20. A reference to anal penetration.

CHALINUS: *[aside]* Goodness, I think they're going to do it right now! This
old man has a habit of going after men even after they've grown beards.

7.16 Quintilian 10.1.100

In his catalogue of Roman authors, Quintilian comes to the comic poet Afranius, who
was active during the latter half of the second century B.C.E.

Afranius excelled in the toga-wearing comedies.[21] If only he had not
stained the plots of his plays by obscene love affairs with boys, thereby
confessing his own habits!

7.17 Polybius 31.25.2–5

Polybius was a Greek historian of the second century B.C.E., whose purpose was to ex-
plain Rome's ascendance to the Greeks. He was a member of the philhellenic intellec-
tual circle gathered around the younger Scipio, to whom he refers here.

Initially, Scipio's[22] eagerness and ambition for good things were directed
toward acquiring a reputation for prudence and surpassing every young
man his age in this regard. Although the crown is great and difficult to
win, at that time in Rome it was easy because the inclinations of most men
were disgraceful. Some of them had given themselves over to their boyfriends among the young men, others to prostitutes, and many to music
and parties, and all the extravagance that comes with them. For they had
quickly been swept up in Greek licentiousness for such things in the war
with Perseus.[23] So great a fever had infected the young men over these
kinds of things that many would pay a talent for a beautiful male slave
and many would pay three hundred drachmas for a jar of Pontic smoked
fish.[24] Outraged at this, M. Cato[25] once said in an address to the people
that he could see the Republic collapsing when he saw good-looking boys
selling for more than fields, jars of smoked fish for more than ox-drivers.

21. The *togata* was a version of romantic and domestic comedy similar to that of Plautus and
Terence, but set in Italian towns.

22. Living from 185 to 129 B.C.E., he was a successful general in the Third Punic War and
subsequently an illustrious Roman statesman.

23. The last Macedonian king of Greece, finally defeated by Rome in 168 B.C.E.

24. A talent was a fortune, three hundred drachmas the equivalent of several months' wages
for a skilled worker. However, it should be noted that a typical container of cured fish could
be as large as four to six gallons.

25. Cato the Censor (234–149 B.C.E.), a famous Roman statesman and advocate of traditional morality. These remarks may have been made while he held the office of censor in 184,
since that magistrate, responsible for maintaining the citizenship rolls, could strike from the
list anyone who was not deemed morally fit to retain their status.

7.18 Aulus Gellius 6.12.4–5

Aulus Gellius wrote a literary and historical miscellany called the "Attic Nights" in the late second century C.E., preserving many notable quotations and anecdotes.

P. Africanus,[26] son of Paullus, was a man endowed with a good education and every virtue, and was clothed in the ancient fashion.[27] Among many other things, he reproached P. Sulpicius Galus, a fastidious man, for wearing tunics that entirely covered his hands.[28] These were the words of Scipio: "A man who wears perfume every day and decks himself out in front of the mirror, who goes about with trimmed eyebrows, a plucked beard and hairless thighs, who, when he was a youth, attended parties in his long-sleeved tunic and bedded down with a lover on the corner of the couch, and who now unduly craves not only wine but men as well—would anyone doubt that such a man did the things that perverts *(cinaedi)* usually do?"

7.19 Aulus Gellius 15.12.2

The following is an excerpt from a speech of the tribune and popular reformer Gaius Gracchus, regarding his behavior as a Roman official in Sardinia in 125 B.C.E.

"In that province, I employed myself in the way I thought beneficial to all of you, not in the way I thought profitable to my own ambition. There was no base tavern at my home, nor were there any exceptionally handsome slaves; but in my company your children behaved more chastely than they did at the general's quarters."

7.20 Plutarch, *Gaius Gracchus* 4.3–4

The following passage refers to Cornelia, the mother of the Gracchi.

Many remarks Gaius made about her when he was attacking one of his enemies in his unpretentious oratorical style have been recorded: "You insult Cornelia, who gave birth to Tiberius?"[29] Since the man who made the abusive remark against her was attacked for being effeminate, Gaius said, "What gall you have to compare yourself to Cornelia! Have you had

---

26. Scipio the Younger. His actual father was L. Aemilius Paullus, but he was adopted by P. Scipio, son of Scipio the Elder, the general of the Second Punic War.

27. In other words, he wore a toga (outer garment) without a tunic (undergarment).

28. The "chirodyte" tunic, a Greek fashion recently introduced into Rome.

29. Tiberius Gracchus was Gaius' older brother and predecessor in advancing popular reforms, assassinated in 133 B.C.E.

as many children as she has? All the Romans know that she had nothing to do with men for longer than you—and you are a man!" His language had this kind of vitriol, and one can find many similar examples in his writings.

7.21 Valerius Maximus 6.1.12

The following event can be dated to 104 B.C.E.

This event[30] motivated the general C. Marius[31] to announce that his sister's son, C. Lusius, a military tribune, had been killed legally by C. Plotius, a frontline soldier, because he had dared to accost him for the purpose of sexual immorality.

7.22 Lutatius Catulus, Fr. 1 *Fragmenta Poetarum Latinorum* = Aulus Gellius 19.9.14

Catulus was the fellow consul of Marius in 102 B.C.E., although he later became a political opponent. He was also a poet of some modest talent.

My soul has fled. I believe, as usual, it has gone
   To Theotimus' house. So it is; it has that refuge.
It's not as if I had not forbidden him to admit the fugitive
   And told him to send it away![32]
We'll go search for it. But I fear that we too may be caught.
   What should I do? Venus, give me advice.

7.23 Apuleius, *Apology* 10

In this passage, the second-century C.E. author Apuleius defends his use of pseudonyms by criticizing the satirist Lucilius, who was active during the final decades of the second century B.C.E.

I criticize Lucilius for prostituting in his poetry the boys Gentius and Macedo with their own names.

---

30. Valerius has just finished narrating the story of Laetorius Mergus (for which see **7.3**).

31. A highly successful Roman general, who enjoyed an unprecedented six consecutive consulships in the last decade of the second century and continued to be a force in Roman politics for many years thereafter.

32. Compare these first two couplets to the first four lines of **6.4**, by Callimachus.

7.24 Lucilius 273–74 Marx

This fragment implies that a praetor can be bought just like a prostitute.

Now the praetor[33] is yours; he will be mine, if Gentius will have left this year.

7.25 Lucilius 866–67 M

This fragment contrasts an unspecified group of males, perhaps male prostitutes or slaves, with women.

. . . who will demand less and will offer themselves much more properly and without disgrace.[34]

7.26 Lucilius 1058 M

Beardless androgynes and bearded pervert-adulterers . . .[35]

7.27 Lucilius 1186 M

This fragment describes the perils of intercourse with each gender.

She covers you with blood and he, on the other hand, covers you with shit.

7.28 Pomponius Bononiensis, *Maccus the Virgin*, Fr. 75–76 Ribbeck

Pomponius wrote Atellan farces, a tradition of comedy featuring stock characters and Italian settings, in contrast with the Greek settings and plots of Plautus. He was active during the earliest decades of the first century B.C.E.

As he walked by, he saw Dossenus[36] in play, not modestly teaching his fellow student, but stroking his butt.

7.29 Pomponius Bononiensis, *The Baker*, Fr. 125–26 R

. . . unless someone should suddenly now come my way, who would bend over and let me plant my boundary-post in a safe place.[37]

---

33. The second highest magistracy in the Roman Republic, associated with judicial as well as military functions.

34. I.e., pregnancy or adultery.

35. The Latin word here is *moechocinaedi*, a compound formed out of the Greek word for adulterer (*moichos*) and *cinaedus*.

36. One of the stock characters of Atellan farce, supposed by some to be a hunchback, by others to be a glutton.

37. A metaphor for anal penetration.

7.30 Pomponius Bononiensis, *The Prostitute*, Fr. 148–49 R

This line may be delivered by a male prostitute who specializes in taking the active role.

I have buggered no citizen through deceit, only the kind who willingly bent over, himself begging me.

7.31 Pomponius Bononiensis, *The Prostitute*, Fr. 151–52 R

The following fragment is also spoken by the prostitute, who plies his trade in order to eat.

I am looking for something to eat, while they are looking for something to shit.[38] It's just the opposite. . . . I consider rumor of little value, as long as there is a stomach I must fill.

7.32 Novius, *The Comic Encore*, Fr. 19 R

Novius was a slightly younger contemporary of Pomponius who also wrote Atellan farces.

As long as they are able to take the passive role, they first depilate their buttocks.

7.33 Novius, *The Comic Encore*, Fr. 20–21 R

No one doesn't know that a boy is better than a woman, and by how much more when his voice begins to crow like a cock's and his branch is already as strong as oak![39]

7.34 Suetonius, *The Deified Julius* 2

Suetonius was a historian of the early second century C.E. *who wrote biographies of the first twelve emperors. The passage is from the first, on Julius Caesar.*

He first served in the army in the province of Asia on the staff of the praetor Marcus Thermus.[40] When Thermus sent him to Bithynia[41] to bring

---

38. In light of **7.27**, this probably refers to a penis being befouled with fecal matter. Alternatively, Pomponius could mean that the repeated insertion and withdrawal of the penis creates a sensation analogous to excretion.

39. I.e., at the age when his voice breaks and his penis becomes capable of full erection.

40. These events transpired in 81–80 B.C.E., when Caesar was 19.

41. A Thracian kingdom in northwestern Asia Minor, allied with the Romans at the time, and ultimately bequeathed to Rome after Nicomedes' death in 74.

back a fleet, he lingered at the court of King Nicomedes, and this gave
birth to the rumor that he had yielded his chastity to the king. This rumor
gained credence when he returned to Bithynia within a few days in order
to exact payment of a debt that was supposedly owed to a certain freedman who was a client of his. He served the rest of this campaign with
better repute and was awarded the civic crown by Thermus at the siege
of Mytilene.[42]

7.35 Suetonius, *The Deified Julius* 49

Besides his relationship with Nicomedes, nothing else damaged his reputation for chastity; that, however, exposed him to unending disgrace and universal reproach. I leave out of discussion Licinius Calvus'[43] famous verses:
"everything that Bithynia had—and Caesar's sodomizer too." I pass over
the orations of Dolabella and Curio Senior,[44] in which Dolabella called
him "the queen's rival and the mattress in the royal litter" and Curio called
him "Nicomedes' whore and Bithynia's brothel." I ignore the edicts of
Bibulus,[45] in which he declared that his colleague was the queen of Bithynia: "Once," he said, "he had desired a king, now he desired a crown."
On that same occasion, according to Marcus Brutus,[46] a certain Octavius,
whose tongue was loosened by his weak mental condition, after he called
Pompey "king" in front of a huge assembly, greeted Caesar as "queen." And
Gaius Memmius[47] even charges that he acted as cupbearer to Nicomedes,
along with other catamites, at a large banquet, where several Roman merchants were present—and he gives their names. Cicero was not content
to have said in certain letters that Caesar had been led into the king's bed-
chamber by attendants; that, dressed in a purple robe, he lay down on a
golden bed; and that "the flower of the youth of Venus' descendant was defiled in Bithynia"; he also, when Caesar was speaking on behalf of Nicomedes' daughter Nysa in the Senate and brought up the causes for his gratitude to the king, said, "Won't you please drop the subject? It is well known
what he did for you—and also what you did for him!" Finally, at the tri-
umphal procession to celebrate his victories in Gaul, his soldiers, among

42. The principal city of Lesbos, which rebelled against heavy Roman taxation in 80.

43. A neoteric poet of Catullus' generation (the 50s B.C.E.).

44. Dolabella was consul in 81 B.C.E. and was later prosecuted by Caesar for corruption;
Curio was consul in 76, and was an active opponent of both Caesar and Cicero until his death
in 53.

45. Bibulus held the offices of aedile, praetor, and consul in the same years as Caesar, but
was a strong opponent of his efforts at hegemony.

46. The onetime ally and eventual assassin of Caesar.

47. The Roman governor of Bithynia in 57 B.C.E., when Catullus was in his service. He eventually reconciled with Caesar and ran for the consulship in 54 with Caesar's support.

the comical songs that they always sing while they follow the victor's chariot, belted out this one, which has come to be proverbial:

Caesar conquered the Gauls, Nicomedes conquered Caesar;
This is the triumph of Caesar, who conquered the Gauls;
Nicomedes does not get a triumph for conquering Caesar.

7.36 Suetonius, *The Deified Julius* 52.3

And in case anyone doubts at all that he was notorious for dissoluteness and adultery, Curio Senior, in one of his orations, calls him "the husband of every wife and the wife of every husband."

7.37 Dio Cassius 43.20.4

Dio Cassius was a Roman statesman of the late second and early third centuries C.E. who wrote, in Greek, a comprehensive history of Rome from the beginnings to his own time. Here he treats Caesar's reaction to his soldiers' criticism and mockery.

He was not, however, aggrieved by their saying these things, but took delight in their availing themselves of so much frankness toward him out of a trust that he would not be angry—except insofar as they abused his intimacy with Nicomedes. For at this he was very angry and was clearly pained; he undertook to defend himself and swore it was not true, and from this action brought even more laughter upon himself.

7.38 Valerius Maximus 9.1.7–8

In this section, Valerius lists several anecdotes illustrating the dangers of luxury and lust.

[7] Moreover, with how much extravagance and lust did the trial of P. Clodius[48] abound! Nights with married women and youths of noble family were bought at great expense and paid out to jurors in lieu of bribes, so that the defendant might be acquitted, even though he was manifestly guilty on the charge of sacrilege. In such a distasteful and complex scan-

---

48. Living from 92 to 52 B.C.E., Clodius Pulcher was a notorious demagogue of the late Republic, who gave up his distinguished aristocratic name to become a commoner, and was Cicero's archenemy. In 61, he was put on trial for sacrilege, in virtue of dressing up as a woman at the rites of the Bona Dea, a goddess whose annual ceremony was open only to women. The jury was bribed by his ally, the future triumvir M. Licinius Crassus, a man of fabulous wealth.

dal, you would not know whom to detest most: the man who devised that species of corruption, or those who allowed their own modesty to become a go-between soliciting perjury, or those who traded their sacred oath as jurors for an immoral sexual act.

[8] Equally scandalous was that party organized for the consul Metellus Scipio[49] and the tribunes of the people, to the embarrassment of the state, by the tribunician messenger Gemellus, a man of freeborn ancestry but lower than a slave in his employment. He set up a brothel in his own house and prostituted Mucia and Fulvia, each illustrious from both her father and husband,[50] and Saturninus, a boy of noble family. Their disgracefully patient bodies were going to be toys of drunken lust. This kind of banquet should not have been attended by a consul and tribunes, but punished by them.

7.39 Catullus 15

Catullus was born in 84 B.C.E. and died at the age of thirty. A series of his polymetric poems concern the boy Juventius and Catullus' rivals (possibly competing poets) Furius and Aurelius. Here he presumes to entrust Juventius to Aurelius' care, possibly before his trip to Bithynia in service under Memmius in 57 B.C.E.

Let me commend me and my boyfriend to you,
Aurelius. I'm asking just one modest favor—
That if you've ever in your heart felt driven
To seek out something chaste and undeflowered,
You'll keep the boy safe for me, and well protected—
Not from the public at large: no, I fear nothing
From folk going to and fro in the piazza,
Brisk, preoccupied, minding their own business.
It's *you* that scares me, you and your great whanger,
A standing threat to boys both good and naughty.   10
Look, wag the damn thing where and how you fancy,
All you've a mind to out there, cocked and ready—
Just leave *him* out of it, make one nice exception!
But should ill-will or mindless madness drive you
To such a state, you bastard, that you're willing
To practice low tricks on me and provoke me,
Ah, *then* you'll feel my dire retaliation,

49. He was consul in 52 B.C.E. An ally of Pompey, he was hated by both Caesar and Cicero.
50. Mucia had been married to Pompey, Fulvia to Clodius, Curio, and Mark Antony.

Feet spread and strapped, back-passage widely gaping,
Reamed all its length with radishes and mullets![51]

7.40 Catullus 16

UP YOURS BOTH, AND SUCKS TO THE PAIR OF YOU,
Queen Aurelius, Furius the faggot,[52]
Who dared judge *me* on the basis of my verses—
They may be raunchy: does that make *me* indecent?
Squeaky-clean, that's what every proper poet's
Person should be, but not his bloody squiblets,
Which, in the last resort, lack salt and flavor
If they're *not* raunchy and rather less than decent,
Just the ticket to work a furious itch up,
I won't say in boys, but in those hirsute   10
Clods incapable of wiggling their hard haunches.
Just because you've read about my countless thousand
Kisses and such,[53] you think I'm less than virile?
UP YOURS BOTH, AND SUCKS TO THE PAIR OF YOU!

7.41 Catullus 21

You, Aurelius, big Daddy of all the hungers—
Not just of these, but of every one hereafter
Or heretofore, in past years or the future:
So you're bent on rogering my darling—
Openly, too! You're with him, swapping stories,
Sticking close up to him, trying every gambit . . .
No good, my friend. If you're plotting to replace me,
I'll fix *you* first, serve you a proper mouthful![54]
If you'd just dined when you did it I'd keep silent;
What *really* ticks me off is that the laddy   10

---

51. Adulterers were traditionally punished by having a variety of unpleasant objects inserted into their anus.

52. In Latin, Aurelius is *pathicus* (usually translated as "sexually passive") and Furius *cinaedus*. Furius may be Catullus' older contemporary Furius Bibaculus, author of anti-Caesarean lampoons and possibly of a mock epic on the Gallic Wars.

53. This could be a reference to two poems of Catullus (5 and 7) in which he exhorts his mistress Lesbia to thousands of kisses or, less probably, to a similar poem (48) addressed to the boy Juventius. Some critics have thought that Furius and Aurelius imputed a lack of masculinity to Catullus because of his weakness and passivity in petitioning Lesbia in those poems.

54. A threat of oral rape.

Will learn from you *that* sort of thirst and hunger.
So—lay off while you decently can, or else you'll
Come to a messy end, mouth crammed to bursting!

7.42 Catullus 24

Hey, Juventius, blossom, best of all your
Blueblood clan,[55] not just the current crop but
Every forebear, each remote descendant—
I'd prefer your shelling out a fortune
On that jerk[56] (who's penniless and slaveless)
To the way you're letting the shit love you!
'What,' you say, 'he's not a dish?' A dish, yes,
But a dish that's penniless and slaveless—[57]
Pooh-pooh that all you like, and blow it off: still,
Still he's got no slaves, and not a penny!   10

7.43 Catullus 28

*Here Catullus addresses his friends Veranius and Fabullus about his disappointing
year in foreign service under Memmius, the governor of Bithynia in 57 B.C.E.*

Dear Veranius, and you, my own Fabullus,
Piso's flacks,[58] poor empty-handed staffers
Loaded up with your piddling little backpacks—
How's life with you, then? Have you had your fill of
Flat wine, cold, and hunger with that bastard?
Do *your* ledgers show a little profit
Paid out, just like mine?[59] When serving *my* chief
I'd chalk up my expenses as net income.
(Memmius, man, you really made me eat that
Yard of yours, laid flat—you took forever!)   10

---

55. The Juventii were an aristocratic family with a consul in their background during the second century B.C.E.; closer to Catullus' time, Juventius Laterensis was praetor in 51 B.C.E. The family also appears to have had a branch in Catullus' native town of Verona.

56. Presumably Aurelius.

57. The substance of a Roman of good class would often be measured in terms of how many slaves he owned.

58. Calpurnius Piso Caesonius was governor of Macedonia from 57 to 55 B.C.E. Veranius and Fabullus were apparently serving under him at the time of this poem's composition.

59. In other words, Catullus' foreign service ended up costing him more money than it gained him. Foreign service could offer opportunities for extravagant profits through extortion and corruption.

Now, so far as *I* can see, you two have
Met the selfsame fate, screwed by no lesser
Yard yourselves! Seek noble friends, they tell us!
May all gods (and goddesses) shower ills on
Those two blots on Romulus and Remus![60]

7.44 Catullus 29

*This poem, probably written in 55 B.C.E., complains of the corruption practiced by
Mamurra, Caesar's principal lieutenant during his campaigns in Britain and Gaul.*

Who, pray, except some gamester, some voracious
Shameless gut would watch this, who could stand it—
Mamurra skimming all the cream from wildwood
Gaul,[61] *and* from Britain, our remotest outpost?
Queen Romulus,[62] can *you* bear such a picture?
Now, I suppose, that arrogant, redundant
Ass will work in turn through every bedroom,
Just like some cute white dove or young Adonis?[63]
Queen Romulus, can *you* bear such a vision?
Then you're a shameless glutton and a gamester!   10
Was this *your* aim, O military Supremo,[64]
While you were in that last isle of the west,
To let this shagged-out prick, your crony, chomp
His way through twenty million, thirty maybe?
What's that but clumsy open-handed waste?
You think he hasn't screwed and chewed his fill?
Look: first he squandered his inheritance,
Next, all his Black Sea pickings,[65] and then, third,
His loot from Portugal—as gold-rich Tagus
Knows:[66] Now Gaul and Britain are in danger   20
Why do you back this no-good? What's his use?
Except to gobble up rich oily patrimonies?[67]

60. In other words, Memmius and Piso both are disgraces to Romulus and Remus, the twin
brothers who founded Rome.
61. The Roman province covering much of what is now France.
62. The Latin epithet here is *cinaedus*. Romulus may stand as a metonym for Rome, although some commentators think that it is specifically Pompey who is addressed in this line.
63. The beautiful youth who was the favorite of Venus, the love goddess.
64. This line is clearly addressed to Caesar, who was in Britain at the time.
65. A reference to Pompey's war against Mithridates in 63 B.C.E.
66. A reference to Caesar's generalship in Spain in 61 B.C.E. The Tagus was a major river in
an area known for gold mines.
67. Olive oil would be used as the base for rich dressings.

Was it for *this,* you ultra-pious couple,
Father and son-in-law,[68] that you blew the takings?

7.45 Catullus 56

Cato,[69] such a ridiculous and comic
Business, *well* worth your notice, sure to get a
Giggle, Cato: laugh, if you love Catullus!
So ridiculous, really too *too* comic—
I just caught my girlfriend's little slave boy
Getting it up for her, and (Venus love me!)
Split *him,* tandem-fashion, with *my* banger!

7.46 Catullus 57

They're well matched, that pair of shameless buggers,[70]
Bitch-queens both of them, Caesar and Mamurra—
Why not? Both display the same disease-spots
(Caught in town by one, abroad by t'other),
Deep pocks, there for life, no scrubbing *them* out.
Twins indeed, both sharing the same sickness,
Two sort-of-well-read dwarfs on one cute couchlet,
Hotshots both as studs for married ladies,
Such close friends—but rivals after nymphets—
They're well matched, that pair of shameless buggers.   10

7.47 Catullus 61.119–48

*The following is from a wedding hymn, in which obscene teasing of the newlyweds as
they proceeded through the streets was conventional. Here some lines are addressed to
the groom's former boy favorite.*

Time, more than time, for the ribald
And cock-a-hoop banter now;   120

68. Even though the younger of the two, Caesar was Pompey's father-in-law in virtue of having cemented their political alliance by giving his young daughter Julia in marriage to Pompey
in 59 B.C.E.

69. It is uncertain whether the Cato addressed here was the critic and poet Valerius Cato or
the more famous Cato Uticensis, who, like his great-grandfather Cato the Censor, was known
for his severe morals. If the latter, the address is clearly ironic.

70. The Latin word here is *cinaedi.* In the next line, "bitch-queen" translates *pathicus* (see
n. 52). The verb *convenire* (well matched) is sometimes used of coitus.

Time for the boy-toy, finding
Himself bereft of his lord
To make over his nuts to the children.[71]
   Nuts to the children, you limp
Boy-toy! It's quite long enough
That *you've* played with nuts; high time
Now to bow out before marriage.
Boy-toy, scatter your nuts!
   Up to today you scorned,
Boy-toy, the rough farm girls: 130
But now your cheeks must be shaved
By the barber, you poor, poor creature!
Boy-toy, scatter your nuts!
   Scented bridegroom, it's rumored
You're finding it hard with smooth boys
To abstain, but abstain you must—
Yo Hymen, Hymeneal yo,
Yo Hymen Hymeneal![72]
   We know you've only indulged in
Licit joys—but for husbands these same   140
Joys are licit no longer—
Yo Hymen, Hymeneal yo,
Yo Hymen Hymeneal!
   You, too, bride, must see that you never
Deny your man what he seeks
Lest he seek out the same elsewhere—
Yo Hymen, Hymeneal yo,
Yo Hymen Hymeneal!

7.48 Catullus 63

This poem tells the story of a young Greek named Attis, who castrates himself and becomes a follower of Cybele, the Asian mother goddess.

Over deep seas Attis, carried on a rapid catamaran,
Eagerly with hurrying footsteps sought that forest in Phrygia,[73]
Penetrated the tree-thick coverts, the Goddess' shadowy habitat,

71. Walnuts were traditionally used in children's games; their scattering at a wedding suggests that it is time to grow up and place childish pursuits aside. A secondary reference to the testicles cannot be ruled out.
   72. A ritual formula chanted at weddings, invoking the marriage god.
   73. A region in northwest Asia Minor.

And there, by furious madness driven, wits adrift in insanity,
Seized a keen flint, slashed away the weight of his groin's double
      complement;
And when she[74] felt the members left her shorn of all their virility
Dropping still a spatter of fresh-shed blood on the ground as she sped
      along,
Quickly with snow-white hand she seized the lightweight rat-a-tat
      tympanum—
Yours the tympanum, O Cybele, yours, great Mother, the mysteries—
And on the hollow drumskin beat a tattoo with delicate fingertips,   10
Making this passionate invocation, body convulsed, to her followers:
"On together with me, you Gallae,[75] seek the high forests of Cybele,
On together, you roving herd of the Dindymenian Domina,[76]
Who, like exiles in pursuit of new and alien territory,
Following me as leader, comrades to my orders obedient,
Bore the salt sea's tidal swiftness, its rough oceanic truculence,
And now have all unmanned your bodies from too great hatred of venery—
By your impetuous wanderings let your mistress' heart be exhilarated!
Purge your spirits of slow reluctance, and all together now follow me
To the Phrygian home of great Cybele, the Goddess' Phrygian forest
      groves,   20
Where the sound of cymbals echoes, and the sharp rattle of kettledrums,
Where the Phrygian player's deep notes boom from the curve of his
      basset-horn,
Where the Maenads,[77] ivy-garlanded, toss their heads in mad ecstasy,
Where with shrilling ululations they act out their ritual ceremonies,
Where the Goddess's roving troupers long have flitted peregrinant—
There is where we now must hasten with our impetuous sarabands!"
As soon as Attis, woman no woman, had uttered these words to her
      followers
An instant cry went up from the quivering tongues of the ululant revelers,
Echoing cymbals clashed, there thudded the light tattoo of the
      tambourines,
As headlong to leafy Ida hastened with scurrying footfall her company. 30
Leading them, breathless, pressing onward, gasping her heart and spirit up,
Threading thick woodlands Attis wandered, the drum-beat still her
      accompaniment,

74. After his self-castration, Attis' gender becomes feminine.
75. A name for the eunuch priests of Cybele.
76. Literally, "the Mistress of Mt. Dindymus" in eastern Phrygia.
77. Ecstatic female followers of Dionysus, whose origins are also sometimes traced to
Phrygia.

Like some heifer, as yet unbroken, fleeing the collar's grim discipline,
While the Gallae crowded hotly after their swift-footed pacesetter.
So when they reached Cybele's precinct, swooning-exhausted,
     woman-faint,
Shot with huge effort, breadless, empty, soon they collapsed into
     somnolence:
Tides of slumber, slow and languorous, closed their eyes, rippled over them:
In soft repose there ebbed to nothing all their minds' rabid delirium.
But when the Sun with his golden orb and eyes of a sharp-dazzling radiance
Lightened the pale white empyrean, harsh Earth, and the sea's liquid
     riotousness,   40
Chasing away Night's gloomy shadows, his fresh steeds' hooves briskly
     clattering,[78]
Then Sleep arose from Attis wakened, fled away swiftly, precipitate,
Sought comfort in the trembling bosom of the goddess Pasithea.[79]
So after slumber, now abandoned by her frenzied paroxysm,
Attis reflected on the deed that she herself had initiated,
Saw where she was, what things she'd lost, mind purged to diaphanous
     clarity.
Back to the shore she forced her footsteps, heart full of simmering
     bitterness,
And there, as she gazed with tear-filled eyes at the ocean's lonely immensity,
Thus she addressed her distant homeland, in saddest accents and
     piteously:
"Ah, dear country that shaped my being, country that bore and
     delivered me,   50
Whom to my misery I abandoned—like some runaway minion
Fleeing his master—and pressed on hotfoot to Ida's wildwooded forestry,[80]
Passed the snowline, made my way to the wild beasts' frost-riven adyta,
Reaching as far, in my mad frenzy, as their remotest covert—ah where,
Where, in which quarter, O my country, must I now look for your territory?
My eyes, unbidden, long to turn their gaze upon you, motherlandwards,
While, for this too-brief space, my mind stays free of its savage insanity.
Ah, am I doomed to these alien forests, far from what's home, what's
     familiar—
Absent from forum and from palaestra,[81] from racecourse and from
     gymnasium?

---

78. The Greeks and Romans imagined that the Sun, Dawn, and the Moon deities all drove across the sky in chariots.

79. One of the three Graces.

80. Ida was the highest mountain in Phrygia.

81. A wrestling school.

Ah wretch, ah wretch, whose life henceforward is nothing but wailing
    and misery!   60
What variation of human figure exists that I haven't appropriated?
This I, now woman, was I the ephebe,[82] the child; this I the young teenager,
This I the gymnasium's finest flower, the glory of oil-smooth athleticism.
For me all thresholds were warm,[83] for me all hallways were crowded with
    visitors,
For me the house was a riot of posies, flowers all looping and garlanded,
When the sun came up and the time was on me to rise and abandon my
    bedchamber.
Am I now to be known as the gods' own handmaid, the serving-girl of
    great Cybele?
Shall I be a Maenad, I but a part of me, I unmanned to sterility?
Am I to dwell on verdant Ida's chill and snowclad escarpments? Shall I
Waste my remaining life span under the lofty columns of Phrygia,   70
There with the hind that roams the forest, there with the boar in his
    timberland?
Now, too late, what I've done appalls me; now, too late, I repent of it!"
As from those rose-red lips there issued with arrowy speed her sharp
    utterance,
Bringing a new report to the ready ears of the gods, those keen listeners,
Cybele then, unyoking the reins that harnessed the lions to her
    chariot-pole,
Goaded the left one, the cattle-killer, kindling its wrath with her urgency:
"Go now, my fierce one, go, pursue him, plague him with savage dementia,
Make the stroke of his frenzy drive him back to the groves of my habitat,
He who yearns so over-freely to shake off my mastering dominance!
Flog your back with your tail in fury, lash yourself into rabidity,   80
Roar till each hidden covert reechoes your fierce and terrifying utterance—
Go, my fierce one, toss the tawny mane on your neck's muscularity!"
So spoke Cybele in rage, and slipped the yoke-pin one-handed. The beast
    took off
In a feral fury, driven wild by its self-incitement to savagery,
Sprang forward roaring, paws in motion sending the brushwood skittering.
But when it neared the sea-damp shoreline, the bright white stretch of the
    littoral,
And there saw delicate Attis standing by the sea's marbled infinity,

---

82. In many Greek cities an ephebe would merely be an adolescent of 15–17, but in Athens after 335 B.C.E., the *ephebeia* became a formalized system of military training and education for 18–20 year olds.

83. An allusion to the topos of a lover camped out on the doorstep of his beloved.

It charged. Demented, she scuttled headlong back to the wild woods,
    a fugitive,
There to remain forever, a lifelong slave-girl, a feminine acolyte.
Goddess, great Goddess, O Cybele, Goddess, mistress of Díndymus,[84]   90
Far from my own house be all your furies, Lady, and madnesses—
Whip up others into frenzy, goad on others to ecstasy!

7.49 Catullus 81

Amid all those crowds, Juventius, was there *no one,*
    Not *one* cute stud to tempt you into love
Except that guest of yours from some seaside snoozepit,
    His complexion more bilious than a bust's stale gilt,
Who's now your darling, whom you've the rind to value
    Above *us?* A factitious fuck-up, don't you think?

7.50 Catullus 99

Juventius, honey-pot, I snatched from you while you were playing
    A tiny kiss, sweeter than ambrosia's sweet.
But no way did I get it for free: an hour or longer,
    As I recall, you had me nailed on the cross
While I made abject apologies, yet all my weeping
    Didn't abate your cruelty one jot.
Oh, the instant I'd done it you dabbed your lips with water,
    Raised a soft hand and knuckled them clean
So that no trace of my mouth should remain, as though expunging
    The filthy saliva of some pissed-on whore.   10
Since then, what's more, you've never quit making my love-life
    A living hell, tormenting me every which way,
So that soon my poor kisslet turned from sweet to bitter,
    Ambrosia no longer, but hellebore.
Well, since such is the penalty for your abject lover,
    Henceforth I will *never* snatch another kiss!

7.51 Catullus 106

Seeing an auctioneer around with some fetching young elf
    One can only assume that he's desperate to sell—himself.

---

84. Here the poet addresses Cybele in his own right.

7.52 Cornelius Nepos, *Preface* 3–5

Nepos was the historian to whom Catullus dedicated his collection of poems. His sole surviving work is a series of biographical sketches of famous Greeks and Romans, which may have been published as late as 34 B.C.E. In the preface to that work he contrasts Greek and Roman customs and argues that the Greeks must be understood in their own context.

For it was not shameful for Cimon, the best man of the Athenians,[85] to marry his sister, given that his fellow citizens did the same thing. But by our standards, this is considered an abomination. Quite young men in Crete are praised for having had as many lovers as they could. No widow in Sparta is very celebrated if she does not come to dinner hired for a wage.[86] Olympic victors generally received great praise in all of Greece, and to enter the stage for public entertainment was not shameful among those same peoples, when for us all of those things are held in some cases as causes of disgrace, in others as base and lacking in dignity.

7.53 Plutarch, *Roman Questions* 274D–E

Here Plutarch discusses why the Romans did not believe in anointing themselves with oil outdoors, as the Greeks regularly did in their gymnastic exercise.

For the Romans used to be very suspicious of rubbing down with oil, and believe that nothing else is so responsible for the Greeks' softness and political enslavement as their gymnasia and wrestling schools, which engender much empty frivolity and wasted time in their cities, as well as pederasty and corruption of the bodies of the young through excessive sleep, walks, rhythmic movements, and prescribed diets. By these practices they have unwittingly fallen away from the practice of arms and love to be called skilled and handsome wrestlers rather than good infantry- and cavalrymen. It is a labor for men who strip in the open to avoid these consequences; but those who anoint themselves and exercise at home do no wrong.

---

85. A conservative Athenian statesman of the 470s and 460s B.C.E., to whom Nepos devotes one of his biographies. Elpinice was his half-sister and lived at his house before being married to Callias; some comic poets implied that Cimon had incestuous relations with her, from which later historians falsely deduced that he had actually married her. In fact, marriage of half-siblings was rare among the Athenians.

86. Although the Spartans did allow women a degree of sexual freedom unusual for other Greek cities, there is no other evidence for the particular custom Nepos here imputes to them.

7.54 Cicero, *On the Republic* 4.3–4

Cicero (106–43 B.C.E.) was the most versatile orator and literary figure of the late Republic, and a statesman who attempted to preserve republican government at a time when it was under threat from many quarters. His Republic, *completed in 51, is a philosophical treatise on the best form of government, but is not preserved in its entirety. In this fragmentary section he discusses Spartan customs.*

[3] . . . by custom those entering the military are assigned guardians under whose control they remain during their first year. . . . not only as it is at Sparta, where boys learn how to plunder and steal. . . . it was disgraceful for adolescent boys not to have lovers. . . .

[4] . . . that a young man be naked. These are the kinds of things that have been traced far back, as though they were some sort of foundation for modesty. But, in fact, how absurd the way their young men exercise in the gymnasia! How lax the military training for their young cadets! How free and unrestricted their amorous fondling! There is no need to even mention the Eleans and the Thebans, for whom lust is granted unrestrained license in amorous relations with their young men of free birth.[87] The Spartans themselves permit it all when it comes to amorous relations with their young men, the one exception being the filthy act itself. An exceedingly thin wall is the only barrier to this excepted act; for they allow lovers to sleep with each other and embrace, just so long as there is covering between them.

7.55 Cicero, *Tusculan Disputations* 4.70–71

This dialogue, written in 45 B.C.E., represents the views of the various philosophical schools on a number of ethical questions. This extract comes from a section discussing love as a disorder of the soul, in which he has quoted a series of poets.

[70] But let us leave the poets to their play, for in their tales we see even Jupiter himself engaged in this shameful behavior. Let us approach the philosophers as teachers of virtue: they deny that love is present in an illicit sexual act,[88] but by doing so, they quarrel with Epicurus, who is not often wrong in my opinion. Indeed, what kind of love is present in friendship? And why does no one love a young man who is ugly or an old man

---

87. See 5.7.182.
88. The Latin word here is *stuprum*. In this context, it is probably meant to denote all physical acts between free males.

who is handsome? It seems to me that this habit was conceived in Greek gymnasia, where these kinds of love were free and acceptable. Thus, Ennius[89] said it well: "The beginning of shameful behavior is public nudity among citizens." As far as I have been able to discover, though these kinds of love are within the bounds of modesty, they are, nevertheless, disquieting and cause distress because only they, and no other, keep themselves in check. [71] And, though we pass over love for women, to which nature gives more freedom, who doubts what the poets mean to say about the rape of Ganymede, or does not understand what Euripides' Laius says and desires?[90] Finally, what do the most educated men and gifted poets say about themselves in their own poems and songs? What things Alcaeus[91] wrote about loving young men, though he was well known in his own country as a brave man! Also, all of Anacreon's poetry is amatory. But it is clear from his writings that Ibycus of Rhegium was inflamed with this kind of love most intensely of all. We see that the love of all these men was lustful. We have come forward as philosophers, with Plato as our founder (whom Dicaearchus[92] accused, and not without reason), and we should attribute authority to love.

7.56 Cicero, *Tusculan Disputations* 5.58

In this section, Cicero discusses the distrustfulness of Dionysius, the tyrant of Syracuse from 406 to 367 B.C.E.

He was born of good parents and respectable rank—though different authors give different accounts—and though he was blessed with friends of equal rank and intimacy with his kinsmen, he still kept certain young men bound by love of the Greek sort. Even so, he trusted none of them, but chose slaves from rich families. After removing the name of slave, he entrusted the care of his person to them, as well as to certain foreigners and wild barbarians.

---

89. An early Roman epic and dramatic poet (239–169 B.C.E.).

90. A reference to Euripides' tragedy *Chrysippus,* dramatizing Laius' pederastic rape of his host's son.

91. A male poet from Lesbos, contemporary with Sappho. Although no explicitly pederastic poem survives among Alcaeus' many extant fragments, the Augustan poet Horace, who appeals to Alcaeus as his principal Greek model, says that he celebrated a boy named Lycus.

92. A pupil of Aristotle who was active in the final decades of the fourth century B.C.E. He wrote a biography of Plato, which may have been unflattering in parts, since at this point the followers of Plato and Aristotle constituted rival schools.

7.57 Cicero, *Against Verres* 2.2.192

The early case that made Cicero's reputation as an advocate and orator was his prose-cution of Verres, the governor of Sicily, for corruption in 70 B.C.E.

One could not produce a lazier and weaker man, someone who is more masculine among women and more unchaste a little lady among men.

7.58 Cicero, *Against Catiline* 2.8

Cicero was consul in 63 B.C.E. and took the lead in suppressing a revolutionary con-spiracy led by his onetime ally, Catiline. This speech was delivered before the general public.

What enticements did any man ever hold out to the young that were so great as his? He himself loved some young men most shamefully, but was a slave most scandalously to the love of others,[93] and promised to some the free enjoyment of their lusts, to others the death of their parents. He not only goaded them, but helped them to accomplish such deeds.

7.59 Cicero, *For Flaccus* 51

In this speech, delivered in defense of a provincial governor of Asia who had been ac-cused of extortion in 59 B.C.E., he attempts to discredit a witness his opponent, De-cianus, plans to call.

And now, Decianus, I come to Lysanias, your special witness, who is from the same city.[94] You knew him as an ephebe[95] at Temnus, and you wanted him to be naked all the time, because his naked body delighted you.[96] You carried him away from Temnus to Apollonis.[97] You loaned the young man money with great profit for yourself, even though you received a fiduciary deposit. You say that this deposit was entrusted to you, and you still have it and enjoy possession of it today. You compelled this witness to give testi-mony by offering him some hope that he could recover his paternal estate.

---

93. This seems to be a way of saying that Catiline took both the active and passive positions sexually.

94. Temnus, a Greek city near the west coast of Asia Minor.

95. See n. 82.

96. Probably what Cicero means is that Decianus encouraged Lysanias' efforts as an athlete. Greek athletes competed naked.

97. A city about thirty miles further inland on the road to Pergamum.

Though he has not yet testified, I anticipate what he will say. I know this type of man, I know their habits, and I know their desires. Therefore, even though I know what he is prepared to say, I shall not say anything in opposition before he has spoken. For he will change everything around and make up other stories, if I speak first.

7.60 Cicero, *After His Return in the Senate* 11

This speech was delivered after Cicero's return from a one-year exile in 57 B.C.E. He attacks the demagogue Clodius Pulcher, whom he holds responsible.

For who could have expected anything good from a man whose earliest years were spent openly available to every lust and every comer, a man who could not stave off the vile lechery of men, not even from the most inviolable part of his body, a man who, after he had squandered his own resources no less vigorously than he would later squander public funds, supported his extravagance and his destitution by pimping whores from his own house, a man who could not have fled the power of the praetor, the mob of his creditors, and the confiscation of his property, had he not sought sanctuary by holding the office of tribune.[98]

7.61 Cicero, *On the Response of the Diviners* 42

In 56 B.C.E. prophets interpreted a strange noise heard outside Rome as evidence, among other things, that a hallowed site had been profaned. Clodius claimed that the site they referred to was Cicero's house, which the Senate had just returned to him after his return from exile. Cicero countered that it was actually a house owned by Clodius. He again attacks Clodius' earlier life.

After the death of his father,[99] he devoted his earliest youth to satisfying the lusts of rich dandies, and when their intemperance had been fulfilled, he turned to domestic and even incestuous sexual acts.[100] Then, after he grew big and strong, he went to the provinces for military service, and after patiently enduring the abuse of pirates, he even satiated the lusts of the Cilicians[101] and barbarians.

---

98. Tribunes were immune from arrest. See **7.5**.

99. This occurred in 76 B.C.E., when Clodius was about sixteen.

100. Cicero and Catullus both charge in other texts that Clodius had sex with his sister, Clodia Metelli.

101. A people living in the southern part of Asia Minor.

7.62 Cicero, *On the Response of the Diviners* 59

Cicero's abuse of Clodius continues.

How great are those crimes he committed against himself and his own
family? Who ever spared an enemy camp less than he did all the parts of
his body? What public ferry in a river was ever made so accessible to all
as his youth was?

7.63 Cicero, *For Milo* 55

*In 52 B.C.E. Milo, a bitter political rival of Clodius, killed him when they met on a
country highway. Cicero wrote this speech in Milo's defense, but did not deliver it. He
argues that Milo acted in self-defense and that it was actually Clodius who set out
intending to kill Milo.*

Come now, compare the travel arrangements of that lightly equipped
highway robber[102] with all the baggage Milo had at the time. Clodius on
previous occasions always traveled with his wife, but then he was without
her. Before, he never traveled except by carriage, but this time he was on
horseback. Before, he had little Greek companions with him wherever he
went, even when on the way to his Etruscan military camps, but this time
there were no such amusements accompanying him. Milo, who never traveled that way, on this occasion happened to be bringing his wife's singing
boys and legions of maids. But Clodius, who always brought along prostitutes, over-age male hustlers,[103] and the lowest brothel whores when he
traveled, then had nobody except the kind of men who would be chosen
by each other for criminal purposes.

7.64 Cicero, *Philippics* 2.44–45

*The Philippics mark Cicero's return to active politics in 43 B.C.E., after a long retire-
ment. He bitterly attacks Mark Antony, who at this point seemed to pose the greatest
threat to republican government after Caesar's assassination. Cicero himself was assassinated on Antony's orders not much later.*

[44] So would you like us to examine your life from childhood up? I think
we should. Let's start from the beginning. You do remember how you
went bankrupt while still a child? "My father is to blame for that," you will

---

102. He means Clodius.
103. These may be identical to the little Greek companions referred to earlier.

say. I grant you that. Certainly your defense is full of filial devotion. Yet you showed your arrogance when you sat in the first fourteen rows of the theater, even though there had been a section specifically set aside for bankrupt men and mandated by the Roscian law, even for someone who had fallen into bankruptcy through bad luck and through no fault of his own.

Then you began to wear the toga of manhood. How quickly you exchanged it for a womanly toga.[104] From the first you have made yourself into a common whore; you fixed the fee for your debauchery, and it was not small!

But Curio[105] soon put an end to this when he seduced you away from your prostitute's trade and, just as though he had given you the gown of a wife, he settled you into a life of matrimonial stability. [45] Never was there a boy, bought for the sole purpose of slaking another man's sexual thirst, who was so much under the power of his master as you were under Curio. How many times did his father throw you out of his house? How many times was a guard stationed to keep you from setting foot inside the door? And yet, under cover of collusive night, under the spur of lust, under the compulsion of profit, they lowered you down over the roof. That house could not stand up under those kinds of shameless acts for very long.

Do you not understand that I am relating events very well known to me? Call to mind now the time when the elder Curio was lying in his bed overcome by grief. His son, prostrated before my feet, in tears, was trying to convince me to protect you. He was begging me to represent him against his own father, if he were to sue his father for six million sesterces;[106] for he was claiming he had posted that much as a guarantee on your behalf. In addition, he himself, inflamed with love, kept promising that he would go into exile, since he could not bear your grievous absence, if you were torn away from him.

7.65 Pliny the Younger, *Letters* 7.4.3–6

Pliny the Younger published a series of literary epistles in the first decade of the second century C.E. The following letter describes an epigram attributed to Cicero concerning his love for his freedman and secretary, Tiro. Since the source Pliny cites is an author hostile to Cicero, the authenticity of the epigram may be open to doubt, as with the epigrams attributed to Plato.

---

104. Prostitutes were the only women who wore a toga. Married women wore a robe.
105. This was the son of the Curio identified in n. 44.
106. This would be the equivalent of about 9000 pounds of silver (i.e., a fortune).

The book of Asinius Gallus comparing his father[107] and Cicero was read to me at my Laurentine villa. Cicero's epigram to his dear Tiro came up in that work. Then when I went to take my afternoon siesta (for it was summer) and sleep failed to come, I began to ponder that the greatest orators praised and took pleasure in this type of exercise. I applied my attention to it and, contrary to my expectation after being so long out of practice, in a very short space of time I scribbled down these verses on that very matter that spurred me to write:

> When I was reading Gallus' book, in which he dared
> To grant his father the palm and glory over Cicero,
> I found a naughty little trifle of Cicero's,
> Remarkable in its genius. For he put aside severity
> And showed that even the minds of great men
> Enjoy humanity, wit, and many varied charms.
> For he complains that Tiro, frustrating his love
> With foul deceit, robbed him of a few nighttime kisses
> After he dined. Reading this, I say,
> "Why after this do we conceal our love affairs   10
> And timidly publish nothing, rather than confess
> That we too have known the deceits of a Tiro,
> The fleeting allurements and infidelities adding new flames of desire?"

107. Asinius Gallus was consul in 8 B.C.E. and a loyal supporter of Augustus. His father was Asinius Pollio, a loyalist of Caesar and Mark Antony, as well as a literary figure of some renown; he was known to have been critical of Cicero's style, as well as being on the opposite side of late republican politics.

CHAPTER 8

Augustan Rome

The Augustan age is defined by the long dominance of Roman politics by Julius Caesar's great-nephew and adopted son, Octavian (after 27 B.C.E. known as "Augustus"), from his initial proclamation as triumvir in 43 B.C.E. to his death in 14 C.E. After Octavian's consolidation of power to the exclusion of his rival triumvir Mark Antony, finalized with the naval victory at Actium in 31, the period was one of relative peace and tranquility, in contrast to the constant political instability and turmoil of the late Republic. Augustus and his lieutenants actively patronized the arts, and the era was one of unparalleled literary creativity in Rome.

The charges of sexual passivity and self-prostitution directed against the young Octavian (**8.1**) are no more to be believed than those aimed at Julius Caesar (**7.34–37**) and Mark Antony (**7.64**). They are topoi of late Republican rhetoric, not dissimilar in spirit from the poetic abuse (**8.3**) addressed to a wealthy man named Luccius in the persona of a former mistress who accuses him of transvestism and sexual passivity in orgiastic religious rituals and even of soliciting sailors in lowly waterfront locales.

Aggressive homosexual imagery of a Catullan stripe was common even in nonelite political discourse, as evidenced by the curious graffiti known as the *glandes Perusinae* (**8.2**), obscene inscriptions on slingshot bullets used by both sides in the Battle of Perugia (41 B.C.E.), a confrontation between Octavian's forces and those aligned with Mark Antony. The bullets were imagined as agents of phallic penetration against the enemy, who are conventionally styled as sexually receptive. This same culture of masculinity defined in terms of phallic aggression against passive opponents is notable throughout the *Carmina Priapea* (**8.5–11**), an anonymous collection of poems written in the persona of the ithyphallic scarecrow god Priapus, found in gardens throughout the Italian countryside. Among the punishments with which Priapus threatens intruders, oral penetration of another male appears to be the worst humiliation possible (see **8.7, 8.10, 8.11**).

At the same time, the Augustan age also bears witness to the rise of a romantically engaged type of pederastic poetry uncommon in the Republic, but more akin to Greek models. Albius Tibullus (c. 55–19 B.C.E.) wrote long subjective elegies primarily on heterosexual themes, but among his work is a cycle of three poems centering upon a boy named Marathus. The name is not Roman, so he is presumably a slave or freedman, but his status is not emphasized in the poems. **8.12** asks the randy Priapus for advice on how to succeed with boys, but the speaker's attempt to set himself up as an authority, armed with Priapus' teachings, founders on his own hopeless devotion to Marathus, which in **8.13** even moves him to help Marathus win the favors of a girl. Some critics, however, see that elegy as ironic and condescending to Marathus' heterosexual ambitions, not unlike Catullus' short poem on catching a slave boy with his mistress (**7.45**); there may be an element here of the "cycle of love" topos observed in archaic and Hellenistic Greek lyric. Although presuming to act as an interested voyeur of the boy's transition from pederastic beloved to active lover of girls, Marathus' lover cannot tolerate a male rival, as **8.14** shows: he curses the rival and dismisses Marathus as a male whore.

Propertius, an elegiac poet coeval with Tibullus, makes a passing reference to pederasty as an easier and less demanding alternative to heterosexual love (**8.15**), but his own poetic concerns are obsessively heterosexual. Later biographical sources (**8.18**) tell us that Vergil (70–19 B.C.E.) was more inclined to the love of boys, and we do find at least two extended treatments of the subject in his work. One of his earliest compositions (**8.4**) is the soliloquy of an enamored shepherd who invites a slave boy from the city to enjoy with him the delights of country living; this poem is modeled on some of Theocritus' bucolic idylls, but has transformed a hopeless and even grotesque heterosexual situation in Theocritus (the love of the one-eyed monster Polyphemus for the beautiful sea nymph Galatea) into a more naturalistic representation of the hopelessness inherent in an age-differential pederastic love, particularly one where the wooer has no real claim to wealth or status.

Of special interest is an episode from Vergil's crowning epic, the *Aeneid*, concerning the man-boy couple Nisus and Euryalus (**8.17**), who are modeled on the sexualized image of Achilles and Patroclus and other warrior-couples in Greek tradition (see **2.14, 5.7.178–79, 5.8.8.32–35**). Critics disagree whether Vergil conceived their relationship as physical or chaste, but this may not be the central question. We are first introduced to the pair earlier in the *Aeneid* (**8.16**) in the context of a footrace where Nisus fouls a competitor to allow his beloved Euryalus to win. However, the later episode (**8.17**) has potentially more serious consequences, in that the two volunteer to carry a message to Aeneas through enemy lines, but become sidetracked from their mission by a desire to impress one another with their courage in (unnecessarily) killing enemy soldiers. When Euryalus is surrounded and caught, but Nisus has the chance to escape and complete his mission, Nisus instead chooses to die, out of loyalty to his beloved. In both episodes, we see the characters' passionate devotion to one another putting them at odds with the common good (good sportsmanship and fair play in **8.16**, conveying the message to Aeneas in **8.17**). In one sense, the episode stands as a critique of the Greek ideal of pederasty in support of a warrior ethos; at the same time, however, we cannot but admire Nisus' courage and self-sacrifice for his beloved. As throughout the *Aeneid,* the individual and the communal come into irresolvable conflict.

Closer to the end of Augustus' long reign, Ovid (43 B.C.E.–17 C.E.) begins the transition from Augustan literary traditions grounded in nationalism and at least the appearance of personal sincerity to the more ironic, rhetorical, and sometimes even antiauthoritarian stance of early imperial (Silver Age) literature. Ovid himself professes a dislike for pederasty because it lacks mutual pleasure (**8.19**). He even speaks with scorn of adult men (married no less) who depilate themselves to appear more attractive to other men (**8.20**). His ambitious mythological miscellany, the *Metamorphoses,* was in many ways intended as an anti-epic countering and deconstructing the *Aeneid.* Among its many episodes stands a short sequence of pederastic myths (**8.22**), but most of these stories end unhappily, with the beloved boy never emerging from his adolescent relationship. **8.21** is the first Roman text to address the question of love between two women, but it allows the possibility only by clothing one of the girls as a boy and ultimately, through divine intervention, granting her a change of biological sex. Moreover, the narrative is divorced from Roman reality by being set in Crete and assigning responsibility for the transformation to an Egyptian goddess. As in Roman assumptions about male homosexuality that characterize the passive partner as somehow weak and feminine, female homosexuality is constructed as necessarily conforming to a heterosexual model of male and female partners.

Bibliographical Note

For a general treatment of homosexuality in the Augustan period, see Meier and de Pogey-Castries (1930) 187–94 and E. Cantarella (1992) 128–48, and on Roman sexual morality more broadly, Robert (1997) 177–242. G. Williams (1962) 38–43 contends that virtually all homosexual references in Augustan poetry are imaginary and influenced by Greek tradition, rather than reflecting the realities of Roman life. Lilja (1983) 62–87 and Griffin (1985) 15–26 argue the opposite position, namely that Augustan poetry does reflect the nature of real sexual practices at the time.

On homosexual themes in the *Priapea*, see Richlin (1992) 120–27 and Hallett (1996) 333–44. Buchheit (1962) favors a single author and a later date for the collection; however, see Richlin (1992) 141–43. For an annotated edition with German translation and introduction, see Kytzler and Fischer (1978); this also includes Priapus poetry outside the *Carmina Priapea*.

On Tibullus' Marathus poems, see Wimmel (1968) 17–120, who regards them as Tibullus' earliest work, and Quinn (1972) 247–49, Bright (1978) 228–59, Cairns (1979) 147–53, McGann (1983). Dawson (1946) and Luck (1969) 92–99 suggest possible Hellenistic models, including **6.7**. Booth (1996) proposes an ironic interpretation of **8.13**. Tadic-Gilloteaux (1965) 249–54 offers a psychoanalytic interpretation of Propertius' work, identifying elements of Oedipal fixation and latent homosexuality.

On the homoeroticism of Vergil's *Eclogue* 2 (**8.4**), see Olliensis (1997) 294–97 and Papanghelis (1999) 44–50. Klein (1978) deals with the poem's influence on later homosexual writers. Hubbard (1998a) 54–68 compares the text closely with Theocritus and sees pederasty as a trope for relationships of poetic influence and succession. The Nisus and Euryalus episode in the *Aeneid* has been the object of much discussion. Lee (1979) 108–13 and Pavlock (1985) see their love as non-physical; Makowski (1989) shows its relation to the traditional Greek model. Many have criticized them for being thoughtless and rash in their pursuit of heroic glory to the detriment of the community good: see Hornsby (1966), Duckworth (1967), Fitzgerald (1972), DiCesare (1974) 161–66, and Cristofoli (1996). However, Lennox (1977) and Potz (1993) take a more sympathetic view and see the couple as a paradigm of personal loyalty as a positive virtue. Putnam (1985) explores the homoerotic overtones of Aeneas' relationship with the young warrior Pallas.

Makowski (1996) sees Ovid's stance toward the homosexual myths of the *Metamorphoses* as parodic and unsympathetic; however, Verstraete (1975) reads the Hyacinthus narrative differently. See also Janan (1988). Wheeler (1997) comments on the sexual significance of the names of Iphis and Ianthe; for the story as an example of patriarchal suppression of mutual female desire, see Pintabone (2002).

8.1 Suetonius, *The Deified Augustus* 68

Suetonius transmits the following charges made against the young Octavian by his poltical rivals.

In his earliest youth he became notorious for shameful conduct of many kinds. Sextus Pompey[1] attacked him as an effeminate. Mark Antony[2] said that he had earned his adoption by his uncle by giving in to lechery; in the same vein Lucius, Mark Antony's brother, said that after Caesar had taken his virginity, he prostituted himself to Aulus Hirtius[3] for 300,000 sesterces,[4] and that he used to singe his legs with red-hot nutshells, so that the hair would grow softer. And once, at the holiday games, when an actor on stage said the following verse about a eunuch priest of the Mother Goddess beating his drum,[5] the whole populace took it as an insult to Augustus and applauded: "Do you see how the pervert (cinaedus) makes the globe resound with a tap of her finger!"

8.2 *Glandes Perusinae* = *CIL* 11.6721

The following obscene inscriptions are found on lead slingshot bullets used in the battle of Perugia during the winter of 41–40 B.C.E. Lucius Antonius occupied the city; Octavian's forces were besieging it.

[7] I seek Octavian's asshole.
[9] Hail Octavian! You suck.
[11] Loose Octavian, sit on this one!
[14] Bald Lucius Antonius and Fulvia,[6] open up your assholes!

8.3 Ps.-Vergil, *Catalepton* 13

This satirical poem is supposed by some scholars to be an early work of Vergil's contemporary Horace, since the style and meter resemble those of his epodes. An abandoned mistress exposes her former lover's secrets.

Do you think you can throw me over,
    Because I can no longer sail the seas as before,

---

  1. Not to be confused with Pompey the Great, Caesar's fellow triumvir and later rival. Sextus was his younger son, born around 67 B.C.E., and a major military threat to Octavian until the defeat of his pirate navy in 36.

  2. Mark Antony's rivalry with Octavian for the succession to Caesar's position as strongman of the Roman state was not completely resolved until the defeat of his and Cleopatra's navy at Actium in 31 B.C.E.

  3. One of Caesar's most trusted loyalists, who later supported Octavian against Antony and died in relieving the siege of Mutina in 43 B.C.E.

  4. About 450 pounds of silver.

  5. This priest would be one of the much-ridiculed Galli, like Attis in **7.48**.

  6. Mark Antony's wife.

Nor bear harsh cold and summer,
    Nor follow the camp of a victorious army?
Healthy, still healthy are my anger and old wrath,
    And the tongue by which I may always be with you,
Whether the topic is the slaves' hut you once shared
    With your prostituted sister—why excite me,
Why, you shameless jerk worthy of Caesar's censure?—
    Or your thefts   10
Or your late parsimony toward your brother
    Who's drunk his estate away,
Or the banquets you as a boy enjoyed in the company of men,
    With your buttocks kept moist through the night
And someone's sudden cries above you,
    "Thalassio, Thalassio!"[7]
Why have you gone pale, lady? Do my jibes hurt?
    Or do you recognize your own acts?
Pretty miss, you won't invite me to the Cotytia[8]
    For the pricks on holiday.   20
Neither will I see you wiggling your loins in your saffron dress,
    Bent over, hands on the altar,
Or calling out to the foul-smelling sailors[9]
    Near the yellow Tiber,[10] where the beached ships
Stand in the shallows, stuck in the filthy mud,
    Struggling with the meager water.
Nor will you take me into the kitchen or the well-anointed
    Compitalia[11] or even low-life feasts.
Filled up with these and drooling,
    You go back home to your fat wife.   30
You let loose your seething bowels
    And, though despised, lick your wife with kisses.
Now abuse me, provoke me, if you can.
    Look! I'll write your name,
Pervert *(cinaedus)* Luccius. Has your wealth now left you
    And do your molars rattle with hunger?

7. A ritual cry at weddings. The sense must be that the boy's lover is pretending to marry him.

8. Ritualized fertility orgies that took place out-of-doors, featuring transvestism and some form of phallic worship. Cotyto was a Thracian goddess associated with sexual license.

9. The implication may be that he makes sexual assignations with the sailors.

10. The river that passed through Rome, called yellow because of its muddiness.

11. A fertility festival celebrated in early January in honor of the patron spirits of country crossroads.

I'll see you when you have nothing left but your lazy brothers,
    An angry guardian spirit,
A belly cracked open from fasting,
    And the swollen feet of an uncle who hits the bottle.   40

8.4 Vergil, *Eclogue* 2

The following pastoral poem imitates Theocritus' bucolic idylls. The Eclogue collection as a whole was published around 35 B.C.E., but this poem is supposed by many scholars to be one of the earliest, possibly written as early as 42.

Corydon the shepherd burned for fair Alexis,
His master's darling, and he hadn't a hope.
The thick-set beeches, with their shady tops,
Were his resort. There, by himself, with pointless
Passion he rambled on to hills and woods.
"Cruel Alexis, don't you like my songs?
Don't you pity me? Will you make me die at last?
Now even cattle seek out shade and coolness,
Green lizards hunt for shelter in a thornbush;
Thestylis pounds thyme, garlic, and pungent herbs[12]   10
For reapers weary in the consuming heat.
But with me shrill crickets, as I trace your steps
Under the burning sun, sound through the trees.
Better put up with Phyllis' moody rages
Or haughty whims—better Menalcas,
Tanned though he was and you all gleaming white.
Don't, lovely boy, stake too much on complexion:
White privets fade, dark blueberries are picked.
You scorn me, never asking who I am—
How rich in flocks, or flowing with snowy milk.   20
A thousand lambs of mine roam Sicily's hills;[13]
Summer or winter, I'm never out of milk.
I sing such songs as, when he called his herds,
Amphion of Thebes on Attic Aracynthus.[14]
Nor am I ugly: once by the shore I saw

12. Ingredients in a rustic salad called *moretum.*
13. Corydon's boast here is excessive. Since he is a slave, the lambs are actually his master's.
14. Amphion was a mythological ruler of Thebes who built the city's wall by charming the stones into place with his lyre. But Corydon overreaches with his learning, as Amphion would be out of place on Mt. Aracynthus, which was not in Attica, but an entirely different region of Greece.

Myself in the wind-calmed sea. I would not fear to
Compete for you with Daphnis:[15] mirrors don't lie.
If only paltry woods and fields could please you!
We would dwell in lowly cottages, shoot deer,
Drive herds of goats with switches cut from greenwood.   30
In the woods with me you'd learn to pipe like Pan—
Pan taught us how to bind close-fitting reeds,[16]
Pan watches over sheep and shepherds both—
And don't begrudge chafing your lips on reeds:
Amyntas would do anything to learn.
I have a well-joined pipe of hemlock stalks
Of different lengths; Damoetas gave it to me
Saying, as he died, 'Now you're its second master.'
He spoke; that fool Amyntas writhed with envy.
Also, a pair of wild kids that I found   40
Deep in a valley, their skins still spotted white;
They suck my she-goat dry; and they're for you.
Thestylis often begs to take them from me—
And so she shall, since all my gifts disgust you.
Come hither, lovely boy: the Nymphs bring baskets
Brimming with lilies; for you fair Naiads,
Plucking bright poppy heads and violets dim,
Will bind narcissus and flowers of fragrant dill;
Then twining cinnamon and pleasant herbs,
Brighten soft blueberries with marigolds.
Myself, I'll gather quinces, young and downy,   50
And chestnuts, which my Phyllis used to love;
I'll toss in waxy plums and honor them too;
And oh you laurels and you myrtles, I'll
Pluck you together, to mingle sweetest smells.
Corydon, you country boy! Alexis scorns
Your gifts—nor could they match Iollas'.
How could I, desperate wretch, want to unleash
Tempests on flowers and boars on crystal springs?
Who do you flee from, madman?[17] Trojan Paris[18]   60

15. A legendary beautiful youth among the shepherds of Theocritus and Vergil.

16. Pan, patron god of shepherds, invented the pan-pipe, or *syrinx*, by chasing after the nymph Syrinx, who was transformed into marsh reeds that he then grabbed and formed into a musical instrument.

17. Here he addresses Alexis again.

18. Paris was a shepherd on Mt. Ida when the three goddesses appeared to him and asked him to judge their beauty.

And gods too dwelt in woods. Let Pallas[19] have
Her citadels, and woods be our delight.
Fierce lions hunt the wolf, the wolf the goat,
The sportive goat seeks out the flowering shrub:
So Corydon you: our pleasures draw us on.
See bullocks drag home plowshares hanging free;
The shadows double as the sun declines;
But love burns me: for how can love know bounds?
Ah Corydon, what madness seizes you?
Your elm tree's leafy, and its vine half-pruned.   70
At least do something useful: supple twigs
Are ready to be woven with soft rushes.
You'll find another lad, if this one's cold."

8.5 *Priapea* 3

The Priapea *is an anonymous collection of epigrams delivered in the persona of the ithyphallic scarecrow god Priapus, who protected gardens against thieves and intruders. They are usually supposed to be Augustan in date, but some scholars think they are much later. This particular poem is attributed to Ovid by Seneca the Elder, writing not long after Ovid's death.*

I could have spoken obscurely. "Give me that which you can
    Always give yet never perishes.
Give me that which one day, perhaps, when the envious beard
    Besieges your sagging cheeks, you will wish in vain to give.
That which the darling boy whom the sacred bird snatched up,
    And who now mixes pleasing cups for his lover, gave to Jove.[20]
That which the foolish virgin gives to her eager husband
    On the first night, when she fears the wounding of the other place."
It's simpler by far in plain English—GIVE ME SOME ASS!
    Well, what can I do? My wit is blunt.

8.6 *Priapea* 5

The law Priapus cited to a boy you'll find
In the following verses I've left behind.
Take whatever my garden has, it's free—
But first, you open your garden to me.

19. An alternative name for Athena/Minerva, the protector of cities, who usually had a temple at the city's highest point.
20. The reference is to Ganymede, lifted up to Olympus by Jupiter's eagle.

8.7 *Priapea* 13

Bugger the boy, fuck the girl;
For the bearded thief the third degree.[21]

8.8 *Priapea* 22

Indemnities for theft by woman, man, or boy:
Her, pussy; him, head; the last, his ass.

8.9 *Priapea* 25

This scepter, cut from a tree,
Has forever shed its viridity.
The scepter lusting women seek,
The scepter kings desire to hold,
The scepter noble Nellies *(cinaedi)* kiss
Will penetrate the innards of the thief
And bury itself in his high-colonic sheath.

8.10 *Priapea* 28

You people with dishonest intentions
Who try to steal from this garden,
You'll be buggered with my yardstick.
If so hard and weighty a punishment
Fails to dissuade, I'll aim higher.

8.11 *Priapea* 35

I'll bugger you, thief, for the first offense.
The second time, into the mouth it goes.
But if you commit a third theft
Your ass will taste my vengeance—
And then your mouth again.

8.12 Tibullus 1.4

Tibullus' first book of elegiac poems was published at some point not long after 27 B.C.E. Although most of the poems are heterosexual, three concern a beloved boy named Marathus. This poem asks the god Priapus for advice on dealing with boys.

---

21. Literally, "a third punishment remains," i.e., forcible oral sodomy.

"Priapus, may a leafy canopy protect
 Your head from harm, from sun and snow! Please, tell me
What's your secret? You know how to catch good-looking
 Boys, but it's not your looks: rough, uncombed,
Beard uncared-for; naked, you endure the freezing
 Winter, and the scorching summer dog-days."
That's what I asked him. The god, the rustic offspring
 Of Bacchus[22] answered, gripping his curved scythe:
"Don't ever trust the tribe of tender boys. Each one
 Will stir your heart with justified enchantment.   10
This one compels, controlling his horse with tight reins;
 Another's snow-white chest divides the waters,
Gliding smoothly through them. You love this one's boldness,
 That one's tender face and virgin blush.
And if at first he says no, don't be discouraged:
 By and by his neck will slide into
The yoke. In time wild lions have been tamed by men;
 In time soft water wears away hard stone;
On sunny hillsides the year brings grapes to ripeness;
 The year's sure change is blazoned in the sky.   20
Don't hesitate to swear oaths: the winds disable
 And scatter the vain perjuries of Venus.
We have Jupiter to thank for this: the father
 Decreed that oaths sworn eagerly by dumb
Love shall have no force. Even Dictynna[23] permits
 False swearing by her arrows, and Minerva[24]
By her lovely hair. Hesitation is your worst
 Possible misstep. Time does not wait.
How quickly the days go by. How quickly the Earth
 Sheds her brilliant colors, and how quickly   30
The stately poplar sheds her luxuriant leaves.
 How slow and lifeless the fastest racehorse turns
When weak senility sets in. I've seen young men
 Grown old, lamenting stupid, wasted days.
The gods are cruel. A serpent can slough off its years,
 But beauty cannot linger very long.

---

22. Priapus is appropriately associated with Bacchus (Dionysus), since he would protect vineyards as well as gardens.

23. Dictynna was a Cretan nymph whose cult was assimilated to that of Artemis (Diana).

24. The Roman equivalent of Athena.

Only Bacchus and Phoebus[25] have eternal youth,
  Gods who glory in their unshorn hair.
Give in to whatever your boy wants. Yield to him.
  Love will often conquer by compliance.   40
Accompany him, however long the journey,
  However parched the fields beneath the dog-star,[26]
Even if the sky is edged with rust-red lace-work,
  A rainbow warning of the coming storm.[27]
If he wants to cleave the dark waves in a small craft,
  Hold the oar yourself, and drive him on.
Don't shrink from undergoing strenuous labor,
  Or wearing out your still uncallused hands.
If he should want to trap game in the wooded vales,
  Oblige him: sling the net across your shoulder.   50
If he wants to spar, you'll take the sword up lightly,
  And often leave an opening for him.
Then he'll be sweet to you, he'll allow you to steal
  Kisses: he'll resist, but he will give them;
Then he'll grow bolder and offer what once you stole;
  And then he'll long to nestle on your neck.
These are bad times. We are mired in corrupted arts.
  Tender boys expect expensive gifts.
As for you, who first taught Venus to sell herself,
  Whoever you are, may the hard earth crush your bones.   60
Boys, you should love the Muses of Pieria
  And learnèd poets more than golden gifts.
Poetry gives life to Nisus' purple tresses;[28]
  Pelops' ivory shoulder[29] could not gleam
Without the Muses. Those whom they love will always
  Live, while there are forests, stars, and streams.
But the one deaf to the Muses, who sells his love,
  Let him follow after Luxury's

---

25. An alternate name for Apollo, literally "the bright one."

26. The dog-star, Sirius, appears in late summer.

27. Curious as the notion seems to us, the ancients believed that rainbows appeared *before* storms.

28. A mythological king of Megara made invincible by his purple lock of hair, which his daughter cut off while he slept, because she loved the leader of an attacking army. The story was told by Callimachus and, during this period, in the epyllion *Ciris,* falsely ascribed to Vergil.

29. Not only is the story of Pelops told by Pindar (**1.87**), but it is mentioned in the works of Vergil and Horace. It, of course, alludes to Poseidon's pederastic love for Pelops.

Idaean chariot,[30] fill three hundred cities
  With his vain footsteps, hack his worthless flesh   70
As Phrygian music blares. Venus loves blandishments,
  Laments, entreaties, desperate lovers' tears."
The god taught me these words to sing to Titius[31]
  But Titius' wife forbids him to remember.
Let him obey her. The rest of you, who suffer
  The deft, well-practiced cruelty of boys,
Hail me as your teacher! To each his own glory:
  Mine will be advising the rejected.
My door is open to all. There will come a time
  When I, an old man spouting Venus' precepts,   80
Will have a tribe of rapt young men escorting me.
  Oh no. Marathus has me on the rack
And wrenches me in a slow agony of love.
  My ruses and well-practiced arts all fail me.
Spare me, I beg you, boy. Don't let me be laughed at,
  Scorned and pitied for my useless teaching.

8.13 Tibullus 1.8

In the second poem of the sequence, Marathus' lover takes a sympathetic interest in the boy's affair with the girl Pholoe.

What whispered words mean, the tilt of a lover's head—
  I am incapable of being fooled.
It's not that I'm a prophet—I can't read omens,
  No bird-song has informed me of the outcome—
Venus herself instructed me, her magic knot[32]
  Binding my wrists behind my bloodied back.
Stop pretending. The god[33] reserves his cruelest fires
  For those who will not take him lying down.
What good does it do you now to have done your hair,
  Arranged each curl, tucked each soft tress in place?   10
What good is it to rouge your cheeks, to trim your nails
  With hands well-versed in the art of manicure?

---

30. The Roman goddess Ops (Plenty/Luxury) is sometimes identified with the Asian mother goddess, Cybele, whose cult is centered on Mt. Ida in Phrygia and whose wandering eunuch devotees play wild, orgiastic music. See **7.48**.

31. A minor poet mentioned by Horace.

32. Knotted threads would sometimes be used to enact erotic binding spells.

33. Eros.

You change your clothes, your look, but those changes don't help:
    A newer cloak, a tighter sandal strap.
She's the one who looks good, though she hasn't put on
    Make-up, or spent hours on her hair.
What's wrong with you? Has some crone in the dead of night
    Turned you pale with herbs or incantations?
Magic spells can draw the crops from a neighbor's field;
    Spells can stop a snake about to strike;   20
Spells have tried to charm the Moon from her chariot
    And would have, if the bronze had not been struck.[34]
But why complain that herbs or spells have done this harm?
    Beauty needs no help from sorcery.
The harm lies in languid kisses, skin touching skin,
    Body to body, thigh entwined with thigh.
And as for you,[35] please don't be too hard on the boy.
    Venus always punishes unkindness.
Don't ask the boy for gifts; ask an older lover
    Who needs to buy himself a little warmth.   30
A young man is worth more than gold—his face is smooth
    And radiant, his kisses do not scratch.
Slide your shining arms around a young man's torso
    And all the wealth of kings seems meaningless.
But Venus finds ways to slip into a boy's bed
    And clasp him in her arms while he's aroused,[36]
And, as he gasps, to kiss him, wrestling tongue to tongue,
    To bite his neck and leave a lasting mark.
No precious stones or jewels can comfort a girl
    Who sleeps alone in the cold, desired by no one.   40
Then it will be too late to call back love and youth,
    When age has stained your head a lifeless gray.
Then you'll take pains with your appearance, change your hair,
    Dye your curls, disguise the effects of time;
Then you'll take care to pull each white hair by the root,
    Peel the years away from your withered face.
For now, while your youth is in its first flowering prime,
    Use it. It will never linger long.
Don't torment Marathus. Save your severity
    For old men. Where's the glory in defeating   50

---

34. It was customary to avert evil spirits by clashing cymbals during an eclipse.

35. Addressed to Pholoe.

36. Another textual reading would yield the following translation: "But Venus finds ways to lie with a frightened boy in secret, while he clings to his soft clothing."

A tender boy? Spare him. He isn't clinically
    Ill, but love has made his skin go sallow.
You should know how he moans at you in your (frequent)
    Absence, how he soaks the place with tears.
"Why aren't you here?" he cries, "guards can be outwitted;[37]
    The god himself grants lovers their deceits.
I know the furtive tricks of Venus, how to breathe
    Quietly, make stolen kisses silent.
No matter how late at night, I can steal softly
    Out to unlock the doors without a sound.   60
What good are wiles when a brutal girl rejects me,
    Abandons her heartsick man in his own bed?
She'll make a promise, break her word in the same breath,
    And leave me to my all-night agony.
I'll imagine that she's on her way, believing
    Each tiny sound was her approaching foot."
Stop crying, child; she's unbreakable. Already
    Your weary eyes are swollen with your tears.
I warn you, Pholoe, the gods hate arrogance,
    And offerings of incense do no good.   70
Marathus himself once trifled with heartsick men
    Not knowing that a god would take revenge.
More than once, they say, he laughed at his victim's tears,
    Prolonged his longing with contrived delays;
Now he can't stand disdainfulness and disapproves
    Of the severity of bolted doors.
Payback awaits, unless you give up your pride.
    You'll wish that prayer could call back this lost day.[38]

8.14 Tibullus 1.9

Here Marathus' lover complains of the boy's infidelity with a wealthy male rival.

Why, if your plan was to break my pathetic heart,
    Did you swear to the gods—oaths to be secretly scorned?
Poor fool. A liar may hide at first, but Punishment
    Will one day creep silently upon him.

---

37. Slaves appointed to guard the door of a house.

38. Addressed to Pholoe, but with obvious reference to the payback Marathus himself has
earned.

Heavenly ones, be merciful: good-looking boys
    Should be excused—just once—from perjury.
In search of gain the farmer yokes his oxen to
    The balanced plow, and cuts through the hard earth;
Through shifting gales the constant stars draw unsteady
    Ships across the waves in search of gain.   10
My boy's heart has been swayed by gifts; I pray the gods
    Will turn those gifts to water and dry ashes.
Soon enough he'll pay the price, his beauty destroyed
    By wind and dust, his locks a tangled mat;
The sun will burn his face and bleach his hair, the long
    Road wear down his soft and fragile feet.
Often I warned you: "Don't let gold pollute your charm—
    A world of unseen harm lies locked in gold.
Venus comes down hard on those who would violate
    A lover's trust, especially for money.   20
I'd sooner have my forehead branded,[39] body chained
    And cut with iron, back lashed black and blue.
And don't delude yourself that you can hide your sins:
    There is a god who makes deceptions known.
The god himself[40] gives license to the silent slave
    To pour his words out freely when he's drunk;
The god himself will urge men in the deepest sleep
    To blurt their secrets out against their will."
Those were my very words. Now I'm ashamed that I
    Threw myself at your tender feet and wept.   30
That's when you swore you would never be unfaithful
    For any price, for gold or heaps of jewels;
You wouldn't sell yourself for a Falernian
    Estate and all its vineyards, or for rich
Campanian soil.[41] I would have believed you then
    If you had said that starlight never shines,
That rivers never rush. You even cried, and I,
    All trusting and naïve, dried every tear.
What can I do? You're in love with a girl yourself.
    May she prove just as traitorous as you.   40

---

39. A punishment of runaway slaves.
40. Either Eros or Bacchus, the god of wine.
41. Campania was the agriculturally rich territory around Naples in southern Italy. Falernus Ager was a coastal region in northern Campania, famous for its wine.

How often I've gone out with you to light the way[42]
    For your private conversations late at night.
Many times, against all hope, I've brought her to you
    Discreetly veiled, waiting behind closed doors.
I died each time; still, poor imbecile that I was,
    I thought you loved me. I fell into your trap.
Delirious, I even sang your praises. Now
    I'm ashamed of all my Muse has done.
I wish those poems could be consumed by Vulcan's[43] flame,
    Dissolved beneath a river's roiling streams.   50
Stay out of my sight, you who would sell your beauty
    To line your pockets, greedy for handfuls of cash.
And you,[44] who have dared to corrupt young boys with gifts:
    May your wife's infidelities be frequent,
Her laughter relentless as she wears out her hot
    Young stud in secret, then lies down with you
Wrapped tightly in her nightclothes, saying she's too tired.[45]
    May many strangers come and leave their mark
Upon your bed; may your doors be always open
    To any man who's yearning for your wife;   60
And may she exceed her sister's prodigious gifts
    For draining older wine and younger men.
They say she often presides over Bacchus' rites
    Until the morning star brings on the day.
She knows how to use the night to her advantage,
    Exploring every novel variation.
Your wife's erotic expertise—her every move—
    Was studied somewhere else, you idiot.
Do you think she has her hair done just for your sake
    And tends it gently with a fine-toothed comb?   70
Is it *your* face that launches her through the doorway
    Swathed in purple, arms entwined with gold?
She dresses up not for you, but for a certain
    Young man, for whom she'd sell out in a second
You and all you have. Why not? A cultivated
    Girl recoils from disease and age.

42. I.e., to carry a torch.
43. Vulcan (Hephaestus) was the god of metallurgy and fire.
44. The speaker here addresses the wealthy rival.
45. Some scholars believe that the wife in question is Pholoe of the previous poem, and thus that Marathus is simultaneously involved with both husband and wife.

And yet my boy lies down with this stiff old relic.
   I could believe he'd mate with snarling beasts.
You've dared, in your insanity, to sell my love
   To someone else, to give away my kisses?   80
You'll be the one to cry, when a new boy has me
   Under his spell, ruling in your place;
And I'll rejoice at your punishment, and offer
   A well-earned golden palm inscribed to Venus:
FREED FROM YOVR DECEPTIVE BONDS OF LOVE, TIBVLLVS
MAKES THIS DEDICATION. PLEASE BE KIND.

8.15 Propertius 2.4.17–22

The second book of Propertius' elegies was published not much later than 26 B.C.E.
In this poem he laments his desperate love sickness from a heterosexual affair.

Let any enemy of ours love girls;
   Let any friend take pleasure in a boy.
You embark on a safe boat in a calm river.
   What harm can the water do with the shore so near?
A boyfriend often changes his heart at a single word;
   A girlfriend will hardly be softened by your very blood.

8.16 Vergil, *Aeneid* 5.293–96, 5.315–44

Vergil's Aeneid, *which was not yet completed to the author's satisfaction at the time*
of his death in 19 B.C.E., tells the story of Italy's settlement by Aeneas and other sur-
vivors of the Trojan War. Here Vergil describes the funeral games Aeneas stages in
Sicily in memory of his father Anchises. One of the events was a footrace.

   Now he called on those
Whom hope for gain led to compete in running,
And set out prizes for them. From all sides
They came up, Teucrians[46] with Sicilians mixed,
Nisus and Euryalus in the lead—
Euryalus exceptional for beauty
And bloom of youth, whom Nisus dearly loved. . . .[47]

---

46. Another name for Trojans.

47. The Latin here specifies *amore pio*, which could mean either "with dutiful love" or "with
honorable love." Some critics accordingly treat this line as evidence that Vergil intended their
relationship to be chaste and Platonic.

*The following lines introduce the other competitors and the prizes which Aeneas sets
for the first three runners.*

                                                  At this
They toed the line; and when they heard the signal,
Suddenly given, broke from the starting post
And made off on the track like an outriding
Rack of storm cloud. As they marked the finish,
Nisus flashed out, sprinting into the lead,
Faster than gale wind or a bolt of thunder.
After him, but far behind, came Salius,   320
And after Salius by a space Euryalus,
Helymus next. But close upon him, look,
Diores in his flight matched stride with stride,
Nearing his shoulder; if more track remained
He would have passed him or come up abreast
In a dead heat. But in the home stretch now
The tired men were making for the finish
When Nisus stumbled by bad luck, in gore—
A slippery place where beasts had been cut down [48]
And blood gushed on the turf soaking the grass.   330
Elated, with the race as good as won,
He staggered there and could not hold his feet
On the trodden ground, but pitched on it headlong
In the mire and blood of offerings. Though beaten,
This man did not forget Euryalus,
His beloved, but surging from the spot
Of slipperiness he tripped up Salius,
And he in turn went tumbling head over heels
To lie flat, as Euryalus flashed past
By his friend's help running to win first place
Amid applause and cheers. Then Helymus
Came in and then Diores, third place now.
At this point the whole banked assemblage rang   340
With Salius' clamor, facing the front-row elders,
For the honor stolen from him by a foul.
The crowd's support and his own quiet tears
Were in Euryalus' favor: prowess
Ever more winning for a handsome form.

Aeneas proceeds to resolve the dispute by offering prizes to all the competitors.

48. Apparently in sacrifice.

8.17 Vergil, *Aeneid* 9.176–449

In this episode, Aeneas' army is besieged by the Rutulians, a hostile neighboring tribe,
while Aeneas is away on a diplomatic mission to secure allies.

Nisus guarded a gate—a man-at-arms
With a fighting heart, Hyrtacus' son. The huntress
Ida had sent him to Aeneas' side,
A quick hand with a javelin and arrows.
Euryalus was his comrade, handsomer
Than any other soldier of Aeneas
Wearing the Trojan gear: a boy whose cheek   180
Bore though unshaven manhood's early down.
One love united them, and side by side
They entered combat, as that night they held
The gate on the same watch. And Nisus said:
"This urge to action, do the gods instill it,
Or is each man's desire a god to him,
Euryalus? For all these hours I've longed
To engage in battle, or to try some great
Adventure. In this lull I cannot rest.
You see how confident the Rutulians are.
Their watch-fire lights wink few and far between,
They've all lain down in wine and drowsiness,
And the whole place is quiet. Now attend   190
To a thought I'm turning over in my mind,
A plan that grows on me. 'Recall Aeneas,'
Everyone, seniors, all our folk, demand:
'Dispatch men to report to him.' Will they
Now promise the reward I ask for you?
The glory of the feat's enough for me.
Below that rise of ground there I can find,
I think, a way through to Fort Pallanteum."[49]
Taken aback, his love of glory stirred,
Euryalus replied to his ardent friend:
"And me? Are you refusing me my place
Beside you in this great affair? Must I
Send you alone into such danger? Born   200
For that, was I, and trained for that, amid
The Argive terror, those hard hours of Troy,

---

49. The city of Evander, a Trojan ally, on the site that would one day become Rome.

By a true fighter, one inured to battle,
My father, Opheltes? Never till now have I
Behaved so at your side, and as a soldier
Pledged to see Aeneas' destiny through.
Believe me, here's a spirit that disdains
Mere daylight! I hold life well spent to buy
That glory you aspire to." Nisus answered:
"Not for a minute had I any qualms
About you on that score. Unthinkable!
Witness great Jupiter—or whoever else
May favor this attempt—by bringing me
In triumph back to you. But if some god
Or accident defeats me—and one sees   210
Miscarriage of bold missions many a time—
You must live on. Your age deserves more life.
If I am dragged free from a fight or ransomed,
Let there be someone who can bury me.
Or if, as often, bad luck rules that out,
Someone who can carry out the ritual
For me, though I'm not there, and honor me
With an empty tomb. Then too, I would not bring
Such grief on your poor mother, one who dared
As many mothers did not, child, to come
This far with you, taking no care for shelter
Behind Acestes' walls." But the boy said:
"Your reasoning is all a waste of breath.
Not by an inch has my position changed.   220
Let us be off." With this he roused the watch,
Men who came up to stand guard in their turn,
As he took his relief, matching his stride
With Nisus', and they sought the prince of Troy.
Earth's other creatures now had given over
Care in sleep, forgetful of their toil,
But the high Trojan captains, chosen men,
Held council on the realm's pressing affairs:
What action should they take? Or who should be
Their messenger to Aeneas? In the open
Midcourt of the camp, leaning on spears,
Gripping their shields, they stood. And Nisus came,   230
Euryalus beside him, eager men
Who begged for a quick hearing, saying how grave
The matter was, worth a commander's time.

Iulus[50] moved first to hear the excited pair,
Ordering Nisus to speak out. He did so,
Saying: "Soldiers of Aeneas, listen
With open minds, and let what we propose
Be looked on without reference to our years.
The Rutulians have quieted down. Their wine
Has put them all to sleep. But we make out
An opening for a sortie where the road
Divides there at the gate nearest the sea,
A gap at that point in their line of fires
With only black smoke rising. If you let us
Take advantage of this to find our way   240
To Aeneas and Pallanteum, you'll see us back
With plunder before long, and slaughter done.
No fear the path will fool us: many times,
Hunting these valleys, we have come in view
Of the town's outposts, and we know the river,
The whole course of it." Bowed by weight of years
And ripe of mind, Aletes here exclaimed:
"Gods of our fathers, in whose shadow Troy
Forever lives, you are not after all
Intent on wiping out the Teucrians,
Seeing you've given our fighters daring souls
And resolute hearts like these." And as he spoke
He took each by the shoulder, took his hand,   250
While tears ran down his cheeks. "What fit rewards
For this brave action, soldiers, shall I reckon
We can make to you? The best of all
The gods will give, and your own sense of duty.
Then our devout Aeneas will recompense you
In other ways, and soon; so will Ascanius,
Young as he is: never will he forget
A feat of this distinction. . . ." Here Ascanius
Broke in: "Never indeed, as my well-being
Wholly depends on Father's coming back.
By our great household gods, by our hearth god,
Lar of Assaracus, by white-haired Vesta's[51]
Holy chapel, Nisus, hear my vow:

50. The adolescent son of Aeneas, who is also called Ascanius.
51. The Lares were patron gods of a clan or household; Assaracus was Aeneas' great-grandfather. Vesta (Hestia) was the goddess of the hearth, and thus another symbol of a household's
identity.

Whatever fortune I may have, whatever   260
Hope, I now commit to both of you.
Recall my father, bring him before my eyes.
With him recovered, nothing can be grim.
Then I shall give two cups well shaped in silver,
Rough with embossing, that my father took
The day Arisba[52] fell; twin tripods, too,
Two gold bars and an ancient wine bowl, gift
Of Dido the Sidonian.[53] More than this:
If it should happen that my father wins
The land and throne of Italy, and divides
By lot the captured booty—well, you've seen
The mount that Turnus rode, the arms he bore,
All golden: I exempt that mount, that shield   270
And crimson-crested helmet from allotment,
Even now, to be your trophies, Nisus.
Father will reward you, too, with twelve
Deep-breasted beauties and twelve captive men,
Each with his armor; beyond these, whatever
Private lands the king, Latinus, owns.
But as for you whose age my own approaches,[54]
Young but so admirable, I embrace you
With my whole heart, and say you'll be my friend
In all future adventures. There shall be
No labor for distinction in my life
In wartime or in time of peace without you.
Whether in speech or action, all my trust
Goes now to you." Euryalus answered him: 280
"The day will never come when I shall prove
Unequal to this kind of mission, hard
And daring as it is—if only fortune
Turns to our benefit and not against us.
One gift above all gifts I ask of you.
My mother comes of the old stock of Priam,
And she is here: poor lady, Ilium,
Her homeland, could not keep her, neither could
Acestes' city walls,[55] from following me.

---

52. A town near Troy, allied with the Trojans.
53. The queen of Carthage, with whom Aeneas had a tragic love affair in *Aeneid* 4.
54. Ascanius at this point addresses Euryalus.
55. Acestes was the king of Sicily, where the Trojans sojourned for a season before sailing on to Italy.

I leave her ignorant of the risks I run,
With no leave-taking. Let the present night
And your sword-arm be witness, I could not
Endure my mother's tears! Will you, I beg,
Console her in her deprivation, help her   290
If she is left without me. Let me take
This expectation of your care along—
I shall face danger with a lighter heart."
This moved the Dardan officers to tears,
Iulus most of all. Thoughts of his own
Devotion to his father wrung his heart.
When he had wept, he said: "Be sure of it.
All here will be conducted worthily
Of the great thing you undertake. That mother
Will be mine—only the name Creusa[56]
Wanting to her—and I shall not stint
In gratitude for parenthood so noble.
Whatever comes of your attempt, I swear,
As once my father did, by my own life   300
That all I promise on your safe return
Holds likewise for your mother and your kin."
So he spoke out in tears, and from his shoulder
Lifted on its belt his gilded sword,
A marvel of craft. It had been forged and fitted
To an ivory sheath by the Cnossian, Lycaon.[57]
To Nisus Mnestheus[58] gave a lion's pelt
And shaggy mane, and steadfast old Aletes
Made an exchange of helmets. Both now armed,
They set out, followed to the gate by all
The company of officers, with prayers
From young and old; and in particular
Princely Iulus, thoughtful, responsible   310
Beyond his years, gave many messages
To carry to his father. These the winds
Of heaven scattered, every one, unheard,
And puffed them to the clouds.
                          The messengers

56. Aeneas' first wife and Ascanius' mother, lost during the evacuation of Troy.

57. An artisan of Cnossus, the chief city of Crete, where Aeneas and his followers had attempted unsuccessfully to found a settlement.

58. One of the two Trojan elders to whom Aeneas entrusted command of the army during his absence.

Now issued from the gate, traversed the trench,
And made their way through darkness toward the encampment
Deadly to them. Still, before the end,
They were to bring a bloody death on many.
Now everywhere they saw in drunken sleep
Lax bodies on the grass, up-tilted chariots
Along the river, forms of men at rest
Amid the reins and wheels, arms lying there
Where wine cups also lay. The first to speak
Was Nisus, and he said: "Euryalus,
Here I must dare to use my sword: the case   320
Cries out for it; our path lies there. But you
Keep watch, keep well alert all round about
For any stroke against us from behind.
Ahead, I'll devastate them right and left
And take you through." He broke off whispering
To lunge at Rhamnes, the proud man propped up
On rugs and snoring loud, lungs full of sleep.
A king himself and augur to King Turnus,
Now by no augury could he dispel
His evil hour. Three of his bodyguards
Who lay nearby at random by their spears
Nisus dispatched, then Remus' armorer
And then his charioteer, discovered prone   330
Under the very horses' feet: the swordsman
Slashed their drooping necks. Then he beheaded
Remus himself, their lord, and left the trunk
To spout dark blood. By the warm blood the ground
And bedding were all soaked. Next Lamyrus
And Lamus died, and so did Serranus,
A handsome soldier who had played at dice
That night for hours and now lay undone
By abundant Bacchus. Lucky this man had been
If he had made his gambling last the night
Unto the dawn. Think of an unfed lion
Havocking crowded sheepfolds, being driven
Mad by hunger: how with his jaws he rends   340
And mauls the soft flock dumb with fear, and growls
And feeds with bloody maw. Euryalus
Carried out equal slaughter, all inflamed,
As he too fell upon the nameless ranks
Of sleeping soldiery. Then he attacked
Fadus, Herbesus, Rhoetus, Abaris,

Unconscious men—but Rhoetus came awake
And took in everything, struck dumb with fear,
Trying to hide behind a huge wine bowl.
Full in the chest as he arose the Trojan
Plunged his blade up to the hilt and drew it
Backward streaming death. Dying, the man
Belched out his crimson life, wine mixed with blood,
As the hot killer like a cat pressed on.   350
He came then to Messapus' company,
Their fires burning low, their tethered horses
Grazing the meadow. But now Nisus spoke
In a curt whisper—for he saw his friend
Carried away by slaughter and lust for blood—
"Let us have done," he said. "The Dawn's at hand
And dangerous. We've made them pay enough,
We've cut our way through." Turning now, they left
A quantity of booty, solid silver
Armor, wine bowls, handsome rugs. Euryalus
Took medals and a golden studded belt
From Rhamnes—gifts the rich man, Caedicus,
In the old days had sent to Remulus   360
Of Tibur as a distant guest-friend's pledge,
And Remulus at death had passed them on
To his own grandson, at whose death in war
The Rutulians had got them. These the boy
Tore off and fitted to his torso—tough
And stalwart as it was, though all in vain—
Then donned Messapus' helm with its high plume
As the marauders put the camp behind them,
Making for safety.
                              At that hour, horsemen
Sent ahead from the city of Latinus[59]—
Other troops being halted on the plain—
Came bringing answers to the prince, to Turnus,
Horsemen three hundred strong, all bearing shields,   370
With Volcens in command. Nearing the camp
And riding toward the rampart, they caught sight
Of the two Trojans over there who veered
On the leftward path. Euryalus' helmet

---

59. The King of Laurentum; the war between the Trojans and Rutulians arose from a dispute between Aeneas and Turnus, the Rutulian king, over marriage to Latinus' daughter.

In the clear night's half-darkness had betrayed him,
Glimmering back, as he had not foreseen,
Dim rays of moonlight. And the horsemen took
Sharp notice of that sight. Troop-leader Volcens
Shouted: "Soldiers, halt! What's this patrol?
Who are you two in arms there, and where bound?"
They offered no reply to him, but made
All speed into a wood, putting their trust
In darkness there. Troopers rode left and right
To place themselves at the familiar byways   380
Until they had the wood encircled, every
Exit under guard. The wood itself
Covered much ground, all bristling underbrush,
Dark ilex, and dense briars everywhere,
The path a rare trace amid tracks grown over.
Deep night under the boughs, and weight of booty,
Slowed Euryalus, and fear confused him
As to the pathway. Nisus, unsuspecting,
Got free of the wood, escaped the foe,
Ran past the places later known as Alban,
Latinus' high-fenced cattle pastures then.
But all at once he stopped and looked around
In vain for his lost friend. "Euryalus,
Poor fellow, where did I lose you? Where shall I   390
Hunt for you? Back all that winding way,
That maze of woodland?" Backward in his tracks,
As he recalled them, now he went, and strayed
Through silent undergrowth. He heard the horses,
Heard the clamor and calls of the pursuit,
And after no long interval a cry
Came to his ears: Euryalus now he saw
Set upon by the whole troop—first undone
By darkness and the treacherous terrain,
Now overwhelmed by the sudden rush of men
Who dragged him off, though right and left he strove.
Now what could Nisus do? What strength had he,
What weapons could he dare a rescue with?
Should he then launch himself straight at the foe,   400
Through many wounds hastening heroic death?
His arm drawn back, hefting his javelin,
He glanced at the high quiet moon and prayed:
"Thou, goddess, thou, be near, and help my effort,
Latona's daughter, glory of the stars

And guardian of the groves.[60] If Hyrtacus,
My father, ever brought gifts to thy altars
Votive gifts for me; if I myself
Have honored thee out of my hunting spoils
With offerings, hung in thy dome or fixed
Outside upon thy sacred roof, now let me
Throw this troop into confusion: guide
My weapon through the air." He made the cast,
With all the force and spring of his whole body.   410
And through the darkness of the night the javelin,
Whipping on, hit Sulmo's back and snapped there,
Putting a splinter through his diaphragm.
The man rolled on the ground and vomited
A hot flood, even as he himself grew chill,
With long convulsions. All the rest peered round
This way, then that way. All the more savagely
The assailant hefts a second javelin
Back to his ear. Now see commotion, hear
The whizzing shaft! It splits the skull of Tagus
Side to side and sticks in the cleft hot brain.
Now Volcens in a wild rage nowhere saw   420
The man who threw the missile, could not tell
In what quarter to hurl himself. "All right,"
He said, "You, then—you'll pay with your hot blood
For both my men." And with his sword unsheathed
He went straight for Euryalus. Now truly
Mad with terror, Nisus cried aloud.
He could not hide in darkness any longer,
Could not bear his anguish any longer:
"No, me! Me! Here I am! I did it! Take
Your swords to me, Rutulians. All the trickery
Was mine. He had not dared do anything,
He could not. Heaven's my witness, and the stars
That look down on us, all he did was care
Too much for a luckless friend." But while he clamored,   430
Volcens' blade, thrust hard, passed through the ribs
And breached the snow-white chest. Euryalus
In death went reeling down,
And blood streamed on his handsome length, his neck

60. In Roman mythology, Diana (Artemis), the goddess of woods and hunting, was also identified with the Moon goddess, considered a quite separate figure in earlier Greek mythology. Latona was the Roman name for Leto.

Collapsing let his head fall on his shoulder—
As a bright flower cut by a passing plow
Will droop and wither slowly, or a poppy
Bow its head upon its tired stalk
When overborne by a passing rain. Now Nisus
Plunged ahead into the crowd of men
And made for Volcens only, of them all,
Concerned only with Volcens. All around him
Enemies grouped to meet him, fend him off   440
To left and right, but onward all the same
He pressed his charge, swirling his lightning blade
Until he sank it in the yelling visage
Straight before him. So he took that life
Even as he died himself. Pierced everywhere,
He pitched down on the body of his friend
And there at last in the peace of death grew still.
Fortunate, both! If in the least my songs
Avail, no future day will ever take you
Out of the record of remembering Time,
While children of Aeneas⁶¹ make their home
Around the Capitol's unshaken rock,
And still the Roman Father governs all.

8.18 Aelius Donatus, *Life of Vergil* 9–11

This biography is found in the fourth-century C.E. commentary of Donatus, but some scholars trace it, in whole or in part, back to the work of Suetonius, who, in addition to composing biographies of the first twelve Roman emperors, wrote lives of famous poets.

[9] His sexual desire was more inclined to boys, among whom he especially loved Cebes and Alexander, whom he names "Alexis" in the *Second Eclogue*.⁶² Alexander was the gift of Asinius Pollio.⁶³ Each boy was educated, and Cebes was even a poet. It is common rumor that there was an affair between Vergil and Plotia Hieria. [10] But Asconius Pedianus⁶⁴

---

61. Figuratively, this designation would refer to all Romans, but it may also have a more specific reference to the Julian family line (including both Julius Caesar and Augustus), who traced their ancestry and name back to Aeneas and his son, Iulus.

62. Such biographical allegorizing was common in later commentaries on Vergil and the other Latin poets. It should not necessarily be accepted.

63. A political associate of Julius Caesar and an early patron of Vergil and other poets, as well as a literary figure of some note in his own right.

64. A grammarian (8 B.C.E.–76 C.E.) who wrote a treatise defending Vergil against his critics.

contends that she herself in her old age was accustomed to tell that Vergil stubbornly refused, even though invited by Varius[65] to become involved with her. [11] In other aspects of his life it is agreed that he was so upright in both speech and soul that he was commonly called "Parthenias"[66] in Naples.

8.19 Ovid, *The Art of Love* 2.683–84

This work was a didactic treatise on seduction, composed in three books of elegiac verse, and published not before 1 B.C.E. The work's concerns are exclusively hetero-sexual, as explained by the following couplet.

I hate sex that doesn't gratify both partners,
    And that is why I'm less enthralled with boys.

8.20 Ovid, *The Art of Love* 3.437–38

Whereas the first two books taught men how to seduce women, the third book, which Ovid says was added later, teaches women how to seduce men.

What can a woman do when her husband has skin
    Silkier than hers and can snare more men?

8.21 Ovid, *Metamorphoses* 9.669–797

The Metamorphoses *are a series of mythological stories involving transformations at the end. Ovid's most ambitious work, it was not yet completely finished at the time of his exile in 8 C.E. The following episode concerns a relationship between two girls, one of whom becomes transgendered.*

                                    Once, in Phaestus,
Not far from Cnossus' kingdom,[67] the rich earth brought forth   670
A poor nobody, free but undistinguished, named
Ligdus, whose wealth did not surpass his ancestry,
Though his life and his integrity were spotless.
To his wife, who was soon to bear their child, he said:
"I wish for two things: that your pains are not too great,
And that the child is male. We can't afford a girl.
Fortune denies us that luxury. Though I hate

---

65. An epic and tragic poet of the Augustan period, praised by both Vergil and Horace.
66. The name means "the maidenly one."
67. Cnossus was the principal city of Crete, Phaestus a city on the south side of the island.

The very thought and shrink from the impiety,
If you by chance should bring to light a female child,
Although it's against my will, she will have to die."
Such was his decree, though he decried it, and he   680
Cried no less than she; both faces were bathed in tears.
Telethusa begs him endlessly, but in vain,
Not to restrict her hopes so narrowly. But no,
Ligdus won't change his mind. Now, with her belly grown
Heavy and ripe for birth, almost too big to bear,
Late at night there comes to her a dream or vision:
Io,[68] with her sacred escort all around her,
Stood, or seemed to stand, before her bed. Her horns
Framed her forehead like the moon, with flashing golden
Spears of grain; her regal dignity was stunning.
With her were the barking Anubis, Bubastis   690
The blessèd, multicolored Apis,[69] and the one
Who urges silence with a finger to his lips;[70]
Sistra[71] were at hand, and there was lord Osiris[72]
—The one who always must be sought for yet again—
And the exotic serpent, veined with sleeping-poison.[73]
The goddess spoke to her as if she were awake
And seeing what was real: "O Telethusa, my
Devotee, lay down your heavy care. Disobey
Your husband's decree, and when Lucina[74] has come
To ease your labor, do not hesitate to raise
Whatever child you have borne. I am a goddess
Who brings help to those who call on her. You'll never
Complain that your devotion was without reward."   700
Her good advice was given, and she left the room.
The Cretan woman rose up joyful from her bed
And stretching her pure hands up to the stars, she prayed

68. A maiden loved by Jupiter and transformed into a cow, who after much suffering gave
birth to a son who became the king of Egypt. Greco-Roman sources often identified her with
the Egyptian goddess Isis, whose cult was popular among Roman women of the Augustan age.
    69. All three were Egyptian gods: Anubis was a god with the head of a dog or jackal, Bubastis
a goddess with a cat's head, Apis a god with a variegated bull's hide and form.
    70. This figure is the Egyptian child god Harpocrates.
    71. Sacred rattles used in the worship of Isis.
    72. Osiris was Isis' consort: he was killed and torn apart, but Isis hunted for him until she
could effect his resurrection. The search for Osiris was reenacted in an annual Egyptian ritual.
    73. Snakes were sacred to Isis' worship, representing both immortality (because they shed
their skin) and the river Nile.
    74. The goddess of childbirth.

For her vision to be really true. Her birth pangs
Came upon her then, and her burden brought itself
Into the open air: a female child, unknown
To her father. Her mother gave her secretly,
To be raised as a boy, to her only trusted
Confidante, a nurse. The father fulfilled each vow
He owed the gods, and gave the child his father's name,
Iphis—named for her grandfather. Her mother was
Delighted, since the name could work for either sex;   710
No need to be dishonest. From these origins
The silent lie continued, and the pious fraud:
She wore boys' clothes and had the kind of face that would
Be called a beauty, masculine or feminine.
Iphis, when you were thirteen years old, your father
Betrothed you to Ianthe, the most praised among
All the girls of Phaestus, with the richest dowry
Of beauty,[75] golden-haired, the daughter of Telestes.
They were alike in age and loveliness, and from
The same teachers they had learned their childhood lessons;
So, naturally, love touched their young hearts equally.   720
The wounds they felt were equal, but their confidence
At total odds: Ianthe longed for her marriage,
The promised wedding torches, and her husband, whom
She believed to be a man. Who wouldn't? Iphis
Loved and longed, but she despaired of ever having
The one she longed for, and this increased her passion,
A girl on fire for a girl. She spoke through her tears:
"What end awaits me, victim of this new, bizarre
Unheard-of spell of Venus? If the gods intend
To spare me, then they should have; if they want me ruined,
They should at least have sent some normal malady.   730
No cow lusts after a cow, or mare for a mare;
The ram inflames the ewes, the doe follows the buck,
And so on: birds, and every type of animal—
No female ever desires another female.
I wish that I didn't exist, or weren't a girl!
Crete has had no shortage of abominations:
The daughter of the Sun[76] desired a bull, but that

75. The implication may be that Ianthe was also from a poor family and beauty was her only
dowry, but made up for the lack of money.

76. Pasiphae, the wife of King Minos, for whom Daedalus constructed a bronze cow in
which she could conceal herself.

At least was male and female, less demented than
My own lust, in all honesty. And she, at least,
Could realize Venus' hope, could embrace her lover:
The counterfeit cow deceived, and received, her stud.   740
But all the world's ingenuity could never
Help me. Let Daedalus himself come flying back
To Crete on wings of wax:[77] what will he do for me,
With all his brains and skill? Turn me into a boy?
Or will he change you, Ianthe? Pull yourself back
Together, Iphis—strengthen your mind, forget this
Stupid, impractical passion. Look! You were born
A girl—don't lie to yourself—and you should seek out
Things that a girl should want, lovers a girl should love.
Love feeds on Hope, and only Hope can capture Love;
Reality itself denies you any shred!   750
No guardian forbids you the caress you crave;
No over-anxious husband, severe patriarch,
Nor even the girl—she's yours for just the asking—
And yet you can't possess her, can't get lucky, not
For all the world, for all that gods and men can do.
Not a single prayer of mine has gone unanswered:
The gods have given all that's in their power to give.
What I want, my father wants; so does my future
Father-in-law, so does my bride-to-be. Nature
Alone says no, and her voice drowns out all the rest,
And she alone subverts me. The day I've longed for,
My wedding day draws near, and soon Ianthe will   760
Be mine, but not belong to me; I'll die of thirst
With water all around. O Juno, protectress
Of brides, O Hymen,[78] why should you attend these rites
That aren't right, where there is no bridegroom; both of us
Are waiting to be carried across the threshold?"
    She ended there; the other girl, no less inflamed
Prayed to you, Hymen, to come soon, without delay.
What she wants, Telethusa dreads, and she puts off
The date by claiming illness, or bad omens, or
Visions, anything—but soon enough she'd used up
Every possible lie. Now the hour of the torch

---

77. The artisan Daedalus eventually escaped Minos' island tyranny along with his son, Ica-
rus, by inventing wings joined to his arms with wax.

78. Juno (Hera), the wife of Jupiter, was especially associated with protecting the importance and sanctity of marriage. Hymen was a lesser spirit whose name was invoked at weddings.

Is at hand, just one day remains. Telethusa   770
Tore the ribbon from her head, and from her daughter's,
Embraced the altar with her hair outspread, and prayed:
"Isis of Paraetonium, Mareotic
Lands, great Pharos, and the seven mouths of the Nile,[79]
Bring help to me, please, and heal my dread. I saw you
Goddess, once, with all your entourage and sacred
Signs, I recognized them all—the torches, the sound
Of sistra—and my mindful soul took note of all
That you commanded: my daughter is alive now,
And I have not been punished; we have you to thank,
The gift of your advice. Take pity on us both: 780
Help us." Tears accompanied her words. The goddess
Seemed to move her altar (and it really did move),
The temple gates trembled, her horns, curved like the moon
Glowed and glittered, and the sistrum rattled loudly.
Still not entirely sure, but feeling much better
Because of this good omen, the mother departs
And following her comes Iphis, her companion,
Whose stride is longer now; her complexion is less
Delicate, her expression sharper; her strength has
Increased, her tousled hair is shorter, and she has
More stamina than usual for a female.   790
The reason, Iphis, is that until this very
Moment you *were* a female, and now you're a boy.
Bring gifts to the temples, rejoice, and have no fear!
They do bring gifts, and they add this verse inscription:
IPHIS THE BOY FVLFILLS VOWS HE MADE AS A GIRL.
The day has dawned; the world is luminous, refreshed.
Venus, Juno, Hymen attend the nuptial fires;
And Iphis, a boy, possesses his Ianthe.

8.22 Ovid, *Metamorphoses* 10.78–219

This extract follows the previous one by a short interval, during which Ovid describes Orpheus' loss of his beloved wife, Eurydice, and his futile attempt to recover her from the Underworld. Like Phanocles, Ovid credits Orpheus with the invention of pederasty and proceeds to tell several other pederastic myths.

---

79. Greco-Roman prayers typically list all the locations associated with a deity. All the sites here are Egyptian, as appropriate for Isis: Praetonium is on the Libyan frontier, Pharos is the island on which the lighthouse of Alexandria was located, and the Mareotic lands are just south of Alexandria.

Titan had ended his third annual circuit
In watery Pisces,[80] and Orpheus had fled
The love of women, either because it had not   80
Gone well for him, or perhaps he'd taken a vow.
Many women were burning with love for the bard;
Many went away disappointed, rejected.
Orpheus first taught the Thracians[81] to love instead
Tender boys, in that brief springtime before they turn
Into young men, when the first new blooms can be plucked.

    There was a hill, and above the hill a spreading
Tableland, green with flourishing grass, but lacking
Any shade. Once the divinely born poet came
To sit there and play on the sounding strings, and then
Shade came to the place:[82] the oak of Chaonia,[83]   90
A grove of poplars, daughters of the Sun;[84] the tall
Italian oak, the tender linden, and the beech;
The still-unmarried laurel, fragile hazel, tough
Spear-handle ash; the smooth-grained pine, and the ilex
Bowed down with acorns; the hospitable plane tree;
The colorful maple, the stream-loving willow;
Water-lotus, evergreen boxwood, tamarisk;
Two-colored myrtle, viburnum with blue berries;
And you came too, lithe-footed ivy, and tendriled
Vines, and elm trees wrapped around with vines; and mountain   100
Ash, and pitch-pine, arbutus laden with red fruit;
Flexible palm, the victor's prize; and the pine tree
With her hair piled high, the Great Mother's beloved,
If the story is true that Cybele's Attis[85]
Exchanged his human form for the rigid pine trunk.

    80. In other words, three years had elapsed since Orpheus' loss of Eurydice: the Sun (Titan) has passed through the twelfth sign of the zodiac (Pisces) three times, and it is now spring again.

    81. Thrace was the area north of the Aegean Sea, populated by comparatively uncivilized tribes, but of considerable colonial interest to the Greeks in historical times.

    82. In other words, Orpheus' music charmed the trees to uproot themselves and come listen.

    83. The oak trees of Dodona in a remote region of northwest Greece (Chaonia) were sacred to Zeus and thought to have the power to speak prophecies.

    84. The *Metamorphoses* had previously told the story of the daughters of the Sun, who were changed into poplar trees when mourning for the fiery death of their brother, Phaethon.

    85. The story of Attis and his devotion to Cybele (the Great Mother of Asia) is related in 7.48. His eventual transformation into a pine tree is otherwise unknown, but pines were sacred in Cybele's cult.

The cypress tree, which is shaped like a turning-post[86]
Came to join this gathering; he was now a tree
But once had been a boy, loved by the god who plies
The lyre's strings, and the strings of the curving bow.[87]
There was a huge deer, sacred to the Carthaean[88]
Nymphs. His antlers spread wide, so extravagantly   110
That they shaded his head. These horns were bright with gold;
From his shapely throat there hung a jeweled necklace
Down to his flanks; a silver charm, delicately
Laced, swayed above his forehead, and a pair of pearls
Of equal vintage, on either side of his face
Hung glittering from his two ears. He seemed to
Have no fear at all. Putting aside the shyness
Natural for his kind, he'd go to people's homes,
Offer his neck to be stroked by anyone's hands;
But, Cyparissus, no one loved him more than you,   120
Most beautiful of all the Ceans. You would lead
The deer to fresh new pastures, clear streams of water;
You'd weave every type of flower through his antlers;
You'd ride on his back, this way and that, pretending
To be a horseman, joyfully guiding his way,
Restraining his soft mouth with a purple bridle.
It was hot—midday—and the hooked arms of Cancer,
The seaside-dweller, seethed in the sun's hot vapor.[89]
The deer lay down his weary body on the grass
Beneath the shady trees, where it was cool. The boy,
Unknowing, struck the deer with his sharp javelin   130
And when he saw him dying from the savage wound
Cyparissus wished to die himself. How many
Words of comfort Apollo spoke, urging the boy
To grieve more moderately, more in keeping with
The magnitude of the loss! But Cyparissus
Would not be consoled. He prayed to the gods for this
Supreme gift: to be allowed to mourn for all time.
And soon enough—his strenuous bouts of weeping
Had drained his body of blood—his limbs turned greenish;
The hair that had hung across his snow-white forehead

86. The conical form of the cypress resembles that of turning posts on ancient race tracks,
around which runners or horses had to negotiate a very tight U-turn.

87. Apollo.

88. Carthaea was a city on the Greek island of Ceos.

89. In other words, it was July, when the Sun was in the sign of Cancer, the crab.

Grew long and wild; he stiffened; now his tapering
Treetop turns its gaze to the star-filled open sky.   140
The saddened god cried, "You'll be lamented by me,
And you'll lament for others, and accompany
All those who grieve."[90]
    Such was the grove that Orpheus
Had drawn around him. He sat among the gathered
Wild beasts, and flocks of birds, and tested his lyre strings
With his thumb; when the different notes came together
In a satisfying sound, he started to sing:
    "Muse, my mother,[91] begin my song with Jupiter[92]
For all things yield to his greatness, and I have sung
Of Jupiter's power often enough before:
In epic mode, I've taken on the great Giants,   150
The Phlegraean plain, blasted with conquering bolts.[93]
But now a lighter theme is called for: let us sing
Of boys whom the gods have loved, and girls who've been struck
By illicit passions, and earned the punishment
For lust.
    The king of gods once found himself on fire
For Phrygian Ganymede. He discovered something
He'd rather be than what he was—now, Jupiter
Would never choose to be any bird other than
The one who could bear his thunderbolts.[94] In a flash
Beating the air with fresh, deceptive wings, he snatched
The Trojan boy, who to this day prepares his cup   160
And, much to Juno's displeasure, serves him nectar.
    Phoebus would have given you a home in the sky,
Amyclides,[95] if the sad fates had allowed it.
Still, what was allowed was done: you are eternal;
Each year, when spring drives winter away, and Aries

---

90. The cypress was a tree especially associated with grave sites and mourning.

91. According to Ovid, Orpheus was the son of the Muse Calliope and Apollo, the god most associated with music.

92. Compare **6.57**.

93. The Phlegraean plain was imagined as the active volcanic area northwest of Naples, where Jupiter supposedly defeated the rebellious Giants in a battle. This is not the only place where Ovid refers to a poem on this theme, but it does not survive. He could be referring to an earlier passage in the *Metamorphoses* (5.318–31), where the Pierides sing a narrative of the battle.

94. The eagle.

95. Phoebus is an alternate name for Apollo, Amyclides for the boy Hyacinthus, who was from Amyclae, a district of Sparta.

Replaces watery Pisces, in the greensward
You rise up and bloom.[96] My father loved you beyond
All others; he would abandon Delphi, the Earth's
Midpoint,[97] and go to spend time with you in Sparta,
The unwalled city by the river Eurotas.
He would neglect his cithara and his arrows,   170
Forget himself, carry hunting nets, handle dogs,
Accompany you along the jagged ridges
Of steep mountains; togetherness stoked his passion.
It was nearly noon: Titan had climbed to the point
That stands halfway between dawn and night's arrival.
They shed their clothes; their bodies sleek with the unguent
Of the rich olive, they decided to contend
With the broad discus. Phoebus threw it first, sent it
Hurtling high into the air, slicing through the clouds.
Its flight was prolonged; it fell back to solid ground   180
Precisely; the god's strength was united with art.
The Spartan boy, impelled by his zeal for the game,
Unknowing, rushed right out to retrieve the discus,
Which the hard earth shot straight back up, Hyacinthus,
Into your face. Apollo went white, no less than
The boy. He cradled your slackened limbs and warmed you,
Stanched your sad wounds, tried bringing your life back with herbs.[98]
His arts were useless; the wound was incurable.
Just as, when someone snaps the stem of a violet,
Or of a poppy in a well-watered garden,   190
Or of lilies, with their long, bristling yellow tongues
—Unstrung, they let drop their suddenly heavy heads,
Unable to sustain their weight, and gaze towards earth—
In just this way your face turned downward as you died;
Your neck, its strength gone, became too great a burden,
Rolled sideways onto your shoulder. Phoebus cried out,
'Descendant of Oebalus,[99] cheated of your youth,
You've fallen, and I see that your wound is my crime.
You are my guilt and my sorrow; my own right hand

---

96. After his death, the boy was transformed into the hyacinth flower (not the same flower as we know by that name).

97. Apollo's oracle in Delphi was at the approximate center of mainland Greece, and was therefore assumed by the Greeks to be at the center of the world.

98. Among his many other functions, Apollo was also a god of healing and medicine.

99. An early king of Sparta. The locution "descendant of Oebalus" commonly refers to any Spartan.

Must be inscribed with your death; I am the author
Of your demise. And yet, what was my great error?   200
Is it wrong to play? Can it be called wrong to love?
If only I could die for you, or die with you!
I'm bound by the laws of fate—but still, you'll always
Be near me: you'll be in my thoughts, and in my words;
My songs, the lyre strings I pluck, will tell of you,
And you will become a flower, my groans engraved
Upon you. The time will come when a great hero
will add himself to this bloom; his grief will be read
from the same petal.' [100] While Apollo prophesied
What was to come, the blood, which had stained the grasses,   210
Ceased to be blood, took on a deeper radiance
Than Tyrian dye, rose up, and assumed the form
Of a lily—except that it was not silver,
But purple. This was still not enough for Phoebus
(The author of the honor): he inscribed AIAI,
The text of his lament, on the flower's petals;
The flower bears this funereal inscription.
Sparta was never ashamed of Hyacinthus,
Whose honor persists to this day: the annual
Hyacinthia [101] and opening procession
Are celebrated in the ancestral manner."

100. The purple flower that the ancients knew as a hyacinth featured a design that resembled the Greek letters alpha and iota (αι), which also corresponds to the Greek cry of lament, *aiai*. Another myth connects the flower's origin to the suicide of the Greek hero Ajax.

101. An annual summer festival of lamentation at Sparta, commemorating the flowers that
died in the summer's heat.

CHAPTER 9

Early Imperial Rome

The imperial age of Rome begins with the death of Augustus (14 C.E.) and continues arguably until the fall of the western empire nearly five centuries later. The earliest stage of that long period, up through the reign of Trajan (98–117 C.E.), is often identified as the "Silver Age" of Latin literature, second in quality to the "Golden Age" of Augustus' reign, but nevertheless a time of great productivity and innovation. Particularly characteristic of literature in this period is a developed rhetorical stance and satirical orientation, even in genres where one might not expect them. The theme of moral and cultural decline also bulks large.

Literature of the first century C.E. bears witness to an increasing polarization of attitudes toward homosexual activity, ranging from frank acknowledgment and public display of sexual indulgence on the part of leading Roman citizens to severe moral condemnation of all homosexual acts, even with slaves. One no longer finds the idealized and romantic images of Vergil and Tibullus, inspired by Greek models, but instead an obsessive interest in the most graphic and salacious aspects of same-sex relations.

Suetonius' reports of Tiberius' scandalous activities with freeborn youths and very young children on Capri (**9.1**) can probably be dismissed as hostile gossip engendered by resentment of the emperor's protracted absence from Rome and speculation about his reasons for remaining out of the public eye. But his account of Nero's same-sex "marriages" and gladiatorial-style sexual performances (**9.7**) may be more deserving of credit, given their public nature and Nero's well-attested penchant for unusual iconoclastic displays.

Petronius was one of Nero's courtiers, who wrote, for the emperor's entertainment, a lengthy picaresque novel (**9.14**) involving the lurid misadventures of an educated but penniless youth and a runaway slave boy whom he loves. The novel's hapless hero, despite all efforts, is impotent with women. The novel inverts the orthodox plot of Greek romance, predicated on a chaste and unfailingly loyal heterosexual couple, by immersing us in a low-life underworld where homosexuality is the norm and no couple is mutually faithful. We see a hypocritical tutor who seduces his only-too-eager young charge, a well-endowed youth who gets picked up by admirers in the public baths, and a wealthy freedman who inherited a fortune after serving as the beloved of his master and who now humiliates his despised wife by publicly kissing his own male slaves in her presence.

9.8 suggests that the native inhabitants in far reaches of the Empire saw Rome in Nero's reign as a culture weakened by homosexual and every other kind of excess, although the quote, attributed to the British queen Boudicca, may be no more than a projection of the fears moralistic Romans had about the weak image a self-indulgent Rome might present to subject populations. Compare Juvenal's remarks at the end of **9.38** about Rome corrupting the virtuous barbarians.

These depictions of Roman life may not be far-fetched. Not long after Nero's reign, in 79 C.E., several towns south of Naples were buried by the sudden volcanic eruption of Mt. Vesuvius and thus preserved virtually intact, affording us an archaeological window into the daily life of the period. Numerous graffiti are found in Pompeii (**9.16**) and attest a thriving homosexual subculture even within this small provincial city. While some are honorific love declarations in the Greek style or boasts of sexual prowess, most are abusive slurs, and oral sex, never mentioned in Greek graffiti, is the most common charge. Even if these are meant as slander rather than assertions of someone's real proclivities, they still attest a culture where such acts were far from unknown and could be imagined as true. Another common type of graffito advertises prices for prostitutes or even specific acts. Many of these prices are surprisingly low, which could either be explained as slander or as an actual reflection of how cheap a slave's services could be. That not everyone approved of the prevailing mores in Pompeii is attested by a single graffito, probably written by a Jew, calling the city "Sodom and Gomorrah." He can only have felt his judgment confirmed by the city's ultimate fate.

Martial, an epigrammatist active at the end of the century, presents a persona reasserting republican standards of acceptable pederasty, inasmuch as he expresses his own attraction to slave boys (**9.22, 9.28**) and lectures a wife not to complain about her husband's activities with their slave boys (**9.31**). A poem of Statius on the death of a favorite slave boy (**9.32**) shows just how deep such relationships could be; compare Pliny's remarks on Cicero's slave Tiro (**7.65**). Slaves could, of course, also be threatened and abused (**9.33**).

Martial bitterly lampoons any form of homosexuality popular opinion might regard as extreme or deviant: a preference for the passive role (**9.20,**

9.21, 9.30), either engaging oneself as a prostitute (**9.24**) or spending one's last dime on prostitutes (**9.19, 9.20**), and worst of all, lesbianism (**9.18, 9.26, 9.27**). Indeed, the literature of this period evinces the first real recognition of female homoeroticism as a phenomenon that occurred in Rome (see also **9.2, 9.5,** and perhaps **9.11**); Ovid (**8.21**) raised the possibility only to deny it. However, virtually all the references to lesbianism are deeply hostile and couched in terms of women taking on men's roles, often using some instrument of penetration (either of other women or, even more extraordinarily, of men).

Deviancy of every type is explored in the texts of this period: Suetonius tells us about the emperor Galba's preference for masculine men (**9.15**), Juvenal exhibits a male concubine hired to penetrate both his wealthy patron and the patron's wife (**9.39**), and Seneca introduces the rich degenerate Hostius Quadra, who enjoyed watching every orifice of his body be penetrated in a boudoir equipped with special distorting mirrors that would exaggerate the endowments of his partners (**9.9**).

Denunciations of such extreme behavior should be contextualized within the growing influence of Stoic philosophy in Roman letters. The Stoics believed in living one's life in accordance with the laws of Nature and not exceeding proper mortal limits. To Seneca, men acting like women (**9.12**) or women acting like men (**9.11**) were examples of rebellion against Nature, as was the common practice of trying to keep male slaves young and attractive looking through depilation and other artificial means (**9.10, 9.12**). His contemporary Musonius Rufus (**9.13**) goes a step further in arguing against any sexual activity outside of married heterosexual intercourse for the purpose of procreation. But both Seneca and Musonius go beyond conventional Roman morality by putting in question even sexual activity with slaves. And at the same time that the philosophers inveighed against sexual immorality, charges of personal hypocrisy were commonly leveled against them, as Juvenal (**9.38**) shows.

The rhetorical tradition also betrays persistently negative judgments. Seneca's father, Seneca the Elder, wrote textbooks with exemplary legal controversies that preserve quotations from famous Augustan and Greek orators: in addition to expressions of abhorrence for lesbianism (**9.2**) and turning slave boys into eunuchs to preserve their androgynous beauty (**9.4**), he also cites a famous line from the orator Haterius (**9.3**) to the effect that homosexuality was an object of censure only to free men, but a necessity for slaves and a duty for freedmen, implying some slaves were manumitted because they had been their master's favorite. However, the elder Seneca also tells us that the line became the subject of almost universal ridicule. The later rhetorician Calpurnius Flaccus summarized two declamations in which violation of a free man's body, whether by rape (**9.36**) or voluntary self-prostitution

(9.37), is considered the worst possible disgrace. Similarly, Quintilian declares such violations so shameful that the victim should not even say anything (9.35). In another part of his treatise on rhetorical education (9.34), Quintilian warns against commingling older and younger boys in the same classroom, lest there should be even an appearance of improper relationships among them.

The coincidence of such severity on the part of moralistic writers with the flagrant and open display of every form of homosexual behavior by Nero and other practitioners indicates a culture in which attitudes about this issue increasingly defined one's ideological and moral position. In other words, homosexuality in this era may have ceased to be merely another practice of personal pleasure and began to be viewed as an essential and central category of personal identity, exclusive of and antithetical to heterosexual orientation. Phaedrus (9.5) tells a fable explaining why both effeminate males and lesbians are physically constituted the way they are: the gods attached the wrong genitals at birth. Petronius' Encolpius (9.14) and Juvenal's Virro (9.39) are men who seem genuinely incapable of erectile performance with women; Martial tells us the same of the "fag hag" Galla's six cinaedic husbands (9.25). Martial notes that some other men with homosexual preferences are forced into heterosexuality only by the most desperate need for money (9.23, 9.29). An interesting graffito from Pompeii (9.16.3932) boasts of converting a man named Rufus into a passive homosexual, thus taking him away from women. From the other side, Juvenal (9.38) shows the courtesan Laronia complaining about homosexual philosophers who want to see the moral laws enforced only against heterosexuals. The stage is clearly being set in this period for the entrenched sexual preference debates we see during the next two centuries.

Bibliographical Note

For surveys of the period, see Meier and de Pogey-Castries (1930) 182–85, 194–202, Boswell (1980) 69–83, E. Cantarella (1992) 155–73, and more generally Robert (1997) 243–85. On legal developments, see Dalla (1987) 101–31. On lesbianism in Roman texts, principally of this period, see Hallett (1997) and Mencacci (1999).

On the unreliability of the anecdotes concerning the emperors, see Krenkel (1980). For homosexual themes in Martial, see Sullivan (1979) and (1991) 185–210, who sees Martial as primarily pederastic in his inclinations and hostile to liberated women, Garrido-Hory (1981), Richlin (1992) 39–44 and 129–41, and especially Obermayer (1998). On the Pompeian graffiti, see Varone (1994) 121–44. On Musonius Rufus' sexual doctrine, see van Geytenbeek (1963) 71–77, Foucault (1986) 150–55, 178–79, and Goldhill (1995) 133–43.

Petronian criticism is divided between those who see the author as a serious moralist critical of the mores he describes, such as Highet (1941) and Arrowsmith (1966), and those who find the work nonjudgmental, such as P. G. Walsh (1974). Wooten (1984) sees the pervasive atmosphere as one of camp. Sullivan (1968) 232–53 finds an authorial preoccupation with themes of scopophilia and exhibitionism; Gill (1973) criticizes this view, finding instead parody and pastiche. Richardson (1984) argues that the novel's homosexual themes reflect Roman sexual realities, not merely the practices of the southern Italian Greek city in which its action is set. Soverini (1976) treats the quarrel of Encolpius and Ascyltos at the beginning of the novel. Bodel (1989a) and (1989b) discusses Trimalchio's background as the sexual favorite of his master, but Pomeroy (1992) downplays the sexual dimension of the relationship; similarly, Schievenin (1976) denies a sexual intent to Trimalchio's attentions to the slave boy. Cervellera (1982) also examines the master-slave relationships in the novel. On the story of the Pergamene boy, see Dimundo (1983) and (1986); Elsner (1993) situates the story in the context of Eumolpus' aesthetic doctrines. On Encolpius' impotence and passivity throughout the novel, see McMahon (1998) 192–215.

On Juvenal 2, see Braund and Cloud (1981), Konstan (1993), Nappa (1998), and Walters (1998). Konstan and Nappa emphasize that it is not homosexual behavior per se that is attacked, but passivity. On Juvenal 9, see Hendry (2000).

9.1 Suetonius, *Tiberius* 43–44

Various debaucheries were attributed to Tiberius (emperor 14–37 C.E.) during the latter part of his reign, when he remained isolated at his palace on the island of Capri.

[43] In his retreat on Capri he designed banquet rooms where he held secret orgies: crowds of girls and of practiced catamites were gathered from all around, as well as contrivers of monstrous couplings, whom he called "sphincters," and they debauched each other in front of him, linked together in chains of three, in order to excite his failing lusts. There were bedrooms all around the palace and he decorated them with images and figurines of the lewdest paintings and statues possible, and he equipped them with books of Elephantis,[1] so that no one, in performing their task, should lack for a model of the positions required. In the woods also and in the groves he laid out specially designed spots for having sex, and in caverns and grottos there were prostitutes of both sexes, dressed as little

---

1. Several sources refer to her as the author of a pseudo-medical treatise on sexual positions.

Pans and nymphs. And thus people openly corrupted the name of the island and called it "Capricorni."[2]

[44] He burned with even greater and more repulsive lust than before, so that it is hardly decent to speak or hear of, much less to believe in, the story. They say that he trained boys of the tenderest age, whom he called "minnows," to swim between his thighs in the water and to play about trying to lick and to nibble him gently, and that further he brought babies who were not newborns, but not yet weaned, to his crotch as if to a breast. Doubtless he was more prone to this form of lust on account both of his age and his nature: this is why, when a painting by Parrhasius, in which Atalanta gratifies Meleager with her mouth, was left to him with the condition that if the subject offended him, he should receive a million sesterces instead, not only did he prefer to keep it, but he set it up in his bedroom.

It is also said that once when he was conducting a sacrifice he was so taken with the looks of the assistant who was carrying the incense-box that he could not keep his hands off him, and when the divine office was hardly finished, right then and there he took the boy aside and raped him and his brother the flute-boy as well; soon afterwards he had the legs of both broken, because they had reproached each other for the shameful act.

9.2 Seneca the Elder, *Controversies* 1.2.23

Seneca the Elder was a rhetorician born around 55 B.C.E. who lived until about the time of Tiberius' death. He is best known for his declamations, rhetorical exercises for the training of orators and jurists. The speeches in his Controversies *attempt to argue both sides of a complicated legal question, often citing the opinions of famous rhetoricians of the past. The following passage gives examples of utterances that are so shameful they are better left out of a speech.*

Hybreas,[3] when he was speaking in the controversy about that man who caught his wife having sex with a woman and killed them both, began to describe the emotions of the husband, who should not have had to perform the shameful examination: "But I examined the man first, to see whether he was born that way or whether it had been stitched on."

Grandaus, an equally Asian-style declaimer,[4] when he spoke in the same

2. Literally "goat horns," since goats had a reputation for being oversexed, and Pan was half goat, half anthropomorphic.

3. A Greek orator of the early Augustan period, prominent in Mylasa, a city of southwestern Asia Minor.

4. The Asianists were orators whose florid style was characterized by long periodic sentences with elaborate parallelism, antithesis, and poetic figures.

controversy, said, "they would not tolerate the killing of adulterers, unless I had caught an adulterer who was not really a man."

In this controversy about a priestess,[5] Murredius spoke no less obscenely: "perhaps when she drove off his sexual impulse, she took it in her hands." One must stay far away from every obscenity in both words and thoughts. It is better to be quiet, even if it damages your case, than to speak if it damages your sense of shame.

9.3 Seneca the Elder, *Controversies* 4.Preface.10

The following is used to illustrate how easily a brilliant and epigrammatic locution can be made to sound ridiculous.

When Haterius[6] was defending a freedman accused of being his patron's male concubine, I remember him saying: "Lack of sexual modesty in a free man is a legitimate charge, but in a slave it is a necessity, and in a freedman a duty." His saying later became a subject of jests: "You're not doing your duty by me" or "That man is much occupied in his duties for this man." From that origin, shameless and obscene men were for some time called "dutiful."

9.4 Seneca the Elder, *Controversies* 10.4.17

Seneca here quotes the Augustan orator Labienus, who spoke in defense of a man who rescued infants abandoned in the woods and then hacked off their limbs so they could help his trade as a professional beggar.

"To think that people have the idle time to worry what a miserable beggar does among beggars, while leading citizens employ their wealth against nature: they have legions of eunuchs and amputate them so they can be apt for a longer passivity toward shameful acts.[7] Because they are ashamed of being men, they bring it about that there should be as few men as possible. Nobody comes to the rescue of those delicate and pretty weaklings."

---

5. The present controversy concerns a woman kidnapped by pirates and sold as a slave to a brothel-keeper; she nevertheless remained a virgin and ultimately killed a soldier who tried to force himself on her. She later tries to become a priestess, but some accuse her of unchastity.

6. A famous orator and declaimer of the Augustan period, known for his powers of improvisation.

7. Castration would keep them boyish-looking longer, and thus more attractive for pederastic purposes.

9.5 Phaedrus, *Fable* 4.16

Phaedrus was an author of versified fables who was active during the reign of Tiberius.

Another asked what cause created
Tribads[8] and soft men, and the old man explained:
"Prometheus, the author of our common clay,[9]
Fragile when it meets the blows of Fortune,
After he had spent a whole day separately molding
Those organs of Nature that Modesty clothes,
Was suddenly invited to dine with Bacchus.
When his veins were full of much wine,
He returned home late at night with uncertain steps.   10
Then with drunken fumbling and a half-slumbering heart,
He fitted the maidens' part to the male race,
And masculine members to women.
And so lust now enjoys perverted pleasures.

9.6 Phaedrus, *Fable* 5.1.12–18

The following describes the comic poet Menander being presented to the late-fourth-century Athenian tyrant Demetrius of Phaleron (perhaps confused with Demetrius Poliorcetes).

Covered with perfume and flowing robes,
He advanced with a slow and delicate gait.
When the tyrant saw this man at the end of the line,
He asked: "Who's that pervert *(cinaedus)* who dares to open
His asshole in my sight?" His courtiers answered,
"This is Menander, the writer." Instantly changed,
The tyrant says, "No man can become more handsome."

9.7 Suetonius, *Nero* 28–29

Nero became emperor at the age of sixteen in 54 C.E. and was overthrown in 68. Stories abounded concerning both his sexual excesses and his penchant for public performance.

---

8. A Greek-derived word for lesbians. It is related to the verb *tribein* (to rub), an apparent reference to manual stimulation.

9. The god Prometheus defied Zeus to give the gift of fire to mankind and was thus always considered a benefactor of human civilization. Some later sources, as here, make him the creator of man.

[28] Along with corrupting freeborn boys and sleeping with married women, he raped the Vestal Virgin Rubria.[10] He came close to making a legitimate marriage with the freedwoman Acte, to which end he had bribed several consuls who were to swear she was of royal birth. He had a boy named Sporus castrated and tried to transform him into an actual woman; he married him in a regular wedding ceremony, with a dowry and a bridal veil, took him home in front of a great crowd, and treated him as his wife. A witty remark that someone made about this is still circulating: that human kind would have been well off, if his father Domitius had had the same kind of wife. He took this boy, Sporus, decked in the trappings of an empress, with him in his litter through the public assemblies and markets of Greece and then in Rome through the figurine-market, kissing him constantly. That he wanted to sleep with his mother[11] but was kept from doing so by her opponents, so that this savage and reckless woman should not come to power through that kind of favor, everyone agrees, because afterwards he added to his concubines a prostitute who, according to rumor, was extremely similar to Agrippina. Indeed, our sources assure us that earlier, every time he rode with this mother in a litter, he had lewd relations with her and that the stains on his clothing betrayed the fact.

[29] He so completely defiled his chastity that when almost all the parts of his body had been violated, he invented a new kind of game (so to speak) in which, dressed in the skin of a wild animal, he was released from a cage and attacked the private parts of men and women who were bound to stakes and, when he had had enough of this savagery, he was finished off (as it were) by his freedman Doryphorus. This Doryphorus he took as his husband, just as Sporus had with him, and in doing so he imitated the cries and wailing of a virgin who is being raped. I have heard from several people that he was absolutely persuaded that no man was chaste or pure in any part of his body, but rather that most people disguised their viciousness and cleverly concealed it; and thus in those who confessed their lewdness to him he pardoned all other crimes as well.

9.8 Dio Cassius 62.6.4

The following are the words of the British queen Boudicca, who incited a revolt of the native tribes against Roman rule in 61 C.E.

10. Vestal Virgins were priestesses of the virgin goddess Vesta (Hestia), goddess of the hearth. Their sexual purity was sacrosanct.

11. It was through the machinations of Agrippina (15–59 C.E.) that Nero, her son by a previous marriage, came into power after the death of the previous emperor, Claudius, her uncle and husband. Many sources say that Claudius was poisoned by her. She was assassinated in 59 on Nero's orders.

"Therefore as the queen of such men and women, I pray to you and ask you for victory, security, and freedom against men who are arrogant, unjust, wanton, and impious, if I must call 'men' those people who bathe in warm water, eat elaborate delicacies, drink unmixed wine, smear themselves with myrrh, take boys who are nearly adults to their luxurious beds, and act like slaves to a bad lyre-player."[12]

9.9 Seneca the Younger, *Natural Questions* 1.16

The son of Seneca the Elder, L. Annaeus Seneca became the young Nero's tutor and later his political advisor, until banished in 62 C.E. From then until his death three years later he devoted his time to writing scientific and moral works, including the following.

[1] Now I want to tell you a little story, so you'll see to what lengths the sexual appetite will use every possible tool for stimulating pleasure and how talented it is at provoking its own frenzied passion. There was this fellow, Hostius Quadra, whose behavior was so indecent it has even been produced upon the stage. When this rich, greedy man, a slave himself to his 100,000,000 sesterces,[13] was killed by his slaves, the emperor Augustus considered his murder not worthy of punishment, and all but declared it a justifiable homicide.

[2] His depravity was not restricted to only one sex, but he was voracious for men and women alike. He had mirrors specially made to reflect distorted images, so that a finger looked longer and thicker than an arm. Moreover, they were set up at angles around the room, so when he was playing bottom he could see all the grindings of his top behind him, and he relished the exaggerated endowment of his own organ as much as if it were real. [3] Quadra actually used to cruise the baths checking peckers, recruiting from the ranks of those who measured up most impressively, but his insatiable perversity was equally entertained by the illusions of his mirrors.

Now go on and tell me the mirror was invented to cultivate taste and refinement. It's horrifying to tell about the things that monster said and did with his drooling, snarling mouth, with his mirrors on every wall, so he could be the audience for his own outrageous crimes against nature. Those secret acts that weigh upon the conscience, the kind all of us would deny, were thrust not just into his mouth but right in his eyes.

12. The reference is to Nero, who was fond of giving public performances of his musical and dramatic skills.

13. An enormous fortune, equivalent to 150,000 pounds of silver.

[4] Yes, indeed, crime trembles before its own reflection. Even among those who have hit rock bottom and have been exposed to every kind of shameful disgrace, the eyes retain a sensitive modesty. Quadra, as if experiences that weren't publicized somehow didn't count, summoned his eyes as witnesses to his crimes, and not content to see the true measurement of his vice, he surrounded himself with mirrors to divide and multiply his scandalous acts. And, since he couldn't see as clearly as he wanted when he burrowed down and gnawed another crotch, he caught glimpses of his chore in the reflection of the mirrors. [5] He would see with his eyes the lust of his mouth; he would see with his eyes the studs he offered his every opening; sometimes shared between a man and a woman, his whole body spread to be taken, he would see with his eyes his unspeakable acts. For why would a morally bereft man leave his activities in the dark? With no fear of the light of day the exhibitionist applauds his own monstrous couplings, when he is exposed in a posture that you might think would be the last one he would want to show off in.

[6] Even prostitutes have a kind of modesty, and though their bodies serve the public debauchery, at least a curtain hides their miserable subjection; a whorehouse still maintains a sense of shame. But for Quadra, the beast, unsightly perversion was show time, and no moonless night was dark enough to blot out his stage-strutting. [7] "I take on a man and a woman at the same time," he says. "I apply my manhood by giving it rough to another with my unoccupied part. Every inch of my body is busy sucking and fucking, so let the eyes have a ball, too; they can be witnesses and supervisors. And when a particular position blocks my line of vision, the ingenious mirrors give me a clear view, in case anyone thinks I don't know what I'm doing. It's nature's big joke to give man such meager tools to achieve his pleasure while she outfits the copulations of other animals so much better. I will find a way to fool my twisted needs into being satisfied. Where's the victim in a crime against nature? I'll surround myself with mirrors cleverly designed to reflect unbelievably massive images. If I could, I'd have that size in the flesh; since I can't, I'll feast on the fantasy. My hardcore lust will see more than it gets and will admire its ability to take it all." Revolting behavior! Perhaps he was killed so quickly that he never saw them coming; he should have been slaughtered in front of his own mirror.

9.10 Seneca the Younger, *Moral Epistles* 47.7

The Moral Epistles *applied Stoic ethical doctrine to a variety of specific situations. This letter laments the various ways in which slaves are mistreated and makes the broader point that we are all slaves to Fortune.*

Another slave, who acts as a wine server, wrestles with his age as he is decked out in feminine attire. He is not allowed to escape boyhood, but is forcibly dragged back to it. A beardless slave with a soldier's stature, his hair rubbed away or plucked out by the roots, he has to remain awake all night and divide his time between his master's drunkenness and lust, a man in the bedroom, but a boy at the feast.

9.11 Seneca the Younger, *Moral Epistles* 95.21

In this letter Seneca discusses women who act like men, which he sees as another form of rebellion against Nature.

Today women equal men in regard to lust, although born to take the passive role—may the gods and goddesses destroy them! So perverse is their new species of invented immodesty: they actually penetrate men! Why then should one be surprised that the greatest physician and natural scientist[14] is caught in a lie, since so many women are now bald and have gout in their feet? They have lost the advantage of their sex through their vices; because of casting off their femininity, they have been condemned to masculine diseases.

9.12 Seneca the Younger, *Moral Epistles* 122.7

This observation forms part of a discussion of vice as living contrary to Nature.

Don't those men who exchange their clothing with women's seem to you to live contrary to Nature? Don't those men who see to it that a boyish appearance shines at a different time of life also live contrary to Nature? What crueler or more wretched thing could happen? Will he never be allowed to become a man, just so he can continue to take the passive role with another man? When his sex ought to have rescued him from such abuse, will not even age release him from it?

9.13 Musonius Rufus 12

Musonius Rufus was a Stoic popular philosopher active in Rome during the time of Nero and his successors. He was banished by Nero in 65 C.E. This discourse is from a short essay titled "On Sexual Matters."

Not the least significant part of the life of luxury and self-indulgence lies also in sexual excess; for example, those who lead such a life crave a variety of loves, not only lawful but unlawful ones as well, not women alone but

---

14. Hippocrates, whom Seneca had earlier quoted as observing that some diseases, such as baldness or gout, belong only to men.

also men; sometimes they pursue one love and sometimes another, and not being satisfied with those which are available, pursue those which are rare and inaccessible, and invent shameful intimacies, all of which constitute a grave indictment of manhood. Men who are not wantons or immoral are bound to consider sexual intercourse justified only when it occurs in marriage and is indulged in for the purpose of begetting children, since that is lawful, but unjust and unlawful when it is mere pleasure-seeking, even in marriage. But of all sexual relations those involving adultery are most unlawful, and no more tolerable are those of men with men, because it is a monstrous thing and contrary to nature. But, furthermore, leaving out of consideration adultery, all intercourse with women which is without lawful character is shameful and is practiced from lack of self-restraint. So no one with any self-control would think of having relations with a courtesan or a free women apart from marriage, no, nor even with his own maid-servant.

Musonius goes on to highlight the fact that men do such things in secret as proof that they know them to be wrong. He also argues that a master having sex with a female slave is no better than a mistress doing so with a male slave.

Would it not seem completely intolerable not only if the woman who had a lawful husband had relations with a slave, but even if a woman without a husband should have? And yet surely one would not expect men to be less moral than women, nor less capable of disciplining their desires, thereby revealing the stronger in judgment inferior to the weaker, the rulers to the ruled. What need is there to say that it is an act of licentiousness and nothing less for a master to have relations with a slave? Everyone knows that.

9.14 Petronius, *Satyricon* 6.1–26.6, 64.2–13, 67.2–69.5, 74.8–87.10, 91.1–99.6

Petronius was a master of entertainments in Nero's court, who eventually fell into disfavor due to false accusations and was forced to commit suicide. He left behind a picaresque novel concerning the adventures of Encolpius (the first-person narrator), a young man cursed with impotence by the god Priapus, and Giton, a slave boy whom he loves. Only excerpts from one part of the novel survive. The setting appears to be southern Italy.

[6] I was listening so intently to Agamemnon[15] I didn't notice that Ascyltos[16] was already gone. As I walked along, absorbed in our heated con-

---

15. A rhetorician and schoolteacher.
16. A more masculine companion of Encolpius and sometime rival for Giton's affection.

versation, a vast throng of students had burst into the portico. Apparently
they'd just heard the speaker after Agamemnon give an extemporaneous
performance. While the students laughed at his sententious style and ridiculed his entire presentation, I managed to sneak away and took off at a
trot after Ascyltos. But I lost my way somehow and had no idea where our
lodgings were. Every turn I took led me back to the same spot until, out
of breath and soaked with sweat, I approached an old woman selling fresh
vegetables.

[7] "Excuse me, Ma'am," I said, "you wouldn't happen to know where
I'm staying, would you?"

Charmed by the polite delivery of my foolish query, she replied "Of
course," and promptly got up and led the way. I thought she must be
divine. . . .

Suddenly, just as we entered an unfamiliar part of town, this street-wise
woman threw back a motley curtain and announced: "You ought to live
here!" I was just about to say I'd never laid eyes on the place, when I
glimpsed a line of naked whores with some customers prowling around
them. I began to grasp—all too slowly—that I'd been led right into a
cathouse. I cursed the woman's tricks, tried to hide my face and dashed
across the room. But when I reached the doorway, I ran smack into Ascyltos, as dead tired as I was; you'd have thought he had the same guide. I
greeted him with a laugh and asked how he ended up in this dive.

[8] Wiping away the sweat with both hands, he said: "If you only knew
what I've been through!"

"What now?" I asked.

"Well," he sighed, as if too tired to speak, "I was wandering all over town
and couldn't even find our lodgings, until a fatherly old man came up and
kindly offered to lead the way. He brought me here by some roundabout
route and then offered to pay me for a quickie. A madam had already collected for the room and this guy had his arm around me. If I hadn't been
stronger than he was, I would have had to pay the price. . . ."

Everyone there looked to me as if they'd drunk satyrion.[17] We joined
forces and defied the troublemaker. . . .

[9] As if in a haze, I spotted Giton standing at the edge of a path and
rushed toward him. . . . When I asked what my lover had gotten us for
lunch, the boy sat down on the bed and brushed away a stream of tears
with his thumb. Troubled at my lover's state, I asked what was wrong. He
didn't want to tell me at first, but when I started to get angry he opened
up: "That lover of yours," he said, "your buddy, just came into our room
a minute ago and wanted to have me then and there. When I started to

17. A kind of aphrodisiac.

scream, he pulled a knife on me and said, 'If you want to play Lucretia, you've found your Tarquin.'"[18]

When I heard this, I shook my fist in Ascyltos' face: "What about it, you male slut, you—with foul breath to match!"

Ascyltos pretended to be shocked at first but a moment later was shaking his fists and shouting even more loudly than I had. "Just shut up," he said, "you filthy gladiator—no, even the arena didn't want you! Just shut up, you sneaking cutthroat! Why, you couldn't even make it with a decent woman when you had the strength! Didn't I play your lover in the garden just as this boy does now in the inn!"

I shot back, "You slunk off while I was talking to the professor."

[10] "What am I supposed to do, stupid, starve to death? Or listen to those pompous epigrams—I'd rather hear bottles broken and dreams interpreted! For god's sake, you're far more shameless than I am. The way you kissed that poet's ass to cop a free dinner . . ." So our ugly quarrel ended in gales of laughter, and we turned calmly to the business at hand. . . .

But I couldn't forget what he had done. "Ascyltos," I said, "it's obvious that we can't get along. Let's split up our things and try to fight off poverty on our own. You're a scholar and so am I; but to stay out of your way I'll try something else. Otherwise we'll quarrel a thousand times a day and scandalize the whole town."

Ascyltos had to admit I was right. "Since we're invited out as scholars tonight, let's not ruin the evening. But tomorrow I'll be more than happy to find my own place—and another lover."

"Gratification delayed is gratification denied," I quipped. . . .

Lust was the cause of this hurried separation. I'd been wanting to get rid of that obnoxious chaperone so Giton and I could live as before. . . .

[11] I looked the whole town over for myself before returning to our little room. At last, I could ask for kisses without looking over my shoulder. I held Giton snug in my arms and was just on the verge of enjoying the most enviable of pleasures. The party was just beginning, when Ascyltos slunk up to the room, forced the bar from the door, and caught us in the act. He filled the little room with his laughter and mock-applause as he pulled off the cloak that covered me. "Well, well, what have we here, my right honorable friend? Isn't this tent a bit small for two, soldier?" He didn't stop there either, but grabbed a strap from his bag and proceeded to give me

---

18. The rape of Lucretia, wife of a Roman citizen, by Sextus, the son of the king, Tarquinius Superbus, was the legendary cause of popular revolt against the Roman kings and the foundation of the Republic in 509 B.C.E. In Roman legend it was a story comparable to that of Harmodius and Aristogeiton in Athenian legend.

a good, thorough thrashing while tossing out taunts like salt on a wound. "Aren't friends supposed to hold all things in common?"

[12] It was just beginning to get dark when we entered the market. There were lots of things for sale—junk for the most part—but the failing light helped to obscure their dubious origins. Since we had the stolen cloak with us, we took advantage of this opportunity to display its border in a corner of the market in the hope that the splendid material might attract a buyer. Almost immediately, a peasant, who looked strangely familiar, walked up with a young woman and began to eye our cloak very carefully. Ascyltos looked him up and down and then suddenly paled and fell silent. Even I couldn't look at him without rubbing my eyes! Of course! This had to be the guy who found our tunic in the middle of nowhere! [19] Yes, this was the guy. But Ascyltos couldn't believe his eyes and, before doing anything rash, walked over like a prospective buyer, lifted the tunic off the man's shoulders and fingered it carefully.

[13] What a marvelous piece of luck! So far the hick's meddlesome paws hadn't touched the seam. Indeed, he proffered it with some distaste —like a beggar's leavings. When Ascyltos saw that our money had not been touched and what a rube the seller was, he pulled me aside. "Brother, do you realize the treasure I was grumbling about has come home again? That little tunic still looks chock full of gold! What are we going to do? How can we reclaim our property legally?"

I was elated—not just because of the treasure, but because I was now relieved of an ugly suspicion. I was against doing anything devious. I thought we should sue him openly, then, if he refused to restore our property, he would find himself facing a court injunction.

[14] But Ascyltos feared the law. "Who in the world knows us here?" he asked. "Who will believe our story? We're much better off if we simply buy it—even if it is ours—and get back our treasure for a few coins instead of risking it in a lawsuit.

> Where cash alone is king, what good are laws,
>   Where no poor man can ever win his cause?
> The Cynics, though they put the times to shame,
>   Will now and then, for pennies, throw the game,
> While law's official guardians sell her dear,
>   The judge presiding as the auctioneer."

The problem was, that except for a single coin—which we would have spent on beans—we were empty-handed. We couldn't let the booty escape,

---

19. This apparently refers to an earlier episode in a portion of the novel that no longer survives.

so we decided to undersell our cloak and accept a little loss for a greater gain. As soon as we unfurled our wares the woman with her head uncovered (who had been standing with the peasant) inspected some marks on the cloak very carefully before grabbing it firmly in both hands and screaming at the top of her lungs: "Stop the thieves!" We were caught completely off guard, but instead of standing there looking stupid, we grabbed that rag of a tunic and shouted back with equal fervor that they were thieves. The argument was absurd. Street dealers attracted by the uproar naturally ridiculed our perverse insistence: while we were laying claim to a rag not worth patching, our rivals were after an obviously costly piece of clothing.

[15] At this point, Ascyltos managed to quell the laughter saying, "Look, everyone likes his own things best: let them return our tunic and they may have their cloak."

A trade was fine all round; but there were already some shady lawyers on hand who wanted to profit from our cloak. They pressed us to deposit both articles with them so that a judge could settle the dispute the next day. There was not, after all, only the issue of ownership at stake, they insisted, but the fact that we were all under suspicion of theft. They were already appointing "trustees"—some street dealer, bald on top, with a forehead positively bristling with warts. He had pled some cases, he said, as he seized our cloak as Exhibit A for the coming trial. The aim of all this was clear enough: to let a pack of thieves get a stranglehold on our cloak in the belief that we would not appear at the appointed time for fear of being charged with a crime. . . .

We were obviously after the same thing and chance helped us both get what we wanted. When we demanded that the old tunic also be treated as evidence, the peasant flew off the handle and threw it in Ascyltos' face. He wanted us to forget the whole thing and for us to return the cloak which had started all the trouble. . . .

With the treasure retrieved, as we thought then, we raced back to our room, shut the door, and had a good laugh at the wiles of those street dealers and con men who so shrewdly recovered our money for us:

I like succeeding by degrees;
"Too easy" spoils the victories.

[16] . . . We were just filling up on dinner, thanks to Giton, when someone banged noisily on the door. . . .

Frightened, we asked who was there, and a voice replied, "Open up and find out!"

Before we could answer, the bar fell from the door, admitting the intruder. It was a woman with her head covered. "Did you think you'd have the last laugh?" she said. "I am the maid of Quartilla whose holy rite you disrupted in front of the grotto.[20] Yes, she herself is coming to your humble lodgings and wishes to have a word with you. Don't worry: her desire is not to blame you for your blunder, nor to punish you. No, in fact, she only wonders what god brought such elegant young men in her direction."

[17] So far we were silent and had agreed to nothing, when the mistress herself entered, accompanied by a young girl. She promptly plopped down on my bed and proceeded to cry for some time. Even then we didn't say a word but sat in astonishment waiting for her tearjerker to end. When this showy storm of tears finally subsided, she unveiled an aristocratic profile, stretched both hands out in front of her, and cracked her knuckles: "Just who do you think you are? And where did you learn to rival the robbers of romance? God knows, I pity you. No one looks with impunity on what it is forbidden to see. Especially since this part of the world is so full of spirits, it's easier to find a god than a man. But don't think I've come here for revenge. I am moved more by compassion for your youth than by the wrong you have done me. You have, quite innocently, I think, committed an irremissible crime. Indeed, on that very night I shook so frightfully with chills that I feared the onset of a fever. So I sought a cure in my dreams. I have been instructed to seek you out and to assuage the on-slaught of illness by the secret method revealed to me. But working a cure is not my only worry; another far greater sorrow drives me to distraction and may mean my death: if in your youthful recklessness you divulge what you saw in the shrine of Priapus and profane the mysteries of the gods, I beg and pray by all that's holy that you not mock our nocturnal rites nor betray those ancient secrets that scarcely three mortals have ever known."

[18] She punctuated this prayer with another burst of tears before roll-ing over face down on my bed, her whole body shaking with sobs. I was torn between pity and fear. I told her to take heart, that she had nothing to fear on either count: no one would profane her rites and, if a god had revealed a remedy to her, we would fill the divine prescription even at our own peril. Almost instantly her mood changed: she leaned over and gave me a wet kiss; laughing through her tears, she gently stroked the hair over my ears. "I will make peace with you and drop the charges I had filed," she announced matter-of-factly. "But if you hadn't agreed to my 'cure,' tomorrow a lynch-mob would have been on hand to avenge the wrong done me and defend my honor.

---

20. Quartilla is a priestess of Priapus. In the lost earlier portion of the novel, Encolpius had apparently intruded on a ceremony she was conducting, and his present impotence is Priapus' punishment.

Neglect is scorn; to rule, a thing of awe;
What I love is to lay down my own law!
Neglected, even a sage can turn to mayhem;
To beat a man in style, girls, never slay him!"

Then she clapped her hands and suddenly sang out in a loud, frightening cackle. Both her maid and young attendant joined in from opposite sides of the room.

[19] The whole place echoed with their stagy laughter, while we stood there wondering what had happened—why this sudden change of mood?—and stared in stupefaction first at each other, then at the women. . . .

"I have forbidden any mortal from setting foot in this inn today in order that you may apply the remedy for my fever without interruption." Thus spoke Quartilla. Ascyltos was momentarily stunned and I felt an alpine chill go up my spine that left me speechless. I would have been even more frightened without my reinforcements. After all, if push came to shove, we were only facing three girls—all three weaklings, presumably. On the other side, we were, if nothing else, physically male. And we were better dressed for a scuffle. I had even matched us up mentally in case of a fight: I would take on Quartilla, Ascyltos the maid, and Giton the girl. . . .

We lost our nerve in a flash, and an unavoidable death loomed before our eyes. . . .

[20] "Please, Ma'am," I said, "if there's anything worse in store for us, get it over with; we didn't commit a crime so great that we deserve to be tortured to death. . . ."

A maid, who was called Psyche, very carefully spread a little blanket on the floor. . . .

She diligently applied herself to my groin, which was now as cold as if it had died a thousand deaths. . . .

Ascyltos covered his head; presumably he had learned how dangerous it was to meddle in other men's secrets. . . .

A maid pulled two scarves from inside her blouse and proceeded to bind our feet with one and our hands with the other. . . .

As our conversation began to run dry, Ascyltos said, "Hey, don't I deserve a drink?"

Responding to my laughter, the maid clapped her hands and said, "I put one right there, young man. Did you drink up the whole dose yourself?"

"What's that?" piped up Quartilla, "Did Encolpius guzzle down all our satyrion? . . ."

A pleasing laugh shook her sides. . . .

Finally Giton couldn't help laughing, especially when the little girl hugged him around the neck and gave him countless kisses without meeting any resistance.

[21] We wanted to cry out in desperation, but there was no one to help. Besides, Psyche stood by with a sharp hairpin, and whenever I was about to call on my fellow citizens for help, she would prick my cheeks while the girl bore down on Ascyltos from the other side with a painter's brush soaked in satyrion. . . .

Finally, a drag queen *(cinaedus)* appeared on the scene decked out in dark green linen, which he had hiked up under his belt. . . . He laid into us with his haunches grinding, then besmeared us with his stinking kisses. At last, Quartilla, with her skirt tucked up, called for an intermission with a wave of her whalebone staff. . . .

Both of us swore by all the religion in us that so dreadful a secret would die with us. . . .

Several masseurs came in and restored us with a rub-down with the usual oil. When we had shaken off our fatigue, we dressed for dinner again and were led into the next room where we found couches set up amid all the accoutrements of a sumptuous banquet. We were invited to take our places and, after tasting some marvelous antipasto, were inundated with the finest Falernian wine. After several courses, we began to feel drowsy. "What is this?" cried Quartilla, "do you intend to sleep when you know this whole night is consecrated to the beneficent powers of Priapus?" . . .

[22] When Ascyltos fell asleep, wrung out by so many trials, the maid whom he had earlier spurned with a blow rubbed a handful of ashes all over his face. Then, while he was still unconscious, she painted his shoulders and sides with phallic symbols.

I was equally exhausted by our Priapic labors and had just gotten my first taste of sleep; the whole household was doing the same thing, inside and out. Some of the servants lay scattered at the feet of sleeping guests, others were propped up against a wall, a couple even slouched head to head in the doorway. As a thin flicker of light shone from the last oil in the lamps, two Syrians in search of plunder stepped into the dining room. While fighting greedily over the silver, they tore a large decanter in two; the table set with silver promptly collapsed and a huge goblet, pitched high in the air, came down with a thud on the head of a servant girl draped across a nearby couch. Her screams succeeded in both betraying the thieves and waking some of the revelers from their drunken sleep. The Syrians had come for profit, but realizing they were caught *in flagrante,* they instantly collapsed side by side behind a couch—you'd have thought they planned it that way—and started snoring as if they'd been asleep there for hours. . . .

By now a steward had gotten up and begun pouring oil into empty lamps while slaves returned to their posts, still rubbing the sleep from their eyes. Then a cymbal-player appeared waking everyone up with her clashing of brass.

[23] The party was reborn: Quartilla exhorted us all to begin drinking again and the festive songs of the cymbal-player added to the merriment. . . .

An old queen *(cinaedus)* came in—a man as thoroughly distasteful as he was clearly worthy of the Villa Quartilla. He was snapping his fingers while he spouted verses like this:

> "Come and get it! Come quickly, you bum-boys outrageous!
>   Get it on! Giddyup! Try to follow!
> All you ace organ-grinders, dude-buggies, glad-handers
>   Old and fey, caponized by Apollo!"

After serving up these verses, he befouled me with a slobbery kiss. Then he got up on my bed and in spite of my resistance forced the covers off me. He labored long and hard over my groin—in vain! The makeup caked on his face melted and streamed off in rivulets; there was so much rouge in his wrinkles you'd have thought of an old wall battered by a rainstorm.

[24] I was at the end of my rope, on the verge of tears, when I managed to say, "Ma'am, didn't I hear you order us an appetizer?"

Quartilla clapped her hands gently and said, "Oh, aren't you a sly one! A fountain of native wit! You mean, you didn't know 'Appetizer' is what we call this queen?"

So my compadre wouldn't get off the hook too easily, I said, "Damn it, is Ascyltos the only one here on vacation?"

"Not at all," replied Quartilla taking my cue, "Ascyltos shall also get his taste of Appetizer." At the sound of her voice the queen changed his mount and rolled over to batter Ascyltos with his buns and lips. Giton stood there in the midst of all this and was about to split a seam, he was laughing so hard. This got Quartilla's attention. She asked very deliberately whose boy he was. When I said that he was my boyfriend, she said, "Then why hasn't he kissed me?" No sooner had she uttered the words than she was leaning into Giton with a kiss. She slipped her hand into his lap and carefully fingered his tender vessel, saying, "This will serve to whet our appetites tomorrow. I don't think I'd enjoy a sardine after today's swordfish!"

[25] With that, Psyche lit up with a broad grin and came over to whisper something to Quartilla. "Yes, yes!" she exclaimed, "What an excellent suggestion! Why not—since this is the perfect occasion—let our girl, Toute-la-nuit,[21] be deflowered?"

A rather pretty girl was produced on the spot. She couldn't have been more than seven. I stood there in amazement as everyone around me applauded the idea and egged on the marriage. I insisted that Giton was

---

21. In the original, the name is Pannychis (Greek for "all night long").

a very modest boy and not up to this kind of kinkiness; nor was the girl of an age to take on the woman's role.

Quartilla objected: "Is she any younger than I was when I had my first man? May Juno desert me if I can even remember when I was a virgin! Even when I was little, I was very naughty with my playmates. Later I applied myself to older boys until I came of age. I guess that's where the old saying comes from: 'Whoever's carried a calf can bear a bull.'"

For fear that something still worse might happen to dear Giton in my absence, I rose to play my part in the marriage ceremony.

[26] Psyche had already dressed the girl in a flame-colored wedding veil. Appetizer led the procession with a torch; drunken women stood clapping in a line after decking the bridal chamber with erotic hangings. These bawdy antics aroused Quartilla who got up, grabbed Giton, and dragged him into the bedroom.

To be sure, Giton was not exactly reluctant; nor, I must say, was the poor girl frightened by the idea of her "wedding night." Once they were ensconced in bed, we all perched on the threshold of the bridal chamber. Quartilla was the first to put an inquisitive eye to an all-too-well-placed crack in the door and spy on their childish sport with all the concentration of a true lecher. Eventually, she pulled me over to take a look. Because we were cheek to cheek in front of the crack, whenever the peeping proved dull, she would move her lips to the side and pepper me with furtive kisses. . . .

Spread on the bed, we spent the rest of the night without fear. . . .

The intervening section describes in detail a sumptuous feast the following evening at the house of Trimalchio, a fantastically rich freedman. The following episode comes toward the end of the feast.

[64] To tell the truth, by this time the lamps seemed to multiply before my eyes and the whole dining room began to blur. Then Trimalchio said, "Say, Plocamus,[22] aren't you going to tell us a story? Won't you entertain us? You used to be a live wire, reciting dialogue and even an occasional poem. How sad it is! The ripe figs have fallen!"

"Yes," he said, "my life in the fast lane ended when I got the gout. But when I was younger, I almost wore myself out with singing. You name it: dance, dialogue, barbershop gossip! I had no peer except Apelles[23] him-

---

22. Another former slave whom Trimalchio has invited to his feast.

23. Apelles was a famous Greek painter of the fourth century, not a musician or performer, as the ignorant Plocamus seems to believe.

self." He then put his hand to his mouth and whistled some god-awful tune he later claimed was "Greek."

Not to be outdone, Trimalchio gave an imitation of trumpeters, and looked round for his favorite, whom he called Croesus.[24] The boy with his bleary eyes and filthy teeth was in the process of wrapping a green handkerchief around an obscenely fat black puppy. He then put a piece of halfeaten bread on the couch and proceeded to stuff it down the little dog's throat until it gagged. This inspired Trimalchio to call for his own dog, Puppy, "Guardian of the home and family."

A hound of enormous size was promptly led in on a chain, and, when ordered to lie down—with a swift kick from the steward—he sprawled right in front of the table. Trimalchio tossed him a piece of white bread and said, "No one in my household loves me more!"

The boy was peeved to hear such praise lavished on Puppy, and so he put his pup on the ground and tried to get her to start a fight. True to his nature, Puppy promptly filled the room with his cacophonous barking and almost tore the head off Croesus' Pearl. The uproar didn't stop with the dogfight either: a candelabrum toppled over one of the tables shattering all the crystal and spattering some guests with hot oil.

Trimalchio tried to make light of the mess, kissed the boy, and told him to climb on his back. Croesus promptly mounted him like a horse, and kept slapping him on his back giggling and shouting, "Bucca, bucca,[25] guess how many fingers I'm holding up?"

After Trimalchio calmed down a bit, he ordered a great bowl of wine to be mixed and drinks served to all the slaves, who were sitting at our feet. "And if anyone turns his drink down," he added, "pour it over his head: daytime is serious, now is for fun!"

In the interval another freedman guest named Habinnas arrives and asks why Trimalchio's wife, Fortunata, is not eating.

[67] "You know how she is," replied Trimalchio, "she won't let water touch her lips until she's gathered up the silver and divided the leftovers among the slaves."

Habinnas responded, "If she doesn't join us, I'm gonna push off." He started to stand up when all the slaves chimed in on cue calling, "Fortunata! Fortunata!" over and over again. She then made her appearance with her skirt hitched up by a yellow sash to reveal a cherry-red slip, ankle bracelets,

24. The original Croesus was a king of Lydia in the sixth century, known for his wealth.
25. A term of abuse for a parasite or sponger.

and gilded Greek slippers. She wiped her hands on a handkerchief tied around her neck and then took her place on the couch, where Scintilla, Habinnas' wife, was reclining. Scintilla was clapping her hands as Fortunata kissed her and asked, as if in disbelief, "Is it really you?"

Fortunata then went so far as to take the jewelry off her beefy biceps and show them to a duly impressed Scintilla. Finally, she even took off her ankle bracelets and golden hair net, which she said was solid gold.

Trimalchio observed these goings on and had the jewelry brought to him. "You see these? A woman's chains!" he said. "This is how we fools get plundered. She must be wearing six-and-a-half pounds of gold! I've even got an arm band myself that weighs almost ten pounds—all made out of what I owe Mercury!"[26] Then, to show he wasn't lying, he had a set of scales brought in and passed around to test the weight.

Scintilla was no better. From her neck she took a golden locket, which she called "Lucky." From the locket she produced two earrings shaped like castanets, which she in turn handed to Fortunata for inspection. Then she remarked, "Thanks to my husband's generosity, no one else has better ones."

"What?" exclaimed Habinnas. "You cleaned me out to buy a glass bean? You know if I had a daughter, I'd cut her ears off! If it weren't for women, we'd think this stuff was just a bunch of rocks. Hell, now we've got to piss hot and drink cold!"[27]

Meanwhile, the wives were getting sloshed, laughing together and exchanging drunken kisses. One chatted on about her virtues as mistress of the house, the other of the boyfriends and vices of her husband. While they gossiped, Habinnas quietly got up, grabbed Fortunata by the ankles, and swung her legs up on the couch. "Oh no!" she shrieked, as her dress flew up over her knees. She then rolled over into Scintilla's lap and buried a hot blush in her handkerchief.

[68] After a brief intermission Trimalchio ordered a dessert course served. The slaves took out the old tables and brought in the new, and they scattered sawdust tinted with saffron and vermillion, and—something I'd never seen before—a glittering powder made of mica. Immediately Trimalchio quipped, "I just might be satisfied with these dessert tables alone—you all have your just desserts now!—but if you have something sweet, bring it on!"

Meanwhile, an Alexandrian boy, who was serving the hot water, started imitating a nightingale, while Trimalchio kept shouting, "Do something else!"

---

26. Among his other functions, Mercury (Hermes) was the god of commerce and luck.
27. In other words money passes through their hands like water through their body.

Then there was another gag: a slave who sat at Habinnas' feet suddenly began to chant the *Aeneid,* evidently at his master's request:

Meanwhile, Aeneas' fleet traversed the main. . . .

A more disgusting sound has never assaulted my ears. Not only did he barbarize the pitch and rhythm of the verse, he also interlarded lines from the Atellan farces.[28] For the first time in my life I actually found Vergil revolting. When he finally got tired and quit, Habinnas boasted, "Can you believe he never went to school? I took care of his education by putting him out with the street people. He has no peer when it comes to mimicking mule-drivers or street musicians. He's damn clever: a cobbler, a cook, a baker, a real 'slave of every muse.' There are just two things that keep him from bein' one in a million: he's circumcised and he snores. Now I don't mind that he's cross-eyed. So's Venus. That's why he's never quiet: one eye is always on the move. I only paid three hundred for him."

[**69**] Scintilla interrupted this paean. "You forgot to mention one of your slave's 'Muses': he's a pimp. And if I have anything to say about it, he'll be branded."

Trimalchio laughed and said, "Oh, I see. A Cappadocian, huh? He doesn't cheat himself out of anything, and I can't blame him for that: no one gives you a good time when you're dead.

"Now don't be jealous, Scintilla. Believe me, we know what you women are like. So help me god, I used to bang my mistress (and how!) until even the master got suspicious. That's why he banished me to the farm. But be quiet, tongue, I will feed you."

As if he'd just been praised to the skies, that worthless slave took a clay lamp out of his pocket and mimicked a trumpeter for more than half an hour, while Habinnas hummed along pressing his lower lip down with his hand. Finally, the slave strode into the middle of the room and did a flute-player with a handful of broken reeds. Then he donned a cloak and whip and did the *Life of a Mule-Driver* until Habinnas called him over, gave him a kiss, and handed him a drink. "Bravo, Massa! I'm gonna give you a pair of boots!"

More dishes are served to the guests, who subsequently take a bath and then return to the dining room for further drinking. A cock crows to signal the approaching dawn.

[**74**] It was then that the party began to go sour. A handsome young boy turned up among our new waiters, and Trimalchio cornered him and proceeded to lavish kisses on him. To assert her wifely rights, Fortunata responded by bad-mouthing Trimalchio, calling him "scum" and "a disgrace" for not controlling his lust. Finally, she called him a "dog." Provoked

28. An Italian form of comedy, quite incompatible with epic. See **7.28–33**.

by her abuse, Trimalchio threw his cup in her face. She screamed as if she had lost an eye and held her trembling hands to her face. Scintilla was also upset and sheltered her shuddering friend on her breast. A dutiful slave held an icy jar to Fortunata's cheek, which she leaned on as she moaned and wept.

But Trimalchio said, "What's all this about? Has this whore forgotten where she was bought? I took her out of the gutter and made her fit for human society. But she puffs herself up like the proverbial bullfrog. She doesn't even spit in her bosom: a blockhead, not a woman! If you're born in a hovel, don't dream of palaces. I'll be damned if I'm going to give in to this 'Cassandra in army boots.'[29]

"And I could have married for millions, penniless as I was. You know I'm not lying. Agatho, the perfumer, took me aside just the other day. 'I beg you,' he said, 'don't let your family die out.' But good-natured fool that I am, I didn't want to seem fickle, so I stuck the axe in my own leg.

"Damn right, I'll make you want to dig me up with your own fingernails! And to show you here and now what you've done to yourself—now hear this: Habinnas,[30] I forbid you to erect a statue of her on my tomb, so at least I won't hear her nagging when I'm dead. And, so she'll know I can hit back—I forbid her to kiss me when I'm dead!"

[75] When his fulminations ended, Habinnas tried to calm him down. "No one's perfect. We're mortals, not gods." Scintilla said the same thing through her tears and, calling him "Gaius,"[31] begged him by his guardian angel to relent.

Trimalchio couldn't hold back the tears any longer. "Please, Habinnas, as sure as you hope to enjoy your own nest-egg, spit in my face if I've done anything wrong. I gave the boy a very frugal kiss—not because he's beautiful—but because he's frugal! He can do division or read a book at sight; he saved enough from his daily allowance to buy a suit of Thracian armor! He's also bought himself an easy chair and two punch ladles! Now doesn't he deserve to be the apple of my eye?

"But Fortunata forbids it! Don't you, my high-heeled Caesar? I warn you, magpie, enjoy what you've got! Don't make me show my teeth, lovebird, or you'll get a piece of my mind. You know me: when I make a decision, it's nailed to the ground. But let's remember the living!

"Please, friends, enjoy yourselves for I, too, was once what you are, but thanks to my native talents I ended up here. Brains make a man, the rest is garbage! I buy low and sell high. Everyone has his own pet wisdom, I guess. I'm just lucky as hell.

29. Cassandra was a Trojan prophetess considered mad by all her contemporaries.

30. Habinnas was a mason and tombstone maker by trade. In the preceding paragraphs, Trimalchio had publicly given him instructions for his own monument.

31. Trimalchio's first name.

"Are you still crying, my snorer? I'll give you something to cry about.

"But—as I was about to say—frugality was the key to my success. When I left Asia I was no bigger than this candelabrum here. In fact, I used to measure myself by it every day and rub its oil on my lips to get a beard on my beak a little sooner! I was still my master's pet for fourteen years. To do your master's bidding is nothing to be ashamed of. And I gave my mistress equal time! You know what I mean. I say no more because I'm no braggart!

[76] "Then I became the master of the house, as the gods willed; I simply had my patron in the palm of my hand. Why waste words? He made me his heir—along with the emperor[32]—and I came into a senator's fortune. But no one is ever satisfied: I just loved doing deals. I won't bore you with the details: I built five ships and loaded them with wine—it was worth more than gold at the time—and shipped it to Rome. Every ship sank. You'd have thought I'd planned it that way. A fact, not a fable. On a single day Neptune gulped down thirty million!

"Do you think I fell apart? No, by god, I didn't even blink. I built more ships—bigger, better, and luckier! No one could deny I was tough. And you know, a big ship is tough, too! I loaded them up again with wine, bacon, beans, perfume from Capua, and slaves. This time Fortunata did the right thing: she sold off all her gold and all her clothes, and put a hundred gold pieces in my hand. This was the seed-money for my fortune. What the gods will happens quickly: I scooped up ten million on a single voyage!

"I promptly bought back all the estates that had belonged to my patron. I built a house and bought up some mules and slaves. Whatever I touched grew like a honeycomb. Once I owned more than the whole country, I threw in the towel. I gave up doing deals and started lending money through my freedmen.

"I already wanted out of handling my own business, and a Greek astrologer named Serapa happened into our town and convinced me. He was on intimate terms with the gods. He even told me things about myself that I had forgotten. He explained me right down to my buttons: he knew my insides. The only thing he didn't tell me was what I'd had for dinner the day before. You'd have thought he'd always lived with me.

[77] "Say, Habinnas, weren't you there when he said, 'You acquired your wife with your wealth. . . . You are unlucky in your friends. . . . No one ever returns your favors. . . . You own enormous estates. . . . You are nursing a viper in your armpit!' And something I should never tell you—right now I have thirty years, four months, and two days to live! And I shall soon come into a legacy. My horoscope says so. If I could only extend my estates to Apulia,[33] I will have gotten somewhere in this life!

---

32. It was conventional to name the emperor in one's will out of respect, since the emperor had the power to abrogate wills if he were displeased.

33. A region of southeastern Italy.

"At least I built this house while Mercury[34] watched over me. As you know, it was a hut; now it's a temple. It has four dining rooms, twenty bedrooms, two marble colonnades, a series of servants' bedrooms, my private bedroom, this viper's lair, and a superb porter's lodge. And there's room enough for a hundred guests. In fact, when Scaurus[35] visited here, he would stay nowhere else, and he has his father's place by the sea. There are lots of other things, which I'll show you in a minute.

"Believe me, if you have a nickel in your pocket, you're worth a nickel. You are what you own. Just like your friend—first a frog and now a king.

"Meanwhile, Stichus, bring out my funeral clothes—the ones I want to be buried in, and bring some perfume and a taste from that jar I want poured over my bones. . . ."

[78] Stichus didn't waste any time: he returned to the dining room carrying a white shroud and a purple-striped toga.[36] . . . Trimalchio urged us to feel if they were made of good wool. Then with a wily smile, he said: "Stichus, make sure no mice or moths get at these—or I'll have you burned alive! I want to have a glorious funeral so that the whole town will shower me with blessings!"

He promptly opened a flask of exotic oil and anointed us all: "I hope I like this as well when I'm dead as I do now!" He then had wine poured in a bowl: "Now pretend you were invited here for my funeral banquet!"

The whole thing was getting positively nauseating when Trimalchio, now sloppily drunk, ordered some trumpeters into the dining room for more entertainment. Propped up on a pile of cushions he stretched out full length along the edge of the couch, saying, "Pretend I'm dead: play something beautiful." The trumpeters blared out a funeral march. One fellow—the slave of the undertaker, who was the most respectable person there—played so loud that he woke up the entire neighborhood. This caused the local fire brigade to think Trimalchio's house was on fire. They promptly broke down the door, and wielding axes and water proceeded as usual to turn everything upside down. We seized this golden opportunity, gave some excuse to Agamemnon, and raced out of there as fast as if it *were* on fire.

[79] We had no torch handy to light our way, and little hope of meeting someone with a light in the dead of night. In addition, we were drunk, not to mention the fact that this neighborhood would have been bewildering to us in broad daylight. So we marched our bleeding feet over sharp rocks and shards of broken pottery for almost an hour until we were finally delivered by Giton's cunning. Our wily boy was afraid of getting lost even in the daytime and so had marked every post and column with chalk; even in

34. See n. 26.
35. A member of an old and prominent senatorial family.
36. Purple was a color worn by the senatorial aristocracy.

the thick of night his marks were visible and their bright color showed the way to us wanderers.

But even when we'd found our lodgings, our sweaty ordeal wasn't over. The old innkeeper had spent so long swilling wine with her lodgers, she wouldn't have noticed if you'd set her on fire! We might have spent the night on her doorstep if one of Trimalchio's couriers hadn't turned up. . . . After making quite a racket, he simply broke down the door and ushered us in. . . .

> Ah, what a night, you gods and goddesses;
> How soft the sheets! We coupled heat to heat
> And lip to lip this way and that we poured
> Our flitting souls. With all your cares,
> Farewell Mortality! So I rehearsed my dying.

My hymn of thanks was premature: as soon as I gave into the wine and loosened my grip, Ascyltos, that master of misdeeds, stole my boy and carried him off to his own bed in the middle of the night! Then after taking a free tumble with someone else's lover—who either didn't mind or pretended not to—he just fell asleep in his arms oblivious of right and wrong.

And so when I woke up and groped for the delight plundered from my bed . . . if you can ever believe a lover, I had half a mind to run them both through with my sword and marry their sleep to death. But I followed a saner plan and woke Giton up with a beating, and looking sternly at Ascyltos said, "Since you've broken faith and raped our friendship, get your things now, and find someplace else to pollute!"

He didn't argue, but after we'd split up our loot very fairly he said, "Okay, now let's divide the boy!"

[80] I thought that would be his parting jest, but then he put his ruthless hand on his sword and said, "You're not gonna be the only one to enjoy this booty you've been hovering over. I'm gonna get my share even if I have to chop it off with my sword!"

I responded in kind—wrapped my cloak around my arm and got ready for a fight. Caught between two desperate lovers the poor boy begged us like a tearful suppliant not to make that shabby inn the setting for a Theban tragedy,[37] or stain the sanctity of a brilliant friendship with each other's blood. "If you must commit a crime," he shouted, "look, my throat is bare, turn your hands to this, bury your blades here! I deserve to die if I've corrupted the sacred bond of friendship!"

At his pleading we put down our swords, and Ascyltos spoke up: "I'll put an end to this quarrel. Let the boy go with whomever he wants; at least he should be free to choose his lover."

---

37. Probably a reference to the fratricide of Oedipus' sons, as staged in works like Aeschylus' *Seven against Thebes* or Euripides' *Phoenissae*.

I had no fears—I thought our longstanding intimacy as good as a tie of blood—on the contrary, I jumped at the offer and happily referred our case to the judge. But as soon as the words were out of my mouth, Giton had stood up and chosen Ascyltos as his lover, without even pretending to deliberate! I was so shattered by this sentence I simply collapsed on the bed. And I would have done myself in then and there if I hadn't begrudged my enemy such a triumph. Ascyltos walked out exulting in his prize and simply abandoned me in despair in a strange town, me who just moments before was his dearest comrade-in-arms, and his mate in misfortune!

> Friendship endures no longer than it pays,
> No longer than a shifting gamepiece stays;
> You stand fast, friends, while fortune keeps its place;
> When *that* gives out, you fall off in disgrace.
> A stage-troupe acts a mime, the father this,
> That one the son; a third "the rich man" is;
> But when the farce that each performs is ended,
> Back to plain truth and off with the pretended!

[81] I didn't indulge myself in tears for long for fear that on top of my other troubles Agamemnon's assistant, Menelaus, would find me alone at the inn. I sadly gathered up my things and took a private room near the beach. There I holed up inside for three days haunted with feelings of loneliness and humiliation. I beat my aching breast and over the din of my own moaning would often shout aloud, "Why couldn't the Earth simply open up and swallow me whole? Or the sea, so cruel to the innocent? Did I escape the law, cheat the arena, and kill my host to end up, after so many proofs of daring, deserted in an inn—a beggar, an alien in some Greek town? And who condemned me to solitude? A boy teeming with filthy desires, deserving exile in his own opinion, a free man—in depravity—well-bred—in depravity—who sold his youth for small change and was hired as a girl even by those who thought him male! And what about his friend? Who came of age in a skirt, not a toga? Whose mother convinced him not to become a man? Who did woman's work in a sweat shop? Who, after he'd gone broke and acquired novel appetites, abandoned his old friend and—most shameless of all—sold out everything for one night in the sack, like some camp follower! Now the lovers lie entwined all night every night! And perhaps, when they've exhausted each other sexually they chuckle over my loneliness. They won't get away with it: for either I'm not a man, let alone a free one, or I'll make them pay for my suffering with their own damn blood!"

[82] In this state of mind I belted on my sword and, to insure my martial vigor, fortified myself with an unusually large lunch. Soon I was out on the street prowling like a madman through all the arcades. Wearing a frankly murderous expression I looked daggers in all directions and frequently

touched the handle of my sword, which I had dedicated to the task, when some soldier—who was probably a con man or a thug—happened to notice me and said, "Say, soldier, what legion are you in? Whose unit?"

I confidently fabricated a legion and a commanding officer. "Well then, tell me, do soldiers in your army go around in Greek slippers?" My guilty look and nervous manner instantly gave me away: he ordered me to hand over my sword and stay out of trouble! Disarmed and deprived of revenge, I went back to my room, but, as soon as I calmed down, I began to feel grateful to that pushy thug! . . .

> Waters waist-deep, undrunk; unplucked the fruit;
>   Poor Tantalus, whom his wishes destitute! [38]
> So mighty rich men fare, their stores immense,
>   Who feed on hunger, fearful of expense.

Don't trust in plans: Fortune has a mind of her own. . . .

[83] I happened into an art gallery with an amazing collection of paintings. I actually saw some originals by Zeuxis,[39] unscathed by all the years, and sketches by Protogenes that so rivaled the truth of nature herself that I trembled to touch them. But when I got to Apelles—the piece the Greeks call "The Goddess on One Knee"—my admiration began to verge on worship. So precisely did the look of his creations conform to nature, you would have thought they were animated! Here a soaring eagle bears Ganymede to heaven; there fair Hylas fights off a wicked Naiad; Apollo damns his own murderous hands and adorns his unstrung lyre with the first hyacinth. Surrounded by these painted lovers I exclaimed as if alone: "Look, even the gods are touched by love! When Jupiter cannot find what he desires in heaven, he harms no one by erring on Earth. The nymph who ravished Hylas would have mastered her desires, had she thought that Hercules would intervene. Apollo invokes his lover's shade in a flower. In all these stories the embraces of love are unimpeded by a rival! But I befriended someone crueler than Lycurgus!"[40]

Even as I contended with the winds, a gray-haired gentleman[41] entered the gallery. His face bore the stamp of experience and seemed to hold out the promise of something great. Not that he was well dressed; in fact, it

---

38. Tantalus' punishment in the Underworld was to stand waist-deep in water that drained away whenever he reached down to drink it, and to have a fruit-laden bough overhead that the wind blew beyond his reach whenever he tried to pluck it.

39. Zeuxis was a Greek painter of the late fifth century, Protogenes and Apelles of the fourth century.

40. It is unclear whether Encolpius here means the legendary Spartan lawgiver or the mythological king of Thrace who suppressed the worship of Dionysus.

41. This is the character Eumolpus, who replaces Ascyltos as Encolpius' chief companion for the rest of the novel.

was plain from his appearance that he was one of those literati rich men love to hate. He walked up and stood beside me. . . .

"I am a poet," he said, "and, one, I hope, of no mean talent, if the garlands of victory still mean anything when favoritism so often crowns the undeserving! 'Then why are you so badly dressed?' you wonder. For just that reason: a passion for beauty never has made a man rich!

> The trafficker at sea brings back a bundle;
> The soldier for his pains wears cloth-of-gold;
> The two-bit yes-man lounges drunk in purple;[42]
> Even the marriage-breaker sins for hire;
> Eloquence alone, left shivering in its rags,
> Invokes forgotten arts with pauper's pleading.

[84] No doubt about it: if any man is averse to all the popular vices and insists on following his own steep path through life, that very fact—his being different—makes him hated. For who really likes what's at odds with himself? So those whose goal in life is to pile up interest-bearing accounts want it believed that there is nothing in the world better than what they themselves possess. So they attack those who love literature however they can in order to make them seem inferior to money, too!" . . .

"I don't know why but the sister of talent is poverty . . . I wish the enemy of my discipline were so harmless that he might somehow be mollified. But in reality, he is a seasoned thief and shrewder than any pimp." . . .

[85] "When I went to Asia to serve on the quaestor's[43] staff, I was put up as a guest in Pergamum. I was happy to stay there, not only because my lodgings were elegant, but also because my host's son was truly beautiful. So I hatched a plan to insure that I would never be viewed with suspicion by the paterfamilias: whenever the conversation at dinner even hinted at the sexual attractions of beautiful boys, I would blush like a virgin and object in the severest tones that my ears were offended by such obscene talk. The mother came to regard me as a veritable philosopher! So I started taking the boy to the gym, I organized his studies; I was his teacher and warned him not to let any sexual predator into the house. . . .

"Once we were lying around the dining room on a holiday when the long hours of play had made us too lazy to retire; around midnight I noticed that the boy was still awake and so, in the softest whisper, I said a prayer: 'Venus, who art in heaven, if I can kiss this boy without his noticing, tomorrow I will give him a pair of doves.'

"When he heard the price of pleasure, the boy started to snore. So I went over to the little faker and stole some kisses. Happy with this begin-

---

42. See n. 36.
43. A Roman treasury official.

ning, I got up early the next morning and, as he expected, brought him a
choice pair of doves, and so fulfilled my promise.

[86] "When the same opportunity arose the next night, I changed my
prayer and said, 'If I can caress this boy with my naughty hands without his
feeling it, I will give him two ferocious fighting cocks for his patience.'

"At this promise the boy came over to me on his own and, I think, he
was even afraid that I had nodded off! I reassured him on this point and
gorged myself on his entire body, stopping just short of the summit of
pleasure. The next morning I gave him what I'd promised and he was
elated.

"When my moment came the third night, I whispered . . . in his ear as
he pretended to sleep: 'Immortal gods, if I could enjoy in full the complete satisfaction of my desires while the boy sleeps, in return for this bliss,
tomorrow I will give him a choice Macedonian thoroughbred, so long as
he has felt nothing!'

"Never has a young man slept more soundly! So, first, I filled my hands
with his milky breasts, then I inhaled kisses, and, finally, all my desires
converged into one.

"In the morning he sat in his room waiting for my usual visit. Well, you
know very well how much easier it is to buy doves and cocks than a thoroughbred. Besides, I was afraid that so extravagant a gift would make my
kind attentions look suspicious. So after wandering around a few hours
I returned home and gave the boy nothing but a kiss. He hugged me
round the neck as he looked about and said, 'Please, sir, where is my
thoroughbred?' . . .

[87] "Because of my broken promise the door I had opened was
slammed shut, so I resorted again to wheedling. A few days later a similar occasion put us in the same lucky situation. Since I could hear his
father snoring I started asking him to be friends again, to let me make it
up to him, and all the other things a swollen libido inspires one to say.
But he was obviously angry with me and only said, 'Go to sleep or I'll tell
my father.'

"There's no obstacle a lack of scruples can't overcome. While he kept
threatening 'to wake up father,' I wormed my way around him and took
my pleasure by force in spite of his half-hearted resistance. He was not
entirely displeased by my ambush, and after he'd complained for some
time that he'd been deceived, and then was laughed at and reviled by his
fellow students (to whom he had boasted of my wealth!), he said, 'But
look, I'm not going to be like you, if you want to, do it again.'

"So with all my sins forgiven I was back in business on friendly terms;
I enjoyed his favors and then slipped off into postcoital slumber. But the
boy was ripe for pleasure—at that age, they're insatiable—and he wasn't
satisfied with a mere repetition. So he woke me up saying, 'Well, don't you

want something?' And I admit, it was no unpleasant task. So somehow I panted, sweated, and banged away till he got what he wanted, then I fell asleep again, exhausted with pleasure. Less than an hour had passed when he started jostling me with his hand and said, 'Why aren't we doing it?'

"I was furious at being woken up so many times, so I gave him a taste of his own medicine. 'Go to sleep,' I warned, 'or I'll tell your father!'"

Encolpius and Eumolpus proceed to discuss the decadence of modern art, and other visitors to the gallery throw stones at Eumolpus after he recites a bad poem. Encolpius takes the poet back to his lodging house for a meal, after which they go to a public bath.

[91] I saw Giton leaning against a wall with rags and scrapers in hand looking sad and confused. You could tell he just didn't take to slavery. Since I could scarcely believe my eyes. . . . As he turned, his face relaxed into a smile, and he said, "Pity me, dear friend! Here where there are no weapons, I can speak openly. Rescue me from this sadistic kidnapper and demand any kind of penance you like from your former judge no matter how brutal! It will be consolation enough for my suffering—just to die in obedience to your will!"

I told him to stop carrying on for fear someone would overhear our plans. We left Eumolpus behind—reciting poetry in the baths—and I quickly led Giton down a dark and dingy little passageway, and then raced back to my room. As soon as the door slammed shut I took him in my arms and brushed my face against the tears on his cheeks. We were both speechless; his lovable breast was still shaking with sobs. "What a disgrace!" I said. "To think that I was abandoned by you whom I love, and there is a gaping wound in my heart, but no scar! But what do you mean taking up with this fly-by-night lover? Do I deserve this kind of treatment?"

After he saw he was still loved, he raised his eyebrows. . . .

"I asked no one but you to judge our love, but I won't complain; I'm ready to forget it all if you repent in good faith."

As I poured out these words sighing and crying, Giton wiped my face with his cloak: "Please, Encolpius, be honest. Did I leave you or did you hand me over? I admit, I'll confess it openly: when I saw two armed men, I sided with the stronger." I fondly kissed that breast so full of wisdom and hugged him round the neck. And to show him that he was forgiven and that our renewed friendship could be counted on, I held him snug in my arms.

[92] It was already getting late and the woman had taken our order for dinner, when Eumolpus banged on the door. I asked, "How many are you?" and tried very hard to peek through a crack in the door to see if Ascyltos had come with him. When I saw my guest was alone, I promptly let him in.

After he'd sat down on the cot and observed Giton setting the table right in front of him, he nodded his head and said, "Say, I like your Ganymede! It should be a nice day!"

This calculated opening did not please me and I was afraid I had hooked up with another Ascyltos. Eumolpus persisted, and when the boy gave him something to drink, he said, "I like you better than the whole bathful," and greedily drained the cup dry. Then he said he had had a singularly unpleasant experience.

"I almost got a beating at the baths just because I tried to share a poem with some people sitting around the edge of the tub. After I was thrown out, I walked up and down every street shouting 'Encolpius!' at the top of my lungs. Out of the blue came a young man, stark naked—he'd evidently lost his clothes—bellowing 'Giton!' with equal ardor. While some boys mocked and mimicked me mercilessly like some kind of madman, an enormous crowd surrounded the young man with applause and a kind of awe: you see, the youth's sexual organs were so oversized that he looked like an appendage to *them*. Talk about a hard worker! I think he must be the kind to start yesterday and finish tomorrow! Anyway, he was soon saved by the cavalry: some Roman knight—a notorious one, I hear—wrapped the vagrant in his own cloak and took him home, in order to enjoy his good fortune alone, no doubt. But I couldn't even have gotten my own clothes back from an officious bath attendant, if I hadn't produced a witness! It just goes to show how much more advantageous it is to have your genius between your legs than between your ears!"

As Eumolpus told his story the expression on my face kept veering from delight—at the misfortunes of my enemy—to sorrow—at his being rescued. But I kept quiet as if I knew nothing about it, and then explained what we'd ordered for dinner. . . .

[93] "What is permitted, I hold cheap; my soul delights in going off the beaten path and finding trouble:

The Black-Sea pheasant and
The guinea-hen delight
Because they're scarce; white geese
And gaudy ducks taste trite.
Hauled home from distant seas
Or scratched from shoals of sand
By way of shipwreck, *these,*
Not *standard* seafood, please.
Far-out and foreign win;
What's out-of-bounds is in."

"Is this how you keep your promise not to versify today?" I said. "Please, spare us, at least: we didn't stone you! If someone drinking in this inn gets even a whiff of a poet, he'll rouse the whole neighborhood and bury us all! Take pity, remember the art gallery and the baths!"

My gentle Giton scolded me for talking this way. He said it was wrong to reproach my elders, to forget the duties of a host, and to spoil with insults the dinner I had so generously provided. He gave much sensible and modest advice of this kind that only served to enhance his beauty still further. . . .

[94] *[Eumolpus to Giton]* "How fortunate your mother was to bear a child like you, what a blessing! The combination of wisdom and beauty is a rarity. And so you won't think all your words were wasted, behold, you have a lover! I will fill my poems with your praises! As your tutor and bodyguard I will follow you beyond the call of duty. Encolpius won't be hurt: he is in love with someone else!"

Eumolpus was lucky that that soldier had taken my sword. Otherwise I would have worked off that rage I had mustered against Ascyltos in Eumolpus' blood. Nor did this escape Giton. He left the room on the pretext of fetching water and his timely exit quelled my anger.

So, after I'd cooled down a bit, I said, "Eumolpus, I would even rather hear you speak in verse than entertain desires like these. Just as I tend to be irate, you are priapic: look how ill-suited our dispositions are! So just consider me a maniac and get out of harm's way: that means, *leave now!*"

Eumolpus was shocked by my outburst, but, instead of asking why I was angry, he promptly left the room and then suddenly slammed the door shut on me. I was caught completely off-guard when he snatched the key and rushed off to look for Giton.

There was no way out, so I decided to end it all and hang myself! I had just tied a belt to the frame of the bed next to the wall and had put the noose around my neck, when Eumolpus and Giton walked in the door and called me back to life from the very verge of death. Giton's grief abruptly converted to rage and he shouted as he pushed me down on the bed with both hands: "You're wrong, Encolpius, if you thought you'd be the first to die. I was first to try: I looked for a sword in Ascyltos' room. And if I hadn't found you the other day, I would have thrown myself headfirst over a cliff! Just so you'll know how near death is for those who really seek it: look at the sight you would have had me behold!"

With that he snatched a razor from Eumolpus' servant, and slashed repeatedly at his throat, before collapsing at our feet. I cried out in horror, rushed to his side, and sought the road to death with the very same blade. But there was not even a trace of a wound on Giton and I felt no pain. The razor was a dummy! It was blunted and safely sheathed for boys to learn barbering. That's why the servant didn't panic when Giton grabbed it, and why Eumolpus hadn't interrupted our comic death scene.

[95] While the lovers were playing out this comedy, the innkeeper came in with the rest of our supper. After observing our filthy wallow, he said, "What are you? Drunks or runaways? Or both? And who tied up that bed? Just what on Earth are you up to? By god, you'd rather run off in the middle of the night than pay your bill, wouldn't you? Well, you won't get away with it: I'll have you know this boarding house doesn't belong to some widow but to Marcus Mannicius!"

"Are you threatening us?" shouted Eumolpus and slapped the man hard in the face with the palm of his hand. The innkeeper responded by lobbing an empty wine jug at the poet's head, cleaving his forehead in mid-scream, and dashing from the room. Eumolpus was not one to suffer insults gladly: he chased after his assailant with a wooden candelabrum and avenged his pride with multiple blows. The whole household was roused now, including a crowd of drunken guests. I seized the opportunity for revenge and locked Eumolpus out. With the tables turned on that ruffian, I enjoyed both the room and the night free of my rival.

Meanwhile the cooks and boarders lit into the poet: one stabbed at his eyes with a spit of sizzling sausages; another threatened him like a gladiator with a fork he'd snatched from the kitchen. Then a bleary-eyed old woman wrapped in a filthy apron and wobbling along on an uneven pair of clogs dragged in an enormous dog on a chain and proceeded to sic him on Eumolpus. But he successfully parried every attack with his candelabrum.

[96] We were watching all this through a hole in the door (where the handle had been before we'd broken it off a little while earlier). I was just delighted to see Eumolpus get this beating. Soft-hearted Giton felt sorry for him though and actually thought we should open the door and rescue him. I was still so angry, I couldn't keep myself from giving Giton's compassionate head a sharp rap with my knuckles! He sat down on the bed in tears, but I kept watching through the hole—first with one eye, then the other, and feasted myself on Eumolpus' suffering just like a fine meal!

I was telling him to get a lawyer, when Bargates, the manager of the house, was interrupted at dinner and had himself carried by two litter-bearers right into the middle of the fight. Evidently, he had gout. He had launched into a rabid denunciation of drunks and runaways in a barbarous voice when he spotted Eumolpus: "Is that you, most eloquent of poets?" he said. "Then these worthless slaves had better quit fighting and get out of here now!" . . .

[Bargates to Eumolpus] "My mistress has taken on airs. So please bad-mouth her in your verse, so she'll show a little respect. . . ."

[97] While Eumolpus was conferring in secret with Bargates, a town crier entered the inn along with a policeman and a fair-sized crowd. Waving a torch that shed more smoke than light, he issued this proclamation:

WANTED: A BOY RECENTLY LOST IN THE PUBLIC BATHS. AGE: ABOUT 16. CURLY-
HAIRED; DELICATE; HANDSOME; CALLED "GITON." WHOEVER TURNS HIM IN OR
REVEALS HIS WHEREABOUTS WILL RECEIVE ONE THOUSAND IN COIN.

Near the crier stood Ascyltos wearing a motley-colored shirt and holding
up the proclamation and the reward money on a silver tray. I told Giton
to jump under the bed and hook his hands and feet in the straps that hold
the mattress to the frame; that way, like old Ulysses clinging to the ram,[44]
he could hang beneath the frame and dodge the hands of the search party.
Giton didn't waste any time. In a split second, he had his hands bound in
place—and Ulysses beaten at his own game! To leave no room for suspicion, I stuffed the bed with clothes and arranged them in the shape of a
man about my size.

Meanwhile, after Ascyltos had gone through everyone's room with an
assistant he reached mine and his hopes rose seeing how carefully the door
was bolted shut. The policeman stuck an axe in the joints and dislodged
the bolts. I knelt before Ascyltos' knees and in memory of our friendship
and all the trouble we'd been through together I begged him to let me at
least see my dear friend. In fact, to make my feigned prayers more credible,
I said, "Ascyltos, I know you've come to kill me. Isn't that why you brought
the axe? So, quench your anger: look, here is my neck! Spill my blood!
That's what you came for under the pretense of this search!"

Ascyltos brushed my charge aside saying that he really sought nothing
but his "runaway" and desired the death of no suppliant, let alone one
whom he had continued to cherish even after a nasty quarrel.

[98] But the cop wasn't so easily handled: he got a cane from the innkeeper, rammed it under the bed, and probed every nick and cranny
along the wall. Giton squirmed out of reach and, while desperately trying
to hold his breath, stuck his face right into the bedbugs. . . .

Next Eumolpus burst in—the broken door couldn't keep anyone out—
talking very excitedly: "I just picked up a thousand in cash! All I have to
do is go after that official and tell him you have Giton—betraying you as
you so richly deserve!"

He persisted in making this threat until I was hugging his knees and
begging him to spare the dying: "Your excitement would be understand-
able, if you knew the boy's whereabouts. But he ran off in the crowd. I
haven't the faintest idea where he went. Be my guest, Eumolpus, bring the
boy back, hand him over to Ascyltos even!"

I'd almost gotten Eumolpus to swallow this, when Giton, who was still

44. In the *Odyssey*, Ulysses (Odysseus) escapes from the Cyclops' cave by tying himself to the
underside of a ram.

holding his breath, suddenly let loose a torrent of sneezes that shook the
bed to its frame. Eumolpus turned toward the commotion and said dryly,
"Bless you, Giton." When the mattress was pulled back, he saw a Ulysses
even a hungry Cyclops would have pitied.

Eumolpus turned on me next: "What is this, you thief? You didn't have
the nerve to tell me the truth even when you were caught red-handed.
No, if god in his wisdom hadn't excited a sneeze from our pendant hero,
I'd be wandering around the local dives on a fool's errand. . . ."

Giton was far smoother than I. First, he treated a cut over Eumolpus' eye
with spider webs soaked in oil. Then he removed Eumolpus' torn jacket
and gave him his own little cloak; finally, he hugged Eumolpus, who was
already softening up, and applied kisses like a soothing salve. "Dearest
father, we are in your hands. If you love your Giton, now is the time to
save him. I wish hungry flames would devour me alone, or a stormy sea
engulf me. I am the motive of all these crimes. I am the cause. If I were
gone, you might be reconciled. . . ."

[99] *[Eumolpus]* "So I have lived in all times and places as if each day I
spent would be my last and never return. . . ."

My eyes brimming with tears I begged and prayed for him to be my
friend again, too. Lovers can't control the madness of jealousy, I insisted,
and I would do my utmost to avoid saying or doing anything else that
would offend him. Only he must heal every sore in his own soul and leave
no scar behind, as befits a man of culture: "Snows linger longer in harsh
uncultivated regions, but where the Earth shines tamed by the plow, a light
frost vanishes as you speak. So it is with anger in our hearts: it obsesses
savage minds but rolls off the cultivated."

"Of course," said Eumolpus, "What you say is true. Look, I kiss my anger
goodbye, so may our affairs prosper! Get your gear together and follow
me, or if you prefer, lead the way."

He was still talking when the door creaked open and a sailor with a
shaggy beard stood in the doorsill: "You're holding us up, Eumolpus, like
you don't know we're in a hurry."

Without a moment's delay, we all stood up and Eumolpus ordered his
man, who had been asleep for sometime, to get his bags. Giton and I
readied what we had for the journey and I boarded the ship with a prayer
to the stars. . . .

9.15 Suetonius, *Galba* 22

*Galba was the Roman general who was declared emperor at the age of 72 after the
death of Nero, but remained in power only three months, until assassinated through
machinations of his ally Otho.*

As for his sexual desires, he was more inclined to males, and among males only to the very strong and experienced. They said that in Spain, when Icelus, one of his long-time kept men, announced Nero's death to him, he not only received him publicly with intense kisses, but begged him to have himself depilated immediately and then took him aside.

9.16 Selected Pompeian graffiti = *CIL* 4

In 79 C.E. the sudden eruption of Mt. Vesuvius covered Pompeii and several other towns south of Naples with lava, ashes, and mud, preserving them virtually intact until modern times. Graffiti is found throughout the town, some of it sexual in nature.

[1256] Beautiful[45] Sabinus, Hermeros[46] loves you.

[1812] Caesius Fidelis loves Mecon from Nuceria.[47]

[1825] Cosmus, Equitia's slave, is a big pervert *(cinaedus)* and cocksucker, with legs spread apart.

[1825a] Narcissus[48] is the biggest cocksucker.

[1882] Whoever fucks a boy on fire hurts his cock.

[2048] SECUNDUS has fucked boys till they hurt.[49]

[2210] I want to fuck a boy.

[2319b] Vesbinus is a pervert *(cinaedus);* Vitalio has fucked him.

[3932] Here I fuck Rufus, dear to . . . Eat your heart out, girls! Farewell, stuck-up cunt!

[4024] Menander, of elegant habits, costs two nickels.

[4917] Albanus is a pervert *(cinaedus).*

[4976] Sodom and Gomorrah.[50]

[5408] Felix sucks for a nickel.[51]

[7339] Felix costs four nickels, Florus ten.

[8483] Dick for sale: $1.

[8512] Januarius, you lick cock.

[8805] On the ninth of September, Q. Postumius asked A. Attius to allow me to fuck him.

45. This epithet transliterates the Greek word *kalos,* found in so many Greek inscribed love acclamations.

46. The name also appears as that of a freedman in Petronius. It is Greek in form.

47. Nuceria was a nearby town to the south of Pompeii. Fidelis could also be an epithet meaning "the faithful."

48. Like Cosmus in the previous fragment, the name is Greek, suggesting servile or freedman status.

49. The name is written in larger letters, suggesting that this inscription was meant as a boast.

50. This inscription attests either a Christian or, more likely, Jewish community at Pompeii that did not approve of the prevailing sexual customs.

51. The monetary values here are relative, based on one *as* equal to five cents.

[**8841**] Martial, you suck Proculus.

[**9027**] Secundus is a cocksucker of rare ability.

[**10232a**] L. Habonius plows Caesonius Felix and puts it in his mouth.

9.17 Greek graffito from Stabiae

Stabiae was a fashionable resort immediately to the south of Pompeii, also destroyed in 79 C.E.

If a beautiful boy doesn't give his ass to be fucked, may he not get a fuck when he falls in love with a beautiful girl.

9.18 Martial 1.90

Martial was a prolific writer of barbed, satirical epigrams on the follies of his time. The first two books were published in 86 C.E., and the remainder at one- or two-year intervals thereafter.

Because I never saw you joined with males, Bassa,
    And no gossip gave an adulterer to you,
But a mob of your own sex always performed
    Every task around you, and no man came near,
You seemed to me, I confess, a real Lucretia;[52]
    But you, disgraceful to say, were fucking women.
You dare to bring twin cunts together
    And your monstrous Venus counterfeits a man.
You have invented a freak worthy of the Theban riddle:[53]
    That here, where no man is, there can be adultery.   10

9.19 Martial 1.92

Often Cestos complains to me, with his dear eyes all tearful,
    That he is being touched by your finger, Mamurianus.
No need for a finger: you can have all of Cestos,
    If nothing else is lacking to you, Mamurianus.
But if you have neither a stove nor a naked futon frame
    Nor a broken-off cup like the one Chione has, or Antiope;
If your coat hangs over your groin like a scribbled-on piece of paper,
    And a Gallic jacket covers your butt halfway,

---

52. In other words, a woman of the utmost sexual integrity. See n. 18.

53. The riddle of the Sphinx, who killed her victims when they could not answer. Oedipus finally solved her riddle and freed Thebes from her depredation.

And you feed on only the steam of a black kitchen
   And you drink dirty water lying on your face with your dog,   10
I'll dig out with my finger your one remaining eye—
   Not your asshole, because it's not an asshole if it never shits.
And you're not going to call me jealous, nor evil-minded, either.
   Just bugger, Mamurianus, when you're full.

9.20 Martial 2.51

Often when there's just one dollar left in your wallet,
   And even it's more worn than your asshole, Hyllus,
Still it's not the baker who'll take it away from you, not the bartender,
   But some guy who's proud of his oversized dick.
Your poor belly just watches the feast for your asshole
   And always goes hungry, while the other one gobbles.

9.21 Martial 3.71

When your boy's prick hurts, Naevolus, along with your asshole,
   I'm no fortuneteller, but I know what you're doing.

9.22 Martial 4.42

If someone by chance would give one to me when I asked,
   I'll tell you, Flaccus, what kind of boy I'd ask for.
First, let this boy be born on the banks of the Nile:
   No country knows better how to get up to mischief.
Let him be whiter than snow: for by dusky Lake Mareotis[54]
   That color is more lovely, the rarer it is.
Let his eyes contest with stars, let his soft locks whip
   His shoulders; curled hair I don't like, Flaccus.
Let his forehead be low, let his nostrils hook just lightly,
   Let his lips be red to rival the roses of Paestum.   10
And let him often force me when I don't want to, and deny me when I do,
   Let him often act more like a free man than his master;
And let him fear boys, and often shut out girls;
   A man to the rest, let him be a boy to me alone.
"Now I know, and you're not wrong; for in my judgment it's the truth.
   Just such a one," you'll say, "was my Amazonicus."

54. A lake at the western edge of the Nile delta.

9.23 Martial 6.33

You've never seen a thing, Matho, more miserable than the bugger
    Sabellus, though before there was nobody happier.
Robbery, runaways, dead slaves, house burned down—troubles
    Beset the man; poor fellow, he even fucks women.

9.24 Martial 6.50

When Telesinus used to hang around with clean friends,
    He walked around dirty in a cold, skinny shirt;
Now that he's started making up to filthy fags *(cinaedi)*,
    He's the one buying silver, tables, country estates.
You want to get rich, Bithynicus? Be in the know.
    Clean kisses will give you nothing, or very little.

9.25 Martial 7.58

Already you have married six or seven fags, Galla,
    While long hair and a combed beard please you excessively.
Finally, when you've experienced their flanks and their groins
    Most like a wet thong, nor made to stand by your weary hand,
You leave unwarlike bedrooms and a soft husband,
    And you fall all over again into the same kind of bed.
Look for some man always talking of the Curii and Fabii,[55]
    Shaggy and savage, with harsh country manners.
You'll find him, but the somber crowd also has its fags:
    It's difficult to marry a real man, Galla.   10

9.26 Martial 7.67

The lesbian Philaenis[56] buggers boys
And, more savage than the hard-on of a husband,
She bangs eleven girls a day.
And she plays ball, wearing gym shorts,
And she gets dirty with the sand of the playing field,
And lifts weights, heavy for fags,[57] with an easy arm,
And, muddy from the dirty wrestling ring,

---

55. Heroes of the early Roman Republic.
  56. Several Greek authors of the third century B.C.E. ascribe to a courtesan of this name a manual of sexual positions.
  57. The Latin word here is *drauci*.

She takes a beating from the oiled instructor.
Nor does she dine or recline before
She has puked up seven pints of undiluted wine;   10
To which she thinks she should return
When she has eaten sixteen steaks.
After all this, when she's feeling sexy,
She doesn't give blowjobs (she thinks this isn't macho enough),
But she just eats the middles of girls.
May the gods give you back your brain, Philaenis,
If you think it's macho to lick cunt.

9.27 Martial 7.70

Philaenis, lesbian of the lesbians themselves,
You rightly call the woman you fuck your "girlfriend."

9.28 Martial 10.98

When a waiter freshens up my wineglass
Who's more languid than the fag of Mt. Ida,[58]
Better dressed than your daughter or your wife
Or your mother or your sister, at the table,
Do you want me to look at the light fixtures,
Or your old mahogany, or your Indian ivory?
To allay your suspicions at dinner,
Give me your field hands, from your dirty plantation,
Crop-haired, shock-headed, crude and no-account,
Sons of some goaty pig-farmer.   10
This anxiety is going to ruin you: Publius,
You can't have these morals and these waiters.

9.29 Martial 11.87

Once you were rich, but then you were a bugger
    And no woman was known to you for a long time.
Now you're chasing old women. What poverty makes us do!
    It even made you fuck women, Charidemus.

---

58. The Latin word is *cinaedus*. The reference is to the Galli, the eunuch devotees of the
Asian mother goddess, whose cult was centered on Mt. Ida in Phrygia.

9.30 Martial 11.88

Charisianus denies that he's been able
To bugger anyone now, for many days.
And when his friends were asking him the reason,
He said it was that he was down with diarrhea.[59]

9.31 Martial 12.96

Since the fidelity and lifestyle of your husband are well known
    To you, nor does any other woman burden or trouble your bed,
Why, like a foolish woman, do you torture yourself about slave-boy rivals,
    Whose love is both brief and transitory?
I will prove to you how the boys do more for you than for their master:
    They see to it that you are the only woman for your husband;
They give what you as a wife do not wish to give. "I do give it," you say,
    "Lest the love of my husband stray wandering from my bedroom."
It's not the same thing. I want a Chian fig, not a *marisca*.[60]
    Lest you doubt which is the Chian, yours is the *marisca*.   10
The wife and woman ought to know their own limits:
    Let boys use their own part, you use yours.

9.32 Statius, *Silvae* 2.6.21–57

This poem consoles the young jurist Flavius Ursus for the loss of his beloved slave Philetas, who died at the age of fifteen. It was published around 92–93 C.E.

What if he were not a slave? I have seen him and marked
His bearing, wanting only you as master. A nobler spirit
Was in his face; his character was clear in his youthful blood.
Greek and Roman brides would wish to conceive
Such a son. Not so beautiful was haughty Theseus,
When the cunning Cretan girl led him back by a thread,[61]
Nor rustic Paris, when off to see a Spartan love,
He set the unwilling pines onto the sea.[62]

59. In other words, he is revealed as a passive rather than active partner.

60. A larger variety of fig. "Fig" and "marisca" are also used as slang terms for hemorrhoids.

61. As a teenage youth, Theseus killed the Minotaur and was led back out of the Cretan labyrinth by the thread of Ariadne, the princess who had fallen in love with him.

62. Ancient ships were typically built out of pine, which was a light wood. The reference here is to Paris' rape of Spartan Helen. Like Theseus, Paris was a mythological example of male beauty.

I kid you not, nor does poetic license lead me astray.
I saw him and still see him, fairer than Achilles, whom   30
Thetis hid on a beach full of girls, only singing of wars,[63]
Fairer than Troilus, when the lance of a Haemonian hand
Caught him, fleeing around cruel Apollo's walls.[64]
What a beauty you were! Fairer by far than all boys
And men, only less fair than your master. His splendor
Alone ranks higher, as the bright moon
And evening star outshine all other fires.
No female adornment was in your face or soft expression
In your brow, like those whose sex is changed
After the crime of doubtful gender,[65] but a manly and strong   40
Ease. Like Parthenopaeus,[66] handsomely visored,
Your gaze was not wanton, but your eyes seductive
With their stern fire. Your hair was carefree in stylish abandon,
Your cheeks not yet besieged, but gleaming
With first down. Such youth does Eurotas rear
With Leda's stream;[67] such a boy, pure in his youth,
Comes to Elis and lays his first years before Jupiter.[68]
With what strain of verse could I trace how modesty,
Calm temperance of character and a spirit more mature
Than his tender age came into his young mind? Often he reproached   50
Even his master and aided him with zeal and lofty
Counsel. With you he was gay or sad; never in his own humor,
He took his countenance from yours,
Worthy of outstripping Haemonian Pylades[69]
And the Athenian friends[70] in his repute. But let his praise
Have what end Fortune allows. No more loyal
Did Eumaeus with aching heart hope for slow Ulysses' return.[71]

---

63. To prevent her son from being taken off to fight in the Trojan War, Thetis dressed the seventeen-year-old Achilles as a girl and hid him on the island of Scyros.

64. Troilus was the most handsome son of Priam, killed by Achilles (who was born in Haemonia = Thessaly). The walls of Troy were built by Apollo and Poseidon.

65. I.e., castration.

66. One of the Seven against Thebes, a fair youth whose name implies a certain androgyny (*parthenos* = maiden).

67. Eurotas was the river that passed through Sparta, of which Leda (the mother of Helen) was the mythological queen. Spartan boys were famous for their strict upbringing and ability to endure hardship.

68. Elis is the region around Olympia. The athletic festival was sacred to Zeus (Jupiter).

69. Pylades was the loyal friend and companion of Orestes through all his travails.

70. Probably Theseus and Pirithous, another pair of renowned companions.

71. In the *Odyssey*, Eumaeus was the loyal swineherd who helped Odysseus (Ulysses) after his return to Ithaca.

9.33 (Anonymous), *Letter to Epaphroditus = P.Oxy.* 3070

The following short letter, written in Greek, was found on a first-century papyrus from Egypt. On the reverse side, it is addressed "give this to our dearest Epaphroditus." It is accompanied by a crude drawing that is captioned "erection and anus."

Apion and Epimas say to our dearest Epaphroditus,[72] "if you give us the opportunity to screw you in the rear, it will be good for you. We will no longer beat you up, if you give us the opportunity to screw you in the rear. Farewell, farewell."

9.34 Quintilian 2.2.14–15

Quintilian was a rhetorician who wrote on the education of an ideal orator. His work was probably published during Domitian's reign (81–96 C.E.). This section discusses the best type of teacher.

[14] I do not approve of younger and older boys sitting together in a classroom. For even if such a man as one would want is set over their studies and character and can keep the young modest, the weak should still be separated from the stronger, and not only the charge of moral turpitude, but even the suspicion of it should be avoided. [15] I have considered that these matters should be briefly noted. That the teacher himself and his school be free from the worst vices I think hardly even needs to be said. And if there is anyone who in selecting a teacher does not avoid obvious moral misconduct, let him know that if this factor has been overlooked, everything else we try to devise for the benefit of the young is utterly futile.

9.35 Quintilian 11.1.84

In the penultimate book of his work, Quintilian considers issues of delivery and performance on the part of an orator.

There is greater trouble when one makes a complaint concerning shameful matters, such as an act of sexual immorality, especially among males, or an act of oral violation. I do not even propose the victim speaking: for what would be appropriate for him other than groans, tears, and cursing of his life, so that the judge could understand his grief rather than hear him describe it. But the advocate will also have to express himself similarly, since it is more shameful for those having suffered this kind of injury to confess it than for those who dared to do it.

72. This is elsewhere always found as a slave name.

9.36 Calpurnius Flaccus, *Declamation* 3

The date of Calpurnius Flaccus is uncertain, but appears most likely to belong to the early second century C.E. This controversy summarizes arguments both in defense and prosecution.

A young soldier of Marius' army killed a relative of Marius, a tribune, because he attempted to rape him.[73] He is a defendant for murder.

[**Defense case**] "A relative of the commander has been killed," he says.[74] Well done, young man! You have delivered Marius from having to do it. Whenever a man's modesty is endangered, he has the law on his side. What were you doing, tribune? Was he not yet a man in your eyes, when he was already a soldier in Marius' view? One who, when asked to undertake an immoral sexual act, merely says no is not far from acquiescing. Believe me, commander,[75] your soldier would have held a low opinion of you, if he had spared the tribune in this case. Verginius avoided this kind of rape by killing his daughter; on account of this disgrace Lucretia stabbed herself.[76] I am ashamed, commander, that I have to defend a soldier with examples of women. Did the man threaten your soldier with an immoral sexual act? What the Cimbri[77] threaten us with is less bad.

[**Prosecution case**] Your soldier, commander, must have some share of immodesty, because he pleases another's immodesty. You[78] stained your sword with the blood of a fellow soldier whom it would have been enough to threaten.

9.37 Calpurnius Flaccus, *Declamation* 20

One of two twin brothers is a prostitute, and the other explains in the Senate the reasons for his wishing to commit suicide:

"Senators, if only my brother wished to die! Why must a modest man like me say things about his own brother that are so disgraceful he is ready to die so as not to see them? You know us, senators. We are, in fact, known to more men than our age and due modesty makes appropriate. My brother has been taken away from me and violated by the most corrupt and worth-

---

73. This is the same incident described in **7.21**.

74. The defense tries to anticipate the arguments of the prosecutor.

75. Here Marius is addressed, who is imagined as the judge in this case.

76. Both were notable legends of the early Republic about the right of citizens to avenge maltreatment by their rulers. On Lucretia, see n. 18. Verginius killed his daughter rather than see her raped by the decemvir Appius Claudius in 449 B.C.E. Both incidents led to citizen rebellions.

77. A warlike tribe from Denmark that invaded Italy in 101 B.C.E. The war against them was the context of this incident.

78. Now he addresses the accused soldier.

less companions. With High Living as his captain and Extravagance rowing, or rather sailing, his ship, he has been thrown onto the rocks of sexual immorality and the shipwreck of his own reputation. By the faith of men and gods! In what kind of state is it possible for a man to be prostituted, but not to die? Do you think it is consistent for this deliberative body to permit a shameful life and prohibit another man from an honorable death? I couldn't bear to live if I saw this even in my sister's case. These men are deviant lechers, who compensate for the loss of their own boyhood by mutual disgrace."

9.38 Juvenal, *Satire* 2

Juvenal was the most vehement of the Roman verse satirists. This poem was probably published at some point during the first decade of the second century C.E.

One longs to escape from here beyond Sarmatia[79] and the frozen
Sea, when some people dare to pronounce on morality—those who
Affect the Curii's[80] style while living a Bacchic orgy.
First, they are ignorant, in spite of the plaster casts of Chrysippus[81]
That fill their houses. The nearest any of them comes to culture
Is to buy a copy of Aristotle's head or Pittacus'[82] image,
Or to have an original bust of Cleanthes placed on their sideboard.
Faces are not to be trusted. Why, every street is just full
Of stern-faced sodomites.[83] How can you lash corruption when *you*
Are the most notorious furrow among our Socratic fairies?[84]   10
Hirsute limbs, it is true, and arms that are stiff with bristles,
Bespeak "a soul of adamant"; but your anus is smooth, as the surgeon
Notes with a grin when he takes a knife to your swollen piles.
Such fellows rarely talk. They've a mighty passion for silence;
And they keep their hair as short as their eyebrows. Peribomius,[85] therefore,
Provides a more honest and genuine case. *That* I put down to

79. An area on the fringe of the civilized world corresponding to southern Russia and the Ukraine.

80. Curius Dentatus was censor in 272 B.C.E. and a stereotypical figure of austere early Republican morality.

81. Active in the late third century B.C.E., the third head of the Stoic school after Zeno and Cleanthes.

82. One of the traditional Seven Sages of archaic Greece.

83. The Latin word here is *obsceni*, literally "obscene men."

84. Despite Socrates' strict abstention from homosexual acts, according to Plato and Xenophon, the pederastic atmosphere surrounding some of the Platonic dialogues led to his characterization as a pederast by later authors.

85. The Peribomii appear to have been a cult society openly professing homosexuality; they may be connected with the Galli of the Asian mother goddess.

The workings of fate.[86] His walk and expression proclaim his disorder.
Such folk, by their candor, call for pity; their very obsession
Secures indulgence. Far worse are those who condemn perversion
In Hercules' style,[87] and having held forth about manly virtue,   20
Wriggle their rumps. As the vile Varillus retorted to Sextus:
"Am I to respect a spaniel like you? You're no better than I am!"
Let the straight-limbed laugh at the cripple, the white at the negro;
But who could endure the Gracchi[88] inveighing against sedition?
Would you not think the sky had fallen and the seas run dry,
If Verres[89] expressed an abhorrence of thieves, and Milo[90] of murderers?
If Clodius[91] railed at seducers of wives, Catiline at Cethegus;[92]
If Sulla's trio of pupils thundered against proscriptions?[93]
Lately we saw such a man—an adulterer stained by a union
Worthy of the tragic stage—reviving harsh legislation   30
Which brought alarm to all, even to Mars and Venus,[94]
At the very time when Julia was relieving her fertile womb
Of so many a fetus, with every lump the image of Uncle.[95]
So isn't it fair and just that the most depraved should be scornful
Of bogus Scauri[96] and, when chastised, should snap in reprisal?

   When one of those grim-faced ascetics was crying "O Julian law,[97]
Where are you now? Wake up!" Laronia[98] could not endure it,

---

86. This passage seems to acknowledge the notion that some men are born effeminate and homosexual.

87. Hercules was an ethical model for the Stoics because he chose a life of hardship and virtue over pleasure and vice.

88. Popular reformers of the late second century B.C.E., accused by their enemies of fomenting mob violence.

89. The governor of Sicily prosecuted by Cicero for extortion (see **7.57**).

90. The murderer of Clodius Pulcher, defended by Cicero (see **7.63**).

91. On Clodius, see **7.38**, **7.60–62**.

92. On Catiline, see **7.58**. Cethegus was a bloodthirsty lieutenant of the dictator Sulla in the 80s B.C.E.

93. The reference is probably to the Second Triumvirate of Octavian, Mark Antony, and Aemilius Lepidus, styled as pupils of Sulla because they adopted his style of mass execution of senatorial opponents.

94. An adulterous couple among the gods. Mars was the father of Rome as the father of Romulus, Venus the mother of Rome as the mother of Aeneas.

95. The reference is to the emperor Domitian (81–96 C.E.), who impregnated his niece Julia and then forced her to have an abortion, from which she died in 89. At about the same time, he renewed the enforcement of old Augustan legislation against adultery.

96. Aemilius Scaurus was censor in 109 B.C.E. and was thus, like Curius, a paradigm of Republican moral austerity.

97. The Augustan law against adultery revived by Domitian.

98. This woman is unknown, but the name is that of a respectable family. She is probably either an adulteress prosecuted by Domitian or a courtesan.

And answered thus with a smile: "It's a happy age that has you, sir,
To reform its morals; Rome had better clean itself up;
A third Cato[99] has dropped from the sky! But seriously, tell me,   40
Where did you get that lovely scent that is wafted in waves
From your hairy neck? You mustn't be shy about naming the shop.
If laws and statutes have to be wakened, you'd better begin, then,
By calling the Scantinian.[100] Turn your attention first to the menfolk,
And scrutinize *them*. What they do is worse, yet they are defended
By their sheer numbers—serried ranks with shields interlocking.
Great unanimity reigns amongst effeminates; women
Provide not a single case of such disgusting behavior.
Tedia doesn't lick Cluvia's body, nor Flora Catulla's.
Hispo accommodates men and is addicted to both perversions.[101]   50
Do any of us plead at the bar, or set up to be experts
In civil law, or disturb your courts by causing an uproar?
Few of us wrestle; few of us feed on fighters' meat.
You card wool; and when you have finished, you carry the fleeces
Back in baskets; you twirl the big-bellied spindle, and finger
The fine-spun thread, Penelope's peer, more deft than Arachne,[102]
Much like that slighted woman who sits, unkempt, on a tree-stump.[103]
Everyone knows why Hister bequeathed his all to a freedman,
And why, when he lived, he showered gifts on his girlish wife.[104]
The woman who sleeps third in a bed is bound to be wealthy.   60
Marry and shut your mouth; the price of silence is rubies.
In view of all this, does our sex deserve the verdict of guilty?
Our censor's rule condemns the doves while acquitting the ravens."[105]

   On hearing such evident truths our Stoic brethren decamped
In disorder; for who could deny what Laronia said? But what

---

   99. Cato the Censor (see **7.17**) and Cato the Younger (who died fighting to save the Republic from Caesar) were both models of Republican moral virtue.
   100. A law against corrupting a Roman youth or sexual passivity on the part of a Roman citizen, first enacted in 149 B.C.E. See **7.5**.
   101. It is unclear whether this means that he was both active and passive or that he enjoyed both oral and anal penetration.
   102. Weaving and spinning were, of course, women's tasks. Penelope is represented in the *Odyssey* as spending countless hours weaving a funeral shroud for her father-in-law, Laertes. Arachne is represented in Ovid's *Metamorphoses* as the most skilled weaver among humans, but is changed by Athena into a spider.
   103. Perhaps a reference to the mythological princess Antiope, in servitude to Dirce, her cruel aunt.
   104. I.e., to buy her silence.
   105. Ravens are not only blacker than doves (and thus more guilty), but popular belief held that they copulated through their mouths; they are accordingly a suitable metaphor for homosexual men.

Will the others stop at when Creticus[106] wears a dress of chiffon,
And, as the audience stares at his clothes, inveighs against wives
Like Procula, say, or Pollitta? Fabulla dishonors her husband.
Condemn Carfinia too, if you wish. But however guilty,
She'll never be seen in a gown like that.[107] "But this is July, dear;   70
I'm hot!" Then plead in your loincloth; lunacy's less degrading.
What a garb for presenting new laws and enactments
Before a community fresh from its triumphs, with wounds still open—
Mountain folk who have left their ploughs to come and hear you!
Think of what you would say if you saw such clothes being worn
By a judge. I question if even a witness should appear in chiffon.
Creticus, fiery and headstrong, master of fearless expression,
You're shining through![108] This plague of yours has been caught through
            contact,
And will spread to others, as in the country a single pig
With scab or mange can cause the collapse of the total herd,   80
And as one grape can develop mold at the sight of another.
Soon you will venture something worse than a matter of clothing.
No one sinks to the bottom at once. Little by little
You will come to be welcomed within the houses of characters wearing
Bonnets with flowing ribbons, and chokers around their necks.
These placate the Bona Dea[109] with a young sow's belly
And a generous bowl of wine. But inverting the normal custom,
They drive all *women* away and forbid them to enter the doorway.
The goddess's altar is only for men. "Away with you, women,
Outsiders all! No girl plays here on a groaning oboe!"   90
Such were the secret torchlight orgies in which the Dippers
Used to disgust the goddess Cotyto in Cecrops' city.[110]
One, with a slanting pencil, lengthens his eyebrows, touching
Them up with moistened soot; raising his fluttering lids,
He blackens the rims. Another drinks from a phallic wine glass,

106. The ancient commentary on Juvenal tells us that there was an orator named Julius Creticus at the time. He is apparently imagined as one of the prosecutors of the adultery law under Domitian.

107. Women condemned for adultery were forced to wear a toga (the same kind of clothing worn by prostitutes and men) instead of the usual matronly *stola*.

108. I.e., the cloth is so thin as to be transparent.

109. See ch. 7, n. 48 for Clodius Pulcher's transvestism at the rites of the Bona Dea. Juvenal implies that there existed a secret society of transvestite men parodying such rituals, normally open only to women.

110. On the orgiastic rites of Cotyto, see ch. 8, n. 8. **8.3** also refers to transvestism and homosexuality in the context of these rites. Eupolis' comedy *Dippers* (c. 416 B.C.E.) may have referred to such rites at Athens (Cecrops' city).

The billowing mass of his hair confined in a golden hairnet.
He wears a blue-checked robe, or a garment of greenish satin;
And his servant swears by his master's "Juno"—a sign of his gender.[111]
A third is clutching a mirror—the gear of Otho the pathic,[112]
Taken off the Auruncan Actor.[113] He saw himself in it,   100
Clad in full armor just as he ordered the troops to advance.
(A kit in a civil war containing a mirror—now *there's*
A thing that rated a mention in the recent annals and history.[114]
It was surely the mark of a supreme commander to eliminate Galba
And to take care of his skin, to aspire to the throne of the emperor
And to put bread on his face, spreading it out with his fingers.
The quivered Semiramis never did *that* in the realm of Assyria,
Nor did the fierce Cleopatra on board her Actian warship.) [115]
No restraint in language here or respect for the table;   110
Here is Cybele's crew, with their uninhibited babel
Of squeaky voices.[116] A crazy old man with snow-white hair
Presides at the rites, a rare and truly remarkable case
Of voracious greed. He ought to be paid to give master classes.
But why hold back? It's time to follow the Phrygian mode:
Just take a knife, and sever the lump of useless meat.
Four hundred thousand[117] is the size of the dowry given by Gracchus[118]
To a cornet-player (or perhaps his horn was the straight variety).
The contract is signed, the blessing pronounced, a numerous party
Is waiting; the newlywed "bride" reclines in the lap of her husband.   120
Shades of our forefathers! Is it a censor we need, or an augur?

111. In addition to being the name of Jupiter's wife, a "Juno" was a woman's guardian spirit, comparable to a man's "Genius."

112. Otho followed Galba as emperor in 69 B.C.E. Suetonius describes him as effeminate in his personal grooming. Men seldom used mirrors.

113. This phrase is lifted from the *Aeneid*, where it refers to Turnus taking a spear off a slain enemy. It could also be an allusion to Nero, who fancied himself an actor and was born in Antium, in the territory of the Aurunci; Suetonius and Martial suggest that Otho and Nero had homosexual relations.

114. Probably a reference to Juvenal's contemporary Tacitus, whose *Annals* chronicled the reigns of Tiberius, Gaius, Claudius, and Nero, and whose *Histories* dealt with Nero's immediate successors.

115. Semiramis was the queen who was believed to have built Babylon; Cleopatra fought at the side of Mark Antony in the decisive naval battle off Actium in 31 B.C.E.

116. The eunuch Galli, like Attis in **7.48**.

117. Four hundred thousand sesterces is the amount necessary to qualify one for equestrian status, i.e., membership in the nonsenatorial elite of Rome.

118. A descendant of the family distinguished by the Gracchi brothers of the second century B.C.E. This Gracchus was apparently one of the Salii, an aristocratic fraternity of priests of Mars who performed ritual dances with shields on specified holidays.

Would you feel more horror, or think it more appalling a portent,
If a woman dropped a calf, or a cow gave birth to a lamb?
A long dress with veil and flounces is worn by a man
Who carried a sacred shield of Mars by its mystic thong,
Sweating beneath the swaying burden. Father of our city,
From where did such evil come to your Latin shepherds?[119] From where
Did this itch arise, O Lord of War, to plague your descendants?
Look—a man of family and fortune—being wed to a man!
Do you not shake your helmet or bang the ground with your spear,   130
Or complain to your father? Away, then; quit the strenuous acres
Of that great Park[120] which you have forgotten. "At dawn tomorrow
I have to keep an appointment, down in Quirinus' valley."[121]
"What's the occasion?" "What do you think? A friend's being married—
A small affair." Such things, before we're very much older,
Will be done in public—in *public,* and will want to appear in the papers!
These brides, however, are racked by one intractable problem:
They cannot conceive, and hold their husbands by having a baby.
It is well that Nature has given no power to their twisted emotions
Over their bodies. They die without issue. For them no assistance   140
Can be had from the bloated Lyde with her box of fertility drugs,
Nor does it help to proffer their hands to the running Luperci.[122]
(Gracchus surpassed even this enormity when, with tunic
And trident, he appeared as a fighter, and was chased across the arena,
A Roman of nobler birth than the Manlii or the Marcelli,
Yes, or the scions of Catulus and Paulus, or the Fabian family,
Or all the onlookers there in their front-row places, including
The man who provided the show where Gracchus cast his net.)[123]
     That there are such things as spirits of the dead and infernal regions,
The river Cocytus, and the Styx with inky frogs in its waters,   150
That so many thousands cross the stream in a single skiff,[124]
Not even children believe, unless they're still in the nursery.
But let's suppose it's true. What does Curius feel,
Or the Scipios twain? What do Fabricius and the shade of Camillus,

---

119. An evocation of Rome's origins as a simple pastoral village.

120. The Campus Martius, where parades and military exercises were held.

121. Quirinus is an alternate name for the deified Romulus. The Roman forum is probably meant here.

122. The priests of Lupercus (a fertility god) ran through the city dressed in loincloths every February and struck anyone they saw, especially women, with strips of goatskin to make them fertile.

123. Gladiators were normally slaves or condemned criminals. The net fighters were considered the lowest even among the gladiators.

124. A reference to Charon's boat, which ferried souls across the rivers of the Underworld.

And Cremera's legion and the valiant lads who fell at Cannae [125]—
The dead of all those wars—when a ghost like this descends
From the world above? They'd insist on purification, if sulfur
And torches were to be had, and a laurel-twig dipped in water.
There, alas, we process in disgrace.[126] Granted, our armies
Have pushed beyond the Irish coast and the recently captured   160
Orkneys, and also Britain with its paltry ration of darkness.
But things go on at the center of our victorious nation
Which are not done by our conquered foes. They tell us, however,
That a Zalaces born in Armenia, even less manly than our
Jeunesse dorée, has given himself to a passionate tribune.
That's what external relations involve. He came as a hostage;
But Rome is where "men" are produced. If lads from abroad are permitted
A longer stay in the city, they'll never be short of lovers.
They'll get rid of their breeches along with their daggers and whips and
        bridles,[127]
And then return to Artaxata [128] carrying our teenage morals.   170

9.39 Juvenal, *Satire* 9

This satire, addressed to the aging male prostitute Naevolus, was published after 118 C.E.

THE SATIRIST: Tell me, Naevolus—why, whenever we meet, do you wear
    A gloomy scowl, like Marsyas when he had lost the contest?[129]
    Why do you have the expression that Ravola had when I caught him
    With his beard still damp from brushing Rhodope's crotch, and I
        gave him
    The kind of thrashing one gives to a slave found licking a pastry?
    Your face is as tragic as that of Crepereius Pollio,[130] who,
    Though he goes around offering triple interest, can't find a person
    Fool enough to take him on. Why, all of a sudden,
    So many wrinkles? You used to ask little of life, and would play
    The provincial squire, an amusing guest who would make remarks   10

125. A catalogue of great Republican military heroes and battles in which many Romans perished.

126. Like a procession of captives in a Roman triumph.

127. Typical accoutrements of eastern warriors.

128. The capital of Armenia.

129. The satyr Marsyas challenged Apollo to a musical contest, with the prize being that the winner could do whatever he wanted with the loser. After Marsyas lost, Apollo skinned him alive.

130. Referred to elsewhere in Juvenal as a man deeply in debt.

With a trenchant wit, urbane as anything born in the city.
Now all is changed. Your expression is grim; your hair is dry[131]
And as wild as a forest; your skin has totally lost that gloss
Produced by bandages plastered with hot Bruttian pitch;[132]
Hairs are sprouting all over your dirty neglected legs.
What does this mean? You're as thin as a patient in whom a quartan
Fever has long resided, ensuring a regular roasting.
You can tell the mental pain that lurks in a sick man's body;
It's the same with joy. The face derives its smiles and frowns
From within. And so you seem to have altered your style of behavior,   20
And to be going against your previous way of life.
Recently, as I recall, you would hang around Isis' temple,[133]
And Peace's Ganymede,[134] and the Palatine shrine of the immigrant
     mother,[135]
And Ceres[136] too (for women are there in every temple).
Aufidius himself was no better known as a hunter of wives;
And (what you don't divulge) you would also mount their husbands.
NAEVOLUS: Many have made a profit from this kind of life, but I
Have had no return for my efforts. Now and again I am given
A greasy cloak to protect my toga (rough and coarse,
And loose in texture, thanks to the comb of a Gallic weaver),   30
Or a piece of brittle silver from an inferior vein.
Men are governed by fate, including those parts which are hidden
Beneath their clothes. For if the stars are not in your favor,
The unheard of length of your dangling tool will count for nothing,
Even though, when you're stripped, Virro[137] stares at you drooling
And sends you a continuous stream of coaxing *billets-doux*.
As Homer said, it's the queer himself that lures a man on.[138]
And yet, what creature is more grotesque than a miserly pervert?[139]

131. In other words, he no longer uses a pomade.

132. Pine pitch, from Bruttium in the toe of Italy, was used as a depilatory agent by men seeking a youthful appearance.

133. Given the popularity of the Isis cult with women (see **8.21**), her temple was a popular cruising spot to pick up women.

134. The temple of Peace built by Vespasian was adorned with numerous works of art, including apparently a statue of Ganymede. The inclusion of this item in the list suggests that these female cruising spots were also frequented by homosexual men.

135. The Asian mother goddess, Cybele, who had a temple on the Palatine hill.

136. The goddess of agriculture (Demeter), the more traditional Greco-Roman mother goddess, many of whose rites were open only to women.

137. The name may be chosen for its ironic pun on *vir* (man). As it turns out, Virro is anything but manly.

138. This parodies *Odyssey* 16.294, substituting *kinaidos* for *sidēros* (steel).

139. The Latin word here is *mollis*, literally "softy."

"I paid you this; I gave you that; and then you got more."
As he tots it up he wriggles his rump. Well, set out the counters;   40
Send for the slaves and the abacus. Put down five thousand[140] in all
As paid to me. And then put down my heavy exertions.
Do you think it's nice and easy to thrust a proper-sized penis
Into a person's guts, encountering yesterday's dinner?
The slave who plows a field has a lighter task than the one
Who plows its owner. But you, of course, used to think yourself
A pretty young lad, fit to become a butler in heaven.[141]
Will people like you show any kindness to a humble attendant
Or to a client, when you will not pay for your sick diversions?
There is the type to whom you should send big amber balls   50
On his birthday, or perhaps a green umbrella in showery weather
In early spring, when he drapes himself on a chaise lounge,
Fingering the stealthy presents which Ladies' Day[142] has brought him!
Tell me, my sparrow,[143] for whom are you keeping those hills and estates
In Apulia, those kites which are weary from flying across your pastures?
Your Trifoline land with its fertile vineyards, the ridge above Cumae,
And Gaurus' cratered hill provide you with ample reserves.[144]
(Does anyone seal more vats of wine that will last for longer?)
How much would it cost to present an acre or two to the organs
Of your worn-out client? But as things are, that child in the country   60
With his mother and little cottage and playmate pup—is it better
That he should be left in your will to a friend who bashes the cymbals?[145]
"It's impertinent of you to beg," he says. But my rent is shouting
"Beg!" and my slave joins in, as solitary as Polyphemus'
Enormous eye, which let the cunning Ulysses escape.[146]
He's not enough; a second will have to be purchased, and both
Of them fed. So what shall I do when the blizzards blow, I ask you,
What shall I say to my lads in December, when their feet and shoulders
Are chilled by the cold north wind? "Hold on, and wait for the
        cicadas?"[147]
    Even though you conceal and ignore everything else,   70
Don't you attach any value to the fact that, had I not been

---

140. Perhaps the equivalent of $1,000 in modern terms, in other words, not much for a
long-term relationship.

141. In other words, another Ganymede.

142. The Matronalia, on March 1, was a day when husbands gave gifts to their wives.

143. A term of endearment, but sparrows were also considered salacious and promiscuous.

144. Apulia is southeastern Italy. Trifolium, Cumae, and Mt. Gaurus are near Naples.

145. A reference to the Galli, the eunuch devotees of Cybele.

146. Polyphemus is the one-eyed Cyclops, whom Odysseus (Ulysses) blinded in the *Odyssey*.

147. Their return was a sign of summer.

A loyal and devoted client, your wife would still be a virgin?
You know right well how often you begged that favor—the tones
Employed, the promises made. Why the girl was actually leaving
When I caught her in my arms. She had torn up the contract and was
    moving out.
I barely managed to save the situation; it took me all night,
While you were wailing outside. The bed is my witness, and you—
You must have heard the creaking of the bed and the mistress's moaning.
A tottering crumbling marriage just on the verge of collapse
Has, in the case of many a house, been saved by a lover.   80
Why prevaricate? How can you frame a respectable answer?
Does it count for nothing, nothing at all, you ungrateful swindler,
That, thanks to me, you possess a little son and daughter?
You rear them as yours, and you like to proclaim in the daily gazette [148]
The proofs of your manhood. Hang a garland over your door;
Now you're a father! I've given you the means of silencing gossip.
Thanks to me, you have parent's rights; you are listed as heir,
You receive whole legacies, and juicy bequests which celibates forfeit. [149]
As well as bequests, you'll enjoy many another advantage,
If I bring your family up to three.   90
                THE SATIRIST: You have every reason
To feel resentful, Naevolus. But what does he say in reply?
NAEVOLUS: He turns a deaf ear and looks for another two-legged donkey.
    I'm telling you this in total confidence; so keep it secret;
Just lock my protests quietly away inside your memory.
It's fatal to antagonize someone who smooths his body with pumice.
The man who has recently told me his secret is angry and hates me.
He suspects I've given away what I know. He will not scruple
To use a dagger, lay open my head with a bludgeon, and set
My door alight. You mustn't dismiss or ignore the fact that,
For wealth like his, the price of poison is never too high.   100
So keep these things to yourself, like the council of Mars in Athens. [150]
THE SATIRIST: Corydon, Corydon, alas! [151] Do you think a rich man's
    secret
Is ever preserved? If his slaves keep quiet, his horses and dog
Will talk, and his doorposts and statues. Fasten the shutters, and cover

---

148. The *Acta Diurna* kept public records of significant legislative and court actions, as well as registering births, marriages, and deaths.

149. Under Roman law, a childless heir could inherit only half of what was left to him.

150. The Council of the Areopagus, a body of senior magistrates that tried murder cases and had other important constitutional functions.

151. A parody of **8.4.69**, which continues, "what madness seizes you?"

The chinks with curtains; close the door and remove the light;
Have all the guests withdraw; let no one sleep within earshot.
Nevertheless, all that he did at second cock-crow
Will be known before dawn to the local barman, along with whatever
Confections the pastry cook may have dreamt up with the aid of the
    carver
And the chief chef. They'll stop at nothing in inventing charges   110
Against their master; for they use such slanders to take revenge
On the straps.[152] And there'll always be someone to track you down in
    the street
And insist on befuddling your luckless ears with his drunken stories.
They are the people you ought to urge to keep dark the matters
On which, just now, you pledged me to silence. But they would *rather*
Betray a secret than drink stolen Falernian vintage
In the quantities that Saufeia would swill when conducting a service.[153]
There are many reasons for living aright, the best one being
That then you can treat with disdain the wagging tongues of your
    servants.   120
The tongue is always the vilest part of a worthless slave.
NAEVOLUS: The advice you have just been giving is sound, but rather
    general.
What should I do right now, in view of my wasted years
And the ruin of my hopes? As a fleeting flower, the paltry portion
Of our sad and straitened life is hurrying on to finish
Its course. As we drink our wine, as we call for perfume and garlands
And girls—old age, unnoticed, is creeping stealthily up.
THE SATIRIST: Courage! So long as these hills stand firm, you will never
    be short   130
Of a passive friend to support you. From every corner of the world
They all converge on Rome in carriage and ship—the fraternity
That scratches its head with a single finger.[154] A second and greater
Hope remains: (like others, seek out a rich old woman),
You'll be her darling, provided you crunch up plenty of rockets.[155]
NAEVOLUS: Quote these cases to luckier souls. My Clotho and Lachesis[156]

152. The whips with which slaves are punished.

153. Saufeia is elsewhere referred to in Juvenal as the drunken wife of a magistrate, who leads the licentious rites of the Bona Dea, a goddess worshipped only by women. Falernian wine is one of the finest.

154. Effeminate men would be concerned not to disturb their elaborate hairstyle by scratching with more than one finger. Some interpret this gesture as a kind of signal homosexual men would use to communicate their orientation to others.

155. Rocket was a salad green thought to have aphrodisiac properties.

156. Two of the three Fates.

Are well content if my organ provides for my belly's needs.
O little household gods of mine, whose aid I am wont
To secure with meal, or grains of incense and a simple garland,
When shall I net a sum that will save me, when I am old,
From the beggar's mat and crutch? An income of twenty thousand[157] 140
From a well-secured principal; some plain silver (a few little pieces,
Which censor Fabricius, however, would ban),[158] a couple of brawny
Moesian[159] porters to take me upon their shoulders, and let me
Ride serenely above the crowd at the noisy racetrack.
I would like, in addition, a stooping engraver, and also an artist
Quick at producing numerous portraits. That is sufficient.
When shall I ever be merely "poor"? A pitiful prayer
Without much hope. When Fortune is prayed to on my behalf,
She always stops her ears with wax obtained from the vessel
Which was pulled away from Sicily's songs by unhearing oarsmen.[160]   150

157. A very modest amount on an annual basis.

158. Fabricius Luscinus, the censor in 275 B.C.E., expelled a former consul from the Senate for owning about ten pounds of silver vessels.

159. The Moesi were a tribe of central Europe.

160. Odysseus had his fellow sailors stop up their ears with plugs of wax so they would not hear the song of the Sirens, who lured sailors to shipwreck on sharp rocks off the Sicilian coast.

CHAPTER 10

Later Greco-Roman Antiquity

This chapter surveys pagan texts of the second, third, and early fourth centuries C.E. With the exception of a few brilliant epigrammatists such as Meleager, Greek literary activity was for the most part undistinguished during the period from the late third century B.C.E. to the early second century C.E. However, the second century bore witness to a new flowering of intellectual, philosophical, and literary culture in both Greece and Hellenized areas of the Roman Empire, in a movement often known as the "Second Sophistic." Teachers of Greek philosophy and rhetoric (sophists) won renewed prestige and many prose authors rejected the simplified *koinē* Greek language commonly in use in favor of a return to pure Attic models of the classical period. The antiquarian writings of Plutarch, Athenaeus, and Pausanias, to which we owe so much of our knowledge about earlier texts, customs, and places, can be seen as part of this renascence of interest in the once proud past of Greek civilization. Although primarily a movement within Greek letters, the antiquarianism of the Second Sophistic also influenced some Latin authors, including Aulus Gellius and Apuleius.

This cultural flowering no doubt received impetus from the patronage of Hellenophile emperors like Hadrian (117–38 C.E.) and his successors, Antoninus Pius (138–61) and Marcus Aurelius (161–80), but its roots may extend as far back as Nero's time. The emperors' attitudes toward homosexuality varied greatly. Hadrian was explicitly and publicly homosexual in his orientation and erected statues and founded cults throughout the empire to his Greco-Bithynian beloved, Antinous, after the handsome young man's death in a swimming accident. On the other hand, Antoninus Pius and Marcus Aurelius both disapproved of pederasty (**10.8**). Later sources characterize Marcus' son Commodus (emperor 180–92) as guilty of grossly immoral conduct, including a predilection for oral sex (**10.21**). Even more extravagant are the stories about the flamboyant emperor Elagabalus (218–22), who supposedly enjoyed dressing as a woman and acting the role of a prostitute (**10.22–23**). Yet other emperors of the same dynasty were so conservative as to wish to curtail male prostitution even on the part of noncitizens: Septimius Severus (193–211) made it illegal to force a slave into prostitution against his will, and Elagabalus' chosen successor, the young Alexander Severus (222–35), decreed that tax revenue collected from prostitutes was so tainted that it should not be commingled with the public treasury (**10.24**). Philip the Arab (244–49) made male prostitution altogether illegal.

The evidence concerning imperial attitudes at wide variance from one regime to the next suggests a continued ethical polarization around the issue, such as we also observed in the first century C.E. Moral and even oratorical texts such as **10.1**, **10.2**, and **10.4** attack active partners as well as passives; indeed, Dio Chrysostom (**10.1**) describes a progression of sexual addiction in which men who grow bored with prostitution turn to adultery, and when bored with adultery, turn to pederasty. For Dio it is a matter of degeneration over time, but other texts express the difference with a concept of fixed and mutually exclusive categories of sexual preference: one loves either women or boys, but not both, as assumed in many earlier texts, both Greek and Roman. A unique feature of this period is the genre of dialogues enacting debates over sexual preference between advocates of heterosexual love and pederasty: the earliest of these is Plutarch's (**10.3**), narrated by his son, whose very presence affirms his own preference for the heterosexual position. Achilles Tatius (**10.18**) stages a shorter debate as an inset piece within his novel; although neither side is declared a winner, the novel's overall context and assumptions are heterosexual. The lengthiest and most heated debate is transmitted as part of Lucian's corpus (**10.37**), although probably not a work of Lucian himself. The debate's judge renders a split verdict, declaring that all men should marry and only philosophers should love boys, but this is somewhat erroneously interpreted as a victory for the pederastic position.

These debates move beyond mere advocacy of one's preference to disgust with and active intolerance of the other side. While the arguments vary slightly in each of the three debates, there are some common threads: basic to the heterosexual position is the characteristic Stoic appeal to the providence of Nature, which has matched and fitted the sexes to each other. The homosexual position responds that Man should be superior to the animals and capable of rising above the dictates of mere natural survival to a higher form of civilization. Again like the Stoics, the heterosexual sees this "higher civilization" as descent into luxury and dissipation. The pederast's appeal to Platonic justifications is ridiculed by the heterosexual as mere pretense. The heterosexual praises women for retaining their beauty longer and affording mutual pleasure, whereas the pederast's position seems in every case to have its origins in a fundamental hatred of women, whose cosmetics and self-adornment are contrasted unfavorably with boys' natural freshness. Interestingly, the Nature/Art opposition is here turned around and the appeal to Nature is appropriated for the homosexual position. That the increasingly liberated status of women was crucial to the polarization of sexual preferences and the (quite new) construction of pederasty as a form of misogyny is suggested by the situation of Plutarch's dialogue: a wealthy and aggressive widow courts an attractive youth, whose male lover argues against the union, only to be preempted by the widow's kidnapping the young man. The scenario would have been unthinkable in Greece of the classical period. Compare the conflict between a courtesan and a pederastic philosopher over a youth's loyalty in **10.10**, or the science fiction utopia on the Moon—where women do not exist and men reproduce by making boys pregnant (**10.11**).

The specter of female independence and self-assertiveness (adumbrated already in texts about masculine women, like **9.11, 9.18, 9.26–27**) is reflected in the growing evidence for lesbian activity, particularly **10.9, 10.5.132–33.** Among the several dozen magical love spells discovered on Greek papyri or inscribed tablets from Greco-Roman Egypt, at least two (**10.34, 10.36**) involve lesbian relations, suggesting that the phenomenon was far from unknown in real life; the other spells mostly involve men pursuing women, with only one reflecting male-male relations (**10.35**). **10.37.28** employs the horror of lesbianism as the heterosexual speaker's crowning argument against sanctioning any form of same-gender love.

Despite the Stoic arguments against homosexuality as a disruption of the natural order, one finds in this period numerous speculations about natural causes or determinants of sexual orientation. The late astrological treatise of Firmicus Maternus (**10.38–41**) explains a range of same-sex behaviors through the conjunction of the stars at the time of one's birth: effeminacy, pederasty, misogyny, passivity, desire for oral sex, male prostitution, and other forms of gender inversion. Longus' novel *Daphnis and Chloe* (**10.19**) describes a rather unattractive character named Gnathon, who is a "pederast by nature." Physiognomic writers (**10.6–7**) describe physiological and facial characteristics that will help reveal even a closeted effeminate or pervert; this theory makes sense only on the assumption that the behavior itself is also physiologically inbred. Caelius Aurelianus (**10.5**), who is for the most part translating or adapting the work of the earlier Greek physician Soranus, adopts an essentially negative and Stoic view of same-gender sexual behavior, which sees it as a disease of the mind rather than of the body, not something that can be blamed on Nature. He nevertheless records other medical explanations that do see it as in some sense either a genetic mutation at birth or an inbred trait received from degenerate ancestors. Curiously, one of his main concerns is to explain how men can be bisexual or sometimes active and sometimes passive. To some extent, this framework may reflect earlier Greek practices, but he also notes, perhaps reflecting observation of his own era, that such individuals tend to be passive in old age as well as in their youth, since the body is most vulnerable to disease at those times of life. What all of these texts reflect is the perception that sexual orientation is something fixed and incurable.

The second and third centuries C.E. saw the flowering of the Greek romance as a literary form. The plots are built around the glorification of heterosexual marriage and fidelity, but the hero and heroine are typically separated throughout most of their adventures and face sexual threats or temptations from a variety of outsiders, sometimes of the same gender. Gnathon's advances threaten Daphnis' impending marriage to Chloe (**10.19**), but in the end the pederast is foiled and disgraced. Xenophon of Ephesus (**10.16**) and Achilles Tatius (**10.17**) both include pederastic inset tales related by minor characters; and in both cases, the beloved boy dies a tragic death indirectly caused by his lover. The tales therefore appear to contrast the ultimately benign outcome of the heterosexual romance with pederastic relations, which seem to arrest a young man's development and deprive him of mature fulfillment; compare the stories of Hyacinthus and Cyparissus in Ovid (**8.22**). The novels of Lucian (**10.11–13**) and the Latin writer Apuleius (**10.15**) are more satirical, but in all these works we find a heterosexual norm contrasted with a homosexual "alternative."

Two texts from this period show sexual orientation as a matter of relative indifference: Artemidorus' *Dream Analysis* (**10.20**) and Philostratus' *Love Letters* (**10.25–33**). The section of Artemidorus' work dealing with sexual dreams freely intermingles heterosexual and homosexual dreams as if it did not even occur to him that these would be useful categories of division. Non-incestuous forms of male homosexual intercourse fall into his category of "according to nature and convention and customary usage"; the incestuous forms are merely "contrary to convention." The only forms of sex he classifies as "against nature" are sex with oneself, bestiality, necrophilia, sex with gods, and lesbianism. There is no note of moral judgment in Artemidorus' analyses of the dreams; even dreams of incest and sex "against nature" are not necessarily portents of ill fortune. However, dreams involving oral sex are always bad.

Philostratus' *Love Letters* is a collection of twenty-three letters addressed to nameless boys, thirty to women, and the rest, mostly non-erotic, to named individuals. Most striking about the collection is its lack of any consistent point of view, as if the letters were models that could be appropriated by different lovers for different addressees. Virtually every letter to a boy has a corresponding "sister" applying the same motif, but with different allusions and exempla, to a beloved woman. Although Philostratus draws heavily on the topoi of Hellenistic epigram, the letters defy conventional expectations: the topos of the mercenary boy is countered by a detailed argument that poor lovers are better (**10.25**), and the flower as a conventional symbol of youth's temporality is countered by its withering in the presence of a youth's greater beauty (**10.26**). While **10.28** assails a boy with the warning that he will soon grow a beard and lose his bloom, **10.29** assures another that more mature youths with their first beards are preferable. **10.32** encourages a youth to shave and wear his hair long to outwit time, whereas **10.31** praises a boy for his lack of attention to appearance. Amid this welter of contradictory sentiments, there is no consistent line between the qualities praiseworthy in a boy and in a woman.

Bibliographical Note

For general discussions of sexual attitudes in this period, see Boswell (1980) 83–87, E. Cantarella (1992) 173–91, and Robert (1997) 287–329. On the sexual preference debates, see Buffière (1980) 481–541, Foucault (1988) 187–232, E. Cantarella (1992) 70–77, and Goldhill (1995) 102–11, 144–61. Foucault sees in these debates a "de-problematization" of sexuality; Goldhill adds some qualifications. On Plutarch specifically, see Capriglione (1999). See Stephens (1996) on Epictetus and Stoic attitudes in this period.

On Greek love charms, see the general discussions of Winkler (1990) 71–98, Montserrat (1996) 180–203, and Faraone (1999), especially 147–49. On same-sex relations in Greco-Roman Egypt, see Montserrat (1996) 116–17, 136–62. For detailed discussion of **10.34** and **10.36**, see Brooten (1996) 77–113; on **10.34** and **10.35**, see Hunt (1929) and Preisendanz (1930), with the latter interpreting them as attempts to divide the couple; on **10.37**, see the edition and commentary of Daniel and Maltomini (1990) 132–53.

On Firmicus Maternus and other astrological theorists' doctrines concerning sexual orientation, see Brooten (1996) 115–41 and Montserrat (1996) 203–9; Barton (1994) 27–94 gives a good general background. On Polemo and physiognomic theory concerning gender deviance, see Barton (1994) 95–131 and Gleason (1995) 21–81. On Soranus' medical discussion of same-sex behavior, see Schrijvers (1985), Halperin (1990) 22–24, and Brooten (1996) 143–73. On Artemidorus' book of dream interpretation, see Foucault (1988) 3–36, Winkler (1990) 17–44, S. R. F. Price (1990), MacAlister (1992), and Brooten (1996) 175–86. For the best modern edition and commentary on **10.2**, see Musurillo (1954) 33–43, 150–60.

On the pederastic narratives as foils within the Greek romance, see Konstan (1994a) 26–30 and (1994b). On the novels' engagement with philosophical accounts of sexuality, see Goldhill (1995) 46–102. On Lucian's dialogue (**10.9**), see Haley (2002).

10.1 Dio Chrysostom 7.148–52

Dio of Prusa, also known as Chrysostom ("golden mouthed"), was a Greek orator active at the end of the first century C.E. and in the first two decades of the second century. This speech is a late work, influenced by Stoicism, in which he contrasts the pure and simple life of Euboean hunters to the moral corruption of city life. This passage follows a diatribe against prostitution and adultery.

[148] Well, in those cities where the condition of the girls is simply such as we have said, what kind of education and training should we expect the boys to receive? [149] Is it possible that this intemperate race would hold off from abuse and corruption of males and impose upon themselves the clear and sufficient limit decreed by Nature?[1] Wouldn't they rather seek another greater and more illicit form of outrage once they had become in every way sated and full of their unrestrained pleasure with women? [150] Female conquests—especially of freeborn maidens—appeared too easy and effortless for one hunting this game with money. Whoever proceeds with Zeus' device, bearing gold in his hands,[2] will never fail even against proud wives and daughters of truly proud men. [151] But the rest becomes obvious, as we see in many examples. The man who is boundless in such desires, when he finds nothing rare or resistant in that race,[3] despises what is easy and devalues the female Aphrodite, since it is readily available and truly altogether feminine.[4] Instead he will cross over to the male side, desiring to commit shameful acts with those who will in the near future be rulers, judges, and generals, [152] finding here a difficult and seldom acquired species of pleasure. He experiences the same thing as hard drinkers and winos, who after long and uninterrupted binges of drinking don't want to drink any more, but intentionally create thirst through steam-baths and the serving of salty or spicy foods.

10.2 (Anonymous), *Against Maximus* = *P.Oxy.* 471.16–135

This fragmentary speech is from the prosecution of C. Vibius Maximus, a Roman official in Egypt accused of bribery, extortion, and abuse of office. This section adds charges of sexual impropriety with a noble youth at Alexandria. The trial took place in Rome around 108 C.E.

---

1. In other words, confining themselves to heterosexual intercourse.
2. Dio had earlier in the speech used the image of Zeus entering Danae's chamber in a shower of gold to describe the widespread seduction of free women and girls through money.
3. I.e., women.
4. Dio must mean "feminine" here as a synonym for "passive."

The last document[5] sets a seal of authenticity on his serious devotion and love toward the youth. . . . (*16 fragmentary lines follow*) . . .

"Berenicianus will be gymnasiarch until the nineteenth year of the emperor's reign, then Anicetus until his twenty-ninth year."[6] For what reason have you kept silent about these things? Will you say that you were deceived or that you took bribes? It is advantageous to confess only the lesser crime. We say that you did not accept payment, but gave it.

What more? A seventeen-year-old boy dined with you every day. Any man who was deemed worthy of your entertainment (and once you became king,[7] you did not dispense such favors readily) has seen the boy at your banquets, both with his father and alone. He has seen both the shameless glance and shameless negotiations of male lovers.

And what else? He was accustomed to greet you with a kiss every day. Those men bear witness, by your good fortune, my lord:[8] while they were waiting to greet Maximus in the morning . . . (*4 fragmentary lines follow*) . . . and were gathered outside his door, they saw the boy coming out of his bedroom alone, all but exhibiting signs of his intimacy with Maximus. Once he had become habituated to shame, this handsome youth of prosperous family grew so affected and arrogant that in everyone's presence he grabbed the hands of the chamberlain Eutychus and played games with him, and burst out in loud and uncontrolled laughter in the midst of the men lined up to pay morning respects to Maximus. He was not naive, but openly advertised to the money-lenders what he did with Maximus.

Why did you,[9] so modest and austere in appearance, not prevent him? But if a poor man in cheap clothing makes a petition to you, you order that his property, his wife's, and that of his friends be confiscated. And you condemned a man to death for sitting in the theater clad in garments that were not white. But this beardless and still . . . and handsome youth you kept in the *palace* all day, no longer sending him to school or to the gymnastic exercises fitting for young men. How much more justly would you have blamed a father who did not attend to his son's pedagogy? . . . (*5 fragmentary lines follow*) . . .

---

5. An affidavit has just been read.

6. These are apparently the words of Maximus' decree concerning the office of supervisor of gymnasia. The nineteenth year of Trajan's reign would begin in 115, the twenty-ninth (had he lived that long) in 125. Maximus is here accused of interfering unlawfully in the selection of gymnasiarchs. This charge may be inserted into the section about his relationship with a noble youth because the office of gymnasiarch was one that demanded high moral integrity to prevent sexual abuse of boys who exercised at the gymnasia (see 2.28). The accuser's implication may be that Maximus appointed individuals whom he could bribe to allow him access to boys.

7. The accuser speaks metaphorically.

8. An oath addressed to the emperor Trajan.

9. The speaker addresses Maximus again.

You traversed all Egypt with the youth. Did he, as a seventeen-year-old boy, not follow you to the rostrum of every marketplace tribunal? Wasn't he with you in Memphis and Pelusium and wherever else you went, Maximus? All the rest of us avoid your travels and tribunals, so that . . .

10.3 Plutarch, *Dialogue on Love* 1–12

Plutarch was a historian and writer of quasi-philosophical dialogues active at the end of the first century and in the first two decades of the second century C.E. This dialogue must be a relatively late work, since it depicts his grown son Autobulus telling a friend about a debate on love at which Plutarch himself was present.

[1] FLAVIAN: It was on Helicon, Autobulus, that you say the conversation on love took place of which at our request you are now going to give us an account? Either you made a record of it or got it by heart from frequent probing of your father.

AUTOBULUS: Yes, Flavian, it was on Helicon, in the shrine of the Muses, while the people of Thespiae were celebrating the Erotidia.[10] This they do every four years in honor of Eros as well as the Muses, with great zeal and splendor.

FLAVIAN: Are you aware of the petition that all of us who have come to you intend to present?

AUTOBULUS: No, but I shall be when you state it.

FLAVIAN: Discard for the moment from your recital the meadows and shady nooks of the poets, the gadding growth of ivy and smilax, and all the other commonplaces on which writers seize, as they endeavor with more enthusiasm than success to endorse their work with Plato's Ilissus, his famous *agnus castus,* and the gentle grass-grown slope.[11]

AUTOBULUS: My dear Flavian, why should my discourse need such preliminaries? The situation that gave rise to the debate merely wants a chorus to sympathize and lacks a stage, for no other element of drama is wanting. Only, let us pray to the Mother of the Muses[12] to be graciously present and help me to resuscitate the story.

[2] A long time ago, before I was born, when my father had only recently married my mother, he rescued her from a dispute that had

---

10. Mt. Helicon, about 6,000 feet high, is the tallest mountain in Boeotia and was considered sacred to the Muses. The nearby town of Thespiae was the principal city of Boeotia in Roman times. Cicero tells us that its colossal statue of Eros was its chief attraction. The Erotidia was a quadrennial festival with athletic and musical contests, perhaps reflecting an original fertility cult.

11. Allusions to the setting of Plato's *Phaedrus* (5.9.229–30).

12. Mnemosyne ("Memory").

broken out between their parents and was so hotly contested that my
father came here to sacrifice to Eros and brought my mother to the
festival; in fact, she herself was to make the prayer and the sacrifice.
His usual friends came with him from home and at Thespiae he found
Daphnaeus, son of Archidamus, the lover of Simon's daughter, Lysandra,
and the most favored of all her suitors. Soclarus, son of Aristion, had
come from Tithora; and there were present also Protogenes of Tarsus
and Zeuxippus of Lacedaemon, friends of his from abroad. My father
said that most of his other Boeotian acquaintances were there.

Now they passed, it seems, the first two or three days in the city, indulging mildly between spectacles in learned conversation in the athletic buildings. After that, routed by a stubborn feud among the harpists
which was preceded by appeals for support and enlisting of partisans,
most of the visitors decamped from the hostile territory and bivouacked
on Helicon as guests of the Muses.

At dawn Anthemion and Pisias joined them, men of some standing
and attached to Bacchon, who was called The Handsome; and because
of their common affection for the youth there was a kind of quarrel between them. You must know that there lived at Thespiae Ismenodora,
a woman conspicuous for her wealth and breeding who led, heaven
knows, over and above this a life of decorum. She had been a widow for
some little time without a word of censure, even though she was still
young and comely. Now Bacchon was the son of an intimate friend of
hers, and Ismenodora, while promoting a marriage between him and a
girl related to herself, had many meetings and conversations with the
youth. The result was that she came to view him with different eyes;
what with hearing, what with saying many kind things about him and
observing the throng of noble lovers who courted him, she was carried
so far as to fall in love with him herself. Her intentions were far from dishonorable: she desired to marry him and be his companion for life. The
situation was startling enough in itself and the boy's mother had mis-
givings that the dignity and splendor of Ismenodora's household were
too grand to suit her loved one. Some of the boy's hunting companions,
moreover, used the discrepancy in ages to deter him. Their making a
joke of the marriage served to counter it more effectively than did the
serious intervention of others. He was still a minor and felt shy of marry-
ing a widow. Nevertheless, he ignored the others and left the decision to
Pisias and Anthemion. The latter was an older cousin of his, while Pisias
was the most sober of his admirers. For this reason, he used his influence against the marriage and took Anthemion to task for surrendering
the young man to Ismenodora. Anthemion, in his turn, found fault with
Pisias, saying that in everything else he was a model, but that as a lover
he was imitating the baser sort in trying to deprive one dear to him of

an estate and an alliance and a great career merely to keep him as long as possible untouched by these matters and a stripping of his clothes in the palaestra.[13]

[3] So to avoid exasperating each other and gradually falling into a rage they had chosen my father and his friends as arbiters and referees and had come to join them. And, just as though it had been arranged in advance, each of them found an advocate in this friendly circle, Anthemion Daphnaeus, Pisias Protogenes. Protogenes, however, set no bounds to his abuse of Ismenodora, at which Daphnaeus exclaimed, "Good heavens, what is one to expect next, if even Protogenes stands by to combat Love, to whom all his time, when he works and when he plays, is devoted, with Love at heart, Love in hand,

Forgetful of learning, forgetful of fatherland?

For it's not just five days' journey, like Laius, that you are away from home.[14] His love traipsed slow, a landlubber, while yours,

Circling on swift wings, flits over the sea[15]

from Cilicia to Athens to look over the handsome lads and make the rounds with them. No doubt it had been some such reason that originally caused Protogenes' journey from home."

[4] This raised a laugh and Protogenes said, "So you think that I'm at war with Love now, do you, and not fighting on his side against lechery and insolence when they try to force the foulest acts and passions into the company of the most honorable and dignified of names?"

"When you say foulest," asked Daphnaeus, "are you referring to marriage, the union of man and wife, than which there has not existed, now or ever, a fellowship more sacred?"

"Why, of course," said Protogenes, "since it's necessary for producing children, there's no harm in legislators talking it up and singing its praises to the masses. But genuine Love has no connection whatsoever with the women's quarters. I deny that it is love that you have felt for women and girls—any more than flies feel love for milk or bees for honey or than caterers and cooks have tender emotions for the calves and fowls they fatten in the dark.

"In a normal state one's desire for bread and meat is moderate, yet sufficient; but abnormal indulgence of this desire creates the vicious habit called gluttony and gormandizing. In just the same way there normally

13. I.e., the wrestling school, frequently a locus of pederastic interaction.
14. The reference to Laius suggests that the line just quoted may be from Euripides' *Chrysippus*, on the exiled Theban king's rape of his host's bastard son.
15. A line of Archilochus.

exists in men and women a need for the pleasure derived from each other; but when the impulse that drives us to this goal is so vigorous and powerful that it becomes torrential and almost out of control, it is a mistake to give the name Love to it. Love, in fact, it is that attaches himself to a young and talented soul and through friendship brings it to a state of virtue; but the appetite for women we are speaking of, however well it turns out, has for net gain only an accrual of pleasure in the enjoyment of a ripe physical beauty. To this Aristippus[16] bore witness when he replied to the man who denounced Lais to him for not loving him: He didn't imagine, he said, that wine or fish loved him either, yet he partook of both with pleasure. The object of desire is, in fact, pleasure and enjoyment; while Love, if he loses the hope of inspiring friendship, has no wish to remain cultivating a deficient plant which has come to its prime, if the plant cannot yield the proper fruit of character to produce friendship and virtue.

"You know the husband in the tragedy who says to his wife:

You hate me? I can lightly bear your hate
And make a windfall of my slighted state.[17]

Yet the man who, not for gain, but for lust and intercourse, endures an evil, unloving woman is no more in love than the husband in the play. Such was the orator Stratocles whom the comic poet Philippides ridiculed:[18]

She turns away: you barely get her braids to kiss.

"If, however, such a passion must also be called Love, let it at least be qualified as an effeminate and bastard love that takes its exercise in the women's quarters as bastards do in the Cynosarges.[19] Or rather, just as there is one eagle, called the true or mountain eagle, which Homer qualifies as 'black' and 'the hunter,' though there are other bastard varieties which catch fish and slow-flying birds in marshes; when they grow hungry, as they often do, they give a famished and plaintive scream —just so: there is only one genuine Love, the love of boys. It is not 'flashing with desire,' as Anacreon says of the love of maidens, or

16. The pupil of Socrates and founder of the Cyrenaic (hedonist) school. Lais was a famous courtesan.

17. Apparently he had married a rich woman. The author of the fragment is unknown.

18. Philippides was a comic poet active in the late fourth and early third centuries B.C.E. Stratocles was a younger opponent of Demosthenes and later a partisan of the tyrant Demetrius Poliorcetes.

19. This gymnasium was the only one in Athens where illegitimate or foreign children were allowed to exercise.

'drenched with unguents, shining bright.' No, its aspect is simple and unspoiled. You will see it in the schools of philosophy, or perhaps in the gymnasia and palaestrae, searching for young men whom it cheers on with a clear and noble cry to the pursuit of virtue when they are found worthy of its attention.

"But that other lax and housebound love, that spends its time in the bosoms and beds of women, ever pursuing a soft life, enervated amid pleasure devoid of manliness and friendship and inspiration—it should be proscribed, as, in fact, Solon did proscribe it. He forbade slaves to make love to boys or to have a rubdown, but he did not restrict their intercourse with women. For friendship is a beautiful and courteous relationship, but mere pleasure is base and unworthy of a free man. For this reason also it is not gentlemanly or urbane to make love to slave boys: such a love is mere copulation, like the love of women."

[5] Though Protogenes would cheerfully have added other arguments, Daphnaeus cut him short. "Good heavens," said he, "many thanks for citing Solon. Let us take him as the criterion of the lover,

> Till he loves a lad in the flower of youth,
> Bewitched by thighs and by sweet lips.

And to Solon you may add Aeschylus, who says:

> You abjured the holy sacrament of the thighs.
> You spurned a profusion of kisses![20]

Others, to be sure, have a good laugh at these gentry for urging lovers to fix their gaze on hams and haunches like priests bent on sacrifice or divination. But I count this as a great argument in favor of women: if union contrary to nature[21] with males does not destroy or curtail a lover's tenderness, it stands to reason that the love between men and women, being normal and natural, will be conducive to friendship developing in due course from favor. For, you see, Protogenes, a woman's yielding to a man was called by the ancients 'favor.'[22] So it was that Pindar declared that Hephaestus was born from Hera 'without favor.' And Sappho addressed a young girl not yet ripe for marriage:

> You seemed to me a small child without favor.

---

20. This line is from the *Myrmidons,* apparently addressed by Achilles to the corpse of Patroclus.

21. The phrase *para physin* might be more accurately translated as "beyond nature" or "not in accordance with nature."

22. The Greek word is *charis.*

And Heracles is asked by someone or other,

> Did you persuade the girl or take your favor by force?

But to consort with males (whether without consent, in which case it involves violence and brigandage; or if with consent, there is still weakness and effeminacy on the part of those who, contrary to nature, allow themselves in Plato's words 'to be covered and mounted like cattle')—this is a completely ill-favored favor, indecent, an unlovely affront to Aphrodite.

"Whence I conclude that those verses I quoted were written by Solon when he was still quite young and 'teeming,' as Plato says, 'with abundant seed.' Here, however, is what he wrote when he had reached an advanced age:

> Dear to me now are the works of the Cyprus-born,[23]
> Of Dionysus and the Muses, works that make men merry,

as though after the pelting storm of his love for boys he had brought his life into the peaceful sea of marriage and philosophy.

"If, then, Protogenes, we have regard for the truth, excitement about boys and women is one and the same thing: Love. But if, for the sake of argument, you choose to make distinctions, you will see that this boy-love of yours is not playing fair: like a late-born son, an aged man's bastard, a child of darkness, he tries to disinherit the Love that is his legitimate and elder brother. It was only yesterday, my friend, or the day before, in consequence of young men's stripping their bodies naked, that he crept furtively into the gymnasia. At first he merely caressed and embraced; then gradually he grew wings in the palaestra and can no longer be restrained. He rails against and vilifies that great conjugal Love which cooperates to win immortality for the human race by kindling afresh through new generations our being, prone as it is to extinction.

"Boy-love denies pleasure; that is because it is ashamed and afraid. It needs a fair pretext for approaching the young and beautiful, so it pretends friendship and virtue. It covers itself with the sand of the wrestling-floor, it takes cold baths, it plays the highbrow and publicly proclaims that it is a philosopher and disciplined on the outside—because of the law. But when night comes and all is quiet,

> Sweet is the harvest when the guard's away.

If, on the one hand, as Protogenes maintains, there is no sexual partnership in pederasty, how can there be any Eros without Aphrodite, whom it is his god-given function to serve and wait upon, as well as to receive

23. Aphrodite.

such portion of honor and power as she bestows? But if, on the other, there is an Eros without Aphrodite, then it is like drunkenness without wine, brought on by a brew of figs and barley. No fruit, no fulfillment comes of the passion; it is cloying and quickly wearied."

[6] During this speech it was obvious that Pisias was full of anger and indignation against Daphnaeus; hardly had the latter ceased when Pisias exclaimed, "Good lord, what coarseness, what insolence! To think that human beings who acknowledge that they are locked like dogs by their sexual parts to the female should dare to transport the god from his home in the gymnasia and the parks with their wholesome fresh-air life in the sun and confine him in brothels with the vanity-cases and unguents and philters of disorderly females! Decent women cannot, of course, without impropriety either receive or bestow a passionate love."

At this point, however, my father relates that he too attacked Protogenes and said, "This word now calls the Argive host to arms.[24] I swear that it's Pisias' lack of moderation that makes me join forces with Daphnaeus. So marriage is to be a loveless union, devoid of god-given friendship! Yet we observe that an alliance, once it is deserted by courtship and 'favor,' can scarcely be held together by such yokes and reins as shame and fear."

"As for me," said Pisias, "I don't take this statement very seriously. But Daphnaeus, I perceive, is acting like copper. It is a fact that copper is not so much affected by fire as it is by molten copper; when this is poured over it, it softens bit by bit and becomes fluid. And it is not Lysandra's beauty that troubles him. Rather by his proximity and contact with one who is all ablaze and burning he is now himself catching fire.[25] It's evident that if he doesn't come running to us, he too will go soft. . . . But I observe," he added, "that the very thing that Anthemion would like best is happening: I myself am offending the judges, so no more."

Anthemion said, "Well and good, since you really ought to have spoken to the point in the first place."

[7] "Well then," said Pisias, "after fair warning to all women that as far as I am concerned, love doesn't exist, I must say that the young man must beware of the lady's wealth. If we were to plunge him into such pomp and high estate, we might unwittingly make him disappear, as tin disappears when mixed with copper. It would be something to brag of if a boy of his age were to marry a simple, unassuming woman and yet keep his quality unchanged in the union, like wine mixed with water.

24. Like the last quotation, this is a line from an unidentified tragedy.
25. In other words, it is Plutarch's influence that makes Daphnaeus defend heterosexuality, not his own love for Lysandra.

But as for this woman, we can see her determination to command and to dominate. Otherwise, she would hardly have rejected so many eminent, noble, and wealthy suitors and be wooing a stripling who has not yet discarded his school uniform, who still needs a tutor.[26] So it comes about that men of sense throw away their wives' excessive fortunes and clip their wings, as it were. For such wealth makes women frivolous, haughty, inconstant, and vain; often it elates them so much that they fly away. Even if they stay, it is better to be fettered 'with the golden chains of Ethiopia'[27] than by a wife's wealth."

[8] "And this you don't mention," said Protogenes, "that we risk being silly and ridiculous to reverse the words of Hesiod if, though he says,

> No marriage much before the age of thirty,
> Nor much after it: this time's the ripe one;
> Let a wife be matured four years, married the fifth—[28]

if, I say, we are going to join a green, immature man to a woman as many years older than he as the bridegroom should be older than the bride —and so follow the example of those who artificially pollinate dates and figs.

"'Yes,' you say, 'for she's in love with him, she's all on fire.' Who, then, prevents her from making revel-rout to his house, from singing the Complaint Before the Closed Door,[29] from putting nosegays on his portraits, from entering the ring with her rivals? These are the actions of true lovers. Let her lower her brow, renounce her easy life, and put on the dress of those who are in the service of passion. But if she is really modest and orderly, let her sit decently at home awaiting suitors, men with serious designs. For if a woman makes a declaration of love, a man could only take to his heels in utter disgust, let alone accepting and founding a marriage on such intemperance."

[9] Protogenes stopped and my father said, "Do you observe, Anthemion, that they are again making a public issue of the matter, forcing a rebuttal from us who neither deny that we are devotees of conjugal love, nor seek to escape from our position?"

---

26. The Greek actually refers to a pedagogue, a slave who accompanies younger boys to school.

27. Herodotus says that the Ethiopians used such chains to confine prisoners, since among them gold was considered a common and valueless metal.

28. This is *Works and Days* 696–98. The fifth year past puberty would be seventeen, since the Greeks reckoned inclusively.

29. This is the conventional *paraclausithyron*, or serenade of the locked-out lover, like **6.14.15–48**.

"Good Lord, yes," said Anthemion. "So now undertake against them a somewhat fuller defense of Love—and put in a word for Wealth, too, of which Pisias is making such use to frighten us."

"What charge," asked my father, "will they not bring against a woman if we are to reject Ismenodora because of her love and her wealth? She does, in fact, live in grandeur and opulence. And what of that if she is beautiful and young? What of her proud and eminent birth? . . . Isn't it true that decent women have a name for being disagreeable and intolerable because of their severity and eagle-beak noses? Aren't they nicknamed Furies[30] because they're always angry with their husbands? So the best plan is to marry a Thracian Habrotonon or a Milesian Bacchis from the market-place without benefit of ceremony and bring her home for a price and a shower of nuts.[31]

"Yet we know a good many men who have been abject slaves of women like this. Samian flute-girls, ballet dancers, women like Aristonica and Oenanthe with her tambourine and Agathoclea[32] have trampled on the crowns of kings. The Syrian Semiramis[33] was the servant and concubine of a house-born slave of the king, Ninus the Great, who one day caught sight of her and fell in love. She grew to have such power and such contempt for him that she asked to be allowed to direct the affairs of state, crowned and seated on his throne, for one day. He granted this and issued orders for everyone to serve and obey her just as they would himself. At first her commands were moderate while she was making trial of the guards; then, when she saw that there was no opposition or hesitation on their part, she ordered Ninus to be seized, put in chains, and finally put to death. When all this was done, she ruled gloriously over Asia for many years.

"Good heavens! Wasn't Belestiche[34] a barbarian female bought in the market place, she to whom now the Alexandrians maintain shrines and temples dedicated through the king's love to Aphrodite Belestiche? And that woman down there who shares a temple and worship with Eros,[35] whose gilded statue stands at Delphi with those of kings and queens, what dowry had she to subjugate her lovers?

---

30. Three goddesses of revenge, represented as old women with snake hair.

31. Habrotonon and Bacchis are typical names for female slaves in New Comedy. Nuts would be thrown at weddings, as in **7.47**, but also to welcome new slaves to the household.

32. Agathoclea was the influential mistress of King Ptolemy IV Philopator of Egypt (221–205 B.C.E.); Oenanthe was her mother.

33. Queen of Assyria and the legendary founder of Babylon, she was, according to Greek accounts, the daughter of the Syrian goddess Derceto.

34. The mistress of King Ptolemy II Philadelphus of Egypt from 283 to 246 B.C.E.

35. Phryne of Thespiae was a famous fourth-century courtesan, for whom the sculptor Praxiteles created a golden statue in Delphi.

"The men these worthless females exploited became their prey unwittingly through their own weakness and softness; yet other men, though poor and obscure, have married rich and noble women and have not been destroyed or lost one particle of dignity; they have enjoyed honor and exercised benevolent authority to the end of their life together. But the man who cramps and diminishes his wife (as a thin man does his ring for fear it may fall off) is like those who shear their mares and then lead them to a river or a pool: when the poor beast sees how she looks in the reflection, ugly and unsightly, they say that she abandons her haughty airs and allows asses to mount her.

"To choose a woman for her wealth rather than for her character or birth would be ignoble and base; but if character and good breeding are added, it be would ridiculous to shun her. Antigonus,[36] to be sure, wrote to the commander of the garrison which had fortified Munychia that it wasn't enough to make the collar strong: the dog must also be made lean. This was in order to drain off the resources of the Athenians. The husband, however, of a rich or beautiful woman must not make her unsightly or poor; rather by his own self-possession and prudence, as well as by his refusal to be overawed by any of her advantages, he must hold his own without servility. The extra weight of his character must turn the scales; thus his wife is controlled and guided with as much profit as justice.

"Moreover, the right age and proper time for marriage are suitably matched as long as both parties are able to procreate. I understand that the lady is in the prime of life, for (he added with a smile at Pisias) she is no older than any of her rivals; nor is her hair gray as is that of some of the gentlemen who try to give their own color to Bacchon. If they are young enough to frequent his company, what is to hinder her looking after the young man better than any young wife in the world? It is true that young people find it difficult to fuse and blend well with each other. Only after a long time do they abandon their stiffness and self-assertion. At the beginning they have stormy weather and struggle with their partners—and still more so if Love is involved. Just as a high wind upsets a boat without a pilot, so Love makes stormy and chaotic a marriage of two people who cannot both command and will not either of them obey.

"The nurse rules the infant, the teacher the boy, the gymnasiarch[37] the youth, his admirer the young man who, when he comes of age, is ruled by law and his commanding general. No one is his own master,

36. Antigonus Gonatas, one of the Macedonian successor kings of Greece in the third century B.C.E. Athens and Sparta revolted against him during the Chremonidean War (267–262), but some historians assign this incident to an earlier period, perhaps around 283–282.

37. An official appointed by the city to oversee the gymnasium. See **2.28**.

no one is unrestricted. Since this is so, what is there dreadful about a
sensible older woman piloting the life of a young man? She will be useful because of her superior intelligence; she will be sweet and affectionate because she loves him.

"To sum up," my father said, "we are Boeotians and so should reverence Heracles and not be squeamish about a marriage of disproportionate ages. We know that he married his own wife, Megara, aged thirty-
three, to Iolaus, who was then only sixteen."[38]

[10] It was at this point in the conversation, said my father, that a
friend rode up from the city with his horse at a gallop bringing a report
to Pisias of a surprisingly audacious occurrence.

It seems that Ismenodora was convinced that, though Bacchon had
no personal antipathy to the marriage, he was embarrassed by its de-
tractors; accordingly, she resolved not to let the young man escape.
She summoned those male friends who were the most vigorous and
most sympathetic to her passion, together with the most intimate of
her women friends, organized them in a disciplined group, and waited
intently for the hour when Bacchon habitually left the palaestra and
walked decorously by her house. On this occasion, freshly annointed, he
approached with two or three companions. Ismenodora met him at the
door and had only to touch his garment when her friends handsomely
snatched up the youth in his cloak and mantle, carried him in a body
into the house, and immediately locked the doors.

At the same time, the women inside snatched off his cloak and put a
wedding garment on him. The servants scurried about and wreathed the
doors with olive and laurel, not only Ismenodora's doors, but Bacchon's
also; and a flute-girl went out and piped her way down the lane.

Now of the Thespians and their guests, some merely laughed, while
others were furious and tried to stir up the gymnasiarchs, for these
maintain a strict control over the young men and pay close attention
to their activities. No one paid any more attention to the contests;[39]
everybody deserted the theater and gathered about Ismenodora's door,
where they engaged in fierce debate.

[11] So when (continued my father) Pisias' friend had come galloping
up as fast as though he were bringing a military dispatch and, in great
excitement, had said no more than that Ismenodora had kidnapped
Bacchon, Zeuxippus began to laugh and, being a great admirer of
Euripides, recited:

38. In this version of the myth, Heracles did not kill Megara in his fit of madness, but only
his children, and he subsequently married her off to his nephew out of fear that his marriage
to her was cursed.

39. Probably the harpists referred to in section 2.

You revel in your wealth, madame:
Keep thoughts upon a mortal plane.

But Pisias jumped up and shouted, "Good heavens! What end will there be to the license that is subverting our town? Now already self-government is on the way to anarchy! Yet it may be absurd to be protesting in defense of laws and statutes when it is the very Laws of Nature that are transgressed when women take over the state. Did even Lemnos[40] see the like? Let's be off!" he cried. "Let's be off and hand over the gymnasium and the Council Chamber to the women since our city is by now completely emasculated!" So Pisias rushed off and Protogenes trailed after him, partly because he shared his anger, partly to calm him.

Anthemion remarked, "Such a bold stroke is certainly a strong action, really Lemnian—we can admit it since we're by ourselves. It shows the hand of a woman very much in love."

Soclarus asked with a little smile, "Do you really think that it's a case of kidnapping and rape? Isn't it rather the plausible counter-stratagem of a sensible young man who has slipped from the clutches of his lovers and deserted to the arms of a rich and beautiful woman?"

"Don't say such things, Soclarus," answered Anthemion. "And don't be putting suspicion on Bacchon. Even if his character were not naturally simple and frank, he certainly wouldn't have concealed it from *me*, with whom he shares every confidence. He sees quite well that in these matters it is I who am Ismenodora's warmest ally. It's Love that it's 'hard to combat,' not 'anger,' as Heraclitus[41] has it: 'whatever it wants, it buys even at the cost of one's life'—and money and reputation, too. Where do you find better behavior in the city than was Ismenodora's? When did any ugly story ever enter her house or any hint of evil-doing ever leave a stain on it? Yes, it's only too plain that some divine impulse, overpowering her common sense, has really taken possession of the poor mortal creature."

[12] And Pemptides laughed and said, "There is, of course, a physical disease which they call the sacred one;[42] so that there's nothing strange about it if some people call the greatest and most frenetic mental affliction sacred and divine.

"Once upon a time in Egypt I saw two neighbors disputing about a snake that had slithered on to the road. They both hailed it as a bringer

40. In Greek myth, the women of Lemnos were afflicted with a foul smell that caused their husbands to cease conjugal relations; they subsequently killed their husbands and all other male inhabitants of the island.

41. A pre-Socratic philosopher active in Ephesus in the late sixth century. His doctrine held that all things were in perpetual flux and strife.

42. Epilepsy.

of good luck, but each wanted to keep it as his own. Similarly, just now, when I observed both parties dragging off Love, some to the men's quarters, others to the women's, while both claimed him as a tremendous and divine blessing, I was not surprised that this passion had acquired all the power and respect that it has, since the very persons who should have been expelling it from every nook and cranny and restricting it were themselves magnifying and exalting it. So I held my peace a while ago, observing that the dispute was more a matter of private than of public concern. But now that Pisias has left us, I should be delighted to hear from you what criterion those who first declared Eros to be a god had in mind when they made the statement."

The dialogue continues with Plutarch himself delivering a long speech on the powers of the god Love.

10.4 Epictetus, *Discourses* 2.10.14–20

As a young slave in Rome, Epictetus heard the lectures of Musonius Rufus. Later he became a famous popularizer of Stoic doctrine in his own right. His lectures were published after his death in 135 C.E.

If, instead of a man, a tame and sociable animal, you became a wild beast, destructive, treacherous and liable to bite, have you lost nothing? No. For you to be damaged, you must, I think, lose a little money. Yet, does not the loss of anything else damage a man? If you had lost your knowledge of grammar or music, you would think yourself damaged by the loss of that knowledge, but if you will lose your modesty, dignity and civility, do you think it is of no consequence? Yet those first things, the grammar and music, are lost through some external and involuntary cause, while these things are lost through their own fault; and while it is neither noble to have those first things, nor shameful to lose them, not to have or to lose these others is a matter of shame and reproach and misfortune. What is lost by the man who endures the fate of the catamite? His manhood. And what is lost by the man who deals that fate? Among many other things, he loses his manhood no less than the other. What does the adulterer lose? His modesty, his self-control, his decency, his ability to be a citizen and a neighbor. What does the angry man lose? Something else. And the fearful man? Something else. No one is base without loss and damage to himself. But if you count loss in terms of coins only, all these are unharmed, undamaged, and perhaps even helped and enriched, if they receive a bit of money from one of their deeds. Note, however, that if you refer everything to monetary gain, not even the man who loses his nose will, according to you, have been harmed.

10.5 Soranus = Caelius Aurelianus, *On Chronic Disorders* 4.9

Soranus of Ephesus was a Greek physician active in Rome during the first half of the second century C.E. Much of his work is preserved in the later Latin translation of Caelius Aurelianus.

[131] No one readily believes that effeminate or sexually passive men (whom the Greeks call *malthacoi*) are actually suffering from a disease. For this behavior does not arise naturally in humans;[43] rather, when modesty has been suppressed, it is lust that coerces to obscene usage body parts that have their own specific function,[44] although there is no limit to desire, no hope of satisfaction when their allotted roles do not suffice for individual parts (for thus divine providence earmarked places in our bodies for specific duties). And then they dress and move and employ other feminine attributes that are not associated with bodily afflictions, but rather are faults of a corrupted mind.[45] [132] For often out of fear or, what is more difficult for them, out of respect for certain men before whom they have occasion to appear, they suddenly change for a little while and try to demonstrate signs of manliness. But because they do not know the parameters of virility, once again they are undermined by excess and do more than befits virtue and involve themselves in greater errors.[46] And in our opinion this is sufficient evidence that these men experience the proper feelings.[47] It is indeed, as Soranus says, an affliction of a despicable and loathsome mind.

For similarly the women called "tribads" (because they have sex with both men and women) rush to mingle with women more than with men and pursue the same women with almost masculine jealousy.[48] When they have been emptied or temporarily relieved of their desire, they seek to cast on others [133] those things that they are known to suffer as an alleviation for their degradation, worn out by the shame of their double sex;

---

43. Aurelianus/Soranus is disputing the type of explanation given in **5.16**. If passive behavior were due to the need to release a build-up of seminal residue, then it could be said to arise naturally, as other diseases do.

44. That is, contrary to **5.16**, the anus is not a locus for seminal collection.

45. Again, contrary to **5.16**, it is not just a question of the need for ejaculation of excess semen.

46. In other words, they go to excess in their heterosexual activities.

47. In other words, their bodies work like everyone else's.

48. On the term "tribad" (one who rubs), see Ch. 9, n. 8. The author's point is that when stimulating another woman sexually, a tribad would rub the same parts of her body that a man would. The desire for another woman, therefore, does not involve the employment of other body parts than those used in heterosexual intercourse. If homosexual desire among women is not caused by physical imperatives that a man is unable to satisfy, homosexual desire among men does not need a physiological explanation either.

just as women corrupted by frequent drunkenness, breaking out into new forms of lust, nourished by their disgraceful habit, rejoice in the injuries of their own sex.[49] So these men are known through a comparison with such women to be troubled by an affliction of the mind.

It is not correct to think that there is any care of the body that should be applied to drive off the affliction; rather the mind that is troubled by so great a stain of transgressions is to be brought under control. For no man has corrected a licentious body by taking the woman's sexual role or alleviated it by contact with a penis, but generally *when such an action brought relief* he soothed a complaint or pain arising from some other material.[50] [134] And so even the account of the cure reported by Clodius[51] is obviously a case of ascarides, which are small worms generated in parts of the rectum, as we have shown in our chapter on intestinal worms.

Parmenides,[52] in the books that he wrote titled *On Nature,* said effeminate or sexually passive men were sometimes generated in the act of conception. Since his work is a Greek poem, I will imitate it in verse. To the best of my ability I have composed Latin verses so that the due proportion of the languages is not confused:[53]

At the same time woman and man mingle together the seeds of love in
    their veins,
A power, shaping from the different bloods,
Preserving proportion, makes well-founded bodies.
[135] For if the powers contend against each other when the seed is mixed
And do not make one when mixed together in the body,
Terribly will they trouble the sex arising from the twin seed.[54]

49. That is, just as alcoholic women derive satisfaction from corrupting other women into drunkenness, even though it does not lead to their own inebriation, so tribads relieve their shame by initiating other women into homosexual practices, even though it does not directly lead to sexual satisfaction for themselves.

50. Than semen. Aurelianus/Soranus is denying the thesis of **5.16** that relief is given to a build-up of semen in the anus; in such a case, there would have to be an ejaculation of semen from the anus of passive homosexuals at the moment of orgasm.

51. A first-century C.E. physician associated with the school of Asclepiades, who apparently reported an emission from the anus after anal intercourse.

52. An early-fifth-century B.C.E. philosopher from Elea in southern Italy. His metaphysical doctrines influenced Plato profoundly.

53. This is not simply an explanation of why he has translated Greek into Latin, but why he has retained the poetic format. Something in the meaning of the Greek will be lost if it is simply translated into prose.

54. See **5.15**. In theories in which material contributions from the parents' bodies accounted for resemblance, an extra mechanism had to be posited to account for the fact that offspring generally belonged to only one sex and did not have their father's penis and mother's breasts, even as they might have their father's nose and mother's eyes. This and comparable

Indeed, he wishes the materials of the seeds to be powers in addition, which, if they mix themselves in such a way as to make one power in the same body, will produce a coherent desire for intercourse. If, however, the powers persist in a separated state when the bodily seed has been mixed, a longing for both sorts of intercourse will follow those born *from this conception.*

Furthermore, many leaders of various schools say it is an inherited disease and on this account enters succeeding generations with the seed. Not that they blame Nature for this, which shows the extent of its purity in other animals (for they are considered to be mirrors of Nature by philosophers), [136] but they do blame the human species, because, having once developed these faults, it has held onto them so that no renewal can cleanse the species, nor has it left any place for a new beginning.[55] And they blame the human species because a mental defect is more serious: although most inherited or acquired diseases are weakened and grow old along with the body (for example, gout, epilepsy, and madness) and on this account indubitably become milder with advancing age, *this is not the case with a mental defect.*[56] For all troublesome things will produce strong effects in the presence of opposing firmness in the underlying material. When this decreases in old people a disease also diminishes, as does their strength. [137] However, the disease under discussion, which produces sexually passive men and effeminates, is the only one which incapacitates men more seriously as their body ages and agitates the body more with unspeakable lust, not indeed without reason. For at other times in their life, as long as the body is healthy and enjoys the natural performance of love, the twin lust is divided in wantonness, the soul of these men being excited sometimes in the active, sometimes in the passive role. But in those men who are weakened through old age and lack the power to play the male role in intercourse, all the lust of the mind is led to the opposite appetite, and on this account they demand the female part more importunately. And so many conjecture that boys are also troubled by this disease from the same cause. For as with old men, they lack the male power; it is not yet present in the one and has passed away from the other.[57]

---

texts divide each sex into an equal number of categories from most masculine to most feminine, but do not feature a hermaphroditic sex partaking of both.

55. That is, the affliction could have been eradicated if those affected had confined themselves to homosexual activity so that their seed would not be passed on to succeeding generations.

56. The author is here contrasting a purely mental defect with epilepsy and madness, which are caused by a physiological excess of phlegm and bile respectively.

57. See ch. 5, n. 163.

10.6 Polemon, *On Physiognomy* 61

Polemon was a sophist and orator active in Smyrna and other Greek cities in the first half of the second century C.E. An epitome of his treatise on physiognomy has been preserved through the Arabic tradition. This chapter is titled "On the Signs of an Effeminate Androgyne."

The sign of such a person is that you see him to be of a moist gaze, lightening fiercely with his eyes, shaking them with a constricted brow, heavily moving his eyebrows and cheeks, neck inclined, frequently moving his back and limbs, as if they were all slack, . . . of frail knees, frequently gazing upon himself and the limbs of his body, his voice thin, sharp, and drawn out, with emphatic movement of the head.

10.7 (Anonymous), *On Physiognomy* 54–55, 74

This treatise of uncertain date discusses similar types.

[54] But when certain people, understanding that they have a weak, flimsy neck, strive and pretend to extend and strengthen their necks with a certain stiffness, they are exposed all the more. For by a trembling of the lips or a turn of the eyes or incongruous and dissonant movements of the feet or a movement of the loins or unsteadiness of the hands or shaking of the voice emitted with effort, they are very easily exposed as effeminates; and even then, the position of the neck in these people is not actually steady, and if you look carefully, you will sometimes see their necks shaking: for all pretense easily fails and slips away.

[55] When the neck is weak, therefore, it should be obvious that its owner is either a fool or an effeminate: naturally the remaining signs guide that determination. When there is a moderate firmness, it indicates the best character. When the upper part of the neck is twisted back it indicates an indolent, harsh, stupid, and worthless person, but one must repeatedly consider and discern through the rest of the signs whether it is due to insanity or to insolence that the neck has been twisted back. When the neck is bent in the direction of the chest, it can indicate a mind occupied by thoughts, it can be a sign of parsimony, or it can be a sign of maliciousness, according to the correspondence of the other signs; you can be sure, however, that it indicates nothing simple or secure or easy. A neck bent to the left side sometimes means an idiot, but more often it means a pervert *(cinaedus)*. Aristotle, however, attributes to perverts a slanting of the head to the right side. . . .

[74] The movement of the body is either natural or affected. There are three types of affected movement. One type is when a man, striving after

status or power or wealth or marriage, arranges himself in a manner that he thinks is most pleasing to the more powerful. He dons the appearance of both extravagance and integrity, he is both haughty and obsequious, he is at once coarse and detached, and sympathetic and diligent, whenever he judges that poverty, coarseness, thriftiness, smallness, and sympathy need to be affected. The second type of affectation belongs to those who strive for beauty and who shape their face and their whole body in order to prey upon maidens or disturb marriages; but also those who are crazy about boys or who actually pass themselves off as women, so that they might be able to attract men to themselves, have a studied and affected body movement. The third type belongs to those who are, in fact, true perverts, but in an attempt to remove suspicion from themselves strive to assume a masculine appearance. For they imitate a young man's gait and they reinforce themselves with a certain hardness, they intensify both their eyes and their voice and they straighten their whole body, but they are easily betrayed by their true nature, which exposes and undoes them. For they frequently slacken their neck and voice, they relax their hands and feet, and there are other momentary indications by which they are easily betrayed. For sudden fear and unexpected joy jolt them from their carefully constructed facade and restore them to their natural state. Yawning too has often caused them to be discovered. All the signs, therefore, which can be gathered from the movements of the body should be related to these four types: to the one that is true and natural, and to the three that we have established as false and contrived.

10.8 Marcus Aurelius, *Meditations* 1.16.1

Marcus Aurelius was born in 121 C.E. and was emperor of Rome from 161 to 180. He was also a Stoic philosopher and jotted down his meditations while on military campaigns.

My father[58] provided me with an example of how to be gentle and to stick calmly by decisions carefully made: of how to be impervious to vanity over what we think of as honors, of industry and application to the task in hand, of how to listen to all those who could offer something of use to the common good, of how to give to each man strictly according to his worth, of the experience to know when to exert oneself and when to relax, and of how to put a stop to all things concerned with the love of boys.

---

58. The reference here is not to his biological father but to Antoninus Pius, who adopted him upon becoming emperor in 138.

10.9 Lucian, *Dialogues of the Courtesans* 5

Lucian of Samosata was Syrian by birth, but wrote works of satire and fiction in a refined classical Greek style. His early dialogues, probably dating to the mid-second century C.E., are prose mimes similar to those of Herondas.

CLONARIUM: We've been hearing strange things about you Leaena. They say that Megilla, the rich Lesbian woman, is in love with you just like a man, that you live with each other, and do goodness knows what together. Hullo! Blushing? Tell me if it's true.

LEAENA: Quite true, Clonarium. But I'm ashamed, for it's unnatural.

CLONARIUM: In the name of Mother Aphrodite, what's it all about? What does the woman want? What do you do when you are together? You see, you don't love me, or you wouldn't hide such things from me.

LEAENA: I love you as much as I love any woman, but she's terribly like a man.

CLONARIUM: I don't understand what you mean, unless she's a sort of woman for the ladies. They say there are women like that in Lesbos, with faces like men and unwilling to consort with men, but only with women, as though they themselves were men.

LEAENA: It's something like that.

CLONARIUM: Well, tell me all about it; tell me how she made her first advances to you, how you were persuaded, and what followed.

LEAENA: She herself and another rich woman, with the same accomplishments, Demonassa from Corinth, were organizing a drinking party and had taken me along to provide them with music. But, when I had finished playing, and it was late and time to turn in and they were drunk, Megilla said, "Come along Leaena, it's high time we were in bed; you sleep here between us."

CLONARIUM: And did you? What happened after that?

LEAENA: At first they kissed me like men, not simply bringing their lips to mine, but opening their mouths a little, embracing me, and squeezing my breasts. Demonassa even bit me as she kissed, and I didn't know what to make of it. Eventually Megilla, being now rather heated, pulled off her wig, which was very realistic and fitted very closely, and revealed the skin of her head which was shaved close, just as on the most energetic of athletes. This sight gave me a shock, but she said, "Leaena, have you ever seen such a good-looking young fellow?" "I don't see one here, Megilla," said I. "Don't make a woman out of me," said she. "My name is Megillus, and I've been married to Demonassa here for ever so long; she's my wife." I laughed at that, Clonarium, and said, "Then, unknown to us, Megillus, you were a man all the time, just as they say Achilles once hid among the girls, and you have everything that a man has, and can play the part of a man to Demonassa?" "I haven't got what you mean," said she, "I don't need it at all. You'll find I've a much pleasanter method of my own." "You're surely not a hermaphrodite," said I, "equipped both as a man and a woman, as many people are said to be?" For I still didn't know, Clonarium, what it was all about. But she said, "No, Leaena, I'm all man." "Well," I said, "I've heard the Boeotian flute-girl, Ismenodora, repeating tales she'd heard at home, and telling us how someone at Thebes had turned from woman to man, someone who was also an excellent soothsayer, and was, I think, called Tiresias.[59] That didn't happen to you, did it?" "No, Leaena," she said, "I was born a woman like the rest of you, but I have the mind and the desires and everything else of a man." "And do you find these desires enough?" said I. "If you don't believe me, Leaena," said she, "just give me a chance, and you'll find I'm as good as any man; I have a substitute of my own. Only give me a chance, and you'll see." Well I did, my dear, because she begged so hard, and presented me with a costly necklace and a very fine linen dress. Then I threw my arms around her as though she were a man, and she went to work, kissing me and panting and apparently enjoying herself immensely.

CLONARIUM: What did she do? How? That's what I'm most interested to hear.

LEAENA: Don't inquire too closely into the details; they're not very nice; so, by Aphrodite in heaven, I won't tell you !

10.10 Lucian, *Dialogues of the Courtesans* 10

This dialogue concerns a courtesan who has lost an attractive young client to a pederastic philosopher.

CHELIDONIUM: Has young Cleinias given up visiting you, Drosis? It's a long time since I've seen him at your house.

DROSIS: Yes, Chelidonium. His tutor has stopped him from coming to see me any more.

CHELIDONIUM: Who's he? Surely not Diotimus, the gymnastics master? He's a friend of mine.

DROSIS: No, but that most accursed of philosophers, Aristaenetus.

---

59. According to Greek myth, Tiresias changed gender when he saw two snakes copulating in the road and knocked them apart with his staff. Based on his experience of intercourse both ways, he was able to referee a dispute between Zeus and Hera about which sex enjoyed intercourse more, and was blinded by Hera as punishment for saying that women received ninetenths of the pleasure.

CHELIDONIUM: Do you mean the grim-looking fellow with the shaggy hair and bushy beard, who's always walking with his boys in the Painted Porch?[60]

DROSIS: That's the hypocrite I mean. I'd like to see him come to a bad end, with the hangman dragging him along by that beard.

CHELIDONIUM: Why ever did he induce Cleinias to act like this?

DROSIS: I don't know, Chelidonium. But although he'd never missed a night with me, since he'd started going with women, and I was his first woman, for three days running he's not even come near our street. Since I was upset, as somehow I'd become rather fond of him, I sent Nebris to have a look at him, while he was in the Agora or the Painted Porch. She said she saw him walking around with Aristaenetus and nodded to him from a distance, but he went red, kept his eyes down and didn't look in her direction again. Then they walked together to the Academy.[61] She followed as far as the Dipylon Gate, but since he'd never even turned in her direction, she came back without any definite information. You can imagine what it's been like for me since that, as I can't think what's come over my boy! "I can't have annoyed him in any way?" I kept asking myself. "Or has he fallen in love with some other woman and hates me now? Has his father prevented his visiting me?" Many thoughts like that kept coming into my poor head, but when it was already late in the afternoon, Dromo[62] came with this note from him. Take it and read it, Chelidonium, for I believe you can read.

CHELIDONIUM: Let us see. The writing's not very clear; it's so slapdash that the writer was obviously in a hurry. He says, "Heaven knows how much I loved you, Drosis."

DROSIS: Alas, poor me! He didn't even start by wishing me well.[63]

CHELIDONIUM: "And now I'm leaving you not because I hate you, but because I'm forced to do so. My father has handed me over to Aristaenetus to study philosophy under him, and Aristaenetus, finding out all about us, gave me a good telling-off, saying it was not at all the thing for a son of Architeles and Erasiclia to associate with a courtesan, for it was much better to prefer virtue to pleasure."

DROSIS: Curse that old driveler for teaching the lad such things!

60. The Stoa Poikile in Athens was famous as the haunt of the Stoic philosophers, and gave its name to their school.

61. The characteristic congregating place of Plato's pupils and the name of his school in later generations. See **2.17**.

62. Apparently a manservant of Drosis. His name means "Runner," as if to imply that his chief function was as a messenger.

63. The usual formula of greeting in Greek and Roman letters.

CHELIDONIUM: "So that I must obey him. He follows me everywhere and keeps a close eye on me. In fact, I'm not allowed even to look at anyone but him. If I live a sober life and obey him in everything, he promises me I'll be completely happy and shall become virtuous through my training in endurance. I've had the greatest difficulty in slipping away to write this to you. I pray that you may prosper, my dear, and never forget Cleinias."

DROSIS: What do you think of the letter, Chelidonium?

CHELIDONIUM: The rest of it might have come from a Scythian,[64] but the part about never forgetting Cleinias shows there's still some hope.

DROSIS: Just what I thought. In any case, I'm dying of love. But Dromo said that Aristaenetus is the sort who's fond of boys, and by pretending to teach them, keeps company with the handsomest youths, and has now got Cleinias on his own and spins him tales, promising of all things that he will make him like a god. Besides that, he's reading with him amorous discourses addressed by the old philosophers to their pupils, and is all wrapped up in the lad. Dromo threatened he'd tell Cleinias' father as well.

CHELIDONIUM: I hope, Drosis, you gave Dromo a good feed.

DROSIS: That I did, though he'll do anything for me, even without that; he's another who is desperate for the love of Nebris.

CHELIDONIUM: Don't worry. Everything will be all right. I think I'll write up on the wall in the Ceramicus,[65] where Architeles often takes a walk, "Aristaenetus is corrupting Cleinias," so that we can charge to the swift support of Dromo's charge.

DROSIS: How can you write it up without being seen?

CHELIDONIUM: By night, my dear. I'll get a bit of charcoal somewhere.

DROSIS: Capital, Chelidonium. If only you can help me fight that old impostor Aristaenetus!

10.11 Lucian, *True History* 1.22

The True History *was a kind of science fiction novella, based on fantastic voyages to faraway places populated by strange races with unique customs.*

I should like to describe the novel and unusual things I noticed during my stay on the Moon. First of all, they are born not of woman but of man; their marriages are of male with male, and they do not even know the word "woman" at all. Up to the age of twenty-five they all act as female

---

64. A wild and barbaric tribe inhabiting the Russian steppes.
65. A district in the northwest part of Athens.

partners, and thereafter as husbands. Pregnancy occurs not in the womb but in the calf of the leg, for after conception the calf grows fat. After a time they cut it open and bring out a lifeless body, which they lay out with its mouth open facing the wind and bring to life. I imagine that this is the origin of the Greek word "calf," inasmuch as on the Moon it is this part of the body that produces young, and not the belly. But I shall tell you about something more marvelous yet. There is on the Moon a kind of men called Treemen, and the manner of their generation is as follows. They cut off a man's right testicle and plant it in the ground; from it there grows an enormous tree of flesh, like a phallus. It has branches and foliage, and its fruit is acorns as long as the forearm. When they are ripe, they harvest them and carve men from them, adding genitals of ivory, or of wood for the poorer ones; these are what they use to consummate their male marriages.

10.12 Lucian, *True History* 2.17–19

This section of the novella describes a visit to the Island of the Blest, a paradise where souls of great men dwelled after death.

[17] I should like also to record the famous people I saw there. . . . There were Lycurgus the Spartan, Phocion and Tellus from Athens, and the wise men except Periander.[66] I also saw Socrates, the son of Sophroniscus, chatting with Nestor and Palamedes;[67] around him were Hyacinthus of Sparta, Narcissus of Thespiae, Hylas, and other handsome youths.[68] He seemed to me to be in love with Hyacinthus—at any rate, he was the one he was arguing most with. I was told that Rhadamanthys[69] was displeased with him and had often threatened to expel him from the island for his nonsense if he didn't drop his self-deprecation and enjoy himself. Plato was the only one missing. They said he was living in the republic he constructed himself, under the constitution and laws of his own devising. . . .[70]

66. After a list of mythological heroes and foreign wise men, Lucian lists famous Greek sages: Lycurgus the lawgiver, Phocion the respected fourth-century general and statesman, and Tellus, an otherwise obscure Athenian praised for his family and courage by Solon. Periander of Corinth, although a great patron of arts and philosophy in the late seventh and early sixth centuries, is excluded because he was a tyrant.

67. Among the Greek heroes at Troy, Nestor and Palamedes were distinguished for their wisdom and intellect.

68. All three were beautiful boys of Greek mythology: Hyacinthus, the beloved of Apollo; Hylas of Heracles; and Narcissus, who fell in love with his own reflection.

69. Rhadamanthys was identified at the beginning of Lucian's description as the judge and ruler of this island.

70. An allusion to Plato's *Republic,* which attempted to construct the constitution of an ideal state. The next paragraph goes on to list other philosophers on the Island of the Blest.

[19] Well, these were the most notable of the company; the most respected members of it are Achilles and, next, Theseus. Their sexual practice is as follows. They make love openly, in the sight of all, with both women and men; this is not considered in any way shameful. Only Socrates had sworn formally that his associations with the young were pure; but everybody thought he was guilty of perjury—Hyacinthus and Narcissus kept saying so, anyway, though he himself denied it. Women are common property, and no one is jealous of his neighbor; they are very Platonic in this respect. Boys submit to anyone who wants them, without any resistance.

10.13 Lucian, *True History* 2.28

After six months on the island, it comes time for Lucian and his crew to leave. Rhadamanthys addresses some final words to Lucian, advising him how to conduct himself if he should return to Earth.

That was all he said. And he pulled up a mallow root and handed it to me, bidding me invoke it at times of greatest danger. He also enjoined me, if ever I reached this world, not to poke fires with a sword, not to eat lupines, and not to associate with boys over eighteen;[71] if I kept these things in mind, he said, I could have hopes of returning to the island.

10.14 Apuleius, *Apology* 74

Born in Madaurus in North Africa, Apuleius was a rhetorician and sophist who developed a distinctive Latin style. This speech, from about 155 C.E., is a self-defense against charges of having seduced his wife by the use of magic. Here, he denounces Herennius Rufinus, whom he blames as the mastermind behind the lawsuit.

I will display this man as he is, out of necessity, and in a few words (with as much restraint as I will be able to muster). If I were completely silent about him, he might be cheated of his labor, that is, the legal trouble he has trumped up against me by his greatest efforts. For this man is the instructor of this little boy,[72] he is the bringer of the charge, he is the gatherer of the lawyers, he is the buyer of witnesses, he is the little furnace of all the calumny, he is the torch and the whip of Aemilianus[73] here, and he

---

71. These instructions parody precepts of purity taught by the Pythagoreans and other mystery religions. Mallow was a regular part of Pythagorean diet. Lupines are perhaps a parodic substitute for beans, which the Pythagoreans always avoided. Both produce flatulence.

72. Sicinius Pudens, the youngest son of the woman Apuleius had just married.

73. Sicinius Aemilianus was his wife's brother-in-law and the official accuser in the case.

glories, without any restraint whatsoever, in the fact that I have been arraigned by virtue of his machinations. And he truly does have affairs on which he may congratulate himself. For he is the fabricator of all lawsuits, the concocter of all perjuries, the architect of all dissimulations, and, indeed, truly the site, the haunt, and the whorehouse of prurient desires and dissipations. Already from an early age he has been openly revealed in all shameful deeds. And this occurred long ago in his boyhood, before he was made ugly by that baldness of his. He was a willing participant in all nameless sins with his emasculators. Soon after, in his youth, he was a dancer upon the stage who was limp and weak enough, but, as I hear, marked by an untrained and uncouth softness. For it is denied that he had anything of what it takes to be an actor except immodesty.

10.15 Apuleius, *Metamorphoses* 8.24–29

The Metamorphoses *or* Golden Ass *is a novel about a man named Lucius (the first-person narrator) who becomes involved with witches and is transformed into an ass, in which guise he suffers many wretched misadventures. He counts the following as one of the worst.*

[24] With jokes of this kind the auctioneer kept the crowd in fits of laughter. But now my cruel Fortune, whom, though I fled never so far afield, I had not been able to escape or appease by all that I had suffered, once again turned her blind eyes on me and, wonderful to relate, produced a buyer who could not have suited my unhappy circumstances more perfectly. Let me describe him: he was a real old queen, bald apart from a few grizzled ringlets, one of your street-corner scum, one of those who carry the Syrian Goddess around our towns to the sound of cymbals and castanets and make her beg for her living.[74] He was keen to buy me and asked the auctioneer where I came from. He pronounced me to be a genuine Cappadocian[75] and quite a strong little beast. Then he asked my age; the auctioneer answered humorously: "Well, an astrologer who cast his horoscope said he was in his fifth year, but the beast himself could tell you better from his tax return. I know I'd be liable to the penalties of the Cornelian law if I sold you a Roman citizen as a slave, but here's a good and deserving servant who can be of use to you both at home and abroad. Won't you buy him?" [25] But my tiresome purchaser persisted with one question after another, wanting particularly to know if he could warrant

74. Variously named Atargatis or Derceto, she is a Syrian version of the Great Mother goddess, known as Cybele in her Anatolian incarnation (see 7.48). Like Cybele, the Syrian goddess had a retinue of mendicant eunuch priests.

75. A region of central Asia Minor known for breeding excellent horses.

me tractable. "Why," said the man, "this here isn't a donkey, it's an old bellwether: he's placid, will do anything you want, he doesn't bite or kick —you'd think it was a well-behaved man dwelling in an ass's skin. You can easily find out—put your face between his thighs, and you'll soon discover the extent of his patience."

These witticisms at the old guzzler's expense were not lost on him, and putting on a great show of indignation he retorted: "You zombie, you stuffed dummy, damn you and your auctioneer's blather, may the almighty mother of all, she of Syria, and holy Sabazius and Bellona and the Idaean Mother and queen Venus with her Adonis[76] strike you blind for the coarse buffoonery I've had to take from you. You bloody fool, do you think I can entrust the goddess to an unruly beast who might suddenly upset the divine image and throw it off, leaving its unfortunate guardian to run about with her hair all over the place looking for a doctor for her goddess lying on the ground?" When I heard this I wondered if I shouldn't suddenly start bucking as if possessed, so that seeing me in a savage temper he would break off the negotiation. However, he was so anxious to buy me that he paid the price down on the nail and nipped that idea in the bud. My master, I suppose, was so pleased to see the last of me that he readily took seventeen denarii for me, and handed me over with a bit of rope for bridle to Philebus, that being my new owner's name.

[26] Taking delivery of this new member of the family he led me off home, where as soon as he got indoors he called out: "Look, girls, at the pretty little slave I've bought and brought home for you." But these "girls" were a troupe of queens, who at once appeared jumping for joy and squealing untunefully in mincing effeminate tones, in the belief that it really was a human slave that had been brought to serve them. When they saw that this was not a case of a hind substituting for a maiden but an ass taking the place of a man, they began to sneer and mock their chief, saying that this wasn't a servant he'd brought but a husband for himself. "And listen," they said. "You're not to gobble up this nice little nestling all on your own— we're your little dovies too, and you must let us have a share sometimes." Exchanging badinage of this sort they tied me up next to the manger. They also had in the house a beefy young man, an accomplished piper, whom they had bought in the market from the proceeds of their street-collections. Out of doors he tagged along playing his instrument when they carried the goddess around, at home he was toyboy in ordinary to the whole establishment. As soon as he saw me joining the household, without

76. Sabazius was an Anatolian god sometimes assimilated to the Greek Dionysus. Bellona was the Roman war goddess, sometimes assimilated to Levantine goddesses like Astarte. The Idaean Mother was Cybele. The myth of Venus and her young lover Adonis also has Near Eastern associations.

waiting for orders he served me out a generous ration of food and welcomed me joyfully. "At last," he said, "here's somebody to spell me in my
loathsome duties. Long life to you! May you please our masters and bring
relief to my exhausted loins!" When I heard this I began to picture to myself the ordeals that lay ahead of me.

[27] Next day they all put on tunics of various hues and "beautified"
themselves by smearing colored gunge on their faces and applying eye
shadow. Then they set forth, dressed in turbans and robes, some saffron-
colored, some of linen and some of gauze; some had white tunics embroidered with a pattern of purple stripes and girded at the waist; and on
their feet were yellow slippers. The goddess, draped in silk, they placed
on my back, and baring their arms to the shoulder and brandishing huge
swords and axes, they capered about with ecstatic cries, while the sound
of the pipes goaded their dancing to frenzy. After calling at a number
of small houses they arrived at a rich man's country estate. The moment
they entered the gates there was bedlam; they rushed about like fanatics,
howling discordantly, twisting their necks sinuously back and forth with
lowered heads, and letting their long hair fly around in circles, sometimes
attacking their own flesh with their teeth, and finally gashing their arms
with the weapons they carried. In the middle of all this, one of them was
inspired to fresh excesses of frenzy; he began to gasp and draw deep
labored breaths, feigning madness like one divinely possessed—as if the
presence of a god sickened and enfeebled men instead of making them
better!

[28] Anyway, let me tell you how heavenly Providence rewarded him.
Holding forth like some prophet he embarked on a cock-and-bull story
about some sacrilegious act he accused himself of having committed, and
condemned himself to undergo the just punishment for his crime at his
own hands. So, seizing a whip such as these effeminates always carry about
with them, its lashes made of twisted wool ending in long tassels thickly
studded with sheep's knucklebones, he laid into himself with these knotted
thongs, standing the pain of the blows with extraordinary hardihood. What
with the sword-cuts and the flogging, the ground was awash with the con-
taminated blood of these creatures. All this worried me a good deal: seeing all these wounds and gore all over the place I was afraid that, just as
some men drink asses' milk, this foreign goddess might conceive an appetite for asses' blood. Finally, however, exhausted or sated with lacerating
themselves, they gave over the carnage, and started to stow away in the
roomy folds of their robes the coppers, indeed, the silver money, that
people crowded round to bestow on them—and not only money but jars
of wine and milk and cheeses and a quantity of corn and wheat; and some
presented the bearer of the goddess with barley. They greedily raked in all

this stuff, crammed it into the sacks that they had ready for these acquisitions, and loaded it on my back, so that I was carrying a double load, a walking barn and temple combined.

[29] In this way they roved about plundering the whole countryside. In one village they enjoyed a particularly lavish haul and decided to celebrate with a banquet. As the price for a fake oracle they got a fat ram from one of the farmers, which they said was to be sacrificed to appease the hungry goddess. Having made all the arrangements for dinner they went off to the baths, whence having bathed they brought back with them to share their dinner a robust young peasant, finely equipped in loin and groin. Dinner was hardly begun and they had scarcely started on the hors-d'oeuvre when the filthy scum became inflamed by their unspeakable lusts to outrageous lengths of unnatural depravity. The young man was stripped and laid on his back, and crowding round him they made repeated demands on his services with their loathsome mouths. Finally I couldn't stand the sight and tried to shout "Romans, to the rescue!"; but the other letters and syllables failed me and all that came out was an "O"—a good loud one, creditable to an ass, but the timing was unfortunate. It so happened that some young men from the next village were looking for an ass that had been stolen that night and were conducting a thorough search of all the lodging-houses. Hearing me braying inside and believing that their quarry was hidden away there, they burst in unexpectedly in a body to reclaim their property then and there, and caught our friends red-handed at their vile obscenities. They immediately called all the neighbors to witness this shocking scene, ironically praising the priests for their spotless virtue.

10.16 Xenophon of Ephesus, *An Ephesian Tale* 3.2

The date of this Greek romance is uncertain, but it is probably to be assigned to the second century C.E. Hippothous, the good-hearted leader of a band of robbers, tells his story.

"I belong," he said, "to one of the leading families of Perinthus, a city close to Thrace. And as you are aware, Perinthus is an important city and its citizens are well-to-do. There while I was a young man I fell in love with a beautiful youth, also from Perinthus, called Hyperanthes.[77] I first fell in love with him when I saw his wrestling exploits in the gymnasium and I could not contain myself; during a local festival with an all-night vigil I

---

77. The names in this story are all significant: Hippothous the robber means "of swift horse;" the beautiful youth Hyperanthes, "of excessive bloom"; the rival Aristomachus, "best in battle."

approached Hyperanthes and begged him to take pity on me. He listened
to me, took pity on me, and promised me everything. And our first steps
in lovemaking were kisses and caresses, while I shed floods of tears. And
at last we were able to take our opportunity to be alone with each other;
we were both the same age, and no one was suspicious. For a long time we
were together, passionately in love, until some evil spirit envied us. One of
the leading men in Byzantium (the neighboring city) arrived in Perinthus:
this was Aristomachus, a man proud of his wealth and prosperity. The moment he set foot in the town, as if sent against me by some god, he set eyes
on Hyperanthes with me and was immediately captivated, amazed at the
boy's beauty, which was capable of attracting anyone. When he had fallen
in love, he could no longer restrain himself but first made overtures to the
young man; when that brought no result (for Hyperanthes would let no
one near him because of his relationship with me), he won over the boy's
father, a villainous man not above bribery. And he made over Hyperanthes
to Aristomachus on the pretext of private tuition, for he claimed to be a
teacher of rhetoric. When he first took the boy over, he kept him under
lock and key, then took him off to Byzantium. I followed, ignoring all my
own affairs, and kept him company as often as I could; but that was seldom,
there were few kisses, and he was difficult to talk to: too many were watching me. At length I could hold out no longer. Nerving myself, I went back
to Perinthus, sold everything I had, got my money together, and went to
Byzantium; I took a sword (Hyperanthes had agreed to this as well), made
my way into Aristomachus' house during the night, and found him lying in
bed with the boy. I was enraged and struck him a fatal blow. All was quiet,
and everyone asleep: I left secretly with Hyperanthes without further ado;
traveling all through the night to Perinthus, I at once embarked on a ship
for Asia, unknown to anyone. And for a while the voyage went well. But a
heavy storm struck us off Lesbos and capsized the ship. I swam alongside
Hyperanthes, gave him support, and made it easier for him to swim. But
night came on, and the boy could not hold on any longer, gave up his
efforts to swim, and died. I was only able to rescue his body, bring it to
land, and bury it. I wept and wailed profusely and removed the relics. I
could only provide a single stone to serve as a memorial on the grave, and
inscribed it in memory of the unfortunate youth with a makeshift epigram.

HIPPOTHOUS FASHIONED THIS TOMB FOR FAR-FAMED HYPERANTHES,
A TOMB UNWORTHY OF THE DEATH OF A SACRED CITIZEN,
THE FAMOUS FLOWER SOME EVIL SPIRIT ONCE SNATCHED FROM THE LAND INTO
    THE DEEP,
ON THE OCEAN HE SNATCHED HIM AS A GREAT STORM WIND BLEW.

After this I decided not to return to Perinthus but made my way through
Asia to Phrygia Magna and Pamphylia. And there, since I had no means of

supporting myself and was distressed at the tragedy, I took to brigandage. At first I was only one of the rank and file, but in the end I got together a band of my own in Cilicia;[78] it was famed far and wide, until it was captured not long before I saw you. This, then, is the misfortune I am telling you about."

10.17 Achilles Tatius, *Leucippe and Clitophon* 1.7–8, 12–14

This Greek romance appears to date to the third quarter of the second century C.E.; it features a more "sophistic" style and greater engagement with intellectual issues than Xenophon's novel. The first-person narrator is the hero Clitophon, a youth of Tyre in Phoenicia, who has just fallen in love with his cousin Leucippe, visiting for the first time.

[7] I had a cousin named Cleinias, whose parents both were dead; he was two years older than myself and already an initiate in the rites of love. His boyfriend was a lad whom he loved to distraction. Recently, when the boyfriend admired a horse he had just bought, Cleinias said, "It's yours," and gave it to him outright. I used to joke with him about his carefree attitude, that he devoted all his time to friendship and was a slave to the pleasures of Eros, and he would smile, shaking his head, and say, "Someday, believe me, you will be such a slave, too."

I went to him now and with a greeting sat down beside him and said: "I am paying the penalty for my jokes: I, too, am Love's slave." With a clap of his hands and a laugh he stood up and kissed me right on the face, where the signs of love's insomnia were all too clear. "You're in love. You're really in love. Your eyes tell the tale."

At that moment Charicles (this was the name of his boyfriend) came running up in great agitation and cried, "O Cleinias, I'm done for!" Cleinias groaned too, and now wholly rapt in Charicles' soul, with a trembling voice said: "You will kill me with silence. Tell me what is hurting you. Who is your enemy?"

And Charicles replied: "My father has arranged a marriage for me, and a marriage with an ugly maiden, so that I have two evils to live with. A wife is a troublesome thing, even a pretty one; but if she also has the bad luck to be ugly, the disaster is doubled. But Father is eager for the match because she is wealthy. I'm being sold for her money. O awful fate—to be a bought husband, married for money!"

[8] At these words Cleinias went pale. Then he sharpened Charicles' will to refuse the marriage with a diatribe against the female sex.

---

78. The southeastern part of Asia Minor.

"So your father has arranged a marriage, eh! What crime have you committed to deserve these chains and fetters? Remember the words of Zeus.

> In lieu of flame I have a gift for men:
> An evil thing and still their heart's delight,
> So all men will embrace their own destruction.[79]

Such is the pleasure of women, like that of the Sirens, who lead men to destruction by the pleasure of their song.[80]

"The extent of the disaster you can understand from the wedding ceremony itself—flutes whining, doors banging, torches waving: noticing such an uproar, someone will say, 'Pity the prospective groom, it looks as if they're sending him off to war.'

"If you were a stranger to culture, you would not know about the dramas involving women, but as it is you could tell others how many plots women have contributed to the stage: Eriphyle's necklace, Philomela's banquet, Stheneboea's accusation, Aerope's theft, Procne's slaughter.[81] Agamemnon desires the beautiful Chryseis, and it brings a plague on the Greeks. Achilles desires the beautiful Briseis and introduces himself to sorrow.[82] Grant that Candaules' wife be fair, yet this same wife killed Candaules.[83] The fiery torch, lit for Helen's marriage, lit another fire hurled against Troy. The wedding of Penelope, chaste creature, was the death of how many suitors?[84] Phaedra loved Hippolytus and killed him; Clytemnestra hated Agamemnon and killed him.[85] Oh, women, women, they stop at nothing! They kill the men they love; they kill the men they hate. Was it right that handsome

---

79. Hesiod, *Works and Days* 57–58, in reference to Pandora, the first woman.

80. In myth, the Sirens are imagined as luring sailors to shipwreck from their perch near a particularly rocky seashore.

81. All of these stories come from tragedy. Eriphyle was bribed to send her husband to war. Philomela and her sister Procne killed Procne's son and fed him to her husband to avenge his rape of Philomela. Stheneboea falsely accused Bellerophon of rape when he repelled her advances. Aerope stole her husband's prized ram and gave it to his brother, with whom she was having an affair.

82. In the *Iliad*, Agamemnon refused to return his concubine, Chryseis, to her father, a priest of Apollo, after which Apollo sent a plague to punish the Greeks. Briseis was Achilles' concubine, whom Agamemnon stole after he was finally forced to give up Chryseis. The ensuing quarrel caused Achilles to withdraw from battle and eventually lose his beloved Patroclus.

83. Herodotus tells the story of Candaules, who allowed his bodyguard Gyges to watch his wife undress. His wife later plotted with Gyges to avenge her honor by killing Candaules.

84. The dispute over Helen was the motivating event in the Trojan War, that over Penelope was part of the plot of the *Odyssey*.

85. Again, these are plots familiar from Athenian tragedy: Phaedra tried to seduce her step-son and then accused him of rape after he rejected her. Her accusation led to his death. Clytemnestra plotted with her lover to kill Agamemnon after he returned from Troy.

Agamemnon be slain, whose beauty was celestial, 'eyes and head like to thundering Zeus'—and a woman, O Zeus, lopped off this fair head.

"All this can be said against beautiful women. They are a sort of mitigated disaster, for beauty does offer some consolation in the midst of calamity, a stroke of luck in a losing streak. But if, as you say, she is not even pretty, it is a catastrophe redoubled. Could any man at all endure this, much less a young man of your beauty? No, Charicles, by all the gods, not you—you'll be a slave and prematurely old, the bloom of your beauty crushed before its time. For marriage has this afterclap as well: the prime of your youth will wither. Please, Charicles, do not wither on the vine; don't let an ugly gardener pluck your lovely rose."

And Charicles replied: "The gods and I will look after this. The wedding is still some days off, and much can happen in a single night. We will discuss it thoroughly at our leisure. But now, I'm off to ride, to enjoy for the first time the wonderful horse you gave me. The exercise will lighten my sorrow." So it was that Charicles departed for his last ride, his first and final feat of horsemanship.

In the intervening sections, Clitophon confesses his love for Leucippe to Cleinias, who counsels him on how to seduce the girl and deal with the god Eros.

[12] While we were thus rapt in deep philosophy concerning the god, one of Charicles' slaves suddenly ran toward us. The expression on his face gave advance warning of bad news. When Cleinias saw him, he exclaimed, "Something has happened to Charicles." Simultaneously the slave exclaimed, "Charicles is dead."

Cleinias froze, stunned and speechless at the news, like a man caught in the eye of a tornado. The slave told the story.

"He mounted on your horse, Cleinias, and rode for a while at a gentle pace. After two or three laps he reined to a halt and began wiping the sweat off the horse, still seated on it and dropping his hold on the reins without a thought. While he was wiping its back, there was a noise from behind, and the horse gave a startled leap straight up into the air and then began to run crazily. Stung to terror, he tossed his head upwards, with the bit still between his teeth, and he performed acrobatic maneuvers, mane flying in the wind. As he ran, it seemed as if his back legs were trying to outrace the front legs, so closely did they follow in pursuit, leap for leap. This persistent bucking up and down of his legs, vying most energetically to outjump each other, made his back arch in rising and falling curves like stormy waves tossing a ship. Poor Charicles bounced to and fro on the alternate surges of this bronco-billow, sliding toward the tail or flung head-first toward the neck. While trying to ride out the squall, he lost control of the rein straps and surrendered himself to the hurricane of his mad career, a plaything of Chance. The horse in headlong flight galloped away from the road toward the woods and suddenly knocked poor Charicles against a tree. He was hurled from his seat as from a catapult, and his face was pelted by the branches, gashed with as many incisions as there were points on the broken wood. The rein thongs were wrapped about his waist and did not pull free but dragged him along, leaving a trail of death. The horse was frightened still further by the falling body, and when it got in the way of his legs, he kicked at the poor corpse, trampling it as an impediment to his progress. He is no longer recognizable as Charicles."

[13] Cleinias was stunned silent for a time. Recovering his senses, he gave a loud moan and started off running toward the body. I followed along, offering such consolation as I could. Charicles was being carried home, a pitiful and grievous spectacle. He was one continuous wound, at the sight of which no bystander could hold back his tears. His father began the mourning with the following distracted outcry.

"O my son, the difference of state between your departure and return! Curses on such riding! Alas for this uncommon death! Alas for your uncomely corpse! Other cadavers preserve at least the trace of their familiar features; they lose the bloom of freshness but retain a recognizable resemblance, consoling our grief by the semblance of sleep. Death takes away the inner life but not its human encasement. Yet Fortune has robbed you of this too, decreeing death (alas!) for body as well as for soul. Even your profile and outline have disappeared. Your soul has fled and I can find no trace of you in these—oh—too mortal remains.

"And when will you marry, my son; when will I make the offerings to sanctify your wedding, O groom and bridegroom—unconsummated bridegroom, unlucky chevalier. Your bridal chamber is the grave, your wedlock is with death, your wedding march a funeral hymn, your marriage song this dirge. I looked to light a different torch for you my son, but envious Fortune extinguished my hope along with your life. Instead, she lights these firebrands of disaster. Oh, how these torches keep wickedly burning—to light the consummation not of your love, but of your life."

[14] So the father spoke his sorrow, while not far off Cleinias uttered his grief privately—lover and father in mournful competition.

"I have lost my master. Why did I give him such a gift? It should have been a golden bowl that he might drink from it and pour libations and use my gift for his revels. Instead—O twisted fate—I gave the lovely boy a wild animal and even decorated the sinful beast with breastplate and frontlet, with silver cheekplates and golden bridle. O Charicles, I put golden trinkets on your murderer. O monstrous horse, you brute insensitive to beauty! He wiped your sweaty withers, promised extra fodder, praised your gait—and you killed him while he flattered you. Did you not love the touch of such a body; weren't you proud to be ridden by such a rider? No, you heartless beast, you trampled his beauty in the dust. O, cruel fate! I bought you your murderer and gave him to you as a gift!"

10.18 Achilles Tatius, *Leucippe and Clitophon* 2.33–38

With the aid of his cousin Cleinias and his servant Satyrus, Clitophon elopes with Leucippe on a ship sailing to Alexandria.

[33] When it was breakfast time, a young man who had settled his belongings next to ours very kindly asked us to eat with him. Satyrus was already serving our breakfast, so we put what we had together in the middle and shared both food and conversation.

I spoke first. "Where do you come from, my young friend, and what is your name?"

"I am Menelaus, born in Egypt. And you?"

"I am Clitophon, and this is Cleinias, both from Phoenicia."

"Why are you traveling?"

"We'd like to hear your story first: then we will tell you ours."

[34] "The principal cause of my travels is the jealousy of Eros and a fateful safari. I was in love with a handsome young man who had a passion for hunting. Often I tried to hold him back, but I could never control him. When he wouldn't be persuaded, I joined him in the chase. We were both on horses, and at first the hunt was successful, as we pursued only smaller creatures. But suddenly a wild boar bolted from the underbrush, and the lad took off in hot pursuit. The boar wheeled about, leveled his tusks at him, and ran straight at him. My boyfriend didn't turn aside, though I called and screamed, 'Hold back; rein aside; he's dangerous.'

"The boar was moving in fast, covering ground by leaps and bounds, making straight for my lover. They were on a collision course, and I was shaking with fright as I watched. Afraid that the boar would strike first and gore the horse, I wound the thongs on my javelin and hurled it at the target without taking careful aim. My lover veered straight into its trajectory and intercepted the weapon.

"What do you think my feelings were then? If I had any feelings at all, they were those of a man dying though still alive. Saddest of all, he reached out his arms to me, just barely breathing, embraced me, and as he lay there dying of that blow I had dealt him, he felt no hatred for me—murderer most foul. And he died in the embrace of the very arms that had killed him.

"The young man's parents brought me to court, and I did not resist. I took the stand and made no defense. Rather I demanded the death penalty for myself. The judges favored clemency and sentenced me to three years in exile, a period that is just now ending. And so I am returning to my own land."

Cleinias wept as he was speaking, "outwardly for Patroclus,"[86] remembering Charicles.

Menelaus said, "Are you weeping for me, or has a similar experience sent you into exile?"

Heaving a great sigh, Cleinias told him all about Charicles and his horse, and I, in turn, related my story.

[35] Since Menelaus was visibly depressed at the memory of his misfortune, and Cleinias silently wept at the thought of Charicles, to liven their spirits and turn their minds from sorrow I turned the discussion in the direction of *jeu d'amour*. Leucippe, of course, wasn't present: she was asleep in a corner of the ship.

I said with a sly smile: "Cleinias always comes out ahead of me. I know he was looking for an opportunity to deliver his diatribe against women as usual, which he could easily do now that he has found a companion who shares his view of love. It does look as if male-directed love is becoming the norm."

"But surely it is much preferable to the alternative," said Menelaus. "Young men are more open and frank than women, and their handsome bodies offer a sharper stimulus to pleasure."

"How can it be sharper? Their beauty no sooner peeps out than it is gone, before the lover has had time to savor it. It often vanishes like Tantalus' pool in the very act of drinking, and the lover goes away thirsty. It is snatched away in the midst of his drinking, before he is satisfied. A lover cannot come to the end of an affair with a boyfriend feeling unqualified gratification, for he is invariably left thirsty for something more."

[36] And Menelaus replied: "Clitophon, you don't know the principal fact about pleasure: to be unsatisfied is always a desirable state. Constant recourse to anything makes satisfaction shrivel into satiation. What can only be snatched is always fresh and blooming—its pleasure never grows old. And as much as beauty's span is diminished in time, so is it intensified in desire. The rose for this reason is lovelier than other plants: its beauty soon is gone.

"There are, I think, two kinds of beauty current among mortals, one heavenly, one vulgar, just like the two goddesses who represent these types of beauty. The heavenly beauty is oppressed at her implication in mortal beauty and seeks quickly to mount to heaven; the vulgar gravitates down-

---

86. This phrase is from *Iliad* 19.302, where the captive Trojan women are forced to mourn for the dead Patroclus, but really weep for their own misfortunes.

wards and luxuriates among bodies. If you would like a poetic testimony to the heavenly ascent of beauty, listen to Homer.

> The gods caught up Ganymede to pour wine for
> Zeus because he was beautiful and they were
> Glad to have him among them.[87]

No woman has ever ascended to the heavens because of her beauty. (Zeus *has* been known to resort to women.) Alcmene became a tearful fugitive; Danae was consigned to the sea in a chest; Semele fed the fire.[88] But when Zeus desired a Phrygian youth, he gave him the sky, that Ganymede might live with him and serve his nectar. The previous occupant of that post was rudely ousted. It was, I believe, a woman."[89]

[37] "One can argue," I said, "that the beauty of women is the more heavenly in that it does not so quickly fade. Timelessness is next to godliness. Anything that changes and fades reflects its mortal nature, and is vulgar rather than heavenly. Zeus lusted, indeed, for a Phrygian youth and brought this Phrygian youth to heaven; but the loveliness of women brought Zeus himself down to earth. To win a woman Zeus has mooed, has capered the satyric high step, has transformed himself to gold.[90] Let Ganymede serve the nectar; let Hebe drink with the gods; let the woman be served by the youth. His rape was not even stylish: a carnivorous bird swooped down, made the snatch, rode roughshod over him—all very undignified, and rather a tasteless spectacle—a young man dangling from those talons. Semele's escort to heaven is nothing to be surprised at. It got Heracles there.[91] You laugh at Danae's chest, but you didn't mention little Perseus in there with her. Alcmene was more than satisfied that Zeus had shanghaied three whole days and spent them all on her.[92]

"If we might pass from this heroic casuistry to speak of the real pleasures involved, though I am only a novice in my experience of women, and that has been restricted to commercial transactions with women of the street, and though another more deeply initiated into their secrets might well have more to say, yet I will speak in their behalf, even though I have no very wide experience.

87. *Iliad* 20.234–35.

88. All three mortal women bore children to Zeus. Alcmene was later persecuted by her nephew, the king of Tiryns; Danae was punished by her father; Semele was consumed in flames when Zeus made love to her.

89. Hebe, the daughter of Zeus and Hera, was formerly the cupbearer to the gods.

90. Zeus transformed himself into a bull to seduce Europa, a satyr to rape Antiope, and a shower of gold to impregnate Danae.

91. Semele and Heracles were both consumed in fire.

92. Zeus stopped the Sun from traversing the sky for three days to prolong his night of pleasure.

"A woman's body is well lubricated in the clinch, and her lips are tender and soft for kissing. Therefore she holds a man's body wholly and congenially wedged into her embraces, into her very flesh; and her partner is totally encompassed with pleasure. She plants kisses on your lips like a seal touching warm wax; and if she knows what she is doing, she can sweeten her kisses, employing not only the lips but the teeth, grazing all around the mouth with gentle nips. The fondled breast, too, is not without its special pleasure.

"When the sensations named for Aphrodite are mounting to their peak, a woman goes frantic with pleasure; she kisses with mouth wide open and thrashes about like a mad woman. Tongues all the while overlap and caress, their touch like passionate kisses within kisses. Your part in heightening the pleasure is simply to open your mouth.

"When a woman reaches the very goal of Aphrodite's action, she instinctively gasps with that burning delight, and her gasp rises quickly to the lips with a love breath, and there it meets a lost kiss, wandering about and looking for a way down: this kiss mingles with the love breath and returns with it to strike the heart. The heart then is kissed, confused, throbbing. If it were not firmly fastened in the chest, it would follow along, drawing itself upwards to the place of kisses.

"Schoolboys are hardly so well educated in kissing; their embraces are awkward; their lovemaking is lazy and devoid of pleasure."

[38] And Menelaus replied: "You seem less like a novice and more like an old, a very old pro at Aphrodite's business, bombarding us with all these fancy refinements devised by women. Now listen to a rebuttal on behalf of boys.

"Women are false in every particular, from coquettish remarks to coy posturing. Their lovely looks are the busy contrivance of various ointments: they wear the borrowed beauty of myrrh, of hair dye, even chemical preparations. If you strip them of their many false attractions, they would be like the fabled jackdaw who lost his feathers.[93] A boy's beauty is not carefully nurtured by the odor of myrrh nor enhanced by other scents of insidious intent. Sweeter than all a woman's exotic oils is the honest day's sweat of an active lad.

"And young men have the privilege, before wrestling under Aphrodite's rules, of grappling on the mat, publicly locking bodies in the gym; and no one says these embraces are immodest. The softer sex are flabby opponents in Aphrodite's ring, but boys' bodies compete on equal terms, striving like athletes whose mutual goal is pleasure.

93. *Phaedrus* 1.3 tells the fable of a jackdaw who planted some peacock feathers among his own and strutted about, only to have the peacocks pull out all his feathers such that he no longer looked even like a jackdaw.

"His kisses, to be sure, are not sophisticated like a woman's; they are no devastating spell of lips' deceit. But he kisses as he knows how—acting by instinct, not technique. Here is a metaphor for a boy's kiss: take nectar; crystallize it; form it into a pair of lips—these would yield a boy's kisses. You could not have enough of these: however many you took, you would still be thirsty for more, and you could not pull your mouth away until the very excess of pleasure frightened you into escaping."

10.19 Longus, *Daphnis and Chloe* 4.11–12, 16–21

Longus is another Greek novelist of the second or third century C.E., probably from the island of Lesbos, where his novel is set. Unlike the other Greek romances, this one is localized within a limited pastoral locale and draws on the bucolic poetry of Theocritus and possibly Vergil. In the last book, the goatherd Daphnis waits for the master to visit his country estate so as to ask him for permission to marry Chloe, but Daphnis must first fend off the advances of Gnathon, the parasitical friend of the master's son, Astylus.

[11] Astylus complimented them on these things and turned his attention to hunting hares, as you'd expect of a rich young man who spent all his time amusing himself and had come to the country to find a new type of pleasure. But all Gnathon[94] knew how to do was to eat and to drink till he was drunk and to have sex when he was drunk. He was nothing but a mouth and a stomach and what lies underneath the stomach. He had paid close attention to Daphnis when he brought the gifts. He had homosexual inclinations,[95] and now that he'd found beauty of a kind you don't get in the city, he decided to make advances, thinking it would be easy to win over Daphnis, who was a goatherd. Having reached this decision, he didn't join Astylus on the hunt but went down to where Daphnis was grazing his herd. He pretended he had come to look at the goats, but actually he was looking at Daphnis. To soften him up, he complimented him on the goats, asked him to play a goatherd's tune on the pipes, and said he would quickly make him a free man, being a person of immense power.

[12] When he saw Daphnis was amenable, he lay in wait for the boy at night when he was driving the goats from the pasture. Gnathon ran up to Daphnis, kissed him first, and then tried to talk him into letting himself be used as he-goats use the she-goats. Daphnis slowly realized what he meant and said that it was all right for he-goats to mount she-goats, but that nobody had ever seen a he-goat mounting a he-goat or a ram mounting a

---

94. The name is related to *gnathos* (jaw or mouth).
95. Literally, "he was a pederast by nature."

ram instead of a ewe or cocks mounting cocks instead of hens. Gnathon then got ready to take him by force and was putting his hands on him, but Daphnis pushed him away and threw him to the ground (the man was drunk and could hardly stand up). Daphnis scampered off like a puppy and left him lying on the ground, needing a man, not a boy, to give him a helping hand. After that Daphnis didn't let Gnathon come near him at all but grazed his goats in different places at different times, avoiding him and looking after Chloe. But Gnathon didn't meddle with him anymore, having found out that he was not only handsome but also strong. But he started looking for an opportunity to talk to Astylus about him and formed the hope of getting him as a present from the young man, who was often willing to do great favors.

The intervening paragraphs describe the arrival of the master and his wife, who are impressed by a display of Daphnis' musical abilities.

[16] Gnathon, on the other hand, was still more inflamed by what had happened at the goat pasture, and thought that life was not worth living if he didn't get Daphnis. He waited until he could catch Astylus walking around the garden, then brought him to the temple of Dionysus, and started kissing his hands and feet. Astylus asked him why he was doing that, told him to say what was on his mind, and swore that he would help him.

"Master," the other said, "this is the end of your poor Gnathon. The one who, until now, loved only your table, who swore that nothing had a finer bloom than a vintage wine, who said that your cooks were better than the young men of Mytilene[96]—now the only thing that I find beautiful is Daphnis! I've lost my taste for expensive food—although there's such a lot being prepared every day, meat, fish, honey cakes—and I'd enjoy turning into a she-goat and eating grass and leaves as long as I was listening to the pipes of Daphnis and was led to pasture by him. Rescue your Gnathon and defeat unconquerable Love. If you don't, I swear by you, my own god, that I will take a dagger, and, filling my stomach with food, I shall kill myself in front of Daphnis's door; and then you'll no longer call me—as you used to, jokingly—'my sweet little Gnathon.'"

[17] Astylus was a generous young man, who had some experience of the pain of love himself, and he could not resist Gnathon when he cried and kissed his feet again. He promised to ask his father to give him Daphnis, and to take the young man to the city as a slave for himself and as a boyfriend for Gnathon. But wanting to induce in the man himself some mis-

96. The principal city of Lesbos, where the master's family lives.

givings, he asked, with a smile, if he wasn't ashamed at being in love with the son of Lamon and at being eager to lie with a young man who looked after goats; and as he said this, he made a gesture of disgust at the stink of the goats. But Gnathon had learned all about love talk in debauched drinking parties; and he did not fail to hit the mark, in his defense of himself and Daphnis.

"Master, nobody in love makes a fuss about things like that. Whatever the body he finds beauty in, he is still captured. That's why some people have fallen in love with a tree, a river, and a wild animal—though who could help feeling sorry for a lover who had to be frightened of the one he loved? I am in love with someone who has the body of a slave but the beauty of a free man. Don't you see how his hair is like a hyacinth, his eyes shine under his brows like a jewel in a golden setting, his face is very rosy, while his mouth is full of white teeth like ivory? What lover would not pray to take sweet kisses from someone like that? And if I've fallen in love with a herdsman, I've done what the gods have done. Anchises was a cowherd; and Aphrodite had him as her lover. Branchus used to graze goats; and Apollo loved him.[97] Ganymede was a shepherd; and the king of the universe snatched him away. We shouldn't look down on a boy who, as we've seen, is obeyed even by his goats, as though they loved him. Instead, we should be grateful to the eagles of Zeus for allowing such beauty to remain on Earth."

[18] Astylus laughed sweetly, especially at this last remark, and said that Love made men into great orators; then he looked out for an opportunity to speak to his father about Daphnis. Eudromus[98] had been secretly listening to this whole conversation. He liked Daphnis, regarding him as an honest young man; and he was annoyed at the thought of such a handsome man becoming the object of Gnathon's drunken lust. So he told everything to Daphnis and Lamon. Daphnis was horrified and resolved to risk an attempt at running away with Chloe or to take her as his companion in death. But Lamon called Myrtale outside the farm and said:

"Wife, we're finished. The time has come to reveal the secrets.[99] You and I will spend our life deserted if I do; the goats will be deserted, and everything else too. But, by Pan and the Nymphs, even if I'm to be left like an ox in the stall (as they say), I won't keep silent about Daphnis's origin. I shall tell how I found him exposed; I shall reveal how I found him being

---

97. Apollo subsequently gave Branchus prophetic powers as a gift, and Branchus founded the oracle of Apollo at Didymas, south of Miletus on the coast of Asia Minor.

98. A servant and messenger of the master Dionysophanes.

99. Lamon and Myrtale are the supposed parents of Daphnis, but their secret is that Daphnis was actually an abandoned child whom they found suckled by a she-goat.

suckled; I shall show the objects left out with him. That revolting Gnathon must know the sort of person he's in love with. Just get the tokens ready for me."

[19] Agreeing on this plan, they went inside again. When his father was unoccupied, Astylus sidled up to him. He asked to be allowed to take Daphnis back to the city; Daphnis, he said, was handsome, too good for the country, and he could quickly be taught the ways of the town by Gnathon. His father gave Daphnis to him with pleasure, and, sending for Lamon and Myrtale, he told them the good news that in future Daphnis would serve Astylus instead of she-goats and he-goats, and promised to give them two goatherds in his place. All the slaves were now crowding round and were pleased that they would have such a handsome fellow slave when Lamon asked permission to speak and started in this way.

"Master, hear the truth from an old man. I swear by Pan and the Nymphs that I shall tell no lies. I am not Daphnis' father, nor has Myrtale ever had the good fortune to be a mother. This child had different parents, who exposed him, perhaps because they had enough older children. I found him exposed, being suckled by my she-goat; when the goat died, I buried it in the yard, loving it because it did the work of a mother. I also found some tokens left out with him—I admit this, master—and I have kept them till now. They are signs of his fortune in life, which is higher than ours. It isn't that I think it's beneath him to become the slave of Astylus, a fine servant for a fine gentleman. But I can't let him become the object of Gnathon's drunken lust—for Gnathon's keen to take him to Mytilene to do the job of a woman."

[20] After saying this, Lamon stopped talking and cried a great deal, while Gnathon blustered and threatened to beat him. Dionysophanes was startled at this statement. He told Gnathon to keep quiet, shooting fierce glances at him, while he questioned Lamon again, telling him to tell the truth and not to make up fabulous tales in an attempt to keep his son with him. But Lamon stood firm and swore by all the gods and offered himself for torture to test if he was lying. So, asking Cleariste [100] to sit on one side and leave him alone, Dionysophanes reviewed what Lamon had said.

"Why should Lamon be lying, when he stands to get two goatherds instead of one? In any case, how could a rustic have made this up? In fact, wasn't it incredible from the start that such a handsome son could have been produced by an old man of that sort and his shabby wife?"

[21] The best thing seemed to be to stop guessing and to look at the tokens to see if they gave signs of a splendid origin and one that was more

100. The master Dionysophanes' wife.

distinguished than Daphnis's present situation. Myrtale went away to bring all the things, which had been put in an old bag for safekeeping. When she had brought them, Dionysophanes saw them first, and once he had seen a purple cloak, a gold clasp, and a dagger with an ivory handle, he gave a great shout of "Oh, Lord Zeus!" and called his wife to come and look. She saw them and also gave a great cry. "Oh, the dear Fates! Aren't these the things we left out with our own child? Wasn't it to these very fields we sent Sophrone, when we told her to carry him off? Yes, these things are nothing other—they are the very things. Dear husband, the child is ours. Your son is Daphnis, and he has been grazing his father's goats."

10.20 Artemidorus, *Dream Analysis* 1.78.1, 7–8, 11–16, 20–21; 1.79.13–14; 1.80.3

In the late second century C.E., *Artemidorus of Ephesus collected for the instruction of his son a book of dreams and their interpretation. The section from which these extracts are taken concerns dreams of a sexual nature, with heterosexual and homosexual dreams intermingled.*

[78.1] The best set of categories for the analysis of intercourse is, first, intercourse according to nature and convention and customary usage, then intercourse against convention, and third, intercourse against nature. . . .[101]

[78.7] To have sex with one's own female slave or male slave is good, for slaves are the dreamer's possessions, therefore taking pleasure in them signifies the dreamer's being pleased with his own possessions, most likely because of their increase in number or value.

[78.8] To be penetrated by one's house slave is not good. This signifies being despised or injured by the slave. The same applies to being penetrated by one's brother, whether older or younger, or *a fortiori* by one's enemy. . . .

[78.11] To be penetrated by an acquaintance is profitable for a woman, depending on what sort of man is entering her. For a man to be penetrated by a richer, older man is good, for the custom is to receive things from such men. To be penetrated by a younger, poorer man is bad, for it is the custom to give to such. The same meaning applies if the penetrator is older but poorer.

---

101. It might be more accurate to translate "convention" and "deviating from nature," since the Greek preposition *para* does not denote opposition, but something beside or beyond. The following paragraphs up through **78.12** illustrate the first category, from **78.13** the second category, and from **80.1** the third category.

[78.12] If a man dreams of manipulating his penis, he will penetrate his male slave or female slave, because the hands applied to his penis are serving him. If he has no servants, he will undergo some penalty because of the useless ejaculation of semen. I know a slave who dreamed he was masturbating his master and he became the chaperon and overseer of his children, for he held in his hands the master's penis, which signifies his children. Again, I know someone who dreamed he was masturbated by his master: he was tied to a pillar and received many blows, thus being beaten off by his master.

[78.13] Concerning intercourse contrary to convention, one must analyze as follows. To penetrate a son under five years of age signifies the child will die, a result which I have often observed. Probably the significant connection is the infant's corruption, for we call death a corruption. If the child is over five but under ten, he will be sick and the dreamer will be foolishly involved in some business and will take a loss. The sickness is signified by the pain of a child being penetrated before the right age and season, the dreamer's loss is through his folly, for it is not the act of a man of sound mind to penetrate his own son or any other boy of that age. If the son is a young adolescent and the father is poor, he will send his son to a teacher and the tuition he pays for his son will be a kind of expenditure into him. If a rich man has this dream, he will give his son many gifts and transfer property to his name, undergoing a loss of substance.

[78.14] To have sex with a son already grown is good for a man who is out of the country, for the dream signifies coming together and abiding together, by the name "sexual union."[102] But for one who is already with his son and living at home it is bad; they will necessarily experience a separation from each other, because the intercourse of men for the most part takes place by one turning his back on the other.

[78.15] To be penetrated by one's son signifies violent injury from the son, an injury which the son too will regret.

[78.16] If a man dreams of penetrating his own father, he will become a fugitive from his fatherland or will develop an enmity with his father. For either the father himself will turn away from him or the whole population, which has the same signification in dreams as one's "pop." . . .

[78.20] To penetrate one's brother, whether older or younger, is good for the dreamer; for he will be above his brother and will look down on him.

[78.21] He who penetrates a friend will develop an enmity with him after inflicting some prior injury. . . .

102. The Greek word for intercourse *(sunousia)* also means "coming together" or "being together."

[79.13] He who is fellated by a friend or a relative or a child who is no longer an infant will develop an enmity with the fellator; he who is fellated by an infant will bury the infant, for it is no longer possible to kiss such a one. He who is fellated by an unknown person will suffer some penalty or other, because of the useless ejaculation of seed.

[79.14] If one dreams of performing oral sex on someone else and that person is an acquaintance, whether man or woman, he will develop an enmity with that person, because it is no longer possible to share mouths. If it is an unknown person, the dream is a bad one for all except for those who earn their living by their mouths, I mean flutists, trumpet-players, rhetors, sophists, and others like them. . . .

[80.4] If a woman penetrates a woman she will share her secrets with her. If she does not know the woman she penetrates, she will undertake useless projects. If a woman is penetrated by a woman, she will be separated from her husband or will be widowed; however, she will nonetheless learn the secrets of the other woman.

10.21 Aelius Lampridius, *SHA Commodus* 1.7, 5.11, 10.1, 10.8–9

Commodus was Marcus Aurelius' son and successor as emperor (180–92 C.E.), but lacked his philosophical temperament and was widely hated. Suetonian-style biographies of earlier emperors written during the time of the Christian emperor Constantine (early fourth century C.E.) are attributed to a shadowy figure named Aelius Lampridius, but the name may have been a fiction.

[1.7] . . . For even from his earliest boyhood he was base, wicked, cruel, lustful, impure in mouth,[103] and stained by debauchery. . . .

[5.11] Nor did he lack the disgraceful reputation of having young men penetrate him. He was impure with his mouth and every part of his body in regard to each sex. . . .

[10.1] Even as a boy he was gluttonous and without sexual modesty. As a youth he disgraced every kind of man who was with him, and was disgraced by all of them. . . .

[10.8] He had among his favorites men who were named after the sex organs of each gender; he gladly kissed them. **[10.9]** He also had a man with a penis larger than even most animals'; he named this man "Donkey" and considered him a very dear friend to himself. Commodus even made him rich and bestowed on him a priesthood of the rural Hercules.[104]

---

103. This phrase usually denotes someone who practices fellatio.

104. Appropriate perhaps because of Hercules' reputation as a hero of superior strength and masculinity.

10.22 Dio Cassius 80.13.1–80.17.1

The Syrian Elagabalus was emperor from 218 to 222 C.E. His attempt to institute worship at Rome of the Syrian sun god and his other strange ways occasioned much controversy.

[**13**] But this Sardanapallus,[105] who considered it proper that even the gods live together according to the custom of marriage, himself carried on very extravagantly. For he married many women and had sex with still many more without any customary protocol. It was not, however, that he himself needed them at all, but so that when sleeping with his lovers he could imitate the action of the women and so that he could acquire comrades in outrage, taking up with them in abandon. Many are the strange things he both did with his body and passively experienced, which no one could stand to speak of or hear. But the most egregious things (and these no one could cover up) are as follows. At night he would go to the taverns wearing a wig and he would work the trade of a barmaid. He would enter the infamous brothels and, driving out the working girls, he would prostitute himself. In the end, he opened a brothel in the palace and there acted licentiously: standing at the door, naked at all times just like the prostitutes, rustling the curtain that was fitted with golden rings, he cooed and offered himself to the passersby with a delicate and ringing voice. Indeed, there were men expressly ordered to perform this task. For, just as in other matters, in this too he had many agents through whom he would solicit those most able to please him with their impurity. He would collect money from them and would exult in his wages. He would argue with his fellow whores, saying that he had more lovers than they did, and that he made more money.

[**14**] He did these things with all those who availed themselves of him in this way, but he also had a favorite man whom he wished to make Caesar because of this. . . . Whenever he presided at court he seemed more or less to be a man; however, in other situations he put on airs with both his actions and the timbre of his voice. Moreover, he would dance not only on the dance floor, but also when walking, sacrificing, being greeted, and giving speeches. Finally, so that I may now return to my original purpose, he was even given away in marriage as a woman; he was called "wife," "mistress," and "queen," and he spun wool, he bound his hair in a net, and he wore makeup on his eyes, applying white lead and red dye to them. Once he even shaved his chin and celebrated a festival for the occasion. After

---

105. An alternate name Dio uses for Elagabalus. The original Sardanapallus was the last king of Assyria in the seventh century B.C.E., infamous for living a life of luxury within his palace at Nineveh, cultivating a feminine appearance in dress and make-up.

this he would be depilated so that from this too he could be effeminate, and he even regularly greeted senators while he was reclining.

[15] "Her" husband was one Hierocles, a Carian slave, formerly the beloved of Gordian,[106] from whom he learned how to drive a chariot. Due to the latter skill he happened to gain the emperor's favor in a most unusual way. For, after falling out of his chariot in a race across from the seat of the emperor Sardanapallus, he lost his helmet in the fall, and he was exposed to the sight of the emperor (he, Hierocles, was still beardless and was adorned with blond hair), and he was ravished away on the spot into the palace. By virtue of his nocturnal deeds, Hierocles enraptured the emperor to a greater extent and he was himself more empowered. As a result he had power even beyond that of the emperor and considered it a trifle that his mother, who was still a slave, had been carried to Rome by soldiers and that she was now reckoned among the wives of former consuls. Indeed, other men also were often honored by Sardanapallus and became powerful, some because they stood together with him in his ascent to power and others because they slept with him in an act of "adultery." For he wished to make it seem as if he were committing adultery so that also in this he could mimic the most wanton of women, and he was frequently even caught in the act by his own design, and, because of this, he was brutally traduced by his husband so that he even had black eyes. He so loved Hierocles, not with a light disposition, but with a vehement and deeply rooted love, that he did not contest such punishment, but, quite to the contrary, he loved him all the more for these very acts, and truly wished to make him Caesar. He even made a threat against his grandmother when she obstructed him in this, and he came into conflict with the soldiers not least because of this man. [16] On account of this, he was soon to perish.

Then Aurelius Zoticus, a man from Smyrna, who was also called "Cook" on account of his father's profession, was both greatly loved and hated by the emperor, and because of this he was also saved. For this man was beautiful all over his body (owing to his athleticism); moreover, he greatly surpassed all others in the size of his genitalia. He was revealed to the emperor by those who were inquiring into these things, and he was immediately snatched away from the games and brought to Rome by an immense procession the size of which neither Augarus in the time of Severus nor Tiridates in the time of Nero had.[107] He held the position of bedroom-

---

106. An ambitious man from an old aristocratic family, who married the great-niece of the emperor Antoninus Pius and held several important magistracies under the following emperors. He later became emperor for a short reign in 238 C.E.

107. Tiridates was crowned king of Armenia by Nero in 66 B.C.E.; Augarus was also known as Abgar IX, King of Osrhoene, a client kingdom in the Upper Euphrates valley (i.e., northeastern Syria). He was brought to Rome by the emperor Septimius Severus in 202 C.E.

watchman before he was even seen by the emperor, and he was honored
with the name of Sardanapallus' grandfather Avitus. He was crowned in
garlands as if at a public festival, and he, illuminated by much torchlight,
came into the palace. The emperor, upon seeing him, jumped up rhyth-
mically; he answered, without hesitation, the usual address, which was
"Hail, Lord and Master," by coyly moving his neck in feminine fashion and
batting his eyes, "Do not call me 'Lord,' for I am 'Mistress.'" The emperor
immediately took a bath with him and, since he found him to be equal to
the rumor, lusted for him all the more when he saw him naked, and he
leaned upon his chest and he took his dinner upon his lap just like some
love-struck woman. Hierocles, however, fearing that the emperor would
be enslaved to this one even more than to himself, and that he might
suffer something terrible of the emperor's doing, such as often happens to
rivals-in-love, made Aurelius Zoticus impotent by means of a certain drug
of the wine stewards, who were friendly to him. And thus, incapacitated
with his impotence for the whole night, Zoticus was divested of everything
that he had acquired and was driven out of the palace and out of Rome,
and, after this, out of Italy completely. And this saved him.

The emperor was driven to such a pitch of sexual deviance that he even
saw fit to ask his physicians to construct a vagina for him by means of a pos-
terior incision, offering them a large compensation for this.

[17] One way or another Sardanapallus was bound to take away a fitting "recompense" in the near future for his own loathsomeness. For,
since he was doing these things and passively experiencing such things,
he was hated by both the people and the soldiers, upon whom he was very
reliant. Finally, he was even slain by them in the camp itself.

10.23 Aelius Lampridius, *SHA Elagabalus* 8.6–7, 10.5–7, 11.7–12.2

[8.6–7] He made a public bath in the royal palace and at the same time
opened to the public the baths of Plautinus so that from this place he
could collect a group of well-endowed men. It was carefully contrived that
those "hung like donkeys" might be sought from the whole city and from
among all the sailors. In this way they designated those who seemed to be
rather "manly." . . .

[10.5–7] He was given away in marriage as a woman and arranged it
so that he even had a matron-of-honor who shouted, "Start your preparations, Cook!" and he did this at the very time when Zoticus was sick.
Then he would inquire of the philosophers and of the most dignified men
whether they themselves in their youth also endured those things which he
was experiencing, and he did this quite shamelessly. For he never checked
himself from using obscene words, and he would show his shamelessness

with finger-signs. Neither did he have any shame in meetings nor when the public was listening to him. . . .

[**11.7–12.2**] Marius Maximus[108] said most of these things in his *Life of Elagabulus.* There were perverse friends of his, certain old men with the mien of philosophers, who would arrange their hair in nets, who claimed to have endured the same perverse things and boasted that they had husbands. These, certain people said, were just feigning their perversity so that they could become more dear to the emperor by their imitation of his vices. He commissioned a dancer who had played the stage at Rome as a prefect of the praetorian guard,[109] and the charioteer Cordius as a prefect of the watchmen, and the barber Claudius as prefect of the yearly wheat crop. To the remaining posts he promoted those who were recommended to him on account of the enormous size of their genitalia. He ordered that a mule-driver, a footman, a cook, and a locksmith take charge as collectors of the five-percent inheritance tax.

10.24 Aelius Lampridius, *SHA Severus Alexander* 24.3–4, 39.2

Alexander Severus was Elagabalus' chosen successor, coming into power as a mere boy and ruling from 222 to 235 C.E. His sexual mores were much more conservative.

[**24.3–4**] He forbade that the tax gathered from pimps, prostitutes, and professional catamites[110] should be deposited into the sacred treasury of the State, but, instead, dedicated it to the restoration of the Theater of Marcellus, Circus Maximus, Colisseum, and Stadium.[111] He had it in mind to eliminate the professional catamites altogether (which Philip later did),[112] but was afraid that an outright prohibition would turn a public disgrace into a matter of private desires,[113] since men who are buffeted by passion always want prohibited vices more than those that are allowed. . . .

[**39.2**] His enjoyment of Venus was moderate and he was so inexperienced with professional catamites that, as we said above, he wanted to pass a law to get rid of them.

108. A contemporary of Elagabalus who continued Suetonius' project by writing biographies of all the emperors from the time of Nerva. He was the major source for much of Aelius Lampridius' work and uncritically recorded gossip about court scandals.

109. The commander of the emperor's elite bodyguard.

110. The Latin word is *exoleti,* used especially of those who were no longer boys.

111. Probably the stadium originally built by Domitian in the Campus Martius. Significantly, all these are places of entertainment and thus appropriately supported by a tax on a different kind of "entertainment."

112. Philip the Arab, emperor from 244 to 249.

113. In other words, men would practice the same acts secretly rather than openly, where their character might be known.

10.25 Philostratus, *Love Letter* 7 Kytzler

Philostratus was a biographer and sophist active in the early third century C.E. Some scholars believe that the erotic epistles ascribed to him may not be his, perhaps the work of his son-in-law or another descendent.

Because I am poor, you think I am less respectable. And yet Eros himself is naked, as are the Graces and the stars. In paintings I see even Heracles clad in an animal's hide[114] and often sleeping on the ground, and Apollo in a mere loincloth throwing the discus, shooting the bow, or running. The Persian kings revel in luxury and sit aloft, giving themselves airs with their abundant gold. On that account they fared badly when conquered by the impoverished Greeks. Socrates was a beggar, but the rich Alcibiades crept under his cloak.[115] Poverty is not a legitimate reproach, nor does each man's fortune excuse his fault in social relations with his fellows. Look at the theater: the crowd consists of poor men. Look at the courts: poor men sit on the juries. Look at military battles: the well-equipped and gilded soldiers leave the ranks, while we excel. As regards relations with the beautiful, look at the difference: the rich man insults the boy who has been seduced, as if he had been bought, whereas the poor man is grateful, as if he had been pitied. The former swaggers at his catch, whereas the latter keeps silent. The man of brilliant station attributes what has happened to the prerogative of his personal power, whereas the poor man attributes it to the humanity and kindness of the boy who bestows the favor. The rich man sends as messenger a flatterer, parasite, cook, or waiters, whereas the poor man sends himself, that he might not deprive his favorite of the honor of personal attention. The rich man is immediately caught when he gives a gift, for the affair is exposed by the number of people who know about it, so that neither neighbors nor even passersby are unaware of the drama. But the boy who enjoys a poor friend escapes detection, for there is not pomp in this man's courtship: he doesn't confess his good fortune, but hides it, so as to avoid the denunciation of outsiders or the emergence of rival lovers among those more powerful than himself. Why should I say more? The rich man calls you his "beloved"; I call you my "master." That man calls you a "servant"; I call you a "god." That man considers you a part of his possessions; I consider you everything. Hence when he falls in love with another, that boy will be just the same to him, whereas a poor man loves only once. Who can remain with you when you are sick? Who can stay up nights with you? Who can go into the army with you? Who can throw

---

114. Heracles was usually depicted with a cape formed by the pelt of the Nemean Lion, whose conquest was his first labor.

115. See **5.7.219**.

himself into the path of an arrow headed toward you? Who can die for
you? In all these regards I am rich.

10.26 Philostratus, *Love Letter* 9 K

What happened to the roses? Before you had them, they were beautiful
and truly roses (for I wouldn't have sent them unless they were worthy
of possession), but after coming to you they immediately withered and
breathed out their last. I don't clearly know the cause, for they didn't want
to tell me anything. It is easy to conjecture that they couldn't bear the
competition with you or being outdone in others' estimation, and as soon
as they touched a sweeter smelling skin they were destroyed. So even a
lamp fades when conquered by a stronger light, and the stars become dull
because they cannot face the Sun.

10.27 Philostratus, *Love Letter* 11 K

How many times have I opened up my eyes for you, that you might run
away, just like hunters who spread open their nets to give animals the possibility of escape? And you just remain seated there, like pesky squatters
who, once they have taken someone else's land, won't hear of moving
on. And again, just as I have been accustomed to do, I lift up my eyelids.
Finally now fly away, break your siege, and become the guest of other eyes!
You aren't listening, and you hold me even more than before, clutching
my very soul. And what is this new inflammation? I am in danger. I ask for
water. No one brings it, because the extinguisher is powerless against a
flame like this one, whether one takes it from a spring or a river. For even
water itself is set on fire by love.

10.28 Philostratus, *Love Letter* 14 K

Greetings, even though you don't want them. Greetings, even if you don't
write, beautiful to others, but haughty toward me. You were not created out
of flesh and the things mixed with it, but out of steel, stone, and Styx.[116]
May I soon have occasion to witness you growing a beard and sitting outside
others' doors.[117] Aye, Eros and Nemesis[118] are swift and inconstant gods!

---

116. A grim river of the Underworld. Its name is related to the verb *stugein* (to hate).

117. A reference to the setting of the *paraclausithyron*, the serenade of the locked-out lover.
See n. 29.

118. The goddess of revenge, elsewhere associated with punishment of unrequited love;
cf. **6.45**.

10.29 Philostratus, *Love Letter* 15 K

Why do you show me your beard, my boy? You are not ending your beauty, but starting it. For although the peak of your youthful season, the part that is flighty and untrustworthy, has passed and is extinguished like a burst of flame, the settled and secure part remains. Time does not embarrass the truly beautiful, but shows them off and bears witness to them more than it begrudges them. Homer, a poet who knows how both to observe and to write about beauty, says that the bearded man is the most lovely.[119] He would never have revealed this unless he himself had first touched and kissed the beard of a beloved. For before they bloomed, your tender and radiant cheeks did not differ from a woman's. But now that you are downy, you are more manly and perfect than your former self. What? Did you want to be no different from a eunuch? Their chins are barren, hard, and stony. These tainted men are at any rate more ashamed of this razor than that one,[120] considering that a secret, this a clear and visible sign of their condition.

10.30 Philostratus, *Love Letter* 18 K

You are delicately disposed, pained by your sandal, as I infer. For new leather is terrible at biting tender flesh. For this reason Asclepius[121] readily heals wounds from war, wild beasts, and all such misfortunes, but he disregards these wounds because they are self-inflicted, occurring more from folly than a spirit's curse. Why don't you go barefoot? Why begrudge the ground? Little slippers, sandals, boots, and shoes are things worn by the old or infirm. At any rate they depict Philoctetes in such protective gear, since he was lame and infirm,[122] but they show barefoot the philosopher of Sinope, Theban Crates,[123] Ajax, and Achilles, and Jason half-barefoot. For it is said that his boot was held by the stream when he was crossing the river Anaurus and the mud laid claim to it.[124] And so one of Jason's feet was set free by Fortune and he was taught what was fitting; not choosing it intentionally, he went away well robbed. Let nothing come between

---

119. *Iliad* 24.348.

120. I.e., the razor that castrated them.

121. The god of medicine.

122. Philoctetes had a festering wound from a snakebite on his foot and was abandoned on the island of Lemnos by the other Greek heroes sailing to Troy.

123. The philosopher of Sinope is Diogenes the Cynic; Crates was his pupil. Since the Cynics rejected all wealth and unnecessary convention, they wore only whatever clothing was physically necessary.

124. This event is significant in the hero's story because the reigning king of Iolcus, Pelias, had been told that he was destined to be overthrown by a man wearing one shoe.

the Earth and your foot. Don't be afraid: the dust will welcome your step like grass, and we shall all kiss your footsteps. Ah, rhythmic steps of dearest feet! New flowers! Plants of the Earth![125] Kiss cast to the ground!

10.31 Philostratus, *Love Letter* 27 K

How ill-tempered and contentious beauty is for you! It blooms more when neglected, like wild plants vigorous by nature and not needing farmers' attention. You don't ride a horse or frequent the wrestling school or lie out in the sun (for a suntan is beautiful boys' flower). But you go about dirty and at war with yourself. You have deceived yourself! You *are* beautiful, even if you don't want to be, just like grape-clusters, apples, and anything else inherently fair. For beautification is a courtesan's art, and one should be ill disposed toward adulterated good looks, as something close to trickery. But unmixed, guileless, uncontrived beauty is the unique possession of those who received it. So even Apollo loved shepherds, Aphrodite cowherds, Rhea rustics, and Demeter those who never knew cities,[126] because everything that is present by nature is truer than what has been contrived by deceit. No one knows of stars, lions, or birds adorned with cosmetics, and the man who decks the face of a horse with gold, ivory, and ribbons doesn't know that he harms the animal's proud spirit and hands over to art the exercise of restoring nature's failings.

10.32 Philostratus, *Love Letter* 58 K

I praise you for matching your wits with Time's and shaving your face. What disappeared by nature remains by art; sweetest is the recovery of things lost. If you obey my advice, keep your hair long and care for your locks, so that some creep down your cheeks a little (anyone will easily brush these away when he wishes) and others lie on your shoulders, just as Homer says the Euboeans wear their hair long in back.[127] For the head blooms more delightfully than Athena's tree, since in fact this acropolis should also not be seen barren and unadorned.[128] However, let your face be bare and let nothing obscure this light, neither cloud nor fog. Just as closed-up eyes

---

125. The plants and flowers are imagined as springing up in the wake of the boy's footsteps.

126. Apollo fell in love with Branchus when herding goats (see **10.19.17** and n. 97); Aphrodite fell in love with Anchises, who was herding cattle on Mt. Ida; Rhea and Demeter were both goddesses of agriculture and therefore preferred the country.

127. *Iliad* 2.542.

128. Athena's tree is the olive, which she gave as a gift to Athens for honoring her as the city's chief god. A sacred olive tree grew on the Acropolis in the vicinity of her temple. A boy's "acropolis" (high point) is, of course, his head.

are no fair sight, so it is with a pretty boy's hairy face. So make your beauty last longer, whether with drugs, sharp razors, nimble fingers, soaps, herbs, or any other device. In this way you will imitate the unaging gods.

10.33 Philostratus, *Love Letter* 64 K

I don't know what to say about the self-restraint on which you vaunt yourself, whether it is a form of savagery opposed to Nature's orders, or a form of philosophy raised on high by boorish stupidity, or a self-chosen cowardice toward pleasures, or a haughty disdain for the better things in life. Whatever it may be and whatever the sophists may think of it, it is fair only in appearance, but rather inhuman in fact. What is noble in being a self-restrained corpse before departing this life? Crown yourself before you entirely wither away, anoint yourself before you rot, win friends before you become eternally alone. It is well to anticipate that night on this night:[129] drink before you are thirsty, eat before you are hungry. Which day do you think is yours? Yesterday? It's dead. Today? You're not using it. Tomorrow? I don't know whether it will be available to you. Both you and those days belong to Fortune.

10.34 Magical Papyrus = *PGM* 32

This spell is recorded on a second-century C.E. Greek papyrus found in Egypt. It attempts to bind one woman in love to another.

I adjure you, Evangelos, by Anubis and Hermes[130] and all the rest down below; attract and bind Sarapias, whom Helen bore, to this Herais, whom Thermoutharin bore,[131] now, now; quickly, quickly. By her soul and heart attract Sarapias herself, whom Helen bore from her own womb, *maei ote elbōsatok alaoubētō ōeio . . . aēn*. Attract and bind the soul and heart of Sarapias, whom Helen bore, to this Herais, whom Thermoutharin bore from her womb, now, now; quickly, quickly.

10.35 Magical Papyrus = *PGM* 32a

Like the preceding example, this spell is also preserved on a second-century C.E. Greek papyrus from Egypt, but it seeks to bind one man to another. The papyrus was tied around a clay figurine, presumably of Ammonius.

---

129. In other words, enjoy yourself tonight in the knowledge of that coming eternal night when there will be no more possibility of pleasure.

130. The Egyptian god Anubis is often syncretized with the Greek Hermes: both escorted souls of the dead. Evangelos ("the good messenger") is appropriately invoked with their names.

131. Herais, the woman casting the spell, has a Greek name, but her mother was apparently Egyptian.

As Typhon is the adversary of Helius,[132] so inflame the heart and soul of that Ammonius whom Helen bore, even from her own womb, *Adōnai abrasax pinouti*[133] and *sabaōs;* burn the soul and heart of that Ammonius whom Helen bore, for love of this Serapiacus whom Threpte bore, now, now; quickly, quickly. In this same hour and on this same day, from this moment on, mingle together[134] the souls of both and cause that Ammonius whom Helen bore to be this Serapiacus whom Threpte bore, through every hour, every day and every night. Wherefore, *Adōnai,* loftiest of gods, whose name is the true one, carry out the matter, *Adōnai.*

10.36 Magical Papyrus = *Supplementum Magicum* 1.42

This lesbian binding spell was inscribed on an oval lead tablet found in Hermoupolis in Egypt. It is third or fourth century C.E. in date.

Fundament of the gloomy darkness, jagged-toothed dog, covered with coiling snakes, turning three heads, traveler in the recesses of the Underworld, come, spirit-driver,[135] with the Erinyes,[136] savage with their stinging whips; holy serpents, maenads, frightful maidens, come to my wroth incantations. Before I persuade by force this one and you, render him immediately a fire-breathing demon. Listen and do everything quickly, in no way opposing me in the performance of this action; for you are the governors of the Earth. *Alalachos allēch Harmachimeneus magimeneus athinembēs astazabathos artazabathos ōkoum phlom lonchachinachana* thou Azael and Lykael and Beliam and Belenea and *sochsocham somochan sozocham ouzacham bauzacham oueddouch.* By means of this corpse-demon inflame the heart, the liver, the spirit of Gorgonia, whom Nilogenia bore, with love and affection for Sophia, whom Isara bore. Constrain Gorgonia, whom Nilogenia bore, to cast herself into the bath-house for the sake of Sophia, whom Isara bore; and you,[137] become a bath-woman. Burn, set on fire, inflame her soul,

---

132. Typhon was the hundred-headed fire-breathing monster who challenged Zeus and the other Olympian gods. He appears to have had origins in Near Eastern mythology. In Egypt, he is identified with Seth, the enemy of Horus, whom some Greek sources identify with Apollo (and thus with the Sun). Interestingly, a Middle Kingdom papyrus (c. 1900 B.C.E.) narrates a story of sexual involvement between Seth and Horus.

133. The last word is Egyptian for "the god."

134. This verb frequently connotes sexual intercourse.

135. Addressed to Cerberus, the three-headed dog who guarded the gates of the Underworld.

136. An alternate name for the Furies, the three old women with serpent hair who pursued criminals as agents of vengeance. They are often represented as residing in the Underworld.

137. Addressed to the corpse-demon conjured up from the Underworld. A bath attendant would be responsible for keeping the fires going to heat the water, hence the imagery of heat and burning.

heart, liver, spirit with love for Sophia, whom Isara bore. Drive Gorgonia, whom Nilogenia bore, drive her, torment her body night and day, force her to rush forth from every place and every house, loving Sophia, whom Isara bore, she, surrendered like a slave, giving herself and all her possessions to her, because this is the will and command of the great god, *iartana ouousio ipsenthanchōchainchoueōch aeēioyō iartana ousiausiau ipsoengeuthadei annoucheō aeēioyō.* Blessed lord of the immortals,[138] holding the scepters of Tartarus and of terrible, fearful Styx and of life-robbing Lethe, the hair of Cerberus trembles in fear of you, you crack the loud whips of the Erinyes; the couch of Persephone delights you, when you go to the longed bed, whether you be immortal Sarapis, whom the universe fears, whether you be Osiris, star of the land of Egypt;[139] your messenger is the all-wise boy; yours is Anubis, the pious herald of the dead.[140] Come hither, fulfill my wishes, because I summon you by these secret symbols, *achaipō thōthō aiē iaē ai ia,* etc. . . . Constrain Gorgonia, whom Nilogenia bore, to cast herself into the bath-house for the sake of Sophia, whom Isara bore, for her. Aye, lord, king of the chthonic gods, burn, set on fire, inflame the soul, the heart, the liver, the spirit of Gorgonia, whom Nilogenia bore, with love and affection for Sophia, whom Isara bore; drive Gorgonia herself, torment her body night and day; force her to rush forth from every place and every house, loving Sophia, whom Isara bore, she, Gorgonia surrendered like a slave, giving herself and all her possessions. Aye, lord, king of the chthonic gods, carry out what is inscribed on this tablet, for I adjure you who divided the entire universe, a single realm,[141] *Thobarabau Semeseilamps sasibēl,* etc. . . . So, do not disobey my request, but cause Gorgonia, whom Nilogenia bore, force her to cast herself into the bath-house for the sake of Sophia, whom Isara bore, for her. Burn, set on fire, inflame the heart, the liver, the spirit of Gorgonia, whom Nilogenia bore, with love and affection for Sophia, whom Isara bore, for a good end. *Bolchozē gonsti ophthē,* burn, set on fire the soul, the heart, the liver, the spirit of Gorgonia, whom Nilogenia bore, with love and affection for Sophia, whom Isara bore, because this is the will of the great god, *achchōr achchōr achchach ptoumi chachchō charachōch chaptoumē . . . Chmouōr Harouēr Abrasax Phnouneboēl ochloba*

---

138. Addressed to Hades, king of the Underworld, husband of Persephone. Tartarus is the place of punishment within the Underworld. Styx and Lethe are subterranean rivers.

139. The Egyptian god Osiris was sometimes syncretized with the Greek Hades in Hellenistic texts, since he was also a ruler of the Underworld. Sarapis was a later god whose worship in Egypt was instituted by the Ptolemies and who took on many of Osiris' attributes.

140. The "all-wise boy" is Hermes, often represented as a precocious child in Greek myth. Anubis is his Egyptian counterpart.

141. Probably a reference to the primordial division of the universe between Zeus, Poseidon, and Hades. Hades would normally be considered the king of the chthonic (i.e., Underworld) gods, but the god here may be invoked as a single divinity with three aspects.

zarachōa baricham who is called *bacham kēbk*. Force Gorgonia, whom Nilogenia bore, to cast herself into the bath-house for the sake of Sophia,
whom Isara bore, for her, so that she love her with passion, longing, unceasing love. *Thēnōrthsi thēnōr Marmaraōth,* etc. . . . burn, set on fire the
soul, the heart, the liver, the spirit of Gorgonia, whom Nilogenia bore,
with love and affection for Sophia, whom Isara bore—with passion, longing, love, *ēnōr thēnōr Abrasax Mithra peuchrē Phrē Arsenophrē abari mamarembō
Iaō Iabōth,* drive, Sun, honey-holder, honey-cutter, honey-producer, *kme.m
Ablanathanalba Akrammachammari Sesengen Barpharaggēs,* drive Gorgonia,
whom Nilogenia bore, to love Sophia, whom Isara bore; burn, set on fire
the soul, the heart, the liver, the spirit of burned, inflamed, tortured Gorgonia, whom Nilogenia bore, until she casts herself into the bath-house
for the sake of Sophia, whom Isara bore; and you, become a bath-woman.

10.37 Ps.-Lucian, *Forms of Love*

*Although transmitted with the corpus of Lucian's works, this dialogue is on stylistic
grounds thought to be the work of a later imitator. The date is uncertain, but the dialogue is usually supposed to come from the third or fourth century* C.E.

LYCINUS: [1] Theomnestus, my friend, since dawn your sportive talk about
love has filled these ears of mine that were weary of unremitting attention to serious topics. As I was parched with thirst for relaxation of this
sort, your delightful stream of merry stories was very welcome to me.
For the human spirit is too weak to endure serious pursuits all the time,
and ambitious toils long to gain some little respite from tiresome cares
and to have freedom for the joys of life. This morning I have been quite
gladdened by the sweet winning seductiveness of your wanton stories, so
that I almost thought I was Aristides being enchanted beyond measure
by those Milesian Tales,[142] and I swear by those Loves of yours that have
found so broad a target that I am indeed sorry that you've come to the
end of your stories. If you think this is but idle talk on my part, I beg
you in the name of Aphrodite herself, if you've omitted mention of any
of your love affairs with a lad or even with a girl, coax it forth with the
aid of memory. Besides we are celebrating a festival today and sacrificing
to Heracles. You know well enough, I'm sure, how impetuous that god
was where love was concerned, and so I think he'll be most delighted to
receive your stories by way of an offering.
THEOMNESTUS: [2] You would find it quicker, my dear Lycinus, to count
me the waves of the sea or the flakes of a snowstorm than to count my

---

142. Aristides of Miletus probably lived around 100 B.C.E., gaining renown as the author of
erotic short stories, similar to the tale of the Pergamene boy in Petronius (9.14.85–87).

loves. For I for my part think that their quiver has been left completely empty and, if they choose to fly off in quest of one more victim, their weaponless right arms will be laughed to scorn. For, almost from the time when I left off being a boy and was accounted a young man, I have been beguiled by one passion after another. One Love has ever succeeded another, and almost before I've ended earlier ones later Loves begin. They are veritable Lernean heads appearing in greater multiplicity than on the self-regenerating Hydra, and no Iolaus can help against them.[143] For one flame is not extinguished by another. There dwells in my eyes so nimble a gadfly that it pounces on any and every beauty as its prey and is never sated enough to stop. And I am always wondering why Aphrodite bears me this grudge. For I am no child of the Sun, nor am I puffed up with the insolence of the Lemnian women or the boorish contempt of Hippolytus that I should have provoked this unceasing wrath on the part of the goddess.[144]

LYCINUS: [3] Stop this affected and unpleasant playacting, Theomnestus. Are you really annoyed that Fortune has allotted you the life you have? Do you think it a hardship that you associate with women at their fairest and boys at the flower of their beauty? But perhaps you'll actually need to take purges for so unpleasant an ailment. For you do suffer shockingly, I must say. Why won't you get all this nonsense out of your system and think yourself fortunate that god has not given you for your lot squalid husbandry or the wanderings of a merchant or a soldier's life under arms? But your interests are in the oily wrestling schools, in resplendent clothes that shed luxury right down to your feet and in seeing that your hair is fashionably dressed. The very torment of your amorous yearnings delights you and you find sweetness in the bite of passion's tooth. For when you have been tempted you hope, and when you have won your suit you take your pleasure, but get as much pleasure from future joys as from the present. Just now at any rate, when you were going through in Hesiodic fashion the long catalogue of your loves from the beginning,[145] the merry glances of your eyes grew meltingly liquid, and, giving your voice a delicate sweetness so that it matched

143. Killing the Hydra of Lerna was the second labor of Heracles. This multi-headed snake regenerated two heads in the place of every head cut off, until Heracles' nephew Iolaus helped him by cauterizing the necks with a torch.

144. Aphrodite punished the Sun for telling her husband, Hephaestus, about her adultery with Ares by making all the female descendants of the Sun fall in love unhappily. The Lemnian women dishonored Aphrodite, so she afflicted them with an unpleasant body odor that made them unattractive to their husbands. Hippolytus dishonored Aphrodite by despising women and remaining chaste.

145. The early epic poet Hesiod wrote catalogue poetry; the *Catalogue of Women* was included among his works in antiquity, although most of it was probably later.

that of the daughter of Lycambes,[146] you made it immediately plain
from your very manner that you were in love not only with your loves
but also with their memory. Come, if there is any scrap of your voyage
in the seas of love that you have omitted, reveal everything, and make
your sacrifice to Heracles complete and perfect.

THEOMNESTUS: [4] Heracles is a devourer of oxen, my dear Lycinus, and
takes very little pleasure, they say, in sacrifices that have no savory smoke.
But we are honoring his annual feast with discourse. Accordingly, as my
narratives have continued since dawn and lasted too long, let *your* Muse,
departing from her customary seriousness, spend the day in merriment
along with the god, and, as I can see you incline to neither type of passion, prove yourself, I beg, an impartial judge. Decide whether you consider those superior who love boys or those who delight in womankind.
For I, who have been smitten by both passions, hang like an accurate balance with both scales in equipoise. But *you,* being unaffected by either,
will choose the better of the two by using the impartial judgment of your
reason. Away with all coyness, my dear friend, and cast now the vote entrusted to you in your capacity as judge of my loves.

LYCINUS: [5] My dear Theomnestus, do you imagine that my narratives
are a matter of sport and laughter? No, they promise something serious
too. I at any rate have undertaken this task on the spur of the moment,
because I've known it to be far from a laughing matter, ever since the
time I heard two men arguing heatedly with each other about these two
types of love, and I still have the memory of it ringing in my ears. They
were opposites, not only in their arguments but in their passions, unlike you who, thanks to your easy-going spirit, go sleepless and earn
double wages, "One as a herdsman of cattle, another as tender of white
flocks."[147] On the contrary, one took excessive delight in boys and
thought love of women a pit of doom, while the other, virgin of all love
of males, was highly susceptible to women. So I presided over a contest
between these two warring passions and found the occasion quite in-
describably delightful. The imprint of their words remains inscribed in
my ears almost as though they had been spoken a moment ago. Therefore, putting aside all pretexts for being excused this task, I shall retail
to you exactly what I heard the two of them say.

THEOMNESTUS: Well, I shall get up from here and sit facing you, "Waiting
the time when Aeacus' son makes an end of his singing."[148] But you must
unfold for us in song the old and glorious lays of the contest of loves.

---

146. Archilochus wrote poems claiming to have seduced the daughters of Lycambes.
147. *Odyssey* 10.84–85.
148. *Iliad* 9.191, referring to Achilles' song.

LYCINUS: [6] I had in mind going to Italy and a swift ship had been made ready for me. It was one of the double-banked vessels which seem particularly to be used by the Liburnians, a race who live along the Ionian Gulf.[149] After paying such respects as I could to the local gods and invoking Zeus, God of Strangers, to assist propitiously in my expedition to foreign parts, I left the town and drove down to the sea with a pair of mules. Then I bade farewell to those who were escorting me, for I was followed by a throng of determined scholars who kept talking to me and parted with me reluctantly. Well, I climbed onto the poop and took my seat near the helmsman. We were soon carried away from land by the surge of our oars and, since we had very favorable breezes astern, we raised the mast from the hold and ran the yard up to the masthead. Then we let all our canvas down over the sheets and, as our sail gently filled, we went whistling along just as loud, I fancy, as an arrow does, and flew through the waves, which roared around our prow as it cut through them.

[7] But it isn't the time to describe at any length the events serious or light of the intervening coastal voyage. But, when we had passed the Cilician seaboard and were in the gulf of Pamphylia, after passing with some difficulty the Swallow-Islands, those fortune-favored limits of ancient Greece, we visited each of the Lycian cities,[150] where we found our chief pleasure in the tales told, for no vestige of prosperity is visible in them to the eye. Eventually we made Rhodes, the island of the Sun God, and decided to take a short rest from our uninterrupted voyaging.

[8] Accordingly our oarsmen hauled the ship ashore and pitched their tents nearby. I had been provided with accommodation opposite the temple of Dionysus and, as I strolled along unhurriedly, I was filled with an extraordinary pleasure. For it really is the city of Helius with a beauty in keeping with that god. As I walked round the porticos in the temple of Dionysus, I examined each painting, not only delighting my eyes but also renewing my acquaintance with the tales of the heroes. For immediately two or three fellows rushed up to me, offering for a small fee to explain every story for me, though most of what they said I had already guessed for myself.

[9] When I had now had my fill of sightseeing and was minded to go to my lodgings, I met with the most delightful of all blessings in a strange land, old acquaintances of long standing, whom I think you also know yourself, for you've often seen them visiting us here, Charicles a young

---

149. The Liburnians actually lived in Dalmatia, the coastal area on the east side of the Adriatic.

150. Apparently Lycinus' ship was sailing from Syria along the southern coast of Asia Minor toward Rhodes, in the southeastern Aegean.

man from Corinth who is not only handsome but shows some evidence
of skillful use of cosmetics, because, I imagine, he wishes to attract the
women,[151] and with him Callicratidas, the Athenian, a man of straight-
forward ways. For he was preeminent among the leading figures in public speaking and in this forensic oratory of ours.[152] He was also a devotee
of physical training, though in my opinion he was fond of the wrestling
schools only because of his love for boys. For he was enthusiastic only for
that, while his hatred for women made him often curse Prometheus.[153]
Well, they both saw me from a distance and hurried up to me overjoyed
and delighted. Then, as so often happens, each of them clasped me
by the hand and begged me to visit his house. I, seeing that they were
carrying their rivalry too far, said, "Today, Callicratidas and Charicles, it
is the proper thing for both of you to be my guests so that you may not
fan your rivalry into greater flame. But on the days to follow—for I've
decided to remain here for three or four days—you will return my hospitality by entertaining me each in turn, drawing lots to decide which of
you will start."

[10] This was agreed, and for that day I presided as host, while on the
next day Callicratidas did so, and after him Charicles. Now, even when
they were entertaining me, I could see concrete evidence of the inclinations of each. For my Athenian friend was well provided with handsome
slave boys and all of his servants were pretty well beardless. They remained with him till the down first appeared on their faces, but, once
any growth cast a shadow on their cheeks, they would be sent away to be
stewards and overseers of his properties at Athens. Charicles, however,
had in attendance a large band of dancing-girls and singing-girls and
all his house was as full of women as if it were the Thesmophoria,[154]
with not the slightest trace of male presence except that here and there
could be seen an infant boy or a superannuated old cook whose age
could give even the jealous no cause for suspicion. Well, these things
were themselves, as I said, sufficient indications of the dispositions of
both of them. Often, however, short skirmishes broke out between them
without the point at issue being settled. But, when it was time for me
to put to sea, at their wish I took them with me to share my voyage, for
they like me were minded to set out for Italy.

151. It is appropriate that the dialogue's advocate of heterosexuality should come from
Corinth, which featured a major cult of Aphrodite, which included female temple prostitutes.

152. Speeches in the law courts, for which Athens was famous since the orators of the late
fifth and fourth centuries B.C.E.

153. Prometheus' deceptions of Zeus on behalf of mankind led Zeus to punish men by creating the first woman, Pandora.

154. An annual festival of Demeter open only to married women.

[11] Now, as we had decided to anchor at Cnidus to see the temple of Aphrodite, which is famed as possessing the most truly lovely example of Praxiteles' skill,[155] we gently approached the land with the goddess herself, I believe, escorting our ship with smooth, calm waters. The others occupied themselves with the usual preparations, but I took the two authorities on love, one on either side of me, and went round Cnidus, finding no little amusement in the wanton products of the potters, for I remembered I was in Aphrodite's city. First we went round the porticos of Sostratus[156] and everywhere else that could give us pleasure and then we walked to the temple of Aphrodite. Charicles and I did so very eagerly, but Callicratidas was reluctant because he was going to see something female and would have preferred, I imagine, to have had Eros of Thespiae[157] instead of Aphrodite of Cnidus.

[12] And immediately, it seemed, there breathed upon us from the sacred precinct itself breezes fraught with love. For the uncovered court was not for the most part paved with smooth slabs of stone to form an unproductive area but, as was to be expected in Aphrodite's temple, was all of it prolific with garden fruits. These trees, luxuriant far and wide with fresh green leaves, roofed in the air around them. But more than all others flourished the berry-laden myrtle growing luxuriantly beside its mistress[158] and all the other trees that are endowed with beauty. Though they were old in years they were not withered or faded but, still in their youthful prime, swelled with fresh sprays. Intermingled with these were trees that were unproductive except for having beauty for their fruit —cypresses and planes that towered to the heavens and with them Daphne, who deserted from Aphrodite and fled from that goddess long ago.[159] But around every tree crept and twined the ivy, devotee of love.[160] Rich vines were hung with their thick clusters of grapes. For Aphrodite is more delightful when accompanied by Dionysus and the gifts of each are sweeter if blended together, but, should they be parted from each other, they afford less pleasure. Under the particularly shady trees were joyous couches for those who wished to feast themselves there.

155. Cnidus was at the end of a peninsula of Asia Minor immediately opposite Rhodes. The fourth-century B.C.E. sculptor Praxiteles represented Aphrodite having just disrobed to take a bath.

156. A famous Cnidian architect, whose porticos supported a series of terraced promenades.

157. Another work of Praxiteles. See n. 10.

158. The myrtle was sacred to Aphrodite.

159. The nymph Daphne fled from Apollo's erotic pursuit and was transformed into a laurel tree.

160. The ivy and grape vine were sacred to Dionysus, the god of wine; as a loosener of inhibitions, he is frequently associated with love.

These were occasionally visited by a few folk of breeding, but all the city rabble flocked there on holidays and paid true homage to Aphrodite.

[13] When the plants had given us pleasure enough, we entered the temple. In the midst thereof sits the goddess—she's a most beautiful statue of Parian marble—arrogantly smiling a little as a grin parts her lips. Draped by no garment, all her beauty is uncovered and revealed, except insofar as she unobtrusively uses one hand to hide her private parts. So great was the power of the craftsman's art that the hard un-yielding marble did justice to every limb. Charicles at any rate raised a mad distracted cry and exclaimed, "Happiest, indeed, of the gods was Ares, who suffered chains because of her!"[161] And, as he spoke, he ran up and, stretching out his neck as far as he could, started to kiss the goddess with importunate lips. Callicratidas stood by in silence with amazement in his heart.

The temple had a door on both sides for the benefit of those also who wish to have a good view of the goddess from behind, so that no part of her be left unadmired. It's easy, therefore, for people to enter by the other door and survey the beauty of her back.

[14] And so we decided to see all of the goddess and went round to the back of the precinct. Then, when the door had been opened by the woman responsible for keeping the keys, we were filled with an imme-diate wonder for the beauty we beheld. The Athenian who had been so impassive an observer a minute before, upon inspecting those parts of the goddess which recommend a boy, suddenly raised a shout far more frenzied than that of Charicles. "Heracles!" he exclaimed, "what a well-proportioned back! What generous flanks she has! How satisfying an armful to embrace! How delicately molded the flesh on the buttocks, neither too thin and close to the bone, nor yet revealing too great an expanse of fat! And as for those precious parts sealed in on either side by the hips, how inexpressibly sweetly they smile! How perfect the pro-portions of the thighs and the shins as they stretch down in a straight line to the feet! So that's what Ganymede looks like as he pours out the nectar in heaven for Zeus and makes it taste sweeter. For I'd never have taken the cup from Hebe if she served me." While Callicratidas was shouting this under the spell of the goddess, Charicles in the excess of his admiration stood almost petrified, though his emotions showed in the melting tears trickling from his eyes.

[15] When we could admire no more, we noticed a mark on one thigh like a stain on a dress; the unsightliness of this was shown up by

---

161. A reference to the capture of Ares and Aphrodite in the act of adultery through a trap constructed in their bed by Hephaestus, Aphrodite's husband.

the brightness of the marble everywhere else. I therefore, hazarding a
plausible guess about the truth of the matter, supposed that what we saw
was a natural defect in the marble. For even such things as these are subject to accident and many potential masterpieces of beauty are thwarted
by bad luck. And so, thinking the black mark to be a natural blemish, I
found in this too cause to admire Praxiteles for having hidden what was
unsightly in the marble in the parts less able to be examined closely.
But the attendant woman who was standing near us told us a strange,
incredible story. For she said that a young man of a not undistinguished
family—though his deed has caused him to be left nameless—who often
visited the precinct, was so ill starred as to fall in love with the goddess.
He would spend all day in the temple and at first gave the impression of
pious awe. For in the morning he would leave his bed long before dawn
to go to the temple and only return home reluctantly after sunset. All
day long would he sit facing the goddess with his eyes fixed uninter-
ruptedly upon her, whispering indistinctly and carrying on a lover's
complaints in secret conversation.

[16] But when he wished to give himself some little comfort from his
suffering, after first addressing the goddess, he would count out on the
table four knuckle-bones of a Libyan gazelle and take a gamble on his
expectations. If he made a successful throw and particularly if ever he
was blessed with the throw named after the goddess herself,[162] and no
dice showed the same face, he would prostrate himself before the goddess, thinking he would gain his desire. But, if as usually happens he
made an indifferent throw on to his table, and the dice revealed an un-
propitious result, he would curse all Cnidus and show utter dejection
as if at an irremediable disaster; but a minute later he would snatch up
the dice and try to cure by another throw his earlier lack of success.
But presently, as his passion grew more inflamed, every wall came to be
inscribed with his messages and the bark of every tender tree told of fair
Aphrodite. Praxiteles was honored by him as much as Zeus and every
beautiful treasure that his home guarded was offered to the goddess.
In the end the violent tension of his desires turned to desperation and
he found in audacity a procurer for his lusts. For, when the sun was
now sinking to its setting, quietly and unnoticed by those present, he
slipped in behind the door and, standing invisible in the inmost part of
the chamber, he kept still, hardly even breathing. When the attendants
closed the door from the outside in the normal way, this new Anchises
was locked in. But why do I chatter on and tell you in every detail the

162. In Greek dice games, the best throw, the "Aphrodite," was the one in which every die
showed a different number.

reckless deed of that unmentionable night? These marks of his amorous embraces were seen after day came and the goddess had that blemish to prove what she'd suffered. The youth concerned is said, according to the popular story told, to have hurled himself over a cliff or down into the waves of the sea and to have vanished utterly.

[17] While the temple-woman was recounting this, Charicles interrupted her account with a shout and said, "Women, therefore, inspire love even when made of stone. But what would have happened if we had seen such beauty alive and breathing? Would not that single night have been valued as highly as the scepter of Zeus?"

But Callicratidas smiled and said, "We don't know as yet, Charicles, whether we won't hear many stories of this sort when we come to Thespiae.[163] Even now in this we have a clear proof of the truth about the Aphrodite whom you hold in such esteem."

When Charicles asked how this was, I thought Callicratidas made a very convincing reply. For he said that, although the love-struck youth had seized the chance to enjoy a whole uninterrupted night and had complete liberty to glut his passion, he nevertheless made love to the marble as though to a boy, because, I'm sure, he didn't want to be confronted by the female parts. This occasioned much snarling argument, till I put an end to the confusion and uproar by saying, "Friends, you must keep to orderly inquiry, as is the proper habit of educated people. You must therefore make an end of this disorderly, inconclusive contentiousness and each in turn exert yourself to defend your own opinion; for it's not yet the time to leave for the ship, and we must employ that free time for enjoyment and also for such serious matters as can combine pleasure and profit. Therefore, let us leave the temple, since great numbers of the pious are coming in, and let us turn aside into one of the feasting-places, so that we can have peace and quiet to hear and to say whatever we wish. But remember that he who is vanquished will never again vex our ears on similar topics."

[18] This suggestion of mine pleased them and after they had agreed to it we left the temple. I was enjoying myself as I was weighed down by no cares, but they were rolling mighty cogitations up and down in their thoughts, as though they were about to compete for the leading place in the processions at Plataea.[164] When we had come to a thickly shaded spot that afforded relief for the summer heat, I said, "This is a pleasant place, for the cicadas chirp melodiously overhead." Then I sat down

163. Where Praxiteles' statue of the beautiful boy Eros is located.

164. Plataea was a village near the border of Attica and Boeotia, where the Persian army suffered its final defeat in 479 B.C.E. Annual rites continued to be held there to celebrate the victory of the Greek forces.

between them in right judicial manner, bearing on my brows all the gravity of the Heliaea[165] itself. When I had suggested to them that I should draw lots to decide who should speak first, and Charicles had drawn this privilege, I bade him begin the debate at once.

[19] He rubbed his brow lightly with his hand and after a short pause began as follows: "To you, Aphrodite, my queen, do my prayers appeal to give help in my advocacy of your cause. For every enterprise attains complete perfection if you shed on it but the faintest degree of the arts of persuasion that are your very own; but discourses on love have particular need of you. For you are their only true mother. Come, you who are the most feminine of all, plead the cause of womankind, and of your grace allow men to remain male, as they were born to be. Therefore do I at the very outset of my discourse call as witness to back my plea the first mother and earliest root of every creature, that sacred origin of all things, I mean, who in the beginning established earth, air, fire, and water, the elements of the universe and, by blending these with each other, brought to life everything that has breath. Knowing that we are something created from perishable matter and that the lifetime assigned each of us by fate is but short, she contrived that the death of one thing should be the birth of another and meted out fresh births to compensate for what dies, so that by replacing one another we live for ever. But, since it was impossible for anything to be born from but a single source, she devised in each species two types. For she allowed males as their peculiar privilege to ejaculate semen, and made females to be a vessel, as it were, for the reception of seed, and, imbuing both sexes with a common desire, she linked them to each other, ordaining as a sacred law of necessity that each should retain its own nature and that neither should the female grow unnaturally masculine nor the male be unbecomingly soft. For this reason the intercourse of men with women has till this day preserved the life of men by an undying succession, and no man can boast he is the son only of a man; no, people pay equal homage to their mother and to their father, and all honors are still retained equally by these two revered names.

[20] "In the beginning, therefore, since human life was still full of heroic thought and honored the virtues that kept men close to gods, it obeyed the laws made by nature, and men, linking themselves to women according to the proper limits imposed by age, became fathers of sterling children. But gradually the passing years degenerated from such nobility to the lowest depths of hedonism and cut out strange and extraordinary paths to enjoyment. Then luxury, daring all, transgressed

165. The principal court of law in Athens.

the laws of nature herself. And whoever was the first to look at the male as though at a female after using violence like a tyrant or else shameless persuasion? The same sex entered the same bed. Though they saw themselves embracing each other, they were ashamed neither at what they did nor at what they had done to them, and, sowing their seed, to quote the proverb, on barren rocks they bought a little pleasure at the cost of great disgrace.

[21] "The daring of some men has advanced so far in tyrannical violence as even to wreak sacrilege upon nature with the knife. By depriving males of their masculinity they have found wider ranges of pleasure. But those who become wretched and luckless in order to be boys for longer remain male no longer, being a perplexing riddle of dual gender, neither being kept for the functions to which they have been born nor yet having the thing into which they have been changed. The bloom that has lingered with them in their youth makes them fade prematurely into old age. For at the same moment they are counted as boys and have become old without any interval of manhood. Thus foul self-indulgence, teacher of every wickedness, devising one shameless pleasure after another, has plunged all the way down to that infection which cannot even be mentioned with decency, in order to leave no area of lust unexplored.

[22] "If each man abided by the ordinances prescribed for us by Providence, we should he satisfied with intercourse with women and life would be uncorrupted by anything shameful. Certainly, among animals incapable of debasing anything through depravity of disposition the laws of nature are preserved undefiled. Lions have no passion for lions, but love in due season evokes in them desire for the females of their kind. The bull, monarch of the herd, mounts cows, and the ram fills the whole flock with seed from the male. Furthermore, do not boars seek to lie with sows? Do not wolves mate with she-wolves? And, to speak in general terms, neither the birds whose wings whir on high, nor the creatures whose lot is a wet one beneath the water nor yet any creatures upon land strive for intercourse with fellow males, but the decisions of Providence remain unchanged. But you who are wrongly praised for wisdom, you beasts truly contemptible, you humans, by what strange infection have you been brought to lawlessness and incited to outrage each other? With what blind insensibility have you engulfed your souls that you have missed the mark in both directions, avoiding what you ought to pursue, and pursuing what you ought to avoid? If each and every man should choose to emulate such conduct, the human race will come to a complete end.

[23] "But at this point disciples of Socrates can resurrect that wonderful argument by which boys' ears as yet incapable of perfect logic are

deceived, though those whose minds have already reached their full powers would not be led astray by them. For they affect a love for the soul and, being ashamed to pay court to bodily beauty, call themselves lovers of virtue. This often tempts me to cackle with laughter. For what is wrong with you, grave philosophers, that you dismiss with scorn what has now long given proof of its quality, and has witnesses to its virtue in its becoming gray hairs and its old age, whereas all your wise love is captivated by the young, though their reasonings cannot yet decide to what course they will turn? Or is there a law that all ugliness should be thought guilty of viciousness but that the handsome should automatically be praised as good? But, indeed, to quote Homer, the great prophet of truth,

> Although one man is worse in looks,
> His frame God crowns with speech, and men rejoice
> To look at him. Unerring does he speak
> With charming modesty, preeminent
> Amid the assembled men; when through the town
> He walks, men look at him as 'twere a god.[166]

And again the poet has spoken with these words:

> You did not then have wits to add to looks.[167]
> Indeed, wise Odysseus is praised more than handsome Nireus.[168]

[24] "How is it then that through you courses no love for wisdom or for justice and the other virtues which have in their allotted station the company of full-grown men, while beauty in boys excites the most ardent fires of passion in you? No doubt, Plato, one ought to have loved Phaedrus for the sake of Lysias, whom he betrayed! Or would it have been right to love the virtue of Alcibiades because he would mutilate statues of the gods and his drunken cries parodied the initiation rites of Eleusis?[169] Who admits to having been in love with the betrayal of Athens, the fortification of Decelea against her, and a life that set its sights on tyranny? But, as godlike Plato says, as long as his beard was not yet fully grown, he was beloved by all. But, after he had passed from boyhood to manhood, during the years when his hitherto immature intel-

---

166. *Odyssey* 8.169–73.

167. *Odyssey* 17.454.

168. Nireus was the most handsome Greek hero at Troy after Achilles, according to *Iliad* 2.673–74.

169. A reference to the scandalous charges that resulted in Alcibiades' disgrace and exile from Athens. He later defected to the Spartans and advised them to build a permanent fort at Decelea, from which they could harass Athenian territory with year-round raids.

lect now had its full powers of reason, he was hated by all. What follows? That it is lovers of youth rather than of wisdom who give honorable names to dishonorable passions and call physical beauty virtue of the soul. But lest I be thought to mention famous men only to vent my hatred, let me say no more on this topic.

[25] "To quit this highly serious plane and descend somewhat to your level of pleasure, Callicratidas, I shall show that the services rendered by a woman are far superior to those of a boy. In the first place I consider that all kinds of enjoyment give greater delight if of longer duration. For swift pleasure flits by and is gone before we can recognize it, but delights are enhanced by being prolonged. How I wish that stingy fate had allotted us long terms of life and it consisted entirely of unbroken good health with no grief preying on our minds. For then we should spend all our days in feasting and holiday. But, since envious Fortune has grudged us these greater benefits, amongst those that we have the sweetest are those that last. Thus from maidenhood to middle age, before the time when the last wrinkles of old age finally spread over her face, a woman is a pleasant armful for a man to embrace and, even if the beauty of her prime is past, yet

> . . . With wiser tongue
> Experience doth speak than can the young.[170]

[26] "But the very man who should make attempts on a boy of twenty seems to me to be unnaturally lustful and pursuing an equivocal love. For then the limbs, being large and manly, are hard, the chins that once were soft are rough and covered with bristles, and the well-developed thighs are, as it were, sullied with hairs. And as for the parts less visible than these, I leave knowledge of them to you who have tried them! But ever does her attractive skin give radiance to every part of a woman and her luxuriant ringlets of hair, hanging down from her head, bloom with a dusky beauty that rivals the hyacinths, some of them streaming over her back to grace her shoulders, and others over her ears and temples curlier by far than the celery in the meadow. But the rest of her person has not a hair growing on it and shines more pellucidly than amber, to quote the proverb, or Sidonian crystal.

[27] "But why do we not pursue those pleasures that are mutual and bring equal delight to the passive and to the active partners? For, generally speaking, unlike irrational animals we do not find solitary existences acceptable, but we are linked by a sociable fellowship and consider blessings sweeter and hardships lighter when shared. Hence was instituted

170. Euripides, *Phoenician Women* 529–30.

the table that is shared, and, setting before us the board that is the mediator of friendship, we mete out to our bellies the enjoyment due to
them, not drinking Thasian wine, for example, by ourselves, or stuffing
ourselves with expensive dishes on our own, but each man thinks pleasant what he enjoys along with another, and in sharing our pleasures we
find greater enjoyment. Now men's intercourse with women involves
giving like enjoyment in return. For the two sexes part with pleasure
only if they have had an equal effect on each other—unless we ought
rather to heed the verdict of Tiresias that the woman's enjoyment is
twice as great as the man's.[171] And I think it honorable for men not to
wish for a selfish pleasure or to seek to gain some private benefit by
receiving from anyone the sum total of enjoyment, but to share what
they obtain and to requite like with like. But no one could be so mad
as to say this in the case of boys. No, the active lover, according to his
view of the matter, departs after having obtained an exquisite pleasure,
but the one outraged suffers pain and tears at first, though the pain
relents somewhat with time and you will, men say, cause him no further
discomfort, but of pleasure he has none at all. And, if I may make a
rather far-fetched point, but one I should make as we are in the precinct of Aphrodite, a woman, Callicratidas, may be used like a boy, so
that one can have enjoyment by opening up two paths to pleasure, but
a male has no way of bestowing the pleasure a woman gives.

[28] "Therefore, if even men like you, Callicratidas, can find satisfaction in women, let us males fence ourselves off from each other; but, if
males find intercourse with males acceptable, henceforth let women too
love each other. Come now, epoch of the future, legislator of strange
pleasures, devise fresh paths for male lusts, but bestow the same privilege upon women, and let them have intercourse with each other just
as men do. Let them strap to themselves cunningly contrived instruments of lechery, those mysterious monstrosities devoid of seed, and let
woman lie with woman as does a man. Let wanton Lesbianism—that
word seldom heard, which I feel ashamed even to utter—freely parade
itself, and let our women's chambers emulate Philaenis,[172] disgracing
themselves with Sapphic amours. And how much better that a woman
should invade the provinces of male wantonness than that the nobility of
the male sex should become effeminate and play the part of a woman!"

[29] In the midst of this intense and impassioned speech Charicles
stopped with a wild fierce glint in his eyes. It seemed to me that he was
also regarding his speech as a ceremony of purification against love

171. See n. 59.
172. See 9.26–27.

of boys. But I, laughing quietly and turning my eyes gently towards the Athenian, said, "It was to decide a sportive piece of fun, Callicratidas, that I expected to sit as umpire, but somehow or other thanks to Charicles' vehemence I've been brought to face a more serious task. For he has shown an extraordinary degree of passion almost as though he were in the Areopagus contesting a case of murder or arson or, indeed, poisoning.[173] Therefore, the present moment, if any time ever did, demands that you should recall one of the speeches made to the people in the Pnyx and in this one speech of yours should expend all the resources of Athens, of Periclean persuasiveness and of the tongues of the ten orators that were marshaled against the Macedonians."[174]

[30] After waiting for a moment, Callicratidas, who, judging from his expression, appeared to me to be most full of fight, began to discourse in his turn and said: "If the assembly and the lawcourts were open to women and they could participate in politics, you would have been elected their general or their champion and they would have honored you, Charicles, with bronze statues in the marketplaces. For hardly even those among them thought preeminent for wisdom could, if given full authority to speak, have spoken about themselves with such zeal, no, not even Telesilla, who armed herself against the Spartiates, and because of whom Ares is numbered at Argos among the gods of the women, no, nor Sappho, the honey-sweet pride of Lesbos, or Theano, that daughter of Pythagorean wisdom![175] Perhaps even Pericles could not have pleaded equally well for Aspasia.[176] But, since it is not improper for men to speak on behalf of women, let us men also speak on behalf of men, and you, Aphrodite, be propitious. For we too honor your son, Eros.

[31] "I thought that our merry contest had gone as far as jest allowed but, since Charicles in his discourse has been minded also to wax philosophical on behalf of women, I have gladly seized my opportunity; for love of males, I say, is the only activity combining both pleasure and virtue. For I would pray that near us, if it were possible, grew that plane-tree which once heard the words of Socrates, a tree more fortunate than

173. The Council of the Areopagus was the Athenian court charged with hearing cases of homicide.

174. The Pnyx was the hill where the Assembly met and orators addressed the entire citizenry of Athens. Pericles was a popular leader of the fifth century B.C.E. known for his oratory, as Demosthenes and the others opposing Philip of Macedon's expansion distinguished the fourth-century oratory.

175. Telesilla was an early-fifth-century Argive poet who, according to legend, rallied the Argive women in battle against the Spartan army. Theano was a philosopher, variously identified as either the wife, daughter, or pupil of Pythagoras.

176. Aspasia of Miletus was an intellectual and the partner of the Athenian statesman Pericles, who defended her against repeated attacks by the comic poets.

the Academy and the Lyceum, the tree against which Phaedrus leaned, as we are told by that holy man endowed with more graces than any other.[177] Perhaps like the oak at Dodona, that sent its sacred voice bursting forth from its branches,[178] that tree itself, still remembering the beauty of Phaedrus, would have spoken in praise of love of boys. But that is impossible,

> For in between there lies
> Many a shady mountain and the roaring sea,[179]

and we are strangers cut off in a foreign land, and Cnidus gives Charicles the advantage. Nevertheless, we shall not be overcome by fear and betray the truth.

[32] "Only do you, heavenly spirit, lend me seasonable help, you kindly hierophant of the mysteries of friendship, Eros, who are no mischievous infant as painters lightheartedly portray you, but were already full-grown at your birth, when brought forth by the earliest source of all life. For you gave shape to everything out of dark confused shapelessness.[180] As though you had removed a tomb burying the whole universe alike, you banished that chaos which enveloped it to the recesses of farthest Tartarus, where in truth,

> Are gates of iron and thresholds of bronze,[181]

so that, chained in an impregnable prison, it may be denied any return. Spreading bright light over gloomy night you became the creator of all things both with and without life. But compounding for mortals the special gift of harmony of mind, you united their hearts with the holy sentiment of friendship, so that goodwill might grow in souls still innocent and tender and come to perfect maturity.

[33] "For marriage is a remedy invented to ensure man's necessary perpetuity, but only love for males is a noble duty enjoined by a philosophic spirit. Anything cultivated for aesthetic reasons in the midst of abundance is accompanied with greater honor than things which require for their existence immediate need, and beauty is in every way superior to necessity. Thus, as long as human life remained unsophisti-

---

177. Plato tells of this spot in **5.9.229**. The Academy was the site of Plato's school, the Lyceum of Aristotle's.

178. The oak trees at the oracle of Zeus in Dodona were imagined to deliver prophecies in a sacred language as the wind rustled through their leaves.

179. *Iliad* 1.156–57.

180. Callicratidas is here alluding to Hesiod's *Theogony*, where Eros is the primordial force enabling the creation of the universe out of Chaos and the first elements.

181. *Iliad* 8.15. Tartarus is the lowest part of the Underworld, where evil spirits are confined.

cated and the daily struggle for existence left it no leisure for improving itself, men were content to limit themselves to bare necessities, and the urgency of their day did not allow them to discover the proper way to live. But, once pressing needs were at an end and the thoughts of each succeeding generation had been released from the shackles of necessity so that they had leisure ever to devise higher things, from that time the arts gradually began to develop. What this process was like we may judge from the more perfected of the crafts. Right from the moment of their birth the earliest men had to search for a remedy against their daily hunger and, under the duress of immediate need, prevented by their helplessness from choosing what was better, fed on any chance herb, digging up tender roots and eating mostly the fruit of the oak.[182] But after a time this was cast before brute animals, and the careful husbandmen discovered how to sow wheat and barley and saw these renew themselves every year. And not even a madman would maintain that the fruit of the oak is superior to the ear of grain.

[34] "Moreover, did not men right from the start of human life, because they needed protection from the elements, skin wild beasts and clothe themselves in their woolly coats? And as refuges against the cold they thought of mountain caves or the dry hollows afforded by old roots or trees. Then, ever improving the imitative skill that started thus, they wove themselves cloaks of wool and built themselves houses, and imperceptibly the crafts that concentrated on these things, being taught by time, replaced simple fabrics with ornate garments of greater beauty, and instead of cheap cottages they devised lofty mansions of expensive marble, and painted the native ugliness of their walls with the luxuriant dyes of color. However, each of these crafts and accomplishments has, after being mute and plunged in deep forgetfulness, gradually risen, as it were, to its own bright zenith after long being set. For each man made some discovery to hand on to his successor. Then each successive recipient, by adding to what he had already learned, made good any deficiencies.

[35] "Let no one expect love of males in early times. For intercourse with women was necessary so that our race might not utterly perish for lack of seed. But the manifold branches of wisdom and men's desire for this virtue that loves beauty were only with difficulty to be brought to light by time, which leaves nothing unexplored, so that divine philosophy and with it love of boys might come to maturity. Do not then, Charicles, again censure this discovery as worthless because it wasn't made earlier, nor, because intercourse with women can be credited with greater

---

182. I.e., acorns.

antiquity than love of boys, must you think love of boys inferior. No, we must consider the pursuits that are old to be necessary, but assess as superior the later additions invented by human life when it had leisure for thought.

[36] "For I came very close to laughing just now when Charicles was praising irrational beasts and the lonely life of Scythians. Indeed, his excessive enthusiasm for the argument almost made him regret his Greek birth. For he did not hide his words in restrained tones like a man contradicting the thesis that he maintained, but with raised voice from the full depth of his throat says, 'Lions, bears, boars do not love others of their own sort but are ruled by their urge only for the female.' And what's surprising in that? For the things which one would rightly choose as a result of thought, it is not possible for those that cannot reason to have because of their lack of intellect. For, if Prometheus or else some god had endowed each animal with a human mind, they would not be satisfied with a lonely life among the mountains, nor would they find their food in each other, but just like us they would have built themselves temples and, though each making his hearth the center of his private life, they would live as fellow citizens governed by common laws. Is it any wonder that, since animals have been condemned by nature not to receive from the bounty of Providence any of the gifts afforded by intellect, they have with all else also been deprived of desire for males? Lions do not have such a love, because they are not philosophers either. Bears have no such love, because they are ignorant of the beauty that comes from friendship. But for men wisdom coupled with knowledge has after frequent experiments chosen what is best, and has formed the opinion that love between males is the most stable of loves.

[37] "Do not, therefore, Charicles, heap together courtesans' tales of wanton living and insult our dignity with unvarnished language nor count Heavenly Love as an infant, but learn better about such things though it's late in your life, and now at any rate, since you've never done so before, reflect in spite of all that Love is a twofold god who does not walk in but a single track or exert but a single influence to excite our souls; but the one love, because, I imagine, his mentality is completely childish, and no reason can guide his thoughts, musters with great force in the souls of the foolish and concerns himself mainly with yearnings for women. This love is the companion of the violence that lasts but a day and he leads men with unreasoning precipitation to their desires. But the other Love is the ancestor of the Ogygian age,[183] a sight vener-

---

183. Ogyges was one of the most ancient mythological kings of Boeotia. "Ogygian age" refers to primeval times.

able to behold and hedged around with sanctity, and is a dispenser of temperate passions who sends his kindly breath into the minds of all. If we find this god propitious to us, we meet with a welcome pleasure which is blended with virtue. For in truth, as the tragic poet says, Love blows in two different ways, and the one name is shared by differing passions. For Shame too is a twofold goddess with both a beneficial and a harmful role.

> Shame which to men does mighty harm and mighty good . . .
> Nor yet are rivalries of one sort. Two kinds
> On Earth there are: the one a man of sense would praise,
> The other's to be blamed, for different is their heart.[184]

It need not surprise us, therefore, that passion has come to have the same name as virtue, so that both unrestrained lust and sober affection are called Love.

[38] "Charicles may ask if I therefore think marriage worthless and banish women from this life, and if so, how we humans are to survive. Indeed, as the wise Euripides says, it would be greatly to be desired if we had no intercourse with women but, in order to provide ourselves with heirs, we went to shrines and temples and bought children for gold and silver.[185] For we are constrained by necessity that puts a heavy yoke on our shoulders and bids us obey her. Though therefore we should by use of reason choose what is beautiful, let our need yield to necessity. Let women be ciphers and be retained merely for child-bearing; but in all else away with them, and may I be rid of them. For what man of sense could endure from dawn onwards women who beautify themselves with artificial devices, women whose true form is unshapely, but who have extraneous adornments to beguile the unsightliness of nature?

[39] "If at any rate one were to see women when they rise in the morning from last night's bed, one would think a woman uglier than those beasts whose name it is inauspicious to mention early in the day.[186] That's why they closet themselves carefully at home and let no man see them. They're surrounded by old women and a throng of maids as ugly as themselves who doctor their ill-favored faces with an assortment of medicaments. For they do not wash off the torpor of sleep with pure clean water and apply themselves to some serious task. Instead numerous concoctions of scented powders are used to brighten up their unattractive complexions, and, as though in a public procession, each maid

---

184. The first line is Hesiod, *Works and Days* 318; the next three are vv.11–13 of the same.
185. This is based on Hippolytus' diatribe against women in *Hippolytus* 618–24. It should not necessarily be assumed to be Euripides' own sentiment, as Callicratidas asserts here.
186. I.e., monkeys.

is entrusted with something different, with silver basins, ewers, mirrors, an array of boxes reminiscent of a chemist's shop, and jars full of many a mischief, in which she marshals dentifrices and contrivances for blackening the eyelids.

[40] "But most of their efforts are spent on dressing their hair. For some pass unfavorable judgment on their own gifts from nature and, by means of pigments that can redden the hair to match the sun at noon, they dye their hair with a yellow bloom as they do colored wool; those who do feel satisfied with their dark locks spend their husbands' wealth on radiating from their hair almost all the perfumes of Arabia; they use iron instruments warmed in a slow flame to curl their hair perforce into woolly ringlets, and elaborately styled locks brought down to their eyebrows leave the forehead with the narrowest of spaces, while the tresses behind float proudly down to the shoulders.

[41] "Next they turn to flower-colored shoes that sink into their flesh and pinch their feet and to thin veils that pass for clothes so as to excuse their apparent nakedness. But everything inside these can be distinguished more clearly than their faces—except for their hideously prominent breasts, which they always carry about bound like prisoners. Need I recount the scandals still more extravagant than these? The Red Sea pearls worth many a talent that hang heavily from the ears, or the snakes round their wrists and arms, which I wish were real snakes instead of gold? Their heads are surrounded with crowns bearing a galaxy of Indian gems, and from their throats hang expensive necklaces, while gold has the misfortune to go right down to the tips of their toes, pinching any part of their ankles left naked—though it's iron with which their legs should by rights be shackled at the ankles! When all their body has been tricked out with the deceptive beauty of a spurious comeliness, they redden their shameless cheeks by smearing on rouge so that its crimson tint may lend color to their pale fat skins.

[42] "How, then, do they behave after all these preparations? They leave the house immediately and visit every god that plagues married men, though the wretched husbands do not even know the very names of some of these, be they Coliades and Genetyllides [187] or the Phrygian goddess and the rout that commemorates an unhappy love and honors the shepherd-boy. [188] Then follow secret initiations and suspicious all-female mysteries and, to put things bluntly, the corruption, of their souls. But when they've finished with these, the moment they're home they have long baths and, by heavens, sumptuous meals accompanied

187. Goddesses of generation and birth.
188. Cybele and her eunuch followers. The shepherd-boy is Attis.

by much coyness towards the men. For when they are surfeited with gorging the dishes in front of them, and even *their* throats can now hold no more, they score each of the foods before them with their fingertips to taste them. Meanwhile, they talk of their nights, their heterosexual slumbers, and their beds fraught with femininity, on rising from which every man immediately needs a bath.

[43] "These then are the signs of an orderly female life; but, should one wish to examine in detail the truth about the more offensive of womankind, he will curse Prometheus in real life and burst out with these words of Menander:[189]

> Then are not painters right when they depict
> Prometheus nailed to rocks? With the brand of fire
> And no other good can he be credited.
> But all the gods, I think, hate what he did,
> In fashioning females, a cursed brood,
> I swear it by the honored gods above.
> Suppose a man weds and marries her,
> She'll spend her time from then in evil
> Furtive lusts and lovers who luxuriate
> On the marriage bed, and poisonings and envy,
> That most terrible of plagues with which
> A woman all her lifetime does consort.

Who goes in quest of boons like these? Who finds so wretched a life acceptable? [44] We ought therefore to contrast with the evils associated with women the manly life of a boy. He rises at dawn from his unwed couch, washes away with pure water such sleep as still remains in his eyes and after securing his shirt and his mantle pins at the shoulder, 'he leaves his father's hearth with eyes bent down' and without facing the gaze of anyone he meets. He is followed by an orderly company of attendants and tutors, who grip in their hands the revered instruments of virtue, not the points of a toothed comb that can caress the hair nor mirrors that without artists' aid reproduce the shapes confronting them, but behind him come many-leaved writing tablets or books that preserve the merit of ancient deeds, along with a tuneful lyre, should he have to go to a music master.

[45] "But, after he has toiled zealously through all the lessons that teach the soul philosophy, and his intellect has had its fill of these benefits of a standard education, he perfects his body with noble exercises. For he interests himself in Thessalian horses. Soon, after he has broken

189. Comic poet of the late fourth century B.C.E. This fragment is from an unknown play. On Prometheus, see n. 153.

in his youth as one does a colt, he practices in peace the pursuits of war, throwing javelins and hurling spears with unerring aim. Next come the glistening wrestling schools, where beneath the heat of the midday sun his developing body is covered in dust; then comes the sweat, that pours forth from his toils in the contest, and next a quick bath and a sober meal suited to the activities that soon follow. For again he has his school-masters and records of deeds of old with hints for the study of such questions as what hero was brave, who is cited for his wisdom, or what men cherished justice and temperance. Such are the virtues which he uses to irrigate his soul while still tender and, when evening brings an end to his activities, he metes out the tribute due to the necessities of his stomach, and then sleeps the sweeter, enjoying a rest that none could grudge after his exertions during the day.

[46] "Who would not fall in love with such a youth? Whose eyesight could be so blind, whose mental processes so stunted? How could one fail to love him who is a Hermes in the wrestling school,[190] an Apollo with the lyre, a horseman to rival Castor, and one who strives after the virtues of the gods with a mortal body? For my part, ye gods of heaven, I pray that it may forever be my lot in life to sit opposite my dear one and hear close to me his sweet voice, to go out when he goes out and share every activity with him. And so a lover might well pray that his cherished one should journey to old age without any sorrow through a life free from stumbling or swerving, without having experienced at all any malicious spite of Fortune. But, if in accordance with the law governing the human body, illness should lay its hand on him, I shall ail with him when he is weak and, when he puts out to sea through stormy waves, I shall sail with him. And, should a violent tyrant bind him in chains, I shall put the same fetters around myself. All who hate him will be my enemies and those well disposed to him shall I hold dear. Should I see bandits or foemen rushing upon him, I would arm myself even beyond my strength, and if he dies, I shall not bear to live. I shall give final instructions to those I love next best after him to pile up a common tomb for both of us, to unite my bones with his and not to keep even our dumb ashes apart from each other.

[47] "Nor will you find my love for those who deserve it to be the first to write such things; rather, were these the laws given by the well-nigh divine wisdom of the heroes, who till their dying day breathed love of friendship. Phocis united Orestes to Pylades right from their

---

190. Hermes was the patron god of gymnasia and wrestling schools, as well as being a paradigm of youthful male beauty like Apollo and Castor.

infancy.[191] Taking the love god as the mediator of their emotions for each other, they sailed together, as it were, on the same vessel of life. Both did away with Clytemnestra as though both were sons of Agamemnon, by both of them was Aegisthus slain. Pylades it was who suffered the more from the Avengers who hounded Orestes,[192] and he stood trial along with him in court. Nor did they restrict their affectionate friendship to the limits of Hellas, but sailed to Scythia at the very ends of the Earth, one of them afflicted, the other ministering to him. At any rate, as soon as they set foot on the land of the Tauri, the Fury of matricides was there to welcome the strangers, and, when the natives stood around them, the one was struck to the ground by his usual madness and lay there, but Pylades

> Did wipe away the foam and tend his frame
> And shelter him with fine well-woven robe,[193]

thus showing the feelings not merely of a lover but also of a father. When at any rate it had been decided that, while one remained to be killed, the other should depart for Mycenae to bear a letter, each wished to remain for the sake of the other, considering that he himself lived in the survival of his friend. But Orestes refused to take the letter, claiming Pylades was the fitter person to do so, and showed himself almost to be the lover rather than the beloved.

> For 'tis a burden sore to me if he be slain,
> For I am captain of this enterprise.

And shortly afterwards he says:

> Give the message to him
> Whom I'll send to Argos; he will thrive.
> But he may take my life, whoever will.[194]

[48] "This too is the case generally. For, when the honorable love inbred in us from childhood matures to the manly age that is now capable of reason, the object of our longstanding affection gives love in return and it's difficult to detect which is the lover of which, since the image of the lover's tenderness has been reflected from the loved one as though

191. When his mother, Clytemnestra, began to plot his father's murder together with Aegisthus, she sent Orestes to stay with the family of Strophius in Phocis. Strophius' son Pylades became his lifelong friend.

192. The Furies, sent to pursue Orestes by his mother's dying curse.

193. Euripides, *Iphigenia in Tauris* 311–12. The events described here relate to this play.

194. The first quotation is *Iphigenia in Tauris* 598–99, the second 603–5 (adapted).

from a mirror. Why then do you censure this as being an exotic indulgence of our times, though it is an ordinance enacted by divine laws and a heritage that has come down to us? We have been glad to receive it and we tend its shrine with a pure heart. For that man is truly blessed according to the verdict of the wise,

> Whoever has boys and whole-hooved steeds,
> That man grows old with greatest ease
> Whom youths do love.[195]

The teaching of Socrates and his famous tribunal of virtue were honored by the Delphic tripod, for the Pythian god uttered an oracle of truth,

> Of all men Socrates the wisest is.

For along with the other discoveries with which he benefited human life did he not also welcome love of boys as the greatest of boons?

[49] "One should love youths as Alcibiades was loved by Socrates, who slept like a father with him under the same cloak. And, for my part, I would most gladly add to the end of my discourse the words of Callimachus as a message to all:

> May you who cast your longing eyes on youths
>   So love the young as Erchius bid you do,
> That in its men your city may be blessed.

Knowing this, young men, be temperate when you approach virtuous boys. Do not for the sake of a brief pleasure squander lasting affection, nor till you've reached manhood show counterfeit feelings of affection, but worship Heavenly Love and keep your emotions constant from boyhood to old age. For those who love thus, having nothing disgraceful on their conscience, find their lifetime sweetest and after their death their glorious report goes out to all men. If it's right to believe the children of philosophy, the heavens await men with these ideals after their stay on Earth. By entering a better life at death they have immortality as the reward for their virtue."

[50] After Callicratidas had delivered this very spirited sermon, Charicles tried to speak for a second time but I stopped him; for it was now time to return to the ship. They pressed me to pronounce my opinion, but, after weighing up for a short time the speeches of both, I said: "Your words, my friends, do not seem to me to be hurried, thoughtless improvisations, but give clear proof of continued and, by heaven, concentrated thought. For of all the possible arguments there's hardly one you've left

195. An adapted version of 1.51.

for another to use. And, though your experience of the world is great, it is surpassed by your eloquence, so that I for one could wish, if it were possible, to become Theramenes, the Turncoat,[196] so that you could both be victorious and walk off on equal terms. However, since I do not think you'll let the matter be, and I myself am resolved not to be exercised on the same topic during the voyage, I shall give the verdict that has struck me as the fairest.

[51] "Marriage is a boon and a blessing to men when it meets with good fortune, while the love of boys that pays court to the hallowed dues of friendship, I consider to be the privilege only of philosophy. Therefore all men should marry, but let only the wise be permitted to love boys, for perfect virtue grows least of all among women. And you must not be angry, Charicles, if Corinth yields to Athens."

[52] After giving this decision hurriedly in a few brief words out of regard for my friend, I rose to my feet. For I saw that he was utterly dejected, almost like one condemned to death. But the Athenian leapt up joyously with a gleeful expression on his face and started to stalk about in front of us most triumphantly, just as if, one would have thought, he had defeated the Persian fleet at Salamis.[197] I derived a further benefit from my verdict when he entertained us to a magnificent feast to celebrate his victory. For his behavior had in other ways, too, shown him to be generous of spirit. As for Charicles, I consoled him quietly by repeatedly expressing my great admiration for his eloquence and his able defense of the more awkward cause.

[53] Well, thus ended our stay in Cnidus and our conversation in the sanctuary of the goddess with its combination of gay earnestness and cultured fun. But now, Theomnestus, you who have evoked these old memories of mine must tell me how *you* would have decided, if *you* had been judge.

THEOMNESTUS: By heaven, do, you think I'm a Melitides or Coroebus[198] to cast a vote in opposition to your just verdict? For through my intense enjoyment of your narrative I thought I was in Cnidus, almost imagining this small chamber to be that temple. But, nevertheless, seeing that nothing said on a festive day is unseemly, and any jesting, even if carried to excess, is thought in keeping with the holiday spirit, I must say I admired the solemnity of the very highbrow speeches evoked by love of boys, except that I didn't think it very agreeable to spend all day with a

196. An Athenian politician known for reversing his positions on issues at the end of the Peloponnesian War.

197. Athens' greatest naval victory, in 480 B.C.E.

198. Foolish men ridiculed by Aristophanes and Lucian.

youth suffering the punishment of Tantalus[199] and, though the waters of beauty are, as it were, almost lapping against my eyes, to endure thirst when one can help oneself to water. For it's not enough to look at the loved one or to listen to his voice as he sits facing you,[200] but love has, as it were, made itself a ladder of pleasure,[201] and has for its first step that of sight, so that it may see the beloved, and, once it beholds, it wishes to approach and to touch. If it only touches with but the fingertips, the waves of enjoyment run into the whole body. Once easily achieving this, love attempts the third stage and tries a kiss, not making it a violent one at first, but lightly bringing lips close to lips so that they part before completing full contact, without leaving the slightest cause for suspicion. Thus it adjusts itself to the success gained and melts into ever more importunate embraces, sometimes gently opening the mouth and leaving neither hand idle. For open embraces of the beloved when clothed give mutual pleasure; or else the furtive hand wantonly glides down into the bosom and squeezes for a moment the breasts swollen past their normal size and makes a smooth sweep to grasp with the fingers the belly throbbing full spate with passion, and thereafter the early down of adolescence, and—

But why recount the thing one should not tell?[202]

Once love has gained so much liberty it begins warmer work. Then it makes a start with the thighs and, to quote the comic poet, "strikes the target."

[54] May I for my part find it my lot to love boys in this way. But may the airy talkers and those who raise their philosophic brows temple-high and even higher beguile the ignorant with the speciousness of their solemn phrases. For Socrates was as devoted to love as anyone and Alcibiades, once he had lain down beneath the same mantle with him, did not rise unassailed. Don't be surprised at that. For not even the affection of Achilles for Patroclus was limited to having him seated opposite

Waiting until Aeacides should cease his song.[203]

No, pleasure was the mediator even of *their* friendship. At any rate, when Achilles was lamenting the death of Patroclus, his unrestrained feelings made him burst out with the truth and say,

199. On Tantalus' punishment, see ch. 9, n. 38.
200. Perhaps a reference to Sappho, **1.9**.
201. The following is clearly a perversion of Diotima's "ladder of love" doctrine in **5.7.211**.
202. Euripides, *Orestes* 14.
203. *Iliad* 9.191.

The converse of our thighs my tears do mourn with duteous piety.

Those whom the Greeks call "revelers" I think to be nothing but ostentatious lovers. Perhaps someone will assert this is a shameful thing to say, but, by Aphrodite of Cnidus, it's the truth.

LYCINUS: My dear Theomnestus, I won't tolerate your laying the foundation of a third discourse, for this one should hear only on a holiday, and further talk should be banished far from my ears. Let us not linger any longer, but go out to the marketplace. For it's now the time when the fire should be lit in honor of Heracles. It's a pleasant sight and reminds those present of what he suffered on Oeta.[204]

10.38 Firmicus Maternus, *Mathesis* 3.6.4–6

This astrological treatise was published around 334–37 C.E. It shows signs of Stoic influence. The author is known to have later converted to Christianity.

[4] Venus on the ascendant by day makes the natives oversexed, unchaste, of ill repute. They will be linen-weavers, embroiderers, or artists in paints, dyers, innkeepers, or tavern-keepers. Saturn in aspect to Venus in any way will make the natives effeminate, homosexuals *(cinaedi)*, or engaged in sedentary activities. Venus on the ascendant promises a wife at an early age. Saturn, however, in strong aspect produces castrates, or weavers, or inventive workers in colors. Jupiter in favorable aspect will make them managers of royal weaving. . . .

[6] Those who have Venus in this house by day will have great reverses of fortune and also late marriages; they will have lawsuits over another woman. Some will be several times widowed. If the Sun or Saturn are in opposition, square aspect, or conjunction with Venus the natives will be sterile, never successful in sexual activity, will never marry, and always be lovers of boys. The misfortunes are less if Venus is in the house or terms of Saturn, Mars, or Mercury.

10.39 Firmicus Maternus, *Mathesis* 5.2.11

Those who have Saturn in these terms in a diurnal chart hate women and marriage. If it is a nocturnal chart, they will be impure and unchaste, not able to accomplish normal sexual intercourse, but trapped in monstrous unnatural vices. They will be in trouble from the changing nature of their

---

204. This festival commemorates Heracles' voluntary incineration on a funeral pyre, when he desired death as a release from the torment of the poisoned robe that his wife Deianeira inadvertently sent him.

plans and will be hated by all respectable people. Jupiter in these terms will make them gentle, sensual, luxury-loving, never cruel in any way, moderate in all their activities. They will be famous artisans and hold high positions in temples.

10.40 Firmicus Maternus, *Mathesis* 6.31.39

The Moon, Saturn, and Venus in the seventh house, that is, on the descendant, make perverts *(cinaedi)* with effeminate softness of body who dance on the stage and act in ancient fables, especially if Mars is in square aspect. For then he makes them addicted to all kinds of base vices; they also practice immoral kinds of intercourse with their wives. If to all these Jupiter is in square aspect from the IMC,[205] together with all these vices he makes them lovers of boys.

10.41 Firmicus Maternus, *Mathesis* 7.25.3–5

[3] If Mercury and Venus are in conjunction in the nineteenth degree of Aries, they make the native impure of mouth.[206] If Venus and the Moon hold the thirtieth degree of any sign and are in square aspect or opposition to each other, they will exercise these vices secretly. But if the rulers of those signs in which the Moon and Venus have the thirtieth degree are in any aspect to these signs, they exercise these vices publicly, without shame.

[4] Mars and Venus in conjunction in a morning rising and in a masculine sign make women shrewish and sterile. In an evening rising in feminine signs, in a man's chart, if Saturn is in any aspect, they make perverts who serve in temple choirs. If this combination is found in Aries or Capricorn, these same afflictions are indicated. But if Venus is in opposition or square aspect and there is no influence of Jupiter, women will be born with masculine character, but men will become castrates or eunuchs or male prostitutes.

[5] If the Moon is in opposition to Saturn, but Mars is so placed that he is in square aspect to them and in opposition to Venus, and all these four are in each other's houses, this combination makes women sterile and shrewish, and makes men male prostitutes. Saturn in conjunction with the Moon will produce male prostitutes.

205. This means from the lowest point in the sky.
206. See n. 103.

WORKS CITED

AJA	American Journal of Archaeology
AJP	American Journal of Philology
BCH	Bulletin de Correspondence Hellénique
BICS	Bulletin of the Institute of Classical Studies
CA	Classical Antiquity
CJ	Classical Journal
CP	Classical Philology
CQ	Classical Quarterly
EMC	Echos du Monde Classique
GB	Grazer Beiträge
GIF	Giornale Italiano di Filologia
GRBS	Greek, Roman, and Byzantine Studies
JHS	Journal of Hellenic Studies
LCM	Liverpool Classical Monthly
MD	Materiali e Discussioni per l'analisi dei testi classici
MH	Museum Helveticum
PCPS	Proceedings of the Cambridge Philological Society
QS	Quaderni di Storia
QUCC	Quaderni Urbinati di Cultura Classica
RFIC	Rivista di Filologia e Istruzione Classica
RhM	Rheinisches Museum
TAPA	Transactions of the American Philological Association
ZPE	Zeitschrift für Papyrologie und Epigraphik

Acosta-Hughes, B. 2002. *Polyeideia: The* Iambi *of Callimachus and the Archaic Iambic Tradition*. Berkeley and Los Angeles.

Adams, D. 1995. "A Socratic Theory of Friendship." *International Philosophical Quarterly* 35: 69–82.

Allen, G., and W. A. Welton. 1996. "An Overlooked Motive in Alcibiades' *Symposium* Speech." *Interpretation* 24: 67–84.

Allen, R. E. 1991. *The Dialogues of Plato*. Vol. 2, *The Symposium*. New Haven.

Arkins, B. 1982. *Sexuality in Catullus*. Hildesheim.

Arrowsmith, W. 1966. "Luxury and Death in the *Satyricon*." *Arion* 5: 304–31.

Barigazzi, A. 1973. "Amore e poetica in Callimaco." *RFIC* 101: 186–94.

Barrett, D. S. 1981. "The Friendship of Achilles and Patroclus." *Classical Bulletin* 57: 87–93.

Barton, T. S. 1994. *Power and Knowledge: Astrology, Physiognomics, and Medicine under the Roman Empire*. Ann Arbor.

Bethe, E. 1907. "Die dorische Knabenliebe: Ihre Ethik und ihre Idee." *RhM* 62: 438–75.

Bodel, J. 1989a. "Trimalchio and the Candelabrum." *CP* 84: 224–31.

———. 1989b. "Trimalchio's Coming of Age." *Phoenix* 43: 72–74.

Bolotin, D. 1979. *Plato's Dialogue on Friendship*. Ithaca.

Bonfante, L. 1989. "Nudity as Costume in Classical Art." *AJA* 93: 543–70.

Booth, J. 1996. "Tibullus 1.8 and 9: A Tale in Two Poems?" *MH* 53: 232–47.

Boswell, J. 1980. *Christianity, Social Tolerance, and Homosexuality*. Chicago.

Braund, S., and J. D. Cloud. 1981. "Juvenal: A Diptych." *LCM* 6: 203–8.

Bremmer, J. 1980. "An Enigmatic Indo-European Rite: Paederasty." *Arethusa* 13: 279–98.

———. 1989. "Greek Pederasty and Modern Homosexuality." In *From Sappho to de Sade: Moments in the History of Sexuality*, 1–14. London.

———. 1990. "Adolescents, *Symposion*, and Pederasty." In *Sympotica: A Symposium on the Symposion*, edited by O. Murray, 135–48. Oxford.

Brenkman, J. 1977. "The Other and the One: Psychoanalysis, Reading, *The Symposium*." *Yale French Studies* 55/56: 396–456.

Brès, Y. 1973. *La psychologie de Platon.*[2] Paris.

Bright, D. F. 1978. *Haec Mihi Fingebam: Tibullus in His World*. Leiden.

Brongersma, E. 1990. "The Thera Inscriptions—Ritual or Slander?" *Journal of Homosexuality* 20: 31–40.

Brooten, B. J. 1996. *Love between Women: Early Christian Responses to Female Homoeroticism*. Chicago.

Brown, C. 1983. "From Rags to Riches: Anacreon's Artemon." *Phoenix* 37: 1–15.

Brown, D. 1977. "Demosthenes on Love." *QS* 3: 79–97.

Brown, M., and J. Coulter. 1979. "The Middle Speech of Plato's *Phaedrus*." In *Plato: True and Sophistic Rhetoric*, edited by K. V. Erickson, 239–64. Amsterdam.

Buchheit, V. 1962. *Studien zum Corpus Priapeorum*. Munich.

Buffière, F. 1980. *Eros adolescent: la pédérastie dans la Grèce antique*. Paris.

Burgess, D. L. 1993. "Food, Sex, Money and Poetry in 'Olympian' 1." *Hermes* 121: 35–44.

Burnett, A. P. 1983. *Three Archaic Poets: Archilochus, Alcaeus, Sappho*. Chicago.

Cairns, F. 1977. "*Erôs* in Pindar's First Olympian Ode." *Hermes* 105: 129–32.

———. 1979. *Tibullus: A Hellenistic Poet at Rome*. Cambridge, England.

Calame, C. 1983. *Alcman: Introduction, texte critique, témoignages, traduction et commentaire*. Rome.

————. 1997. *Choruses of Young Women in Ancient Greece.* Trans. D. Collins and J. Orion. Lanham.

Cantarella, E. 1992. *Bisexuality in the Ancient World.* Trans. C. Ó Cuilleanáin. New Haven.

Cantarella, R. 1975. "Agathon und der Prolog der 'Thesmophoriazusen.'" In *Aristophanes und die alte Komödie,* edited by H.-J. Newiger, 324–38. Darmstadt.

Capriglione, J. C. 1999. "L'amore è un dardo: le ragioni dell'omosessualità in Aristótele e Plutarco." In *Plutarco, Platón y Aristóteles,* edited by A. P. Jiménez, J. C. López, and R. M. Aguilar, 567–81. Madrid.

Carey, C. 1978. "Sappho Fr. 96 LP." *CQ,* n.s., 28: 366–71.

————. 1989. *Lysias: Selected Speeches.* Cambridge, England.

Cartledge, P. 1981. "The Politics of Spartan Pederasty." *PCPS,* n.s., 27: 17–36. Also in *Spartan Reflections,* 91–105. Berkeley and Los Angeles.

Cerri, G. 1989. "Il carme 56 di Catullo e un' iscrizione greca di recente publiccazione." *QUCC* 60: 59–65.

Cervellera, M. A. 1982. "Omosessualità e ideologia schiavistica in Petronio." *Index* 11: 1–15.

Clark, C. A. 1996. "The Gendering of the Body in Alcman's *Partheneion* 1: Narrative, Sex, and Social Order in Archaic Sparta." *Helios* 23: 143–72.

Clarke, W. M. 1978a. "Achilles and Patroclus in Love." *Hermes* 106: 381–96.

————. 1978b. "Problems in Straton's Παιδικὴ μοῦσα." *AJP* 99: 433–41.

————. 1984. "Observations on the Date of Straton of Sardis." *CP* 89: 214–20.

————. 1994. "Phallic Vocabulary in Straton." *Mnemosyne* 47: 466–72.

Clavaud, R. 1974. *Démosthène: Discours d'Apparat.* Paris.

Clay, J. S. 1995. "Catullus' Attis and the Black Hunter." *QUCC* 79: 143–55.

Cody, J. M. 1976. "The Senex Amator in Plautus' *Casina.*" *Hermes* 104: 453–76.

Cohen, D. 1991. *Law, Sexuality, and Society: The Enforcement of Morals in Classical Athens.* Cambridge, England.

Cohen, E. E. 2000. *The Athenian Nation.* Princeton.

Connor, W. R. 1971. *The New Politicians of Fifth-Century Athens.* Princeton.

Cornford, F. M. 1950. *The Unwritten Philosophy.* Cambridge, England.

Cristofoli, R. 1996. "Note di lettura agli episodi di Eurialo e Niso." *GIF* 48: 261–68.

Crotty, K. M. 1982. *Song and Action: The Victory Odes of Pindar.* Baltimore.

Cummins, W. J. 1981. "Eros, Epithumia, and Philia in Plato." *Apeiron* 15: 10–18.

Dalfen, J. 1986. "Literarische Fiktion—Funktion von Literatur: Zum 'Lysiastext' in Platons *Phaidros.*" *GB* 12–13: 101–30.

Dalla, D. 1987. *"Ubi Venus mutatur": Omosessualità e diritto nel mondo romano.* Milan.

Daniel, R. W., and F. Maltomini. 1990. *Supplementum Magicum.* Vol. 1. Opladen.

Davidson, J. 2001. "Dover, Foucault, and Greek Homosexuality: Penetration and the Truth of Sex." *Past and Present* 170: 3–51.

Dawson, C. M. 1946. "An Alexandrian Prototype of Marathus?" *AJP* 67: 1–15.

De Jean, J. 1989. *Fictions of Sappho, 1546–1937.* Chicago.

Devereux, G. 1970. "The Nature of Sappho's Seizure in Fr. 31 LP as Evidence of Her Inversion." *CQ,* n.s., 20: 17–31.

De Vries, G. J. 1969. *A Commentary on the* Phaedrus *of Plato.* Amsterdam.

De Vries, K. 1997. "The 'Frigid Eromenoi' and Their Wooers Revisited: A Closer

Look at Greek Homosexuality in Vase Painting." In *Queer Representations: Reading Lives, Reading Cultures*, edited by M. Duberman, 14–24. New York.

DiCesare, M. A. 1974. *The Altar and the City: A Reading of Vergil's* Aeneid. New York.

Dimundo, R. 1983. "Da Socrate a Eumolpo: Degradazione di personaggi e delle funzioni nella novella del fanciullo di Pergamo." *MD* 10–11: 255–65.

———. 1986. "La novella dell' Efebo di Pergamo: Struttura del racconto." In *Semiotica della novella latina: Atti del seminario interdisciplinare "La novella latina" (Perugia 11–13 Aprile 1985)*, 83–94. Rome.

Dodd, D. B. 2000. "Athenian Ideas about Cretan Pederasty." In *Greek Love Reconsidered*, edited by T. K. Hubbard, 33–41. New York.

Döpp, S. 1983. "Der Verfasser des Erotikos in Platons 'Phaidros.'" *Glotta* 61: 15–29.

Dorter, K. 1969. "The Significance of the Speeches in Plato's *Symposium*." *Philosophy and Rhetoric* 2: 215–34.

Dover, K. J. 1965. "The Date of Plato's *Symposium*." *Phronesis* 10: 2–20.

———. 1966. "Aristophanes' Speech in Plato's *Symposium*." *JHS* 86: 41–50.

———. 1978. *Greek Homosexuality*. London.

———. 1988. *The Greeks and Their Legacy*. Oxford.

du Bois, P. 1985. "Phallocentrism and Its Subversion in Plato's *Phaedrus*." *Arethusa* 18: 91–103.

———. 1995. *Sappho Is Burning*. Chicago.

Duckworth, G. E. 1967. "The Significance and Function of Nisus and Euryalus for *Aeneid* IX–XII." *AJP* 18: 129–50.

Ebert, J. 1965. "Παῖδες Πυθικοί." *Philologus* 109: 152–56.

Edmonds, R. G., III. 2000. "Socrates the Beautiful: Role Reversal and Midwifery in Plato's *Symposium*." *TAPA* 130: 261–85.

Edmunds, L. 1987. "Foucault and Theognis." *Classical and Modern Literature* 8: 79–91.

Effe, B. 1978. "Die Destruktion der Tradition: Theokrits mythologische Gedichte." *RhM* 121: 48–77.

———. 1992a. "Die Homoerotik in der griechischen Bukolik." In *Homoerotische Lyrik: 6. Kolloquium der Forschungsstelle des Mittelalters*, edited by T. Stemmler, 55–67. Tübingen.

———. 1992b. "Die Hylas-Geschichte bei Theokrit und Apollonios Rhodios: Bemerkungen zur Prioritätsfrage." *Hermes* 120: 299–309.

Ehrenberg, V. 1956. "Das Harmodioslied." *Wiener Studien* 69: 57–69.

Elsner, J. 1993. "Seductions of Art: Encolpius and Eumolpus in a Neronian Picture Gallery." *PCPS*, n.s., 39: 30–47.

Faraone, C. A. 1999. *Ancient Greek Love Magic*. Cambridge, Mass.

Fehr, B. 1984. *Die Tyrannentöter, oder Kann man der Demokratie ein Denkmal setzen?* Frankfurt am Main.

Ferrari, G. R. F. 1987. *Listening to the Cicadas: A Study of Plato's* Phaedrus. Cambridge, England.

Fisher, N. 2001. *Aeschines: Against Timarchos*. Oxford.

Fitzgerald, G. J. 1972. "Nisus and Euryalus: A Paradigm of Futile Behavior and the Tragedy of Youth." In *Cicero and Virgil: Studies in Honour of Harold Hunt*, edited by J. R. C. Martyn, 114–37. Amsterdam.

Fitzgerald, W. 1992. "Catullus and the Reader: The Erotics of Poetry." *Arethusa* 25: 419–43.

Flacelière, R. 1961. "A Propos du Banquet de Xénophon." *Revue des Études Grecques* 74: 93–118.

Foley, H. P. 1998. "'The Mother of the Argument': Eros and the Body in Sappho and Plato's *Phaedrus*." In *Parchments of Gender: Deciphering the Body in Antiquity*, edited by M. Wyke, 39–70. Oxford.

Ford, A. 1999. "Reading Homer from the Rostrum: Poems and Laws in Aeschines' *Against Timarchus*." In *Performance Culture and Athenian Democracy*, edited by S. Goldhill and R. Osborne, 231–56. Cambridge, England.

Foucault, M. 1986. *The History of Sexuality*. Vol. 2, *The Use of Pleasure*. Trans. R. Hurley. New York.

———. 1988. *The History of Sexuality*. Vol. 3, *The Care of the Self*. Trans. R. Hurley. New York.

Fowler, R. L. 1996. "How the *Lysistrata* Works." *EMC*, n.s., 15: 245–49.

Furiani, P. L. 1987. "Omofilia e androcrazia nella società maschile di Stratone di Sardi." *Euphrosyne* 15: 217–26.

———. 1991. "Intimità e socialità in Nosside di Locri." In *Rose di Pieria*, edited by F. de Martino, 179–95. Bari.

Garlan, Y., and O. Masson. 1982. "Les acclamations pédérastiques de Kalami (Thasos)." *BCH* 106: 3–21.

Garrido-Hory, M. 1981. "La vision du dépendant chez Martial à travers les relations sexuelles." *Index* 10: 298–315.

Gauthier, P., and M. B. Hatzopoulos. 1993. *La loi gymnasiarchique de Beroia*. Athens.

Gentili, B. 1988. *Poetry and Its Public in Ancient Greece*. Trans. A. T. Cole. Baltimore.

Gerber, D. E. 1982. *Pindar's Olympian One: A Commentary*. Toronto.

Giangrande, G. 1968. "Sympotic Literature and Epigram." In *L' épigramme grecque: Entretiens sur l' antiquité classique 14*, 91–177. Geneva.

———. 1969. "Callimachus, Poetry and Love." *Eranos* 67: 33–42.

———. 1971. "Theocritus' Twelfth and Fourth Idylls: A Study in Hellenistic Irony." *QUCC* 12: 95–113.

———. 1992. "Deux passages controversés: Theocrite, *Id.* XXIII, vv. 26–32 et Nossis, *A.P.*, 170." *Antiquité Classique* 61: 213–25.

Gigante, M. 1974. "Nosside." *Parola del Passato* 29: 22–39.

———. 1981. "Il manifesto poetico di Nosside." In *Letterature comparate: Studi in onore di E. Paratore*, edited by V. Ussani et al., vol. 1, 243–45. Bologna.

Gill, C. 1973. "The Sexual Episodes in the *Satyricon*." *CP* 68: 172–85.

———. 1990. "Platonic Love and Individuality." In *Polis and Politics: Essays in Greek Moral and Political Philosophy*, edited by A. Loizou and H. Lesser, 69–88. Aldershot, England.

Gleason, M. W. 1995. *Making Men: Sophists and Self-Presentation in Ancient Rome*. Princeton.

Glidden, D. K. 1981. "The *Lysis* on Loving One's Own." *CQ*, n.s., 31: 39–59.

Golden, M. 1984. "Slavery and Homosexuality at Athens." *Phoenix* 38: 308–24.

———. 1998. *Sport and Society in Ancient Greece*. Cambridge, England.

Goldhill, S. 1987. "The Dance of the Veils: Reading Five Fragments of Anacreon." *Eranos* 85: 9–18.

———. 1995. *Foucault's Virginity: Ancient Erotic Fiction and the History of Sexuality*. Cambridge, England.

Gonfroy, F. 1978. "Homosexualité et idéologie esclavagiste chez Cicéron." *Dialogues d' histoire ancienne* 4: 219–36.

Görgemanns, H. 1998. "Ein neues Argument für die Echtheit des lysianischen Erotikos." *RhM* 131: 108–13.

Gould, T. F. 1963. *Platonic Love.* New York.

Gow, A. S. F., and D. L. Page. 1965. *The Greek Anthology: Hellenistic Epigrams.* Cambridge, England.

Greene, E. 1996a. *Reading Sappho: Contemporary Approaches.* Berkeley and Los Angeles.

———. 1996b. *Re-reading Sappho: Reception and Transmission.* Berkeley and Los Angeles.

———. 2002. "Subjects, Objects, and Erotic Symmetry in Sappho's Fragments." In Rabinowitz and Auanger (2002) 82–105.

Griffin, J. 1985. *Latin Poets and Roman Life.* London.

Griffiths, A. 1972. "Alcman's *Partheneion:* The Morning after the Night Before." *QUCC* 14:7–30.

Grimal, P. 1986. *Love in Ancient Rome.* Trans. A. Train. Norman, Okla.

Griswold, C. L. 1996. *Self-Knowledge in Plato's* Phaedrus. University Park, Pa.

Gutzwiller, K. J. 1998. *Poetic Garlands: Hellenistic Epigrams in Context.* Berkeley and Los Angeles.

Hackforth, R. 1952. *Plato's* Phaedrus. Cambridge, England.

Hague, R. 1984. "Sappho's Consolation for Atthis, fr. 96 LP." *AJP* 105: 29–36.

Haley, S. P. 2002. "Lucian's 'Leaena and Clonarium': Voyeurism or a Challenge to Assumptions?" In Rabinowitz and Auanger (2002) 286–303.

Hallett, J. P. 1979. "Sappho and Her Context: Sense and Sensuality." *Signs* 4: 447–64. Also in Greene (1996a) 125–49.

———. 1996. "*Nec Castrare Velis Meos Libellos:* Sexual and Poetic *Lusus* in Catullus, Martial and the *Carmina Priapea.*" In *Satura Lanx: Festschrift für Werner Krenkel zum 70. Geburtstag,* edited by C. Klodt, 321–44. Hildesheim.

———. 1997. "Female Homoeroticism and the Denial of Roman Reality in Latin Literature." In *Roman Sexualities,* edited by J. P. Hallett and M. B. Skinner, 255–73. Princeton.

Halperin, D. M. 1985. "Platonic Eros and What Men Call Love." *Ancient Philosophy* 5: 161–204.

———. 1986. "Plato and Erotic Reciprocity." *CA* 5: 60–80.

———. 1990. *One Hundred Years of Homosexuality.* New York.

———. 1992. "Plato and the Erotics of Narrativity." In *Methods of Interpreting Plato and His Dialogues,* edited by J. C. Klugge and N. D. Smith, 93–129. Oxford.

Hani, J. 1982. "Le mythe de l' androgyne dans le Banquet de Platon." *Euphrosyne* 11: 89–101.

Harris, E. M. 1995. *Aeschines and Athenian Polititcs.* New York.

Harris, W. V. 1997. "Lysias III and Athenian Beliefs about Revenge." *CQ,* n.s., 47: 363–66.

Henderson, J. 1975. *The Maculate Muse: Obscene Language in Attic Comedy.* New Haven.

Hendry, M. 2000. "Excluded Husband and Two-Legged Ass: Two Problems in Juvenal 9." *EMC,* n.s., 19: 85–90.

Henrichs, A. 1979. "Callimachus *Epigram* 28: A Fastidious Priamel." *Harvard Studies in Classical Philology* 83: 207–12.

Highet, G. 1941. "Petronius the Moralist." *TAPA* 72: 176–94.

Hiller von Gaertringen, F. 1897. *Die archaische Kultur der Insel Thera.* Berlin.

Hindley, C. 1994. "*Eros* and Military Command in Xenophon." *CQ,* n.s., 44: 347–66.

———. 1999. "Xenophon on Male Love." *CQ,* n.s., 49: 74–99.

Hornsby, R. 1966. "The Armor of the Slain." *Philological Quarterly* 45: 347–59.

Howie, J. G. 1983. "The Revision of Myth in Pindar *Olympian* 1: The Death and Revival of Pelops (25–27, 36–66)." *Papers of the Liverpool Latin Seminar* 4: 277–313.

Hubbard, T. K. 1987. "The 'Cooking' of Pelops: Pindar and the Process of Mythological Revisionism." *Helios* 14: 3–21.

———. 1998a. *The Pipes of Pan: Intertextuality and Literary Filiation in the Pastoral Tradition from Theocritus to Milton.* Ann Arbor.

———. 1998b. "Popular Perceptions of Elite Homosexuality in Classical Athens." *Arion,* ser. 3, 6.1: 48–78.

———. 2000. "Pederasty and Democracy: The Marginalization of a Social Practice." In *Greek Love Reconsidered,* edited by T. K. Hubbard, 1–11. New York.

———. 2002. "Pindar, Theoxenus, and the Homoerotic Eye." *Arethusa* 35: 255–96.

———. 2003. "Were Athlete-Trainer Relationships Pederastic?" *Intertexts* 7.

Hubner, U. 1996. "Kallimachos' 28. Epigramm ohne Lysanias." *Philologus* 140: 225–29.

Hug, A. 1874. "Aeschines und Plato." *RhM* 29: 434–44.

Hunt, A. S. 1929. "An Incantation in the Ashmolean Museum." *Journal of Egyptian Archaeology* 15: 155–57.

Hunter, R. 1993a. *The Argonautica of Apollonius: Literary Studies.* Cambridge, England.

———. 1993b. "One Party or Two? Simonides 22 West^2." *ZPE* 99: 11–14.

———. 1996. *Theocritus and the Archaeology of Greek Poetry.* Cambridge, England.

Hupperts, C. A. M. 1988. "Greek Love: Homosexuality or Pederasty? Greek Love in Black Figure Vase-Painting." In *Proceedings of the Third Symposium on Ancient Greek and Related Pottery,* edited by J. Christiansen and T. Melander, 255–68. Copenhagen.

Huss, B. 1999. *Xenophons Symposion: Ein Kommentar.* Stuttgart.

Hyland, D. A. 1968. "*Eros, Epithymia,* and *Philia* in Plato." *Phronesis* 13: 32–46.

Instone, S. 1990. "Love and Sex in Pindar: Some Practical Thrusts." *BICS* 37: 30–42.

Inwood, B. 1997. "Why Do Fools Fall in Love?" In *Aristotle and After,* edited by R. Sorabji, 57–69. London.

Irigaray, L. 1994. "Sorcerer Love: A Reading of Plato's *Symposium,* Diotima's Speech." In *Feminist Interpretations of Plato,* edited by N. Tuana, 181–95. University Park, Pa.

Janan, M. 1988. "The Book of Good Love? Design versus Desire in *Metamorphoses* 10." *Ramus* 17: 110–37.

Jocelyn, H. D. 1980. "A Greek Indecency and Its Students: *ΛΑΙΚΑΖΕΙΝ.*" *PCPS,* n.s., 26: 12–66.

Joó, M. 1997. "Die Liebe zum Ähnlichen (Platonischer Eros und Feminismus)." *Gymnasium* 104: 131–55.

Kahn, C. H. 1987. "Plato's Theory of Desire." *Review of Metaphysics* 41: 77–103.

Kakridis, J. T. 1930. "Die Pelopssage bei Pindar." *Philologus* 85: 463–77.

Keller, E. F. 1985. *Reflections on Gender and Science.* New Haven.

Kelly, S. T. 1979–80. "On the Twelfth Idyll of Theocritus." *Helios* 7: 55–61.

Kilmer, M. 1997. "Painters and Pederasts: Ancient Art, Sexuality, and Social History." In *Inventing Ancient Culture: Historicism, Periodization, and the Ancient World,* edited by M. Golden and P. Toohey, 36–49. London.

Kinsey, T. E. 1966. "Catullus 16." *Latomus* 25: 101–6.

Klein, T. M. 1978. "The Greek Shepherd in Vergil, Gide, Genet, and Barthes." *Helios* 6: 1–32.

Koch-Harnack, G. 1983. *Knabenliebe und Tiergeschenke: Ihre Bedeutung im päderastischen Erziehungssystem Athens.* Berlin.

Koehl, R. B. 1986. "The Chieftain Cup and a Minoan Rite of Passage." *JHS* 106: 99–110.

Koenen, L. 1993. "The Ptolemaic King as a Religious Figure." In *Images and Ideologies: Self-Definition in the Hellenistic World,* edited by A. Bulloch et al., 25–115. Berkeley and Los Angeles.

Köhnken, A. 1965. *Apollonios Rhodios und Theokrit: Die Hylas- und die Amykosgeschichten beider Dichter und die Frage der Priorität.* Göttingen.

———. 1974. "Pindar as Innovator: Poseidon Hippios and the Relevance of the Pelops Story in Olympian 1." *CQ,* n.s., 24: 199–206.

———. 1996. "Paradoxien in Theokrits Hylasgedictht." *Hermes* 124: 442–62.

Konstan, D. 1993. "Sexuality and Power in Juvenal's Second Satire." *LCM* 18: 12–14.

———. 1994a. *Sexual Symmetry: Love in the Ancient Novel and Related Genres.* Princeton.

———. 1994b. "Xenophon of Ephesus: Eros and Narrative in the Novel." In *Greek Fiction: The Greek Novel in Context,* edited by J. R. Morgan and R. Stoneman, 49–63. London.

Kosman, L. A. 1976. "Platonic Love." In *Facets of Plato's Philosophy,* edited by W. H. Werkmeister, 53–69. Assen, Netherlands.

Krafft, P. 1977. "Zu Kallimachos' Echo-Epigramm (28 Pf.)." *RhM* 120: 1–29.

Krenkel, W. 1980. "Sex und politische Biographie." *Wissenschaftliche Zeitschrift der Wilhelm-Pieck-Universität Rostock, Gesellschaftliche und sprachwissenschaftliche Reihe* 29.5: 65–76.

Kwintner, M. 1992. "Plautus *Pseudolus* 782: A Fullonious Assault." *CP* 87: 232–33.

Kytzler, B., and C. Fischer. 1978. *Carmina Priapea: Gedichte an den Gartengott.* Munich.

Lambert, M., and H. Szesnat. 1994. "Greek 'Homosexuality': Whither the Debate?" *Akroterion* 39: 45–63.

Lang, M. 1976. *The Athenian Agora XXI: Graffiti and Dipinti.* Princeton.

Lardinois, A. 1994. "Subject and Circumstance in Sappho's Poetry." *TAPA* 124: 57–84.

Lasserre, F. 1944. "Ἐρωτικοὶ λόγοι." *MH* 1: 169–78.

———. 1974. "Ornements érotiques dans la poésie lyrique archaïque." In *Serta Turyniana: Studies in Greek Literature and Palaeography in Honor of Alexander Turyn,* edited by J. L. Heller, 5–33. Urbana.

Latacz, J. 1985. "Realität und Imagination: Eine neue Lyrik-Theorie und Sapphos *phainetai moi kênos*-Lied." *MH* 42: 67–94.

Lavelle, B. 1986. "The Nature of Hipparchus' Insult to Harmodius." *AJP* 107: 318–31.

Lee, M. O. 1979. *Fathers and Sons in Virgil's* Aeneid. Albany, N.Y.

Leitao, D. 2002. "The Legend of the Sacred Band." In *The Sleep of Reason: Erotic Experience and Sexual Ethics in Ancient Greece and Rome,* edited by M. Nussbaum and J. Sihvola, 143–69. Chicago.

Lennox, P. G. 1977. "Virgil's Night Episode Re-Examined (*Aeneid* IX, 176–449)." *Hermes* 105: 331–42.

Levine, D. B. 1985. "Symposium and the *Polis.*" In *Theognis of Megara,* edited by T. J. Figueira and G. Nagy, 176–96. Baltimore.

Levy, D. 1979. "The Definition of Love in Plato's *Symposium.*" *Journal of the History of Ideas* 40: 285–91.

Lewis, J. M. 1985. "Eros and the *Polis* in Theognis, Book II." In *Theognis of Megara,* edited by T. J. Figueira and G. Nagy, 197–222. Baltimore.

Lilja, S. 1983. *Homosexuality in Republican and Augustan Rome.* Helsinki.

Livrea, E. 1996. "Per l'esegesi di due epigrammi callimachei (8 e 41 Pf.)." *Philologus* 140: 63–72.

Luck, G. 1969. *The Latin Love Elegy.*[2] London.

Ludwig, W. 1963. "Plato's Love Epigrams." *GRBS* 4: 59–82.

———. 1968. "Die Kunst der Variation im hellenistischen Liebesepigramm." In *L' épigramme grecque: Entretiens sur l' antiquité classique 14,* 297–348. Geneva.

MacAlister, S. 1992. "Gender as Sign and Symbolism in Artemidorus' *Oneirokritika:* Social Aspirations and Anxieties." *Helios* 19: 140–60.

Mace, S. 1996. "Utopian and Erotic Fusion in a New Elegy by Simonides (22 West[2])." *ZPE* 113: 233–47.

MacMullen, R. 1982. "Roman Attitudes to Greek Love." *Historia* 31: 484–502.

Makowski, J. F. 1989. "Nisus and Euryalus: A Platonic Relationship." *CJ* 85: 1–15.

———. 1996. "Bisexual Orpheus: Pederasty and Parody in Ovid." *CJ* 92: 25–38.

Mastronarde, D. J. 1968. "Theocritus' Idyll 13: Love and the Hero." *TAPA* 99: 273–90.

Maxwell-Stuart, P. G. 1972. "Strato and the *Musa puerilis.*" *Hermes* 100: 215–40.

McEvilley, T. 1978. "Sappho, Fragment Thirty-One: The Face Behind the Mask." *Phoenix* 32: 1–18.

McGann, M. J. 1983. "The Marathus Elegies of Tibullus." *Aufstieg und Niedergang der römischen Welt* II.30.3: 1976–99.

McKay, K. J. 1974. "Bird-watching in Theognis and a Callimachean Echo." *GB* 2: 105–19.

McMahon, J. M. 1998. *Paralysin Cave: Impotence, Perception, and Text in the Satyrica of Petronius.* Leiden.

Meier, M.-H.-E., and L. R. de Pogey-Castries. 1930. *Histoire de l' amour grec dans l' antiquité.* Paris.

Mencacci, F. 1999. "Päderastie und lesbische Liebe: Die Ursprünge zweier sexueller Verhaltensweisen und der Unterschied der Geschlechter in Rom." In *Rezeption und Identität: Die Kulturelle Auseinandersetzung Roms mit Griechenland als europäisches Paradigma,* edited by G. Vogt-Spira and B. Rommel, 60–80. Stuttgart.

Merkelbach, R. 1957. "Sappho und ihr Kreis." *Philologus* 101: 1–29.

Meulder, M. 1989. "Timarque, un être tyrannique dépeint par Eschine." *Les Études Classiques* 57: 317–22.

Miller, S. G. 1979. "Excavations at Nemea, 1978." *Hesperia* 48: 73–103.

Monoson, S. S. 1994. "Citizen as *Erastes:* Erotic Imagery and the Idea of Reciprocity in the Periclean Funeral Oration." *Political Theory* 22: 253–76.

———. 2000. "The Allure of Harmodius and Aristogeiton." In *Greek Love Reconsidered,* edited by T. K. Hubbard, 42–51. New York.

Montserrat, D. 1996. *Sex and Society in Graeco-Roman Egypt.* London.

Moretti, L. 1982. "Sulla legge gimnisiarchica di Berea." *RFIC* 110: 45–63.

Muecke, F. 1982. "A Portrait of the Artist as a Young Woman." *CQ,* n.s., 32: 41–55.

Musurillo, H. A., S.J. 1954. *The Acts of the Pagan Martyrs: Acta Alexandrinorum.* Oxford.

Nappa, C. 1998. "*Praetextati Mores:* Juvenal's Second Satire." *Hermes* 126: 90–108.

Natalicchio, A. 1998. *Eschine: Orazioni. Contro Timarco; Sui misfatti dell' ambasceria.* Milan.

Nethercut, W. 1984. "The Interpretation of Theocritus 12.1–9." *Helios* 11: 109–15.

Neumann, H. 1965. "Diotima's Concept of Love." *AJP* 86: 33–59.

Nicholson, G. 1999. *Plato's Phaedrus: The Philosophy of Love.* West Lafayette.

Nicholson, N. 1998. "The Truth of Pederasty: A Supplement to Foucault's Genealogy of the Relation between Truth and Desire in Ancient Greece." *Intertexts* 2: 26–45.

———. 2000. "Pederastic Poets and Adult Patrons in Late Archaic Lyric." *Classical World* 93: 235–59.

Nicolai, W. 1998. "Zur platonischen Eroskonzeption." *GB* 22: 81–100.

Nola, R. 1990. "On Some Neglected Minor Speakers in Plato's *Symposium:* Phaedrus and Pausanias." *Prudentia* 22: 54–73.

Nussbaum, M. 1980. "Aristophanes and Socrates on Learning Practical Wisdom." *Yale Classical Studies* 26: 43–97.

———. 1986. *The Fragility of Goodness: Luck and Ethics in Greek Tragedy and Philosophy.* Cambridge, England.

———. 1994. "Platonic Love and Colorado Law: The Relevance of Ancient Greek Norms to Modern Sexual Controversies." *Virginia Law Review* 80: 1515–1651.

———. 1995. "Eros and the Wise: The Stoic Response to a Cultural Dilemma." *Oxford Studies in Ancient Philosophy* 13: 231–67.

Obermayer, H. P. 1998. *Martial und der Diskurs über männliche "Homosexualität" in der Literatur der frühen Kaiserzeit.* Tübingen.

Ogden, D. 1996. "Homosexuality and Warfare in Classical Greece." In *Battle in Antiquity,* edited by A. B. Lloyd, 107–68. Newburyport, Mass.

Olliensis, E. 1997. "Sons and Lovers: Sexuality and Gender in Virgil's Poetry." In *The Cambridge Companion to Virgil,* edited by C. Martindale, 294–311. Cambridge, England.

Osborne, C. 1994. *Eros Unveiled: Plato and the God of Love.* Oxford.

Paduano, G. 1989. *Antologia Palatina: Epigrammi Erotici: Libro V e Libro XII.* Milan.

Papanghelis, T. D. 1999. "Eros Pastoral and Profane: On Love in Virgil's *Eclogues.*" In *Amor: Roma. Love and Latin Literature,* edited by S. M. Braund and R. Mayer, 44–59. Cambridge, England.

Parker, H. N. 1993. "Sappho Schoolmistress." *TAPA* 123: 309–51.

Patzer, H. 1982. *Die griechische Knabenliebe.* Wiesbaden.

Pavlock, B. 1985. "Epic and Tragedy in Vergil's Nisus and Euryalus Episode." *TAPA* 115: 207–24.

Pedrick, V. 1993. "The Abusive Address and the Audience in Catullan Poems." *Helios* 20: 173–96.

Pender, E. E. 1992. "Spiritual Pregnancy in Plato's *Symposium*." *CQ*, n.s., 42: 72–86.

Penwill, J. L. 1978. "Men in Love: Aspects of Plato's *Symposium*." *Ramus* 7: 143–75.

Percy, W. A., III. 1996. *Pederasty and Pedagogy in Archaic Greece*. Urbana.

Pintabone, D. T. 2002. "Ovid's Iphis and Ianthe: When Girls Won't Be Girls." In Rabinowitz and Auanger (2002) 256–85.

Plass, P. C. 1978. "Plato's 'Pregnant' Lover." *Symbolae Osloenses* 53: 47–55.

Podlecki, A. J. 1966. "The Political Significance of the Athenian 'Tyrannicide'-Cult." *Historia* 15: 129–41.

Pomeroy, A. J. 1992. "Trimalchio as *Deliciae*." *Phoenix* 46: 45–53.

Potz, E. 1993. "*Fortunati ambo:* Funktion und Bedeutung der Nisus/Euryalus Episode in Vergil's *Aeneis*." *Hermes* 121: 325–34.

Preisendanz, K. 1930. Review of "An Incantation in the Ashmolean Museum," by A. S. Hunt. *Philologische Wochenschrift* 50: 748–49.

Pretagostini, R. 1984. "La rivalità tra Comata e Lacone: Una paideia disconosciuta (Theocr. 5, 35–43. 116–119)." *MD* 13: 137–41.

———. 1997. "L'omosessualità di Agatone nelle Tesmoforiazuse di Aristofane e la figura del *Keletizein* (v. 153)." In *Mousa: Scritti in onore di Giuseppe Morelli*, edited by P. D'Alessandro, 117–22. Bologna.

Price, A. W. 1981. "Loving Persons Platonically." *Phronesis* 26: 25–34.

———. 1989. *Love and Friendship in Plato and Aristotle*. Oxford.

———. 1991. "Martha Nussbaum's *Symposium*." *Ancient Philosophy* 11: 285–99.

Price, S. D. 1990. "Anacreontic Vases Reconsidered." *GRBS* 31: 133–75.

Price, S. R. F. 1990. "The Future of Dreams: From Freud to Artemidoros." In *Before Sexuality: The Construction of Erotic Experience in the Ancient Greek World*, edited by D. M. Halperin, J. J. Winkler, and F. I. Zeitlin, 365–87. Princeton.

Prins, Y. 1999. *Victorian Sappho*. Princeton.

Privitera, G. A. 1969. "Ambiguità antitesi analogia nel fr. 31 LP." *QUCC* 8: 37–80.

Putnam, M. C. J. 1985. "Possessiveness, Sexuality, and Heroism in the *Aeneid*." *Vergilius* 31: 1–21.

Quinn, K. 1972. *Catullus: An Interpretation*. London.

Rabinowitz, N. S., and L. Auanger. 2002. *Among Women: From the Homosocial to the Homoerotic in the Ancient World*. Austin.

Race, W. H. 1989. "Sappho, fr. 16 L.-P. and Alkaios, fr. 42 L.-P.: Romantic and Classical Strains in Lesbian Lyric." *CJ* 85: 16–33.

Radici Colace, P. 1971. "La tecnica compositiva dell' ἐραστής pseudo-teocriteo." *GIF* 23: 325–46.

Rainer, J. M. 1986. "Zum Problem der Atimie als Verlust der bürgerlichen Rechte insbesondere bei männlichen homosexuellen Prostituierten." *Revue Internationale des Droits de l'Antiquité* 33: 89–114.

Rankin, H. D. 1976. "Poem 16 of Catullus." *Symbolae Osloenses* 51: 87–94.

Reshotko, N. 1997. "Plato's *Lysis:* A Socratic Treatise on Desire and Attraction." *Apeiron* 30: 1–18.

Richardson, T. W. 1984. "Homosexuality in the *Satyricon*." *Classica et Mediaevalia* 35: 105–27.

Richlin, A. 1992. *The Garden of Priapus: Sexuality and Aggression in Roman Humor.*[2] New York.

———. 1993. "Not before Homosexuality: The Materiality of the *Cinaedus* and the Roman Law against Love between Men." *Journal of the History of Sexuality* 3: 523–73.

Rist, J. M. 1997. "Plato and Professor Nussbaum on Acts 'Contrary to Nature.'" In *Studies in Plato and the Platonic Tradition: Essays Presented to John Whittaker,* edited by M. Joyal, 65–79. Aldershot, England.

Robbins, E. 1994. "Alcman's *Partheneion:* Legend and Choral Ceremony." *CQ,* n.s., 44: 7–16.

Robert, J.-N. 1997. *Eros Romain: Sexe et morale dans l' ancienne Rome.* Paris.

Roochnik, D. L. 1987. "The Erotics of Philosophical Discourse." *History of Philosophy Quarterly* 4: 117–29.

Rosen, S. 1968. *Plato's* Symposium. New Haven.

———. 1979. "The Non-lover in Plato's *Phaedrus.*" In *Plato: True and Sophistic Rhetoric,* edited by K. V. Erickson, 223–37. Amsterdam.

Rossetti, L. 1992. *Understanding the* Phaedrus: *Proceedings of the II Symposium Platonicum.* Sankt Augustin.

Rowe, C. J. 1986. *Plato: Phaedrus.* Warminster.

———. 1990. "Philosophy, Love, and Madness." In *The Person and the Human Mind: Issues in Ancient and Modern Philosophy,* edited by C. Gill, 227–46. Oxford.

Sandy, G. N. 1971. "Catullus 16." *Phoenix* 25: 51–57.

Santas, G. 1988. *Plato and Freud: Two Theories of Love.* Oxford.

Saylor, C. 1990. "Group vs. Individual in Vergil IX." *Latomus* 49: 88–94.

Scanlon, T. F. 2002. *Eros and Greek Athletics.* Oxford.

Schievenin, R. 1976. "Trimalcione e il *puer non inspeciosus* (Petron. 75,5)." *Bollettino di Studi Latini* 6: 295–302.

Schindel, U. 1978. "Doppeltes Recht oder Prozeßtechnik? Zur Aischines' erster und dritter Rede." *Hermes* 106: 100–111.

Schofield, M. 1991. *The Stoic Idea of the City.* Cambridge, England.

Schrijvers, P. H. 1985. *Eine medizinische Erklärung der männlichen Homosexualität aus der Antike.* Amsterdam.

Schwinge, E.-R. 1980. "Poetik als praktizierte Poetik: Kallimachos' Echo-Epigramm (28 Pf.)." *Würzburger Jahrbücher für die Altertumswissenschaft,* n.s., 6A: 101–5.

Scott, W. C. 1969a. "Catullus and Calvus (Cat. 50)." *CP* 64: 169–73.

———. 1969b. "Catullus and Cato (Cat. 56)." *CP* 64: 24–29.

———. 1971. "Catullus and Caesar (Cat. 29)." *CP* 66: 17–25.

Selden, D. 1992. *"Ceveat Lector:* Catullus and the Rhetoric of Performance." In *Innovations of Antiquity,* edited by R. Hexter and D. Selden, 461–512. New York.

Sergent, B. 1986. *Homosexuality in Greek Myth.* Trans. A. Goldhammer. Boston.

Shapiro, H. A. 1981. "Courtship Scenes in Attic Vase Painting." *AJA* 85: 133–43.

———. 1992. "Eros in Love: Pederasty and Pornography in Greece." In *Pornography and Representation in Greece and Rome,* edited by A. Richlin, 53–72. Oxford.

———. 2000. "Leagros and Euphronios: Painting Pederasty in Athens." In *Greek Love Reconsidered,* edited by T. K. Hubbard, 12–32. New York.

Sier, K. 1997. *Die Rede der Diotima: Untersuchungen zum platonische Symposium.* Darmstadt.

Skinner, M. B. 1979. "Parasites and Strange Bedfellows: A Study in Catullus' Political Imagery." *Ramus* 8: 137–52.

———. 1989. "Sapphic Nossis." *Arethusa* 22: 5–18.

———. 1991a. "Aphrodite Garlanded: *Erôs* and Poetic Creativity in Sappho and Nossis." In *Rose di Pieria*, edited by F. de Martino, 77–96. Bari. Also in Rabinowitz and Auanger (2002) 60–81.

———. 1991b. "Nossis *Thelyglossos:* The Private Text and the Public Book." In *Women's History and Ancient History*, edited by S. B. Pomeroy, 20–47. Chapel Hill.

———. 1993. *"Ego Mulier:* The Construction of Male Sexuality in Catullus." *Helios* 20: 107–30.

Slater, W. J. 1978. "Artemon and Anacreon: No Text without Context." *Phoenix* 32: 185–94.

Snyder, J. M. 1974. "Aristophanes' Agathon as Anacreon." *Hermes* 102: 244–46.

———. 1989. *The Woman and the Lyre: Women Writers in Greece and Rome*. Carbondale.

———. 1997. *Lesbian Desire in the Lyrics of Sappho*. New York.

Soverini, P. 1976. "Le perversioni di Encolpio (Per una nuova possibilità di interpretazione di Petr. 9,8 s.)." *Materiali e contributi per la storia della narrativa greco-latina* 1: 97–107.

Stanzel, K.-H. 1995. *Liebende Hirten: Theokrits Bukolik und die alexandrinische Poesie*. Stuttgart.

Stehle, E. 1997. *Performance and Gender in Ancient Greece*. Princeton.

Stein, E. 1992. *Forms of Desire: Sexual Orientation and the Social Constructionist Controversy*. New York.

Steinbichler, W. 1998. *Die Epigramme des Dichters Straton von Sardes*. Frankfurt am Main.

Steiner, D. T. 1996. "For Love of a Statue: A Reading of Plato's *Symposium* 215 A–B." *Ramus* 25: 89–111.

———. 1998. "Moving Images: Fifth-Century Victory Monuments and the Athlete's Allure." *CA* 17: 123–49.

Stephens, W. O. 1996. "Epictetus on How the Stoic Sage Loves." *Oxford Studies in Ancient Philosophy* 14: 193–210.

Stewart, A. 1997. *Art, Desire, and the Body in Ancient Greece*. Cambridge, England.

Stohn, G. 1993. "Zur Agathonszene in den 'Thesmophoriazusen' des Aristophanes." *Hermes* 121: 196–205.

Stokes, M. C. 1986. *Plato's Socratic Conversations: Drama and Dialectic in Three Dialogues*. Baltimore.

Storey, I. 1995. "Philoxenus . . . of Doubtful Gender." *JHS* 115: 182–84.

———. 1998. "Poets, Politicians, and Perverts: Personal Humour in Aristophanes." *Classics Ireland* 5: 85–134.

Sullivan, J. P. 1968. *The Satyricon of Petronius: A Literary Study*. London.

———. 1979. "Martial's Sexual Attitudes." *Philologus* 123: 288–302.

———. 1991. *Martial: The Unexpected Classic*. Cambridge, England.

Svenbro, J. 1984. "La stratégie de l' amour: Modèle de la guerre et théorie de l' amour dans la poésie de Sappho." *QS* 19: 57–79.

Tadic-Gilloteaux, N. 1965. "A la recherche de la personnalité de Properce." *Latomus* 24: 238–73.

Taillardat, J. 1983. *"ΜΥΙΚΚΟΣ 'ΑΓΡΕΟΣ* ou *'ΑΓΡΙΟΣ*?" *BCH* 107: 189–90.

Tarán, S. L. 1979. *The Art of Variation in the Hellenistic Epigram*. Leiden.

———. 1985. "*ΕΙΣΙ ΤΡΙΧΕΣ*: An Erotic Motif in the Greek Anthology." *JHS* 105: 90–107.

Taylor, R. 1997. "Two Pathic Subcultures in Ancient Rome." *Journal of the History of Sexuality* 7: 319–71.

Thesleff, H. 1978. "The Interrelation and Date of the *Symposia* of Plato and Xenophon." *BICS* 25: 157–70.

Thorp, J. 1992. "The Social Construction of Homosexuality." *Phoenix* 46: 54–61.

Too, Y. L. 1997. "Alcman's *Partheneion:* The Maidens Dance the City." *QUCC* 85: 7–29.

van Geytenbeek, A. C. 1963. *Musonius Rufus and Greek Diatribe.* Trans. B. L. Hijmans, Jr. Assen, Netherlands.

Varone, A. 1994. *Erotica Pompeiana: Iscrizioni d' amore sui muri di Pompei.* Rome.

Versenyi, L. 1975. "Plato's *Lysis.*" *Phronesis* 20: 185–98.

Verstraete, B. C. 1975. "Ovid on Homosexuality." *EMC,* o.s., 19: 79–83.

———. 1980. "Slavery and the Social Dynamics of Male Homosexual Relations in Ancient Rome." *Journal of Homosexuality* 5: 227–36.

Vetta, M. 1980. *Theognis: Elegiarum Liber Secundus.* Rome.

Veyne, P. 1985. "Homosexuality in Ancient Rome." In *Western Sexuality: Practice and Precept in Past and Present Times,* edited by P. Ariès and A. Béjin, trans. A. Forster, 26–35. Oxford.

Vlastos, G. 1973. *Platonic Studies.* Princeton.

von der Mühll, P. 1964. "Weitere pindarische Notizen." *MH* 21: 168–72.

Wallace, R. W. 1997. "On Not Legislating Sexual Conduct in Fourth-Century Athens." In *Symposion 1995: Vorträge zur griechischen und hellenistischen Rechtsgeschichte,* edited by G. Thür and J. Vélissaropoulos-Karakostas, 151–66. Cologne.

Walsh, G. B. 1990. "Surprised by Self: Audible Thought in Hellenistic Poetry." *CP* 85: 1–21.

Walsh, P. G. 1974. "Was Petronius a Moralist?" *Greece and Rome* 21: 181–90.

Walters, J. 1998. "Juvenal, Satire 2: Putting Male Sexual Deviants on Show." In *Thinking Men: Masculinity and Its Self-Representation in the Classical Tradition,* edited by L. Foxhall and J. Salmon, 148–54. London.

Wheeler, S. M. 1997. "Changing Names: The Miracle of Iphis in Ovid's *Metamorphoses* 9." *Phoenix* 51: 190–202.

White, F. C. 1989. "Love and Beauty in Plato's *Symposium.*" *JHS* 109: 149–57.

———. 1990. "Love and the Individual in Plato's *Phaedrus.*" *CQ,* n.s., 40: 396–406.

Wilkinson, L. P. 1967. "Callimachus, *A.P.* xii.43." *Classical Review,* n.s., 17: 5–6.

Williams, C. A. 1999. *Roman Homosexuality: Ideologies of Masculinity in Classical Antiquity.* Oxford.

Williams, G. 1962. "Poetry in the Moral Climate of Augustan Rome." *Journal of Roman Studies* 52: 28–46.

Williamson, M. 1995. *Sappho's Immortal Daughters.* Cambridge, Mass.

Wills, G. 1967. "The Sapphic 'Umwertung aller Werte.'" *AJP* 88: 434–42.

Wimmel, W. 1957. "Zum Verhältnis einiger Stellen des xenophontischen und platonischen Symposions." *Gymnasium* 64: 230–50.

———. 1968. *Der frühe Tibull.* Munich.

Winkler, J. J. 1990. *The Constraints of Desire.* New York.

Winter, T. N. 1973. "Catullus Purified: A Brief History of *Carmen* 16." *Arethusa* 6: 257–65.

Winterling, A. 1990. "Symposion und Knabenliebe: Die Männergesellschaften in archaischen Griechenland." In *Männerbande Männerbünde: Zur Rolle des Mannes im Kulturvergleich,* edited by G. Völger and K. von Welck, vol. 2, 15–22. Cologne.

Wohl, V. 1999. "The Eros of Alcibiades." *CA* 18: 349–85.

Wooten, C. 1984. "Petronius and 'Camp.'" *Helios* 11: 133–39.

———. 1988. "Clarity and Obscurity in the Speeches of Aeschines." *AJP* 109: 40–43.

INDEX

abortion, 432

abuse, sexual, 260

Academy of Athens, 73, 95, 174, 470, 519–20

Achilles, 70n32, 76, 78, 147, 182–83, 201, 217–18, 284, 345, 428, 454n20, 468, 473, 500, 507n148, 516n168, 530–31

Achilles Tatius, 3, 444–46, 479–87

Acusilaus, 181

Addaeus, 296

Adonis, 307, 475

adultery, 87, 98, 190, 256, 258–59, 264–65, 311, 322, 325, 327n51, 329–30, 360, 395, 423, 432n95, 432n97, 432n98, 434, 438, 444, 448, 495

aedile, 315

Aelian, 55–56, 69

Aelius Lampridius, 493, 496–97

Aeschines, 7, 92n9, 119–21, 131–55

Aeschylus, 76, 78, 183, 454

Afranius, 309, 319

Agamemnon, 480–81, 527. *See also* Argynnus

Agathon, 6, 86–87, 89, 101–10, 164, 166, 180, 183n30, 192–94, 218, 290

age, 5–6, 19–20, 22–23, 49, 57–58, 69, 95, 114, 119–20, 137–38, 163, 172, 177, 183, 212–13, 228, 230n111, 234–35, 249, 260, 266–67, 269–70, 284–85, 299, 302, 304–6, 308, 319, 357, 403–4, 437–38, 441, 446, 451, 457, 459–60, 465, 473, 478, 491–92, 500, 515–17, 527

Agesilaus, 56, 67–68

agora, 92, 140, 143, 470

Ajax, son of Oileus, 40

Ajax, son of Telamon, 207, 500

Alcaeus Comicus, 88

Alcaeus Lyricus, 106, 283, 288n45, 338

Alcaeus of Messene, 291–92

Alcestis, 182, 201

Alcibiades, 12, 57, 63–65, 122–23, 164, 166–67, 169, 204–7, 212n67, 212n70, 265, 498, 516–17, 530

Alcman, 5, 16, 21–24, 26–29

Alexander of Aetolia, 59

Alexander the Great, 56, 75n49, 79, 150–51, 154–55, 268

Alexander Severus, 444, 497

Alexandria. *See* Egypt

Alexis, 88, 114–15, 290

Alpheius of Messene, 296–97

Amphis, 115

Anacreon, 12, 16, 20, 22–25, 36–38, 106, 229, 306, 307n103, 338, 453–54

Anacreontea, 306–7

anal penetration, 11, 19–20, 82, 84–85, 87–88, 90–91, 93, 98, 101, 262–64, 296, 300, 303–4, 309–10, 317n14, 317n16, 318n18, 318n20, 322–23, 327, 349, 352–53, 402, 422–24, 427, 429, 431, 433n101, 439, 464, 491–92, figs. 5a–5b, 8, 14, 26a–26b

Anaxandrides, 115

Compositor: G&S Typesetters, Inc.
Text: 10/12 New Baskerville
Display: Joanna